Sovereignty disputes and the United Nations Convention on the Law of the Sea

Manchester University Press

MELLAND SCHILL STUDIES IN INTERNATIONAL LAW

General editors, Iain Scobbie and Jean D'Aspremont

MELLAND SCHILL Studies in INTERNATIONAL LAW

Founded as a memorial to Edward Melland Schill, a promising scholar killed during the First World War, the Melland Schill Lectures (1961–74) were established by the University of Manchester following a bequest by Edward's sister, Olive B. Schill, to promote the understanding of international law and implicitly lessen the possibilities for future conflict. Dedicated to promoting women's employment rights and access to education, Olive's work is commemorated in both the Melland Schill series and the Women in International Law Network at the University of Manchester.

The Melland Schill lecture series featured a distinguished series of speakers on a range of controversial topics, including Quincy Wright on the role of international law in the elimination of war, Robert Jennings on the acquisition of territory, and Sir Ian Sinclair on the Vienna Convention on the Law of Treaties.

In the 1970s, Gillian White, the first woman appointed as a Professor of Law in mainland Britain, transformed the lectures into a monograph series, published by Manchester University Press. Many of the works previously published under the name 'Melland Schill monographs' have become standard references in the field, including: A.P.V. Rogers' *Law on the battlefield*, which is currently in its third edition, and Hilary Charlesworth and Christine Chinkin's *The boundaries of international law*, which offered the first book-length treatment of the application of feminist theories to international law.

Closely linked to the Melland Schill Classics and Melland Schill Perspectives series, Melland Schill Studies in International Law has become a home for exceptional academic work from around the world.

To buy or to find out more about the books currently available in this series, please go to: https://manchesteruniversitypress.co.uk/series/melland-schill-studies-in-international-law/

Sovereignty disputes and the United Nations Convention on the Law of the Sea

A public order perspective

Thomas D. Grant

MANCHESTER UNIVERSITY PRESS

Published by Manchester University Press
Oxford Road, Manchester, M13 9PL

www.manchesteruniversitypress.co.uk

British Library Cataloguing-in-Publication Data
A catalogue record for this book is available from the British Library

ISBN 978 1 52619060 4 hardback

First published 2026

EU authorised representative for GPSR:
Easy Access System Europe, Mustamäe tee 50, 10621 Tallinn, Estonia
gpsr.requests@easproject.com

Typeset
by New Best-set Typesetters Ltd

Contents

Preface

This book involves three matters. One of them is settlement of disputes under the United Nations (UN) Convention on the Law of the Sea 1982 (UNCLOS), in particular where disputes admix territorial and maritime questions. Another is the contemporary crisis in international public order that arises from the recrudescence of armed aggression against the territorial integrity of states. And the third is legal method, which is to say the body of techniques that international lawyers, whether as advocates, adjudicators, or social scientists, apply in our work.

Each of these matters I have had occasion to consider during the thirty years that I have been a lawyer, most of that time practicing as an international lawyer as well as teaching and writing about international law. In this book, I suggest that all three are interconnected. Their interconnection has come into focus over the past decade in a series of decisions under UNCLOS.

The dispute settlement provisions of UNCLOS display their connection to public order in unusually vivid form in a jurisdictional decision that an UNCLOS Annex VII tribunal adopted in early 2020 in a case that Ukraine had instituted against Russia in regard to Ukraine's rights as the coastal state on the Black Sea, Sea of Azov, and Kerch Strait.[1] To refer to Ukraine's rights as rights of *the* coastal state the alert reader will note has a conclusory purport. It implies that, whatever the content of the rights might be, there is no dispute that Ukraine, as the coastal state, is the state that holds them. Indeed, until March 2014 there was no dispute. It was common ground that the international boundary between Russia and Ukraine was settled. But what Justice Holmes said of human affairs in general—'repose is not the destiny of man'[2]—is true of international affairs in particular: Change

1 *Dispute concerning Coastal State Rights in the Black Sea, Sea of Azov, and Kerch Strait (Ukraine v. Russian Federation)*, Permanent Court of Arbitration (PCA) Case no. 2017–06, UNCLOS Annex VII (Paik, President; Bouguetaia, Gómez-Robledo, Lowe, and Golitsyn, arbitrators), Award on Preliminary Objections (21 February 2020).

2 Holmes, 'The Path of the Law' (1897) 10 HLR 457, 464.

in legal relations is a reality of international life. It is change, or assertion that there has been a change, that instigates legal incidents, including those that parties seek through third-party procedures under international law to resolve.

It might be said that *any* legal dispute entails a change in legal relations, or at least an assertion, on the law and facts, that they *should* change. Parties bring contentious cases in order to obtain relief, and a binding decision will constitute a change in legal relations if the claimant prevails. The decision will establish, under the secondary rules of responsibility, that the respondent (defendant) owes the applicant (claimant) reparation in some form, whether of restitution, compensation, satisfaction,[3] or two or all of these combined.[4] The duty to make reparation, as established in the decision, is new in the legal relations of the parties.[5] Even where the claimant does not prevail, a change in the parties' legal relations might result—for example, where, if it can and does, the adjudicator imposes costs.[6] Whichever party prevails and on whatever terms, so long as the terms entail a final resolution of the legal claims raised in the case the legal relations that the invocation of claims had placed in question are now ascertained and a dispute thus quieted.[7] In short, a final and binding decision that resolves legal claims brings about a change in the parties' legal relations.

Though bringing about a change in legal relations is the object of legal proceedings, it is not mainly in adjudication that legal relations change. They change much more in the world at large than in the formal setting of dispute settlement procedure. It therefore is no surprise that, in some cases,

3 *Pulp Mills on the River Uruguay (Argentina v. Uruguay)*, Judgment, 20 April 2010, ICJ Rep. 2010 p. 18, pp. 103–104, ¶ 273 and to the same effect ARSIWA Arts. 34–37.

4 ARSIWA Art. 34, Comment (2), ILC Yearbook 2001, vol. II, Part Two, p. 95. See *Responsibilities and Obligations of States Sponsoring Persons and Entities with Respect to Activities in the Area*, Case No. 17, Seabed Disputes Chamber, Advisory Opinion, 1 February 2011, ITLOS Rep. 2011 p. 10, pp. 62–63, ¶¶ 196–197.

5 See ARSIWA Art. 1, Comment (1), ILC Yearbook 2001, vol. II, Part Two, p. 32: 'The term "international responsibility" covers the *new legal relations* which arise under international law by reason of the internationally wrongful act of a State' (emphasis added). See also ARSIWA, *General commentary*, Comment (3)*(f)*: ILC Yearbook 2001, vol. II, Part Two, p. 31.

6 Under treaty-based dispute settlement, costs awards are most familiar in investment arbitration, as to which see Franck & Roe, 'The Cost Award' in Gómez & Titi (eds.) (2024) 59–77.

7 Such being the result of the application of the principle of *res judicata* and the goal that both parties (might, but do not necessarily) pursue in the course of litigation. See, for example, *Dispute over the Status and Use of the Waters of the Silala (Chile v. Bolivia)*, Judgment, 1 December 2022, ICJ Rep. 2022 p. 614, p. 635, ¶ 44; and *ibid*. Declaration of Judge Charlesworth, ICJ Rep. 2022 at p. 676, ¶ 22.

a party asserts that a change in legal relations has already taken place, that is to say before the adjudicator resolves the case and even before proceedings were instituted. Where an opposing party disagrees, and maintains that there has been no change in legal relations, other than that which is intrinsic to the institution of legal proceedings,[8] this question itself—that is, whether or not the parties' legal relations have remained otherwise stable—an adjudicator might be called upon to resolve.

International adjudicators from time to time, in the course of adjudicating disputes that turn on the application of a treaty to facts, have been called upon to say whether, between the disputing parties, the treaty still applies.[9] Adjudicators in that situation are mindful of the principle of stability of treaty relations, a fundamental principle of international law.[10] So prevalent is the principle that parties seldom convince adjudicators that a treaty, once accepted to be in force, has since ceased to be by some event or process other than consent of its parties or as its terms otherwise expressly provide. The stability of legal relations embodied in a boundary settlement is even more deeply entrenched than the stability of legal relations under treaties in general.[11]

At the heart of the *Coastal State Rights* case—as the Black Sea, Sea of Azov, and Kerch Strait matter is titled—is a question about stability and change in legal relations. The question is whether, before Ukraine instituted proceedings concerning maritime rights, a legal dispute had arisen between Ukraine and Russia over which state is sovereign in Crimea, the territory to which the relevant maritime areas appertain. The 2020 decision, which I address in Chapters 6 and 7, concluded that a dispute had arisen. According

8 While instituting proceedings has legal effects, and all the more so where the adjudicator finds that there is a receivable claim, the legal effect of discontinuing proceedings is not necessarily precisely opposite to these effects, as to which see Wegen, 'Discontinuance and Withdrawal: Article 88 of the Rules' in Zimmermann, et al. (eds.) (2019) p. 1611, ¶ 66. Even where proceedings have ended, claims—and doubts—might endure.

9 Consider, e.g., pleas of *rebus sic stantibus* under a treaty, including as expressed in Art. 62 VCLT, such as Hungary's against Slovakia in *Gabčíkovo-Nagymaros Project (Hungary/Slovakia)*, Judgment, 25 September 1997, ICJ Rep. 1997 p. 7, pp. 59–60, ¶ 95; or of invalidity or breach, such as Nicaragua's against Colombia in regard to a 1928 territorial settlement by treaty: *Territorial and Maritime Dispute (Nicaragua v. Colombia)*, Preliminary Objections, Judgment, 13 December 2007, ICJ Rep. 2007 p. 832, p. 857, ¶ 74. Hungary in *Gabčíkovo-Nagymaros* also pleaded termination by breach: ICJ Rep. 1997 at pp. 60–62, ¶ 96.

10 *Gabčíkovo-Nagymaros Project (Hungary v. Slovakia)*, Judgement, 25 September 1997, ICJ Rep. 1997 p. 7, p. 65, ¶ 104. See also *Temple of Preah Vihear (Cambodia v. Thailand)*, Judgment, 15 June 1962, Sep. Op. Judge Sir Gerald Fitzmaurice, ICJ Rep. 1962 at p. 57.

11 For example, as reflected in Art. 62(2)*(a)* VCLT. See generally Grant (2015) 116–119.

to the decision, a legal dispute had arisen in 2014 as to which state holds sovereign title to Crimea. The decision adverts to an often-invoked prerequisite for the existence of a legal dispute, namely that two parties have asserted contradictory claims about their legal relations. However, because the legal relations of two states embodied in a peacefully settled boundary are specially entrenched, such relations differ from others under international law. To say that a dispute now exists as to a boundary that was peacefully settled is to say that the legal relations of the two states have changed in an unusual way. For a party to demonstrate that *those* legal relations have changed, the party must do more than assert that they have. As to the following two propositions, international practice is clear: formal assertion does not constitute a claim to sovereignty in every case; assertion by armed force does not constitute a claim to sovereignty in any case.

The Annex VII tribunal in *Coastal State Rights* was silent in regard to what constituted the change in legal relations that Russia posited had introduced a legal dispute as to sovereignty over Crimea. A layperson familiar with the general outline of events between Russia and Ukraine might think it obvious that a change in legal relations took place in 2014 between them: Ukraine before that had effective control of Crimea; Russia had it after. The layperson might surmise that a change in effective control over a territory necessarily brings with it certain changes in legal relations, and an international lawyer would agree. However, the international lawyer would insist on a caveat: a change in effective control does not necessarily entail a change in sovereignty. Nor does a change in effective control necessarily entail a dispute as to which state is sovereign. There is no legal dispute in respect of a given matter unless there are contradictory legal claims in respect of the matter. To demonstrate that a state has a legal claim to a territory, more is needed than the fact that the state controls the territory. It was in respect of Russia's assertion that a sovereignty dispute had arisen that the *Coastal State Rights* tribunal was silent—except for its conclusion that one had. Much in the tribunal's award rested on the conclusion that that particular change in legal relations had occurred—not that a change *in abstracto* had occurred, but that a sovereignty dispute had arisen. The conclusion is remarkable, because the sovereign boundaries of Ukraine had not been disputed at any time in the state's modern existence—up to practically the moment Russia took control of Crimea. The tribunal's silence as to what gave rise to the putative dispute—that is, how a contradictory claim emerged when for decades the parties had been in accord—gives occasion to consider certain problems of legal principle. It also gives occasion to consider certain elements of legal method.

To start, because change in a peacefully settled boundary between states under modern international law requires consent of the states concerned, it is unusual for a party to contend that there has been a change, where the party presents no evidence that there has been consent to change. Russia's argument was that Ukraine's consent was irrelevant in the matter, because, Russia said, Ukraine was responsible for extreme human rights abuse, including genocide, and this misconduct, in effect, led to 'developments' in the region that could only be addressed through a change of international boundaries, and, thus, Russia's sovereign claim arose. If one accepts such an argument at face value, then one invites two serious consequences. First, it would be the case that mere argument, without fact evidence, can place settled boundaries in doubt. Second, it would be the case that a party, though it gave its consent to jurisdiction, has the power by its own later act to create a legal situation in which a tribunal will refrain from exercising jurisdiction, because, in the received view, UNCLOS does not confer compulsory and binding jurisdiction over 'any unsettled dispute concerning sovereignty ... over continental or insular land territory.'[12]

Adjudicators in future cases can avert both consequences. One way to avert them would be to temper the received view about sovereignty disputes and UNCLOS jurisdiction. Chapters 2 and 3 suggest that the text, drafting history, and object and purpose of UNCLOS support tempering the received view. However, to avert the consequences—the destabilization of boundaries and the ineffectiveness of party consent to UNCLOS jurisdiction—no change in how we interpret the Convention is needed. To avert them, I argue, a tribunal only need apply ordinary methods of evidentiary scrutiny and ordinary approaches to resolving differences between parties as to the scope of a tribunal's jurisdiction. The *Coastal State Rights* tribunal in its 2020 decision, I suggest, did neither.

Among the questions that the 2020 decision raises are questions about inconsistencies between conclusions of fact that different international institutions, including courts and tribunals, as well as intergovernmental political organizations, reach. It also raises questions about how an adjudicator should address 'mixed' claims—that is to say, claims in which matters that the adjudicator's jurisdiction does not embrace are admixed with matters that it does. Relevant here is the long-running contestation among jurists as to the relation between applicable law and jurisdiction. Relevant too is the scope of an adjudicator's power to consider ancillary or incidental matters, whether of fact, of law, or of both, in order to determine the scope of its jurisdiction to settle matters on the merits. Among the elements of

12 UNCLOS Art. 298(1)(a)(i), though, as will be seen, in the central case in which the matter is addressed, the focus of the reasoning was Art. 288(1): see *Chagos Marine Protected Area*, ¶¶ 213–221, 307–318; United Kingdom argument, Final Transcript 654: 17–19, quoted in Award of 18 March 2015, ¶ 170.

legal method that adjudicators employ to address these questions, and that the 2020 decision seems to place in doubt, are those concerned with fact-finding, allocation of burden of proof, and exposition of reasons, all of these being familiar to adjudicators when they consider cases that parties have entrusted them to settle.

* * *

I first turned my mind to the relation between land territory disputes and the dispute settlement provisions of UNCLOS, which the Convention sets out in its Part XV, section 2, when working with the late James Crawford, then the Whewell Professor of International Law at Cambridge and an international law practitioner whose docket of sovereign matters at that time was one of the most extensive of any lawyer in the field. It was some time after the completion of the second edition of Crawford's *Creation of States in International Law*,[13] in 2006, that we were called on in a practice setting to consider how in light of the jurisdictional constraints a state might deal with concurrent land territory disputes and maritime disputes. I later turned to similar questions when engaged as an advisor to the government of Vietnam from 2010 to 2019, a period during which I served as legal counsel to Vietnam in that state's participation as an observer in the *South China Sea* Annex VII proceedings between the Philippines and China.

By the start of that period, academic writers already had recognized that the scope and limits of UNCLOS Part XV, section 2, in regard to land territory disputes are of intrinsic legal interest and carry considerable practical implication. Referring chiefly to the text of UNCLOS, the Convention's drafting history, and teleological considerations, an extensive body of writings addressed the matter.[14] No judgment or award yet had addressed it. In a short space of time, however, in 2015 and 2016, awards in two major cases did so. The first of the cases, and the more influential in regard to the interpretation of the territorial sovereignty provision of Part XV, section 2, is *Chagos Marine Protected Area (Mauritius v. United Kingdom)*. The tribunal constituted under UNCLOS Annex VII in that case adopted its final award on 18 March 2015.[15] The second case is that in which I served as

13 Crawford, *Creation of States in International Law*, 2nd edn. (2006) viii; Wood (2006) 55(4) ICLQ 994.
14 I consider the pre-2015 literature, *passim*, in Chapters 2 and 3.
15 *Chagos Marine Protected Area (Mauritius v. United Kingdom)*, PCA Case No. 2011–03 (Shearer, President; Greenwood, Hoffman, Kateka, and Wolfrum, arbitrators), Award, 18 March 2015, with dissenting and concurring opinion of Judges Kateka and Wolfrum.

an observer state's legal counsel, *South China Sea (Philippines v. China)*.[16] The Annex VII tribunal constituted in *South China Sea* adopted an award on jurisdiction and admissibility on 29 October 2015 and a final award on 12 July 2016. Chapters 4 and 5 consider *Chagos Marine Protected Area* and *South China Sea*, respectively. The two cases address the territorial sovereignty question under UNCLOS in different ways. I argue in Chapter 5 that writers—and adjudicators—have overstated the teachings of *South China Sea* in regard to that question. Both cases nevertheless have implications for international public order beyond the four corners of UNCLOS dispute settlement procedure.

Diverse participants in international relations, international lawyers among them, recognize that a crisis has arisen for international public order.[17] W. Michael Reisman, who taught me international law when I was a student at Yale (1991–1994) devoted a considerable part of his writing over six decades to problems of public order in international law; an International Court of Justice (ICJ) case in which I served as counsel with Reisman, *Macedonia v. Greece*, arose out of a public order question—enlargement of NATO.[18] Questions of public order were plainly in view as well, in the ICJ advisory proceedings on *Kosovo*, in which I served as counsel for the United Kingdom,[19] and in the *Temple of Preah Vihear* interpretation proceedings, in which I served as counsel for the Kingdom of Thailand.[20] A Security Council resolution, SCR 1244 (1999), was centrally important in the former proceedings;[21] the border clashes that instigated the latter led the Security

16 *South China Sea (Republic of Philippines v. People's Republic of China)*, PCA Case No. 2013–19 (Mensah, President; Cot, Pawlak, Soons, and Wolfrum, arbitrators).

17 Among international lawyers, see the Preface to Professor McLachlan's *Principle of Systemic Integration*, in which the theme of crisis is prevalent: McLachlan (2024) v–vi, ix. For an illustration of consensus as to the challenge, see the US executive branch's chief statement on national security under the Trump and Biden Administrations, administrations which in most respects diverged on judgments of policy. *National Security Strategy of the United States of America* (2017) 27: '[China and Russia] are contesting our geopolitical advantages and trying to change the international order in their favor,' 27; *National Security Strategy* (2022) 11: '[China] presents America's most consequential geopolitical challenge ... [and] Russia poses an immediate and ongoing threat to the regional security order in Europe.'

18 Application of the Interim Accord of 13 September 1995 (the former Yugoslav Republic of Macedonia v. Greece), Judgment, 5 December 2011, ICJ Rep. 2011 p. 644.

19 *Accordance with International Law of the Unilateral Declaration of Independence in Respect of Kosovo*, Advisory Opinion, ICJ Rep. 2010 p. 403 (22 July).

20 *Request for Interpretation of the Judgment of 15 June 1962 in the Case concerning the* Temple of Preah Vihear (Cambodia v. Thailand) *(Cambodia v. Thailand)*, Judgment, 11 November 2013, ICJ Rep. 2013 p. 281.

21 ICJ 2010 at pp. 439–452, ¶¶ 85–121 (22 July).

Council to call for a permanent ceasefire.[22] Public order questions exist in the near background in many cases,[23] but these are examples in which the questions were in the foreground.

Over the years, I have spent time in parts of the world beset by public order crises—Georgia in 2001, when the consequences of the civil war in the country's first years of independence remained visible even while more aggressive foreign intervention had yet to come; northern Cyprus in 2001 and 2002, where a final settlement still eluded the parties decades after constitutional breakdown and armed intervention; Sri Lanka in 2009 just after its internal armed conflict had ended; Bahrain in 2011 in the aftermath of the Arab Spring (and a decade after that kingdom's dispute with Qatar over maritime delimitation and territorial issues); Iraq in 2017 as the forces of the government and its allies were at last suppressing Islamic State in Mosul; and Ukraine in 2015 and 2018, as that country dealt with the consequences of armed intervention of Russia in Crimea and Donbas, and again in 2023, in the midst of the full-scale war that Russia started on 24 February 2022. The situations in these places each involved immediate or near-term questions of the stability of territorial dispositions that earlier all parties had taken to be settled.

It is almost a commonplace to refer to UNCLOS as a 'constitutional' instrument, in one form of words or another to attribute significance to it for purposes of public order. Thus, for example, the United Kingdom's ambassador, Barbara Woodward, in the 2023 General Assembly meeting on the law of the sea said that UNCLOS 'is critical to the rules-based international system' and 'has made a significant contribution to global peace, prosperity, and security by providing consistency and certainty concerning the governance of the ocean.'[24] When the ICJ delimited the maritime area around Colombia's San Andrés Islands in 2012, it took care to avoid cut-off effects that would have fragmented Colombia's exclusive economic

22 Provisional Measures, Order, ICJ 2011 p. 537, p. 549 ¶ 48 (18 July); Rpt. of SC to GA (1 August 2010 to 31 July 2011) 26.

23 Among such cases in which I have served as party counsel, see *Chevron Corporation, Texaco Petroleum Company v. Republic of Ecuador*, PCA Case No. 2009–23 (UNCITRAL [UN Commission on International Trade Law]) (Veeder, President; Grigera Naón and Lowe, arbitrators), Third Interim Award on Jurisdiction and Admissibility, 27 February 2012; as advisor on background issues of public international law relevant to the case, *Peeples & othrs v Secretary of State for Northern Ireland & othrs* [2023] UKSC 5.

24 Amb. Barbara Woodward, UK statement at the UN General Assembly, 5 December 2023: www.gov.uk/government/speeches/the-un-convention-on-the-law-of-the-sea-is-a-major-achievement-of-diplomacy-and-international-law-makinguk-statement-at-the-un-general-assembly

zone. The Court stated that 'the delimitation ... must take into account the need of contributing to the public order of the oceans.'[25] These expressions of the point are located at opposite ends of a spectrum between generality and specificity—one serving to affirm political support for the Convention in a multilateral forum, the other applying considerations of public order to arrive at a dispositive result (lines of delimitation) in a maritime dispute adjudicated in court between two states. But what, if anything, does public order have to do with this area of law in other settings? Between the general and the specific, what insight does a public order perspective on UNCLOS supply?

UNCLOS contains a system for dispute settlement, set out in Part XV, section 2, that states may employ to address some of the most sensitive disputes that arise in their international relations. The importance of resources in the seas increases over time.[26] The sensitivity of disputes over maritime entitlements increases at least proportionately. The public order significance of UNCLOS is demonstrable in the present-day disputes that parties might adjudicate under its procedures.

The Convention also reflects the particular state of international public order that prevailed at the time of its drafting and adoption.

The UNCLOS dispute settlement system came into being during the Cold War, which is to say a time of Great Power contestation. Geopolitical risks were conspicuous during the Cold War. However, this was also a time of stability.[27] The boundaries of states were in large part settled by the time the Cold War began. The colonial territories that had not become states would keep the boundaries they had when they did. The cases of postcolonial partition, especially that of India, were exceptional and, even there, boundaries with *third states* largely stayed the same. Moreover, a combination of rules, institutions, and political reality ensured that states respected and preserved the boundaries that they had settled. The USSR in particular championed stability of international boundaries.[28] The main concern of that state was

25 *Territorial and Maritime dispute (Nicaragua v. Colombia)*, Judgment, 19 November 2012, ICJ Rep. 2012 p. 624, p. 716, ¶ 244. Note: I assisted with the written submissions (for Colombia) in the merits phase.

26 Fish, oil, and natural gas are of critical importance. Anticipated to gain importance are polymetallic nodules in the Area, to be exploited through deep seabed mining, as to which see *Activities in the Area*, ITLOS Rep. 2011 p. 10, *passim*.

27 Ford, 'Arms Control and Strategic Stability' in Colby & Gerson (eds.), *Strategic Stability* (2013) 201, 204.

28 See, for example, the USSR's termination of support for Somalia when, in the Ogaden war, Somalia pursued forcible change of boundaries against Djibouti and Ethiopia: Roy Lyons, 'The USSR, China and the Horn of Africa' (May–August 1978) *Review of African Political Economy* 5, 10–11.

with boundaries in Europe,[29] but its legal position, which aligned with its approach to geopolitics, was widely shared. States in Latin America and newly independent states in Africa and South Asia, for their own reasons and in the distinct circumstances of decolonization, favored a presumption that boundaries of the colonial era become the international boundaries of new states,[30] and that a boundary, once peacefully settled between states, remains where it is settled, unless the states concerned consent to its modification. Even where there were misgivings, as in Africa in the last years of colonialism and first years of independence, territorial stability in the main prevailed.[31]

There had been a long epoch in which states routinely used force and threat to modify their spatial relations. By the time of the UN Conferences on the Law of the Sea, that epoch had passed. In place of a law that had accommodated the forcible change of boundaries, even accepted it as routine, there came a law that prohibited—absolutely—forcible change of a boundary between states where the boundary had been peacefully settled.

The law of the sea was not the only domain of international law in which the rules and institutions underwent rapid development in the new epoch of spatial stability. An enormous outgrowth of international law began after the end of World War II and intensified after the end of the Cold War.[32] Ingrid Brunk and Monika Hakimi, coeditors-in-chief of the *American Journal of International Law*, observe that 'territorially-defined states have … been the building blocks of the international order.'[33] For definition to have utility, however, it must be reliable over time. It is not only that states have come to be the prevalent actors of international law and have come to have clear spatial definition. It is also that their spatial definition has come to be presumptive and thus predictably endures. The relation between spatial stability and the efflorescence of modern international law is undertheorized, but that the two are correlated is unmistakable.[34]

29 Movchan (1977) 154 Hag. Rec. 4, 8–12. See also Grant (2014) 25(4) *Security and Human Rights* 383–405.

30 *Case concerning the Frontier Dispute (Burkina Faso/Republic of Mali)*, Judgment (Chamber: Bedjaoui, President; Judges Lachs, Ruda; Judges *ad hoc* Luchaire, Abi-Saab), 22 December 1986, ICJ Rep. p. 554, p. 564, ¶ 19; *Case concerning Territorial and maritime Dispute between Nicaragua and Honduras in the Caribbean Sea (Nicaragua v. Honduras)*, Judgment, 8 October 2007, ICJ Rep. 2007 p. 659, p. 706, ¶ 151.

31 See, for example, ILC discussion on boundary régimes established by a treaty, Comment of Morocco, ILC Yearbook 1974 vol. II, Part One, p. 76. See generally Ahmed, *Boundaries and Secession in Africa* (2015) 47–74.

32 For my reflections, see (2022) 13(1) JIDS 41–53.

33 See Brunk & Hakimi (2024) 118(3) AJIL 417, 466.

34 Professor Bardonnet thought that the definitiveness and stability of borders 'at least *prima facie*' was a contributing 'factor to peace and security in the relations among neighboring States.' Bardonnet (1976) 153 Hag. Rec. 15, 30.

The dispute settlement system of UNCLOS is no guarantor of world peace. Its effects are modest when compared to geopolitical convulsions such as the world wars or the end of the USSR. It nevertheless exists as part of a particular public order. It is a system of law and procedure surrounded by a larger system of sometimes coexisting, sometimes clashing, sovereigns. If one believes that UNCLOS influences public order, then one would counsel those who operate its dispute settlement system not to ignore that, through UNCLOS, they, too, influence public order: when adjudicators exercise the dispute settlement function, they influence the public order in which the dispute settlement procedure exists. If instead one takes the formalist's view, and one maintains that the Convention and its procedures are not to be understood as a 'constitutional' order but, instead, as rules and tools that an adjudicator applies one case at a time—which, for practical purposes, for the most part, is how one indeed must understand them—then one nevertheless ought to reach much the same conclusion: the UNCLOS adjudicator should keep public order in view, because, past a point, where that order goes, UNCLOS necessarily in time will follow. Moreover, judges who compose International Tribunal for the Law of the Sea (ITLOS) and arbitrators who compose UNCLOS Annex VII tribunals are not the only international law decision-makers. Others, too, are called on to reach decisions relevant to public order—politicians, civil servants, and soldiers, to name a few—and it would be as naïve to think that these decision-makers pay no heed to the judgments and awards of adjudicators as it would be to think that every one of them in every situation scrupulously adheres to the international adjudicator's every command. The importance of the full range of actors involved in international law decision-making equally suggests that we should take care about the system around the system.

Yet, whether or not a dispute entails considerations of public order, adjudicators called on to settle a dispute must apply ordinary methods of legal reasoning. Adjudicators called on to say whether a state's conduct in a maritime area accords with another state's rights under UNCLOS are involved in the international relations of two sovereigns. Latent in disputes that sovereigns submit to UNCLOS procedures are matters of public order that seldom surface in a dispute between commercial parties over, say, the delivery of a cargo of sugar. (Though even a dispute such as that might have a public order element.)[35] Parties expect adjudicators to employ much

35 Thus, in the famous pre-State Immunity Act 1978 (UK) case, *I Congreso del Partido*, Cuba's counsel argued that '[t]he act of Cuba was a classical act of one sovereign state against another to mark detestation of its character … in effect [a declaration of] economic war.' *I Congreso del Partido* [1983] 1 A.C. at 251, but, having examined the evidence, the House of Lords (divided 3 to 2) decided that the disputed transactions were commercial and thus not embraced by sovereign immunity. *Ibid.* at 276 (Lord Diplock), 278 (Lord Keith), 279 (Lord Bridge).

the same methods regardless of the particulars of jurisdiction, procedure, or substantive claim. True, an UNCLOS adjudicator is not a commercial court judge. At the same time, recognizing the adjudicator's identity and function within the system is not to call for subjecting UNCLOS cases to special methods. To the contrary. The prescription that I argue in this book emerges is that adjudicators who apply UNCLOS should aim to use the methods of decision-making that, in at least a general way, parties expect adjudicators under all legal procedures to use.

This leads to the third matter that the book addresses. Whether one calls them a 'method' or a 'technique' or 'the tools of the trade,' certain practices and habits of mind are indispensable in law. This includes law as advocacy, law as decision-making, and law as social science. Under international law, method arguably performs an even more important function than it does in other branches of law. The relative importance of method in international law becomes evident when we consider one of the salient characteristics of international law: its incompleteness as a legal system. H. L. A. Hart's verdict that international law is not a complete system of law lingers over the discipline and its practice.[36] The apprehensions that international law is not complete law are not isolated or transitory. However, even the most acid skeptics of international law, when the matter is put to them rigorously, are likely to concede that in at least one respect what we do is very much *law*: we use methods of analysis, scrutiny, and reasoning that are characteristically legal. Whether we are advising as counsel, arguing as advocates, reasoning as adjudicators, or discoursing as academics, we are doing much the same as our colleagues in other branches of law.

It is to be suggested, as my friend and colleague Campbell McLachlan does,[37] and as the UN International Law Commission (ILC) has done as well, in particular in its work on methods for identifying rules of customary

36 Hart, *The Concept of Law* (2012; 1961) 214: 'The absence of these institutions [legislature, courts with compulsory jurisdiction, and centrally organized sanctions] means that the rules for states resemble that simple form of social structure, consisting only of primary rules of obligation, which, when we find it among societies of individuals, we are accustomed to contrast with a developed legal system.' See further Payandeh (2010) 21(4) EJIL 967–995.

37 Professor McLachlan indeed describes the 'principle of systemic integration,' which is the subject of his magisterial 2024 study on that matter, as 'provid[ing] a legal reasoning *technique*' (emphasis added). McLachlan (2024) p. 5, § 1.05. He takes as a necessary starting point 'methods and techniques' for dealing with the 'collisions' among 'norms and regimes and the rules' of international law: *ibid.*, quoting Martti Koskenniemi, Chairman, Report of the Study Group on Fragmentation of International Law: Difficulties arising from the Diversification and Expansion of International Law, 2006 ILC Yearbook, vol. II Part One, p. 100, ¶ 493 (13 April 2006).

international law,[38] that legal method is the sinew that holds diverse parts of international law together. Françoise Hampson, whose work Professor McLachlan highlights in the introduction to *The Principle of Systemic Integration*, suggested in 2012 that researchers would uncover important insights into the 'conundrum' of legal fragmentation by focusing on 'the horizontal collisions in international law and the tools available and substantive principles relevant to their determination.'[39] Professor McLachlan, for his part, suggests that we will gain insight '[a]t the level of *legal technique*' by considering 'how the principle of systemic integration actually works in practice … where it fits within a broader set of techniques of interpretation and application of rules.'[40] Put in slightly different terms, if the conflicts and contradictions that have arisen in international law in its recent decades of enlargement are to be conciliated, then legal method is to be the conciliator.

A corollary follows from the proposition that it is legal method that supplies coherence to international law. If the proposition is credible, and I believe that it is, that coherence in international law comes from method, then we should be alert to signs of methodological lapse.[41] We as international lawyers are not in a system that can count on hierarchy to impose order. That insight is central to understanding the challenge of legal fragmentation and is one of the main conclusions of the ILC's 2006 report on the matter—'no homogenous, hierarchical meta-system is realistically available to do away' with the problems of fragmentation in international law.[42] It is in international law that Austin's model of law—equating law to the effective power to impose compliance with command[43]—is least convincing. Either that, or

38 Draft conclusion on identification of customary international law, with commentaries (2018), ILC Yearbook 2018 vol. II, Part Two, p. 122, General comment (2): 'The present draft conclusions concern *the methodology* for identifying rules of customary international law' (emphasis added). Lest one mistakenly infer from the numbering that this point of substance is second in sequence, one should note that General comment (2) is the Commission's first substantive comment on the topic. General comment (1) is confined to the ordinary notice that the draft conclusions 'are to be read together with the commentaries.'

39 Hampson in Sheeran & Rodley (eds.), *Routledge Handbook of International Human Rights Law* (2013) 185, 194, quoted at McLachlan (2024) p. 5 § 1.05.

40 McLachlan (2024) p. 5 § 1.06 (emphasis added).

41 As adjudicators in recent cases are. See *Embassy of Mexico in Quito (Mexico v. Ecuador)*, Request for Provisional Measures, Order, 23 May 2024, ICJ Rep. 2024, Declaration of Judge Nolte, ¶¶ 11–14.

42 Martti Koskenniemi, Chairman, Report of the Study Group on Fragmentation of International Law: Difficulties arising from the Diversification and Expansion of International Law, 2006 ILC Yearbook, vol. II, Part One, p. 100, ¶ 493 (13 April 2006).

43 Austin, *Province of Jurisprudence* (1995; orig. 1832), Lecture I, pp. 18–37, *passim* and esp. at p. 33 on 'imperfect laws.'

the premise that 'international law' is law is unconvincing. For that reason—because no institution has effective power over all who are subject to international law—legal method has special centrality to international law. Method is important to all branches of law, but international law is the branch in which it is most important. Lose the method, and, in international law, you lose the law.

The chapters that follow concern UNCLOS jurisdiction as parties invoke it in a time of public order crisis. Within the confines of that jurisdiction, it well may be that the boldest ambitions for international law are best served when lawyers apply our most familiar methods.

Acknowledgments

In spring and summer 2023, two law firms each known for work in international investment arbitration and sovereign-to-sovereign disputes invited me to address their lawyers on a topic of my choosing. My own work in these areas of practice over nearly thirty years, along with my academic writings, suggested the topic of sovereignty disputes and law of the sea. The basic idea for this book emerged from those talks at Volterra Fietta at its annual retreat in Oxfordshire, UK, and Three Crowns LPP at its offices in Washington, DC and from my ongoing work and reflection on the challenges that present-day geopolitics creates for the practice of law in this field.

The book profits from comments from a number of friends and colleagues who saw it in draft, including Alberto Alvarez-Jimenez, Oude Elferink, Markus Gehring, Monika Hakimi, Neil Kaplan CBE KC SBS, Avidan Kent, Bjørn Kunoy, Hayk Kupelyants, Juliette McIntyre, Cameron Miles, Omri Sender, Yoshifumi Tanaka, Kevin Toh, Jamie Trinidad KC, and Noam Zamir.

The Lauterpacht Centre for International Law, where I have been a fellow since 2002, continued to furnish a lively and supportive environment during the period in which I worked on the manuscript that became this book.

I thank Siobhán Poole, senior commissioning editor, and Humairaa Dudhwala, assistant editor for law, at Manchester University Press, for their effort to bring this work to press, and Professors Iain Scobbie and Jean d'Aspremont, the series editors for the Melland Schill Studies in International Law, for their confidence in the project from the start. I also thank the anonymous referees who supplied helpful reports on the text in draft.

Any error or opinion in the book is mine, and nothing herein necessarily reflects the view of any organization or individual besides my own. The presentation of legal materials in the book is current up to January 2025.

Dr. Thomas D. Grant,
Cambridge University,
25 February 2025

Abbreviations

AdV	Archiv des Völkerrechts
AJIL	American Journal of International Law
ARSIWA	2001 ILC draft Articles on Responsibility of States for Internationally Wrongful Acts
Asian YBIL	Asian Yearbook of International Law
ASIL Proc	Proceedings of the American Society of International Law
BIICL	British Institute of International and Comparative Law
BIOT	British Indian Ocean Territory
BIT	bilateral investment treaty
BYIL	British Yearbook of International Law
Can. YBIL	Canadian Yearbook of International Law
CERD	Convention on the Elimination of All Forms of Racial Discrimination
Colum. LR	Columbia Law Review
C(T)YBIL	Chinese (Taiwan) Yearbook of International Law and Affairs
ECtHR	European Court of Human Rights
EEZ	exclusive economic zone
EHRR	European Human Rights Reports
EJIL	European Journal of International Law
GAR	UN General Assembly resolution
Hag. Rec	Recueil des cours de la Haye (Collected Course of the Hague Academy)
HILJ	Harvard International Law Journal
HLR	Harvard Law Review
ICC	International Chamber of Commerce
ICCPR	International Covenant on Civil and Political Rights
ICJ	International Court of Justice
ICLQ	International & Comparative Law Quarterly
ICSFT	International Convention for the Suppression of the Financing of Terrorism

ICSID	International Centre for Settlement of Investment Disputes
IJMCL	The International Journal of Marine and Coastal Law
ILA	International Law Association
ILC	UN International Law Commission
ILM	International Legal Materials
ILR	International Law Reports
ISNT	informal single negotiating text
ITLOS	International Tribunal for the Law of the Sea
JIDS	Journal of International Dispute Settlement
Leiden JIL	Leiden Journal of International Law
LQR	Law Quarterly Review
LTE	low-tide elevation
Melbourne JIL	Melbourne Journal of International Law
MLR	Modern Law Review
MPA	marine protected area
NAFTA	North American Free Trade Agreement
Neth. YBIL	Netherlands Yearbook of International Law
ODIL	Ocean Development & International Law (journal)
PACE	Parliamentary Assembly of the Council of Europe
PCA	Permanent Court of Arbitration
PCIJ	Permanent Court of International Justice
Pol. YBIL	Polish Yearbook of International Law
RIAA	UN Reports of International Arbitral Awards
SCR	UN Security Council resolution
UAE	United Arab Emirates
UN	United Nations
UNCITRAL	UN Commission on International Trade Law
UNCLOS	UN Convention on the Law of the Sea 1982
UNGA	United Nations General Assembly
UNTS	United Nations Treaty Series
VCLT	Vienna Convention on the Law of Treaties 1969
Virg. LR	Virginia Law Review
WTO	World Trade Organization
YLJ	Yale Law Journal
YJIL	Yale Journal of International Law
ZaöRV	Zeitschrift für ausländisches öffentliches Recht und Völkerrecht

Judgments and awards

Accordance with International Law of the Unilateral Declaration of Independence in respect of Kosovo, Advisory Opinion, ICJ 2010 p. 403 (22 July).

Aegean Sea Continental Shelf Case (Greece v. Turkey), Judgment, ICJ 1978 p. 3 (19 December).

Aeroport Belbek LLC and Mr. Igor Valerievich Kolomoisky v. the Russian Federation, PCA Case No. 2015–07 (Dupuy, President; Bethlehem and Mikulka, arbitrators), Decision on Jurisdiction (24 February 2017).

Aeroport Belbek LLC and Mr. Igor Valerievich Kolomoisky v. the Russian Federation, PCA Case No. 2015–07 (Dupuy, President; Bethlehem and Mikulka, arbitrators), Partial Award (liability) (4 February 2019).

Ahmadou Sadio Diallo (Republic of Guinea v. Democratic Republic of the Congo), Merits, Judgment, ICJ 2010 p. 639 (3 November).

Alabama v. King & Boozer, 314 U.S. 1, 9 (1941).

Allegations of Genocide under the Convention on the Prevention and Punishment of the Crime of Genocide (Ukraine v. Russian Federation), Provisional Measures, Order, ICJ 2022 p. 211 (16 March).

Allegations of Genocide (Ukraine v. Russian Federation: 32 States intervening), Preliminary Objections, ICJ 2024 (2 February).

Al-Skeini v. UK, (2011) 53 EHRR 18.

Alvarez-Machain v. U.S., 331 F. 3d 604 (9th Cir. 2003) (vacated, 374 F.3d 1384 (2004)).

Appeal relating to jurisdiction of the ICAO Council (India v. Pakistan), ICJ 1972 p. 46 (18 August).

Application of the Convention on the Prevention and Punishment of the Crime of Genocide (Bosnia and Herzegovina v. Yugoslavia (Serbia and

Montenegro)), Further Requests for the Indication of Provisional Measures, Sep. Op. Judge Shahabuddeen, ICJ 1993 p. 353 (13 September).

Application for Revision of the Judgment of 11 July 1996 in the Case concerning Application of the Convention on the Prevention and Punishment of the Crime of Genocide (Bosnia and Herzegovina v. Yugoslavia), Preliminary Objections (Yugoslavia v. Bosnia and Herzegovina), Dis. Op. Judge Dimitrijević, ICJ 2003 p. 53 (3 February).

Application of the Convention on the prevention and punishment of the crime of genocide (*Bosnia and Herzegovina v. Serbia and Montenegro*), ICJ 2007 p. 43 (3 February).

Application of the International Convention on the Elimination of All Forms of Racial Discrimination (Qatar v. *United Arab Emirates)*, Provisional Measures, Dis. Op. Judge *ad hoc* Cot, ICJ 2019 p. 402 (14 June).

Application of the Convention on the Prevention and Punishment of the Crime of Genocide (Bosnia and Herzegovina v. Serbia and Montenegro), Judgment, ICJ 2007 p. 43 (26 February).

Application of the Convention on the Prevention and Punishment of the Crime of Genocide (Croatia v. Serbia), Judgment, ICJ 2015 p. 3 (3 February).

Application of the International Convention for the Suppression of the Financing of Terrorism and of the International Convention on the Elimination of All Forms of Racial Discrimination (Ukraine v. Russian Federation), Order, Indication of Provisional Measures, ICJ 2017 p. 104 (19 April).

Application of the International Convention for the Suppression of the Financing of Terrorism and of the International Convention on the Elimination of All Forms of Racial Discrimination (Ukraine v. Russian Federation), Preliminary Objections, ICJ 2019 p. 558 (8 November).

Application of the International Convention for the Suppression of the Financing of Terrorism and of the International Convention on the Elimination of All Forms of Racial Discrimination (Ukraine v. Russian Federation), Judgment, ICJ 2024 (31 January).

The 'ARA Libertad' (Argentina v. Ghana), Provisional Measures, Order, ITLOS 2012 p. 332 (15 December).

The 'ARA Libertad' Case (Argentina v. Ghana), Provisional Measures, Joint Sep. Op. Wolfrum and Cot, ITLOS 2012 p. 363 (15 December).

Arbitral Award of 3 October 1899 (Guyana v. Venezuela), Preliminary Objection, ICJ 2023 p. 262 (6 April).

Arbitral Award of 3 October 1899 (Guyana v. Venezuela), Preliminary Objection, Declaration of Judge *ad hoc* Wolfrum, ICJ 2023 p. 300 (6 April).

Arbitral Award of 3 October 1899 (Guyana v. Venezuela), ICJ 2023, Provisional Measures, Order (1 December).

Arctic Sunrise (Netherlands v. Russia), PCA Case No. 2014–02, Award on Jurisdiction (26 November 2014).

Arctic Sunrise (Netherlands v. Russia), PCA Case No. 2014–02, Annex VII tribunal (Mensah, President; Burmester, Soons, Symonides, and Székely, arbitrators), Award, Merits, (14 August 2015).

Armed Activities in the Territory of the Congo (New Application: 2002) (Democratic Republic of the Congo v. Rwanda), ICJ 2006 p. 6 (3 February).

Armed Activities on the Territory of the Congo (Democratic Republic of the Congo v. Uganda), Reparations, Sep. Op. Judge Yusuf, ICJ 2022 p. 145 (9 February).

Arrest Warrant of 11 April 2000 (Democratic Republic of Congo v. *Belgium)*, Judgment, ICJ 2002 p. 3 (14 February).

Barbados/Trinidad and Tobago, Case 2004–02, UNCLOS Annex VII (Schwebel, President; Brownlie, Lowe, Orrego Vicuña, and Watts, arbitrators), Award (11 April 2006).

Barcelona Traction, Light and Power Company, Limited (New Application: 1962) (Belgium v. Spain), Preliminary Objections, ICJ 1970 p. 3 (5 February).

Bay of Bengal Maritime Boundary Arbitration (Bangladesh v. *India)* (Wolfrum, President; Cot, Mensah, Rao, and Shearer, arbitrators) Award (7 July 2014).

Belhaj v. Straw [2017] UKSC 3.

Cambodia Power Company v. Kingdom of Cambodia, Electricité du Cambodge, ICSID Case No ARB/09/18 (Kaplan, President; Beechey and Landau, arbitrators), Award on Jurisdiction (22 March 2011).

CEAC Holdings v. Montenegro, ICSID Case No. ARB/14/8 (Hanotiau, President; Park & Stern, Arbitrators), Award (26 July 2016).

Certain Activities carried out by Nicaragua in the Border Area (Costa Rica v. Nicaragua), Request for Provisional Measures, Order, ICJ 2011 p. 6 (8 March).

Certain activities carried out by Nicaragua in the Border Area (Costa Rica v. Nicaragua)/Construction of a Road in Costa Rica along the San Juan River (Nicaragua v. Costa Rica), Judgment, ICJ 2015 p. 665 (16 December).

Certain German Interests in Polish Upper Silesia (Preliminary Objections), 1925 PCIJ Ser A No 6 (25 August).

Certain Norwegian Loans (France v. *Norway)*, Sep. Op. Judge Sir Hersch Lauterpacht, ICJ 1957 p. 34 (6 July).

Chagos Marine Protected Area Arbitration (Mauritius v. United Kingdom), UNCLOS Annex VII/PCA Case. No. 2011–03 (Shearer, President; Greenwood, Hoffmann, Kateka, and Wolfrum, members) (Kateka and Wolfrum dissenting in part), Award (18 March 2015).

Continental Shelf (Libya/Malta), Judgment, ICJ 1985 p. 13 (3 June).

Continental Shelf (Tunisia/Libya), Judgment, ICJ 1982 p. 18 (24 February).

Continental Shelf (Tunisia/Libya), Sep. Op. Judge Jímenez de Arechaga, ICJ 1982 p. 100 (24 February).

Convention on the Prevention and Punishment of the Crime of Genocide (Croatia v. Serbia), ICJ 2015 p. 3 (3 February).

Corfu Channel (United Kingdom v. Albania), Judgment, ICJ 1949 p. 4 (9 April).

Delimitation of the maritime boundary between Ghana and Côte d'Ivoire in the Atlantic Ocean (Ghana/Côte d'Ivoire), Provisional Measures, Order, ITLOS 2015 p. 146 (25 April).

Delimitation of the maritime boundary between Ghana and Côte d'Ivoire in the Atlantic Ocean (Ghana/Côte d'Ivoire), Judgment, ITLOS 2017 p. 4 (23 September).

Delimitation of the Maritime Boundary in the Gulf of Maine (Canada/United States of America), Judgment, ICJ 1984 p. 246 (12 October).

Delimitation of the Maritime Boundary between Mauritius and Maldives in the Indian Ocean (Mauritius/Maldives), Preliminary Objections, Special Chamber (Judge Paik, President; Judges Jesus, Pawlak, Yanai, Bouguetaia, Heidar, and Chadha, members; Judges *ad hoc* Oxman and Schrijver), ITLOS 2021 p. 16 (28 January).

Dispute concerning delimitation of the maritime boundary between Mauritius and Maldives in the Indian Ocean (Mauritius/Maldives), Preliminary Objections, Sep. & Dis. Op. Judge *ad hoc* Oxman, ITLOS 2021 p. 118 (28 January).

Dispute concerning delimitation of the maritime boundary between Mauritius and Maldives in the Indian Ocean (Mauritius/Maldives), Merits, Special Chamber, ITLOS Case No. 28 (28 April 2023).*Dispute Concerning Coastal*

State Rights in the Black Sea, Sea of Azov, and Kerch Strait (Ukraine v. Russia), Annex VII/PCA Case No. 2017–06 (Paik, President; Bouguetaia, Gómez Robledo, Lowe, and Golitsyn, arbitrators), Preliminary Objections (21 February 2020).

Dispute concerning delimitation of the maritime boundary between Bangladesh and Myanmar in the Bay of Bengal (Bangladesh/Myanmar), Judgment, ITLOS 2012 p. 4 (14 March).

Dispute concerning the detention of Three Ukrainian Naval Vessels (Ukraine v. Russian Federation), Provisional Measures, Order, ITLOS 2019 p. 283 (25 May).

Dispute concerning the Detention of Ukrainian Naval Vessels and Servicemen (Ukraine v. the Russian Federation), PCA Case No. 2019–28 (McRae, President; Eiriksson, Wolfrum, Golitsyn, and Greenwood, arbitrators), Procedural Order No. 1 (22 November 2019).

Dispute concerning the Detention of Ukrainian Naval Vessels and Servicemen, PCA Case No. 2019–28, UNCLOS Annex VII tribunal (McRae, President; Eiriksson, Wolfrum, Golitsyn, and Greenwood, members), Award on Preliminary Objections (27 June 2022).

Duzgit Integrity Arbitration (Malta v. São Tomé and Príncipe), PCA Case No. 2014–07, UNCLOS Annex VII tribunal (Soons, President; Kateka and Treves, arbitrators), Award (5 September 2016).

East Timor (Portugal v. Australia), ICJ 1995 p. 90 (30 June).

EEOC v. Arabian American Oil Co., 499 U.S. 244 (1991).

Electricity Company of Sofia and Bulgaria (Belg. v. Bulg.), Interim Measures of Protection, Order, 1939 PCIJ Ser. A/B No. 79 p. 193 (5 December).

The 'Enrica Lexie' Incident (Italy v. India), Provisional Measures, Order, ITLOS 2015 p. 182 (24 August).

Enrica Lexie (Italian Republic v. Republic of India), PCA Case No. 2015–28, Annex VII Tribunal (Golitsyn, President; Paik, Robinson, Francioni, and Rao, members), Award (21 May 2020).

Enrica Lexie, Concurring and Dissenting Opinion, Dr. P. S. Rao, (21 May 2020).

Eritrea/Ethiopia, PCA Case No. 2001–02, Eritrea-Ethiopia Claims Commission (van Houtte, President; Aldrich, Crook, Paul, and Reed, arbitrators), *Jus ad Bellum* (Ethiopia's Claims no. 1–8), Partial Award (19 December 2005).

Eritrea/Yemen, PCA Case No. 1996–04, Tribunal constituted under Arbitration Agreement of 3 October 1996 (Jennings, President; Schwebel, El-Kosheri, Highet, and Higgins, members), First Stage, Territorial Sovereignty and Scope of the Dispute, Award (9 October 1998).

Eritrea/Yemen, PCA Case No. 1996–04, Second Stage, Maritime Delimitation, Award (17 December 1999).

Everest Estate LLC et al. v. the Russian Federation, PCA Case No. 2015–36 (Rigo Sureda, President; Reisman and Knieper, arbitrators), Decision on Jurisdiction (19 March 2017).

Everest Estate LLC et al. v. the Russian Federation, PCA Case No. 2015–36, Award on the Merits (2 May 2018).

Fisheries Jurisdiction (Spain v. Canada), Jurisdiction, ICJ 1998 p. 432 (4 December).

Frontier Dispute (Burkina Faso/Republic of Mali), ICJ 1986 p. 566 (22 December).

Gabčíkovo-Nagymaros Project (Hungary/Slovakia), Judgment, ICJ 1997 p. 7 (25 September).

Government of the Province of East Kalimantan v. PT Kaltim Prima Coal, Rio Tinto PLC, BP P.L.C., Pacific Resources Investments Limited, BP International Limited, Sangatta Holdings Limited, and Kalimantan Coal Limited, ICSID Case No. Art/07/03 (Kaufmann-Kohler, President; Hwang & van den Berg, Arbitrators), Award on Jurisdiction (28 December 2009).

Groupe Danone v. Commission of the European Communities, Case C-3/06 P, Opinion of the Advocate General (Poiares Maduro) (16 November 2006).

Guyana v. Suriname, PCA Case No. 2004–4, UNCLOS Annex VII (Nelson, President; Franck, Smit, Shearer, and Hossain, arbitrators), Award (17 September 2007).

Guzzardi v. Italy, ECtHR, App. no. 7367/76, Dis. Op. Judge Sir Gerald Fitzmaurice (6 November 1980).

Hrvatska Elektroprivreda d.d. v. Republic of Slovenia, ICSID Case No. ARB/05/24 (Williams, President; Paulsson and Brower, arbitrators), Decision on the Treaty Interpretation Issue (12 June 2009).

Içkale Insaat Limited Sirketi v. Turkmenistan, ICSID Case No. ARB/10/24 (Heiskanen, President; Lamm and Sands, arbitrators), Award (8 March 2016).

Immunities and Criminal Proceedings (Equatorial Guinea v. France), Judgment, ICJ 2020 p. 300 (11 December).

In the matter of an arbitration under the Arbitration Agreement between the Government of the Republic of Croatia and the Government of Slovenia, Signed on 4 November 2009 (Croatia/Slovenia), PCA Case No. 2012–04 (Guillaume, President; Einar Fife, Lowe, Michel, and Simma, arbitrators), Final Award (29 June 2017).

Interpretation of the Greco-Turkish Agreement of December 1st, 1926 (Final Protocol, Article IV), Advisory Opinion, 1928 PCIJ Ser. B No. 16 p. 20 (28 August).

J. H. Rayner (Mincing Lane) Ltd v. Department of Trade and Industry [1990] 2 AC 418 (Templeman LJ).

The King v. Turner (1816) 5 Maule and Selwyn 206, 210 (Lord Ellenborough C.J.).

Land and Maritime Boundary between Cameroon and Nigeria (Cameroon v. *Nigeria: Equatorial Guinea intervening)*, Judgment, ICJ 2002 p. 303 (10 October).

Land Reclamation by Singapore in and around the Straits of Johor (Malaysia v. Singapore), Provisional Measures, Order, ITLOS 2003 p. 10 (8 October).

Legal Consequences arising from the Policies and Practices of Israel in the Occupied Palestinian Territory, Including East Jerusalem, ICJ 2024, Advisory Opinion (19 July).

Legal Consequences arising from the Policies and Practices of Israel in the Occupied Palestinian Territory, Including East Jerusalem, ICJ 2024, Dissenting Opinion of Vice-President Sebutinde (19 July).

Legal Consequences of the Construction of a Wall in the Occupied Palestinian Territory, Advisory Opinion, ICJ 2004 p. 136 (9 July).

Legal Consequences of the Separation of the Chagos Archipelago from Mauritius in 1965, Advisory Opinion, ICJ 2019 p. 95 (25 February).

Lotus (France v. Turkey), 1927 PCIJ Ser. A. No. 10 at 18–19 (7 September).

M/V 'Louisa' (Saint Vincent and the Grenadines v. Kingdom of Spain), Judgment, ITLOS 2013 p. 4 (28 May).

M/V 'Louisa' (*Saint Vincent and the Grenadines v. Kingdom of Spain)*, Sep. Op. Judge Ndiaye, ITLOS 2013 p. 57 (28 May).

M/V 'Saiga' (Saint Vincent and the Grenadines v. *Guinea), Prompt Release*, Judgment, ITLOS 1997 p. 16 (4 December).

M/V 'Saiga' (No. 2) (Saint Vincent and the Grenadines v. Guinea), Judgment, ITLOS 1999 p. 10 (1 July).

M/V 'Virginia G' Case (Panama/Guinea-Bissau), ITLOS 2014 p. 4 (14 April).

M'Culloch v. *Maryland*, 22 U.S. (4 Wheat.) 316, 307 (1819) (Marshall, CCJ).

Malaysian Historical Salvors SDN BHD v. Government of Malaysia, ICSID Case No. ARB/05/10 (Schwebel, President; Shahabuddeen and Tomka, *ad hoc* committee members), Decision on the Application for Annulment (16 April 2009).

Maritime Delimitation and Territorial Questions between Qatar and Bahrain (Qatar v. Bahrain), Merits, ICJ 2001 p. 40 (16 March).

Maritime Delimitation in the Black Sea (Romania v. Ukraine), Judgment, ICJ 2009 p. 61 (3 February).

Maritime Delimitation in the Indian Ocean (Somalia v. Kenya), Judgment, ICJ 2021 p. 206 (12 October).

Maritime Dispute (Peru v. Chile), Judgment, ICJ 2014 p. 3 (27 January).

Mavromatis Palestine Concessions, Judgment on Objection to Jurisdiction, 1924 PCIJ Ser. A No. 2 p. 11 (30 August).

Methanex Corp. v. United States of America, NAFTA/UNCITRAL (Veeder, President; Christopher and Rowley, arbitrators), Partial Award, Jurisdiction and Admissibility (7 August 2002).

Military and Paramilitary Activities in and against Nicaragua (Nicaragua v. United States of America), Merits, ICJ 1986 p. 14 (27 June).

Military and Paramilitary Activities in and Against Nicaragua (Nicaragua v. United States of America), Dis. Op. Judge Oda, ICJ 1986 p. 212 (27 June).

Monetary Gold Removed from Rome in 1943 (Italy v. France, U.K., U.S.), ICJ 1954 p. 19 (15 June).

Niko Resources (Bangladesh) Ltd. v. Bangladesh Oil Gas and Mineral Corp. (Petrobangla) and Bangladesh Petroleum Exploration and Production Co. Ltd. (BAPEX), ICSID Case No. ARB/10/18 (Schneider, President; McLachlan and Paulsson, members), Decision on Jurisdiction (18 August 2013).

Niko Resources (Bangladesh) Ltd. v. Bangladesh Oil Gas and Mineral Corp. (Petrobangla) and Bangladesh Petroleum Exploration and Production Co. Ltd. (BAPEX), ICSID Case No. ARB/10/18 (Zuleta, President of the *ad hoc* Committee; Annacker and Ali Khan, members), Decision on Annulment (12 October 2023).

Niko Resources (Bangladesh) Ltd., ICSID Case No. ARB/10/18, Dis. Op. Makhdoom Ali Khan (12 October 2023).

NJSC Naftogaz of Ukraine, PJSC State Joint Stock Company Chornomornaftogax, PJSC Ukrgasvydobuvannya and others v. Russian Federation, PCA Case No. 2017–16 (Binnie, President; Stanivuković and Poncent, arbitrators), Partial Award (22 February 2019).

North Sea Continental Shelf (Federal Republic of Germany/Denmark; Federal Republic of Germany/Netherlands), Judgment, ICJ 1969 p. 3 (20 February).

Northern Cameroons (Cameroon v. United Kingdom), Preliminary Objections, ICJ 1963 p. 15 (2 December).

Norway—Restrictions on Imports of Apples and Pears, L/6474– 36S/306, GATT, Panel Report, 22 June 1989.

Obligation to Negotiate Access to the Pacific Ocean (Bolivia v. Chile), Preliminary Objections, ICJ 2015 p. 592 (24 September).

Obligation to Prosecute or Extradite (Belgium v. Senegal), ICJ 2012 p. 422 (20 July).

Obligations concerning Negotiations relating to Cessation of the Nuclear Arms Race and Nuclear Disarmament (Marshall Islands v. India), Jurisdiction and Admissibility, ICJ 2016 p. 255 (5 October).

Obligations concerning Negotiations relating to Cessation of the Nuclear Arms Race and Nuclear Disarmament (Marshall Islands v. Pakistan), Jurisdiction and Admissibility, ICJ 2016 p. 552 (5 October).

Obligations concerning Negotiations relating to Cessation of the Nuclear Arms Race and Nuclear Disarmament (Marshall Islands v. *United Kingdom)*, Preliminary Objections, ICJ 2016 p. 833 (5 October).

Oil Platforms (Islamic Republic of Iran v. United States of America), Merits, Judgment, ICJ 2003 p. 161 (6 November).

Oil Platforms (Islamic Republic of Iran v. United States of America), Merits, Sep. Op. Judge Kooijmans, ICJ 2003 p. 246 (6 November).

Oil Platforms (Islamic Republic of Iran v. United States of America), Merits, Sep. Op. Judge Simma, ICJ 2003 p. 324 (6 November).

Oschadbank v. Russian Federation, PCA Case No. 2016–14 (Williams, President; Brower and Perezcano Díaz, arbitrators), Award (26 November 2018).

Panhandle Oil Co. v. Mississippi ex rel *Knox,* 277 U.S. 218, 223 (1928) (Holmes, J., dissenting).

PJSC CB PrivatBank and Finance Company Finilon LLC v. the Russian Federation, PCA Case No. 2015–21 (Dupuy, President; Bethlehem and Mikulka, arbitrators), Interim Award (27 March 2017).

PJSC CB Privatbank and Finance Company Finilon LLC v. Russian Federation, PCA Case No. 2015–21, Partial Award (Dupuy, President, Bethlehem and Mikulka, arbitrators) (4 February 2019).

Pulp Mills on the River Uruguay (Argentina v. Uruguay), Judgment, ICJ 2010 p. 14 (20 April).

The Queen on the Application of Melli Bank Plc v. HM Treasury & Foreign and Commonwealth Office [2008] EWHC 1661 (Admin) (Moses LJ).

Request for an Advisory Opinion submitted by the Commission of Small Island States on Climate Change and International Law, ITLOS Case No. 31, Advisory Opinion (21 May 2024).

Request for an Advisory Opinion submitted by the Sub-Regional Fisheries Commission (SRFC), Advisory Opinion, Sep. Op. Judge Lucky, ITLOS 2015 p. 88 (2 April).

Request for Interpretation of the Judgment of 15 June 1962 in the Case concerning the Temple of Preah Vihear (Cambodia v. Thailand) *(Cambodia v. Thailand)*, Provisional Measures, Order, ICJ 2011 p. 537 (18 July).

Request for Interpretation of the Judgment of 15 June 1962 in the Case concerning the Temple of Preah Vihear (Cambodia v. Thailand) *(Cambodia v. Thailand)*, Judgment, ICJ 2013 p. 281 (11 November).

Request for Interpretation of the Judgment of 23 May 2008 in the case concerning Sovereignty over Pedra Branca/Pulau Batu Puteh, Middle Rocks and South Ledge (Malaysia/Singapore) *(Malaysia v. Singapore)*, Order (discontinuance), ICJ 2018 p. 288 (29 May).

Responsibilities and Obligations of States Sponsoring Persons and Entities with respect to activities in the Area, Advisory Opinion, Seabed Disputes Chamber, ITLOS 2011 p. 10 (1 February).

Rights of Nationals of the United States of America in Morocco (France v. USA), ICJ 1952 p. 176 (27 August).

Russia—Measures concerning traffic in transit (Ukraine v. Russian Federation), Panel (Abi-Saab, Chair; Araki and Saeed, members), Report of the Panel, WT/DS512/R (5 April 2019).

Russia—Measures concerning traffic in transit, Interim Review, WT/DS512/R/Add.1 p. 112, Annex E-1 (5 April).

Salant Corporation v. United States, 25 C.I.T. 162, 166 (U.S. Court of International Trade) (2001).

Siag v. Egypt, ICSID Case No. ARB/05/15 (Pryles, President; Williams and Orrego Vicuña, arbitrators) (Vicuña, dissenting), Decision on Jurisdiction (11 April 2007).

South China Sea arbitration (Republic of the Philippines v. People's Republic of China), PCA Case No. 2013–19, UNCLOS Annex VII tribunal (Mensah, President; Cot, Pawlak, Soons, and Wolfrum, arbitrators), Award on Jurisdiction and Admissibility (29 October 2015).

South China Sea arbitration, Award (12 July 2016).

South West Africa Cases (Ethiopia v. South Africa; Liberia v. South Africa), Preliminary Objections, ICJ 1962 p. 319 (21 December).

Southern Bluefin Tuna (New Zealand v. Japan; Australia v. Japan), Provisional Measures, Order, ITLOS 1999 p. 280 (27 August).

Southern Bluefin Tuna (New Zealand-Japan, Australia-Japan), Annex VII tribunal (Schwebel, President; Feliciano, Keith, Tresselt, and Yamada, members), Award on Jurisdiction and Admissibility, XXIII RIAA 1 (4 August 2000).

Southern Bluefin Tuna (New Zealand-Japan, Australia-Japan), Sep. Op. Justice Sir Kenneth Keith, XXIII RIAA 49 (4 August 2000).

Sovereignty over Pedra Branca/Pulau Batu Puteh, Middle Rocks and South Ledge (Malaysia/Singapore), ICJ 2008 p. 12 (23 May).

Sovereignty over Pulau Ligitan and Pulau Sipadan (Indonesia/Malaysia), Application by the Philippines for Permission to Intervene, ICJ 2001 p. 575 (23 October).

Sovereignty over Pulau Ligitan and Pulau Sipadan (Indonesia/Malaysia), Application by the Philippines for Permission to Intervene, Sep. Op. Kooijmans, ICJ 2001 p. 626 (23 October).

Sovereignty over Pulau Ligitan and Pulau Sipadan (Indonesia/Malaysia), Application by the Philippines for Permission to Intervene, Sep. Op. Judge Weeramantry, ICJ 2001 p. 630 (23 October).

Sovereignty over Pulau Ligitan and Pulau Sipadan (Indonesia/Malaysia), Application by the Philippines for Permission to Intervene, Sep. Op. Judge *ad hoc* Franck, ICJ 2001 p. 652 (23 October).

Stabil et al v. the Russian Federation, PCA Case No. 2015–35 (Kaufmann-Kohler, President; Price and Stern, arbitrators), Award on Jurisdiction, (26 June 2017).

Stabil v. Russian Federation, Final Award (12 April 2019).

Status and Use of the Waters of the Silala (Chile v. *Bolivia)*, Decl. Judge Charlesworth, ICJ 2022 p. 667 (1 December).

Temple of Preah Vihear (Cambodia v. Thailand), Merits, ICJ 1962 p. 6 (15 June).

Territorial and Maritime Dispute (Nicaragua v. Colombia), Preliminary Objections, ICJ 2007 p. 832 (13 December).

Territorial and Maritime Dispute (Nicaragua v. Colombia), Judgment, ICJ 2012 p. 624 (19 November).

Territorial and Maritime Dispute between Nicaragua and Honduras in the Caribbean Sea (Nicaragua v. Honduras), Judgment, ICJ 2007 p. 659 (8 October).

Territorial and Maritime Dispute between Nicaragua and Honduras in the Caribbean Sea (Nicaragua v. Honduras), Sep. Op. of Judge Ranjeva, ICJ 2007 p. 765 (8 October).

Territorial Dispute (Libya/Chad), Judgment, ICJ 1994 p. 6 (3 February).

Texaco v. Libya (Dupuy, sole arbitrator), Award on the Merits (19 January 1977).

Timor Sea Conciliation (Timor-Leste v. Australia) (Conciliation Commission: Taksøe-Jensen, Chair; Balkin, Koroma, McRae, and Wolfrum, members), Report and Recommendations (9 May 2018).

Ukraine and the Netherlands v. Russia (MH17 case), ECtHR, Applications nos. 8019/16, 43800/14 and 28525/20), Decision (25 January 2023).

Ukraine v. *Russia (re Crimea)*, ECtHR, Applications nos. 20958/14 and 38334/18, decision on admissibility (16 December 2020).

United States Diplomatic and Consular Staff in Tehran (United States of America v. Iran), Judgment, ICJ 1980 p. 3 (24 May).

United States v. Stuart, 489 U.S. 353 (1989).

Western Sahara Campaign UK v. Commissioners for Her Majesty's Revenue and Customs, Secretary of State for Environment, Food and Rural Affairs, Court of Justice of the European Union, Case C-266/16, Opinion of Advocate General Wathelet (10 January 2018).

Western Sahara, Advisory Opinion, Sep. Op. Judge Dillard, ICJ 1975 p. 116 (16 October).

World Duty Free Co. Ltd. v. Republic of Kenya, ICSID Case No. ARB/00/7 (Judge Guillaume, President; Rogers and Veeder, arbitrators), Award (4 October 2006).

Treaties and other international instruments (selected)

1945	26 June	UN Charter 1945
		Art. 2(3)
		Art. 18
		Art. 27(3)
		Art. 33(1)
		Art. 73
1945	24 October	Statute of the ICJ
		Art. 36(2)
		Art. 38
1947	30 October	General Agreement on Tariffs and Trade (GATT)
		Art. XXI(b)(iii)
1948	9 December	Convention on the Prevention and Punishment of the Crime of Genocide
		Art. IX
1950	4 November	European Convention on Human Rights
		Art. 35
1952	18 August	Santiago Declaration (Chile-Ecuador-Peru)
1954	4 December	Special Maritime Frontier Zone Agreement 1954 (Chile-Ecuador-Peru)
1955	15 August	Treaty of Amity, Economic Relations and Consular Rights (Iran-USA)
1956	21 January	Treaty of Friendship, Commerce and Navigation (Nicaragua–USA)
1960	14 December	Declaration on the Granting of Independence to Colonial Countries and Peoples, GAR 1514 (XV)
1961	18 April	Vienna Convention on Diplomatic Relations
		Art. 1*(i)*
		Art. 22
1965	18 March	ICSID Convention
		Art. 25(1)

1969	23 May	VCLT
		Art. 29
		Art. 31
		Art. 32
		Art. 62(2)
1970	24 October	Friendly Relations Declaration, GAR 2625 (XXV)
1978	14 April	ICJ Rules of Court
		Art. 79
1978	23 August	Vienna Convention on the Succession of States in respect of Treaties
		Art. 2(1)*(b)*
		Art. 11
1982	10 December	UNCLOS
		Art. 2(3)
		Art. 7
		Art. 11
		Art. 13
		Art. 15
		Art. 32
		Art. 33
		Art. 46
		Art. 47
		Art. 49(1)
		Art. 56(2)
		Art. 58(2)
		Art. 60(8)
		Art. 74
		Art. 74(3)
		Art. 75
		Art. 76
		Art. 77
		Art. 80
		Art. 83
		Art. 83(3)
		Art. 121
		Art. 121(3)
		Art. 124
		Art. 125
		Art. 160
		Art. 189
		Art. 237(1)

		Art. 279
		Art. 286
		Art. 287
		Art. 288(1)
		Art. 288(2)
		Art. 288(4)
		Art. 292
		Art. 293(1)
		Art. 296
		Art. 297
		Art. 298(1)(a)*(i)*
		Art. 300
		Art. 301
		Art. 304
		Art. 305(a)(e)
1982	10 December	Resolution III, Final Act, UNCLOS III
1986	12 February	Treaty of Canterbury (France–UK)
1995	28 September	Israeli–Palestinian Interim Agreement on the West Bank and the Gaza Strip
1998	17 July	Statute of the International Criminal Court
		Art. 15 *bis*
		Art. 15 *ter*
2001	12 December	ARSIWA 2001
		Art. 40
		Art. 41
2022	1 July	ICSID Arbitration Rules (2022)
		Rule 41
2023	19 June	Agreement on Marine Biodiversity of Areas Beyond National Jurisdiction
2024	3 October	UK and Mauritius Joint Statement (regarding the Chagos Archipelago)

Introduction

Questions concerning sovereign title to territory and questions concerning a sovereign's entitlements in adjacent areas of the sea are closely connected both in principle and in practice. Ad hoc tribunals and the International Court of Justice (ICJ) have settled such questions together in a number of cases.[1] States have negotiated such questions together.[2] Many disputes exist today in which those questions go hand in hand.[3] Yet, under the prevalent view, the treaty which provides the widest scope for adjudication of maritime questions, the UN Convention on the Law of the Sea 1982 (UNCLOS),[4]

1 For example, *Eritrea/Yemen*, PCA Case No. 1996–04, Tribunal constituted under Arbitration Agreement of 3 October 1996 (Jennings, President; Schwebel, El-Kosheri, Highet, and Higgins, members), First Stage, Territorial Sovereignty and Scope of the Dispute, Award, 9 October 1998; Second Stage, Maritime Delimitation, Award, 17 December 1999; *Maritime Delimitation and Territorial Questions (Qatar v. Bahrain)*, Merits, Judgment, ICJ 2001 p. 40 (16 March); *Territorial and Maritime Dispute between Nicaragua and Honduras in the Caribbean Sea (Nicaragua v. Honduras)*, Judgment, ICJ 2007 p. 659 (8 October).

2 For example, under the (unpublished) Brunei–Malaysia Exchange of Letters, 16 March 2009, about which see Jeffrey J. Smith, 'Brunei and Malaysia Resolve Outstanding Maritime Boundary Issues' (2010) 1 *LOS Reports* (American Society of International Law). See also Franckx, 'Eastern Baltic Sea' (1998) 13 IJMCL 274–284. As to the role of compromise in boundary matters (including in adjudication and arbitration), see Munkman, 'Territorial and Boundary Disputes' (1972–1973) 46 BYIL 1.

3 See van Logchem, *The Rights and Obligations of States in Disputed Maritime Areas* (2021) 239.

4 Preferences vary as between two acronyms for the 1982 Convention, 'UNCLOS' and 'LOSC,' but the preponderant use today is of the former. Churchill, Lowe & Sander, *The Law of the Sea*, 4th edn. (2022) xvii. Using the former, however, one should take care to distinguish between the 1982 Convention and *conferences* at which law of the sea was the topic and, eventually, the 1982 Convention was drafted, these conferences each having been titled a 'United Nations Conference on the Law of the Sea,' and sometimes abbreviated 'UNCLOS' with a roman numeral suffix to denote which in the sequence, thus UNCLOS I (the 1958 Conference or 'First Conference'), UNCLOS II (the 1960 Conference or 'Second Conference'), and UNCLOS III ('Third Conference,' this having met from 1973 to 1982).

provides little or no scope for the concurrent consideration of territorial questions. The prevalent view would seem to find reinforcement in a series of decisions between 2015 and 2022. In those decisions, adjudicators indicated that it would have exceeded the scope of UNCLOS jurisdiction for them to have addressed questions of territorial sovereignty.

The most striking among the decisions in which the matter has arisen is that which has attracted the least general comment, that of 21 February 2020 by an UNCLOS Annex VII tribunal in *Coastal State Rights*, a case instituted by Ukraine against Russia to seek relief in regard to Russia's conduct in the Black Sea, Sea of Azov, and Kerch Strait, maritime areas appurtenant to Crimea. In *Coastal State Rights*, Russia grounded its objection to the exercise of jurisdiction by the tribunal on the observation that maritime entitlements concerned in the case derive from sovereignty over the territory of Crimea—and on the assertion that sovereignty over the territory of Crimea is in dispute. The decision in the *Coastal State Rights* case, in which the tribunal agreed with Russia that a legal dispute exists between Russia and Ukraine as to which state is sovereign over Crimea, holds interest for its interpretation and application of the jurisdictional provisions of UNCLOS and, moreover, for the consequences for public order that follow from the particular interpretation and application that the tribunal applied. The decision also illustrates certain methodological problems that arise for an adjudicator when a party asserts the existence of a factual or legal circumstance that, if it were found to exist, would prevent the exercise of jurisdiction over another party's claims. The methodological problems affect dispute settlement procedure in practically any situation where an adjudicator functions under a consent-based jurisdiction subject to limits and exceptions, and, so, they merit concern beyond the confines of UNCLOS jurisdiction.

UNCLOS jurisdiction in a time of public order challenge

A proposition central to the present book is that, where only the use or threat of armed force lies behind a party's assertion against another that it, and not the other, is sovereign in a certain territory, then the assertion constitutes no claim to territory for purposes of international law. The proposition is variously articulated as a prohibition of the acquisition of territory by force or of the forcible change of peacefully settled boundaries, or as a rule that no assertion of title to territory based solely on force shall be recognized. Jurists express the proposition in different ways. The linguistic variation reflects a degree of analytic imprecision which, as we will see, can lead to difficulties in practical application. Chapter 1 argues, the difficulties notwithstanding, that the proposition is of central importance in present-day international law.

To set out a second proposition, with a corollary: it takes at least two parties to have a dispute, and, so, where only one party has a claim to sovereignty over a territory for purposes of international law, there is no dispute as to sovereignty over the territory. Substituting terms, we reach this conclusion: where only use or threat of force lies behind one party's assertion against another that it, and not the other, is sovereign in a particular territory, there is no dispute between them as to sovereignty over that territory.

What authority would a tribunal with compulsory and binding jurisdiction constituted under UNCLOS have to get to grips with this matter? The view that currently prevails is that such a tribunal has no jurisdiction to deal with territorial disputes, except, perhaps, in 'minor' cases,[5] an exception that, as posited, remains both equivocal and undefined. With or without the exception, the prevailing view has consequences for the adjudication of maritime disputes. It is upon a state's sovereignty over territory appurtenant to a maritime area that the state's entitlements, or potential entitlements,[6] as well as its authority, or potential authority,[7] in the maritime area, in the main,[8]

5 *Chagos Marine Protected Area Arbitration (Mauritius v. United Kingdom)*, UNCLOS Annex VII/PCA Case. No. 2011–03 (Shearer, President; Greenwood, Hoffmann, Kateka, and Wolfrum, members) (Kateka and Wolfrum dissenting in part), Award, 18 March 2015, ¶ 221.

6 For example, UNCLOS Art. 2 (Legal status of the territorial sea, of the air space over the territorial sea and of its bed and subsoil).

7 For example, under UNCLOS Art. 21 (Laws and regulations of the coastal State relating to innocent passage), Art. 33 (Contiguous zone), Art. 41 (Sea lanes and traffic separation schemes in straits used for international navigation); Art. 42 (Laws and regulations of States bordering straits relating to transit passage).

8 The qualifying phrase '[i]n the main' is required, because there exist entitlements, such as access to traditional fishing grounds on the basis of historical practice, that do not necessarily derive directly from the geographic relationship between a state's land territory and the maritime area in which the state exercises the entitlements, though, even there, a relationship in most instances exists between the maritime area and land territory of the state concerned. See, for example, the provisions on archipelagic waters concerning 'rights' and 'legitimate interests' of 'an *immediately* adjacent neighbouring State' (emphasis added): UNCLOS Art. 47(6), Art. 51(1). In a different context, see *Eritrea/Yemen*, First Stage, Territorial Sovereignty and Scope of the Dispute, Award, 9 October 1998, ¶ 526, where the Tribunal required Yemen to 'ensure that the traditional fishing regime of free access and enjoyment for the fishermen of both Eritrea and Yemen shall be preserved.' See also Award in the Second Stage of the Proceedings (Maritime Delimitation), 17 December 1999, ¶ 87. See generally the discussion on 'historic rights short of sovereignty' in Kopela, 'Historic Titles and Historic Rights' (2017) (48)(2) ODIL 181, 188–194.

depend:[9] 'the land dominates the sea.'[10] Accordingly, a dispute as to which state has sovereignty over territory appurtenant to a maritime area casts in doubt which state holds entitlements, or potential entitlements, in the maritime area. Under the view of UNCLOS jurisdiction that currently prevails, if a dispute exists as to which state is sovereign in the territory appurtenant to the maritime area concerned in a maritime dispute, then, by and large, the tribunal must refrain from exercising jurisdiction over the maritime dispute.

In the chapters that follow, I trace the emergence of the view that UNCLOS tribunals have little or no jurisdiction to deal with territorial disputes. I argue that we should question that view, and that on a plain reading of the relevant provisions of UNCLOS, and in light of the drafting history as well, adjudicators have the authority to address territorial questions that parties raise in connection with maritime disputes that they have consented to compulsory and binding procedures under UNCLOS to settle.[11]

Teleological considerations are not necessary to this conclusion, but, as I suggest, they, too, support decision-makers reaching certain questions of territorial sovereignty.[12]

Territorial sovereignty and more particularly the stability of agreed boundaries and title bring us to public order, which is one of the central concerns in this book. Armed aggression against the territorial integrity of states is one of the central concerns of public order. Extra-legal claims

9 Provisions of UNCLOS reflecting the dependency when read together with Art. 5 (Normal baseline) include Art. 3 (Breadth of the territorial sea), Art. 57 (Breadth of the exclusive economic zone), and Art. 76 (Definition of the continental shelf). The last of these, the provision for the definition of the continental shelf, Art. 76, embraces 'the submarine areas that extend beyond [the coastal state's] territorial sea throughout the natural prolongation of its land territory, or to a distance of 200 nautical miles from the baselines from which the breadth of the territorial sea is measured where the outer edge of the continental margin does not extend to that distance,' and, thus, it provides two methods whereby a state might identify the area concerned: measurement from the baselines, which requires reading Art. 76 in conjunction with Art. 5, and determination of 'the natural prolongation of its land territory,' which entails a methodology defined in Art. 75, ¶¶ 4–7. As to differences of view in applying the methodology and problems in defining the terms on which it relies, see summary of the jurisprudence, Parson 'Article 76' in *Proelss Commentary* (2017) 592–598.

10 *North Sea Continental Shelf Cases (Federal Republic of German/Denmark; Federal Republic of Germany/Netherlands)*, Judgment, ICJ 1969 p. 3, p. 51 ¶ 96 (20 February). For the maxim as stated in a mixed territorial–maritime dispute, see, e.g., *Territorial and Maritime Dispute between Nicaragua and Honduras in the Caribbean Sea (Nicaragua v. Honduras)*, Judgment, ICJ 2007 p. 659, p. 702 ¶ 135 (8 October); *Maritime Delimitation and Territorial Questions between Qatar and Bahrain (Qatar v. Bahrain)*, Judgment, ICJ 2001 p. 40, p. 97 ¶ 185 (16 March).

11 See below Chapter 3, pp. 102–118.

12 See below Chapter 1, pp. 28–35, 49–54; Chapter 4, pp. 139–143; Chapter 8, pp. 323–325.

to revise long-settled international boundaries have proliferated in recent practice. International law and its organized expression through procedures such as compulsory and binding dispute settlement under UNCLOS are not intended to prevent a general breakdown in public order or to repair the damage if such a breakdown occurs. They are, however, expected to apply the law, including the ordering principles that impart law consistency and predictability.

The prevailing view that questions of territorial sovereignty have little or no place in binding and compulsory proceedings under UNCLOS is convenient. Applying that view, an adjudicator readily avoids addressing geopolitical collisions that armed aggression creates. It might be thought that such avoidance is for the better, because it focuses the adjudicator on particular problems that arise in legal disputes that the adjudicator can solve, rather than on public order problems that arise in international relations that the adjudicator cannot. This reasoning is sound—as far as it goes. It falls short when a public order problem encompasses a legal problem. When the public order problem has a discrete legal manifestation that lends itself to ordinary methods of legal reasoning and legal procedure, the adjudicator should pause before choosing avoidance. The approach that elides problems that are precisely those that adjudicators are intended to solve is not readily reconciled with the adjudicator's function.

It is timely to reconsider the prevailing view that Part XV, section 2, the dispute settlement section of UNCLOS, excludes from compulsory and binding procedure disputes 'concerning sovereignty or other rights over continental or insular land territory.' I am going to call into question the prevailing view that the exclusion of issues of territorial sovereignty is a *general* exclusion, rather than one confined to narrow circumstances. I argue that, at the very least, whatever its scope under Part XV, section 2, an adjudicator must interpret and apply *that* exclusion consistently with a prior and imprescriptible one—the exclusion of claims to revise the spatial entitlements of states by force.[13] The adjudicator's function here necessarily entails looking at an assertion of sovereignty closely enough to discern whether or not it is one that modern international law might accept. Assertions of sovereignty with nothing behind them other than force or threat are not assertions that modern international law accepts.[14]

This book explores the interplay between use of force and Convention rights. It also explores the jurisdictional architecture of UNCLOS, where the exclusion of territorial issues from dispute settlement resides in that architecture, and how adjudicators have addressed the exclusion in practice.

13 See below Chapter 1, pp. 25–58.
14 See below Chapter 6, pp. 206–246.

Interpreting and applying the limits of jurisdiction

Adjudicators under UNCLOS so far have considered issues of territorial sovereignty in only a handful of decided cases. As I argue, in *Coastal State Rights*, the arbitral tribunal accepted an exaggerated interpretation of the scope of the exclusion of territorial issues. Accepting that interpretation led to a dubious result. The putative issue of territorial sovereignty in *Coastal State Rights*, on the better view of the facts, had nothing behind it other than Russia's use of force in 2014 against Ukraine.[15] Because a settled international boundary is not cast in legal doubt by use of force,[16] and because Russia and Ukraine had settled their international boundary,[17] I argue that the arbitrators in *Coastal State Rights* should have reached the conclusion that no sovereignty dispute existed.

My argument here involves two interrelated but distinct tasks that an adjudicator might be called on to perform under UNCLOS Part XV, section 2. It involves identifying the limits of UNCLOS jurisdiction. And it involves distinguishing situations that are embraced within the limits from those that are not. The latter task relates to the former, because the answer that an adjudicator gives to a jurisdictional objection in a particular case refines our understanding of the jurisdictional limits. If a certain situation is embraced within the limits of jurisdiction in one case, then a similar situation, all else being equal, ought to be as well.

The task of distinguishing among situations that parties raise in their jurisdictional objections relates to the former task—the task of identifying the limits of jurisdiction—in a further way. The manner in which the adjudicator approaches that task—that is to say, the manner in which the adjudicator determines whether a party objecting to jurisdiction has demonstrated that jurisdiction does not embrace the other party's claim—indirectly identifies the jurisdictional limits. For example, to which party the adjudicator assigns burden of proof, and how it calibrates standard of proof, affects the likelihood that a jurisdictional objection succeeds. How the adjudicator carries out fact-finding—the forensic process—also can affect the outcome of an objection. A jurisdictional limit is identified not only by adjudicators interpreting it in abstract terms; it is identified by adjudicators applying the terms to concrete examples of jurisdictional objection.[18]

The manner in which the Annex VII tribunal in *Coastal State Rights* reached the decision to accept the jurisdictional objection—that is, the

15 See below Chapter 6, pp. 194–196, 220, 229–234.
16 See below Chapter 1, pp. 25–58.
17 See below Chapter 7, pp. 252, 271–272.
18 See below Chapter 7, p. 246; Chapter 8, p. 287.

objection that asserted that a territorial sovereignty dispute existed and thus prevented adjudication of certain maritime claims—should raise as much concern as the decision itself. In two respects, the 2020 award in *Coastal State Rights* merits critique. First, the award relied upon an exaggerated interpretation of the territorial sovereignty exclusion in UNCLOS Part XV, section 2. As I argue in Chapters 2 and 3, the jurisdictional scheme, on the better reading, allows adjudicators to address disputes over territorial sovereignty at least in some cases. And, second, whatever interpretation one places on the land territory provisions of UNCLOS, there are well-tested methods that adjudicators use to decide objections to jurisdiction, but the *Coastal State Rights* tribunal did not use them. Striking in the 2020 award, when presented with the fact—which both the parties acknowledged—that *no* dispute existed as to which state was sovereign in Crimea before March 2014,[19] the arbitrators declined to consider evidence at their disposal that would have satisfied a reasonable finder of fact that there still was no dispute. We shall see that in other cases adjudicators, by contrast, did consider evidence and decided that a sovereignty dispute had not sprung into existence, notwithstanding a party's insistence that one had. The essentially passive approach to fact evidence that the *Coastal State Rights* tribunal took, if imitated generally, would jeopardize the future operation of any international dispute settlement procedure that is faced with territorial crises of the kind that present-day geopolitics, sadly, augur and will vex international relations in the years to come.

Starting with the unremarkable premise that an international adjudicator has authority to determine the scope of its own jurisdiction—*compétence de la compétence*—I recall that in certain circumstances adjudicators have exercised authority to consider ancillary or incidental matters, in particular when these have been necessary to address an objection that a party has raised to jurisdiction. The ancillary or incidental matters include matters of evidence and of the plausibility (or reasonableness or credibility) of the factual assertions that are necessary predicates to a party's jurisdictional objection. When a party objecting to the exercise of jurisdiction has asserted that a sovereignty dispute exists, the adjudicator under Part XV, section 2, has the competence—and I argue the duty—to carry out such inquiry as is needed to reach a well-grounded conclusion as to the question whether the putative dispute indeed exists. As we will see, an exaggerated interpretation of the territorial sovereignty exclusion invites the adjudicator to refrain from subjecting a jurisdictional objection to the scrutiny that it deserves. Interpreting the territorial exclusion as an absolute exclusion of territorial questions affects the method that the adjudicator applies to fact-finding and

19 See below Introduction, p. 14 and n. 41; Chapter 6, p. 177 and n. 19, p. 216.

to scrutiny of party assertion. Instead of the ordinary method of testing evidence and scrutinizing party assertion, the adjudicator approaches the matter with such lightness of touch as to leave it practically in the hands of the objecting party. Interpreting the territorial exclusion to mean, in effect, that the adjudicator shall not scrutinize a party's assertion that a territorial dispute exists, the adjudicator in effect equips the party with a tool for auto-revocation of jurisdictional consent.[20]

International adjudicators take appropriate care to keep their decision-making within the limits of the jurisdiction that parties have consented to grant them. In doing so, adjudicators must discern the limits reliably. A tribunal misjudges a jurisdictional limit when it concludes that it has jurisdiction to address a matter that it does not have. A tribunal also misjudges a jurisdictional limit when it concludes that it does *not* have jurisdiction to address a matter that it *does* have. Distinguishing cases that it shall adjudicate from cases that it shall not requires the adjudicator to engage in legal analysis and, where parties disagree as to the facts, also to engage in fact-finding. In applying UNCLOS Part XV, section 2, an adjudicator accepts a party's jurisdictional objection if, after subjecting it to appropriate scrutiny, the adjudicator finds that the objection has merit.

The procedural right to object is not a substantive power to withdraw an extant consent to jurisdiction. UNCLOS Article 288, paragraph 4, is clear that the adjudicator is duty-bound to determine whether it has jurisdiction when jurisdiction is in dispute.[21] The cases with which this book is concerned involved objections to jurisdiction under UNCLOS, where the premise of the objections was that a sovereignty dispute constituted the real substance of the claim that an applicant sought to adjudicate. But, to discern reliably whether a claim is located within the limits of its jurisdiction, a tribunal does not accept an objection to jurisdiction without first applying scrutiny to the premise on which the objection relies. The adjudicator's task here is not a mere formal exercise. The objecting party likely will assert grounds, in fact or law or both, that it says support its premise. It will characterize some incident or event, perhaps some instrument or other legal act, and say that the premise therein finds its support. The objecting party might also suggest that whatever ground or grounds it has asserted involve matters over which the adjudicator has no jurisdiction and, thus, the adjudicator *must* accept these as the objecting party has characterized them, *must* accept the premise that the objecting party says the asserted grounds support, and thus *must* decline to adjudicate the other party's claim. The circularity of this approach is obvious when one boils it down to its essentials: the

20 See below Chapter 8, p. 309, Conclusion, p. 341.
21 See below Chapter 2, pp. 62–66.

objecting party has argued that there is no jurisdiction—because there is no jurisdiction to say whether there is jurisdiction. The adjudicator's appropriate response is to apply the ordinary legal and forensic methods that all parties are entitled to expect an adjudicator to apply. The adjudicator is to test the grounds on which the objecting party has premised its objection.

The adjudicator also must satisfy itself, not only that the assertions of the objecting party might be validated in the abstract, but that those assertions might be validated *on the international law plane* in particular. An adjudicator that refuses to test the factual or legal assertions that the objecting party says supply the grounds for its jurisdictional objection and fails to hold those assertions to the requirements of the applicable law effectively confers on the objecting party a unilateral power of jurisdictional avoidance. This is the tool of auto-revocation that UNCLOS adjudicators will have fashioned if they continue to accept the territorial exclusion in its furthest-reaching form.

To exaggerate the scope of the territorial exclusion has policy implications as well. It poses the risk of surprise to treaty parties and, in turn, may drive parties away from UNCLOS. The supposed territorial exclusion, after an UNCLOS Annex VII tribunal adopted it in the *Chagos Marine Protected Area* case in 2015, quickly acquired an almost talismanic quality. But UNCLOS adjudicators will not necessarily consider the exclusion to bind them in every future case. For one thing, there is the exception concerning 'minor' territorial issues to which the *Chagos* tribunal alluded. Even putting the 'minor' exception aside—it is hardly clear what situations the exception, as posited, would embrace—a problem of predictability remains. Adjudicators in other international dispute settlement systems have exhibited a tendency to enlarge their jurisdiction even where the texts of the applicable jurisdictional instruments supply little or no support to do so. World Trade Organization (WTO) dispute settlement is an oft-remarked example of a jurisdiction that adjudicators have enlarged; the exercise of jurisdiction by the WTO Appellate Body has instigated a crisis.[22] The development of the jurisprudence of the European Court of Human Rights (ECtHR) is another example.[23] If a state

22 Invoking 'repeated failure of the Appellate Body to apply the rules of the WTO agreements in a manner that adheres strictly to the text of those agreements,' see United States Trade Representative, *Report on the Appellate Body of the World Trade Organization* (February 2020) 121. Cf. Marceau, 'Evolutive Interpretation by the WTO Adjudicator' (2018) 21 *Journal of International Economic Law* 791–813; Shaffer, Elsig & Puig, 'WTO Appellate Body' (2016) 79 *Law and Contemporary Problems* 237–273.

23 For the critical response, see generally Lord Hoffmann, 'The Universality of Human Rights' (2009) 125 LQR 416; Lord Hoffman, 'Human Rights and the House of Lords' (1999) 62 MLR 159; Lord Sumption, 'The Limits of Law,' Sultan Azlan Shah Law Lectures 2013: www.sultanazlanshah.com/pdf/2021/SAS_Lecture_27.pdf

participates in UNCLOS on the assumption that sovereignty issues will *not* be addressed under Part XV, section 2, then the state participates on shaky ground. No bold 'evolutive jurisprudence' is needed to address sovereignty issues under UNCLOS. As I argue, all that is needed, when a case with the requisite shape is presented, is that judges and arbitrators apply the Convention as written.

The facts of geography, where they meet the facts of global competition for resources and the law of the sea, suggest that cases with the requisite shape will not be lacking. Differences concerning sovereignty over territory intersect with differences concerning the rights of states in appurtenant maritime areas in many places. Writing in 2022 about islands, Donald Rothwell ventured that 'international law has entered an age of islands. Never before have islands demanded such attention from international law. They are in the global legal spotlight in multiple different contexts and international law is continuing to develop around them.'[24] The posited limits to dispute settlement under UNCLOS will challenge, even frustrate, parties that seek to 'develop' international law 'around' islands, which is to say in the maritime areas around them. Islands are relevant here as one kind of land territory. The developmental impetus arises just as much from continental territory as from insular. The cases are many and widespread that might come to test the posited limits to dispute settlement.

Another curious aspect of the proposition that questions of territorial sovereignty fall outside the competence of adjudicators under UNCLOS Part XV, section 2, is that, in spite of its widespread acceptance by doctrinal writers, the proposition finds surprisingly few examples in practice to sustain it. There is no great corpus of decided cases to justify an adjudicator refusing to exercise merits jurisdiction, much less to refuse to exercise *compétence de la compétence*, over questions of territorial sovereignty that a party has raised. Professor Bernard Oxman, serving as Judge *ad hoc* in *Mauritius/Maldives*, dissented from the judgment of the Special Chamber of the International Tribunal for the Law of the Sea (ITLOS), that judgment having determined that no territorial dispute exists between Mauritius and the United Kingdom in regard to the Chagos Archipelago, a territory that the United Kingdom has administered since 1965 as the British Indian Ocean Territory (BIOT). According to Judge *ad hoc* Oxman, to address the 'merits with respect to the Chagos Archipelago … would require adjudicating the merits of the claims to the islands, which would run counter to the

24 Rothwell, *Islands and International Law* (2022) 261.

jurisdictional limitations recognized *by the existing jurisprudence*.'[25] The 'existing jurisprudence' to which Judge *ad hoc* Oxman referred consisted of one jurisdictional decision, that in *Chagos Marine Protected Area (Mauritius v. United Kingdom)*, in which an UNCLOS Annex VII tribunal, split three-to-two, indicated only a qualified exclusion of territorial disputes, and in which the dissenting arbitrators drew attention to the lack of support for the majority's interpretation in the treaty text; the *Coastal State Rights* award of 21 February 2020 in which an Annex VII tribunal repeated the *Chagos Marine Protected Area* majority's conclusion, without acknowledgment, much less analysis, of the difficulties that the majority's view entails; and a decision in another case, *South China Sea (Philippines v. China)*, in which no dispute between states as to sovereignty over a territory needed to be settled and, thus, in which the Annex VII tribunal constituted to adjudicate the case had no reason to address the scope of the putative territorial exclusion, and, in fact, on a careful reading of its award on jurisdiction and admissibility did not address it.

The 'jurisprudence' of a general exclusion of sovereignty issues from the compulsory dispute settlement procedures in UNCLOS is thin at best. However, since the Third Conference on the Law of the Sea, at which the delegates of states completed the text that states adopted as the United Nations Convention on the Law of the Sea in 1982, legal writers have stubbornly insisted that the text, or if not the text the drafting history, or if not the drafting history teleological considerations, compel the interpretation that territorial disputes are all but categorically excluded from the purview of UNCLOS adjudicators.[26] In this book, I consider the text, the drafting history, and the object and purpose behind the Convention. The picture that emerges is considerably more nuanced than a general exclusion of sovereignty issues. UNCLOS is intimately concerned with the *territorial* authority of states.[27] Its provisions in many cases are difficult or impossible to apply without a clear definition of the geographic limits of the territorial sovereignty of states. But the maxim that 'the land dominates the sea' is not the main reason that we should be skeptical of a view that demands the clinical isolation of territorial disputes from maritime disputes and the exclusion of the former from UNCLOS jurisdiction. The putative territorial

25 *Dispute concerning delimitation of the maritime boundary between Mauritius and Maldives in the Indian Ocean (Mauritius/Maldives)*, Preliminary Objections, Sep. & Dis. Op. Judge *ad hoc* Oxman, ITLOS 2021 p. 118, p. 129 ¶ 32 (28 January) (emphasis added).

26 See below Chapter 3, pp. 110–117.

27 See below Chapter 2, pp. 88–99.

exclusion, I show, is lodged in a subsidiary exception that expressly limits the exclusion to a special case. Its positioning there, the drafting history records, was carefully negotiated and deliberate.[28]

The exponents of a *general* exclusion of territorial disputes from UNCLOS procedures, as I relate, have attempted to shift the matter to the general jurisdictional provision, Article 288(1), which provides that jurisdiction extends to 'any dispute concerning the interpretation or application of [UNCLOS] which is submitted to [a court or tribunal] in accordance with [Part XV, section 2].'[29] But to find the exclusion *there* requires that the exclusion be a premise, an assumption antecedent to the text. It is, in other words, only an act of inference that would identify a general exclusion in Article 288(1), a provision expressed only in affirmative terms and stipulating that jurisdiction embraces a wide range of disputes. Finding an exclusion *there* is an uphill battle.

Tellingly, even as expressed in *Chagos Marine Protected Area*, the seeming *locus classicus* of the territorial exclusion such as it is, the exclusion is qualified. The majority in *Chagos Marine Protected Area* stated, by way of dictum, that 'minor [sovereignty] issues ... ancillary to a [maritime] dispute,'[30] might be adjudicated under Part XV, section 2. The majority did not say what factual and legal circumstances would allow adjudicators to distinguish land sovereignty issues as 'minor' and 'ancillary,' but the majority plainly were not prepared to shut the door on possible adjudication when a case presents sovereignty issues. The territorial exclusion, even posited with the 'minor' and 'ancillary' qualification, nevertheless has had dubious results where adjudicators have applied it.

Chapter outline and cross-cutting themes

This book, in addition to its Preface and the present Introduction, contains eight chapters, followed by a Conclusion.

Chapter 1 addresses the prohibition of forcible changes to international boundaries. The prohibition is arguably the most important achievement of modern international law and the starting point from which much else in international law has developed. Yet a long time elapsed without practitioners

28 See below Chapter 3, pp. 108–110.

29 See below Chapter 2, pp. 96–99.

30 *Chagos Marine Protected Area Arbitration (Mauritius v. United Kingdom)*, UNCLOS Annex VII/PCA Case. No. 2011–03 (Shearer, President; Greenwood, Hoffmann, Kateka, and Wolfrum, members) (Kateka and Wolfrum dissenting in part), Award, 18 March 2015, ¶ 221.

or writers giving much thought to it or to the difficulties that would result if it were to fall away. That the prohibition applies equally as between terrestrial and maritime boundaries follows from principle and also finds reflection in practice.[31] Chapter 1 recalls the central importance of the prohibition and notes the evidence of its erosion in face of armed aggression.

The book proceeds in Chapter 2 to an overview of the familiar jurisdictional provisions of UNCLOS Part XV, section 2. Several readily observed elements of Part XV, section 2, merit particular note: the open-textured terms of Article 288(1);[32] the requirement, articulated in Article 288(4), that tribunals determine the scope and limits of their own jurisdiction;[33] and the practice of tribunals under which Article 293 has permitted the adjudication of issues that general international law addresses even though UNCLOS itself does not.[34] This last element has drawn reasoned critique, including from Sir Michael Wood, former Foreign and Commonwealth Office Legal Advisor,[35] and Peter Tzeng, the latter in the 2016 volume of the *Yale Law Journal*,[36] but, as a matter of positive law, it is a visible part of UNCLOS jurisprudence and so is not to be set aside on purely formal grounds.

Whatever one makes of Article 293, it is clear that Article 298(1)(a)*(i)*, *fons et origo* of the premise that territorial issues are subject to a general jurisdictional exclusion, has nothing to do with territorial issues outside the narrow circumstances to which that provision's exclusion clause is confined. Chapter 3 considers the territorial exclusion in its setting. In Chapter 3, I recall the distinction between the consent to jurisdiction that UNCLOS expresses in global terms ('any dispute concerning the interpretation or application of this Convention') and the specifically enumerated *limits* to jurisdiction set out under Article 297,[37] before turning to examine Article 298(1)(a)*(i)* and its territorial exclusion.[38]

The book then considers the first three cases in which UNCLOS Annex VII tribunals directly addressed territorial issues and their effect on dispute settlement jurisdiction. The *Chagos Marine Protected Area Arbitration* is the first of these. It occasioned a sharp split among the arbitrators over how a tribunal is to characterize a dispute that raises both territorial and maritime

31 See below Chapter 1, pp. 49–54.
32 See below Chapter 2, pp. 60–62.
33 See below pp. 62–66.
34 See below pp. 66–88.
35 Wood, 'The International Tribunal for the Law of the Sea and General International Law' (2007) 2 IJMCL 351, 356–357.
36 Tzeng, 'Jurisdiction and Applicable Law Under UNCLOS' (2016) 126 YLJ 242.
37 See below Chapter 3, pp. 101–102.
38 See below pp. 102–117.

questions and over the scope of UNCLOS jurisdiction.[39] I consider *Chagos Marine Protected Area* in Chapter 4.

Turning in Chapter 5 to the *South China Sea Arbitration (Philippines v. China)*, I observe that territorial issues arise under a number of substantive provisions of UNCLOS but that not every territorial issue entails determining what state is sovereign in a territory. The Annex VII tribunal in *South China Sea* demonstrated that such issues do not necessarily implicate disputes over sovereignty as such, even when the parties agree that disputes over sovereignty do exist between them. In subsequent cases adjudicators have suggested that *South China Sea* supports the broad exclusion of disputes over sovereignty from Part XV, section 2, procedures. Reading a broad exclusion from *South China Sea*, however, is unconvincing. The Philippines, as claimant, was explicit that it asked for no adjudication of the territorial disputes that exist in the region, and the Annex VII tribunal avoided any language in its *dispositif* and in its reasoning that might suggest that it was purporting to settle those disputes. Moreover, a close reading of its two awards shows that the tribunal maintained cautious ambiguity, rather than clearly taking a side, in the controversy as to the scope and limits of jurisdiction under Part XV, section 2, in respect of territorial issues.[40] Adjudicators who have prayed in aid *South China Sea* for a maximalist interpretation of the territorial exclusion have imputed more to the awards in that case than they support.

Chapters 6 and 7 consider the most problematic among the cases: *Coastal State Rights*. To assert, as Russia did, that a sovereignty dispute exists in regard to Crimea is surprising, because Ukraine, the country that controlled Crimea until the beginning of 2014, and Russia, Ukraine's neighbor closest to Crimea, from December 1991 to March 2014, agreed that *no* dispute as to sovereignty existed there.[41] In February and March 2014, in the space of a few weeks, and without trace of an antecedent legal claim, Russia took control and declared that Crimea is part of Russia. The Annex VII tribunal constituted to hear the *Coastal State Rights* case alluded to 'developments' at that time, which the tribunal left unnamed.[42] The 'developments,' if one accepts the tribunal's conclusion, gave rise to a 'sovereignty dispute' for purposes of international law. Chapters 6 and 7 present a detailed critique of *Coastal State Rights*.

39 See below pp. 144–148.

40 See below Chapter 5, pp. 162–165.

41 See Written Observations and Submissions of Ukraine on Jurisdiction, 27 November 2018, ¶ 26. In addition to Russia's acknowledgment of the point in *Coastal State Rights*, see *Oschadbank v. Russian Federation*, PCA Case No. 2016–14 (Williams, President; Brower and Díaz, arbitrators), Award, 26 November 2018, ¶ 198.

42 See below Chapter 5, pp. 162–165.

Other tribunals, so far, have not expressly criticized the 21 February 2020 award in *Coastal State Rights*, but in cases where parties have pleaded it, judges acting under various jurisdictional instruments have approached it with a degree of reserve. At the ECtHR, decisions on preliminary objections in the *Crimea* and *MH17* cases, dated 16 December 2020 and 25 January 2023 respectively,[43] said nothing about the award, except (in the earlier decision) to mention it in passing.[44] A Special Chamber of ITLOS in its judgment of 28 January 2021 on preliminary objections in *Delimitation of the Maritime Boundary between Mauritius and Maldives in the Indian Ocean* referred to *Coastal State Rights*,[45] and said that it accepts the conclusion, reached in *Chagos Marine Protected Area* and repeated in *Coastal State Rights*, that UNCLOS Part XV, section 2, procedures are generally excluded from addressing territorial issues.[46] The Special Chamber proceeded, however, to give detailed consideration to—and to declare settled—the question of sovereignty over the Chagos Archipelago, the territorial issue that the Maldives pleaded should have barred the Special Chamber from adjudicating the merits of Mauritius' maritime boundary claim.[47] These decisions since *Coastal State Rights* suggest an effort at damage control.

Also of interest are awards in a number of investment cases instituted against Russia by Ukrainian parties under the Ukraine–Russia bilateral investment treaty (BIT). The BIT proceedings were running at the same time as the *Coastal State Rights* Annex VII proceedings. Some of the awards in the investment cases pre-date the 2020 *Coastal State Rights* award, but these only began to enter the public domain recently. They hold interest for the particular approaches that the investment tribunals took to sovereignty in Crimea. I consider them as well in Chapter 8.[48]

The *Coastal State Rights* award contains serious deficiencies in its treatment of questions of sovereignty in law of the sea dispute settlement. Categorical abstention from the exercise of jurisdiction over disputes involving questions of sovereignty poses a risk to general public order, as does a rigidly formal approach that accepts on the basis of mere assertion that a question of that

43 *Ukraine v. Russia (re Crimea)*, ECtHR, Applications nos. 20958/14 and 38334/18, decision on admissibility, 16 December 2020; *Ukraine and the Netherlands v. Russia (MH17 case)*, ECtHR, Applications nos. 8019/16, 43800/14, and 28525/20, Decision, 25 January 2023.

44 *Ukraine* v. *Russia (re Crimea)*, decision of 16 December 2020 at ¶ 244.

45 *Mauritius/Maldives*, ITLOS Special Chamber (Judge Paik, President; Judges Jesus, Cot, Yanai, Bouguetaia, Heidar, and Chadha, and Judges *ad hoc* Oxman & Schrijver, members), preliminary objections, 28 January 2021, ¶¶ 224, 225.

46 *Ibid.* at ¶¶ 134, 139, 214, 246.

47 *Ibid.* at ¶¶ 246, 247–248.

48 See below pp. 302–308.

kind exists in a given case. However, in conclusion, I suggest grounds for cautious optimism in light of the post-*Coastal State Rights* decisions, and because judges and decision-makers in other settings have not resiled from the challenge that an armed aggressor presents to public order and to the formal systems of adjudication that states have constituted to moderate their relations.[49]

Running through the chapters, and in particular Chapters 6, 7, and 8, are five themes. *First*, use of force is a reality of international affairs, and dispute settlement procedures, unlikely to expunge force from statecraft, must operate within that reality in a manner that does the most to preserve, and where possible advance, pacific settlement of disputes. The three cases that I address in this book at chapter length concern maritime claims where a party has contended that territorial sovereignty disputes are involved and should prevent adjudication. In each of the sovereignty disputes, use of force is either immediately involved or in the near background. The *Chagos Marine Protected Area* case concerns a legacy of the era when Great Britain and other European states established far-flung outposts of their sovereignty, either through armed force or with the threat plainly in view. The question whether territorial change was coerced or given with free consent was the central question in the case. The *South China Sea* case addresses incursions by China that threatened the Philippines and other littoral states and were part of an armed presence that China since has enlarged in a maritime region where competing territorial claims complicate the orderly management of maritime disputes. The Philippines' apprehensions about a future of armed imposition of *faits accomplis* were a key factor motivating the Philippines to institute UNCLOS Annex VII proceedings in the matter.[50] Finally, the *Coastal State Rights* case proceeds against the backdrop of the first forcible seizure of territory across a peacefully settled boundary between states in Europe since 1945. As I have sketched in summary form in this Introduction, the preliminary objections award of 2020 in that case raises troubling questions for the resilience of third-party dispute settlement in an era of increasing geopolitical stress.

Second, there are many 'mixed' territorial-maritime disputes, and in the fraught geopolitics of our time possibilities exist for more. Law of the sea dispute settlement thus must come to grips with its own jurisdictional limits and ask what role it will play as states seek ways to resolve such disputes. Russia's assertions in regard to Crimea and China's in the South China Sea by no means complete the catalogue of attempted revisions in the spatial

49 See below pp. 343–346.

50 *South China Sea Arbitration (Republic of the Philippines v. People's Republic of China)*, PCA Case No. 2013–19, UNCLOS Annex VII tribunal (Mensah, President; Cot, Pawlak, Soons, and Wolfrum, arbitrators), Award, 12 July 2016, ¶ 1177.

relations among states that endanger political stability and might complicate, or exclude, application of UNCLOS Part XV, section 2, under the prevailing view of the territorial exclusion. There is Iran's seizure in 1971 of Abu Musa and the Greater and Lesser Tunbs, islands of the United Arab Emirates in the Gulf which continue to this day under Iran's armed control.[51] The Hala'ib Triangle on the Red Sea coast has been a matter of difference between Egypt and Sudan since 1958.[52] Venezuela in 2023 escalated its irredentist assertions against Guyana in respect of the Essequibo region. This included threatening an invasion of Guyana and holding a referendum in Venezuela inviting Venezuelans to express their view that the territory should be incorporated into Venezuela. The referendum was held on 3 December 2023 and is hard to reconcile with an ICJ provisional measures order of 1 December 2023 that had been animated by Guyana's concerns over the threats and then-impending referendum, and by which the Court required Venezuela to 'refrain from taking any action which would modify the situation that currently prevails in the territory in dispute.'[53]

Guatemala, at length, consented to submit the matter of its extensive claims against the territory and maritime entitlements of Belize to the ICJ.[54] Argentina continues to assert (against the United Kingdom) that it is the rightful sovereign in the Falkland Islands (Islas Malvinas),[55] and Spain makes a similar assertion for its own part in regard to Gibraltar.[56]

The ICJ in 2024 declared in an advisory opinion that Israel's presence in the West Bank and Gaza is unlawful.[57] The situation in Israel differs from other territorial questions in a number of respects, including the lack of

51 www.uae-embassy.org/discover-uae/foreign-policy/occupied-uae-islands

52 See Dzurek (with Schofield), *Red Sea* (2001) 4–6.

53 *Arbitral Award of 3 October 1899 (Guyana v. Venezuela)*, ICJ, Provisional Measures, Order, 1 December 2023, ¶¶ 7, 45 (2). Guyana drew the Court's attention to statements 'indicating that Venezuela's armed forces [were] ready and determined to "recover our Guyana Esequiba"': *Ibid.* at ¶ 31. Cf. the Joint Declaration of Argyle for Dialogue and Peace between Guyana and Venezuela, 14 December 2023: www.foreign.gov.bb/the-joint-declaration-of-argyle-for-dialogue-and-peace-between-guyana-and-venezuela/

54 By Special Agreement of 8 December 2008, the two states had consented to the jurisdiction of the ICJ but subject to ratification under national procedures involving simultaneous referenda: Art. 7. The referenda were long-delayed. The two states submitted the Special Agreement to the Court on 22 August 2018 and 7 June 2019, respectively. Second-round pleadings (Reply and Rejoinder) were scheduled for 8 December 2022 and 8 June 2023. See Order, ICJ 2022 p. 474, p. 475 (24 June).

55 See Joint Statement of 19 October 1989 Re-establishing Consular Relations between Britain and Argentina, and Agreeing a Framework on Sovereignty, ¶ 2(1)(b); Special Committee on Decolonization, 2023 Sess., 7th mtg., GA/COL/3371 (20 June 2023).

56 www.exteriores.gob.es/en/PoliticaExterior/Paginas/Gibraltar.aspx

57 *Legal Consequences arising from the Policies and Practices of Israel in the Occupied Palestinian Territory, Including East Jerusalem*, ICJ 2024, Advisory Opinion, ¶ 285(3) (19 July).

peacefully settled boundaries and the presence of only one party that is undoubtedly a state. Moreover, in that situation, the territorial issues *stricto sensu* are hardly the only issues: long-running challenges of national security, and at times during the history of the state of Israel existential threats, pervade the situation. Nonetheless, the territorial aspect is sufficiently discrete to allow some reflections about what it says about territorial disputes in general. I consider the 2024 ICJ advisory opinion in Chapter 1.[58]

Third, problems both in practice and principle arise from the prevailing view that UNCLOS requires the clinical separation of territorial disputes from those in maritime areas when parties seek to adjudicate these under Convention procedures.[59] Dispute settlement under the Convention risks a loss of confidence among states if the prevailing view is not tempered.

Fourth, persuasive grounds exist to temper the prevailing view, and these are both formal and teleological.[60] The purposes of UNCLOS are better served by a more open approach to territorial disputes than adjudicators have taken to date. And the more open approach is more faithful to the text of the Convention than the prevailing view.

Fifth, lateral approaches, through which parties use dispute settlement procedure to address problems of international public order, sometimes overstep the limits of jurisdiction, but adjudicators should take care not to err the other way. Directly related to this theme, it is an adjudicator's duty to exercise a jurisdiction conferred.[61] The cases considered in Chapters 4, 5, 6, and 7 offer a vivid test of Sir Chris Greenwood's celebrated 'glass slipper/ungainly foot' analogy. With the analogy, Greenwood had in mind parties invoking a limited jurisdictional instrument (a 'glass slipper') to pursue a claim that really concerns, not a bilateral legal dispute that the jurisdictional instrument was intended to embrace, but a different, often much less concise, dispute, in some cases concerned with international public order at large (thus the 'ungainly foot').[62] Yet the circumstance that a claim involves a larger question does not in itself exclude the claim from adjudication.[63] It surely cannot be the case, or else little will remain of compulsory binding procedure, that the mere *ipsa dixit* of an objecting party suffices to demonstrate the existence of a question that bars the exercise of merits jurisdiction.

58 See below pp. 35–49.
59 See below Chapter 2, pp. 88–99.
60 See below Chapter 3, pp. 102–127.
61 See below Chapter 2, pp. 62–66.
62 See below Chapter 4, p. 146; Conclusion, pp. 338–340.
63 *United States Diplomatic and Consular Staff in Tehran (United States of America v. Iran)*, Judgment, ICJ 1980 p. 3, p. 20 ¶ 37 (24 May).

Because it supplies a remarkable illustration of these main themes, the *Coastal State Rights* award of 2020 merits a thorough-going account. The award elucidates a number of further points as well that are of enduring significance to international dispute settlement, including but extending beyond territorial and maritime disputes. These include:

- the proper performance of an international adjudicator's forensic function (fact-finding method);[64]
- the testing of party assertions (burden of proof, standard of proof);[65]
- the determination of ancillary or incidental questions (especially questions necessary to the task of determining the scope of a tribunal's jurisdiction);[66]
- the relation in a treaty between its jurisdictional provisions and its substantive provisions (especially the degree to which, if at all, the latter affect the proper interpretation and application of the former);[67]
- the drawing of distinctions among related but distinct matters in law, including, where appropriate, distinguishing matters decided (*res judicata*) from matters not *(dicta)*;[68]
- the distinction between political action (including use of force), on the one hand, and legal dispositions (including sovereignty) and legal claims, on the other;[69]
- plausibility, reasonableness, and good faith in international claims practice;[70]
- the relevance of decided cases;[71]
- the relevance of other related international practice (e.g., resolutions of international organizations);[72] and
- the contribution, if any, of eye witness testimony to our understanding of the drafting history of a treaty.[73]

The *Coastal State Rights* award contains idiosyncrasies that are striking in their departure from well-recognized approaches. Unusual, and, as Chapters 6 and 7 relate, in my view unsatisfactory are the approaches that the arbitrators took in connection with each of the points to which I have just adverted. The case is significant as well for its subject matter, the applicant, Ukraine, having asked for relief in respect of Russia's violations of UNCLOS in the

64 See below Chapter 6, pp. 206–222.
65 See below pp. 239–244.
66 See below Chapter 2, pp. 66–88, Chapter 6, pp. 185–188, 214, 245–246, Conclusion, p. 335.
67 See below Chapter 2, pp. 75–76.
68 See below Chapter 8, pp. 317–320.
69 See below Chapter 6, pp. 199–202.
70 See below pp. 223–228, 229–234.
71 See below Chapter 2, p. 81; Conclusion, pp. 336–337.
72 See below Chapter 7, pp. 258–281.
73 See below Chapter 8, pp. 308–313.

Black Sea, Kerch Strait, and Sea of Azov, and having struggled with the concomitant issue of Russia's armed presence in the territory to which those waters appertain.

Use of terms

I use the term 'adjudication' in this book to refer to the decision-making process that judges or arbitrators carry out when they apply compulsory and binding third-party dispute settlement procedures, including procedures under UNCLOS Part XV, section 2. The distinction is elementary between adjudication *stricto sensu* (i.e., dispute settlement by judges serving on a permanent court such as the ICJ or ITLOS constituted as a standing institution available to settle a range of as-yet-unidentified disputes) and arbitration (i.e., dispute settlement by an arbitrator or arbitrators comprising a tribunal such as an UNCLOS Annex VII tribunal constituted as a temporary organ to settle a specific dispute). Parties and tribunals use the word 'adjudication' to refer to the decision-making process under both, however, in part, perhaps, because to use the phrase 'adjudication or arbitration' (or 'to adjudicate or to arbitrate') when the distinction is not critical to the purpose at hand would be pedantic, as well as prolix.[74]

The terms 'methodology' and 'method,' both of which I use in the chapters that follow, in particular where I address aspects of the 2020 *Coastal State Rights* award that I argue are unsatisfactory in their departure from ordinary methodology, are used in legal settings to denote a number of different things. In international legal settings, the terms 'method' and 'methodology' are often associated with the equidistance method of maritime delimitation and the 'usual methodology' of successive steps of adjustment, following the identification of a provisional equidistance line.[75] The term, in international

74 See, for example, Note Verbale from the Department of Foreign Affairs, Republic of the Philippines, to the Embassy of the People's Republic of China in Manila, No. 13–1585 (9 May 2013), quoted at *South China Sea Arbitration*, Award (12 July 2016), ¶ 1118; Coastal State Rights in the Black Sea, Sea of Azov, and Kerch Strait (Ukraine v. Russia), Annex VII/PCA Case No. 2017–06, Preliminary Objections (21 February 2020) ¶ 181 (and regarding Annex VIII, *ibid.* at ¶ 437); Chagos Marine Protected Area Arbitration (Mauritius v. United Kingdom), Annex VII/PCA Case. No. 2011–03, Award (majority) (18 March 2015), ¶ 217. Cf. use of the term 'courts' to refer to both courts and tribunals: Churchill, Lowe & Sander (2022) 306.

75 As to their use in reference to the equidistance method, see *North Sea Continental Shelf*, Judgment, ICJ 1969 p. 3, p. 23 ¶ 23; and as to the provisional equidistance line and the 'usual methodology' (or 'standard method'), see *Maritime Dispute (Peru v. Chile)*, Judgment, ICJ 2014 p. 3, p. 66, ¶ 184 (27 January); *Territorial and Maritime Dispute (Nicaragua v. Colombia)*, Judgment, ICJ 2012 p. 624, pp. 697–698, ¶¶ 198–199 (19 November).

law usage, has a wider meaning than that, however. For example, there is a natural affinity between the study of 'general questions of methodology' and evidentiary matters, such as judging 'the relative weight to be accorded to empirical research into State practice, as against deductive reasoning,' an example that Sir Michael Wood gave as United Nations (UN) International Law Commission (ILC) Special Rapporteur for identification of customary international law.[76]

Though used throughout the ILC's project on identification of customary international law, the term 'methodology' or 'method' does not seem to have been given a definition in that setting. The *Oxford English Dictionary* gives as its first among several definitions, '[a] procedure for attaining an object,' and as another, '[a] special form of procedure or characteristic set of procedures employed (more or less systematically) in an intellectual discipline or field of study as a mode of investigation and inquiry, or of teaching and exposition.'

A (very provisional) definition, for the purpose to which I am putting the term here, would be that a legal method is a practice of legal reasoning, legal exposition (whether of argument or of decision), fact-finding, or the conduct of dispute settlement procedure, that is not necessarily codified but that is observed by advocates, adjudicators, governments, or other parties involved in formal dispute settlement procedure or other formal legal discourse, with such regularity as to create an expectation that, in like settings, they will continue to observe the practice and, if they depart from it, they will give reasoned explanation for doing so. It is, hopefully, adequate for present purposes to leave this as a stipulative definition and reserve for another time a study of empirical evidence of the use of the term.[77]

The subtitle of this book, 'a public order perspective,' might bring to mind the *ordre public* exception(s) that national courts sometimes apply to prevent or limit the recognition and enforcement of international arbitral awards,[78] or the public order that arbitrators have invoked *in extremis* to

76 Sir Michael Wood, Special Rapporteur, First report on formation and evidence of customary international law, 17 May 2013, A/CN.4/663, p. 121 ¶ 21).

77 See also *Norway—Restrictions on Imports of Apples and Pears*, General Agreement on Tariffs and Trade, Panel Report, 22 June 1989, ¶ 3.16 ('normal legal method,' based on public documents, for discerning the relationship between an international trade obligation of Norway and the State's municipal law).

78 See, for example, de Bailleul & Kerc, 'Defining Violations of International Public Policy Under French Law,' *Baker McKenzie Global Arbitration News*, 13 December 2023. See also Grant, 'Arbitration, Corruption and Post-award Control in French and English Courts' (2022) 71(2) ICLQ 481–496; Grant, 'Fraud and the Integrity of Arbitration: Part 1' (2022) 25(3) *International Arbitration Law Review* 177, 183–8, 187–88, 192; *ibid.* 'Part 2' (2022) 25(4): 259, 275–76.

protect the dispute settlement process from identified abuse.[79] Readers schooled in international law will also think of the New Haven School of international law. Its original exponents, Myres McDougal and Harold Lasswell, described their way of thinking about international law as a 'policy-oriented jurisprudence.'[80] An early observer—none other than John Norton Moore, who later would play a significant role in US policy on law of the sea—described the 'McDougal–Lasswell system' as one that 'utilizes a specialized vocabulary for theorizing about law and for exploring and analyzing the role of law in social process.'[81] The 'specialized vocabulary'—a 'meta-language,' by which is meant a language for talking about a language—Moore identified as the system's strength and as its weakness.[82] Practitioners a half century later continue to object that the 'specialized vocabulary' of the New Haven School in instances obscures more than it clarifies.

The 'public order perspective' in this book does not use a 'meta-language.' I intend that my prose be accessible to lawyers and laypersons alike! Then what is the reason for a 'public order perspective' in this setting? One reason is to keep in view the complexity of the relationship between law and the social reality that law seeks to regulate. The complexity stems from law's double character in that relationship: law shapes social reality, but, at the same time, social reality shapes law. In a settled geopolitics, such as prevailed from 1945 to sometime in the recent past, the environment was congenial to international law, and the law and its institutions grew in scope and depth. It is not by happenstance that international human rights law, world trade law, and international investment law (and investor–state dispute settlement) experienced their most impressive development under conditions of general stability in public order. To observe that stability in public order has begun to erode is not to speak in abstruse formulae of international relations theory. Armed invasion with the declared aim of overthrowing the settled boundaries between states is today no mere theory but a concrete fact. We thus face a change in the social conditions that had allowed international law to flourish. In light of international law's dependence on these social conditions, the change warrants international lawyers' concern.

79 See International Chamber of Commerce (ICC) case no. 1110 (Lagergren, sole arbitrator), Paris, 1963, ¶ 20 (reprinted with redactions in 1994 *Arbitration International* 282 *et seq.*); *World Duty Free Co. Ltd. v. Republic of Kenya*, ICSID Case No. ARB/00/7 (Judge Guillaume, President; Rogers and Veeder, arbitrators), Award, 4 October 2006, ¶¶ 179–181 and note esp. ¶ 190 on costs and observing that 'in this case there can be no successful party on the merits in the traditional sense.'

80 Lasswell & McDougal, 'Jurisprudence in Policy-Oriented Perspective' (1966–1967) 19 *University of Florida Law Review* 486, 491.

81 Moore, 'Myres McDougal and Harold Lasswell' (1968) 54(4) Virg. LR 662, 665–666.

82 *Ibid.* at 665.

A further reason for a public order perspective in this book is that international law practitioners indeed are coming to recognize its relevance, even urgency. To give a small, but revealing, example, in the space of less than a week in autumn 2024, a casual survey of publicity materials for international investment arbitration conferences disclosed not fewer than three, organized with leading practitioners from major law firms, in which geopolitics was centrally involved.[83] Few lawyers heretofore were interested in geopolitics,[84] but some of us now recognize that geopolitics is interested in us. Thus the public order perspective in this book.[85]

'Sovereignty' has abundant meanings traversing several disciplines in addition to law. The meaning that I attribute to the term for purposes of this book is a legal meaning, though even within the law the term has more than one sense.[86] For example, units of federations, for the purposes of federal law, sometimes have 'sovereignty' within the limits of the federal legal order.[87] For international law purposes, 'sovereignty' means the aggregate of all legal rights that any legal person might have and that states, as the principal legal persons under international law, have to plenary extent.[88] A 'sovereignty dispute' is a dispute as to the identity of the state that holds that aggregate of rights in respect of a given territory and thus has full competence to govern the territory and to control the relations of the territory with other

83 Symposium, University of Vienna, ICSID, and Herbert Smith Freehills LLP, *The Winds of Change: ICSID in the Geopolitical Arena* (27 November 2024); Australian Arbitration Week 2024, Norton Rose Fulbright LLP, *Once BIT-ten, Twice Shy: Managing Political Risk and Optimising Value in Foreign Investments during Turbulent Times* (16 October 2024) ('an engaging and topical conversation looking at how to manage and mitigate political risk in foreign investments in a time of geopolitical uncertainty'); ICC New York Conference on International Arbitration, *Contracting and Arbitrating with States and State-Owned Entities: Emerging Trends, Challenges and Best Practices* (26 September 2024), in which one participant, Jonathan C. Hamilton, co-head of the international arbitration practice of Paul Hastings LLP, referred to 'the importance of legal stability and the rule of law.'

84 An exception that proves the rule, W. Michael Reisman, came to be the chief representative of the New Haven School. See, for example, Reisman, 'In Defense of World Public Order' (2001) 95(4) AJIL 833–835. In that editorial comment, weeks after the terror attacks of 11 September 2001 on New York, New York and Arlington, Virginia, USA, Reisman identified the far-reaching goals of the attackers as a threat to world public order.

85 For one of the many critical appraisals of the New Haven School, see Chimni, *International Law and World Order*, 2nd edn. (2017) 104–178.

86 See Crawford, *Creation of States,* 2nd edn. (2006) 32–33.

87 See Jennings & Watts (eds.), *Oppenheim's International Law, vol. 1, Peace*, 9th edn. (1992) 249–255.

88 Crawford, *Brownlie's Principles of Public International Law*, 9th edn. (2019) 432–433; Crawford (2006) 33.

sovereigns, and the right to insist that others respect its competence to that extent.[89] A state can be 'sovereign' in this sense whether in fact it exercises its rights or not for the time being, the negative case arising, for example, during voluntary subjection of a territory to certain (reversible) obligations under treaty or involuntary subjection under armed occupation.[90]

Finally, I use the word 'spatial' in the chapters that follow as an adjective to describe the entitlements, claims, rights, boundaries, etc. of a state on land and also in maritime areas. My intention in using the word is to embrace a category of legal incidents that one must relate to the state's geographic—that is, spatial—limits in order to define, and to distinguish between the category as a whole and its parts that pertain only to one geographic area or the other. (Some writers, by contrast, to embrace maritime and land areas as a whole, have referred, for example, to 'a law of *territory*.')[91] In an early example of usage of the term 'spatial' in the maritime setting, P. E. Corbett in Hague lectures in 1954 (which is to say well before the law of the sea settled the matter that he was addressing) referred to 'a *spatial limit* upon territorial waters which has no agreed measurement in miles or meters.'[92] The earliest example in an ICJ judgment appears to be in *Aegean Sea Continental Shelf*, where the Court referred to the 'geographical—the spatial—extent of Greece's rights over the continental shelf in the Aegean Sea.'[93]

89 For ICJ usage, see *Obligation to Negotiate Access to the Pacific Ocean (Bolivia v. Chile)*, ICJ 2015 p. 592, p. 603 ¶ 29 (24 September); *Maritime Dispute (Peru v. Chile)*, ICJ 2014 p. 3, 52 ¶ 131 (27 January); *Sovereignty over Pedra Branca/Pulau Batu Puteh, Middle Rocks and South Ledge (Malaysia/Singapore)*, ICJ 2008 p. 12, p. 51 ¶ 122 (23 May); *Territorial and Maritime Dispute (Nicaragua v. Colombia)*, Preliminary Objections, ICJ 2007 p. 832, p. 849 ¶ 42 (13 December).

90 Crawford (2006) 33, 73 (belligerent occupation); 89 (distinction between political and legal sense of the term in relation to treaty limits).

91 See Milano & Papanicolopulu, 'State Responsibility in Disputed Areas on Land and at Sea' (2011) 71 ZaöRV 587, 588 (emphasis added).

92 Corbett, *Social Basis of a Law of Nations* (1954) 85 Hag. Rec. at 471 (emphasis added).

93 *Aegean Sea Continental Shelf Case (Greece v. Turkey)*, Judgment, ICJ 1978 p. 3, p. 33 ¶ 80 (19 December).

1

Use of force and settled boundaries

Disputes between states in regard to sovereignty over territory arise from time to time in which no maritime issues are involved. The settlement of sovereignty disputes, particularly disputes as to the delimitation of boundaries between states in relatively localized areas, is a mainstay of international practice.[1]

Parties from time to time distinguish between claims to territories and claims to the precise location of a boundary.[2] Though usage is not strict and juridical categories also less than precise, territorial claims, typically, concern the larger areas—provinces, islands, regions—whereas claims as to the geographic coordinates that a border traces, typically, concern only the smaller. Territorial claims also might be described as claims to title and be said *not* to involve boundaries at all, because the territory which the claim concerns is of agreed scope and contour.

And yet, as a matter of geometry and ordinary parlance, even if disputing parties agree as to the geographic limits of a territory, a dispute as to which of them is sovereign still concerns a boundary. Each claims a boundary that will encompass the territory within its own spatial domain and outside the other's. The distinction between 'territorial disputes' and 'boundary disputes' is not in itself consequential in the present connection, though jurists have adverted to it in others, and it well might have consequences for the application of the law of self-determination and for fact-finding.[3] For purposes of this

1 See, for example, Chukwurah, *Boundary Disputes* (1968).

2 See *Territorial Dispute (Libya/Chad)*, Judgment, ICJ 1994 p. 6, pp. 14–15 ¶ 19 (3 February). For general comment, see Thirlway, 'Territorial Disputes' (2018) 31 Leiden JIL 117, 120–121.

3 See *Sovereignty over Pulau Ligitan and Pulau Sipadan (Indonesia/Malaysia)*, Application by the Philippines for Permission to Intervene, 23 October 2001, Sep. Op. Franck, ICJ 2001 at p. 651 ¶ 2; p. 653 ¶ 4: '[T]he Philippine claim is to North Borneo ... and not to bits of it. This is not a boundary dispute to which evidence of historic title and evidence of texts and efficacies might well be relevant. This is, in effect, a claim by the Philippines to one of the federated states of Malaysia. It is in essence a claim to a territory that had been administered as a British dependency, an interest in reversing that territory's decolonization almost 40 years ago.'

chapter, the terms 'territorial dispute' and 'boundary dispute' are applicable whether the area be large or small that a question about a boundary affects.

There was a time when international lawyers said that war changed boundaries and was, indeed, the source of title over entire countries. As unimpeachable authority as Oppenheim, as late as 1911, called it 'a generally recognized rule of law' that it is open to a state to carry out 'annexation after effective conquest.'[4] The rule, as thus stated, mirrored a volatile international relations in which one state might use force to try to change a border, and the other state typically would resist. Not that the state using force wanted it that way. Clausewitz quipped, 'The aggressor is always peace-loving (as Bonaparte always claimed to be); he would prefer to take over our country unopposed.'[5] Whether use of force met forcible resistance or not, and even where only the threat of force was involved, under international law at an earlier stage in the development of that law an international boundary might change through the unilateral act of one state and without the consent of the other.

Since 1945, however, states have observed a new principle: boundaries peacefully settled change only with the consent of the states concerned. The General Assembly famously stated the principle in its Friendly Relations Declaration in 1970: 'The territory of a State shall not be the object of acquisition by another State resulting from the threat or use of force. No territorial acquisition resulting from the threat or use of force [since entry into force of the UN Charter] shall be recognized as legal.'[6] Professors Klein and Koutroulis, writing in 2018, observe that '[t]he evolution of international law in the course of the twentieth century resulted in the design of a totally different framework with the unequivocal effect of ruling out

4 Oppenheim, *The Future of International Law* (1921) 57 ¶ 68. (Oppenheim published the work originally in 1911 in the German language as *Die Zukunft des Völkerrechts*. James Brown Scott, 'Introductory Note' at *ibid.* v). See the earlier formulation of the leading publicist of imperial Russia, F. F. Martens: 'This most ancient method of acquisition remains up to the present the most frequently applied.' Martens, *Sovremennoe mezhdunardodnoe parvo tsivilizovannykh narodov*, 2nd edn. (St. Petersburg: Tipo. Ministerstva putei soobschcheniia, 1887), I, 353, as quoted by Tunkin, *Theory of International Law* (Butler, trans.) (1974) 405 and extensive reference to other nineteenth- and early twentieth-century writers, *ibid.* 405–408.

5 Von Clausewitz, *On War*, Book VI, chapter 5 (1976) (Howard & Paret, eds. & trans.) (original *Vom Kriege* (1832)) 370.

6 UN General Assembly resolution (GAR) 2625(XXV) (Friendly Relations Declaration), 24 October 1970, Annex. As to general observance of the principle, see Grant, *Aggression against Ukraine* (2015) 1, 5; Alvarez-Jimenez, 'Boundary Agreements' (2012) 23 EJIL 495, 496 (referring to the 'undisputed character of consent as the pillar of boundaries'); Yiallourides, Gehring & Gauci (2018) 71 ¶ 139, 73 ¶ 143.

the use of forcible means to acquire new territories or to resolve territorial disputes.'[7] Whether it resulted from 'design,' happenstance of geopolitics, or some happy confluence of factors, Professors Klein and Koutroulis are right to emphasize the 'framework' character of the principle and its novelty. Observance of the principle has imparted predictability to territorial entitlements under international law that they earlier had lacked.[8]

States do not frequently choose to change their boundaries. When they do, including through consent-based adjudication,[9] under international law today the effects of change are identified and agreed, rather than uncertain and open to general contestation. The shift to a law of spatial stability does not exclude disputes over whether a boundary agreement exists,[10] or about the precise scope and meaning of an agreement.[11] Parties sometimes have such disputes, and adjudicators address them on the law and facts. However, under law, the grounds of contestation today are narrowed, and force is excluded as a method of contestation and, *a fortiori*, as a means of settlement.

This new and stable state of affairs, in turn, has fostered the development of international law well past its earlier limits. International law writers,

7 Klein & Koutroulis, 'Territorial Disputes and the Use of Force' in Kohen & Hébié (eds.), *Research Handbook on Territorial Disputes in International Law* (2018) 235.

8 Others, too, have noted the novelty of the present-day state of legal affairs, in which states define their borders thoroughly and the definitions they adopt are by and large stable. Tracing the emergence of definitiveness and permanence in interstate boundaries under modern international law, see Bardonnet, *Les frontières terrestres et la relativité de leur trace (Problèmes juridiques choisis)* (1976) 153 Hag. Rec. 15, 19–31.

9 The consent of states may extend to accepting as binding the determination of a boundary by a third-party decision-maker, e.g., a court or arbitral tribunal. Such a determination is no exception to the rule that settled interstate borders change only by consent: it manifests the rule. See Hugh Thirlway, 'Territorial Disputes and their Resolution in the Recent Jurisprudence of the International Court of Justice' (2018) 31(1) Leiden JIL 117, 119.

10 Alvarez-Jimenez (2012) 23 EJIL at 498–509, 509–513 (as to disputes over the existence of boundary agreements; and to the validity of boundary agreements).

11 For a case in which the parties disputed the scope of a territorial settlement earlier indicated in a judicial decision, see *Request for Interpretation of the Judgment of 15 June 1962 in the Case concerning the Temple of Preah Vihear* (Cambodia v. Thailand) *(Cambodia v. Thailand)*, Judgment, ICJ 2013 p. 281, p. 310 ¶ 49 (11 November). (Note: I served as counsel to the Kingdom of Thailand in the *Interpretation* case.) As to disputes concerning the content of special régimes and entitlements under boundary settlements, see Saliternik, 'Critical Geography' (2021) 50(1) *Vanderbilt Journal of Transnational Law* 113.

by and large, have had little to say about the relationship between the principle that boundaries do not change by force and the development of international law, and international law practitioners still less.[12] Those most concerned with international law took the principle for granted, and nobody seemed likely to challenge it. In the past decade of international relations, however, it has been challenged. Reflection therefore is timely on the importance of the principle that boundaries peacefully settled between states do not change by force or threat.

The teleological ground: states, spatial authority, and stability

States are the chief actors in international relations,[13] and they are the chief legal persons in international law.[14] The centrality of states in public international order is relative and probably has been since the emergence of the modern interstate system with the Peace of Westphalia in 1648;[15] but the existence of international actors besides states has not displaced states from their central role, a reality that owes to the continued power of states to determine which actors might participate, and on what terms, in international legal relations.[16]

The authority of a state is intrinsically spatial.[17] Alberto Alvarez-Jimenez, writing in the *European Journal of International Law* in 2012, rightly observed

12 Some go as far as to say that to talk about the relationship is a distraction. See Daniel Bethlehem, "Inaugural Sir Elihu Lauterpacht Lecture: The End of Geography; The Changing Nature of the International System and the Challenge to International Law" (2014) 25 EJIL 9.

13 Lake, 'The State in International Relations' in Reus-Smit & Snidal (eds.), *The Oxford Handbook of International Relations* (2008) 41–61.

14 Its 'plenary competence' (Crawford's term) being one of the distinguishing features of the State: Crawford (2006) 40–41 and as to legal personality *ibid*. 28–31.

15 McDougal, Lasswell & Reisman, 'The World Constitutive Process of Authoritative Decision' in Black & Falk (eds.), *The Future of the International Legal Order, vol. 1, Trends and Patterns* (1969) 73, 81 (noting that 'there has always been a wide discrepancy between … doctrine and practice' regarding the exclusivity of States as international legal actors).

16 As to the continued role of states as the 'gatekeepers' of international legal relations, see Grant, 'Gatekeepers' (2022) 13 JIDS 41, 45, 47–52. See also Alvarez, 'State Sovereignty' in Cassese (ed.), *Future of International Law* (2012) 26, 29–32; de Brabandere, 'Non-state Actors in International Dispute Settlement' in d'Aspremont (ed.), *Participants in the International Legal System* (2011) 342, 346 ('What is important is that the direct access to international arbitration is part of the protection offered to foreign investors *by states*' (emphasis added)).

17 For the *locus classicus* on the limitation of the state's legislative powers to its own territory, see *'Lotus' (France v. Turkey)*, 1927 PCIJ Ser. A. No. 10 at 18–19

that '[b]oundaries are a key element of the exercise of states' power and sovereignty, for they determine the extent of their territory—with all the attached social, political, economic, and human dimensions—and of states' jurisdiction.'[18] Parties sometimes claim that a state has responsibility for conduct outside its territory,[19] and a state sometimes asserts that its legislation and its enforcement powers extend beyond its territory.[20] A state sometimes even has responsibility for the international relations of a territory other than its own.[21] But the scope of action of a state is usually centered *in* its territory,[22] and the responsibility of a state for the international relations of territory usually means of *its* territory.[23] When parties—whether states or other actors—have relations with a state, in most instances they know that the state has a defined territory and exercises authority therein.[24]

(7 September), cited, e.g., by Lord Sumption in *Belhaj v. Straw* [2017] UKSC 3 at ¶ 236; *Alvarez-Machain v. U.S.* (9th Cir. 2003), 331 F. 3d 604, 616, n. 8 (vacated, 374 F.3d 1384 (2004)).

18 Alvarez-Jimenez (2012) 495.

19 And courts sometimes agree, as the ECtHR famously did: *Al-Skeini v. UK* (2011) 53 EHRR 18 (holding the UK responsible for deaths both in custody and during patrols by UK troops in Iraq on grounds that the UK exercised 'control and authority over' the individuals concerned). In *Belhaj*, the allegation was that the UK was complicit in misconduct outside the UK. See Lord Mance, [2017] UKSC 3 at ¶ 1. See also Karagiannis, 'Treaties and Territory' in Hollis (ed.), *The Oxford Guide to Treaties*, 2nd edn. (2020) 309, 321–334.

20 See, for example, *EEOC v. Arabian American Oil Co.*, 499 U.S. 244 (1991) ('Both parties concede, as they must, that Congress has the authority to enforce its laws beyond the territorial boundaries of the United States'). Cf. Knox, 'Extrajurisdictionality' (2010) 104 AJIL 351.

21 For example, as did France for Morocco's: *Rights of Nationals of the United States of America in Morocco (France v. USA)*, ICJ 1952 p. 176, 188 (27 August).

22 For example, its tax enforcement activities, and thus the need for international cooperation if one state seeks enforcement measures in support of enforcement action outside its territory, a matter that led to the dispute in *United States v. Stuart*, 489 U.S. 353 (1989).

23 That this is the usual situation finds reflection, e.g., in the Vienna Convention on the Succession of States in respect of Treaties, Art. 2(1)*(b)* ('"succession of States" means the replacement of one State by another in the responsibility for the international relations of territory'), and in the widespread practice by which application of a treaty beyond a state party's territory, or its disapplication *within* that territory, is indicated as an express exception. As to disapplication, VCLT Art. 29 is explicit ('Unless a different intention appears from the treaty or is otherwise established, a treaty is binding upon each party in respect of its entire territory'). As to the 'predictable' territorial principle behind treaties, see Karagiannis in Hollis (ed.) (2020) 310–321.

24 While incomplete as a definition (see Grant, 'Defining Statehood: The Montevideo Convention and its Discontents' (1999) 37 *Columbia Journal of Transnational Law* 403, 437–447), the Montevideo Convention (Convention on the Rights and Duties

Without clear definition of the spatial limits of the state, a great deal else becomes uncertain. Routine exercises of state power, such as the provision of public security and enforcement of regulatory rules; relations with other states, such as negotiation and conclusion of treaties; episodic encounters with persons subject to state power, such as actions by the state against the property rights of a foreign investor—all these (and more) take place with reference to a state's spatial limits.[25] Actors benefit from clear articulation of the limits.[26] International investment, international trade, and international human rights by definition involve legal and physical relations across state borders, but concretely identifiable practice in these matters takes place *in a place*—which is to say, for the overwhelming majority of activity, it takes place within the boundaries of a state.[27] Certainty as to the limits of a state's spatial jurisdiction is essential to the flourishing of activity that we associate with international law as it has developed in recent decades. This is a teleological ground for the rule of stability embodied in the prohibition of forcible change of boundaries and the principle that a state does not establish sovereignty over territory by force. The presumption of the spatial stability of the limits to a state's power has advanced a range of values that law seeks to implement.

of States, 26 December 1933, 165 UNTS 19 (1934) 28 AJIL (Supp.) 75) reflects the widespread expectation that a state has a territory in which it reliably exercises authority. See American Law Institute, *Restatement (Third) Foreign Relations Law of the United States*, §201, Comment *b.* ('*Defined territory*') and Comment *d.* ('*Government*') 73 (1987).

25 For a history that traces state power to early modern efforts at rationalization of control over resources in a state's territory (including, in particular, forests), see Scott, *Seeing Like a State* (1998) 11–22. Scott illustrates the connection between certainty over the disposition of territory, which States fostered, e.g., through mapping internal property boundaries, and the exercise of State power. See, for example, *ibid.* 37–52 (on cadastral maps). See also Bardonnet (1976) 153 Hag. Rec. 15, *passim*.

26 See Ezenwajiaku, *State Territory and International Law* (2020) (arguing that respect for territorial boundaries 'provides a template within which a person's freedom is realized') 184.

27 Grant (2015) 130, 160. This includes activity that takes place in the maritime jurisdiction of a state—that is, within the state's maritime boundaries (as to which see UNCLOS Part II (Territorial Sea and Contiguous Zone) (Arts. 2–33); Part III (International Straits) (Arts. 34–45); Part V (Exclusive Economic Zone) (Arts. 55–75); Part VI (Continental Shelf) (Arts. 76–85). The only activity that might lack contact with an area within the spatial limits of a state is activity in outer space or other common areas, which principally are the Antarctic, the high seas (as to which see UNCLOS Part VII (High Seas) (Arts. 86–120)), and the deep seabed (as to which see UNCLOS Part XI (The Area) (Arts. 133–191)).

International law treats the presumption of spatial stability as central. So central is the presumption of spatial stability to international law that a treaty settling an interstate border creates a legal regime of general—that is, not just *inter partes*—application, and the regime survives the disappearance of the treaty.[28] Thus the law of treaties—and other framework rules of international law, such as the law of state succession—ensure the stability of interstate borders.[29] Article 62, paragraph 2, of the Vienna Convention on the Law of Treaties 1969 provides that '[a] fundamental change of circumstances may not be invoked as a ground for terminating or withdrawing from a treaty: *(a)* If the treaty established a boundary.'[30] When Nicaragua asked the ICJ to infer that a sovereignty dispute existed in respect of Colombia's islands of San Andrés, Providencia, and Santa Catalina, the ICJ recalled that 'it is a principle of international law that a territorial régime established by treaty "achieves a permanence which the treaty itself does not necessarily enjoy" and the continued existence of that régime is not dependent upon the continuing life of the treaty under which the régime is agreed.'[31] Article 11 of the Vienna Convention on Succession of States in respect of treaties 1978 provides that '[a] succession of States does not as such affect: (a) a boundary established by a treaty; or (b) obligations and rights established by a treaty and relating to the régime of a boundary.'[32] As the tribunal in the proceedings between Croatia and Slovenia in respect of the delimitation of their maritime area observed, '[i]n accordance with established principles of customary law reflected in Article 11 of the Vienna Convention on the Succession of States in respect of Treaties, a succession of States does not as such affect a boundary established by treaty.'[33] These treaty rules, and their application by adjudicators, reflect the stability of settled boundaries.

28 *Territorial and Maritime Dispute (Nicaragua v. Colombia)*, Preliminary Objections, ICJ 2007 p. 832, p. 861 ¶ 89 (3 December), quoting *Territorial Dispute (Libya/Chad)*, Judgment, ICJ 1994 p. 6, p. 37 ¶ 73 (3 February).
29 As to the law of treaties, see Grant (2015) 116–117; as to state succession, *ibid.* 117–118.
30 1155 United Nations Treaty Series (UNTS) at 347.
31 *Territorial and Maritime Dispute (Nicaragua v. Colombia)*, Judgment, ICJ 2007 p. 832, p. 861 ¶ 89 (13 December), quoting *Territorial Dispute (Libya/Chad)*, Judgment, ICJ 1994 p. 37 ¶¶ 72–73 (3 February).
32 1946 UNTS at 10.
33 *In the matter of an arbitration under the Arbitration Agreement between the Government of the Republic of Croatia and the Government of Slovenia, Signed on 4 November 2009 (Croatia/Slovenia)*, PCA Case No. 2012–04 (Guillaume, President; Einar Fife, Lowe, Michel, and Simma, arbitrators), Final Award, 29 June 2017, ¶ 9.

Reflecting the central importance of the stability of boundaries, the law identifies the attempt to change a boundary by force as the main case of international aggression,[34] the 'crime of crimes' in international law.[35]

Only a consent-based transaction with change as its object supersedes a peaceful boundary settlement between states.

A question, to which I turn in the next section of this chapter in connection with the 2024 *Israeli Practices* advisory opinion, is whether, and if so how and to what extent, the principle that boundaries do not change by force applies to boundaries other than those peacefully settled between states. The principle of territorial integrity of states is not precisely the same as the principle of stability that concerns us here, but the two are sufficiently related that the received understanding of the former is suggestive of certain limits in the latter. When asked to hold whether the long-running crisis in the then-Serbian province of Kosovo, which started in 1989, escalated in 1998, and eventually, in 2008, involved the territory declaring its independence from Serbia, entailed a violation of the territorial integrity of Serbia, the ICJ said that the principle of territorial integrity did not have application in those circumstances. 'The principle of territorial integrity,' said the Court, 'is confined to the sphere of relations *between States*.'[36]

The principle that use of force does not throw a settled boundary into legal doubt is to be distinguished from the rule prohibiting use of force to settle a doubted boundary.[37] Writers and jurists naturally associate the two with one another. But they require individuation. The former, which we also may express as a principle of non-acquisition of title to territory by force, concerns the identity of the state that is sovereign of a territory. It concerns a legal conclusion, opposable to all states, that the identity of the sovereign

34 Grant (2015) 136.

35 See, for example, Mégret, 'International Criminal Justice' (2018) 29 EJIL 835; Barriga, 'Amendments on the Crime of Aggression' in Barriga & Kreβ (eds.), *The Travaux Préparatoires of the Crime of Aggression* (2012) 4; Weisbord, 'Conceptualizing Aggression' (2009) 20 *Duke Journal of Comparative and International Law* 1, 1; Coracini & Wrange, 'The Specificity of the Crime of Aggression' in Kreβ & Barriga (eds.), *The Crime of Aggression: A Commentary* 338 (2017). While often associated with the crime of genocide, see, e.g., Zelman, 'A Crime Universally Acknowledged' (2020) 51 *Georgetown Journal of International Law* 727, 744, aggression as 'crime of crimes' encompasses a distinct violation of law: 'These [genocide, crimes against humanity, and war crimes] are all concepts ... that are not included within the current definition of the crime of aggression,' Judge Sanji Mmasenono Monageng (2017) 58 HILJ 79, 81–82.

36 *Accordance with International Law of the Unilateral Declaration of Independence in respect of Kosovo*, Advisory Opinion, ICJ 2010 p. 403, p. 437 ¶ 80 (22 July) (emphasis added). Cf. *Restatement (Third), Foreign Relations Law of the United States* at §202 p. 80, Reporters' Note 1. ('*Statehood and recognition*').

37 See Mikanagi, 'Establishing a Military Presence in a Disputed Territory: Interpretation of Article 2(3) and (4) of the UN Charter' (2018) 67 ICLQ 1021, 1034.

has not changed, and the consequent requirement that nobody recognize a state as sovereign in a territory purchase over which the state has gained from another only by force. The latter, by contrast, is a specific instance of the prohibition of use of force. When the prohibition is applied (in light of the facts and subject to exceptions, including self-defense), and when found to have been breached, the result is the international legal responsibility of the state that has breached it. The legal responsibility of a state for an unlawful use of force says nothing in itself as to a claim to sovereignty, though, as I suggest a little later in this chapter, the unlawfulness of a use of force might have evidentiary value if one is called on to say whether a sovereignty claim is valid. An assertion of sovereignty with no foundation *other than* use of force is invalid per se.

Where a boundary is in legal dispute, the prohibition of use of force of course applies. Use of force to settle a disputed boundary also brings into play the obligation to seek to settle disputes by peaceful means.[38] The relation between the two, it would seem, is no more or less proximate than that between the prohibition of use of force, as such, and the peaceful settlement rule.[39] Be that as it may, both are dependent on an antecedent circumstance, namely the existence of a dispute: the rule that prohibits use of force to settle a dispute and the rule obliging peaceful settlement, alike, only apply where a dispute exists.

Another part of the general framework of international law that identifies attempts to change boundaries by force as raising special, arguably paramount, concern is the law of state responsibility. When the ILC expounded the consequences under the law of state responsibility that follow specially from a serious breach of a peremptory norm,[40] the main cases that it adduced

38 UN Charter Arts. 2(3), 33(1). Franchini and Buchan cite as indicative of the customary status of the obligation *Military and Paramilitary Activities* and the *Temple interpretation* case: Franchini & Buchan, 'The Obligation of Peaceful Settlement of International Disputes' in Buchan, Franchini, & Tsagourias (eds.), *International Dispute Settlement* (2023) 15, 19 n. 18.

39 Though see the admonition about 'conflation of the principles': Franchini & Buchan at 16, citing (with skepticism) Pellet 'Peaceful Settlement of International Disputes' in Peters (ed.), *Max Planck Encyclopaedia of International Law* (2013) ¶ 5.

40 As to which see Conclusion 3, Draft conclusions on identification and legal consequences of peremptory norms of general international law (*jus cogens*), A/77.10 p. 2 (2022) (forthcoming in ILC Yearbook 2022, vol. II, Part Two). For judicial use, see, e.g., *Obligation to Prosecute or Extradite (Belgium v. Senegal)*, ICJ 2012 p. 422, p. 457 ¶ 99 (20 July) and the understanding that, more typically, the peremptory character of a norm breached does *not* affect the application of general framework rules (e.g., the rules establishing the jurisdiction of a court or tribunal): *Convention on the Prevention and Punishment of the Crime of Genocide (Croatia v. Serbia)*, ICJ 2015 p. 3, 45 ¶ 85 (3 February); *ibid.* 47, ¶ 88 (with references to earlier jurisprudence).

are acts of aggression intended to change by force the boundaries between states.[41] The conclusion that special consequences follow from a serious breach of a peremptory norm is remarkable in the law of state responsibility, because that law otherwise refers to no primary (i.e., substantive) obligation, providing only for consequences that follow from breaches irrespective of the primary obligation breached.[42] The special consequences that follow from a serious breach of a peremptory norm are that states shall withhold recognition from the situation created by the serious breach, shall deny any legal effects to the situation, and shall cooperate through lawful action to reverse it.[43] The law of state responsibility is open to the possibility that other substantive obligations have peremptory character and thus the possibility that their breach, too, attracts these special secondary obligations. But in the inductive process of identifying the consequences of breaches of peremptory norms,[44] the ILC found far and away the strongest evidence in the practice concerning aggression to change the boundaries between states.

The rule of non-recognition of attempts to change boundaries by force reflects a further teleological ground for the prohibition of forcible change. The rule removes an incentive by states to go to war to change a boundary.

Wars to change boundaries were frequent before the mid-twentieth century. International relations writers have adduced evidence that aggrandizement of the state's spatial domain had been one of the chief goals in war-making.[45] It could be that seizing a territory for the strictly negative purpose of keeping another state from having it serves a state interest but,[46] at least in the

41 See ARSIWA, Art. 41, Comments (6) (Japan's invasion of China and purported severance of Manchuria) and (7) (Iraq's invasion and purported annexation of Kuwait) and the possible exception, but if an exception then one that proves the rule, Comment (8) (South Africa's purported partitioning of its own territory in furtherance of the apartheid regime).

42 For a critique, see Chimni, 'Articles on State Responsibility' (2020) 31 EJIL 1211, 1213.

43 ARSIWA Art. 41. The obligation of non-recognition and reversal applies, *mutatis mutandis*, to international organizations. See Draft articles on the responsibility of international organizations, Arts. 41 and 42: 2011 ILC Yearbook, vol. II, Part Two, 82, 83.

44 The inductive process is visible throughout the ILC's work and occasionally mentioned by name. See, for example, Mr. Ago (Special Rapporteur), State responsibility, 1976 ILC Yearbook, vol. I at 9, ¶ 13 and *ibid.* 12, ¶ 15, Mr. Hambro's affirmation that 'all the members approved of [the Special Rapporteur's] inductive method of dealing with the topic.'

45 See p. 57 n. 142.

46 The negative interest might involve absorbing the territory into an autarchic system from which other states already are excluded. A distinction fundamental to geopolitics is involved here, that between the maritime ('rimland') powers and the Eurasian ('heartland') powers. Professor Sarah Paine explained that the two kinds of powers

interconnected world that emerged over the past eighty years, much the more prevalent interest in having effective control over a territory has been to involve the territory (and its inhabitants) in far-reaching social and economic relations. Such relations and thus the modern interest in territory are frustrated, if other states refuse to treat the state as lawfully in the territory for general social and economic purposes. In most cases, to be lawfully in a territory in that way means to be sovereign in the territory. And, so, the rule that denies that the state is sovereign whose only presence is based on force is an incentive against use of force. In short, if a state can effect no change of legal title by using force, then an incentive to use force is lacking. A public order in which that incentive is lacking, in turn, is more pacific and more stable than one in which it exists.

Taking a sociological view of the matter, one finds reason to believe that the law's presumption of spatial stability has roots deep in patterns of human interaction. Surabhi Ranganathan observes that entrepreneurs and technologists have attempted in the first decades of the twenty-first century to create new social formats that would function independently from the jurisdiction of states and not be fixed at any particular spatial locus. Their efforts have been halting at best. Professor Ranganathan notes the irony that some of the most avant garde venturers in this direction have come to concede that people in fact do not want 'dynamic geography, and unimpaired freedom for residents to innovate legal and political arrangements.'[47] There is as yet no Silicon Valley start-up company poised to turn the principle of stable boundaries obsolescent! The challenge to this fundamental principle in the relations of states does not come from actors outside the traditional framework of international law and relations. It comes from within. It comes from states.

The principle of non-acquisition by force, its scope, and consequences: the 2024 *Israel* advisory opinion

At its uncontroversial core, the principle that boundaries do not change by force applies to a peacefully settled boundary between states. Questions

pursue 'fundamentally different world orders: one of mutually exclusive spheres of influence, and the other a world governed by universal rules.' Sarah C. M. Paine, Sims University Professor of History and Grand Strategy, U.S. Naval War College, 'The 2022 George C. Marshall Lecture in Military History—Centuries of Security: Chinese, Russian and U.S. Continental versus Maritime Approaches' (2022) 86 *The Journal of Military History* 813, 836.

47 Ranganathan, 'Seasteads, Land-Grabs and International Law' (2019) 32 Leiden JIL 205, 209.

arise where parties seek to apply the principle in other situations. Difficulties arise where, alongside the principle, parties also invoke the prohibition of use of force. The more complex the factual circumstances, the more acute the difficulties.

The ICJ advisory proceedings in 2024 in respect of *Legal Consequences Arising from the Policies and Practices of Israel in the Occupied Palestinian Territory, Including East Jerusalem* addressed a situation that, arguably, does not involve two states and that it is common ground does not involve peacefully settled boundaries.[48] Violence has vexed the relationship between Israel and its Arab neighbors for decades, and a final overall disposition, including in regard to boundaries, remains elusive. As it had done twenty years before in the *Wall* advisory proceedings,[49] the ICJ in 2024 affirmed that territory is not acquired by use of force under modern international law.[50] If one were to confine one's reading of the advisory opinion to this point, then the advisory opinion would seem unexceptionable. Confining one's reading to the one point about territorial acquisition, however, would be artificial, because the advisory opinion ignores three further points, each fundamental to the question that instigated the advisory proceedings. The fundamental points are these: responsibility for use of force is analytically distinct from the principle of non-acquisition by force; the prohibition of use of force is subject to the exception of self-defense; and advisory opinions are not a device to adjudicate disputes without party consent.

Let us start with the principle of non-acquisition of territory by force—which the advisory opinion is unexceptionable in having restated—and then turn to the points that the Court ignored and, by having ignored, deprived the advisory opinion of persuasive effect.

Among states participating in the proceedings that did not object to the Court entertaining the General Assembly's question, nearly all invoked the prohibition of forcible acquisition of territory. Turkey, for example, said that 'acquisition of territory by military conquest is inadmissible under international law.'[51] Russia referred to 'the principle of inadmissibility of acquisition of territory by force.'[52] Japan, too, referred to the principle in

48 *Legal Consequences arising from the Policies and Practices of Israel in the Occupied Palestinian Territory, Including East Jerusalem*, ICJ, Advisory Opinion, 19 July 2024.

49 *Legal Consequences of the Construction of a Wall in the Occupied Palestinian Territory*, Advisory Opinion, ICJ 2004 p. 136, p. 171 ¶ 87 (9 July).

50 Advisory Opinion of 19 July 2024, ¶ 175.

51 Written Statement submitted by the Republic of Türkiye, 20 July 2023, p. 5.

52 Written Statement by the Russian Federation, 24 July 2023, p. 22, ¶ 72.

the same terms.[53] Other states used a variety of terms to express much the same proposition.[54]

The Court's advisory opinion and separate opinions of a number of judges alike acknowledged the prohibition of the acquisition of territory by force. The Court said that '[armed] occupation can under no circumstances serve as the source of title to territory or justify its acquisition by the occupying Power'[55] and that 'security concerns' do not 'override the principle of the prohibition of the acquisition of territory by force.'[56] With reference to Security Council practice, the Court referred to the 'inadmissibility of the acquisition of territory by force.'[57] In a joint declaration, Judges Nolte and Cleveland stated that 'the threat or use of force to seek to permanently acquire territory is prohibited—indeed, it is absolutely prohibited.'[58] Judges

53 Written Statement of Japan, 25 July 2023, ¶ 8. Japan's Written Statement reviewed State practice on the point in detail. See *ibid.* ¶¶ 5–17.

54 See Written Statement of the Hashemite Kingdom of Jordan, 25 July 2023, ¶¶ 3.11, 4.58, 4.75, 4.82; Written Statement of the Republic of Namibia, 21 July 2023, ¶ 143; Written Statement by the Cooperative Republic of Guyana, 25 July 2023, ¶¶ 8, 21; Written Statement of the Arab Republic of Egypt, 25 July 2023, ¶¶ 78–79, 261; Written Statement of the Government of the People's Democratic Republic of Algeria, p. 17; Written Statement of the Government of Norway, 7 July 2023, p. 2; Written Statement of Lebanon, 24 July 2023, ¶ 56; Written Statement of Japan, 25 July 2023, ¶¶ 7–8; Written Statement of the Republic of Maldives, 25 July 2023, ¶¶18, 22; Written Statement of the Republic of Yemen, 25 July 2023, ¶¶ 19, 33; Written Statement of the Swiss Confederation, 17 July 2023, ¶ 46; Written Statement of the Kingdom of Saudi Arabia, 25 July 2023, ¶ 26; Written Statement of the State of Qatar, 25 July 2023, ¶ 3.2; Written Statement Submitted by the Government of the Republic of South Africa, 25 July 2023, ¶¶ 54, 125; Written Statement Submitted by the Islamic Republic of Pakistan, 25 July 2023, ¶¶ 109–110; Written Statement of the Federative Republic of Brazil, 25 July 2023, ¶ 43; Written Statement of the Republic of the Gambia, 25 July 2023, ¶ 1.18; Written Statement of the People's Republic of China, 25 July 2023, ¶¶ 26; Statement issued by the State of Kuwait, 25 July 2023, ¶ 26; Written Statement of the Republic of Mauritius, 25 July 2023, ¶ 7; Written Statement of the Plurinational State of Bolivia, 25 July 2023, pp. 4–5; Written Statement of Belize, 25 July 2023, ¶¶ 48, 50, 59; Statement of Ireland, 25 July 2023, ¶¶ 30, 36, 41; Written Statement of Cuba, 25 July 2023, pp. 5–6; Written Statement of Malaysia, 25 July 2023, ¶¶ 28, 70; Written Statement of the Government of Senegal, 21 July 2023, p. 3; Written Statement of the Republic of Djibouti, 25 July 2023, ¶¶ 11, 15; Written Statement submitted by the Government of the Republic of Indonesia, 25 July 2023, ¶ 41. See also CR 2024/7, Public Sitting, 21 February 2024, Mr. Visek (for the United States), p. 56, ¶ 32.

55 Advisory Opinion of 19 July 2024, ¶ 253.

56 *Ibid.* at ¶ 254.

57 *Ibid.* at ¶ 276.

58 Joint Declaration of Judges Nolte and Cleveland, ¶ 7. See also Written Statement of the African Union, 25 July 2023, ¶ 121: 'the prohibition of the acquisition of territory by force is a rule that admits no exceptions.'

Tomka, Abraham, and Aurescu in their joint opinion wrote to similar effect.[59] Judge Iwasawa identified '[t]he prohibition of forcible acquisition of territory' as 'a principle of customary international law.'[60] Judge Cleveland, writing in a separate opinion, agreed.[61] So the Court and judges writing separately broadly concurred in their understanding that a prohibition exists against the acquisition of territory by force.

But the advisory opinion reflects uncertainty as to the relation between *that* prohibition and the prohibition of use of force as such. The Court said that 'to seek to acquire sovereignty over an occupied territory … is contrary to the prohibition of the use of force in international relations and its corollary principle of the non-acquisition of territory by force.'[62] Though now restated in a number of settings,[63] the dictum is doubtful that the 'principle of the non-acquisition of territory by force' is a 'corollary' to the prohibition of use of force.

A 'corollary,' the dictionary tells us, is a 'proposition appended to another which has been demonstrated, and following immediately from it without new proof.'[64] Let us consider whether the principle of non-acquisition of territory by force is a proposition that is appended to the prohibition of use of force 'following immediately from it without new proof.'

A prominent feature of the prohibition of use of force is that it is a qualified prohibition. Under the prohibition, significant areas of doubt exist, and factual questions make particular cases difficult to judge. Nevertheless, though in a given case it is likely to be contested whether use of force is lawful, it is not doubted that there are situations in which it is. Does it 'corelate' that, having engaged in a lawful use of force, a state might annex a territory belonging to another state and, in so doing, acquire the territory for purposes of international law? The received view is that the putative

59 Joint Opinion of Judges Tomka, Abraham and Aurescu, ¶ 22.

60 Separate Opinion of Judge Iwasawa, ¶ 15.

61 Separate Opinion of Judge Cleveland, ¶ 28. See also Declaration of President Salam, ¶ 37; Separate Opinion of Judge Yusuf, ¶ 1; Declaration of Judge Tladi, ¶ 2; Separate Opinion of Judge Gómez Robledo, ¶ 21; Declaration of Judge Xue, ¶ 3; Declaration of Judge Charlesworth, ¶ 26.

62 Advisory Opinion of 19 July 2024, ¶ 179.

63 Prior to the Advisory Opinion of 19 July 2024, which refers at its ¶ 179 to 'non-acquisition of territory by force' as a 'corollary principle' of the prohibition of use of force, the ICJ already in the *Wall* advisory opinion of 9 July 2004 had referred to the non-acquisition principle as a 'corollary principle': *Legal Consequences of the Construction of a Wall in the Occupied Palestinian Territory,* Advisory Opinion, ICJ 2004 p. 136, p. 171 ¶ 87. See also *Policies and Practices* advisory proceedings, Written Statement of the Hashemite Kingdom of Jordan, 25 July 2023, ¶¶ 4.4, 4.36, 4.78, 5.6; Written Comment of Pakistan, 25 October 2023, ¶ 6.

64 *Oxford English Dictionary*, 'corollary.'

acquisition would be null and void. The principle of non-acquisition of territory by force, in the received view, as Judges Nolte and Cleveland suggested, is absolute. Attempting to transpose these observations onto the dictionary definition, we find that they do not fit. The proposition that use of force generates no change in title to territory does not 'follow [...] immediately from' the demonstrated proposition that use of force in some circumstances is lawful and others not. The two propositions are not mutually exclusive, but they do not relate to one another in a corollary fashion.[65]

The consequences of breaches of the two rules do not 'correlate' either. The consequences are of juristically different kinds. A breach of the prohibition of use of force results in responsibility of the state in breach; it has, in itself, no other necessary result. By contrast, where force is the putative basis of territorial claim, the result is *not* necessarily legal responsibility for the use of force. The use of force, as such, might have been lawful and, thus, in itself, not a wrongful act attracting legal responsibility. The necessary result of the attempted forcible acquisition, instead, is that the territorial claim by the state attempting it is null and void. Judge Tomka, in a declaration appended to the advisory opinion, aptly criticized the Court for having failed 'clearly [to] distinguish between the nullity, which affects the act in question, depriving it of its validity in international law, and the responsibility that affects the state author of the act which is null.'[66]

The Court's failure in this regard calls to mind a remark by Enrico Milano and Irini Papanicolopulu, writing in the *Zeitschrift für ausländisches öffentliches Recht und Völkerrecht* thirteen years before the advisory opinion. They remarked that the relation between 'the law of State responsibility and the rules on contested territory and maritime areas' is an unresolved problem in international dispute settlement for which 'a consistent and thorough elaboration by international tribunals, together with further scholarly analysis, is especially due.'[67] Professors Milano and Papanicolopulu well might add today as a postscript that 'consistent and thorough' elaboration remains due—the 2024 advisory opinion having not delivered it but, instead, having confused matters more.

To say whether or not an act that a state performs with the intention of asserting a boundary or title will fulfill that intention, and to say whether the

65 Without driving the point to tedium, one can nevertheless remark that, even if one understands the prohibition of use of force itself to *incorporate* and *contain* a rule that force shall not be used to acquire territory, the rule is not a 'corollary' to the prohibition; it is part of it. On that understanding, stating the non-acquisition rule one merely restates part of the use of force rule. Correlation requires a logical step or inference, not mere restatement.

66 Declaration of Judge Tomka, ¶ 6.

67 Milano & Papanicolopulu (2011) at 590.

act is in accord or not with other rules, including the prohibition of use of force, and thus whether the act does or does not attract legal responsibility, are two different things, requiring two different operations of legal logic. As Professors Brunk and Hakimi observe, '[r]egulating the use of force does not by itself resolve questions about the transfer of title to territory following the use of force.'[68] Brunk and Hakimi similarly doubt that the principle of non-acquisition of territory by force is a 'corollary' of the prohibition of use of force.[69]

The absence in the 2024 advisory opinion of a satisfactory elaboration of how use of force relates to the prohibition of forcible acquisition was not just a missed opportunity to bring clarity to legal doctrine. It distorted the Court's approach to the facts. Missing from the advisory opinion was the reasoned consideration that one would have expected of the long course of armed attacks from and across Palestinian areas, including by states and by Palestinian military and paramilitary formations, from which Israel has defended itself from practically the day of its independence. Judges Tomka, Abraham, and Aurescu were struck by the Court's omission. They noted, for example, that Hamas, which perpetrated large-scale atrocities against Israel on 7 October 2023, 'denies the very legitimacy of the existence of the State of Israel'[70] and that, though Israel's occupation has been long, one must consider the occupation 'in light of the exceptionally complex history and nature of the Israeli–Palestinian conflict and the many successive attempts at resolution, the failure of which [the judges said] cannot be attributed to a single party.'[71] Judge Sebutinde recalled the Arab states' repeated rejection of peace settlements in respect of Israel and the series of wars[72] by which those states and Palestinian groups sought to gratify their 'openly expressed ... desire to see the State of Israel ... wiped off the face of the earth.'[73] Self-defense is not unlawful, and armed occupation is not either, when conducted for purposes of self-defense.[74]

68 Brunk & Hakimi (2024) 118(3) AJIL at 420.
69 *Ibid.* at 419–420.
70 Joint Opinion of Judges Tomka, Abraham and Aurescu, ¶ 36. It was for Israel, in its Statement to the Court, dated 24 July 2023, to note that, in the aftermath of Israel's withdrawal from Gaza in 2005, Hamas conducted massive missile attacks on Israel. Statement of the State of Israel Pursuant to the Court's Order of 3 February 2023 Relating to the Advisory Proceedings Initiated by UN General Assembly Resolution 77/247, p. 2.
71 *Ibid.* ¶ 35.
72 Dissenting Opinion of Vice-President Sebutinde, ¶¶ 14–20.
73 *Ibid.* ¶ 56.
74 However, see the debate among writers on whether it is lawful for the defending state to reoccupy territory that is its own (or that it claims is) after a long period of ceasefire. Tom Ruys and Felipe Rodriguez Silvestre argue that it is not:

Judges Tomka, Abraham, and Aurescu concurred with the Court's 'assertion that "[t]he annexation of occupied territory by an occupying Power is unlawful" … and that "occupation can under no circumstances serve as the source of title to territory."'[75] But they '[did] not see how we can go from the finding that the annexation policy pursued by the occupying Power is illegal to the assertion that the occupation itself is illegal. Yet that is exactly what the Opinion does, without any explanation of even minimal legal substantiation [*sans aucune explication ayant un tant soit peu de consistance juridique*].'[76] Judges Tomka, Abraham, and Aurescu here convincingly took the Court to task. The Court ignored the distinction between the prohibition of use of force and the principle that a state does not acquire territory by force. Concluding that Israel is in breach of the latter, the Court seems to have reasoned that such a breach necessarily entails a breach of the former. Judge Tomka in his separate declaration took the Court to task on this point as well. He 'agree[d] that all States are under an obligation to not recognize' any putative acquisition of territory by force (i.e., 'annexation'), but '[did] not share the Court's view that Israel's continued presence in the Occupied Palestinian Territory is unlawful.'[77]

Having entangled the (qualified) prohibition of use of force and the (absolute) principle of non-acquisition by force, the Court entered a thicket of confusion. It ignored the distinction between lawfulness of a use of force, or of an armed occupation, and particular incidents that might arise from the use of force or from the occupation. The distinction is basic to the law concerning use of force. A state engaged in a lawful war of self-defense might engage in violations of humanitarian law. The violations of humanitarian law attract legal responsibility, but they do not transform the lawful act—self-defense—into a breach.

In seeming to identify the prohibition of use of force as the logically sufficient predicate to the principle that a state does not acquire territory by force, the Court obscures the distinct purposes of the latter. Among the

www.justsecurity.org/73310/the-nagorno-karabakh-conflict-and-the-exercise-of-self-defense-to-recover-occupied-land/ (10 November 2020). Dapo Akande and Antonios Tzanakopoulos broadly disagree with Ruys and Rodriguez Silvestre but propose a different question. According to Professors Akande and Tzanakopoulos, 'an occupation resulting from an armed attack on another state is … a continuing armed attack' and then ask whether 'the attacked state' loses 'its right to self-defence simply because of passage of time.' They argue, convincingly, that it does not: www.ejiltalk.org/use-of-force-in-self-defence-to-recover-occupied-territory-when-is-it-permissible/ (18 November 2020).

75 Joint Opinion of Judges Tomka, Abaham and Aurescu, ¶ 22.

76 *Ibid.* ¶ 22.

77 Declaration of Judge Tomka, ¶ 8.

purposes of the principle of non-acquisition is to deter attempts to use force to reorder the spatial relations of states. By denying legal effect to any such attempt, the prohibition removes an incentive to embark on it. A state using force typically does so to pursue a result. The state might pursue any number of results by using force, some lawful (e.g., fulfilling a Chapter VII Security Council mandate), others not (e.g., committing atrocities against civilians). A state that attempts to acquire a territory attempts to change legal title to the territory: either it attempts to gain title from an existing sovereign or it attempts to establish title where there is none to start.[78] The attempt to acquire territory might be through conduct that is lawful; it might not be. However, when a state attempts to acquire territory by use of force, the law has a concern to deny legal effect to the attempted acquisition. That concern is analytically distinct from the concern to attribute responsibility for the use of force.

The invalidity of an attempt by force to acquire territory and illegality of a use of force are separate categories. Analytic clarity recommends their separation, as do the public order considerations that ground them. The invalidity of an attempted acquisition and its nullity as a legal claim do not result from the illegality of the use of force; they are invalid and null regardless of whether the use of force was lawful or not.[79] Conversely, the invalidity and nullity say nothing in themselves of the lawfulness of the use of force or the legal responsibility of the state that has used force. The principle that territory is not acquired by force is not one that says what a state shall or shall not do. It is one that says whether a certain legal effect—acquisition—follows from what a state has done.

The distinctiveness of the two categories—the prohibition of use of force and the principle that a state does not acquire sovereignty by force—by no means entails that the lawfulness, or otherwise, of a use of force is irrelevant to a question of sovereignty. The circumstances in which a state has used force well might be relevant for purposes of evidence, for example where, as in the 2024 advisory proceedings, it is contended that annexation lurks behind conduct that does not include *formal* annexation. If, as the Court did, one accepts that de facto annexation runs foul the prohibition as much

78 The latter case—an attempt to assert title where no state already has done so—is a residual one. Establishing title over *terra nullius* is a possibility of essentially historical interest, though evidence of title so established might still be relevant in settling modern disputes. See Huh, 'Original Title and *Terra Nullius*' (2015) 26(3) EJIL 709–725.

79 Thus, e.g., Professors Klein and Koutroulis, who observe that a prohibition of acquisition by force applies 'in the event of *any* use of force, be it lawful or unlawful': Klein & Koutroulis in Kohen & Hébié (2018) 239 (emphasis added).

as does its *de jure* variant,[80] then one invites assessment of the full range of factual circumstances.[81] Where a state offers no evidence of military necessity to justify its conduct in the occupied territory, one might be readier to infer from the state's conduct that the state aims to acquire the territory. If there really were no defensive purpose in the occupation (and putting aside Security Council mandates that might require a state to be in a territory), then why would the state remain there?

The merits of existing legal claims in regard to the territory, and the manner in which the other party has sought to vindicate its legal claims, might affect an assessment of the matter as well.

The two categories—the prohibition of use of force and the prohibition of forcible acquisition—are not entirely divorced from one another, but it is a mistake to view the latter as a mere correlate, or logical derivation, from the former. Even if one agrees that there have been 'violations by Israel of the prohibition of the acquisition of territory by force'[82] (not every judge agreed),[83] it does not follow that the 'violations' have 'direct impact on the legality of the continued presence of Israel, as an occupying Power.'[84] The Court said that 'sustained abuse by Israel of its position as an occupying

80 The Court said that 'although differing in terms of the means through which the annexation is carried out, both types of annexation share the same objective—the assertion of permanent control over the occupied territory.' Advisory Opinion of 19 July 2024, ¶ 160. It then said that '[a]gainst this background, the Court must examine whether, through its conduct, Israel establishes its permanent control over the Occupied Palestinian Territory, *in a manner that would amount to annexation*' (emphasis added). *Ibid.* at ¶ 161. See also Separate Opinion of Judge Cleveland, ¶ 28: 'The critical question … is what constitutes an unlawful "acquisition" of territory that could place the conduct of an occupying Power in violation of this fundamental norm. "Annexation" in this sense can be (mis)understood as involving the assertion of formal sovereignty over a territory or the incorporation of foreign territory into a State's own territory—neither of which is required for a violation of the prohibition of the acquisition of territory by force.' This distinction—between formal and *de facto* annexation—is hardly immune from doubt.

81 In the view of several of the judges who wrote separately, and on a fair reading of the advisory opinion, the Court did not consider the facts adequately. The Court's omission of any considered assessment of Israel's self-defense has been noted already. See above pp. 40–41. Judges Tomka, Abraham, and Aurescu, in their Joint Opinion, also regretted that the Court introduced terminological confusion by referring to *de jure* and *de facto* annexation, as well as to 'gradual' or 'creeping' annexation.' Joint Opinion of Judges Tomka, Abraham and Aurescu, ¶ 31.

82 Advisory Opinion of 19 July 2024, ¶ 261.

83 See Dissenting Opinion of Vice-President Sebutinde, who comprehensively rejects the Court's approach, and differs from its conclusions, including in respect of the illegality of settlements on the West Bank: Dissenting Opinion of Vice-President Sebutinde, *passim* and ¶ 89.

84 Advisory Opinion of 19 July 2024, ¶ 261.

Power, through annexation and an assertion of permanent control over the Occupied Palestinian Territory and continued frustration of the right of the Palestinian people to self-determination' is what 'renders Israel's presence in the Occupied Palestinian Territory unlawful.'[85] This is a jumble of legal categories, and it is difficult to make sense of it.

The Court's silence as to a further legal category—self-defense—makes the Court's reasoning even harder to follow. A number of judges writing separately criticized the Court, some sharply, for failing to address Israel's self-defense.[86] As the legality of a use of force does not render legal a forcible seizure of territory, so too the unlawful pursuit of annexation or other breaches of the law applicable to occupation of territory do not suspend the state's right of self-defense. There is no doctrine of 'unclean hands' under which a state that conducts its self-defense without full regard for the laws of war loses its right to defend itself. Yet something much along those lines is what the Court seems to have posited, where, silent regarding Israel's self-defense, it concluded that Israel's continued presence in the territories is unlawful and that Israel must end its presence there 'as rapidly as possible.'[87]

If the right to self-defense were to dissipate in that way, then a state, concerned with a continuing question of unsettled sovereignty, might well ask whether other rules relevant to use of force might do so as well. In face of an intransigent counterparty that rejects negotiations or other peaceful means, does the prohibition of acquisition by force apply the same way as it does among states with peacefully settled borders? What of a situation where there is no effective counterparty at all? To the extent that stability is lacking—for example, where a boundary remains disputed between states, where a self-determination community has yet to elect the final status of

85 Advisory Opinion of 19 July 2024, ¶ 261.

86 See Dissenting Opinion of Vice-President Sebutinde, ¶¶ 12–20, 56–58; Joint Opinion of Judges Tomka, Abraham, and Aurescu, ¶¶ 33, 36–37. See also Separate Opinion of Judge Cleveland, ¶ 3.

87 Advisory Opinion of 19 July 2024, ¶ 285 (3) and (4). Judge Cleveland stated the matter in a separate opinion like this: 'Instrumentalizing an occupation to achieve the acquisition of territory, as Israel has done in East Jerusalem and the West Bank, renders such presence unlawful, irrespective of any self-defence justification a State may have.' Separate Opinion of Judge Cleveland, ¶ 14. And Judges Nolte and Cleveland in their Joint Declaration posited that 'any possible justification [for an occupation of territory] is necessarily lost if such a presence is abused for the purpose of annexation and suppression of the right to self-determination.' Joint Declaration of Judges Nolte and Cleveland, ¶ 8. It is to be asked whether Judges Nolte and Cleveland would have concluded, assuming that the fire bombing of Dresden were illegal, that that act would have suspended the right of Britain and the United States of self-defense and thus required the cessation of armed activities by those States in Europe in February 1945.

the territory it inhabits, or where an interlocutor capable of negotiating and adhering to resultant settlements does not exist—it is not altogether clear that the prohibition of forcible change of boundaries should apply exactly the same way as it does to a peacefully settled boundary between states. The prohibition of forcible change of boundaries serves the function of stability. Stability is relative, but there is no function of stability to serve where there is no stability and none in prospect. More relevant in that setting would be the prohibition of use or threat of force, humanitarian constraints on the use of force, and the duty to seek pacific settlement of disputes.[88]

This last consideration—the duty to seek pacific settlement—is especially salient in the situation that the Court's advisory opinion addressed. Among the states that made written submissions in the proceedings, a number urged the Court to refrain from adopting an advisory opinion.[89] Influential in the

88 The 1970 Friendly Relations Declaration (GAR 2625 (XXV), 24 October 1970) appears to reflect the distinction. Principle 1 of the Declaration, in its paragraph 4, identifies a 'duty to refrain from the threat or use of force to violate the existing international boundaries of a State or as a means of solving international disputes, including territorial disputes and problems concerning frontiers of States' and, in its paragraph 5, makes clear that the duty applies to 'international lines of demarcation, such as armistice lines'—which is to say, in situations where parties have not yet reached a final peaceful settlement of their boundary. Separately, in its paragraph 10, Principle 1, the Declaration expresses the prohibition of acquisition by force—but expresses it as a prohibition of acquisition of the 'territory *of a State*' (emphasis added). Its next clause says that '[n]o territorial acquisition resulting from the threat or use of force shall be recognized as legal,' which embraces a wider set of circumstances, including not only attempts to acquire territory by force from a state but also, it would appear, from non-state entities. The reason for the two variants in wording, side by side, is unclear. A distinction is also visible between the Declaration on the granting of independence to colonial countries and peoples (GAR 1514 (XV), 14 December 1960) and the Friendly Relations Declaration. The Colonial Declaration referred to 'countries' as the units protected against the disruption of territorial integrity; the Friendly Relations Declaration, to 'the territorial integrity or political unity of *sovereign and independent States*' (emphasis added). The UK and Mauritius traded competing views on the matter in the *Chagos* advisory proceedings (see Written Statement of the United Kingdom, 15 February 2018, ¶ 8.48; Written Comments of the Republic of Mauritius, 15 May 2018, ¶ 3.60), but the Court, in its advisory opinion, gave priority to the earlier declaration without addressing the limiting language of the latter: *Legal Consequences of the Separation of the Chagos Archipelago from Mauritius in 1965*, Advisory Opinion, ICJ 2019 p. 95, p. 134 ¶ 160 (25 February). See also discussion in Pobjie, *Prohibited Force* (2024) 109–111.

89 See, for example, Written Statement of Hungary, 25 July 2023, ¶¶ 41–42; Written Statement of the Government of the Republic of Togo, 24 July 2023, ¶ 9; Written Statement of the United Kingdom, 20 July 2023, ¶ 81; Written Statement of Canada, 14 July 2023, ¶ 22; Written Statement of Fiji, 25 July 2023, p. 8. See also the convenient summary of statements by other states, UK Written Statement, ¶¶ 38. The United States, curiously, did not frontally request that the Court refrain from addressing

reasoning of those states was that Israel and the Palestinian party have agreed, and the Security Council has directed, that they shall negotiate a final settlement of their long-running and complex differences and, thus, it is not for the Court through its advisory procedure to address them.[90] The very political character of the main questions that persist in the situation indeed suggests that judicial procedure here is inapt. It will be recalled that judicial procedure, under UN Charter Article 33(1), which indicates pacific settlement of disputes to be obligatory, is not the only method of pacific settlement, nor does it enjoy any general priority.

The question of the status of territories inhabited by Palestinians—that is, whether these belong to a state of Palestine—divides writers and states. When James Crawford addressed the matter in 2005, he drew particular attention to the retained powers of Israel in the territories, the open question of final status, and the centrality of the search for a negotiated settlement, all embodied in the Oslo Accords, and concluded that the limitations on the Palestinian Authority, in particular 'the exclusion of substantive powers in the field of foreign relations,' made the case for the existence of a state of Palestine 'unpromising.'[91] Even before the Oslo Accords, some hundred states recognized Palestine as a state,[92] and more have since.[93] Others have not, including three permanent members of the Security Council—France, the United Kingdom, and the United States. The General Assembly in 2024

the questions posed but, instead, seemed resigned to the likelihood that the Court *would* address them. The United States' Written Statement aimed to narrow and guide the Court in addressing the questions, rather than to block it from addressing them entirely. The United States concluded by positing that 'the referral questions should be understood as a request for advice aimed at facilitating the General Assembly's proper role and function in promoting a negotiated resolution to the conflict within the established framework. The Court's opinion should advance that objective.' Written Statement of the United States, 25 July 2023, ¶ 5.7. In somewhat similar vein, see Written Statement of Italy, 25 July 2023, ¶ 5. In its oral statement, the United States went so far as to say that '[t]he Court has an important role to play' in the matter through its advisory proceedings. CR 2024/7, Public Sitting, 21 February 2024, Mr. Visek (for the United States), heading at p. 52.

90 See, for example, Written Statement of Canada, 14 July 2024, ¶¶ 5–7; Written Statement of the United Kingdom, 25 July 2024, ¶¶ 9, 14–19 (regarding the Oslo Accords). See also Written Statement of the United States, 25 July 2023, ¶¶ 3.22, 5.1–5.7; Written Statement of Zambia, 4 August 2023, p. 2.

91 Crawford (2006) 444.

92 *Ibid.* 438.

93 A UK House of Commons Library Research Briefing in 2022 said that 139 UN member states recognized a 'State of Palestine' at that time, though the UK did (and does) not. *UK Government recognition of the State of Palestine alongside the State of Israel,* 21 February 2022: https://commonslibrary.parliament.uk/research-briefings/cdp-2022–0039/

adopted a resolution recommending that the Security Council vote to admit the state of Palestine as a UN member state.[94] Nine member states voted against the resolution; twenty-five abstained.[95] International opinion remains divided on the matter and consensus elusive.

As to the boundaries concerned in Israel's relations with the Palestinians, the position is closer to consensus in one respect: It is a shared view that the parties have not peacefully settled their boundaries. The ICJ, in the 2024 advisory opinion, recalled that the Peace Treaty between Israel and Jordan of 26 October 1994 'fixed the boundary between the two States according to the lines set under the Mandate for Palestine ... but provided that with regard to the "territory that came under Israeli Military government control in 1967" [i.e., East Jerusalem and the West Bank], the boundary with Jordan would be considered "administrative".'[96] The Oslo Accords, too, provide that borders remain to be settled.[97] The Security Council in resolution 2735 (2024) referred to its 'vision' that there will be a two-state solution 'where two democratic States, Israel and Palestine, live side by side in peace within secure and recognized borders,' a form of words that does not evince a view that Palestine is already a state, or that 'secure and recognized borders' already have been agreed.[98]

ICJ judges adding separate opinions to the 2024 advisory opinion recalled the unsettled character of Israel's boundaries. Judge Sebutinde, Vice-President of the Court, in a dissenting opinion, recalled that the armistice agreements following the 1948 Arab invasion of Israel 'were clear in stating that the armistice lines were not boundaries and that the parties retained their claims to territorial sovereignty,'[99] and even the one armistice line that coincided with the Palestine Mandate's boundary—that with Lebanon—the parties stipulated was without prejudice to territorial sovereignty.[100] The Oslo Accords, Judge Sebutinde recalled, are clear that final status negotiations must be concluded before the borders are finalized.[101] Judges Tomka, Abraham, and Aurescu observed as well, in passing, that the settlement of Israel's borders is one of the issues that remains open.[102] Judge Gómez Robledo

94 GAR ES-10/23, 10 May 2024.
95 A/ES-10/PV.49, 10 May 2024.
96 Advisory Opinion of 19 July 2024, ¶ 63.
97 Borders are identified as one of the issues 'that will be negotiated in the permanent status negotiations': Israeli-Palestinian Interim Agreement on the West Bank and the Gaza Strip, 28 September 1995, Art. XVII(1)(a). A/51/889—S/1997/357 p. 22. See also *ibid.* Article XXXI(5).
98 UN Security Council resolution (SCR) 2735 (2024), 10 June 2024, ¶ 6.
99 Dissenting Opinion of Vice-President Sebutinde, ¶ 74.
100 *Ibid.* ¶ 75. See also *ibid.* ¶ 67.
101 *Ibid.* ¶ 60. See further *ibid.* ¶¶ 67–73.
102 Joint Opinion of Judges Tomka, Abraham and Aurescu, ¶ 45–46.

said that 'what is important now is to consolidate the State of Palestine and make it viable, including by settling *through negotiations* [*inter alia*] the question of boundaries.'[103]

It might be objected that to confine the application of the principle that boundaries do not change by force to peacefully settled boundaries between states would diminish the principle's effective meaning. Surely, the objector would say, if a boundary is already peacefully settled, then the purpose of law in the matter has been served and there is nothing left for law to do. This objection would be too formal by half. As a matter of law 'on a given day,'[104] a boundary settlement resolves the matter: the boundary, unlike an as-yet-only-emergent customary rule, requires no further legal incident to give it clarity. As a matter of geopolitics, outside the law, however, a party might well attempt to overturn the settlement. States (and others[105]) today are attempting to overturn long-settled borders, not by legal argument or process but by force. In respect of the boundaries of Ukraine and Russia, where nobody doubted that two states existed and that their boundaries were settled, Russia attacked a boundary settlement by force and then asserted that a sovereignty dispute has arisen. Nor does the law itself finish with a boundary the day that the boundary is settled. Law continues to enshrine the stability of the boundary, not least of all against claims to have changed it by force, and law communicates to all states and to non-states parties too which sovereign is responsible in which territory.

From these considerations, one may suggest some conclusions about boundaries and use of force, some cautious, some confident. As to the scope of application of the prohibition of acquisition by force, it may be that the prohibition applies even where stability is lacking. The ICJ and it would seem all of the Court's judges agree on this point. Some caution, however, is called for on that point. Extending the principle to situations where stability is lacking would seem viable only to the extent that a party or parties exist that have the legal capacity and functional effectiveness to agree to an eventual pacific settlement of the boundary or other final disposition of the territories concerned. Moreover, the consequence of applying the principle is not the legal responsibility of the party that has attempted to effect a

103 Separate Opinion of Judge Gómez Robledo, ¶ 16 (emphasis original).

104 With apologies to James Crawford & Thomas Viles, 'International Law on a Given Day' in James Crawford, *International Law as an Open System: Selected Essays* (Cameron May, 2002) 69.

105 For example, Islamic State, one of the striking features of which was its attempt to change borders by force.

territorial acquisition by force. *That* consequence—legal responsibility—results, or not, depending on the application of the prohibition of use of force (including the right of self-defense), and probably too of the rule requiring pacific settlement of disputes.[106] The consequence of applying the principle that territory is not acquired by force is, instead, that the attempted acquisition has no legal effect.

Finally—and here one may conclude confidently—the principle that a state does not acquire territory by force applies to a peacefully settled boundary between states.

Stability of boundaries at sea

I suggested at the start of this chapter that the stability of boundaries emerged as a principle of international law in connection with disputes concerning terrestrial boundaries.

The stability of boundaries, at least as a matter of principle, applies in much the same way to maritime boundaries.

When serving as judge *ad hoc* in the Indian Ocean maritime boundary case between Mauritius and the Maldives in 2023, Nico Schrijver described the adjudication of a maritime boundary as '"freez[ing]", so to speak, the physical reality at the time of the delimitation and fix[ing] the boundary upon the basis of contemporary evidence.'[107] Judge *ad hoc* Schrijver understood that, '[i]n doing so, judicial decisions contribute to the stability and permanence of boundaries in the same vein as the exclusion of boundary agreements from the rule of fundamental change of circumstances does (article 62, paragraph 2 (a), of the Vienna Convention on the Law of Treaties).'[108] Other jurists have stated the matter in a similar way in other settings. For example, Rüdiger Wolfrum at the American Society of International Law in 2020,

106 As to which in connection with boundary disputes, see Milano & Papanicolopulu (2011) at 597–599; Yiallourides, Gehring, & Gauci (2018) 93–101.

107 *Mauritius/Maldives*, 28 April 2023, Declaration of Judge *ad hoc* Schrijver, ¶ 4.

108 *Ibid.* The concern that Judge *ad hoc* Schrijver addressed was the recession of coastlines, as to which see also Bogdan Aurescu and Nilüfer Oral, Co-Chairs of the Study Group on Sea-Level Rise in Relation to International Law, *Sea-Level Rise in Relation to International Law*, UN Doc. A/CN.4/740 (28 February 2020) at p. 54, ¶ 141(b). Further to the exclusion of boundary agreements from the rule of fundamental change of circumstances, see Lisztwan, 'Stability of Maritime Boundary Agreements' (2012) 37 YJIL 153, 192; Purcell, *Geographical Change and the Law of the Sea* (2019) 151. See also Schofield & Freestone, 'Sea Level Rise and Insular Status' (2019) 34 IJMCL 391, 398–399.

noted that 'a new state … is bound by the agreements concerning boundaries as well as the boundaries declared by the previous state' and '[t]his rule applies to maritime boundaries as well.'[109] According to Judge Wolfrum, '[b]oundaries are to be protected against changes; states should be able to trust in the permanence of boundaries since disputes about boundaries may lead to belligerent conflicts.'[110]

To give an example from many years before, Judge Jímenez de Arechaga, in the Tunisia/Libya *Continental Shelf* case, noted that 'Tunisia has accepted that the principle of stability of African colonial frontiers as well as the principle of State succession apply to this delimitation, *despite the fact that this is a maritime boundary*.'[111] This was also Cameroon's position in regard to the maritime boundary established under the Maroua Agreement, which the Court accepted. According to Cameroon (as summarized by the Court), 'international law comes down unequivocally in favour of the stability and permanence of boundary agreements, whether land or maritime.'[112]

States in the Sixth Committee in 2023, discussing the effect of anticipated sea level rise on boundaries, referred to the 'intangibility of boundaries' as a matter of 'fundamental importance' and thought that *uti possidetis*, though not directly applicable, 'could be used as a source of inspiration.'[113] It was suggested that 'the principle of "legal stability" should equally apply to baselines and maritime zones derived from islands and rocks pursuant to article 121 of [UNCLOS].'[114]

Rothwell, considering sea level rise and its effects in particular on islands, takes a less categorical position. Rothwell acknowledges that '[t]he potential unravelling of well entrenched maritime boundaries due to [sea level rise] would impact on the certainty and stability of the maritime order and international law in general' but identifies the fixing of baselines as '*[o]ne*

109 'Remarks by Rüdiger Wolfrum: Shifting Baselines—Shifting Maritime Boundaries?' (2021) 114 ASIL Proc. 386, 387.
110 *Ibid.*
111 *Continental Shelf (Tunisia/Libya)*, Sep. Op. Judge Jímenez de Arechaga, ICJ 1982 at p. 131 ¶ 101 (emphasis added).
112 *Land and Maritime Boundary between Cameroon and Nigeria (Cameroon* v. *Nigeria: Equatorial Guinea intervening)*, ICJ 2002 at p. 426 ¶ 253. Cf. Sep. Op. of Judge Ranjeva in *Territorial and Maritime Dispute between Nicaragua and Honduras in the Caribbean Sea (Nicaragua* v. *Honduras)*, ICJ 2007 at p. 769 ¶ 10 ('The plotting of the provisional line must add to the element of stability and permanence which characterizes a boundary delimitation exercise') and *ibid.* at p. 786 ¶ 16, quoting *Frontier Dispute (Burkina Faso/Republic of Mali)*, ICJ 1986 p 566 ¶ 23 (22 December).
113 Topical summary of the discussion held in the Sixth Committee of the General Assembly, seventy-eighth sess., 6 February 2024; A/CN.4/763 p. 19 ¶ 89.
114 *Ibid.* at ¶ 88.

response' that state practice supports, which is to say not the only one.[115] An objection to fixing baselines as against sea level rise (or fixing the outer limits of maritime boundaries to similar effect), says Rothwell, is that, while these solutions 'are to the benefit of the relevant coastal States,' they are 'not necessarily to the benefit of the international community.'[116] Rothwell nevertheless acknowledges that 'certainty and stability of ... international law in general' is at least a *desideratum*. To the extent that they migrate, migration of maritime boundaries diminishes certainty and stability.

In its advisory opinion on *Obligations of States in Respect of Climate Change*,[117] which the Court adopted just as this book went to press, the ICJ considered that 'States parties to UNCLOS are under no obligation to update… charts or lists of geographical co-ordinates' that show the baselines and outer limit lines of their maritime zones once these have been 'duly established in conformity with the Convention.'[117a] The Court noted that 'many participants [in the advisory proceedings] voiced strong concerns about sea level rise and its implications, especially for the stability of maritime zones.'[117b]

As for ITLOS, its advisory opinion of 21 May 2024 noted that the Commission of Small Islands States on Climate Change and International Law, which had requested the advisory opinion,[118] 'explained that questions relating to consequences of sea level rise upon maritime zones, entitlements and boundaries are not before the Tribunal.'[119] ITLOS, examining the request, concluded that 'if the Commission had intended to solicit an opinion on the consequences of sea level rise for base points, baselines, claims, rights or entitlements to the maritime zones established under the Convention, or maritime boundaries, and the corresponding obligations, it would have expressly formulated the request accordingly.'[120]

115 Rothwell (2022) 248 (emphasis added).

116 *Ibid.*

117 *Obligations of States in Respect of Climate Change*, Advisory Opinion, ICJ 2025 (23 July). See GAR 77/276, 29 March 2023 (Request for an advisory opinion of the International Court of Justice).

117a ICJ 2025 ¶ 362.

117b *Ibid.* ¶ 355. And see also the Court's view that disappearance of a state's territory 'would not necessarily entail the loss of its statehood.' *Ibid.* ¶ 363.

118 Commission of Small Islands States on Climate Change and International Law, Letter transmitting to Registrar of ITLOS Request for an Advisory Opinion, 12 December 2022: www.itlos.org/fileadmin/itlos/documents/cases/31/Request_for_Advisory_Opinion_COSIS_12.12.22.pdf

119 *Request for an Advisory Opinion submitted by the Commission of Small Island States on Climate Change and International Law*, ITLOS Case No. 31, Advisory Opinion, 21 May 2024, ¶ 149.

120 *Ibid.* ¶ 150.

Nevertheless, a number of states in the ITLOS proceedings made written submissions arguing that ITLOS should not accept that a rise in sea level necessarily would change the state's maritime boundaries. Japan stated that 'it is permissible for coastal states to preserve the existing baselines and maritime zones established in accordance with UNCLOS, notwithstanding the regression of coastlines caused by the climate change-related sea level rise.'[121] Micronesia thought that there is a 'growing internal consensus' at the ILC that UNCLOS does not 'impose an obligation on coastal States' to review their maritime baselines and change them if a coast recedes.[122] Chile went somewhat further, positing that 'baselines drawn in accordance with the Convention and customary international law are permanent and *cannot* be affected by sea-level rise.'[123] Other states in the advisory proceedings took the same or a similar position or at least alluded to it.[124] The Agreement for the Establishment of the Commission of Small Island States on Climate Change and International Law (the parties to which are Antigua and Barbuda, Niue, Palau, St. Kitts and Nevis, St. Lucia, St. Vincent and the Grenadines, Tuvalu, and Vanuatu) '[a]ffirm[s]' that maritime zones established in accordance with UNCLOS continue 'without reduction, notwithstanding any physical changes connected to climate change-related sea-level rise.'[125]

No doubt distinct issues arise in the adjudication of maritime boundaries, in particular issues concerning the modern legal construction of maritime entitlements. In the ILC Study Group on sea level rise in relation to international law, opinion was divided on whether maritime boundaries are subject to the principle of 'immutability and intangibility.' 'Some Study Group members noted that the intangibility of boundaries was a fundamental principle of international law, and called upon the Study Group to place more emphasis on it. At the same time, [others said] that the legal stability of boundaries had limited application in the … law of the sea.'[126]

121 Written Statement of Japan, 15 June 2023, p. 2 n. 2.
122 Written Statement of the Federated States of Micronesia, 16 June 2023, ¶¶ 53–54.
123 Written Statement of Chile, 16 June 2023, ¶ 100 (emphasis added).
124 See, for example, Written Statement of Nauru, 15 June 2023, ¶ 4 n. 7; and Indonesia and Rwanda, see note 125.
125 Agreement for the establishment of the Commission of Small Island States on Climate Change and International Law, Edinburgh, 31 October 2021, preamble, UNTS Reg. no. 56940 p. 4. Note reference in Indonesia's written statement, 15 June 2023, ¶ 17, in the ITLOS *Climate Change* advisory proceedings; and in Rwanda's written statement, 17 June 2023, ¶ 35(c).
126 Sea-level rise in relation to international law, ILC 2023 session: A/78/10, p. 95 ¶ 165. Cf. regarding *uti possidetis* and maritime boundaries, see Bogdan Aurescu and Nilüfer Oral, Co-chairs of the Study Group on sea-level rise in relation to international law, Additional paper, 13 February 2023, A/CN.4/761 at pp. 45–47, ¶¶ 106–110.

In *Maritime Delimitation in the Black Sea (Romania v. Ukraine)*, the ICJ cautioned that

> a maritime boundary delimiting the continental shelf and exclusive economic zones is not to be assimilated to a State boundary separating territories of States. The former defines the limits of maritime zones where under international law coastal States have certain sovereign rights for defined purposes. The latter defines the territorial limits of State sovereignty.[127]

The ICJ thus distinguished between maritime and terrestrial boundaries. The offshore zones of which maritime boundaries mark the spatial limits are subject each to a particular and limited regime of national jurisdiction, each regime being a modern legal construction. The territory of which a terrestrial boundary marks the spatial limits is subject to the totality of state power, that power being embodied in the long-standing concept of sovereignty. The difference the Court understood to justify the conclusion that maritime boundaries are 'not to be assimilated to a State boundary separating territories of States.'

Consistent with its conclusion that the two kinds of boundaries are to be kept conceptually distinct, the Court has hesitated to award a state an all-purpose maritime boundary on the basis of agreements that the state adopted before or in the formative stages of the international consensus on the scope and substantive content of maritime entitlements. The ICJ gave only limited effect to the 1952 Santiago Declaration between Peru, Ecuador, and Chile, deciding that the parties' agreed boundary was confined to maritime zones around certain near-shore islands.[128] In the same case, the Court considered a 1954 Special Maritime Frontier Zone Agreement,[129] and certain practical arrangements from the late 1960s, but found that they, too, 'do not indicate the extent and nature of [the] maritime boundary.'[130] In considering their earlier transactions, the Court noted that 'both Parties [Chile and Peru] recognized that their claim ... did not correspond to the international law of that time.'[131]

So in the maritime setting, special problems arise when an adjudicator must decide whether parties agreed a maritime boundary and, if so, for what purposes, when expressed against the backdrop of a still-evolving

127 *Maritime Delimitation in the Black Sea (Romania v. Ukraine)*, ICJ 2009 at p. 130 ¶ 217.

128 *Maritime Dispute (Peru v. Chile)*, ICJ 2014 at p. 29 ¶¶ 60–62, p. 31 ¶ 70 (27 January). See generally Fietta and Cleverly (2016) 533–549.

129 ICJ 2014 at p. 39 ¶ 92.

130 *Ibid.* at p. 41 ¶99.

131 *Ibid.* at p. 47 ¶ 116. As to earlier practice that does not accord with the Convention, see Churchill, Lowe, & Sander (2022) 294–295.

law of maritime entitlements. It is to be submitted that this, not doubt as to immutability as such, accounts for much of the observed hesitation to cross-apply the principle of immutability of boundaries from the terrestrial setting to the maritime. With appropriate adaptation or qualifiers, the principle plausibly applies at sea.

The Annex VII tribunal in *Bangladesh v. India* in 2014 largely agreed. It stated the matter like this:

> [M]aritime delimitations, like land boundaries, must be stable and definitive to ensure a peaceful relationship between the States concerned in the long term ... '[i]n general, when two countries establish a frontier between them, one of the primary objects is to achieve stability and finality' ... The same consideration applies to maritime boundaries.[132]

Indeed, as far back as 1978, in the *Aegean Sea* case, the ICJ affirmed that, '[w]hether it is a land frontier or a boundary line in the continental shelf that is in question, the process ... inevitably involves the same element of stability and permanence, and is subject to the rule excluding boundary agreements from fundamental change of circumstances.'[133]

Again, where adjudicators have hesitated to apply the principle of stability this has been where parties have disputed, not the principle, but the purposes that agreed or putative delimitations serve or their consistency with the modern rules defining the potential geographic scope and substantive content of maritime entitlements. The cases in which adjudicators have not applied the principle have tended, thus, to confirm the principle: they pertain to situations where boundaries that fully stabilize the relations of the parties in accordance with the law have yet to be defined. It does not derogate or impugn a stability principle to decline to apply it where the thing that it exists to stabilize is lacking.

Stability redux

When Russia, in 2014, used force to take hold of Crimea and to separate parts of the Donetsk and Luhansk provinces from Ukraine's effective control,

132 *Bay of Bengal Maritime Boundary Arbitration (Bangladesh v. India)* (Wolfrum, President; Cot, Mensah, Rao, and Shearer, arbitrators) Award, 7 July 2014, at ¶ 216, quoting *Temple of Preah Vihear (Cambodia v. Thailand)*, Merits, ICJ 1962 at p. 34.

133 *Aegean Sea Continental Shelf Case (Greece v. Turkey)*, ICJ 1978 at pp. 35–36 ¶ 85. Cf. *Mauritius/Maldives*, ITLOS Case No. 28, Preliminary Objections, 28 January 2021, Sep. and Dis. Op. Judge *ad hoc* Oxman, ¶ 35: 'Land and maritime boundaries share the characteristics of formality and finality, whatever the conceptual distinctions between them.'

the boundary settlement that had long prevailed in Europe was ruptured. Russia's attack took place against long-settled boundaries on a continent where, more than any other, it was supposed that states had put the geopolitics of conquest to rest. Russia escalated its invasion in 2022 and declared that Ukraine has no right to exist as a state. In Russia's ambitions, one notices similarity to those that the states on Israel's borders pursued in the past and that others pursue today.

Before 2022, there were writers who drew attention to the central importance of settled boundaries,[134] but most, and in particular the most active practitioners of international dispute settlement, placed the emphasis on the large outgrowth of international rules and institutions, not on the stability of spatial entitlements between states that supplied the necessary conditions for the outgrowth and sustained it.[135] Understandably, as Ukraine itself sought to add a 'lawfare' dimension to its self-defense, it turned to the rules and institutions.[136] The procedures to which Ukraine turned, from the ICJ, to UNCLOS Annex VII, to investment arbitration, would not have achieved the vitality that they have if settled sovereignty had not prevailed over the earlier law of conquest and the geopolitics of armed aggression. And they are unlikely to survive solely through their own operation.

A shift is now in progress toward wider acknowledgment that modern international law starts with settled sovereignty. Some trace of the shift, of stability redux, is even visible among adjudicators, as Chapter 8 relates. In a high-profile example in international law scholarship, Professors Brunk and Hakimi, the coeditors-in-chief of the *American Journal of International Law*, in October 2022 agreed that Russia's aggression 'rejects *the* foundational principle of the post-World War II order—namely, that international boundaries may not be changed with force alone.'[137] According to the coeditors,

134 See esp. Grant (2015). See also Wuerth (2017).

135 See regarding Sir Daniel Bethlehem's declaration that international lawyers are paying too much attention to 'notions of territoriality,' Grant (2015) 158–159, quoting Bethlehem, 'End of Geography' (2014) 25 EJIL 9, 17–18. Consider, too, the Western legal team that acted for Russia in the *Coastal State Rights* proceedings (i.e., after the invasion and seizure of territory of 2014). They withdrew in the first weeks following 24 February 2022, when Russia extended its aggression to the whole of Ukraine. See Pomson, 'Russian Preliminary Objections at the ICJ' *Articles of War* (13 October 2022): https://lieber.westpoint.edu/russian-preliminary-objections-icj-case-must-go-on/

136 Miles, 'Lawfare in Crimea' (2022) 38 *Arbitration International* 135–150.

137 Brunk & Hakimi, 'Russia, Ukraine, and the Future World Order' (2022) 116(4) AJIL 687, 688 (emphasis added). See also Brunk & Hakimi, 'The Prohibition of Annexations and the Foundations of Modern International Law' (2024) 118(3) AJIL 417, 448 n. 197, quoting Grant, *Aggression against Ukraine* (2015) 9: 'the preservation of the territorial settlement among States—that is, the maintenance of the proposition that boundaries are not to be changed by force—is a foundational value of the international law system.' One of the co-editors, Professor Brunk, as

'the prohibition of forcible annexation of foreign territory' is '*the* norm at the core of the UN Charter system on the use of force.'[138] As they further observed, jettisoning that foundational principle, ignoring that 'norm,' removes any 'limiting condition' on the use of force, because it opens the door to the use of force anywhere 'people continue to harbor historical grievances about the internationally recognized borders that they have inherited.'[139] One may add that such grievances are many and that, in any case, opportunists can manufacture a grievance tomorrow where it is absent today.[140] Settled

early as 2017 rightly had placed emphasis on the prohibition of forcible seizure of territory as the core principle of international law: Brunk, 'International Law in the Post-Human Rights Era' (2017) 96 *Texas Law Review* 279, 201–06. See also Bering, 'The Prohibition on Annexation' (2017) 49 *New York University Journal of International Law and Policy* 747, 758–62. The centrality of the prohibition is the main thesis of Grant (2015), in which see also 103–131. *Compare* Hathaway & Shapiro, *The Internationalists* (2018), who connect the emergence of modern international law to the prohibition of change of international borders by force (*ibid.* 167–179, 188–190) but argue that the core principle is a prohibition of use of force *per se* (*ibid.* 223–224). Their argument is the more difficult to sustain in light of evidence of what states do and what they say the law permits them to do.

138 Brunk & Hakimi (2022) at 689 (emphasis added). The authors further elaborated their thinking to observe that the rule against forcible change of international borders connects not only to the prohibition of use of force but also to the 'territorial basis of international law' and to self-determination: (2024) 118(3) AJIL at 443–445 (use of force), 445–448 ('Territorial Entrenchment and Self-determination').

139 Brunk & Hakimi (2022) at 689.

140 Grant (2015) 160. Lauri Mälksoo, in the welcome second edition of *Illegal Annexation and State Continuity*, draws attention to the general threat to peace and security that opening historical territorial issues would create a 'Pandora's box of mutual claims.' Mälksoo, *Illegal Annexation and State Continuity*, 2nd rev. edn. (2022) 223–224. See also, positing that 'normative' influences, which would include narratives about 'historical justice' are as or more influential in fomenting territorial disputes than 'power-political' considerations, Forsberg 'Explaining Territorial Disputes: From Power Politics to Normative Reasons,' (1996) 33(4) *Journal of Peace Research* 433, 445. Historical narrative was at the base of the Philippines' assertions in respect of North Borneo too: see *Sovereignty over Pulau Ligitan and Pulau Sipadan (Indonesia/Malaysia)*, ICJ, Application for Permission to Intervene by the Government of the Philippines (13 March 2001) p. 4, ¶ 4. For Malaysia's reply, see Observations of Malaysia on the Application for Permission to Intervene by the Government of the Republic of the Philippines (2 May 2001) pp. 3–7, ¶¶ 5–13. The Philippines' assertion of a claim to North Borneo was relatively innocuous, as the Philippines did not use armed force to attempt to give it substance, but it nevertheless was disruptive in the *Indonesia/Malaysia* proceedings. The Court, in eventually rejecting the Philippines' application to intervene, made note of the incongruence between the territory over which the Philippines asserted a sovereignty claim and the territorial scope of the dispute that Indonesia and Malaysia and instituted proceedings to settle. ICJ 2001 at p. 600 ¶ 66. However, the Court also indicated that the Philippines' assertions were improbable in their substance, a point to which I return in Chapter 6.

sovereignty—'the holy grail of the post-World II order'[141]—took centuries of searching, and two world wars, to find. It might take considerably less time to lose.

In notable symmetry with international law and its modern development, empirical evidence suggests that conflicting assertions of sovereignty over territory are the most prolific cause of war and that the abeyance of interstate war owes in large part to their diminishing frequency.[142] Conflicting assertions of sovereignty over territory 'are more prone to escalation and armed conflict than any other kind of dispute.'[143] As I suggested earlier in this chapter, a teleological ground for the principle that boundaries do not change by force is that a resolute refusal to recognize any claim to acquire sovereign title that a state asserts by use of force removes an incentive for states to use force.

These insights, as I argue in Chapters 6 and 7, evidently had no influence on the Annex VII tribunal in *Coastal State Rights*. It is my purpose in Chapters 6 and 7, and in this book as a whole, to apply the main insight—that the long-established stability of spatial relations among states is the foundation on which the rich growth of international law since 1945 rests—to a particular and powerful instance of that rich growth, the modern law of the sea as embodied in UNCLOS. The Annex VII tribunal's award in *Coastal State Rights* concluded that a legal dispute exists as to sovereignty in Crimea, and, thus, that the tribunal cannot address maritime claims that depend on Ukraine's continued jurisdiction over maritime areas appurtenant to Crimea. The award thus treated an assertion of sovereignty based on an armed seizure of territory as a legal claim rather than as the nullity that modern international law identifies it to be.

141 (Wuerth) Brunk & Hakimi (2022) 689. See also Brunk & Hakimi (2024) 439–442.

142 See, for example, Vasquez & Barrett, 'Comparing the Democratic and Territorial Peace' (2015) 2 *Journal of Territorial and Maritime Studies* 5, 6–8; and, with references to an extensive literature, Duffy Toft, 'Territory and War' (2014) 51(2) *Journal of Peace Research* 185–198. See also among earlier studies Forsberg (1996) 433; Kocs, 'Territorial Disputes and Interstate War, 1945–1987' (1995) 57(1) *The Journal of Politics* 159–175. There is also evidence that, where borders do change, the change causes the least difficulty where the new border is only a newly *internationalized* border: borders that, in accordance with *uti possidetis*, emerge from existing national or subnational delimitations are less likely to be the subject of armed conflict than those that are completely new: Carter & Goemans, 'New Borders and the Emergence of Interstate Conflict' (2011) 65(2) *International Organization* 275–309. See also Zacher, 'The Territorial Integrity Norm' (2001) 55(2) *International Organization* 215–250. For an international lawyer who agreed, see Bardonnet (1976) 153 Hag. Rec. at 30.

143 Yiallourides, Gehring, & Gauci (2018) 101 citing Gibler, 'Territorial Issues in Militarized Interstate Disputes, 1816–2001' (2017) 24(2) *Conflict Management and Peace Science* 194, 196.

The tribunal's award in *Coastal State Rights* discloses that the tribunal failed to appreciate the damage to general public order that this conclusion entails. Perhaps, one might say, a tribunal should not be blamed for a failure such as that: parties do not appoint arbitrators to serve as guardians of public order. However, the tribunal also failed to exercise the dispute settlement function in accordance with the formal terms of UNCLOS Part XV, section 2. The proper function of an adjudicator under a limited jurisdictional instrument is not to repair an imperfect legal system. It *is* to apply the authority that parties have conferred upon it. Parties also expect adjudicators to use ordinary tools for evaluating evidence and ordinary standards for measuring the credibility of assertions that the adjudicators hear in the course of proceedings.[144] Certain general principles, such as the distinction between legal claim and political assertion, likewise apply in every proceeding and are particularly important to apply in proceedings between states under treaty. These and related issues are some that the chapters that follow address.

* * *

Before turning to the main UNCLOS cases in which adjudicators have considered the relation between UNCLOS jurisdiction and questions of sovereignty (Chapters 4, 5, 6, 7, and 8), let us consider the overall architecture of jurisdiction under UNCLOS (Chapter 2); and let us consider the limitations and optional exceptions to UNCLOS jurisdiction (Chapter 3). I consider in particular how the exclusion of certain sovereignty disputes from conciliation under Article 298(1)(a)*(i)* has come to be interpreted, and I argue that the doctrinaire exclusion of sovereignty issues from consideration in *all* circumstances and for *all* purposes is not in accord with the text, the context, the drafting history, or the objects and purposes of the Convention.

144 See Park, 'Arbitrators and Accuracy' (2010) 1(1) JIDS 25, 34–42.

2

Jurisdiction under UNCLOS Part XV, section 2: the framework

Further to set the scene for the cases that Chapters 4, 5, 6, 7, and 8 address, let us consider the basic architecture of dispute settlement under UNCLOS.

Article 286, the first article in Part XV, section 2, of UNCLOS, provides for the application of the Convention's dispute settlement procedures in the following terms:

> Article 286
>
> Application of procedures under this section
>
> Subject to section 3, any dispute concerning the interpretation or application of this Convention shall, where no settlement has been reached by recourse to section 1, be submitted at the request of any party to the dispute to the court or tribunal having jurisdiction under this section.[1]

As Mathias Forteau elegantly describes it, Article 286 '*fait office de charnière entre les deux premières sections de la partie XV*' ('serves as a hinge between the two first sections of Part XV').[2] Section 1 of Part XV privileges existing dispute settlement agreements and requires the parties to a dispute to attempt to settle it by exchange of views (i.e., negotiated settlement at the diplomatic level).[3] Only on fulfillment of the condition—that 'no settlement has been reached by recourse to section 1'—does the door open to section 2. If we were to extend the hinging metaphor, then we might describe section 3 of Part XV as a series of locks, some in-built, some optional: Article 297 sets out the limitations to jurisdiction which are automatic—the built-in locks,

1 1833 UNTS at 509. See generally Forteau, 'Le règlement des différends' in Forteau & Thouvenin (eds.), *Traité de droit international de la mer* (2017) 989–992; Treves, 'Article 286' in *Proelss Commentary* at 1844–1849; Churchill, Lowe, & Sander (2022) 863–866.

2 Forteau, 'Le règlement des différends' in Forteau and Thouvenin (eds.) (2017) at 991; Merrills & De Brabandere, *Merrill's International Dispute Settlement*, 7th edn. (2022) 263–265, 269.

3 As to Part XV, section 1, generally, see Klein, *Dispute Settlement in the UN Convention on the Law of the Sea* (2009) 31–52.

if you will; and then we turn to Article 298 for the optional ones, exceptions to jurisdiction that apply only if a party elects one or more of them. The overall framework of jurisdiction under UNCLOS thus 'is encapsulated in Article 286.'[4]

Article 286 having encapsulated the overall framework of Part XV—by relating section 2 to the constraints set out in sections 1 and 3—it is to further provisions of section 2 that we turn for terms by which parties have consented to an adjudicator exercising jurisdiction over a dispute.

Article 288(1) and the scope of merits jurisdiction

Provided that the dispute in question is not excluded by operation of section 1 or section 3 of Part XV, the scope of application of the dispute settlement apparatus of the Convention is identified by Article 288, paragraph 1, which belongs to section 2 of Part XV and is titled '*Jurisdiction.*' Article 288, paragraph 1, reads as follows:

> Article 288
>
> Jurisdiction
>
> 1. A court or tribunal referred to in article 287 shall have jurisdiction over any dispute concerning the interpretation or application of this Convention which is submitted to it in accordance with this Part.[5]

Article 287 refers to the ITLOS, the ICJ, an arbitral tribunal constituted in accordance with UNCLOS Annex VII, and 'a special arbitral tribunal constituted in accordance with Annex VIII for one or more of the categories of disputes specified therein' (Article 287(1)(d)).[6] These are the courts or tribunals having jurisdiction over 'any dispute concerning the interpretation or application' of UNCLOS to which Article 288(1) refers.

Paragraph 2 of Article 288 potentially enlarges Part XV, section 2, jurisdiction. Article 288(2) indicates that a procedure referred to in article 287

4 *South China Sea Arbitration (Philippines v. China)*, Award on Jurisdiction and Admissibility, 29 October 2015, ¶ 1087. See also Klein (2009) 29–124.

5 1833 UNTS at 510. See generally Forteau in Forteau & Thouvenin (eds.) (2017) at 1006–1009; Treves, 'Article 286' in *Proelss Commentary* (2017) at 1848; Churchill, Lowe, & Sander (2022) at 865–866.

6 1833 UNTS at 509–510. See generally Klein (2009) 52–59; Forteau in Forteau & Thouvenin (eds.) (2017) at 1007–1009; Treves, 'Article 287' in *Proelss Commentary* (2017) at 1849–1857; Tanaka, *Peaceful Settlement of Disputes* (2018) 236–237; Churchill, Lowe, & Sander (2022) at 870–875; Merrills & De Brabandere (2022) 269–270; Klein & Parlett (2022) 101–103.

'shall also have jurisdiction over any dispute concerning the interpretation or application of an international agreement related to the purposes of [the] Convention, which is submitted to it in accordance with the agreement.' Rosenne and Sohn in the *Virginia Commentary* said that Article 288(2) 'extends the jurisdiction of any court or tribunal functioning under article 287 beyond disputes relating to the interpretation or application' of the Convention.[7]

Thus the dispute settlement apparatus of UNCLOS Part XV, section 2, is not a general international dispute settlement apparatus. Nor, however, is it confined to disputes concerning only particular enumerated terms of UNCLOS, or to disputes that are submitted exclusively in reference to UNCLOS rights and obligations. Jurisdiction under that apparatus reaches 'any dispute concerning the interpretation or application' of UNCLOS and, potentially, to a wide range of disputes arising under other instruments 'related to the purposes' of UNCLOS.

From the *travaux*, it is clear that careful deliberation preceded the decision to adopt the 'any dispute' approach in Article 288. The Third Conference considered '[a]nother approach'—that is, a 'functional [approach], based upon the reference of specific categories of disputes to special procedures of settlement.'[8] The 'functional approach' is not the one that the Third Conference adopted. Instead of 'specific categories of disputes,' Article 288 addresses 'any dispute.'

Courts and tribunals under Part XV, section 2, are directed by Article 293 to apply the rules contained in UNCLOS and also to apply 'other rules of international law not incompatible' with UNCLOS. Adjudicators have read Article 293 to allow them to adjudicate disputes involving a range of matters, including use of force, that UNCLOS contains few or no specific terms to address. As we will see later in this chapter, writers have criticized this reading, which they say confuses the relation between applicable law and jurisdiction.

The provisions of Part XV, section 1, which, as noted, privilege existing dispute settlement agreements and require the parties to a dispute to attempt to settle it by exchange of views, are important limiting provisions. Failure to fulfill those provisions, to the extent that they apply, is fatal to a party's

7 Nordquist (gen. ed.), Rosenne & Sohn (eds.), *The United Nations Convention on the Law of the Sea 1982: A Commentary*, vol. V (1989) p. 47 §288.3. See also Georgoula, 'The LOSC Renvois as a Source of Untapped Jurisdiction' (2023) 38 IJMCL 228–248; Bankes, 'The Jurisdiction of the Dispute Settlement Bodies of the Law of the Sea Convention with Respect to Other Treaties' (2021) 52 ODIL 346–380.

8 Letter dated 1 May 1975 from the Co-chairmen of the Informal Working Group on Settlement of Disputes: Platzröder, vol. XII, p. 194.

claim.[9] However, section 1 does not concern the main question of UNCLOS jurisdiction that this book addresses, and, so, I leave it to one side. The limitations on and optional exceptions to jurisdiction contained in Part XV, section 3, do concern that question. I turn to section 3 in Chapter 3. For the purposes of the present chapter, two further provisions of section 2 call for consideration. One of these is a further paragraph of Article 288: paragraph 4, under which the Convention affirms the authority—and the duty—of judges and arbitrators under Part XV, section 2, to determine the scope of their jurisdiction. The other is Article 293(1), which gives rise to the controversy to which I just alluded about adjudicating questions of use of force.

Article 288(4) and *compétence de la compétence*

Article 288, paragraph 4, provides as follows: 'In the event of a dispute as to whether a court or tribunal has jurisdiction, the matter shall be settled by decision of that court or tribunal.'[10]

Article 288(4), with this brief statement, affirms that adjudicators seised of a dispute under Part XV possess *compétence de la compétence*. Article 58 of the ITLOS Rules of Procedure expresses the same rule in respect of 'a dispute as to whether [ITLOS] has jurisdiction.'[11]

The affirmation that adjudicators decide whether they have jurisdiction is unremarkable in view of the generality of the proposition that an international court or tribunal both must satisfy itself that it has jurisdiction before it proceeds to adjudicate the merits of a dispute and is duty-bound to determine the scope of its jurisdiction if a party has placed jurisdiction in dispute. Thus the Permanent Court as far back as 1928 in the Advisory Opinion on *Interpretation of the Greco-Turkish Agreement of 1 December 1926* referred to 'the principle that, as a general rule, any body possessing jurisdictional powers has the right in the first place itself to determine the

9 For analysis, including of the limitations of the requirements of Part XV, section 1, see *Southern Bluefin Tuna (New Zealand v. Japan; Australia v. Japan)*, Award on Jurisdiction and Admissibility, 4 August 200, XXIII RIAA 1, 42–43 ¶ 55; *Southern Bluefin Tuna*, Provisional Measures, Order, ITLOS 1999 p. 280, p. 295 ¶ 6 (27 August); *Land Reclamation by Singapore in and around the Straits of Johor (Malaysia v. Singapore)*, Provisional Measures, Order, ITLOS 2003 p. 10, p. 19 ¶ 47 (8 October).

10 1833 UNTS at 510. See Treves, 'Article 288' in *Proelss Commentary* (2017) at 1862–1863. Cf. *M/V 'Louisa' (Saint Vincent and the Grenadines v. Kingdom of Spain)*, Judgment, ITLOS 2013 p. 4, pp. 28–29 ¶ 73 (28 May); *Delimitation of the Maritime Boundary between Mauritius and Maldives in the Indian Ocean (Mauritius/Maldives)*, ITLOS Case No. 28, ITLOS Special Chamber, Prelim. Obj. ¶ 190.

11 ITLOS/8, 17 March 2009.

extent of its jurisdiction.'[12] The provision for *compétence de la compétence* in UNCLOS drew little comment from the glossators or, evidently, in the negotiations leading to the adopted text.[13] Professor Ranjeva (as he then was) described Article 288(4) as a 'reiteration of the principle that the court or tribunal shall decide on its own jurisdiction'; he said that it is 'not an innovatory feature.'[14] Judge Treves notes the resemblance between UNCLOS Article 288(4) and Article 36(6) of the Statute of the ICJ.[15] Professors Rosenne and Sohn in the *Virginia Commentary* described *compétence de la compétence*, in the context of the law of the sea, as a rule of customary international law.[16] That Article 288(4) is no innovation, however, does not make it any the less important to the functioning of dispute settlement procedures under Part XV.

An ITLOS Special Chamber in its judgment of 28 January 2021 on jurisdictional objections in *Mauritius/Maldives* placed considerable weight on Article 288(4). The case presented a dispute as to whether the Special Chamber had jurisdiction to adjudicate the maritime boundary between Mauritius and the Maldives.[17] The potential maritime entitlements of the state that is sovereign over the Chagos Archipelago overlap with the potential maritime entitlements of the Maldives.[18] The Maldives took the position that a sovereignty dispute exists between Mauritius and the United Kingdom concerning the Chagos and, on that basis, argued that it was not open to

12 *Interpretation of the Greco-Turkish Agreement of December 1st, 1926 (Final Protocol, Article IV)*, Advisory Opinion, 28 August 1928, PCIJ Ser. B No. 16, p. 20.

13 See the observations by Treves in the *Proelss Commentary*, which, like Rosenne and Sohn's in the *Virginia Commentary*, are sparse: Treves, 'Article 288' in *Proells Commentary* (2017) 1862.

14 Ranjeva, 'Settlement of Disputes' in Dupuy & Vignes (eds.), *Handbook on the New Law of the Sea*, vol. 1 (1991) 1333, 1375.

15 Treves in *Proelss Commentary* at 1862–1863.

16 Rosenne & Sohn in *Virginia Commentary* at 48, §288.5. In respect of Article 36 of the ICJ Statute, see Sir Hersch Lauterpacht's classic statement: *Certain Norwegian Loans (France* v. *Norway)*, Sep. Op. Judge Sir Hersch Lauterpacht, ICJ 1957 p. 34 at pp. 43, 44 (6 July).

17 *Mauritius/Maldives,* Prelim. Obj., ITLOS 2021 p. 16, p. 44 ¶ 81 (indispensable third party objection); p. 49 ¶ 101 (objection against adjudicating a sovereignty dispute) (28 January).

18 See *Delimitation of the Maritime Boundary between Mauritius and Maldives in the Indian Ocean (Mauritius/Maldives)*, ITLOS Case No. 28, ITLOS Special Chamber, Merits, Judgment, 28 April 2023, Sketch-map No. 2 (at p. 43) and ¶ 102 and the Special Chamber's conclusion that 'the north-facing coastline of Peros Banhos Atoll and Salomon Islands Atoll'—that is, atolls belonging to the Chagos—'generat[e] projections that overlap with projections from the coast of the Maldives.' *Ibid.* ¶ 109.

the Special Chamber to treat the Chagos coast as belonging to Mauritius.[19] Mauritius maintained that there is no sovereignty dispute over the Chagos and that the Chagos belong to Mauritius.[20] The Maldives' position would seem to have been the better grounded: the *Chagos Marine Protected Area* tribunal[21] had acknowledged in 2015[22] that a 'long-standing' sovereignty dispute exists in respect of the Chagos.

The Special Chamber, however, rejected the Maldives' position. The Special Chamber concluded that the Chagos indeed belong to Mauritius, a territorial dispute no longer exists, and, thus, the Special Chamber had jurisdiction to adjudicate the Mauritius/Maldives maritime delimitation.[23] We return to *Mauritius/Maldives* in Chapter 8 to consider its implications for the methodology that adjudicators apply when a party presents an objection to jurisdiction, but for present purposes the point of interest is the reliance that the Special Chamber placed on Article 288(4).

According to the Special Chamber:

> 1. Under article 288, paragraph 4, of the Convention, the Special Chamber has the competence to decide its own jurisdiction. In this regard, whether the [ICJ] *Chagos* advisory opinion [2019] has clarified the legal status of the Chagos Archipelago is a question central to the jurisdiction of the Special Chamber. Accordingly, the Special Chamber is competent to assess the Parties' dispute as to the consequences of the advisory opinion to the extent necessary to determine its jurisdiction.[24]

As I suggest in Chapter 8, referring the matter to the ICJ advisory opinion was a formal sleight of hand. It served to distance the Special Chamber

19 *Mauritius/Maldives* (Prelim. Obj.) ¶ 114.

20 *Ibid.* ¶ 108. See also *ibid.* ¶ 113 (stating Mauritius's premise that the Chagos coast, which is opposite the Maldives, is under Mauritius's sovereignty).

21 See Chapter 4, pp. 131–132.

22 For the Maldives' pleading of the point in *Mauritius/Maldives (Prelim. Obj.)*, see *ibid.* at ¶ 104 and the Special Chamber's observation that, at least at one time, a Mauritius-UK dispute existed: *ibid.* at ¶ 242. See *Chagos Marine Protected Area*, Award, ¶ 209 (concluding that the territorial dispute had existed 'at least [since] 1980'); and *Mauritius/Maldives* (Prelim. Obj.) at ¶ 134 (acknowledging the *Chagos Marine Protected Area* Annex VII tribunal's conclusion).

23 *Mauritius/Maldives* (Prelim. Obj.) at ¶¶ 247–248, 249–251.

24 *Mauritius/Maldives* (Prelim. Obj.) ¶ 190, referring to *Legal Consequences of the Separation of the Chagos Archipelago from Mauritius in 1965*, Advisory Opinion, ICJ 2019 p. 95 (25 February) (hereinafter *Chagos Adv. Op.*) See also *Mauritius/Maldives* (Prelim. Obj.), ¶ 115: 'the legal status of the Chagos Archipelago is at the core of the disagreement between the Parties with respect to the second preliminary objection'—that is, the Maldives' second objection to the exercise of jurisdiction by the Special Chamber. This statement, importantly, characterized the matter as a dispute as to jurisdiction, thus setting the stage for the Special Chamber to settle it in accordance with Art. 288(4). See further below Chapter 8, pp. 293–300.

from the territorial dispute and reflects an excess of sensitivity to the putative bar against addressing issues of territorial sovereignty under Part XV, section 2. Even when exercising *compétence de la compétence*, the ITLOS judges evidently were discomfited by the thesis, which we explore further in Chapter 3,[25] that territorial disputes are forbidden ground. In effect, and in logic, however, the Special Chamber 'assessed the Parties' dispute'—and not just, or even mainly, their dispute about the advisory opinion: the Special Chamber, as we will see, engaged with the parties' dispute *about the Chagos*.

A brief observation is in order here about the Special Chamber's approach and its relation to UNCLOS jurisdiction. The task for the adjudicator in *Mauritius/Maldives* was to determine, in light of the Maldives' objection, whether it had jurisdiction to address the merits. In other words, it was the adjudicator's task to fulfill the duty placed upon it by Article 288(4). In international dispute settlement, to invoke a different tribunal's conclusion to reach a determination such as that required under Article 288(4) is not the complete answer that it might be under a rule of binding precedent. One tribunal constituted to deal with one case under international law does not bind another tribunal constituted to deal with another case. So for one tribunal to rely on another tribunal's decision falls short of a complete answer, even when the one tribunal is addressing questions similar to those that the other tribunal settled. To invoke a non-binding advisory opinion is even further from a complete answer. The Special Chamber therefore needed to do more than merely invoke the ICJ's *Chagos* advisory opinion. It needed to engage actively with the Chagos territorial dispute. In light of its conclusion that there is *no* dispute—on a matter that the United Kingdom and Mauritius were actively engaged in negotiations to resolve[26]—one may doubt whether the Special Chamber engaged actively enough. Nevertheless, the Special Chamber is to be commended: it did not merely accept at face value the objecting party's assertion that a sovereignty dispute stood in the way of adjudication. The Special Chamber instead applied Article 288(4) and inquired whether the 'territorial dispute' that the objecting party had asserted exists really does exist.

The conclusion that the Special Chamber reached in *Mauritius/Maldives* in regard to the Chagos stands in stark contrast to that which the Annex VII tribunal reached in *Coastal State Rights* in regard to Crimea. The Special Chamber concluded that the United Kingdom, which originally had established its presence in Mauritius in the nineteenth century under a very different international law and then negotiated the continuation of its presence in

25 See Chapter 3, pp. 100–127.

26 For the (possible) resolution or path to the same, see UK and Mauritius Joint Statement, 3 October 2024: www.gov.uk/government/news/joint-statement-between-uk-and-mauritius-3–october-2024

the Chagos with the pre-independence authorities of Mauritius, could not possibly be the sovereign in the Chagos. As we will see in Chapter 6, the Annex VII tribunal in *Coastal State Rights* concluded that Russia, which had invaded Crimea and forcibly stripped the territory from Ukraine in 2014, might be the sovereign. The methodologies that the two dispute settlement organs applied were also very different. The Special Chamber exercised its competence under Article 288(4) to determine the scope of its own jurisdiction and thereby scrutinized the objecting party's assertion that a territorial dispute stood in the way of adjudication. I return in Chapter 6 to *Coastal State Rights*, where the adjudicators, unlike in *Mauritius/Maldives*, refused to look behind the assertion that a territorial dispute exists.

Article 293(1) and the use of force cases

As I recalled above, UNCLOS Article 293(1) provides that '[a] court or tribunal having jurisdiction under … [Part XV, section 2] shall apply this Convention and *other rules of international law not incompatible with this Convention*.'[27] The second clause of Article 293, paragraph 1, reflects, in its 'other rules' formulation, that the Convention is not an exhaustive catalogue of rules that courts and tribunals might apply when settling disputes. It seems self-evident that, even if the Convention did not have Article 293(1), at least *some* 'other rules' would have to apply. The Seabed Disputes Chamber in its Advisory Opinion of 1 February 2011 on *Responsibilities and Obligations of States Sponsoring Persons and Entities with Respect to Activities in the Area* without much comment made clear, for example, that the law of treaties applies.[28] The negotiating history of Article 293 'is sparse,'[29] but

27 1833 UNTS at 512 (emphasis added). See generally Ranjeva, 'Settlement of Disputes' in Dupuy & Vignes (eds.) vol. 2 (1991) 133–1341; Ferrara, 'Article 293' in *Proelss Commentary* (2017) at 1893–1896; Foreteau, 'Le règlement des différends' in Foreau & Thouvenin (eds.) (2017) 996; Churchill, Lowe, & Sander (2022) 35. See also Parlett, 'Scope of Jurisdiction of Law of the Sea Tribunals' (2017) 48 ODIL 284, 286–290.

28 ITLOS 2011 p. 10, p. 28 ¶ 57. The Advisory Opinion recited Art. 293 five paragraphs before (*ibid.* at p. 27 ¶ 52) but did not mention it as the grounds for the conclusion at ¶ 57 that 'the Chamber is bound to apply' the law of treaties. See also *Arctic Sunrise*, where the Annex VII tribunal affirmed its authority to apply secondary rules of general international law *without* reference to Art. 293; and primary rules *with* reference to Art. 293: *Arctic Sunrise*, PCA Case No. 2014–02, Judgment, Merits, 14 August 2015 at ¶¶ 190, 191.

29 Walker, *Definitions for the Law of the Sea: Terms not Defined by the 1982 Convention* (2011) §132 p. 270.

commentators have thought it evident that 'other rules' also include the rules regulating use of force.[30]

It is to Article 293(1) that tribunals in a series of UNCLOS cases have referred when settling disputes concerning use of force, and in further cases tribunals have addressed issues of human rights and sovereign immunity, matters, like use of force, about which the Convention itself has little to say. This practice has drawn criticism, but its scope is sufficient to identify it as an important feature of UNCLOS jurisprudence. Let us consider the use of force cases (and the homologous human rights and sovereign immunity cases) and the argument of one of their more thoughtful critics, before turning to section 3 of Part XV, the limitations and optional exceptions to jurisdiction.

The M/V 'Saiga' *(No. 2) line of cases*

M/V 'Saiga' (No. 2), the merits phase of the first ITLOS case, and the first in which a court or tribunal applying UNCLOS addressed a claim regarding use of force,[31] was instituted by Saint Vincent and the Grenadines after Guinea had arrested the M/V *'Saiga,'* a vessel flying the Saint Vincent and the Grenadines' flag.[32] Saint Vincent and the Grenadines instituted proceedings and requested relief under UNCLOS Article 292, the provision requiring the prompt release of vessels.[33] In addition to requesting relief under Article 292 for alleged unlawful delay in release of the vessel, Saint Vincent and the Grenadines also requested relief for alleged injuries suffered as a consequence of the use of force by Guinea in the arrest. The prompt release provision of UNCLOS, Article 292, says nothing about use of force. No provision of UNCLOS does, or at least not in terms. Notwithstanding the

30 *Ibid.* at p. 269.

31 Incidents involving use of force and UNCLOS occur that do not reach any third-party dispute settlement procedure. Indeed, most such incidents do not. For some examples, and also examples of use of force at sea in vindication of a coastal State's rights before conclusion of UNCLOS, see Pobjie, *Prohibited Force* (2024) 180–186.

32 *M/V 'Saiga' (No. 2) (Saint Vincent and the Grenadines v. Guinea)*, Judgment, ITLOS 1999 p. 10 (1 July). See generally Pobjie (2024) 207–208; de la Fayette, 'Saga of the Saiga' (2000) 15 IJMCL 355–392; Oxman & Bantz, 'The M/V "Saiga" (No.2)' (2000) 94 AJIL 140–150. As to the prompt release phase, see *M/V 'Saiga' (Saint Vincent and the Grenadines v. Guinea)*, Judgment, ITLOS 1997 p. 16 (4 December), and for comment Oxman, 'The M/V "Saiga"' (1998) 92 AJIL 278–282. See also Anderson, 'Coastal State Jurisdiction and High Seas Freedoms in the EEZ in Light of the "Saiga" case' in Symmons (ed.) (2011) 105–115; Churchill, Lowe, & Sander (2022) 42.

33 For an overview of prompt release jurisdiction, see Merrills & De Brabandere (2022) 295–296.

paucity of rules in UNCLOS regarding use of force, ITLOS nevertheless entertained Saint Vincent and the Grenadines' claim.

According to ITLOS:

> Although the Convention does not contain express provisions on the use of force in the arrest of ships, international law, which is applicable by virtue of article 293 of the Convention, requires that the use of force must be avoided as far as possible and, where force in unavoidable, it must not go beyond what is reasonable and necessary in the circumstances. Considerations of humanity must apply in the law of the sea, as they do in other areas of international law.[34]

As this extract suggests, ITLOS's decision in *M/V 'Saiga' (No. 2)* found much of its support in the interpretation of Article 293. By eighteen votes to two, ITLOS decided that 'while stopping and arresting the *Saiga* Guinea used excessive force contrary to international law and thereby violated the rights of Saint Vincent and the Grenadines.'[35]

The *M/V Saiga* judgment, adopted in 1999, which is to say in the first decade of UNCLOS as a treaty in force, is not an anomaly. An Annex VII tribunal in *Guyana v. Suriname* relied on *M/V Saiga* to hold that it had jurisdiction to address Guyana's allegation that Suriname had engaged in unlawful use or threat of force against an oil rig and drill ship in the maritime area disputed between the states.[36] On the merits, the tribunal held that Suriname's expulsion of the rig and ship from the area in dispute constituted a threat of the use of force in breach of UNCLOS.[37] The tribunal went no further than that; it rejected Guyana's request for an order forbidding repetition and for compensation. The larger point however was clear. A dispute settlement organ under UNCLOS Part XV may exercise jurisdiction over a claim that a state's conduct constitutes an unlawful use of force, where the claim is ancillary to a claim that the state's conduct constitutes a breach of one of the express obligations of the Convention. The Annex VII tribunal in *Guyana v. Suriname* found that the issues regarding use of force 'can be considered as subsumed within the main dispute,' the main

34 *M/V 'Saiga' (No. 2) (Saint Vincent and the Grenadines v. Guinea)*, Judgment, ITLOS 1999 p. 7, pp. 61–62 ¶ 155 (1 July).

35 *Ibid.* at p. 72 ¶ 183 (9).

36 *Guyana v. Suriname*, PCA Case No. 2004–4, UNCLOS Annex VII (Nelson, President; Franck, Smit, Shearer, and Hossain, arbitrators), Award, 17 September 2007, ¶ 487(ii). See generally Fietta & Cleverly, *Maritime Boundary Delimitation* (2016) 439–452. For critical observations, see 'Remarks by Loretta Malintoppi' (2017) 111 ASIL Proc. 131, 133; Forteau, 'Applicable Law Before International Tribunals' in Wolfrum & Gätzschmann (eds.), *International Dispute Settlement* (2013) 417, 437.

37 *Guyana v. Suriname*, at ¶ 488(2). Thoughtful writers have asked whether the tribunal was correct to find Surinam's conduct constituted an unlawful use of force or even excessive force for purposes of law enforcement: Milano & Papanicolopulu (2011) at 623 n. 118.

dispute having been a maritime boundary delimitation dispute.[38] The tribunal relied on ITLOS's holding in regard to Article 293 in *M/V 'Saiga,'* which I quoted above.

In 2014, in *M/V 'Virginia G' (Panama v. Guinea-Bissau)*,[39] ITLOS again reasoned that a claim regarding use of force in connection with the arrest of a vessel falls within the Tribunal's jurisdiction. ITLOS, reaching Panama's use of force claim on the merits, found that Guinea-Bissau did not use excessive force when boarding and impounding the *M/V 'Virginia G.'*[40] ITLOS, in adjudicating the merits of the use of force claim, applied 'the standards referred to by the Tribunal in the *M/V 'Saiga' (No. 2)* case.[41] The Tribunal did not offer fresh reasoning in regard to the jurisdictional basis for reaching the merits of the use of force claim, resting on the passage in *M/V 'Saiga' (No. 2)* in which the Tribunal had invoked UNCLOS Article 293.[42]

Two provisions of UNCLOS seemingly just as relevant to use of force as Article 293, if not more so, received no comment either by ITLOS in *M/V 'Saiga'* or in *M/V 'Virginia G'* or by the Annex VII tribunal in *Guyana v. Suriname*. Article 279 (Obligation to settle disputes by peaceful means) provides as follows:

> 1. States Parties shall settle any dispute between them concerning the interpretation or application of this Convention by peaceful means in accordance with Article 2, paragraph 3, of the Charter of the United Nations and, to this end, shall seek a solution by the means indicated in Article 33, paragraph 1, of the Charter.

Article 301 (Peaceful uses of the seas) provides:

> 2. In exercising their rights and performing their duties under this Convention, States Parties shall refrain from any threat or use of force against the territorial integrity or political independence of any State, or in any other manner inconsistent with the principles of international law embodied in the Charter of the United Nations.[43]

38 *Guyana v. Suriname* ¶ 410.

39 *M/V 'Virginia G' Case (Panama/Guinea-Bissau)*, ITLOS 2014 p. 4 (14 April). For comment see Oxman & Cogliati-Bantz, 'The M/V "Virginia G"' (2014) 108 AJIL 769–775; Scanlon, 'The Legality of Vessel Confiscation under the LOSC After the *M/V "Virginia G" Case*' (2018) 33 IJMCL 166–198.

40 ITLOS 2014 at pp. 100–103 ¶¶ 350–362; p. 125 ¶ 452 (13).

41 *Ibid.* at p. 103 ¶ 362.

42 *Ibid.* at p. 101, ¶ 359, quoting *M/V 'Saiga' (No. 2)* at ¶ 155.

43 Tzeng draws attention to the curious omission of these provisions in the tribunals' reasoning: 126 YLJ at 256. As to the possible invocation of Art. 301 in maritime disputes where a party has unlawfully used force in respect of a relevant territory, see Kunoy, 'Preservation of Territorial Integrity: A Substantive Rule under UNCLOS?' *EJIL: Talk!* (23 April 2024), www.ejiltalk.org/preservation-of-territorial-integrity-a-substantive-rule-under-unclos/

In *M/V 'Saiga,'* the parties' pleadings were rather muted in regard to use of force. Saint Vincent and the Grenadines in its final submissions made no reference to Article 279 or Article 301, or for that matter to Article 293, the UNCLOS provisions that one might have thought would serve a state seeking an award relating to the use of force.[44] Curiously, Saint Vincent and the Grenadines in its final submissions did not request a holding in respect of unlawful use of force. In its Memorial, Saint Vincent and the Grenadines made some general observations about use of force at sea, but it did not connect those observations to any specific UNCLOS provisions there either.[45] In its Reply, Saint Vincent and the Grenadines set out factual matter relating to the alleged excessive use of force,[46] but again without reference to specific UNCLOS provisions and without legal argument about how ITLOS might exercise jurisdiction in regard to allegations of unlawful use of force. ITLOS nevertheless set out an interpretation of Article 293, as quoted above, and determined that Guinea's use of force against the *M/V 'Saiga'* had been excessive and thus in violation of international law rights of Saint Vincent and the Grenadines.

In *Guyana v. Suriname*, the parties presented more developed pleadings on use of force than had the parties in *M/V 'Saiga,'* but only to a point. Guyana in its Statement of Claim expressly requested relief for injuries that it alleged it had suffered as a consequence of Suriname's use of force.[47] It invoked Article 279 in support of this element of its request.[48] It developed its argument on Article 279 in its Memorial, adding observations in regard to Article 301[49] and also invoking Article 293.[50]

In *M/V 'Virginia G,'* Panama, the vessel's flag state, alleged that Guinea-Bissau's authorities boarded the vessel 'violently ... as though it were an assault' and pointed firearms at the crew.[51] Panama stated that '[i]nternational law—applicable by virtue of Article 293 UNCLOS, requires that the use of force must be avoided as far as possible and, where force is unavoidable,

44 www.itlos.org/fileadmin/itlos/documents/cases/case_no_2/merits/C02_Final_Submission_SVG_EN.pdf

45 Saint Vincent and the Grenadines Memorial, ¶¶ 96–99: www.itlos.org/fileadmin/itlos/documents/cases/case_no_2/merits/memorial_svg.pdf

46 Saint Vincent and the Grenadines Reply, ¶¶ 117–120: www.itlos.org/fileadmin/itlos/documents/cases/case_no_2/merits/reply_svg_eng.pdf

47 Guyana, Statement of Claim (24 February 2004), ¶ 33(2): https://pcacases.com/web/sendAttach/903

48 *Ibid.*

49 Guyana, Memorial, ¶¶ 10.1–10.11: https://pcacases.com/web/sendAttach/904

50 *Ibid.* at ¶¶ 7.29, 7.30.

51 Panama, Submission of Dispute to Arbitration, 2 June 2011, p. 21 ¶¶ 17, 18. See also Panama, Memorial, 23 January 2012, p. 101 ¶ 372.

it must not go beyond what is reasonable or necessary in the circumstances.'[52] Panama requested that ITLOS declare that Guinea-Bissau 'used excessive force,'[53] a request which, as noted, ITLOS rejected.[54]

Human rights and immunity of a warship

The *Arctic Sunrise Arbitration* occasioned an Annex VII tribunal to consider whether, exercising jurisdiction under Part XV, section 2, it might apply certain human rights and freedoms belonging to general international law and expressed in the International Covenant on Civil and Political Rights (ICCPR).[55] The Netherlands had instituted Annex VII proceedings against Russia after Russia, in 2013, arrested a Netherlands-flagged Greenpeace vessel, *Arctic Sunrise*, and detained its crew.[56] In its claim, the Netherlands alleged that Russia 'prevented the Kingdom of the Netherlands, the vessel and the crew members from exercising and enjoying their rights, notably the freedom of navigation, and human rights and fundamental freedoms.'[57] The Netherlands argued that Article 293, in its provision requiring UNCLOS tribunals to apply 'other rules of international law,' required on the facts of the Netherlands' case that the Annex VII tribunal apply ICCPR and customary international law.[58]

The *Arctic Sunrise* tribunal stated that 'Article 293(1) does not extend the jurisdiction of a tribunal.'[59] However, in saying what it understood Article 293(1) *not* to do, the tribunal also said what Article 293(1) *does*:

52 Panama, Submission of Dispute to Arbitration, 2 June 2011, p. 34 ¶ 197. See also Panama, Memorial, 23 January 2012, p. 103 ¶ 382 and, quoting *M/V 'Saiga' No. 2*, *ibid.* at p. 104 ¶ 383.

53 Panama, Memorial, 23 January 2012, p. 117, ¶ 442(10).

54 See p. 69 n. 40.

55 *Arctic Sunrise (Netherlands v. Russia)*, PCA Case No. 2014–02, Annex VII tribunal (Mensah, President; Burmester, Soons, Symonides, and Székely, arbitrators), Award, Merits (14 August 2015); Award on Jurisdiction (26 November 2014). See also *ibid.* Award on Compensation (10 July 2017); and *The 'Arctic Sunrise' Case*, Provisional Measures, Order, ITLOS 2013 p. 228 (22 November). For comment, see James Harrison, 'The Arctic Sunrise Arbitration (Netherlands v. Russia): Background to the Arbitral Proceedings' (2016) 31 IJMCL 145–159; Kontorovich, 'Arctic Sunrise' (2016) 110 AJIL 96–102; Oude Elferink, 'The *Arctic Sunrise* Incident' (2014) 29 IJMCL 244–289; Guilfoyle & Miles, 'Provisional Measures' (2014) 108 AJIL 271–287.

56 The Netherlands, Notification and Statement of Claim, 4 October 2013: https://pcacases.com/web/sendAttach/1314

57 *Ibid.* at ¶ 5.

58 *Ibid.* at ¶¶ 28–30.

59 *Arctic Sunrise (Netherlands v. Russia)*, PCA Case No. 2014–02, Annex VII tribunal (Mensah, President; Burmester, Soons, Symonides, and Székely, arbitrators), Award, Merits, ¶ 187 (14 August 2015).

'it ensures that, in exercising its jurisdiction under the Convention, a tribunal can give full effect to the provisions of the Convention.'[60] Describing Article 293(1) this way, the *Arctic Sunrise* tribunal seemed sure to have set the stage for future skirmishes over the provision's effect on UNCLOS jurisdiction. The tribunal's affirmative description of Article 293(1) is capacious. The *Arctic Sunrise* tribunal proceeded to observe that Article 293 'makes ... possible' the application of 'relevant rules of international law.'[61] It noted ITLOS's application in *M/V 'Saiga' No. 2* of the general international law rules on use of force.[62] Concluding on the point, the tribunal determined that it would 'have regard to the extent necessary to rules of customary international law, including international human rights standards.'[63]

Interestingly, two years before *'Arctic Sunrise,'* though having determined that it lacked jurisdiction to adjudicate the applicant's claim, ITLOS in *M/V 'Louisa' (Saint Vincent and the Grenadines v. Kingdom of Spain)* felt that 'it [could not] but take note of the issues of human rights' that the case raised.[64] Whether or not ITLOS was justified in articulating this dictum under the circumstances (and there were doubts),[65] *M/V 'Louisa'* suggests that certain issues that arise under fundamental rules of international law are difficult to isolate and exclude from dispute settlement procedure. True, 'to have regard' for rules and to do even that only 'to the extent necessary' (as the *'Arctic Sunrise'* tribunal formulated its approach) or merely to 'take note of the issues' (as ITLOS did in *M/V 'Louisa'*) supplies no precise account of what the adjudicator is doing. But the adjudicators in those cases were doing *something* about the 'rules' and 'issues' concerned. Though they maintained studied ambiguity, they did not pass by the 'rules' or 'issues' in silence.

Another case relevant in this connection concerned the immunity of a warship. In *ARA Libertad*, Argentina instituted Annex VII proceedings against Ghana after Ghana had detained an Argentine warship. Argentina asserted that Ghana's conduct constituted a violation, *inter alia*, of 'well-established general or customary international law rules' regarding the immunity of

60 *Ibid.*

61 *Ibid.* at ¶ 191.

62 *Ibid.*, quoting M/V 'Saiga' (No. 2), Judgment, ITLOS 1999 p. 10, p. 61 ¶ 155 (1 July).

63 *Arctic Sunrise*, Award, Merits, ¶ 198. See also *M/V 'Louisa' (Saint Vincent and the Grenadines* v. *Kingdom of Spain)*, Judgment, ITLOS 2013 at p. 46 ¶ 154–155 (28 May).

64 *M/V 'Louisa' (Saint Vincent and the Grenadines v. Kingdom of Spain)*, Judgment, ITLOS 2013 at p. 46 ¶ 154 (28 May). As to aspects of the case generally, see Yoshifumi Tanaka, 'A Note on the M/V Louisa Case' (2014) 45 ODIL 205–220.

65 See Sep. Op. Judge Ndiaye, ITLOS 2013 at pp. 67–68 ¶ 38.

warships.[66] Argentina took the position that, under general international law, a warship enjoys immunity from arrest.[67] Ghana argued that Article 288(1) does not confer jurisdiction on an Annex VII tribunal to consider disputes over the interpretation or application of general international law.[68] Argentina and Ghana settled the matter by an agreement,[69] upon which the Annex VII proceedings were terminated,[70] and no definitive holding was issued as concerns the applicability of a general international law rule of warship immunity. However, ITLOS granted provisional measures prior to the constitution of the Annex VII tribunal, and Ghana released the warship after ITLOS granted provisional measures. The Tribunal's provisional measures order merits a brief word.

Under UNCLOS Article 290, paragraph 5, ITLOS may grant provisional measures 'if it considers that *prima facie* the tribunal which is to be constituted would have jurisdiction.'[71] (Judge Treves describes the *prima facie* requirement 'as a consolidation or codification of the law developed previously by the practice of the ICJ.')[72] ITLOS concluded that Argentina had articulated 'a basis on which *prima facie* jurisdiction of the Annex VII arbitral tribunal might be founded.'[73] ITLOS then, among other points, stated that 'in accordance with general international law, a warship enjoys immunity.'[74] Because ITLOS made this statement within the limits of a provisional measures order, there was no final and dispositive decision here as to the parties' claims and defenses. However, with this statement, ITLOS addressed a point of law—warship immunity under general international law—that, according to Ghana, Article 288(1) did not permit ITLOS to address. ITLOS rejected Ghana's argument about Article 288(1), that is, ITLOS rejected the argument that Article 288(1) *prima facie* does not confer jurisdiction to consider a dispute in regard to the existence of a rule of warship immunity under

66 Argentina, Notification, 29 October 2012, p. 3 ¶ 6(1): https://pcacases.com/web/sendAttach/424
67 *Ibid.* at p. 341 ¶ 44. Argentina articulated its position with reference to UNCLOS Art. 32, which provides that, subject to express exceptions elsewhere in the Convention, 'nothing in this Convention affects the immunities of warships and other government ships operated for non-commercial purposes.'
68 *The 'ARA Libertad' (Argentina v. Ghana)*, Provisional Measures, Order, ITLOS 2012 p. 332, p. 343 ¶ 58 (15 December).
69 Agreement between Argentina and Ghana, 27 September 2013: https://pcacases.com/web/sendAttach/429
70 See Termination Order, 11 November 2013: https://pcacases.com/web/sendAttach/432
71 In *'ARA Libertad,'* ITLOS addressed Argentina's request for provisional measures, as the Annex VII tribunal had yet to be constituted: ITLOS 2012 at p. 339 ¶ 32.
72 Treves, 'Art. 290' in *Proelss Commentary* (2017) 1866, 1870.
73 ITLOS 2012 at p. 344 ¶ 66.
74 *Ibid.* at p. 348 ¶ 95.

general international law. In the provisional measures order, ITLOS did not mention Article 293.[75]

Together with the use of force cases, *Arctic Sunrise* and *ARA Libertad* reflect the readiness of UNCLOS tribunals to reach legal and factual matters that connect to UNCLOS rules but that UNCLOS rules do not expressly embrace.

The Tzeng critique and a tentative reply

Peter Tzeng, writing in the *Yale Law Journal* in 2016, offered a critique of the '*M/V "Saiga"* line of cases.'[76] Tzeng argued that the UNCLOS tribunals in those cases 'effectively invoked Article 293(1) to expand their jurisdiction,'[77] a step that he argued was 'legal error.'[78] Tzeng cautioned against adjudicators exercising jurisdiction in excess of that to which the parties have consented.[79] In the *Chagos Marine Protected Area Arbitration*, which I consider in detail in Chapter 4, Mauritius and the United Kingdom concurred that 'Article 293 does not, of itself, constitute a basis of jurisdiction,'[80] and tribunals such as the Annex VII tribunal in *Arctic Sunrise*, which I quoted above, have said much the same. A 2007 partial award in the *Eurotunnel Arbitration*, a case under the Treaty of Canterbury, not UNCLOS, has become a point of reference on the matter. The *Eurotunnel* tribunal admonished that applicable law provisions are not jurisdictional provisions.[81] Adjudicators under UNCLOS have noted the admonition.[82] Tzeng refers to the 'well-established principle

75 Judges Wolfrum and Cot, writing separately and in effect in dissent on the point, were clear that it was Art. 293—a misapplication of Art. 293, in their view—on which ITLOS founded its determination regarding warship immunity: *'ARA Libertad' Case*, Joint Sep. Op. Judges Wolfrum and Cot, ITLOS 2012 at pp. 364–365 ¶ 7. For comment on *'ARA Libertad,'* see generally Kraska, 'The "ARA Libertad"' (2013) 107 AJIL 404–410; Tanaka, 'ARA Libertad Case' (2013) 28 IJMCL 375–388.

76 Tzeng's description: Tzeng (2016) 243.

77 *Ibid.* at 243.

78 *Ibid.* at 258.

79 *Ibid.* at 259.

80 *Chagos Marine Protected Area (Mauritius v. United Kingdom)*, ¶ 181.

81 *Channel Tunnel Grp. Ltd. v. Sec'y of State for Transp. of the Gov't of the U.K.*, Tribunal constituted under Treaty of Canterbury, Art. 19 (Crawford, President; Fortier, Paulsson, Guillaume, and Millett, members) Partial Award of 30 January 2007, 132 ILR 1, ¶¶ 152–153.

82 For example, *Arctic Sunrise*, Merits, at ¶ 188 n. 179. Though without reference to *Eurotunnel*, see *Duzgit Integrity Arbitration (Malta v. São Tomé and Príncipe)*, PCA Case No. 2014–07, Annex VII tribunal (Soons, President; Kateka and Treves, arbitrators), Award (5 September 2016), ¶ 208; and the warning to similar effect by Dr. Rao: *'Enrica Lexie' Incident*, PCA Case No. 2015–28, Annex VII tribunal (Golitsyn, President; Paik, Robinson, Francioni, and Rao, members), Concurring and Dissenting Opinion, Dr. P.S. Rao, 60 ILM 185, 248 ¶ 46 (21 May 2020).

of international law that applicable law provisions do not expand the jurisdiction of international courts and tribunals.'[83] Tzeng is by no means alone in identifying the point as a principle.[84]

However, as with many principles, including 'well-established' ones, the difficulty with the 'principle ... that applicable law provisions do not expand ... jurisdiction' is not ascertaining that it exists; it is applying it on particular facts in particular legal settings. In the *Chagos* Annex VII proceedings, the parties differed as to how Article 293 interacts with jurisdiction against the backdrop of a long-standing territorial issue. Tribunals in other situations have combined confident invocations of the principle with ambivalence about its application.

Tzeng's account acknowledges that all is not pellucid clarity here. We detect the ambivalence both in cases in which tribunals invoked Article 293(1) to exercise jurisdiction (Tzeng says 'to expand' it) and in cases in which tribunals declined to exercise jurisdiction after a party had pleaded Article 293(1) in the hopes of convincing them to exercise it. In the former cases, adjudicators have not offered very precise guidance as to how Article 293(1) affects the proceedings, much less a principled account of how to give full expression to the applicable law provision without ignoring the consent-based limits of jurisdiction.[85] In the latter cases, while there are examples of tribunals rejecting claims, in particular in the early—and emphatic—rejection of 'non-UNCLOS' claims in *Mox Plant (Ireland v. United*

83 Tzeng (2016) at 242, citing *Eurotunnel* (as 'Channel Tunnel Grp.'), *ibid.* at 242 n. 4.

84 Among jurists who express the point much the same way, see former ITLOS judge, David H. Anderson, 'Peaceful Settlement of Disputes under UNCLOS' in Barrett & Barnes (eds.), *Law of the Sea: UNCLOS as a Living Treaty* (2016) 385. See also, e.g., Wood, 'The International Tribunal for the Law of the Sea and General International Law' (2007) 2 IJMCL 351, 356–357; 'Remarks by Loretta Malintoppi' (2017) 111 ASIL Proc. 131, 132; Forteau, 'Le règlement des différends' in Forteau & Thouvenin (eds.) (2017) 996 and works cited *ibid.* at n. 4263. And see Judge Ndiaye's mild rebuke to ITLOS for having touched on human rights questions, though in that case, ITLOS had decided that it lacked any merits jurisdiction at all: *M/V 'Louisa' (Saint Vincent and the Grenadines v. Kingdom of Spain)*, Sep. Op. Judge Ndiaye, ITLOS 2013 at pp. 67–68 ¶ 38. For a different nuance on the matter, see Boisson de Chazournes, 'Plurality in the Fabric of International Courts and Tribunals' (2017) 28 EJIL 13, 34. See also Merrills & De Brabandere (2022) 271–275; Parlett, 'Jurisdiction of Law of the Sea Tribunals' (2017) 48 ODIL 284, 285–286. Tzeng's *Yale Law Journal* article merits the focus here, first, because it is unusual in recent decades for a major American law review to address detailed analyses of points of international law; second, because Tzeng is a practitioner in law of the sea matters as well as a writer; and, finally, because it is not to present purpose to ventilate in its entirety the large literature on the relation between applicable law and jurisdiction.

85 See Tzeng (2016) 248–251.

Kingdom) (2002),[86] attempts after that to conciliate a restrictive reading of Article 293(1) with the *M/V 'Saiga'* line of cases resulted in a muddle.[87]

One rightly queries when the principle at issue here—the distinction between choice of law and jurisdiction—came to be fully established in regard to Articles 288(1) and 293(1), or whether it even has. Ranjeva, considering Article 293 in 1991, thought that the provision 'means that the concepts of interpretation and application of the Treaty must be understood in *the broadest sense*.'[88] After thoughtful consideration, Kupelyants and Waibel, writing in 2022, concluded that 'the exact interaction between jurisdiction and applicable law under UNCLOS remains contested.'[89]

Yet not all here is contestation and ambivalence either. The Annex VII tribunal constituted in *Enrica Lexie* spoke plainly. It decided to adjudicate Italy's claim that India had breached Italy's immunity when India had arrested, detained, and prosecuted a pair of Italian Marines in connection with the killing of two Indian fishermen. Italy referred to a general international law rule of immunity and argued with reference to Article 293.[90] India argued strenuously that to apply the immunity rule as Italy had pleaded it would overstep the bounds of jurisdiction.[91] The tribunal, in its award of 21 May 2020 (which is to say some years after Tzeng's commentary), concluded as follows: '[W]hile the Convention may not provide a basis for entertaining an independent immunity claim under general international law, the Arbitral Tribunal's competence extends to the determination of the issue of immunity of the Marines that necessarily arises as an incidental question in the application of the Convention.'[92]

Finding that the 'issue of the immunity of the Marines is an incidental question that necessarily presents itself' in connection with the UNCLOS

86 Statement by the President, 13 June 2003, ¶ 5.

87 See Tzeng (2016) 251–258.

88 Ranjeva, 'Settlement of Disputes' in Dupuy & Vignes (eds.), *A Handbook on the New Law of the Sea* (1991) vol. 2, p. 1333, 1341 (emphasis added).

89 Kupelyants & Waibel, 'Applicable Law' in Ruiz Fabri (ed.), *Max Planck Encyclopedia of International Procedural Law* (2022).

90 Italy, Notification under Article 287 and Annex VII and Statement of Claim (26 June 2015) p. 12 ¶ 29(g) www.pcacases.com/pcadocs/Notification/Italys%20 Notification%20(Redacted).pdf

91 *Enrica Lexie (Italian Republic v. Republic of India)*, PCA Case No. 2015–28, Annex VII Tribunal (Golitsyn, President; Paik, Robinson, Francioni, and Rao, members), Award, 21 May 2020, ¶¶ 740–755.

92 *Ibid.* at ¶ 809. See generally Devaney & Tams, '"Enrica Lexie" Incident' (2021) 115 AJIL 513–519. Devaney and Tams are critical of the tribunal's reasoning. See *ibid.* 517–518. See also Fisler Damrosch, 'The Sources of Immunity Law: Between International and Domestic Law' in Ruys, Angelet, & Ferro, *The Cambridge Handbook of Immunities and International Law* (2019) 40, 57.

claims that Italy advanced, the tribunal determined that it had jurisdiction to deal with the issue.[93] As Professor Kunoy says, 'This finding defined the case.'[94]

Enrica Lexie is of a piece with the *M/V 'Saiga'* line of cases. It suggests an admonition in the opposite direction of *Eurotunnel* and of Tzeng's critique. If we might generalize, then the *Enrica Lexie* award suggests as follows: presented with assertions that stand in the way of a party's otherwise credible UNCLOS claim, and even where UNCLOS contains no dispositive rules that an adjudicator might apply to evaluate the assertions on their substance, a tribunal nevertheless shall address the assertions and decide whether it accepts them. To the extent that *Enrica Lexie* gets the relation right between incidental issues and the exercise of UNCLOS jurisdiction, the approach that the Annex VII tribunal took would seem appropriate with regard to a wide range of incidental issues. Incidental issues that a party raises that implicate fundamental international law rules would seem, at least in a general way, all the more plainly to call for a tribunal's considered treatment.

In the *Enrica Lexie* proceedings, there were suggestions that an adjudicator might treat certain issues of public order directly, rather than incidentally. Italy invoked Article 2(3) for the stipulation in that provision that the sovereignty of a coastal state in the territorial sea 'is exercised subject … to other rules of international law'; and Article 56(2) and Article 58(2), for the stipulation in those provisions that 'rights and duties of other States' and 'other pertinent rules of international law' apply in the exclusive economic zone (EEZ).[95] Italy here sought to convince the tribunal that the immunity rule applies as part of Articles 2(3), 56(2), and 58(2). Having considered the factual evidence, the tribunal concluded (albeit in a three-to-two split) that these provisions were inapplicable. They were inapplicable because India arrested the Italian marines only when the vessel was in port—that is, in internal waters, not in the territorial sea or EEZ.[96] It remains an open

93 *Ibid.* at ¶ 811. See Harris, 'Incidental Determinations in Proceedings under Compromissory Clauses' (2021) 70(2) ICLQ 417, 434 who agrees with the *Enrica Lexie* tribunal that a jural basis of the adjudicator's authority to reach incidental determinations may be found in *Certain German Interests in Polish Upper Silesia* (Preliminary Objections), 1925 PCIJ Ser A No 6, 18 (25 August). See also Kunoy, 'Jurisdiction of Courts and Tribunals under the UN Convention on the Law of the Sea over Disputed Land Areas' (2024) 39 IJMCL 345, 355. See *Enrica Lexie* award at ¶ 808. Defining 'incidental' for these purposes remains a challenge for adjudicators. For a useful *Problemstellung*, see Ben Love, 'Jurisdiction over Incidental Questions in International Law' (2017) 111 ASIL Proc. 316, 321.

94 Kunoy (2024) 358.

95 *Enrica Lexie*, Award, 21 May 2020, ¶ 797.

96 *Ibid.* ¶ 798. President Golitsyn and arbitrators Paik and Francioni adopted this conclusion; arbitrators Robinson and Pemmaraju Sreenivasa Rao rejected it. *Ibid.* ¶ 1094A(4).

question whether on different facts a state might invoke the 'other rules' or 'pertinent rules' provisions to apply a regime such as the immunity regime.

There was also India's claim under Article 301—the provision obliging states to 'refrain from any threat or use of force against the territorial integrity or political independence of any State, or in any manner inconsistent with the principles of international law embodied in the Charter of the United Nations.' The tribunal said that Article 301, reflecting as it does Article 2(4) of the Charter, 'would not seem to add anything to the obligations of States that existed prior to [UNCLOS].'[97] But Article 301 does add something. It is in part a *renvoi* to the Charter, and it is in part more than that as well. It spells out certain terms expressly—those concerning 'the territorial integrity or political independence of any State.' In so doing, Article 301 entails that those terms, where there is credible evidence that a state party has breached them, would give rise to claims potentially subject to UNCLOS jurisdiction. And jurisdiction exercised on that basis in no way could be impugned as an enlargement based on 'other rules': the rules concerned are not 'other rules'; they are UNCLOS rules. As to the point of legal interpretation, it appears that India and Italy agreed that Article 301 indeed could apply the way India argued it does.[98] On the fact evidence, the *Enrica Lexie* tribunal concluded that Italy's marines had acted consistently with international law concerning the prevention of piracy and so had not breached India's rights when they fired upon an Indian fishing boat.[99]

In his critique of the enlargement of jurisdiction by reference to substantive rules, Tzeng was writing before *Enrica Lexie* and so did not address it at the time. Tzeng did address *Arctic Sunrise*. He said that the tribunal there 'rejected an expansion of jurisdiction under Article 293(1).'[100] Tzeng's characterization of *Arctic Sunrise* merits a closer look. It is true that the tribunal rejected the Netherlands' claims under the ICCPR.[101] However, as recalled above, the tribunal affirmed that it could 'have regard to the extent necessary to rules of customary international law, including international human rights standards, not incompatible with the Convention, in order to assist in the interpretation and application of the Convention's provisions that authorize the arrest or detention of a vessel and persons.'[102] Nobody posits that Article 293(1) allows a tribunal to reach a dispositive decision on a subject matter bearing no link to an UNCLOS claim. (In much the

97 *Enrica Lexie*, ¶ 1071.
98 *Ibid.* ¶ 1047.
99 *Ibid.* ¶¶ 1076–1077.
100 Tzeng (2016) 253.
101 *Arctic Sunrise*, Merits, at ¶ 197.
102 Ibid. at ¶ 198.

same way, when one invokes Article 31(3)*(c)* of the VCLT, the 'relevant rules of international law' that one thus might plead in aid of interpretation must apply in the relations between the parties concerned under the treaty concerned in the case concerned.) But, if positing that the *Arctic Sunrise* tribunal did not apply general human rights law in a manner that extended its exercise of jurisdiction, then one must say with specificity what it meant for that law to have 'assist[ed] in the interpretation and application of the Convention's provisions.' That is what the Annex VII tribunal in *Arctic Sunrise* said that the law did. It is to be submitted that the *Arctic Sunrise* tribunal, with this phrase, was clothing (if not quite cloaking) its exercise of jurisdiction over human rights matters—that is to say, carrying out 'an expansion of jurisdiction.'

Similar considerations lead me to doubt whether the Annex VII tribunal in *Duzgit Integrity* rejected the '*Saiga* line' of cases as plainly as Tzeng suggests.[103] In *Duzgit Integrity*, Malta alleged that São Tomé and Príncipe breached 'fundamental human rights' when it boarded the vessel *Duzgit Integrity*, allegedly in carrying out 'enforcement measures.' The *Duzgit Integrity* Annex VII tribunal was cautious about Malta's human rights claims. Reciting the doctrine, the tribunal said that '[t]he combined effect of [Articles 288(1) and 293(1)] is that the Tribunal does not have jurisdiction to determine breaches of obligations not having their source in the Convention (including human rights obligations)';[104] 'Article 293(1) does not extend a tribunal's jurisdiction.'[105] However, the tribunal did extend its consideration of 'enforcement measures.' It found that São Tomé, in the manner in which it carried out enforcement measures, had violated Article 49 of the Convention: São Tomé's enforcement measures had been 'unreasonable and disproportionate when considering the original wrong committed by the vessel.'[106]

The Convention does not define 'enforcement measures.' '[R]easonable and proportionate' is not a Convention term at all.[107] Therefore, if confining oneself to rules expressed in UNCLOS in regard to 'enforcement measures,' one would not find the limiting term that the *Duzgit Integrity* tribunal applied to 'enforcement measures'; one would not find that enforcement measures shall be 'reasonable and proportionate.' It was to Article 293(1)

103 See Tzeng (2016) 243–244.

104 *Duzgit Integrity Arbitration (Malta v. São Tomé and Príncipe)*, PCA Case No. 2014–07, Annex VII tribunal (Soons, President; Kateka and Treves, arbitrators), Award (5 September 2016), ¶ 207.

105 *Ibid.* at ¶ 208.

106 *Duzgit Integrity*, ¶ 256.

107 Standing on its own, 'reasonable' appears in the Convention repeatedly—some four dozen times—and 'fair and reasonable' ten times, in several different connections, but not in Art. 49.

that the *Duzgit Integrity* tribunal referred in order to find a limiting term and thus to impart definition to the expression 'enforcement measures.' According to the tribunal, '[w]hile Article 293(1) does not extend a tribunal's jurisdiction, it ensures that a tribunal can give full effect to the provisions of the Convention.'[108] The tribunal borrowed this wording on 'full effect' from *Arctic Sunrise*. Reasoning further, the *Duzgit Integrity* tribunal said that 'in order properly to interpret and apply particular provisions of the Convention, it may be necessary for a tribunal to resort to foundational or secondary rules of general international law.'[109] It even may be necessary, according to the tribunal, '[i]n the case of some broadly worded or general provisions ... to rely on primary rules of international law other than the Convention.'[110]

Turning to the scope of 'enforcement powers,' the tribunal then said as follows:

> The exercise of enforcement powers by a (coastal) State in situations where a State derives these powers from provisions of the Convention is also governed by certain rules and principles of general international law, in particular the principle of reasonableness. This principle encompasses the principles of necessity and proportionality. These principles do not only apply in cases where States resort to force, but to all measures of law enforcement. Article 293(1) requires the application of these principles. They are not incompatible with the Convention.[111]

And later in the award: 'Under international law, enforcement measures taken by a coastal State in response to activity within its archipelagic waters are subject to the requirement of reasonableness, which encompasses the general principles of necessity and proportionality.'[112]

Here, then, to reach a conclusion on a merits issue, a tribunal found in Article 293(1) a powerful tool to complete the meaning of a Convention term and to limit the term's application. A coastal state has enforcement powers, but those powers allow a state to do only that which under general international law is necessary and proportionate. The tribunal, in elaborating

108 *Duzgit Integrity* at ¶ 208.
109 *Ibid.*
110 *Ibid.*
111 *Duzgit Integrity*, ¶ 209. Internal citation (to *Arctic Sunrise* and *M/V Saiga (no. 2)* omitted). Churchill, Lowe, and Sander think that the application of 'certain rules and principles of general international law' here is 'important': Churchill, Lowe, & Sander (2022) 163. Cf. *ibid.* Judge Kateka's dissent, ¶ 9, evidently agreeing with the tribunal as to the legal interpretation—that is, that 'certain rules and principles' shall apply—but differing with the tribunal as to their application to the facts of the case.
112 *Duzgit Integrity*, ¶ 254.

the Convention text, referred both to *Arctic Sunrise* and *M/V 'Saiga' (no. 2)*.[113]

Tzeng acknowledged that the Convention is not silent on use of force entirely.[114] I would go further than that. The Convention plays a role in the wider legal setting to which it belongs. UNCLOS serves to ensure 'the public order of the oceans,' a phrase that is not mere rhetoric, but one which adjudicators invoke as a reason for substantive outcomes.[115] There is also the fact of the decided cases. Courts and tribunals that interpret and apply UNCLOS have adopted dispositive conclusions on use of force. As conclusions reached under consent-based jurisdiction between states, their holdings do not bind judges and arbitrators in future cases, but the existence of the jurisprudence that they have developed is an objective fact. The jurisprudence emerges from claims that have undoubted bases in UNCLOS, and, even if it pushes against the limits of UNCLOS jurisdiction, it sits comfortably with public order considerations that motivated the drafters of the Convention and that adjudicators have acknowledged to be relevant in settling particular disputes.

The *Duzgit Integrity* tribunal understood the 'resort to foundational … rules of general international law' to be permissible, even necessary. This understanding accords with a constitutional conception of the Convention. It also accords with a formal requirement, that of effective interpretation. Without the foundational rules, provisions of central importance to the Convention would be difficult or impossible effectively to interpret.

The readiness of tribunals to exercise jurisdiction in respect of maritime disputes involving use of force is particularly salient to sovereignty disputes and UNCLOS jurisdiction. As I said in Chapter 1, it is fundamental to modern

113 *Duzgit Integrity*, ¶ 209 n. 285. For an interesting definition problem in a older treaty, see Denk, 'Interpreting a Geographical Expression in a Nineteenth Century Cession Treaty and the Senkaku/Diaoyu Islands Dispute' (2005) 20 IJMCL 97–116.

114 Tzeng (2016) 249.

115 For example, where the ICJ used the phrase, it did so as part of the reasoning for its merits judgment that delimited overlapping maritime areas between Nicaragua and Colombia in a manner that avoided cutting off either State from part of its entitlement to an EEZ and continental shelf. *Territorial and Maritime Dispute (Nicaragua v. Colombia)*, ICJ 2012 at p. 716 ¶ 244 (19 November). Cf. *'Enrica Lexie' Incident*, Dr. Rao, Concurring and Dissenting Opinion, ¶¶ 42, 43 (connecting the constitutional character of the Convention to Article 293 and the scope of dispute settlement jurisdiction). American lawyers might recall the expression from *M'Culloch v. Maryland*, 22 U.S. (4 Wheat.) 316, 307 (1819) (Marshall, CCJ) 'we must never forget, that it is a *constitution* we are expounding,' which, for better or worse, lawyers many times have repeated. For critique, see Antonin Scalia, 'Essay: Assorted Canards of Contemporary Legal Analysis' (1989) 40 *Case Western Reserve Law Review* 581, 594–596.

international law—the foundational rule of foundational rules—that changes to territorial title between states are not brought about by threat or use of force.[116] UNCLOS adjudicators, in adjudicating UNCLOS claims, have been ready to apply the law governing use of force, for example by applying principles of proportionality or reasonableness that that law embraces. *Duzgit Integrity, 'Saiga' (No. 2)* and other cases that I have considered in the present chapter illustrate the readiness of UNCLOS tribunals not only to address questions of use of force as matters necessary to adjudicating UNCLOS claims but to adjudicate those questions themselves. The practice of UNCLOS adjudicators, and of international adjudicators generally, is well established in applying other rules for more modest purposes. Such purposes include discerning the meaning of terms that might otherwise be in doubt. To discern the meaning, which includes identifying the limits, of a phrase such as 'unsettled dispute concerning sovereignty,' it is surely open to UNCLOS adjudicators to apply other rules, such as those governing use of force, self-determination, and the stability of boundaries between states.

Addressing a question of use of force, self-determination, or the stability of boundaries is *a fortiori* within the scope of UNCLOS jurisdiction when it is a respondent's jurisdictional objection that gives rise to the question. Article 288, paragraph 4, which I considered earlier in this chapter, is clear in its direction to UNCLOS tribunals. Settling a question as to the scope of its jurisdiction is not a discretionary function of the tribunal. It is a function that the tribunal shall perform. Moreover, in answer to Tzeng's concern that a tribunal not invoke Article 293(1) to overextend its exercise of jurisdiction, a tribunal should note, as the *Arctic Sunrise* Annex VII tribunal did, and as the *Duzgit Integrity* Annex VII tribunal did as well,[117] that Article 293(1) 'ensures that ... a tribunal can give full effect to the provisions of the Convention.'[118] Reading Article 293(1) together with the mandatory direction of Article 288(4), when a party invokes a 'sovereignty dispute' as a bar against the exercise of jurisdiction, but the putative 'dispute' is closely connected to use of force and stability of boundaries, an UNCLOS tribunal should apply the modern international law rules concerning use of force and stability of boundaries. At the very least, the rules should inform the tribunal's understanding of what constitutes a 'sovereignty dispute' in

116 Brunk & Hakimi (2022) 688–689; Brunk & Hakimi (2024) 448 n. 197; Grant (2015) 103–131.

117 *Duzgit Integrity* at ¶ 208 quoting *Arctic Sunrise*.

118 *Arctic Sunrise (Netherlands v. Russia)*, PCA Case No. 2014–02, Annex VII tribunal (Mensah, President; Burmester, Soons, Symonides, and Székely, arbitrators), Award, Merits, ¶ 187 (14 August 2015).

the modern law, and the tribunal should test the evidence in the case at hand against that definition. I return to this matter in Chapter 6.[119]

Use of force in other settings: some observations by analogy

The ICJ in notable cases has reached decisions regarding allegations of use of force notwithstanding the absence of merits jurisdiction to reach them. The decisions have drawn criticism but are a reality of the ICJ's jurisprudence. *Military and Paramilitary Activities in and against Nicaragua* and *Oil Platforms* are relevant for present purposes, but not because of their subject matter. The parties' claims were not UNCLOS claims. The cases are relevant because they illustrate that an international court can address questions of use of force in a variety of ways in a variety of procedural settings, even where the parties have not consented to the adjudicator settling the questions. These cases are further relevant because they illustrate that an international court knows full well how to scrutinize assertions that a respondent makes in defense against an applicant's claims.

In *Military and Paramilitary Activities,* the ICJ applied, *inter alia*, the Nicaragua–United States Treaty of Friendship, Commerce and Navigation of 1956. Article XXI(1)*(d)* of the Treaty provided that the Treaty 'shall not preclude the application of measures ... necessary to fulfil the obligations of a Party for the maintenance or restoration of international peace and security, or necessary to protect its essential security interests.' The Court interpreted this provision to be subject to the judgment of the Court, and, thus, not a matter of auto-appreciation by either state party.[120]

After an extended exercise in fact-finding, the Court concluded that countries in Central America over whom it exercised no jurisdiction, and one of which, El Salvador, it had refused to let intervene in the case,[121] were not under armed attack.[122] One area of factual evidence that the Court considered was the diplomatic record. Considering the diplomatic record, the Court concluded that none of the states that the United States said were under armed attack by Nicaragua—El Salvador, Honduras, and Costa Rica—had conducted themselves in a manner 'consistent with such a situation,

119 See Chapter 6, pp. 173–247.

120 ICJ 1986 at p. 116 ¶ 222. See Michael Reisman's trenchant critique: W. Michael Reisman, 'The Other Shoe Falls: The Future of Article 36(1) Jurisdiction in Light of *Nicaragua*' (1987) 81 AJIL 166, 167–168.

121 Order, ICJ 1984 at p. 216 (4 October).

122 See esp. conclusions at ICJ 1986 p. 86 ¶ 160 (stating that only 'an intermittent flow of arms' took place to El Salvador from Nicaragua); and p. 128 ¶ 252 (concluding that no 'activities in El Salvador attributed to the Government of Nicaragua' could justify the United States' intervention in Nicaragua).

either at the time when the United States first embarked on the activities which were allegedly justified by self-defence, or indeed for a long period subsequently.'[123] Even El Salvador's plain statements in the UN Security Council that it was a victim of armed attack did not satisfy the Court, those statements having been made (the Court said) too late to support the United States' contention that the United States was acting in accord with the right of self-defense.[124] The Court's rejection of El Salvador's submissions on this point was pivotal to the case. The United States, in response to Nicaragua's claims, had argued that assistance to armed groups opposing Nicaragua was justified under the right of collective self-defense. The Court in rejecting the evidence of Nicaragua's armed incursions against states in Central America, including the evidence that El Salvador adduced to support its request to intervene in the proceedings, rejected the United States' defense.

Oil Platforms is another case in which the United States as respondent pleaded that use of force was justified as self-defense. In *Oil Platforms*, Iran instituted proceedings against the United States for alleged breaches of the Iran–United States Treaty of Amity, Economic Relations and Consular Rights of 1955. Iran argued that armed measures that the United States had taken against certain Iranian oil platforms in the Gulf constituted breaches of the Treaty. The Treaty's compromissory clause does not embrace disputes arising out of use of force. However, Article XX(1)*(d)* of the Treaty, in terms practically the same as those of Article XXI(1)*(d)* of the Nicaragua–United States Treaty of 1956, contains a savings clause that affirms each Party's right to use force in certain circumstances. According to Article XX(1)*(d)*,

> The present Treaty shall not preclude the application of measures:
>
> *(d)* necessary to fulfil the obligations of a High Contracting Party for the maintenance or restoration of international peace and security, or necessary to protect its essential security interests.[125]

The United States, in reply to Iran's claims, adduced evidence to show that Iran had authored armed attacks in the Gulf, and pleaded that its own resort to force was a lawful response to the attacks—in short, 'measures necessary to protect its essential security interests.'

The Court's answer to the United States' plea needed to say whether or not the United States' measures were 'necessary' in the Article XX(1)*(d)* sense. The Court, however, went further than that. The Court said that its jurisdiction to interpret and apply Article XX(1)*(d)* 'extends, where appropriate, to the determination whether action alleged to be justified under that

123 ICJ 1986 at p. 120 ¶ 233.
124 *Ibid.* at pp. 120–121 ¶ 233.
125 8 United States Treaties and Other International Agreements 901, 912.

paragraph was or was not an unlawful use of force, by reference to international law applicable to this question, that is to say, the provisions of the Charter of the United Nations and customary international law.'[126] The Court concluded that the United States' armed actions against the Iranian platforms 'constituted recourse to armed force not qualifying, under international law on the question, as acts of self-defence.'[127] The Court reached its conclusion after carrying out an inquiry into the facts. The Court was rather selective in its inquiry, but it did not omit entirely to inquire. The necessary inference from the Court's conclusion was that the United States had violated the prohibition of use of force under general international law. This matter was plainly not one that the 1955 Treaty empowered the Court to decide, but that did not stop the Court from deciding it.

Judge Buergenthal wrote separately in *Oil Platforms*, in effect in dissent, that the judgment of the Court overstepped the Court's jurisdiction when it 'stigmatize[d] the actions of the United States as a breach of international law on the use of force without having the requisite jurisdiction to make such a ruling.'[128] Judge Kooijmans concurred with the three main conclusions of substance in the *dispositif* of the judgment 'but with considerable hesitation.'[129] Judge Higgins, noting that Iran made no request at any phase of the proceedings for the Court to adopt any finding under Article XX(1)*(d)*,[130] thought that the Court, in addressing the legality of the United States' armed measures in the *dispositif*, overstepped the limits of the *ultra petita* rule.[131] In short, there were good reasons for the Court to have refrained from addressing the allegations of unlawful use of force in the case, but the Court did not find any of those reasons persuasive.

In Judge Simma's view, the Court should have gone further and stated outright that the United States had violated the general international law prohibition and the UN Charter prohibition of use of force.[132] It took no great act of inference, however, to read the judgment as having gone a long way in the direction that Judge Simma wanted it to. The inference from the judgment that the United States had engaged in an illegal use of force is precisely what drew Judge Buergenthal and Judge Higgins to rebuke the Court and Judge Kooijmans to express hesitation. It is to be submitted that the Court would have averted at least some of the criticism, if it had crafted

126 ICJ 2003 at pp. 182–183 ¶ 42.
127 *Oil Platforms (Islamic Republic of Iran v. United States)*, ICJ 2003 at p. 199 ¶ 78.
128 Sep. Op. Judge Buergenthal, ICJ 2003 at p. 278 ¶ 19.
129 Sep. Op. Judge Kooijmans, ICJ 2003 at p. 246 ¶ 2.
130 Sep. Op. Judge Higgins, ICJ 2003 at p. 228 ¶ 12.
131 *Ibid.* at p. 231 ¶ 24.
132 Sep. Op. Judge Simma, ICJ 2003 at p. 327 ¶ 6.

a more reserved dispositive paragraph,[133] and left its conclusions about self-defense in the reasoning that came before.

Undefined terms and incidental rules

Judge Kooijmans, in his separate opinion in *Oil Platforms*, observed that the Court could not apply Article XX(1)*(d)* by reference to the terms of the 1955 Treaty alone, because 'neither Article XX, paragraph 1*(d)*, itself nor any other provision of the Treaty contains elements which enable the Court to apply the legality test with regard to the question whether measures, taken to protect the essential security interests, are necessary indeed.'[134] It was true, Judge Kooijmans acknowledged, that the Court's 'jurisdiction [was] limited to the interpretation and application of the ... Treaty.' Nevertheless, given the lack of any 'elements which enable the Court to apply the legality test,' the Court had 'no choice but to rely for this purpose on the body of general international law.'[135] In short, the logic of the treaty rendered '[g]eneral international law ... indispensable as a standard of interpretation of the provisions of the ... Treaty.'[136] The reliance on general international law, it will be noted, Judge Kooijmans was careful to qualify was '*for this purpose*'—that is to say, the limited purpose of evaluating the United States' contention concerning 'essential security interests.'

Situations such as that which the Court and Judge Kooijmans addressed are numerous, in which a treaty term, the interpretation or application of which is indispensable to interpreting or applying other treaty terms, is ambiguous or undefined in the treaty. In those situations, courts and tribunals look to other sources of law and examine facts, even when their jurisdiction does not embrace differences between the parties as to the other sources of law or facts. To recall, invoking UNCLOS Article 293(1), the Annex VII tribunal in *Duzgit Integrity* said that an adjudicator under UNCLOS might have to consider 'foundational or secondary rules of general international law,' because without those rules it will not be able 'properly to interpret and apply particular provisions of the Convention.'[137] The *Arctic Sunrise* tribunal relied on similar reasoning.[138]

To give a more terrestrial, if not prosaic, example than maritime enforcement actions gone awry, France and Equatorial Guinea fell into dispute

133 Esp. at ICJ 2003 at p. 218 ¶ 125(1), in which it is not obvious that the Court needed to say anything at all about the 'essential security interests' defense.
134 Sep. Op. Judge Kooijmans, ICJ 2003 at p. 261 ¶ 48.
135 *Ibid.*
136 *Ibid.* at ¶ 49.
137 *Duzgit Integrity* at ¶ 208.
138 *Arctic Sunrise*, Merits, ¶ 187 (14 August 2015).

over France's seizure of property from a building in Paris that Equatorial Guinea asserted was a 'premises of the mission' for purposes of Article 1*(i)* of the Vienna Convention on Diplomatic Relations. The dispute required the ICJ to interpret and apply Article *1(i)*. If the building was a 'premises of the mission,' then the building was inviolable under Convention Article 22 and France had no right to enter it. At issue in the dispute was whether Equatorial Guinea's act of designating the building as a diplomatic premises was one which for the purposes of the Convention and in the circumstances of the case France must accept.[139] The problem for the Court was that neither Article 1*(i)* nor any other provision in the Convention gave much 'assistance in determining the circumstances in which a property acquires the status of "premises of the mission."'[140] Nor did the drafting history shed light on the matter.[141] Instead, the Court turned to sources outside the Convention, including the unobjected state practice under which receiving states assert that their approval is required in order for a sending state's designation of a building as 'premises of the mission' to take effect.[142] The Court concluded on the point that a receiving state that makes timely objection to the designation of a building as 'premises of the mission,' where the objection is neither arbitrary nor discriminatory, thus prevents the building from acquiring protected status for purposes of the Convention.[143]

Lorand Bartels some years ago drew attention to provisions that, like Article XX(1)*(d)* of the 1955 Iran–US Treaty and Article 1*(i)* of the 1961 Vienna Convention, contain terms that the instrument of which they are part does not define. Under such provisions, the decision-maker, if she refuses to consider 'incidental' rules—fearful that, because disputes about them are not subject to jurisdiction, *any* application of them will exceed the bounds of jurisdiction—might well find that she has no way to interpret certain rules that the treaty expressly calls on her to apply.[144] The result will be gaps in the application of the dispute settlement procedure which, arguably, the parties did not intend. One need not seek to expunge *non liquet* as an operative international law category to be wary nevertheless of an interpretative theory that categorically refuses to consider incidental rules in these situations. It is one thing to indulge in a doctrinaire insistence that the adjudicator never leave a gap in a treaty. It is quite another to insist on an

139 *Immunities and Criminal Proceedings (Equatorial Guinea v. France)*, Judgment, ICJ 2020 p. 300, pp. 316–319 ¶¶ 47–60 (11 December).
140 *Ibid.* at p. 319 ¶ 62.
141 *Ibid.* at p. 323, ¶ 70.
142 *Ibid.* at p. 322, ¶ 69.
143 *Ibid.* at p. 324, ¶¶ 74–75.
144 Bartels, 'Applicable Law and Jurisdiction Clauses' in Broude & Shany (eds.), *Multisourced Equivalent Norms in International Law* (2011) 115, 134.

interpretive theory that will leave treaties rife with gaps, even when the straightforward application of well-known principles would close them.

Nothing in UNCLOS says what constitutes a sovereignty dispute for purposes of Article 298(1)(a)*(i)* or for any other purpose. But among the 'incidental' rules that an adjudicator might consult in forming a view as to the matter is the fundamental rule that use of force is not a source of sovereign title—or a basis to assert a claim to sovereign title—under modern international law. If it is allowable for an adjudicator to refer to the general international law principles of 'reasonableness,' 'necessity,' and 'proportionality' to impart meaning—and define a limit—to the UNCLOS term 'enforcement measures,' as the Annex VII tribunal did in *Duzgit Integrity*, then an adjudicator may apply the principle of stability of territorial entitlement to limit the term 'sovereignty dispute.'[145] That principle, like the rules concerning use of force as such, forms part of the framework in which UNCLOS jurisdiction functions.

In answering a question that it *must* answer, a tribunal sometimes touches on a question that it must *not*. The better approach is for the tribunal to answer the question that it must answer in the manner that does the least to prejudice the other, while at the same time answering the question for the purposes of the case at hand. Distinguishing between matters decided and matters *not* decided is a method that adjudicators employ when a case presents this sort of difficulty. Under the widespread view that UNCLOS Part XV, section 2, entails that an adjudicator must *not* answer questions about territorial sovereignty, the method has particular salience in proceedings under UNCLOS where a party has interposed a question about territorial sovereignty. I return to this point in Chapter 8.

Land territory in UNCLOS: 'the land dominates the sea' (or UNCLOS comes ashore)

A line of reasoning that emerged in some of the cases that I discuss later in this book, in particular *Chagos Marine Protected Area*, which is the concern of Chapter 4, is that the exclusion of territorial sovereignty issues from Part XV, section 2, procedures is *not* found in Article 298 but, instead, inheres in the affirmative expression of the scope of jurisdiction found in Article 288(1). Let us call this the 'Article 288(1) argument.' According to the Article 288(1) argument, jurisdiction extends to disputes 'concerning the interpretation or application' of the Convention but—according to the argument—disputes about territorial sovereignty issues are not disputes

145 *Duzgit Integrity Arbitration*, ¶ 209.

'concerning the interpretation or application' of the Convention. In short, if the argument is accepted, then sovereignty issues do not belong to the Part XV, section 2, framework at all, and so one need look no further to recognize that UNCLOS adjudicators cannot address them.

It is certainly true that UNCLOS is a 'law of the sea treaty' and not a 'law of the land' treaty. The difficulty with the Article 288(1) argument is that beyond that point, which is trite, one searches in vain for such a clinical separation of territory from UNCLOS as would establish the putative inherence of a territorial exclusion in Article 288(1). Instead, connections are readily observed between territory and UNCLOS's main provisions. The connections, quite the opposite of establishing that it is inherent in Article 288(1) that territory is *not* an UNCLOS concern, tend to show that it is.

'*Il est frappant de constater*,' says Maurice Kamto, '*à quel point le territoire terrestre exerce un impact sur le droit de la mer*' ('It is striking to note... to what extent land territory has an impact on the law of the sea').[146] The most obvious, and most important, impact of land territory in UNCLOS is upon the existence and scope of potential maritime entitlements of states. A coastal state holds jurisdictional rights (and obligations) in respect of maritime zones appurtenant to land, meaning land under the sovereignty of the coastal state. Where there is no land, there are no such rights over the sea. This follows from—or is the source of the validity of—the famous maxim 'the land dominates the sea.' The ICJ, since first setting it down in the *North Sea Continental Shelf* cases,[147] has invoked the maxim numerous times.[148] The ITLOS and Annex VII tribunals have invoked it as well.[149] A maritime entitlement can be no more sound than the title to territory

146 Kamto, 'Les différentes catégories d'Etat' in Forteau & Thouvenin (eds.) (2017) 235, 237.

147 *North Sea Continental Shelf (Federal Republic of Germany/Denmark; Federal Republic of Germany/Netherlands),* Judgment, ICJ 1969 p. 3, p. 51 ¶ 96.

148 See, for example, *Continental Shelf (Tunisia/Libya)*, Judgment, ICJ 1982 at p. 61 ¶ 73 (24 February); *Territorial and Maritime Dispute between Nicaragua and Honduras in the Caribbean Sea (Nicaragua* v. *Honduras),* Judgment, ICJ 2007 at p. 661, p. 696 ¶ 113 (8 October); *Maritime Delimitation and Territorial Questions between Qatar and Bahrain (Qatar* v. *Bahrain)*, Merits, ICJ 2001 p. 40, p 97 ¶ 185 (16 March). See also the Chamber decision in *Delimitation of the Maritime Boundary in the Gulf of Maine (Canada/United States of America)*, Judgment, ICJ 1984 p. 246, p. 312 ¶ 157 (12 October).

149 *Dispute concerning delimitation of the maritime boundary between Bangladesh and Myanmar in the Bay of Bengal (Bangladesh/Myanmar)*, Judgment, ITLOS 2012 p. 4, p. 56 ¶ 185 (14 March). *Bay of Bengal Maritime Boundary (Bangladesh/India)*, Annex VII (Wolfrum, President; Cot, Menash, Rao, and Shearer, members) Award, 7 July 2014, ¶ 279 ('it is axiomatic ... that the "land dominates the sea"'). Cf. *South China Sea (Philippines v. China)*, Award on Jurisdiction and Admissibility, 29 October 2015, where the parties concurred as to the applicability of the maxim: ¶ 143.

on which it is claimed. Maritime jurisdiction is concomitant to territorial sovereignty.

The land–sea link

We see this relation between maritime jurisdiction and territorial sovereignty—their concomitance—very clearly in key provisions of UNCLOS.

Article 2, paragraph 1, indicates the legal status of the territorial sea by stating that '[t]he sovereignty of a coastal State extends, beyond its land territory and internal waters ... to an adjacent belt of sea.' So the rights of the state in the territorial sea are expressed in terms of the sovereignty which starts in 'its land territory.' By necessary implication, the régime of the EEZ under Article 55 also emanates from land, starting as the EEZ does from the same baselines as the territorial sea (Article 57). The Convention defines the continental shelf of the state (in the first instance) as comprising 'the seabed and subsoil of the submarine areas that extend beyond its territorial sea throughout the natural prolongation of its land territory' (Article 76, paragraph 1).

We also may advert in this connection to the Convention's rules on straight baselines (Article 7), including the requirement that 'the sea areas lying within the lines must be sufficiently closely linked to the land domain to be subject to the régime of internal waters.'[150] Opinion is divided as to the degree to which internal waters are juristically assimilated into the land territory of the state. In *'ARA Libertad,'* the question came to the fore, because Argentina asserted that the immunity of a warship applies to the warship when it visits another state's port—that is, when it is in the state's internal waters. UNCLOS Article 32 provides, subject to certain exceptions (not in themselves determinative of the internal waters question), that 'nothing in [UNCLOS] affects the immunities of warships and other government ships operated for non-commercial purposes.' Argentina contended that Article 32 of the Convention applies in internal waters and thus renders a foreign warship there immune to host state enforcement measures. Ghana—the host state—disagreed. In Ghana's view, internal waters are so closely assimilated with land territory that the Article 32 régime does not reach internal waters and, thus, a warship in port is not immune.[151] Judges Wolfrum and Cot agreed with Ghana. In their separate opinion, Judges Wolfrum and Cot said that 'limitations of the coastal States' sovereignty over internal waters cannot be assumed.'[152] By contrast, the ITLOS majority in its provisional measures

150 1833 UNTS at 401. As to internal waters, see generally Churchill, Lowe, & Sander (2022) 110–129.

151 ITLOS 2012 at p. 344 ¶ 65.

152 *'ARA Libertad' (Argentina v. Ghana)*, Provisional Measures, Joint Sep. Op. Judges Cot and Wolfrum, ITLOS 2012 at p. 370 ¶ 25 (15 December).

order found plausible that internal waters are subject to the UNCLOS régime of immunity.[153] Churchill, Lowe, and Sander say that Judges Cot and Wolfrum 'cogently argued' that Article 32 does not apply.[154] Studying the colloquy between Judges Cot and Wolfrum and the ITLOS majority, other writers, for example Professor Tanaka, instead agree with the majority's conclusion.[155] That the land–sea relation here is ambiguous enough to elude consensus tends further to suggest caution toward a categorical separation of land from sea.

The observation that land and sea are intimately related in UNCLOS may be extended to archipelagic waters. The Convention permits a state that meets the definition of 'archipelagic State,' under Article 46,[156] to draw 'archipelagic baselines' joining the state's constituent features, subject to limitations specified under Article 47.[157] The waters enclosed by archipelagic baselines—'archipelagic waters'—in accordance with Article 49(1) are under '[t]he sovereignty of [the] archipelagic State.' In other words, at least certain incidents of state authority that otherwise are restricted to land territory embrace this maritime area. Further linkage between land territory and archipelagic waters is explicit in the limitations under Article 47. Under Article 47(1), the archipelagic state's right to draw archipelagic baselines is defined (and limited) by a formula of ratios between 'area of water' and 'area of the land.' Where the ratio of area of water to area of land 'is between 1 to 1 and 9 to 1,' it is open to the archipelagic state to draw archipelagic baselines; outside that range, it is not.[158]

153 ITLOS 2012 at pp. 343–344 ¶¶ 60–67.
154 Churchill, Lowe, & Sander (2022) 123.
155 Tanaka, '*ARA Libertad* and *Ukraine* v. *Russia* cases' (2020) 96 *International Law Studies* 223, 242–245. Similarly, Professors Kohen and Gómez Pulisich understand the immunities regime to extend landward under UNCLOS into internal waters: Kohen & Gómez Pulisich, 'Typologie des espaces marins' in Forteau & Thouvenin (eds.), *Traité de droit international de la mer (CEDIN)* (2017) 341, 350–355. Cf. Dupuy, 'The Sea under National Competence' in Dupuy & Vignes, vol. 1 (eds.) (1991) at 249–253.
156 1833 UNTS at 414. As to the definition, see Redgwell & Tzanakopoulos, 'The Interaction of Treaty and Custom in the Concept of Offshore Archipelagos' (2023) 72 ICLQ 573, 581–582, 587.
157 1833 UNTS at 414–415. As to the emergence of the archipelagic regime at the Third Conference, see Redgwell & Tzanakopoulos (2023) 578–581. See generally Rothwell (2022) 101–141.
158 As to the legal regime of archipelagic waters, see generally Churchill, Lowe, & Sander (2022) 187–205; Roach, 'Offshore Archipelagos Enclosed by Straight Baselines: An Excessive Claim' (2018) 49 ODIL 176–200; Whomersley, 'Offshore Archipelagos Enclosed by Straight Baselines: A Reply to J. Ashley Roach' (2018) 49 ODIL 203–207; Office of the Staff Judge Advocate, U.S. Indo-Pacific Command, 'Archipelagic States' (2021) 97 *International Law Studies* 12–16.

If a dispute arises concerning any of these maritime areas that the Convention defines, then, in an essential way, the dispute concerns the land territory from which maritime jurisdiction is generated. Without a settled understanding of where the land territory is, and under what state's sovereignty it lies, the terms 'archipelagic waters,' 'territorial sea,' 'exclusive economic zone,' and 'continental shelf' remain to a degree abstract or incomplete. These are not minor terms within the scheme of the Convention. The familiar provisions of UNCLOS defining the territorial sea, the EEZ, and the continental shelf in particular reflect crucial developments in the law of the sea generally and are a central feature in UNCLOS. It is simply incorrect to have asserted, as one writer did in 1980, that 'substantive articles of the Convention do not relate to such matters [as the status of land territory].'[159] The Convention *does* 'relate to such matters.' The relation is all the more vital in its setting, because states at the time of the negotiation and adoption of the Convention understood their territorial entitlements to be a largely fixed quantity, subject to be sure to adjustment through consent-based decisions, but settled and secure enough to justify seeking a new and comprehensive settlement of concomitant maritime rights. Stable expectation of territorial entitlement is not a mere incidental feature of the setting in which UNCLOS emerged. It is essential to the modern law of the sea, for, without it, the drafting effort and political investment that led to the adopted text would have been to no avail. The modern elaboration of the law of maritime jurisdiction was worth the trouble because a modern law of stable territorial boundaries had emerged.

The Convention relates to land territory in other ways in addition to defining national rights over archipelagic waters, territorial sea, EEZs, and the continental shelf. Article 33 provides that a state in its contiguous zone (i.e., the zone extending a further twelve nautical miles from the outer limit of the territorial sea) 'may exercise the control necessary to: (a) prevent infringement of its customs, fiscal, immigration or sanitary laws and regulations within its territory or territorial sea; (b) punish infringement of the above laws and regulations committed within its territory or territorial sea.'

So the Convention is expressly concerned with infringement of national law, where the infringement originates within the territory of a state, not just within the territorial sea. Similarly, Article 216 requires states to enforce '[l]aws and regulations adopted in accordance with this Convention ... for the prevention, reduction and control of pollution of the marine environment by dumping' not just in respect to acts at sea but also in respect to 'acts of loading wastes or other matter occurring within its territory' (Article 216,

159 Irwin, 'Settlement of Maritime Boundary Disputes: An Analysis of the Law of the Sea Negotiations' (1980) 8 ODIL 105, 114.

subparagraph 1(c)). These rules address acts on the land territory of a state. The Convention is not an instrument for the regulation of the land territory of the state as such; but, by the same token, the Convention does not eschew contact to land. A number of provisions of the Convention concern maritime matters that have a close connection to the state's jurisdiction over land. In those provisions, the Convention expressly involves itself in the state's jurisdiction over land. Perhaps UNCLOS does not come entirely ashore, but it touches the land in many ways.

There are still further examples in the Convention of provisions concerned with issues connected to the land territory. The Convention is concerned with landlocked states and rights of transit over the land territory of transit states. Article 124 defines a 'land-locked State' as one 'which has no sea-coast' and 'transit State' as one 'situated between a land-locked State and the sea, through whose territory traffic in transit passes' (Article 124, subparagraphs 1(a), (b)). It is to be asked whether there is no dispute concerning the interpretation or application of Article 124, where a state's only potential sea coast is on land territory which it claims from another state. And what if the transit route from the landlocked state to the sea passes over territory disputed in some way between the transit state and a third state? Is the dispute in respect of that territory unconcerned with the interpretation or application of Article 124? As for Article 125, its first paragraph provides that 'land-locked States shall enjoy freedom of transit through the territory of transit States by all means of transport.' If a dispute arises concerning transit arrangements, then is this a dispute concerning Article 125 and, if so, is it a dispute subject to dispute settlement under the Part XV, section 2, mechanisms? It is far from obvious that it is not.

A group of landlocked states early in the Third Conference addressed the draft provision on maritime access. These states said that 'this provision shall not be construed as prejudicing territorial disputes of any kind.'[160] The landlocked states were saying, in effect, that the existence of a conventional right of access should not affect the settlement of a dispute over other rights concerning the territory, including sovereignty over it. The landlocked states' purpose, understood in this way, was to limit the effects of the substantive provision. Their statement was a cautionary declaration to make certain that a territorial claim of a landlocked state, wherever that state might bring its claim, would not be prejudged by reference to the state's acceptance of

160 Afghanistan, Bhutan, Bolivia, Botswana, Burundi, Czechoslovakia, Hungary, Laos, Lesotho, Mali, Mongolia, Nepal, Paraguay, Swaziland, Uganda, Upper Volta, and Zambia: explanatory paper on the draft articles relating to land-locked States in document A/AC.138/93, Third UN Conference, First and Second Sessns., 30 July 1974, A/CONF.62/C.2/L.29: III *Official Records* 209.

a right of transit.[161] It indeed would have been an unhappy outcome for a landlocked state to have agreed to UNCLOS Article 125, motivated by the freedom of transit that Article 125 promises, only to have Article 125 invoked against it by a state seeking to curtail either an existing (pre- or non-UNCLOS) transit right or to prejudge a territorial dispute concerning the area in which a transit right is concerned. In any event, the landlocked states' declaration had to do with the substantive content of Article 125; it does not seem to limit the dispute settlement provisions of the Convention.

Another consideration that is relevant to the competence of Part XV, section 2, procedures is the close—and dependent—relation of maritime jurisdiction to the characteristics of land, in particular of islands.

The relation is particularly clear in Article 121, wherein is set down the régime of islands.[162] According to Article 121:

> 1. An island is a naturally formed area of land, surrounded by water, which is above water at high tide.
>
> 2. Except as provided for in paragraph 3, the territorial sea, the contiguous zone, the exclusive economic zone and the continental shelf of an island are determined in accordance with the provisions of this Convention applicable to other land territory.
>
> 3. Rocks which cannot sustain human habitation or economic life of their own shall have no exclusive economic zone or continental shelf.

Courts and tribunals applying Article 121, paragraph 1, have had no hesitation to enter into the threshold question: is a contested feature an island—that is, 'a naturally formed area of land, surrounded by water, which is above water at high tide'—and thus capable of appropriation as sovereign territory?[163]

161 Cf. Mrs. Chibesakunda (Zambia), Third UN Conference, Second Sess., 32nd plen. mtg., 8 July 1974, A/CONF.62/SR.32: I *Official Records* 131, ¶ 48.

162 For review and discussion of Art. 121 and related dispute settlement practice, as well as pre-UNCLOS background, see Rothwell, *Islands and International Law* (2022) 10–18.

163 See *Territorial and Maritime Dispute (Nicaragua* v. *Colombia)*, Judgment, ICJ 2012 p. 624, pp. 641–645, ¶¶ 25–38; *Maritime Delimitation and Territorial Questions (Qatar* v. *Bahrain)*, Merits, Judgment, ICJ 2001 at p. 102 ¶ 206. In *Nicaragua v. Colombia*, sharp contestation arose in respect of a series of small features constituting a bank, Quitasueño. Nicaragua contended that there were no features there above water at high tide—that is, no islands. Colombia disagreed. The factual evidence established that at least one feature is an island: '[T]he Court concludes that the feature referred to as QS 32 is capable of appropriate'—a conclusion that, in turn, generated a territorial sea entitlement for Colombia at the Quitasueño bank. See ICJ 2012 at pp. 642–645 ¶¶ 27–38; pp. 692–693 ¶¶ 181–183. See *ibid.* at p. 714 (Sketch-map No. 11). (Note: I served on the legal team for Colombia in the merits phase of *Territorial and Maritime Dispute.*)

For the Convention dispute settlement procedures to apply to the question of whether a given feature is a permanent dry feature constituting an island is necessarily to enter into questions of sovereignty over land territory: where there is no land, there is no sovereignty over land; where land exists, sovereignty over land may follow. Writers who have considered the point seem to agree that Article 121 entails the question of whether land exists and that that provision is not excluded from the dispute settlement system.[164]

Interpreting and applying Article 121 in this way is not the same as deciding whether a given land feature belongs to *state A* or to *state B*, but it is also not the same as disclaiming the competence to say anything about land sovereignty. Adjudicators under Part XV, section 2, very well may decide that the sovereignty of *neither* state is concerned. This is the decision that adjudicators in fact have reached with respect to maritime spaces where there is no land. The putative bar against adjudicating sovereignty issues, if it serves a purpose, would seem to insulate a state's sovereignty claims from adjudication. The argument against adjudicating the issues rests on the assertion that the states parties to UNCLOS have not consented to courts or tribunals adjudicating them. But at least in this negative posture, courts and tribunals have reached decisions that do settle sovereignty issues.

The Convention also addresses artificial features and excludes them from treatment as territory. Thus, '[o]ff-shore installations and artificial islands shall not be considered as permanent harbour works' for purposes of Article 11. In accordance with Article 60, paragraph 8, artificial islands, installations, and structures 'do not possess the status of islands' and, thus, have no territorial sea of their own.[165] As Chapter 5 considers,[166] the Annex VII tribunal in *South China Sea (Philippines v. China)* applied these provisions. It settled questions as to whether certain features are islands (and thus susceptible to sovereignty) or LTEs (and thus not); whether certain features are natural (and thus potentially generate the full (or fuller) extent of legal effects in regard to appurtenant maritime areas) or artificial (and thus influence those areas only to a much lesser extent).

These questions concerning land territory are threshold questions, because other questions that parties under UNCLOS Part XV, section 2, might ask tribunals to settle depend on the answers that they receive. An adjudicator should exercise caution when interpreting and applying the jurisdictional instrument from which the adjudicator's authority flows. It could be that

164 See, for example, Hong, *UNCLOS and Ocean Dispute Settlement: Law and Politics in the South China Sea* (2012) 93.

165 Under Art. 80, the limitation on artificial features in the EEZ applies *mutatis mutandis* to artificial features on the continental shelf. 1833 UNTS at 430.

166 See pp. 150–172.

some threshold questions are beyond the scope of jurisdiction and, because they cannot be settled, the adjudicator cannot exercise jurisdiction over other questions. But there is risk as well in the *negative* determination—that is, the determination that the maritime question is, in effect, not ripe for adjudication because some non-maritime question first needs to be settled but cannot be resolved. In reaching *that* determination, the adjudicator does not necessarily leave the juristic landscape undisturbed. Before proceedings began, it might not have been clear that the threshold question even existed. Saying that it does exist, the adjudicator not only eschews settlement of the claim that the applicant instituted proceedings to settle but it also leaves the applicant with a new question that it might not have known that it had. Parties expect adjudicators to settle questions of jurisdiction, even the thorniest ones, not reflexively decline to adjudicate. There are threshold questions that are so closely involved in the main questions that denying an incidental power to deal with them is not to exercise due caution but, instead, begins to partake of artificiality or avoidance.

The inherency of sovereignty questions and the problem with the Article 288(1) argument

These considerations—the risk of encumbering a party with claims that it did not face when proceedings began, and the risk of failing in the duty to adjudicate claims properly instituted—were at least in the background when the ICJ in *Nicaragua v. Honduras* addressed the question of sovereignty over certain islands in the Caribbean. The sovereignty question had not been part of the applicant state's original request to the Court. Nicaragua, in its application, had requested only that the Court determine 'the course of the single maritime boundary between the areas of territorial sea, continental shelf and exclusive economic zone appertaining respectively' to the two parties.[167] The 'claim relating to sovereignty over the islands in the maritime area in dispute ... [was] a new claim.'[168] That the claim was new potentially excluded the Court from adjudicating it. The Court in numerous cases has rejected as inadmissible 'new claims,' where these 'would have transformed the subject of the dispute originally brought before it under the terms of the Application.'[169] However, here, the Court judged that the sovereignty question did *not* 'transform [...] the subject of the dispute.' It is worth recalling the Court's reasoning on the point.

167 ICJ 2007 at p. 694 ¶ 104.
168 *Ibid.* at p. 695 ¶ 109.
169 *Ibid.* at p. 695 ¶ 108, with citations to judgments.

According to the Court:

> To draw a single maritime boundary line in an area of the Caribbean Sea where a number of islands and rocks are located the Court would have to consider what influence these maritime features might have on the course of that line. To plot that line the Court would first have to determine which State has sovereignty over the islands and rocks in the disputed area. The Court is bound to do so *whether or not a formal claim has been made in this respect.* Thus the claim relating to sovereignty is *implicit in and arises directly out of* the question which is the subject-matter of Nicaragua's Application …
>
> In light of the foregoing, the Court concludes that the Nicaraguan claim relating to sovereignty over the islands in the maritime area in dispute is admissible *as it is inherent in* in the original claim relating to the maritime delimitation.[170]

This passage in *Nicaragua v. Honduras* deserves attention. It is to be remarked that, under the *ultra petita* principle, the Court adjudicates questions only to the extent that they belong to the subject matter that the parties have presented to it for adjudication. As surely as the absence in the jurisdictional instrument of an indication of the parties' consent to the adjudication of a question bars its adjudication, so does the absence of the question in the parties' claims. When the Court said that it is 'bound' to determine 'which State has sovereignty over the islands and rocks' regardless of 'whether or not a formal claim has been made in this respect,' the Court was not rejecting *ultra petita* as a principle that limits the conduct of the judicial function! It would not have been for the Court to do that. Instead, the Court was characterizing the dispute that Nicaragua had originally presented. The Court was characterizing that dispute as encompassing, at once, the maritime delimitation claim and the sovereignty question that had to be settled in order to settle the maritime delimitation claim. The sovereignty question was 'implicit in and ar[ose] directly out of' the maritime delimitation claim. The former was open for the Court to settle, 'as it [was] inherent in' the latter. The Court's reasoning was founded on the juristic ties between modern maritime jurisdiction and territorial sovereignty.

Herein lie further grounds to question the received view of the land territory exclusion and, in particular, the imputation of that exclusion to Article 288(1). The legal rights of states in maritime areas under UNCLOS are in large part inseparable from territorial sovereignty. The relation of land questions to maritime questions is, to borrow the ICJ's term, one of inherency, and the inherency is pervasive. No maritime jurisdiction—no

170 *Ibid.* at p. 697 ¶¶ 114–115 (emphasis added).

territorial sea, EEZ, or continental shelf—exists except with reference to sovereignty over land. True, the provisions of the Convention which define certain rights in common areas—that is, in the areas beyond the limits of national jurisdiction—can largely be understood without knowing which states have sovereignty over land. The common areas are an exception that proves the rule: they are areas that no state 'may validly purport to subject ... to its sovereignty' (Article 89). The much more extensive provisions in UNCLOS are concerned with areas proximate to states' coasts where the law recognizes that a state may exercise certain elements of national jurisdiction.[171] In the historical development of the law of the sea, the larger concern was precisely with those proximate areas—that is to say, with crystallizing the rules to govern, and to limit, the projection of national jurisdiction in the form of maritime entitlements appurtenant to land.[172] Moreover, in the areas near land, the law imposes on coastal states certain obligations toward other states. Such obligations are difficult or impossible to apply without a settled picture of land rights. It is by no means obvious why a question as to sovereignty over a coast (whether insular or continental) could never belong to a dispute 'concerning the interpretation or application' of the provisions setting down the coastal state's obligations. The identification of states' obligations (and rights) in the areas appurtenant to their terrestrial domain is a central purpose of the Convention. An unresolved dispute over territory frustrates that purpose.[173]

Again, UNCLOS was not adopted to furnish a new jurisdiction to address land-related disputes, but it is unsupportable to contend that UNCLOS is silent as to land territory and the exercise of state power over land territory. Significant provisions of the Convention address precisely those matters. It is far from self-evident that disputes concerning the interpretation or application of those provisions of the Convention are *not* to be adjudicated or arbitrated under Part XV, section 2.

The Article 288(1) argument, in sum, may be stated thus: as much as territory and sovereignty *are* concerns of many provisions of the Convention, the words 'any dispute concerning the interpretation or application of this

171 There are also traditional rights of use, such as those that the *Eritrea/Yemen* tribunal memorably affirmed, which are rather abstracted from sovereignty over land. See Introduction, n. 8.

172 See the overview of historical development of maritime entitlements by Dupuy, 'The Sea under National Competence' in Dupuy and Vignes, vol. 1 (eds.) (1991) 247–249.

173 Donald Rothwell noted some time ago that in the Asian-Pacific region unresolved territorial sovereignty disputes stood in the way of maritime boundary dispute settlement: Rothwell, 'The Law of the Sea in the Asian-Pacific Region' (1994–1995) 13 C(T)YBIL 81, 86–88. This was also the issue that the ICJ addressed in *Nicaragua v. Honduras*, as just noted.

Convention' do not embrace a dispute concerned with territory and sovereignty. The Article 288(1) argument is unconvincing. A territorial exclusion is impossible to distill from the open-textured language of Article 288(1). To the extent that issues of territorial sovereignty are excluded from UNCLOS jurisdiction, their exclusion is to be found someplace else.

It was open to the drafters to exclude sovereignty questions from dispute settlement jurisdiction *grosso modo*. However, as we will see in Chapter 3, they did not do so. As recalled here, they adopted provisions related to territory and provisions central to the maritime subject matter of the Convention that an adjudicator cannot fully interpret or apply without a settled understanding of the physical extent of territory and of state sovereignty over territory. Considering Article 288(1), which provides that jurisdiction extends to 'any dispute concerning the interpretation or application of this Convention'; considering Article 288(2), which provides that jurisdiction extends as well to 'any dispute concerning the interpretation or application of an international agreement related to the purposes of this Convention'; and considering Article 288(4), which *requires* that, '[i]n the event of a dispute as to whether a court or tribunal has jurisdiction,' the adjudicator settle the matter; the contention, if it is to be convincingly maintained, that territorial issues are generally excluded needs more support than has been adduced for it so far. To posit that '[i]ndeed, disputes concerning territorial sovereignty are not the disputes "concerning the interpretation or application of this Convention"'[174] is question-begging: it draws further attention to the question which itself remains to be answered but offers no *reasoned* answer to that question, only assertion.

A striking element in the discourse over this matter is the persistence of those who expound the complete exclusion of territorial issues from UNCLOS jurisdiction. I say more below about the view that UNCLOS somehow excludes any and all territorial issues from dispute settlement. But, first, let us turn to the text of Article 298(1)(a)*(i)*, which, as we will see, concerns a limited exception to jurisdiction, not the far-reaching one that the exponents of the territorial exclusion long have contended.

174 Jia & Talmon, 'Introduction' in Talmon & Jia (eds.), *The South China Sea Arbitration: A Chinese Perspective* (2014) 1, 9.

3

Jurisdiction under UNCLOS Part XV, section 2: limitations and optional exceptions

In Chapter 2, I considered familiar provisions of UNCLOS under which the Convention establishes a potential jurisdiction over any dispute concerning the interpretation or application of the Convention. I considered the controversy that tribunals have provoked by applying Article 293 to reach questions concerning use of force in maritime disputes.

I also considered the argument that a limitation on jurisdiction inheres in Article 288(1) of such scope as to bar adjudicators from addressing sovereignty questions. Article 288(1) is not the obvious place to look for limitations on jurisdiction. The obvious place to look is in the provisions that expressly define the limitations. This chapter considers those provisions. It also considers the land territory exclusion in Article 298 which some jurists maintain is a general exclusion preventing Part XV, section 2, procedures from reaching questions of land territory.

Limitations and optional exceptions distinguished

As recalled above, Part XV, section 2, addressing compulsory procedures of dispute settlement entailing binding decisions, allows a party to submit a dispute after the party has satisfied the requirements of section 1 (absence of agreements to use other dispute settlement procedures, exchange of views, etc.) and where none of the limitations or exceptions to the applicability of section 2 set out in section 3 apply. Section 3 contains Articles 297 and 298.[1] Article 297 expresses the limitations on applicability of section 2; Article 298 provides for the optional exceptions. Each merits a brief overview,

1 Along with Art. 299, a savings clause making clear that parties to a dispute that on one ground or another is otherwise excluded from jurisdiction are not prevented from agreeing to a dispute settlement procedure or from settling their dispute through other amicable means.

before we turn to consider Article 298(1)(a)*(i)* and its optional exception for territorial disputes.

Article 297: the specified limits on jurisdiction

Having resulted from heated negotiations at the Third United Nations Conference on the Law of the Sea, the expression in Article 288(1) of the parties' consent to jurisdiction over 'any dispute concerning the interpretation or application' of UNCLOS reflects a considered drafting choice.[2] Consistent with that choice, the states parties, in the provision that became Article 297, adopted exclusions from jurisdiction 'over *specified categories* of issues.'[3] It was said at the Conference that the language expressing exclusions from jurisdiction must be narrow and specific, because, otherwise, a 'loop-hole' would open.[4] Rosenne and Sohn, studying the negotiating history, relate that '[m]any ... speakers took a similar position, emphasizing that they would prefer to have no exceptions, but that if there must be some, every proposed exception should be formulated very clearly, and its scope and application should be interpreted restrictively.'[5]

While far from the model of the draftsman's art,[6] Article 297 largely reflects the Conference delegates' intention to confine exceptions to jurisdiction to narrow and specific terms. The affirmation of jurisdiction in Article 297 over certain categories of disputes, at first glance, looks out of keeping with the drafting architecture. For example, the first clause of Article 297(3)(a) reads, '[d]isputes concerning the interpretation or application of the provisions of this Convention with regard to fisheries shall be settled in accordance with section 2.'[7] On inspection, however, the function of this textual device becomes clear: it serves to frame the concomitant exclusions and to maintain their specificity.[8]

2 Rosenne & Sohn, Article 297 in Nordquist (gen. ed.), *Virginia Commentary*, p. 88, §297.2.

3 Rosenne & Sohn at p. 88 (emphasis added). Further to the background and drafting, see the summary by Serdy in the *Proelss Commentary* 1906, 1910–1912. See also Klein (2009) 125–126, 140–144; Forteau in Forteau & Thouvenin (eds.) (2017) 1001–1002; Churchill, Lowe, & Sander (2022) 866–867; Allen, 'Article 297' (2017) 48 ODIL 313–330.

4 Rosenne & Sohn at p. 92, §297.6.

5 *Ibid.*

6 Professor Kunoy notes the 'convoluted drafting techniques' visible in the provision: Kunoy (2021) 103.

7 1833 UNTS at 514.

8 See *'Enrica Lexie' Incident*, PCA Case No. 2015–28, Annex VII tribunal (Golitsyn, President; Paik, Robinson, Francioni, and Rao, members), ¶ 802 (rejecting Italy's argument that Art. 297(1)(b) supplied a further basis for jurisdiction over Italy's claims) (21 May 2020).

Article 298: the optional exceptions to jurisdiction

The second article of Part XV, section 3, Article 298, indicates certain optional exceptions to jurisdiction, one or more of which a state party may elect by written declaration.[9] The optional exceptions to jurisdiction exclude compulsory dispute settlement only in regard to those categories of claims that Article 298(1) identifies and only to the extent that a party elects.

Of the provisions in Article 298, one in particular attracts disagreement when it is asked whether, and if so to what extent, an UNCLOS tribunal might address issues of territorial sovereignty. This is subparagraph (1)(a)*(i)* of Article 298, which the balance of this chapter considers.

Article 298(1)(a)*(i)* and its sovereignty disputes clause

It is an enduring puzzle why much of the commentariat concerned with UNCLOS insist that the clause in Article 298(1)(a)*(i)* that refers to 'dispute[s] concerning sovereignty or other rights over continental or insular land territory' entails an omnibus exclusion of territorial issues from dispute settlement under the Convention. As a careful reading of the provision shows, the sovereignty clause is limited on its terms to one dispute settlement procedure—non-binding conciliation under UNCLOS Annex V[10]—in one circumstance: where a party has made submission to Annex V conciliation against a party that has elected an optional exception.[11] That is the extent of the application of the sovereignty clause in Article 298(1)(a)*(i)*. There is no other sovereignty or territorial exclusion clause in UNCLOS.

Against this limited exclusion of territorial disputes, there is the general statement in Articles 286 and 288 extending jurisdiction to 'any dispute.' On the prevalent view today, however, jurisdiction under UNCLOS procedures—not just under Annex V conciliation but under the entire suite

9 1833 UNTS at 515–516. For a summary of states that as at 2021 had made declarations under Article 298, see Churchill, Lowe, & Sander (2022) 868–869. As to Article 298 generally, see Klein (2009) 227–315; Serdy in *Proelss Commentary* (2017) 1918; Forteau in Forteau & Thouvenin (eds.) (2017) 1002–1005; Kunoy (2021) 117. See also Ye & Zou, 'Article 298' (2017) 48 ODIL 331–344; Merrills & De Brabandere (2022) 277–281.

10 As to conciliation procedure generally, see Merrills & De Brabandere (2022) 281–283.

11 For the first, and to date only, use of Annex V conciliation, see *Timor Sea Conciliation (Timor-Leste v. Australia)* (Conciliation Commission: Taksøe-Jensen, Chair; Balkin, Koroma, McRae and Wolfrum, members), Report and Recommendations, 9 May 2018. For comment, see Tamada, 'The Timor Sea Conciliation' (2020) 31 EJIL 321–344; Merrills & De Brabandere (2022) 283–284.

of procedures and under *all* circumstances—does not extend to disputes which 'necessarily involve' issues of territorial title, even where these issues are concurrent with maritime questions. Budislav Vukas, who served as Vice-President of ITLOS from 2002 to 2005, expressed the prevalent view as follows: 'Disputes concerning sea boundary delimitations that involve the concurrent consideration of issues concerning sovereignty or other rights over continental or insular land territory could be submitted to the ICJ, *but not to the other procedures* [under Part XV, section 2].'[12]

Other writers have taken a still more categorical view of the matter. On their view, territorial questions, including those that are ancillary to a dispute concerning the interpretation or application of UNCLOS, are beyond the scope of jurisdiction even if the parties elect to submit their dispute to the ICJ—that is to say, to the principal judicial organ of the United Nations, which is not an organ constituted by UNCLOS.[13] What passes now for mainstream opinion on the matter thus ranges from a view that the ICJ might have jurisdiction to consider territorial issues but that none of the other procedures available under UNCLOS Article 287 do, to a view that in dispute settlement under UNCLOS a territorial exclusion exists tantamount to an absolute jurisdictional bar.

But if disputes over territory cannot be settled by adjudication or arbitration under ITLOS or Annex VII procedures, or Annex VIII, and perhaps even at the ICJ, why, precisely, would that be the case? Judge Vukas suggested, in the quotation above, that a dispute referred to the ICJ in accordance with UNCLOS Part XV, section 2, *could* include a dispute involving 'the concurrent consideration of issues concerning sovereignty or other rights over continental or insular land territory.' The grounds for the late Judge Vukas's view—excluding territorial issues, where the parties have referred

12 Vukas, 'The Definition of the Law of the Sea' in Ando, McWhinney, Wolfrum, & Baker Röben (eds.), *Liber Amicorum Judge Shigeru Oda* (2002), vol. 2, pp. 1303, 1310 (emphasis added).

13 In connection with the South China Sea disputes, see Beckman, 'UNCLOS Part XV and the South China Sea' in Jayakumar, Koh, & Beckman (eds.), *The South China Sea Disputes and Law of the Sea* (2014) 229, 233; Beckman, 'International Law, UNCLOS and the South China Sea' in Beckman et al. (eds.), *Beyond Territorial Disputes in the South China Sea* (2013) 47, 89; Hong, *UNCLOS and Ocean Dispute Settlement: Law and Politics in the South China Sea* (2012) 54–55, 92–93; Talmon & Jia, 'Introduction' in Talmon & Jia (eds.), *The South China Sea Arbitration: A Chinese Perspective* (2014) 1, 9; *ibid.*, Talmon, 'The South China Sea Arbitration: Is There a Case to Answer?' 15, 31, 78; *ibid.*, Sheng-Ti Gau, 'Issues of Jurisdiction in Cases of Default of Appearance,' 81, 92–93, 101; *ibid.*, Jia, 'The Issue of Admissibility in Inter-State Arbitration,' 107, 126; *ibid.*, Zhang & Mi, 'Jurisprudential Tenability of the Philippines v. China Arbitration on South China Sea Disputes?' 137, 146.

the dispute under the same convention—are not clear. However, the difficulty here is not only one of internal consistency. As will be seen, grounds are elusive as well for the absolute view—the view that holds that *no* dispute settlement mechanism to which a party refers a maritime dispute under UNCLOS has jurisdiction to address concurrent territorial issues.

The plain text of Article 298(1)(a)(i)

Article 298(1)(a)*(i)*, under the particular circumstances that the provision identifies, excepts from conciliation 'any dispute that necessarily involves the concurrent consideration of any unsettled dispute concerning sovereignty or other rights over continental or insular land territory.' As the numbering of the provision would suggest, this exception is nested within other provisions. In fact, it is an exception nested within two antecedent exceptions. The structuring of the exception in this way makes its analysis somewhat involved. Let us consider the exception step by step.

Article 298, paragraph 1(a), provides that states may except from the jurisdiction of 'any one or more of the procedures' identified in Part XV, section 2, the following: 'disputes concerning the interpretation or application of articles 15, 74 and 83 relating to sea boundary delimitations, or those involving historic bays or titles.'

In accordance with Article 298(1)(a)*(i)*, then, it is open to states to elect to remove one or more defined categories of disputes from the jurisdiction that otherwise would apply under Part XV, section 2. Namely, these are disputes concerning the interpretation or application of articles 15, 74, and 83,[14] or those involving historic bays or titles. To recall, the jurisdiction that otherwise would apply under Part XV, section 2, is that embracing the category identified in Article 288(1)—*inter alia* 'any dispute concerning the interpretation or application of this Convention which is submitted to it in accordance with [Part XV].'

So the first necessary antecedent, if the possibility is to arise that the land territory exception be activated, is that a party elect an Article 298(1)

14 But not necessarily articles 15, 74, and 83 taken *grosso modo*. For a dispute to be removed from jurisdiction, it must also be a dispute 'relating to sea boundary delimitations.' Thus, arguably, disputes arising under article 15, 74 and 83 might be disputes *not* relating to sea boundary delimitations. Take, for example, Art. 74(3), which obliges states, '[p]ending agreement' to delimit the EEZ between them, to 'make every effort to enter into provisional arrangements of a practical nature and, during this transitional period, not to jeopardize or hamper the reaching of the final agreement.' Under these terms well could arise a dispute not 'relating to sea boundary delimitations,' though much here would turn on the scope one ascribes to the word 'relating.'

optional exception. In other words, a party must have chosen to give itself the benefit of an exception, before the question of a land territory exception might arise.

Then there is a second step, the first exception-within-an-exception. The *chapeau* of Article 298(1) having invited a state to declare that it does not accept any one or more of the procedures provided for in Part XV, section 2, in respect to one or more of the enumerated kinds of disputes, then adds a proviso:

> [P]rovided that a State having made such a declaration [i.e., a declaration excepting from jurisdiction disputes concerning the interpretation or application of articles 15, 74 and 83 relating to sea boundary delimitations, or those involving historic bays or titles] shall, when such a dispute arises subsequent to the entry into force of this Convention and where no agreement within a reasonable period of time is reached in negotiations between the parties, at the request of any party to the dispute, accept submission of the matter to conciliation under Annex V, section 2.

Reading the *chapeau*, we thus see that it is open to states to elect an exception to maritime boundary delimitations and disputes involving historic bays or titles; but conciliation under Annex V, section 2, is excepted from that exception. It is 'provided that' conciliation, a non-binding procedure, is available against a state even though the state has opted out of some, or all, of the other dispute settlement procedures in regard to some, or all, of the named categories of disputes.

And, finally, there is an exception within *that* exception. When a party invokes the provision in the *chapeau* and makes a submission to conciliation under Article 298(1)(a)*(i)*, it is 'further provided that any dispute that necessarily involves the concurrent consideration of any unsettled dispute concerning sovereignty or other rights over continental or insular land territory shall be excluded from such submission.'

This provision is unique in UNCLOS. It is the only UNCLOS provision that excludes disputes 'concerning sovereignty or other rights over continental or insular land territory' from dispute settlement. Indeed, it is the only provision in UNCLOS that excludes land-related disputes in terms. It excludes them as an exception to an exception to an exception. And it excludes them only in respect to one of the Part XV, section 2, procedures: non-binding conciliation.

To summarize, Article 298 provides for specific and limited exceptions to the dispute settlement system. These are the exceptions that, if a state elects them all, apply to the system as a whole. Article 298 then provides an exception to one class of excepted disputes: it allows a party having a dispute belonging to that class to submit that dispute to conciliation even where the other party has elected to except disputes belonging to that class from all other mechanisms; and, finally, it provides an exception to that exception by barring the submitting party from submitting a particular type of dispute to conciliation—that is, a 'dispute that necessarily involves the concurrent consideration of any unsettled dispute concerning sovereignty or other rights over continental or insular land territory.' In short, Article 298(1)(a)*(i)* makes non-binding conciliation compulsory, even in face of a party that has elected the maximum scope of exclusions permitted under Article 298, but it narrows the material scope of conciliation by excluding from that procedure the land territory issues, as specified.

From this structure, the following conclusion is to be drawn: if it were the case that the disputes which Article 298(1)(a) addresses did not include disputes in respect of land sovereignty—that is, if 'such a dispute' did not include disputes in respect of land sovereignty—then the land territory exception would be to no purpose. The phrase 'such a dispute' merits close attention here. The phrase denotes that the dispute which the party may submit to conciliation is—almost—the same as the dispute that was excluded from other mechanisms under Article 298(1)(a)*(i)*. It is only *almost* the same, because the dispute, now excluded from other dispute settlement mechanisms, is subject to the *ratione materia* exclusion specified in the 'further provided' clause of the sub-subparagraph. That is what '*such a* dispute' means in this context. The phrase 'such a dispute' refers back to the antecedent phrase, which here is 'disputes concerning the interpretation or application of articles 15, 74 and 83 relating to sea boundary delimitations, or those involving historic bays or titles.' Where a party has elected the exception that withholds jurisdiction from one or more of those disputes, the party nevertheless is obliged to accept submission of such disputes to conciliation, subject to the 'further provided' clause—that is, the clause that excludes the specified type of dispute related to land. The structure here, while complex, is not unclear. It has a plain meaning.

Except for the territorial dispute exclusion, nothing in the sub-subparagraph that obliges conciliation changes the scope *ratione materiae* of the disputes subject to the powers of the conciliation commission. The only disputes subject here to the obligation of conciliation are 'such' disputes as were excluded from the mechanisms of Part XV, section 2. The conciliation commission inherits, as it were, the disputes passed down to it from the general dispute settlement provision after a party has elected one or more of the optional exceptions. The Article 298(1)(a)*(i)* exclusion of land-related disputes would have been a strange drafting choice if the general provision—Part XV, section 2—already had excluded land-related disputes. This is the implicit but necessary conclusion that results from the 'reading *a contrario* of article 298, paragraph 1(a)' to which Rüdiger Wolfrum (as President of

ITLOS) drew attention,[15] and to which I return in Chapter 4. Considering the wording and structure of Article 298(1)(a)*(i)*, there is no ground to conclude that land-related disputes are excluded from jurisdiction of Part XV, section 2, mechanisms, at least to the extent that such disputes are properly characterized as concerning the interpretation or application of other provisions of the Convention.[16]

If the textual analysis of Article 298(1)(a)*(i)* is intricate, then that is a reflection on the text. One commentary on the Convention opined that '*ratione materiae* jurisdiction [under UNCLOS Part XV] [is] confusing and complex'; the text 'reflect[s] the very difficulties which had arisen during negotiations.'[17] The jurisdictional scheme is no doubt 'complex'; confusion, if any, depends in part on what those who interpret and apply the scheme make of it.

To summarize so far, the following points of interpretation are evident on a plain reading of the text:

1. The territorial exclusion applies by the express terms of Article 298(1)(a)*(i)* only to such submission as a party might make to Annex V conciliation against a party that has elected an optional exclusion under Article 298(1)(a)*(i)*;
2. The territorial exclusion would be to no purpose and thus in conflict with the principle of effective interpretation if a like exclusion applied to the procedures of Part XV, section 2, as a whole.
3. The location of the territorial exclusion in Article 298(1)(a)*(i)* as part of an optional exception to the applicability of Part XV, section 2, accords with the structure and organization of the provisions of Part XV that express the scope of jurisdiction in open and general terms (Article 288(1): '*any* dispute concerning the interpretation or application of the Convention'); and the scope of limitations on applicability (Article 297) and of optional exceptions (Article 298) in specific, limited terms.

15 ITLOS, 'Statement of President Wolfrum,' Statement Given to the Informal Meeting of Legal Advisers of Ministries of Foreign Affairs (New York, 23 October 2006) 6. To similar effect, see Judge Tullio Treves, 'What Have the United Nations Convention and the International Tribunal for the Law of the Sea to Offer as Regards Maritime Delimitation Disputes?' in Lagoni & Vignes (eds.), *Maritime Delimitation* (2006) 77.

16 Cf. Judge Albert Hoffmann, Asian-African Legal Consultative Organisation, 46th sess., Cape Town, 2–6 July 2007: www.itlos.org/fileadmin/itlos/documents/statements_of_president/wolfrum/hoffmann_aalco_050707_eng..pdf; Judge P. Chandrasekhara Rao, 'Delimitation Disputes under the United Nations Convention on the Law of the Sea: Settlement Procedures' in Ndiaye & Wolfrum (eds.), *Liber Amicorum Judge Thomas A. Mensah* (2007) 877, 890–891.

17 Ranjeva, 'Settlement of Disputes' in Dupuy & Vignes (eds.), *A Handbook of the New Law of the Sea* (1991) 1333, 1361.

Drafting history of Article 298(1)(a)(i)

From the considerations set out above, a clear jurisdictional scheme emerges. Territorial disputes are excluded in that scheme only on the specific terms of Article 298(1)(a)*(i)*. Those terms do not denote a general exclusion of territorial disputes from Part XV, section 2, procedures.

The drafting history of the Convention does not evince a general territorial exclusion. To the contrary. It further suggests that the territorial clause has only a narrow compass.

The deliberate placement of the land territory exclusion

The compulsory conciliation provision of Article 298(1)(a)*(i)* was the subject of contentious exchanges in the Third Conference on the Law of the Sea. The *Virginia Commentary* notes that at one stage forty-five drafting variants were on the table, a mass of competing texts too large to be comprehended and ultimately, in frustration it would seem, boiled down to a (still long) series of consolidations.[18] As the Conference was negotiating an advanced draft in 1980, it was proposed that the clause excluding disputes relating to sovereignty over land or insular territories from conciliation be moved. Instead of locating the clause in Article 298(1)*(a)*, the suggestion was that it be located in 'article 296 with the other exceptions in that article.'[19] These are the exceptions that finally were adopted as Article 297—'Limitations on applicability of section 2.' They are the limitations that extend to the entire dispute settlement system of Part XV, section 2.

If the Conference had accepted the proposal to locate the clause excluding disputes relating to sovereignty over land and insular territory in draft article 296 (adopted Article 297), then the change would have been consequential. The consequence that that change would have had, if the drafters had adopted it, is evident from the text. Article 297 is an architectural provision. It addresses the design of the compulsory dispute settlement system of UNCLOS as a whole. To have added an exclusionary clause to that provision would have limited the applicability of the system as a whole in respect of whatever subject matter the exclusionary clause might have contained. There is little doubt that those who proposed relocating the territorial disputes exclusionary clause to Article 297 sought precisely that effect—a complete ouster of land disputes from all Part XV, section 2, dispute settlement

18 Nordquist, Rosenne, & Sohn (eds.), *The United Nations Convention on the Law of the Sea 1982: A Commentary* (1989) 126. For a summary of the labyrinthine path to the adopted text of Art. 298(1)(a)(i), see *ibid.* 122–133.

19 Report of the President on the work of the informal plenary meeting of the Conference on the settlement of disputes, A/CONF.62/L.59, 23 August 1980: XIV *Official Records* 130, ¶ 6.

procedures. According to the representative of Venezuela: 'The problem was one of placement, since those provisions did not belong under article 298: it was not a question of optional exceptions but rather of limitations on the applicability of section 2 of Part XV.'[20]

The aim behind the proposed change of 'placement' was to remove the exclusion of disputes relating to sovereignty over land and insular territory from the 'optional' section where it related to conciliation only and place it instead in the section on general limitations. The aim was to enlarge the 'limitations on the applicability of section 2 of Part XV'—that is, to limit the dispute settlement apparatus as a whole in this further way. The proposed change, as is evident in the adopted text, was not accepted.[21]

In fact, the suggestion to apply the exclusion of disputes relating to sovereignty over land or insular territories to Part XV, section 2, as a whole was rejected emphatically. According to the Official Records: 'The President had stressed, both in [a prior conference document] and at the commencement of these negotiations, that changes of substance should be avoided, in particular, any changes concerning the texts of article 296, paragraphs 2 and 3.'[22]

Avoiding 'changes of substance' was not merely a matter of convenience. '[D]elicate compromises that had been very carefully negotiated are contained in that article' and it was for this reason that 'any attempt to raise these questions should be avoided.'[23] The President's admonition underscores that the exclusions from compulsory procedure indicated in Article 297 are complete. It makes it hard to see how the positioning of the exclusion of disputes relating to sovereignty over land or insular territories was anything but deliberate: declining to locate the one territorial exclusion with the global exclusions was a considered decision, taken to preserve 'delicate compromises that had been very carefully negotiated.'

20 Mr. Aguilar (Venezuela), Third UN Conference, Summary Records of the Plenary, Eleventh Sess., 158th mtg., 30 March 1982, A/CONF.62/SR.158: XVI *Official Records* 15, ¶ 13. Cf. Louis B. Sohn's proposal of 27 March 1979: Platzöder (ed.), *Third United Nations Conference on the Law of the Sea: Documents* (1982), 438, 440.

21 Nor was a special colonial Part, which might have been read to exclude territorial disputes as well. Regarding informal single negotiating text (ISNT) draft art. 136, ¶ 2, see below pp. 118–120.

22 XIV *Official Records* p. 130, ¶ 7 (A/CONF.62/L.59): Report of the President on the work of the informal plenary meeting of the Conference on the settlement of disputes (23 August 1980). The prior conference document in which the President had stressed the finality of draft article 296 was document SD/3.

23 *Ibid.* As to the difficulties that required the compromises, see, e.g., Report of the Chairman of negotiating group 7, 22 August 1979, Reports to the plenary Conference, A/CONF.62/91: XII *Official Records* 108.

And to recall, for avoidance of doubt: in order to arrive at the conclusion that the territorial disputes exclusion is a limited one, one does not need to refer to this episode at the Third Conference. As argued above, the text on its own leads to the same conclusion.

The exponents of the territorial exclusion and their strained readings of the drafting history

The plain text of Article 298(1)(a)*(i)*, in a fair view, should be the end of the matter. The plain text read in context should underscore the finality. Add to that the negotiating history, and the argument should be rejected and put to rest that UNCLOS contains a general exclusion of land territory disputes from its jurisdictional apparatus. However, a number of writers long have expounded a general exclusion.

Even before UNCLOS opened for signature in 1982, writers in the field began to suggest that Article 298(1)(a)*(i)* was imprecise or even mistaken. Bernard Oxman, for example, wrote as follows: 'While the exclusion for land territory disputes is drafted so that it does not literally apply to adjudication or arbitration under the Convention when a state does not elect to reject such procedures, it would seem that this is a mere drafting point.'[24]

In its usual sense, the expression 'mere drafting point' refers to a point that is only a small matter of form, a slip of the drafter's pen. Professor Oxman, however, in noting that the exclusion of territorial disputes '*does not literally apply*' to the dispute settlement apparatus as a whole, offered no reason to think that this was the slip of a pen. We saw in the drafting history that the provision resulted from negotiation and careful choices. Nor did Oxman identify linguistic ambiguity here. The effect of the adopted wording is clear, and Oxman acknowledged it to be: the adopted wording means that no territorial exclusion applies to Part XV, section 2, as a whole. It is dubious to say that such a literal meaning in a text is to be ignored—or rewritten—when the literal meaning is as clear as Oxman acknowledged it to be.

Perhaps, then, the effect, if we insist on the text's literal meaning, is in some way absurd or unreasonable. Is it absurd or unreasonable to say that the interpretation or application of certain provisions of UNCLOS relates to issues of sovereignty over land territory? Under the canons of interpretation, one would have to make the case that it is, if one were to invoke other sources, such as the drafting history, to overwrite those provisions. I recalled in Chapter 2 that the Convention is replete with provisions relating to land territory. To say that land territory has nothing to do with UNCLOS is a

24 Oxman, 'The Third United Nations Conference on the Law of the Sea: The Ninth Session (1980)' (1981) 75 AJIL 211, 233 n. 109.

canard. To say that it would be absurd or unreasonable for jurisdiction under Part XV, section 2, to embrace land territory questions is equally unsound. Oxman, to open the door to a non-textual approach to interpretation, would have to have argued that land territory is so remote from the terms of UNCLOS that Article 288(1) could not possibly embrace land territory issues. Oxman did not say what ground would justify the radically inventive approach to interpretation that he insisted upon. He gave no reason why an exclusion that 'does not literally apply' ought nonetheless to apply.

Oxman's failed attempt to dismiss the literal meaning of the text as a 'mere drafting point' should have had no followers, but it did. Moreover, the exponents of a general exclusion of territorial disputes from Part XV, section 2, have been persistent. A notable example is Stefan Talmon. According to Professor Talmon, writing in 2014, which is to say some thirty-four years after Oxman: 'Indeed, the subject-matters of sovereignty and other rights over land territory are actually misplaced in Article 298 UNCLOS. They are not optional exceptions, but rather part of the general limitations on the compulsory jurisdiction under section 2 of Part XV of UNCLOS.'[25]

But the provisions of Article 298(1) *are* optional exceptions! They are exceptions that a state may opt for, subject to an option carved out for other states to submit certain disputes to Annex V conciliation against that state. By the terms of Article 298(1)(a)*(i)*, it is when a state exercises the option carved out to allow it to submit certain disputes to Annex V conciliation against the state that opted for one or more of the Article 298 optional exceptions that certain land territory issues are excepted from jurisdiction. The land territory clause, in its own subordinate way, thus is just as much an optional exception as the others. What Talmon refers to as 'general limitations' are the specific enumerated exceptions found under Article 297. It is indeed only there that the jurisdictional scheme expresses limitations having general application across the scheme as a whole. And *there* is not where the territorial exclusion is located.

The placement of the territorial exclusion where it is—in Article 298—presents no difficulty such as would require resort to supplementary means of interpretation. Even if the interpreter judged that he should resort to the drafting history to elucidate Article 298, the drafting history only confirms that the placement of the territorial exclusion in Article 298 was a considered choice. The Venezuelan proposal, which I recalled above, was based on the view that the territorial sovereignty clause should have been located elsewhere—namely, in Article 297. This proposal was not an after-the-fact way of explaining some occluded or obscure meaning of Article 298. It was a way of seeking a consequential drafting change in favor of excluding

25 Talmon in Talmon & Jia (2014) 15, 46.

territorial sovereignty disputes from all Part XV, section 2, dispute settlement procedures. The drafting change was not adopted. It was rejected. There is no reasoned basis—in the text, in its context, or in the drafting history—to read the territorial exclusion in Article 298 as curtailing the jurisdiction of the other dispute settlement procedures of Part XV, section 2.

The exponents of a generalized exclusion of territorial disputes from Part XV, section 2, having despaired of finding it through ordinary legal analysis, abandon legal analysis altogether and declare the exclusion as actually adopted 'misplaced.' This is the logic of art criticism, not of legal analysis. An art critic well might say of a painting, 'The milk cart doesn't belong on the footpath. It should be in the meadow with the cows.' Art criticism has a logic of its own. Interpreting a treaty requires a different logic. And, yet, even if it is with aesthetics that we are concerned, instead of with ordinary legal analysis, the territorial exclusion *still* is not in any discernible way 'misplaced.' The territorial exclusion, nested in Article 298(1)(a)*(i)*—part of the '[o]ptional exceptions to applicability of section 2'—is itself part of the system of optional exception and, thus, correctly placed.

Other writers, including Beckman, contend that the Third Law of the Sea Conference adopted a generalized exclusion of territorial questions from Part XV, section 2, because states would have rejected the Convention if such an exclusion had not been adopted.[26] This is a hybrid of counterfactuals and bald assertion. A generalized exclusion was *not* adopted, and, it goes without saying, the Convention was not rejected. In contrast to Talmon, who adopts the persona of art critic, Beckman devolves into pure hectoring: it *cannot* be the way it is, Beckman in effect says, because nobody would have had it that way! As an argument, this is unconvincing, because it is mere assertion. It fails completely when held up against the facts. There is, first, the fact that the Convention does not contain the generalized exclusion that Beckman insists that it must. The text simply does not contain it. Second, there is the drafting history that reflects that certain states very much wanted it precisely the way it is. As much as some states said that territorial disputes should not be subject to jurisdiction, others said that they saw no reason to exclude such disputes. Ambassador Rosenne, for example, speaking on behalf of Israel's delegation, 'saw no inherent difference between disputes over land frontiers and disputes over maritime boundaries.'[27] Pakistan, noting that the 'compulsory third-party dispute settlement procedure enjoyed widespread

26 See, for example, Beckman (2014) at 241.

27 Mr. Rosenne (Israel), Third UN Conference, Eighth Sess., Second Comm., 57th mtg., 24 April 1979, A/CONF.62/C.2/SR.57: XI *Official Records* 61, ¶ 50. To similar effect, see Mr. Hollander (Israel), Third UN Conference, Eighth Sess., 112th plen. mtg., 25 April 1979, A/CONF.62/SR.112: XI *Official Records* 11, ¶ 25.

support,' said that that procedure should contain 'no differentiation between land-related and sea-related disputes.'[28] Chile said that 'almost all the proposals submitted ... contained a compulsory dispute settlement element' and thought it unfortunate that the *compulsory conciliation clause* would enable a party to exclude disputes with a 'territorial element.'[29] Chile's observation accords with the adopted text, the exclusion of territorial disputes indeed being confined on the terms of Article 298(1)(a)*(i)* to the particular circumstance of Annex V conciliation after a state opts for one or more of the Article 298 optional exceptions. Colombia, associating itself with Chile's position, said that placing the territorial exclusion in Article 297, where it would have applied not just to conciliation but to *all* dispute settlement procedures, would have been 'completely unacceptable.'[30]

One state recorded to have said the opposite or something close to it—that the text *as actually written* was unacceptable—was Venezuela. Venezuela said that the absence of a global exclusion 'would make it difficult, if not impossible, for a number of States to ratify the convention.'[31] Venezuela said this in an earlier iteration of its proposal to move the territorial exclusion from the Article 298 optional exceptions to the Article 297 limitations on applicability of section 2[32]—that is, the proposal that, as we have seen, the Conference eventually rejected on considered grounds.[33] In the end, states that favored the widest dispute settlement procedures and states that wanted none at all adopted the Convention. It is unconvincing to infer from this negotiating history a generalized territorial exclusion that the adopted text does not contain. Colson and Vohrer say that they 'cannot believe that knowingly, and *without comment* in their approval of the Convention, [states] determined that these long-standing territorial sovereignty disputes would henceforth be subject to the dispute settlement regime of the Convention.'[34] Colson and Vohrer seem to ignore the drafting history: states *did* comment, and the record shows that they knew full well what they were doing.

28 Mr. Mahmood (Pakistan), Third UN Conference, Eighth Sess., 112th plen. mtg., 25 April 1979, A/CONF.62/SR.112: XI *Official Records* 13, ¶ 43.
29 Mr. Zegers (Chile), Third UN Conference, Eighth Sess., 112th plen. mtg., 25 April 1979, A/CONF.62/SR.112: XI *Official Records* 11, ¶ 28.
30 Mr. Samper (Colombia), Third UN Conference, Eighth Sess., 112th plen. mtg., 25 April 1979, A/CONF.62/SR.112: XI *Official Records* 12, ¶ 31.
31 Mr. Falcón Briceño (Venezuela), Third UN Conference, Summary Records of the Plenary, Ninth Sess., 135th plen. mtg., 25 August 1980, A/CONF.62/SR.135: XIV *Official Records* 21, ¶ 17.
32 Ibid, pp. 20–21, ¶ 17.
33 See above pp. 108–109.
34 Colson & Vohrer, 'In re Chagos Marine Protected Area (Mauritius v. United Kingdom' (2015) 109 AJIL at 851 (emphasis added).

Admitting to the jurisdictional system of UNCLOS maritime disputes in which certain territorial issues are concerned introduces no obvious discordance with any provision of Part XV, section 2. Nor is it at variance with the object and purpose of the Convention. There are direct connections in UNCLOS between land territory and maritime areas; the Convention as a whole does not merely mention land territory; it identifies land territory as integral to substantive legal régimes that it contains. Many of the rules concerning maritime jurisdiction are difficult or impossible to apply without considering the land and the states that have sovereignty over land. The literal reading of the Article 298(1)(a)*(i)* exclusion—that is, that the exclusion reaches only Annex V conciliation and even then only when a party submits a dispute to that procedure against a party that has opted out of other Part XV, section 2, procedures—is perfectly coherent on its own and in the context of the Convention as a whole.

Yet the exponents of a general territorial exclusion repeat their position with little or no new evidence or argument to sustain it. Some of them have suggested that, during negotiations, a separate provision was proposed which would have expressly conferred jurisdiction over disputes concerning territorial sovereignty, and that the rejection of such a provision is tantamount to an express exclusion of jurisdiction in the adopted Convention. Nong Hong, for example, says that 'during the negotiation at UNCLOS III, a drafted article concerning sovereignty disputes over islands was deleted from the draft of UNCLOS.'[35] Nong Hong's reference here is not to the negotiating texts or UNCLOS III proceedings, however. The reference is to Robert Smith at the Seventeenth Annual Conference of the Law of the Sea Institute in 1983 (i.e., the year after the Convention was opened for signature).[36] Smith, under the title 'The Effect of Extended Maritime Jurisdiction on Land Sovereignty Disputes,'[37] in fact said as follows: 'To have attempted to place sovereignty issues in a law of the sea treaty most likely would have failed.'[38]

But this is to state the obvious: UNCLOS is a law of the sea treaty, not a law of the land treaty. It equally 'likely would have failed' if parties had attempted, for example, to 'place [*war*] issues' in the clauses identifying the kinds of disputes over which the parties consented to jurisdiction in the Nicaragua–US and Iran–US treaties that the ICJ applied in *Military and Paramilitary Activities* and in *Oil Platforms*. Yet, as I recalled in Chapter

35 Hong (2012) 54.
36 *Ibid.* 97 n. 74.
37 See volume table of contents, which reflect the full title.
38 Smith, 'The Effect of Extended Maritime Jurisdiction on Land Sovereignty Disputes' in Koers, Oxman, & Østreng (eds.), *The 1982 Convention on the Law of the Sea: Proceedings, Law of the Sea Institute Seventeenth Annual Conference* (1984) 336, 343.

2, the ICJ reached those issues. As I also recalled, tribunals under UNCLOS itself have not hesitated to address questions of use of force either. The drafters of UNCLOS did not expressly confer jurisdiction on Part XV, section 2, mechanisms to adopt merits decisions addressing such questions *in particular*,[39] but that has not stopped adjudicators from addressing them.

Even if Nong Hong identified a record from the drafting history showing that the parties had rejected a provision extending jurisdiction to disputes over sovereignty over islands, such a record would not necessarily demonstrate anything about the adopted text.[40] The negotiators might have rejected a proposed provision expressly addressing disputes over sovereignty over islands for any number of reasons. One reason that they might have rejected such a proposed island sovereignty provision is that islands occasioned difficult debates on other points, for example the eligibility of small islands for EEZ and continental shelf entitlements, the effect of near-shore islands on maritime delimitation, and the distinction between islands and LTEs.[41] And, so, if the drafters rejected a special island territory dispute settlement clause, then this would have been to avert a further potential complication. Another reason not to have accepted a provision specifically extending jurisdiction to island sovereignty disputes *in particular* is that, read together with silence about other sovereignty disputes, such a provision would have implied that jurisdiction reaches *only* island sovereignty disputes. If the negotiators in fact rejected an island sovereignty jurisdiction clause, then that equally would support the inference that they intended jurisdiction to reach sovereignty issues more broadly.

Also relevant here is the overall architecture of Part XV, section 2. As noted, Part XV, section 2, does not enumerate a list of specific categories of disputes over which dispute settlement procedures may exercise jurisdiction. Instead, Article 288(1) as noted above, indicates that jurisdiction is '*over any dispute* concerning the interpretation or application of this Convention.'[42] By contrast, the limitations on applicability of section 2, under Article 297, *are* an enumerated list of specific situations.[43] This architecture—identifying

39 See Chapter 2, pp. 59–99.

40 For interesting observations about the need to verify references to historical materials in law of the sea disputes, see Hayton, 'Unreliable Evidence' (2017) 48 ODIL 17–34.

41 For overview of some of the debates, see Talmon, 'Article 121: Regime of Islands' in *Proelss Commentary* (2017) 858, 860–861. For a thorough review of the debates in drafting work, dating to the 1930 Hague Codification Conference, see Terasaki, 'The Regime of Islands in International Conventions (Part 1),' *The OPRI Center of Islands Studies* (13 March 2014).

42 Art. 288(1) (emphasis added).

43 It is true that Article 297 contains a paragraph of affirmative cases—paragraph 1—but these serve to delineate the bounds of the limitations and thus to prevent their over-extension, not to constitute independent heads of jurisdiction.

in global terms disputes that are *included*, and identifying in specific and limited terms disputes that are *excluded*—was evidently deliberate. An approach that would have specified disputes subject to jurisdiction was proposed in an early draft, but the approach was not accepted.[44] To have adopted a specific clause to include territorial questions in the dispute settlement system would have contradicted a considered drafting decision, and it would have detracted from the overall drafting scheme.

In any event, Smith at the Seventeenth Annual Conference seems to have been addressing a hypothetical point—that is, whether the states parties to the Third Law of the Sea Conference could have agreed to include a separate provision expressly indicating that the Convention's dispute settlement procedures establish jurisdiction to settle disputes concerning 'sovereignty issues.' Smith believed that they could not have. But he was referring to an attempt that, in his view, *would* have failed—if it had been made. As far as I am aware, Smith did not refer to a specific attempt that in fact had been made. He identified no reference in the *travaux* to a proposal to adopt a dispute settlement provision in those precise terms.

A proposal that was in fact made was to adopt a provision that would have done precisely the opposite. Excluding land sovereignty disputes in Article 297 would have resulted in the global exclusion of such disputes that Smith and others attribute to the Convention. The failure of *that* proposal is not a matter of speculation. The proposal in fact was made; and it in fact failed. This is a matter on the record in the *travaux*.

From these considerations, it follows that the Conference's rejection of a proposed inclusion under the jurisdictional system (if such an inclusion had been proposed) and its rejection of a proposed exclusion (there is no doubt that such an exclusion was proposed) are not symmetric. Rejecting a proposed inclusion of a specified subject matter in a system that deliberately identifies jurisdiction in global, not specific, terms would have been in the interest of preserving the drafting scheme—in other words, to borrow Professor Oxman's phrase, a drafting point. By contrast, rejecting a proposed *exclusion* of a specified subject matter in a system that deliberately identifies exclusions from jurisdiction in specific terms evinces an intention not to exclude the specified subject matter. *That* rejection, in short, is *not* a drafting point but an episode in the negotiations reflecting a consequential choice.

One is reminded of Judge Nelson's warning about 'proposals which have not been accepted by the Conference ... somehow still remain[ing] like shades waiting to be summoned, as it were, back to life.'[45] The placement

44 See ISNT, draft part XI, art. 137: A/CONF.62/WP.8/Part II, printed in IV *Official Records* 171.

45 *M/V 'Saiga' (No. 2)*, Sep. Op. Judge Nelson, ITLOS 1999 p. 116, p. 124 (1 July).

of an exclusion of sovereignty disputes in Article 297 was a proposal not accepted. It should not 'be summoned' to overwrite the Convention as actually adopted.

Agreement on Marine Biodiversity of Areas beyond National Jurisdiction (2023) and its non-effect

A brief word is in order here about the Agreement on Marine Biodiversity of Areas beyond National Jurisdiction adopted on 19 June 2023.[46] Article 60 of the Agreement provides as follows:

> 9. Nothing in this Agreement shall be interpreted as conferring jurisdiction upon a court or tribunal over any dispute that concerns or necessarily involves the concurrent consideration of the legal status of an area as within national jurisdiction, nor over any dispute concerning sovereignty or other rights over continental or insular land territory or a claim thereto of a Party to this Agreement, provided that nothing in this paragraph shall be interpreted as limiting the jurisdiction of a court or tribunal under Part XV, section 2, of the Convention.

Here, then, is a relatively plain exclusion of jurisdiction over sovereignty claims. Paragraph 9 of Article 60 is not confined in its application to only one part of the Agreement. It is however confined in its application *to the Agreement*: '[N]othing in … paragraph [9] shall be interpreted as limiting the jurisdiction of a court or tribunal under Part XV, section 2.' When a court or tribunal interprets the scope of jurisdiction under Part XV, section 2, in respect of sovereignty disputes, the Agreement does nothing to widen it or to narrow it.[47] Paragraph 9 is clear as to this non-effect.

Professors Guilfoyle and Mossop suggest that the drafting of the Agreement reflected 'a degree of nervousness about the extent to which UNCLOS dispute settlement has infringed upon territorial and sovereignty disputes.'[48] And yet, as they note, the parties expressly limited the effects of the Agreement, so that it 'does not constitute subsequent practice evidencing the parties' interpretation of jurisdiction under Part XV generally.'[49] In other words, '[a]ny implicit criticism in paragraph 9 of the approach taken by

46 An Intergovernmental Conference on Marine Biodiversity of Areas Beyond National Jurisdiction adopted the Agreement: A/CONF.232/2023/4 (19 June 2023). The General Assembly had convened the Conference by GAR 72/249, 24 December 2017. As of October 2024, the Agreement had 105 signatories, of which, fourteen parties.

47 See also Art. 6 and Art. 60(10) of the Agreement.

48 Guilfoyle & Mossop 'The Extent and Legitimacy of the Judicial Function in UNCLOS Dispute Settlement' (2024) 73(3) ICLQ 641, at 666.

49 *Ibid.*

various tribunals to their jurisdiction under Part XV is therefore only prospective in operation and confined to disputes arising under the Agreement.'[50]

The drafting of the 2023 Agreement was an opportunity to supply parties in future cases with an argument to narrow the interpretation of Part XV. The drafters did not use the opportunity. Instead, they expressly limited Article 60(9) and, thus, pre-empted invocation of the provision to such ends. If anything, the without-prejudice provision in the Agreement suggests that Part XV, section 2, does not exclude sovereignty disputes entirely, for, if it did, then the intended non-effect of paragraph 9 would itself be of no effect.

Other territorial exclusion arguments

For the sake of completeness, a few words are in order here in regard to three further arguments that one might make for a broad territorial exclusion from UNCLOS procedures.

Draft article on territorial disputes and self-determination

A draft provision, which the Third Conference in the end did not adopt, would have addressed 'Territories under foreign occupation or colonial domination.' The draft provision would have required that certain territorial disputes be settled as a precondition for the application of other convention rules. The draft was as follows:

> *Article 136*
>
> 1. The rights recognized or established by the present Convention to the resources of a territory whose people have not attained either full independence or some other self-governing status recognized by the United Nations, or a territory under foreign occupation or colonial domination, or a United Nations Trust Territory, or a territory administered by the United Nations, shall be vested in the inhabitants of that territory, to be exercised by them for their own benefit and in accordance with their own needs and requirements.
>
> 2. Where a dispute over the sovereignty of a territory under foreign occupation or colonial domination exists, the rights referred to in paragraph 1 shall not be exercised until such dispute is settled in accordance with the purposes and principles of the Charter of the United Nations.
>
> 3. In no case may the rights referred to in paragraph 1 be exercised, profited or benefited from or in any way infringed by a metropolitan or foreign power administering or occupying such territory or purporting to administer or occupy such territory.

50 *Ibid.* 664.

4. References in this article to a territory include continental and insular territories.[51]

The main effect of the draft article would have been to suspend the application of the Convention's substantive provisions concerning natural resources in maritime areas related to 'territory under foreign occupation or colonial domination.' The suspensive effect would have continued until a territory achieved deoccupation or decolonization (draft article 136, paragraph 1). 'Where a dispute over the sovereignty of a territory under foreign occupation or colonial domination exists,' the suspensive effect would have continued until 'such dispute is settled in accordance with the purposes and principles of the Charter of the United Nations' (draft article 136, paragraph 2). This said nothing as to the scope of the competence of courts or tribunals under the convention dispute settlement régime, except, perhaps, to suggest that the specified colonial disputes were to be settled elsewhere—that is, 'in accordance with the purposes and principles of the Charter ... [but not here].'[52] So it might be posited that draft article 136, paragraph 2, would have excluded disputes over occupied territory or colonial territory from the convention's dispute settlement régime. If that position is taken, then the rejection of the draft, if anything, is a further illustration that the negotiating parties did not reach agreement to adopt such an exclusion of territorial disputes.

If it is posited, instead, that the draft article took no position as to the mechanisms under which territorial disputes are to be settled, then there is still the rejection of the proposed suspensive effect over the Convention's substantive rules. The draft article would have suspended certain substantive rules of the Convention, rendering them inoperative, until disputes had been settled (whether under the Convention dispute settlement system or elsewhere). The draft provision was rejected, and thus no such suspensive effect was adopted.

This episode in the drafting history is relevant for present purposes to the following extent: it suggests that there was no agreement that the convention's rules should be held in suspense by the existence of an unsettled

51 ISNT art. 136 (as sole provision of 'Part X: Territories under Foreign Occupation or Colonial Domination'): A/CONF.62/WP.8/Part II, set out in IV *Official Records* 171. See also informal composite negotiating text, rev. 1, unnumbered 'Transitional Provision' (under 'Part XVI: Final Clauses'): A/CONF.62/WP.10/Rev.1, set out in VIII *Official Records* 139.

52 Though New Zealand expressed itself in favor of conferring jurisdiction upon convention mechanisms in respect of abuses by an administering Power against a colonial territory: Mr. Templeton (New Zealand), Second Committee, 38th mtg., 13 August 1974, ¶ 69: II *Official Records* 278. New Zealand, perhaps not incidentally, was one of the former Nauru mandatories.

dispute over territorial rights.[53] As to the law regarding use of force and occupation of territory, the rejection of the draft article on 'Territories under foreign occupation or colonial domination' obviously supports no inference that the drafters intended UNCLOS to contradict the existing rules that regulate the conduct of a state that occupies another's territory. Rules of such fundamental importance as those would not fall away on mere inference from a text addressing a different subject matter. The drafting history in regard to 'Territories under foreign occupation or colonial domination' supports little, if any, inference about the adopted text. To the extent that something might be inferred from the history, it is confirmatory of the adopted text.

Oxman's resolution III argument

An argument based on resolution III of the Third Conference may be treated here as well. Judge *ad hoc* Oxman in *Mauritius/Maldives* argued that one should infer from resolution III a limiting effect on UNCLOS jurisdiction. According to Judge *ad hoc* Oxman, because 'questions regarding the right of self-determination and decolonization were addressed … in resolution III rather than in the text of the Convention,' 'such matters are beyond the scope of the substantive and dispute settlement obligations accepted by the States parties' to the Convention.[54]

Resolution III of the Final Act of the Third UN Conference on the Law of the Sea provides as follows:

> *The Third United Nations Conference on the Law of the Sea,*
>
> Having regard to the Convention on the Law of the Sea,

53 Support for the draft, interestingly, was not universal among newly independent states. See, for example, Mr. Scotland (Guyana), 136th plen. mtg., 26 August 1980, ¶ 74: XIV *Official Records* 36. In contrast, see, e.g., Mr. Ballah (Trinidad and Tobago), Second Committee, 39th mtg., 14 August 1974, ¶ 47: II *Official Records* 282–283; Mr. Nandan (Fiji), *ibid.*, ¶ 51, p. 283; Mr. Slade (Western Samoa), Second Committee, 24th mtg., 1 August 1974: II *Official Records* 189–190. Few if any of the supporters said anything about possible implications for the dispute settlement régime; they were concerned with preserving the rights of colonial peoples in maritime resources pending decolonization. The concern in particular was that a colonial power might dispose of a people's resources (including by means of delimitation) without consultation: see esp. in this regard Mr. Venchard (Mauritius), Second Committee, 40th mtg., 14 August 1974, ¶ 32: II *Official Records* 288.

54 *Mauritius/Maldives*, Preliminary Objections, Sep. & Dis. Op. Judge *ad hoc* Oxman, ITLOS 2021 p. 118, pp. 129–130 ¶ 33 (28 January). For resolution III, see Final Act of the Third United Nations Conference on the Law of the Sea, Annex I, p. 183.

> Bearing in mind the Charter of the United Nations, in particular Article 73 [under Chapter XI: Declaration Regarding Non-Self-Governing Territories]
>
> 1. Declares that:
>
> (a) In the case of a territory whose people have not attained full independence or other self-governing status recognized by the United Nations, or a territory under colonial domination, provisions concerning rights and interests under the Convention shall be implemented for the benefit of the people of the territory with a view to promoting their well-being and development.
>
> (b) Where a dispute exists between States over the sovereignty of a territory to which this resolution applies, in respect of which the United Nations has recommended specific means of settlement, there shall be consultations between the parties to that dispute regarding the exercise of the rights referred to in subparagraph (a). In such consultations the interests of the people of the territory concerned shall be a fundamental consideration. Any exercise of those rights shall take into account the relevant resolutions of the United Nations and shall be without prejudice to the position of any party to the dispute. The States concerned shall make every effort to enter into provisional arrangements of a practical nature and shall not jeopardize or hamper the reaching of a final settlement of the dispute.
>
> 2. Requests the Secretary-General of the United Nations to bring this resolution to the attention of all Members of the United Nations and the other participants in the Conference, as well as the principal organs of the United Nations, and to request their compliance with it.[55]

It is hard to see why the affirmation in resolution III concerning 'a territory whose people have not attained full independence or other self-governing status ... or a territory under colonial domination' has the limiting effect on UNCLOS jurisdiction that Oxman posited. To scholars and practitioners concerned with decolonization, the content of paragraph 1(a) of resolution III is familiar. Article 73, to which the preamble of the resolution refers, long ago affirmed that 'the interests of the inhabitants of these territories

55 Final Act of the Third UN Conference on the Law of the Sea, 183. See generally Churchill, Lowe, & Sander (2022) 261. See Portugal's Declaration to apply Resolution III to East Timor (3 November 1997): reprinted in Hayashi & Lee (eds.), 2 *New Directions in the Law of the Sea: Regional and National Developments* § 9:2; Argentina's Declaration to disapply Resolution III to 'the "Question of the Falkland Islands (Malvinas)"' (18 October 1995): reprinted in *ibid.* at § 11:2; and Spain's Declaration to disapply Resolution III to Gibraltar (15 January 1997): reprinted in *ibid.* at § 6:7. As to Western Sahara and Resolution III, see *Western Sahara Campaign UK v. Commissioners for Her Majesty's Revenue and Customs, Secretary of State for Environment, Food and Rural Affairs*, Court of Justice of the European Union, Opinion of Advocate General Wathelet (10 January 2018), Case C-266/16, ¶ 256.

are paramount' and that the 'well-being of the inhabitants' is a responsibility of administering powers, which 'accept' that they are, *inter alia*, to 'develop self-government [in such territories]' and 'to assist them in the progressive development of their free political institutions.' The substantive propositions in resolution III thus derive from UN Charter Article 73. It would be a surprising interpretation to say that a treaty conference, by having repeated such propositions in its final act and thus affirmed that they apply to the legal relations concerned, removed disputes relating to those propositions from the dispute settlement provisions of the treaty adopted. It is far from clear how Oxman got from the substantive propositions in resolution III to a general exclusion of territorial issues from Part XV, section 2.

Then there is paragraph 1(b) of resolution III, addressing dispute settlement. This is not an omnibus dispute settlement clause. Instead, it applies only '[w]here a dispute exists between States over the sovereignty of a territory to which this resolution applies, *in respect of which the United Nations has recommended specific means of settlement*' (emphasis added); and, even in that situation, the only constraint that it lays down is that the states shall conduct 'consultations ... regarding the exercise of the rights referred to in subparagraph (a)' and treat in those consultations 'the interests of the people of the territory concerned ... [as] a fundamental consideration.' Relevant here is UNCLOS Article 279, which itself is a reiteration of general international law, invoking as it does the '[o]bligation to settle disputes by peaceful means ... in accordance with Article 2, paragraph 3, of the Charter ... and, to this end [to] seek a solution by the means indicated in Article 33, paragraph 1, of the Charter.' Resolution III in its subparagraph 1(b) reiterates the position set out in the Charter on dispute settlement. If in so doing it were to exclude the dispute settlement provisions of UNCLOS Part XV, section 2, then UNCLOS jurisdiction would be illusory: nothing would be left of it, if these terms of general application regarding the duty to seek pacific settlement of disputes somehow, as Oxman would have it, place the 'matters [they address] ... beyond the scope of the substantive and dispute-settlement obligations accepted by the States parties.' The better reading of resolution III is that it affirms the distinct interest of the peoples of non-self-governing and certain other dependent territories as a legal interest that the states parties to a dispute over the sovereignty of such a territory shall not ignore: 'In such consultations the interests of the people of the territory concerned shall be a fundamental consideration.' To read more into subparagraph 1(b) of resolution III than that is not supported by the text.

At risk of pedantry, it is to be noted that Oxman was not accurate, to the extent that he suggested that UNCLOS has nothing to say about decolonization. (It appears that he indeed said that UNCLOS has nothing to say about decolonization, when he said that 'questions regarding the right of self-determination and decolonization were addressed … in resolution III *rather than* in the text of the Convention' (emphasis added).) UNCLOS does say things about decolonization. There is UNCLOS Article 305(1)(e). That provision opens the Convention for signature by territories which, though they 'enjoy full internal self-government, recognized as such by the United Nations,' and 'have competence over the matters governed' by UNCLOS, 'have not attained full independence in accordance with General Assembly resolution 1514 (XV) [Declaration on the Granting of Independence to Colonial Countries and Peoples].' There is also Article 160, concerning the Assembly of the International Sea-Bed Authority. Article 160(2)(f)*(i)* provides that among the powers of the Assembly is 'to consider and approve … the rules, regulations and procedures on the equitable sharing of financial and other economic benefits derived from activities in the Area and the payments and contributions made pursuant to article 82' and that the Assembly is to exercise this power 'taking into particular consideration the interests and needs of [*inter alia*] … peoples who have not attained full independence or other self-governing status.' Under Article 162(2)(o)*(i)*, the Council of the International Sea-Bed Authority, too, is to take into 'particular consideration' those 'interests and needs.' True, these are not provisions for the general disposition of all remaining colonial interests! Just as UNCLOS is not a 'law of the land treaty,' it is not a colonial dispute settlement treaty. But that is just as much to state a truism. Nobody says that an UNCLOS tribunal may address such territorial issues in the absence of a law of the sea issue. The question is whether in a case in which they are conjoined with a law of the sea issue such issues effectively oust the jurisdiction of the tribunal. Oxman's proposed inference from resolution III of the Final Act does not supply a convincing argument that they do.

Absence of substantive provisions as grounds for jurisdictional abstention?

Chapter 2 considered the practice under Part XV, section 2, in which adjudicators, referring to Article 293(1), reasoned that, under certain circumstances, they may address issues concerning use of force and human rights. Chapter 2 also considered the view, which Peter Tzeng and others articulated,[56] that the adjudicators were in error for having addressed such issues. Tzeng recalled the axiom that applicable law does not enlarge the scope of jurisdiction.

Writers have posited, however, that the *absence* of substantive law *reduces* the scope of jurisdiction. According to one of the prominent exponents of the land territory exclusion, quoting another, '"it would be beyond the

56 See Chapter 2, p. 75, n. 84.

substantive scope of the convention to determine the status of land territory,"' and, for that reason, beyond the jurisdiction of courts and tribunals.[57] Similar reasoning is visible in other early writings that asserted a categorical exclusion of land territory disputes: 'As substantive articles of the Convention do not relate to such matters, *it would certainly be inappropriate for the dispute settlement provisions to cover them.*'[58]

An initial response to those who contend that the exercise of jurisdiction over a given issue is precluded, because substantive law is lacking in a treaty on the issue, is that their contention collides with the critique noted above, which contends that substantive law does not act as a basis for jurisdiction. Let us for convenience call this the 'substance-jurisdiction critique.' If one accepts the substance-jurisdiction critique—that is to say, if one accepts that substantive law does not affect the scope of jurisdiction—then the reflexive proposition would seem valid as well: the absence of substantive law does not, in itself, affect the scope of jurisdiction either.

One might also say, as I suggested in Chapter 2, that the premise is doubtful that UNCLOS contains no substantive provisions concerning territorial issues. UNCLOS is replete with provisions concerning territorial issues.

However, even if one accepts the substance-jurisdiction critique as many do (e.g., the *Channel Tunnel* arbitrators, Tzeng), and even if one ignores that UNCLOS contains provisions concerned with territory, one yet finds weakness in the contention that the contours of the Convention's substantive law reflect an intention to exclude territorial issues from adjudication under UNCLOS. The weakness in the contention is visible on two considerations.

First, similar to Articles 74 and 83 which make general international law applicable in negotiated settlements of EEZ and continental shelf boundaries, Article 293, paragraph 1, identifies the law to be applied by a court or tribunal having jurisdiction under Part XV, section 2, to be 'this Convention *and other rules of international law not incompatible with this Convention*' (emphasis added).

Under Article 293, paragraph 1, therefore, the applicable rules, when a dispute is submitted to a Part XV, section 2, procedure, are those contained in the Convention and also those of international law to the extent not

57 Smith, 'The Effect of Extended Maritime Jurisdiction' in Koers, Oxman, & Østreng (eds.), *The 1982 Convention on the Law of the Sea: Proceedings, Law of the Sea Institute Seventeenth Annual Conference* (1984), quoting Irwin, 'Settlement of Maritime Boundary Disputes: An Analysis of the Law of the Sea Negotiations' (1980) 8 ODIL 104, 114 (emphasis added). See also Talmon (2014) 46; Beckman (2014) 233; and www.interaksyon.com/article/36782/unclos-cant-settle-philippine-territorial-disputes-with-china—expert

58 Irwin (1980) 8 ODIL at 114 (emphasis added).

incompatible with the Convention. ITLOS has had no difficulty applying other rules of international law (e.g., those concerning 'the immunity enjoyed by [a] warship under general international law'),[59] nor has an Annex VII tribunal hesitated to 'have regard to' other rules (e.g., those concerning human rights).[60] As Chapter 2 recalled, UNCLOS tribunals have reached decisions concerning a party's claims that another party had engaged in unlawful use of force as well.[61] It is beyond question that the general international law rules concerning use of force are compatible with UNCLOS: the law of the sea has not overturned the general rules of public international order. Much the same may be said regarding the rules regarding territorial entitlement and the presumption of the stability of boundaries between states, rules that arguably are even more fundamental to general public order than the regulation of use of force as such.[62] As Chapter 1 recalled, boundaries settled between states remain so, unless and until the states concerned agree to change them. This is a part of international law that UNCLOS has not superseded, and its compatibility with UNCLOS is not to be doubted. An exclusion of territorial issues, whatever its scope, does not exclude such a part of international law as that. The principle that a state does not change its international boundaries by force must apply in any event.

The second fault with this objection to adjudication of territorial issues is that it can be directed equally against the adjudication of maritime boundaries. Nobody says that UNCLOS does not confer jurisdiction on courts and tribunals to settle maritime boundary disputes—they do in fact settle maritime boundary disputes[63]—yet the substantive provisions in UNCLOS for settling such disputes are extremely slim. Churchill, Lowe, and Sander rightly call those provisions 'laconic.'[64] Article 74 concerning delimitation of overlapping EEZs and Article 83 concerning delimitation of overlapping continental shelves say nothing at all as to the methods of delimitation, except that states should negotiate a boundary by reference

59 *The 'ARA Libertad' (Argentina v. Ghana)*, Provisional Measures, Order, ITLOS 2012 p. 332, p. 349 ¶ 98 (15 December). Ghana had maintained the contrary—that is, that ITLOS did *not* have jurisdiction to address 'the interpretation or application of general international law': *ibid.* at p. 343 ¶ 58.

60 *Arctic Sunrise (Kingdom of the Netherlands v. Russian Federation)*, PCA Case No. 2014–02, Annex VII tribunal (Judge Mensah, President; Burmester, Soons, Symonides, and Székely, arbitrators), Award on the Merits, ¶¶ 197–198 (14 August 2015).

61 See Chapter 2, pp. 67–71.

62 Grant (2015) 103–131; (Wuerth) Brunk & Hakimi (2022) at 688; Brunk & Hakimi (2024) at 442.

63 For examples of completed or ongoing delimitation cases under Part XV, section 2, procedures (as of 2021) see Churchill, Lowe, & Sander (2022) at 308 nn. 20, 21.

64 *Ibid.* at 42.

to international law, as defined in Article 38 of the Statute of the ICJ, 'in order to achieve an equitable solution.'[65]

Failing agreement as to delimitation, Articles 74 and 83 call for the submission of the delimitation to a mechanism under Part XV. Those articles provide no guidance as to the rules to be applied in judicial or arbitral settlement. True, Article 15 provides for delimitation of potentially overlapping territorial sea entitlements with special reference to the median line between the states with opposite or adjacent coasts—that is, the line 'every point of which is equidistant from the nearest points on the baselines from which the breadth of the territorial seas of each of the two States is measured.' However, this is not a self-contained rule of delimitation; it is a starting point, a principle to be applied but then adjusted by reference to, for example, 'special circumstances.' As Prescott and Schofield have noted, these provisions open the door 'for radically differing interpretations as to which factors and methods of delimitation are appropriate to a particular case, and therefore potential for dispute and deadlock in delimitation negotiations.'[66] Smith noted that the Convention lacks 'concrete guidance' as to the rules for settling maritime boundary disputes, providing instead an 'ambience of understanding and cooperation.'[67] The Convention text addressing maritime delimitation supplies little substantive law. Indeed, Malcolm Evans writes that '[t]he chief virtue of this formulation is that it avoided any mention of the terms which at [the] time [of drafting] were a source of controversy—equidistance, equitable principles, special circumstances, or relevant circumstances—and is virtually devoid of substantive content ... It is of next to no practical utility at all for those seeking to better understand how to delimit a boundary.'[68]

In short, the Convention articulates no well-developed rules for maritime delimitations, yet UNCLOS tribunals have adjudicated maritime delimitations. Therefore, to assert that, because it says little in relation to territorial disputes, the Convention does not supply jurisdiction to adjudicate territorial disputes is unconvincing. The syllogism would be sound, only on the premise that the rules for maritime delimitations are well-developed. But that premise is faulty. UNCLOS in truth tells the adjudicator practically nothing of substance about how to settle maritime disputes. To rely on the

65 The 'lack of specificity' as to rules for delimitation owes to sharp controversies at the Third Conference, as to which see Caflisch, 'The Delimitation of Marine Spaces between States with Opposite or Adjacent Coasts' in Dupuy & Vignes (eds.), vol. 1 (1991) 425, 477–479.

66 Prescott & Schofield, *The Maritime Political Boundaries of the World*, 2nd edn. (2005) 246.

67 Smith (1984) 348–349.

68 Evans, 'Maritime Boundary Delimitation' in Rothwell, Oude Elferink, Scott, & Stephens (eds.), *The Oxford Handbook of the Law of the Sea* (2015) 254, 258.

substantive law provisions as an interpretative device for the jurisdictional provisions in the way that the exponents of the territorial exclusion would do (i.e., to rely on the lack of substantive law regarding territorial issues to support the contention that jurisdiction does not embrace those issues) requires a contrast between the substantive law in respect of territorial issues and the substantive law in respect of maritime issues (i.e., paucity in respect of one, sufficiency in respect of another). Where the substantive law is not spelled out in respect of either, and jurisdiction exists in respect of one, it is not convincing to say that the lack of substantive law means lack of jurisdiction over the other.

4

A question of coasts: Chagos Marine Protected Area Arbitration (Mauritius v. United Kingdom)

The Chagos Archipelago was a dependency of Mauritius. Mauritius was a colony of the United Kingdom. Mauritius became an independent state on 12 March 1968. Before Mauritius became an independent state, the United Kingdom, as colonial administrator, concluded the Lancaster House Undertakings with the local administration in Mauritius. In accordance with the Lancaster House Undertakings, the United Kingdom separated the Chagos from the colony of Mauritius and constituted the archipelago as the BIOT. The separation of the Chagos and its constitution as the BIOT took place in November 1965. The United Kingdom continued to administer the BIOT after Mauritius became an independent state. Around 1980, Mauritius began to object to the separation of the Chagos. On 1 April 2010, the United Kingdom created by UK statute a 'marine protected area' (MPA) around the BIOT extending to a distance of 200 nautical miles from the baselines of the Chagos Archipelago.[1] Mauritius on 20 December 2010, asserting that the United Kingdom, by having created and maintained the MPA, violated UNCLOS, instituted Annex VII proceedings against the United Kingdom.

Mauritius's claims against the United Kingdom rested, broadly, on two arguments: first, that, owing to alleged irregularity of the separation of the Chagos Archipelago from Mauritius in 1965, the United Kingdom is not the 'coastal State' in the Chagos and therefore had no authority to declare the MPA; and, second, in the alternative, that the MPA violated the undertakings that the United Kingdom made to Mauritius in 1965.[2] The United Kingdom objected on jurisdictional grounds to all parts of Mauritius's claims.[3]

1 *Chagos Marine Protected Area Arbitration (Mauritius v. United Kingdom)*, PCA Case No. 2011–03, Annex VII tribunal (Shearer, President; Greenwood, Hoffmann, Kateka, and Wolfrum, members), Award, 18 March 2015, ¶¶ 1–5 (hereinafter '*Chagos Marine Protected Area*').

2 *Ibid.* at ¶ 7.

3 *Ibid.* at ¶ 11.

As to Mauritius's argument that the United Kingdom is not the 'coastal State,' the United Kingdom objected, in effect, that Mauritius was asking the tribunal to adjudicate a territorial dispute and that the tribunal had no jurisdiction to do so. In its objection, the United Kingdom relied chiefly on the 'any dispute' clause in Article 288(1),[4] and, having argued that a 'general exclusion' of territorial issues emerges from that clause, maintained that the territorial exclusion in Article 298(1)(a)*(i)* 'does no more than clarify that the general exclusion of consideration of unsettled territorial sovereignty disputes from compulsory dispute settlement also applies in the context of conciliation.'[5] It is with this objection, which the Annex VII tribunal decided to uphold, that the present chapter is concerned.[6]

The United Kingdom's objection to jurisdiction over the territorial issue

The United Kingdom argued that Articles 286 and 288 of UNCLOS entail implicit limitations to Part XV, section 2, jurisdiction. In particular, the United Kingdom argued that it is 'self-evident ... that a dispute concerning sovereignty over land territory is not a dispute concerning the interpretation or application of the law of the sea convention.'[7] If the limitation were 'self-evident,' as the United Kingdom described it, then the limitation would be found without further inspection or analysis. As I suggested above, considering Article 288(1) in particular, limitations are not 'self-evident' in the Convention's global statement of jurisdiction.

The United Kingdom noted that a dispute over sovereignty over the Chagos Archipelago had been (in the tribunal's words) 'a longstanding point of contention' and it was only very recently that Mauritius had asserted a maritime dispute in connection with that dispute over land territory.[8] In drawing attention to the duration of the land territory dispute, the United

4 *Chagos Marine Protected Area*, Preliminary Objections to Jurisdiction submitted by the United Kingdom, 31 October 2012, ¶¶ 3.37–3.57.

5 *Ibid.* ¶ 3.51.

6 For comment on the *Chagos Marine Protected Area* award, see Colson & Vohrer, 'In re Chagos Marine Protected Area (Mauritius v. United Kingdom' (2015) 109 AJIL 845–851; Talmon, 'The Chagos Marine Protected Area Arbitration: Expansion of the Jurisdiction of UNCLOS Part XV Courts and Tribunals' (2016) 65 ICLQ 927–951; Forteau in Forteau & Thouvenin (eds.) (2017) at 1006–1007; Serdy, 'Article 298' in *Proelss Commentary* (2017) at 1925–1927; Guilfoyle, 'The Chagos Archipelago before International Tribunals' (2021) 21 Melbourne JIL 749–771; Rothwell (2022) 64, 229.

7 Final Transcript 654: 17–19, quoted in the Award of 18 March 2015, ¶ 170.

8 Award, ¶ 172.

Kingdom argued that Mauritius was attempting artificially to link that dispute—which taken on its own would not be subject to Part XV, section 2, jurisdiction—to the question, which state is the 'coastal State' facing the maritime area in question, 'coastal State' being a term in UNCLOS and, thus, a term that, at least potentially, might be subject to interpretation in a Part XV, section 2, proceeding.[9] The long duration of the land territory dispute in respect of the Chagos is a point to which I return below, because it presents a stark contrast to the third case that I consider: the *Coastal State Rights* case between Ukraine and Russia.

One might think that, in arguing that an issue of land territory falls outside Part XV, section 2, jurisdiction, the United Kingdom faced a difficulty in the manifest readiness of UNCLOS tribunals to 'address [...] some issues beyond the strict confines of the Convention itself.'[10] As I noted in Chapter 2, tribunals have addressed, and settled, 'some issues' with which the Convention does not deal, or with which the Convention deals only in passing. In particular, there are the cases in which tribunals have addressed and settled issues relating to use of force and to human rights. The United Kingdom argued that those cases are inapposite. The United Kingdom characterized them as having chiefly concerned maritime issues and as having touched on others as merely 'some incidental issue[s].'[11]

In this connection, the United Kingdom said that Article 293, in line with doctrine, has no bearing on the proper interpretation of the jurisdictional provisions of the Convention.[12] One might think that on this point in particular the United Kingdom would have run into difficulty. As I recalled in Chapter 2, the tribunals in the *Saiga* line of cases had found merit in the argument that Article 293 enables a tribunal to consider a range of international law rules not contained in the Convention and, on the basis of such rules, the tribunals proceeded to adjudicate issues concerning use of force. However, agreeing with the United Kingdom, the *Chagos Marine Protected Area* tribunal did not find Article 293 to supply a means to address the territorial question that Mauritius's claim had raised.

The United Kingdom argued that Article 298(1)(a)*(i)* had little to do with the case either. The United Kingdom observed that Article 298(1)(a)*(i)* concerns only a certain category of 'mixed disputes'—namely, ones in which delimitation of maritime boundaries involve concurrent issues of land sovereignty.[13] As I argued in Chapter 3, the obvious conclusion to have

9 Award, ¶ 172.
10 Award, ¶ 173.
11 Award, ¶ 173, quoting Final Transcript, 668:9–13.
12 Award, ¶ 184.
13 Award, ¶ 174.

drawn from the specific and limited language of Article 298(1)(a)*(i)* is that, because that provision does not articulate a general exclusion of territorial issues, and because there is no other territorial exclusion clause in the Convention, the Convention does not generally exclude territorial issues. The United Kingdom, of course, did not draw that conclusion; it instead merely repeated its main assertion—that is, that a general exclusion exists elsewhere in the Convention.[14] The United Kingdom conceded that Article 298(1)(a)*(i)* is not 'an implicit exclusion of all land sovereignty matters.'[15] The United Kingdom did not venture to say precisely how far the exclusionary effect of Article 298(1)(a)*(i)* goes or, for that matter, what purpose the provision serves. The United Kingdom offered only the rather anemic suggestion that 'article 298(1)(a)(i) does no more than clarify … the general exclusion … in the context of conciliation,' a suggestion tantamount to saying that Article 298(1)(a)*(i)* has no effect. The United Kingdom plainly wished to shift the analysis somewhere else.

The majority opinion: shifting the issue to 'relative weight' and Article 288(1)

The tribunal opened its analysis of jurisdiction and land territory disputes with a platitude: it observed that UNCLOS provides no 'guidance on the identification of the "coastal State" in cases were sovereignty over the land territory fronting a coast is disputed.'[16] Nobody would say the contrary, just as nobody would say that UNCLOS provides 'guidance on the identification of [state responsibility for use of force or for violations of human rights].' Nor for that matter does UNCLOS provide guidance, or at least not much guidance, as to the settlement of maritime delimitation disputes, but those disputes are a mainstay of Part XV, section 2, jurisdiction. As I noted in Chapter 3, UNCLOS tribunals have addressed issues which the Convention contains few substantive rules to address. Maritime delimitation cases supply the main examples.[17] The *Chagos* tribunal did not say why absence of rules in regard to territory precludes jurisdiction, whereas absence of rules in regard to other issues does not. In short, the tribunal's observation that UNCLOS provides no 'guidance' on the matter is accurate but unhelpful. It provides no logical support for the conclusion that the tribunal eventually reached.

14 See *Chagos Marine Protected Area*, Preliminary Objections to Jurisdiction submitted by the United Kingdom, 31 October 2012, ¶ 3.51.
15 Award, ¶ 174, quoting Final Transcript, 1168:18–24.
16 Award, ¶ 203.
17 See pp. 88–99.

The *Chagos* tribunal also said that UNCLOS makes no provision 'for circumstances of war or secession in which a coast might effectively be occupied by authorities exercising *de facto* governmental powers.'[18] This is *dictum* far beyond the boundaries of the parties' claims in the *Chagos* case, but, as we will see, it held portent for Ukraine's claims several years later against Russia in the Black Sea and Sea of Azov.

As for the jurisdictional question that the *Chagos* case did present, Mauritius argued that identifying the 'coastal State' in the Chagos is a matter of interpreting and applying the Convention and, thus, a matter that Article 288(1) embraces. The tribunal did not accept Mauritius's argument. Instead, the tribunal espoused what I referred to in Chapter 2 as the 'Article 288(1) argument.' This is the argument that holds that jurisdiction extends to disputes 'concerning the interpretation or application' of the Convention but that disputes about territorial sovereignty are not disputes 'concerning the interpretation or application' of the Convention. As I suggested, the Article 288(1) argument is question-begging: it states as a premise the very question that calls for a reasoned answer.

Proceeding on the premise that Article 288(1) does not embrace territorial sovereignty disputes, the tribunal asked whether, in fact, a territorial sovereignty dispute exists between Mauritius and the United Kingdom. The tribunal's analysis on that question is the strongest and most convincing part of the *Chagos* award. Crucial in its analysis, the tribunal drew attention to the material evidence of a dispute, including the long duration of exchanges between Mauritius and the United Kingdom in regard to the Chagos. On the basis of the evidence, the tribunal concluded that the dispute had existed '[s]ince at least 1980.'[19] The existence of a territorial dispute having been established, the task for the tribunal next was to determine whether Mauritius's maritime claims constituted a dispute concerning the interpretation and application of UNCLOS.

The tribunal reasoned that, in order to determine whether a dispute is one concerning the interpretation and application of UNCLOS, one must determine 'where the relative weight of the dispute lies.'[20] The presence of *some* territorial issue, the tribunal suggested, does not necessarily entail that 'the relative weight of the dispute lies' outside the scope of Article 288(1). By contrast, where 'the Parties' dispute *primarily* concern[s] sovereignty' (emphasis added), and the interpretation or application of the Convention term (the term 'coastal State' in the case at hand) 'merely represent[s] a manifestation of that dispute,' the relative weight of the dispute lies outside the scope of Article 288(1). In short, if the 'relative weight' is with the

18 Award, ¶ 203.
19 Award, ¶ 209.
20 Award, ¶ 211.

territorial issue, and not with the contestation of a Convention term, then the dispute is a 'sovereignty dispute' in the relevant sense and, thus, it is a dispute over which an UNCLOS adjudicator does not have jurisdiction. The tribunal estimated that, on the facts of the *Chagos* case, the question where the relative weight of the dispute lay 'all but answer[ed] itself': it lay with the territorial dispute.[21]

In this reasoning, we see the tribunal performing a familiar operation of the adjudicator: it ascertained the quality of a thing as a whole by considering the relation among the thing's disparate parts. As a matter of the adjudicator's method, this is an eminently reasonable operation to perform. However, one may ask whether the tribunal's invocation of 'relative weight' is quite satisfactory in the circumstances of the *Chagos* case. The tribunal placed considerable emphasis on Article 288(1), saying that that provision entails a general exclusion of territorial issues from UNCLOS jurisdiction. But if Article 288(1) entails a *general* exclusion of territorial issues, then why would 'relative weight' enter the picture? As I consider later in this chapter, neither Article 288(1) nor any other UNCLOS provision provides a textual basis for the tribunal to introduce the concept of 'relative weight.'

Let us assume, nevertheless, that the tribunal was justified in referring to 'relative weight.' As a matter of principle, there is nothing wrong with an adjudicator weighing a matter in that fashion. As I suggested, legal method is familiar with situations that call for judgment as to the relation between disparate elements that comprise a particular phenomenon. Such situations raise a question, however: what standard is an adjudicator to apply in measuring 'relative weight'? The relationship between the two parts in Mauritius's claims—the relationship between the territorial and maritime parts—was a matter of appreciation. Relationships between such elements are susceptible to widely different measurement by different decision-makers. Where a thing is all one thing or all another, the task is easy: there is no relationship between disparate parts to measure. Where the thing has two parts, measuring the relationship between them calls for judgment, and exercising judgment calls for a standard to guide the judge. The *Chagos* tribunal's concept of 'relative weight' called for a standard, but the tribunal did not identify any.

It is to be submitted that a better approach would be to require that a territorial issue, if it is to be subject to UNCLOS jurisdiction, be connected to a maritime dispute in a manner articulated in an UNCLOS provision. As I noted at the end of Chapter 2, UNCLOS contains many provisions concerning territory—and each of these connects in its own way to provisions concerning the sea. It is true that an adjudicator, if asked to say whether two things are connected, must also engage in appreciation—how much

21 Award, ¶ 211.

connection suffices?—and, so, a 'connection' approach does not remove all doubt. But it would ground the tribunal's reasoning more firmly in the Convention text than the 'relative weight' approach that the *Chagos* tribunal applied. Another way of expressing the matter is to say that a tribunal must judge whether a relationship is closely enough related—that is, connected enough—to a Convention term to supply a basis for jurisdiction. This was the concept—not 'relative weight'—that the Annex VII tribunal in *Southern Bluefin Tuna* applied: 'it is for this Tribunal to decide whether the "real dispute" between the Parties does or does not reasonably (and not just remotely) relate to the obligations set forth in the treaties whose breach is alleged.'[22] An approach that measures connection or relation to specific treaty terms is preferable to an approach that measures 'relative weight.' It grounds the adjudicator's decision on the applicable terms and, thus, applies the ordinary methods of textual interpretation that are a mainstay of the adjudicator's function.

Be that as it may, having concluded that the 'relative weight' of Mauritius's claim lay with the land territory issue, having affirmed the United Kingdom's objection under Article 288(1), and having treated that objection as dispositive, the tribunal would seem to have given a complete answer as to jurisdiction. In light of its further statement that 'much of [the parties'] argumentation [about Article 298(1)(a)*(i)*] misses the point,' it is all the more surprising that the tribunal nevertheless devoted a further section of its award to Article 298(1)(a)*(i)*. Doubling back in this way, the *Chagos* tribunal came to the most dubious parts of its reasoning.

From Article 298(1)(a)*(i)* and back again: the majority opinion in disarray

Curiously for a text that, while complicated, expresses its meaning clearly and produces no absurd or unreasonable result, Article 298(1)(a)*(i)* drew the *Chagos* tribunal into a series of reflections on the negotiating history.

22 *Southern Bluefin Tuna (New Zealand-Japan, Australia-Japan)*, Annex VII tribunal (Schwebel, President; Feliciano, Keith, Tresselt, and Yamada, members), Award, 4 August 2000, ¶ 48: (2006) XXIII RIAA 1, 39. Judge Keith evidently agreed with this part of the award, his famous dissent having concerned a different issue (the one that is more often written about, and on which Australia and New Zealand lost the case) that is, whether the other treaty—the Convention for the Conservation of Southern Bluefin Tuna–precluded all other dispute settlement procedures. See Sep. Op. Justice Sir Kenneth Keith, XXIII RIAA at p. 49, ¶ 1, as to which see, e.g., Kunoy, 'The Scope of Compulsory Jurisdiction and Exceptions Thereto under the United Nations Convention on the Law of the Sea' (2021) 58 Can. YBIL 78, 85–86.

In addressing Article 298(1)(a)*(i)* in that way, the tribunal considered 'that the simple explanation for the lack of attention to this question [of territorial sovereignty] is that *none of the Conference participants* expected that a long-standing dispute over territorial sovereignty would ever be considered to be a dispute "concerning the interpretation or application of the Convention."'[23] The tribunal's characterization of the matter is hard to reconcile with the negotiating record. As I recalled in Chapter 3, there had been a skirmish at the Conference, and the states that wanted an express exclusion of territorial sovereignty issues lost. Those states knew what they wanted, and they knew what they did not get. Their adversaries in the debate knew what *they* wanted, and they go it: a convention that leaves open the possibility of adjudication of at least *some* territorial sovereignty issues.

In turning back again to Article 298(1)(a)*(i)*, the tribunal implicitly conceded that Article 288(1) is *not* the source of a limitation on jurisdiction. As the text and structure of UNCLOS reflect, and as the argumentative structure of the *Chagos* majority opinion implicitly acknowledges, the limitations and the optional exceptions to Part XV, section 2, jurisdiction are contained in Part XV, section 3, not in Article 288(1). Notwithstanding the pride of place it gave in its analysis to Article 288(1), the tribunal indeed reasoned that the exclusion of territorial issues follows from Article 298(1)(a)*(i)*. The tribunal said as follows:

> 216. [...] Given the inherent sensitivity of States to questions of territorial sovereignty, the question must be asked: if the drafters of the Convention were sufficiently concerned with the sensitivities involved in delimiting maritime boundaries that they included the option to exclude such disputes from compulsory settlement, is it reasonable to expect that the same States accepted that more fundamental issues of territorial sovereignty could be raised as separate claims under Article 288(1)?
>
> 217. In the Tribunal's view, had the drafters intended that such claims could be presented as disputes 'concerning the interpretation or application of the Convention', the Convention would have included an opt-out facility for States not wishing their sovereignty claims to be adjudicated, just as one sees in Article 298(1)(a)(i) in relation to maritime delimitation disputes.[24]

The tribunal, in these paragraphs, started from an unobjectionable premise: the states parties created an optional exception to jurisdiction over delimitation disputes in Article 298(1)(a)*(i)*.[25] The premise nobody doubts; the optional exclusion is explicit in the text, and tribunals observe it with care. From

23 Award, ¶ 215 (emphasis added).
24 Award, ¶¶ 216–217.
25 The tribunal referred only to delimitation disputes. It did not mention the optional exclusion of disputes involving historic bays or titles.

the premise, the tribunal concluded that if the states parties had understood that jurisdiction exists over territorial issues, then they would have created an optional exception to jurisdiction over territorial issues, too. The tribunal's reasoning relies on an *a fortiori* proposition: territorial issues are more important than maritime issues—they are the 'more fundamental' issues—and, so, states would not consent to jurisdiction over the former if they did not consent to jurisdiction over the latter. The tribunal's reasoning also relies on a certain reading of Article 288(1): namely, that if UNCLOS jurisdiction embraces territorial issues, then territorial issues 'could be raised as *separate claims* under Article 288(1)' (emphasis added).

Quite apart from which kind of issue is 'more fundamental,' the tribunal's reasoning here is unconvincing. It is unconvincing because, in its rhetorical question—'is it reasonable to expect that the same States accepted that more fundamental issues of territorial sovereignty could be raised as separate claims under Article 288(1)?'—the tribunal presented a straw man. The straw man is found in the tribunal's reading of Article 288(1): nobody contends that a territorial issue on its own as a 'separate claim' is subject under UNCLOS to compulsory and binding procedure. It is only in connection with a maritime dispute that the possibility arises under UNCLOS that jurisdiction might apply to a territorial issue. Thus, where a party has excluded jurisdiction over the maritime dispute, the possibility of jurisdiction over a territorial dispute connected with that maritime dispute disappears.

Article 298(1)(a)*(i)* provides the optional exception that the tribunal insists is absent and the supposed absence of which is the basis of the tribunal's reasoning. The states parties provided for the optional exception of delimitation disputes (and of historic bay and title disputes), and, by having so provided, they assured that a state party that does not wish to be subject to compulsory and binding procedure in relation to one or more such disputes, by electing the optional exception, will not be. Any territorial dispute connected with a maritime dispute that a party elects to except is itself excepted too.

It is true that, even having elected the full extent of the optional exceptions under Article 298(1), a party is still subject to jurisdiction in regard to *other* disputes concerning the interpretation or application of the Convention—and it would follow that the party is still subject to jurisdiction in regard to territorial issues connected to one or more such disputes. There is nothing implausible per se in a drafting solution that provides optional exceptions to *some* issues but not to others: Article 298(1)(a)*(i)* provides optional exceptions to some issues but not to others. A significant number of participants in the Third Conference wanted no exceptions at all. The adopted Convention text is complex and its jurisdictional architecture the product in particular of hard-fought controversies and pragmatic solutions. To note these realities of UNCLOS does not in itself answer particular interpretative questions, but the realities caution against a perfectionist's reading. The *Chagos* tribunal's reading, under which the tribunal insisted that optional exceptions must sweep the table clean of any territorial issues, is a perfectionist's. It does not accord with the adopted text, which provides optional exceptions in regard to some matters but not to others.

I return in a moment to this matter—the residuum of maritime disputes subject to jurisdiction even after a state elects the Article 298(1) exceptions. I agree with the *Chagos* majority that the residuum carries with it the implication that connected territorial disputes, too, are potentially subject to jurisdiction. I disagree with the *Chagos* majority that the 'more fundamental' character of territorial disputes entails that we must read into UNCLOS a general exclusion of territorial disputes so as to avoid the implication. The grounds for my disagreement on this point I elaborate by reference to the majority's reasoning about the so-called *a contrario* argument.

The *a contrario* argument is an argument that Judge Wolfrum had articulated some years before the *Chagos* case in extrajudicial capacity and that he and Judge Kateka, as we will see, adopted in dissent in the *Chagos* case. The *a contrario* argument observes that, if territorial issues were subject to a general exclusion from jurisdiction, then the particular exclusion of territorial issues in Article 298(1)(a)*(i)* would be without purpose.[26] The *Chagos* majority grudgingly allowed that the *a contrario* argument demonstrates that jurisdiction might exist in respect of territorial issues connected with *delimitation* disputes (and with disputes involving historic bays or titles), but the tribunal then insisted that the argument goes no further than that: 'At most, an *a contrario* reading ... supports the proposition that an issue of land sovereignty might be within the jurisdiction of a Part XV court or tribunal if it were genuinely ancillary to a dispute over a maritime boundary or a claim of historic title.'[27] Article 298(1)(a)*(i)* is an optional exception to delimitation disputes (and disputes involving historic bays and titles), and so, the tribunal insisted, the presence in Article 298(1)(a)*(i)* of the territorial exclusion demonstrates at most that jurisdiction might exist in regard to territorial issues connected with those kinds of disputes.

The tribunal's position here has two formal defects and a teleological one.

Misreading the a contrario *argument*

To read the *a contrario* argument correctly, one must take care to observe the argument's essentially negative valance. The *a contrario* argument supports the proposition that UNCLOS Part XV, section 2, jurisdiction does not

26 See the dissenting opinion of Judges Kateka and Wolfrum, ¶ 40.
27 Award, ¶ 218.

completely exclude land sovereignty issues. It was the United Kingdom's position—that Article 288(1) somehow does completely exclude territorial issues—that Mauritius contested. And that is the position that the *a contrario* argument impugns. The *a contrario* argument demonstrates that examples of territorial dispute exist that are subject to jurisdiction and, thus, demonstrates that Part XV, section 2, jurisdiction does not completely exclude territorial disputes. It is in this way that the *a contrario* argument, as the moniker suggests, is an essentially negative demonstration.

It is true that the argument relies on an affirmative demonstration to arrive at the negative, and it is further true that the *particular* affirmative demonstration visible in Article 298(1), and to which Judges Kateka and Wolfrum drew attention, concerns only disputes 'over a maritime boundary or a claim of historic title.' But once the negative is arrived at—that is, once it is demonstrated by counterexamples that a complete exclusion is not inferable from Article 288(1)—the door is open to more. Whatever the limit to jurisdiction might be, jurisdiction extends *at least* as far as to embrace the counterexamples. With the words '[a]t most,' the majority suggested that the *a contrario* argument entails a *limit* to jurisdiction. This was a misreading. The logic of the argument entails not a limit but a starting point. The argument demonstrates what Article 288(1) does *not* mean; it does not demonstrate, in itself, the limits of what Article 288(1) means.

The contradiction between the tribunal's conclusion and Article 288(1)

The tribunal, where it concluded that a *general* exclusion of territorial issues is found in Part XV, but conceded that *some* territorial issues might *not* be subject to the exclusion, introduced a puzzle that it did not solve. The puzzle is the scope of the exceptions to the supposed general exclusion and their textual basis.

Article 288(1) is a general jurisdictional clause. It does not particularize. It does not segment. If it has any limiting effect on the scope of jurisdiction, then that effect is general across the jurisdictional system of which it is the capstone. The tribunal, however, in conceding that *some* territorial issues are subject to jurisdiction and insisting that others are not, particularized and segmented. Put another way, the tribunal read into Article 288(1) a limiting effect that the provision does not contain. It is as if the tribunal detected in Article 288(1) a kind of background radiation that renders the environment of UNCLOS as a whole inhospitable to dispute settlement jurisdiction over territorial issues. And yet the tribunal said that *some* territorial issues are subject to jurisdiction. What part of the Convention protects *those* territorial issues from the supposed limiting effect but not the others?

The limiting effect in Article 288(1) that supposedly bars adjudication of territorial issues—call it what you will: a presumption, a teleological preference, a felt need of public policy, etc.—has no express existence in the text. And it has no fixed target. The generality of Article 288(1) has an important consequence for any jurisdictional exclusion that one attributes to Article 288(1). The generality of Article 288(1) means that a jurisdictional exclusion, if the source of the exclusion is Article 288(1), applies to every substantive provision of the Convention. The effect does not reach only specific parts of the Convention, for how could it? Nothing in Article 288(1) distinguishes between parts of the Convention. A stringent test thus emerges for the thesis that an exclusion exists that derives from Article 288(1). If the exclusion exists, then it applies to the Convention as a whole. If, by contrast, one observes that there are parts of the Convention to which the exclusion does *not* apply, then the thesis has to be rejected: Article 288(1) is not the source of a partial or selective exclusion.

The supposed generality of the exclusion is the strength of the Article 288(1) argument, but it is also its weakness. The argument is only as strong as its weakest link. If *any* substantive provision of UNCLOS is observed to be free from the exclusion, then a necessary inference is that there is no exclusion at all, at least on the basis of Article 288(1), a provision that has *only* general effect. The *a contrario* argument supplies the negative demonstration: it demonstrates that certain provisions of the Convention are *not* subject to an exclusion with regard to territorial issues. The *Chagos* tribunal conceded that they are not. By necessary inference, following the *Chagos* tribunal's logic, *no* provision of the Convention is subject to a territorial disputes exclusion.

All that remains of the tribunal's theory, then, is a recitation of the oft-repeated protest that it is unlikely that the drafters of UNCLOS would have intended territorial issues to be subject to UNCLOS adjudication. As I argued in Chapter 3, the protest is unconvincing, because it finds no support in either text or *travaux*.

*The residuum of UNCLOS disputes, connected territorial disputes, and a procedural incentive not to aggravate disputes: an answer to the anti-*a contrario *argument*

But what of the residuum of disputes: those disputes that remain subject to UNCLOS jurisdiction even for a party declaring that it does not accept 'disputes concerning the interpretation or application of articles 15, 74 and 83 relating to sea boundary delimitations, or those involving historic bays or titles'? Even after electing the maximal extent of exclusions under Article 298, a party still is subject to UNCLOS jurisdiction in respect of some disputes. If Judges Kateka and Wolfrum were correct in their reading of Article 298(1)(a)*(i)*, or if I am correct in my reading of Article 288(1), then territorial disputes connected to *those* kinds of disputes—the residual UNCLOS disputes—are also potentially subject to UNCLOS jurisdiction. This observation was the starting point for the *Chagos* majority's attempted refutation of the *a contrario* argument. The *Chagos* majority (in what we might call the anti-*a contrario* argument) maintained that the necessary inference from Judges Kateka and Wolfrum's argument (the inference that territorial disputes, if connected with such residual UNCLOS disputes, remain subject to jurisdiction) demonstrates that the Judges Kateka and Wolfrum are wrong.

To give some examples of the residuum of UNCLOS disputes, there are disputes arising under Articles 56, 58, and 77.[28] To take one of these provisions, in respect of the EEZ Article 56 provides for the coastal state's

> sovereign rights for the purpose of exploring and exploiting, conserving and managing the natural resources, whether living or non-living, of the waters superjacent to the sea-bed and of the sea-bed and its subsoil, and with regard to other activities for the economic exploitation and exploration of the zone, such as the production of energy from the water, currents and winds.[29]

The sovereign rights here follow from the maritime entitlement. And delimiting the maritime entitlement might well be excluded from UNCLOS jurisdiction. It is a state's right to exclude delimiting maritime entitlements.

Taken on its own, the maritime entitlement is a relative abstraction. It is in the sovereign rights—that is to say, rights to engage in certain conduct and activities—that a state finds practical substance in the maritime entitlement. Disputes concerning conduct and activities are *not* disputes that a state has an omnibus right to exclude from UNCLOS jurisdiction. *Those* disputes, or at least some of them, remain subject to jurisdiction. It is in that observation—the observation that a range of disputes concerning conduct remain subject to jurisdiction—that the exponents of an exclusion of territorial disputes suggest that we find a demonstration of the drafters' intent. Surely, say the exponents of an exclusion of territorial disputes, it could not have been the drafters' intent to allow territorial disputes connected to *those* kinds of UNCLOS disputes to be adjudicated. That is the ground on which the *Chagos* majority rejected Judge Kateka and Judge Wolfrum's *a contrario* argument.

The majority's logic, however, is not entirely sound. The majority, in effect, reasoned on the basis of an unproved assertion about the drafters' intent: namely, that because of the gravity of territorial disputes as a matter of public policy, it could not possibly have been the drafters' intent to allow

28 See *South China Sea*, Merits, ¶ 1203 (8), (9), (10).
29 1833 UNTS 418.

adjudication of territorial disputes when they are connected with one or more residual UNCLOS disputes. The unproved part is not the part about the gravity: it should be common ground that territorial disputes are important (see Chapter 1). The unproved part concerns the drafters' intent as such. The *Chagos* majority spoke insistently about what the drafters intended, saying that the drafters could not have intended jurisdiction to embrace territorial disputes associated with residual disputes, unless they had 'included an opt-out facility for States not wishing their sovereignty claims to be adjudicated.' This was at paragraphs 216 and 217 of the award, which I quoted earlier.[30] To sustain the anti-*a contrario* argument, one would have to show that the drafters' intent could not possibly have been to allow the adjudication of territorial disputes—and that they included no 'opt-out facility.' I think that, when we consider situations in which territorial disputes might exist in connection with residual UNCLOS disputes, we see that the more convincing conclusion is that the drafters very well *could* have intended jurisdiction to embrace such territorial disputes—and that they did include an 'opt-out facility,' or at least a ready path for a party to avoid the relevant UNCLOS dispute and thus any connected territorial dispute.

Let me enlarge on these points by starting with a question. In what situations would a territorial dispute exist connected to one of these other kinds of UNCLOS disputes—that is, connected to a maritime dispute that a party cannot exclude by means of an Article 298 declaration? The chief examples have these characteristics: (1) a territory is in dispute; (2) a maritime area appurtenant to the territory is also in dispute, owing to the open question as to which state is sovereign in the territory; (3) a party, instead of exercising restraint, has engaged in conduct in the disputed maritime area (e.g., it has pursued fisheries exploitation or it has granted oil block concessions and promoted hydrocarbon exploration); and (4) the party's conduct has instigated a further dispute—that is, a dispute arising from its conduct—in the disputed maritime area.

Here is the reason that the drafters would *not* have excluded the territorial dispute from UNCLOS jurisdiction: *including* the territorial dispute gives the parties a procedural incentive not to aggravate the maritime dispute. We see, conversely, that if the territorial dispute were excluded from UNCLOS jurisdiction, then an aggressive state would have the opposite incentive: it would have the incentive to impose itself in the disputed maritime area, knowing that, in light of the territorial dispute, nobody will challenge its conduct under an UNCLOS procedure. The armed incident that erupted between Guyana and Surinam illustrates that there is good reason to give

30 See p. 135.

states an incentive to moderate their conduct in disputed areas, or to refrain from certain conduct in disputed areas altogether.[31]

The drafters of UNCLOS elsewhere in the text formally require states to avoid conduct in disputed areas that might lead to friction. In respect of disputed areas of potential EEZ entitlement, Article 74(3) provides that '[p] ending agreement ... the States concerned, in a spirit of understanding and co-operation, shall make every effort to enter into provisional arrangements of a practical nature and, during this transitional period, not to jeopardize or hamper the reaching of the final agreement.'[32] Article 83(3) provides the same in respect of disputed areas of potential continental shelf entitlement.[33] These provisions accord with general international law, under which a party to a dispute is obliged to refrain from conduct that would aggravate the dispute. I say something more about non-aggravation in Chapter 8.[34]

Territorial disputes that are connected with maritime disputes belonging to the jurisdictional residuum (i.e., maritime disputes that a party does not have the right to exclude by Article 298 declaration), too, will remain largely quiet as far as the UNCLOS dispute settlement system is concerned—so long as a party does not engage in conduct in the relevant maritime area likely to lead to a maritime dispute. The underlying maritime dispute—that is to say, the dispute as to the boundaries of the maritime entitlement—the party has the right to exclude from jurisdiction. The party excludes the underlying maritime dispute from jurisdiction by electing one or more of the Article 298 exclusions. Territorial disputes associated with the underlying maritime dispute the party has the right to exclude from jurisdiction as well—by the same means. By electing an Article 298 exclusion, the party *ipso facto* excludes any territorial issue connected to the maritime dispute thus excluded. *Other* maritime disputes—those arising out of *conduct,* not merely out of the entitlement claim—the party has the means to avoid as well. It avoids *those* disputes by exercising self-restraint. In regard to its conduct in the disputed maritime area, the party refrains from imposing itself on the area. This is the ready path to which I alluded, by which a party avoids creating an UNCLOS dispute and thus avoids exposing itself to the adjudication of a connected territorial dispute.

Observing restraint in the disputed maritime area, the party largely avoids the risk that an adversary will bring a claim about its conduct in the maritime area. Restraint also avoids the risk of a claim about the appurtenant territory. Nobody says that an UNCLOS adjudicator has the authority to address a territorial claim without a maritime claim. To open the door to the exercise

31 See above Chapter 2, pp. 68–69.
32 1833 UNTS at 428.
33 1833 UNTS at 431. As to Arts. 74(3) and 83(3), see Milano & Papanicolopulu (2011) at 611–621, 638.
34 See below Chapter 8, pp. 325–328.

of jurisdiction under Part XV, section 2, a territorial claim needs a maritime claim, and, where a party has elected the maximal extent of jurisdictional exclusions under Article 298, a maritime claim subject to jurisdiction will arise only if conduct in the disputed maritime area presents grounds for it. In answer to the *Chagos* majority's assertion that the UNCLOS drafters could not possibly have intended to allow adjudication of territorial disputes in association with residual UNCLOS claims, I suggest that they very well might have. They very well might have intended to supply not just a formal rule but also a procedural deterrent to prevent aggravation of disputes.[35]

With these considerations in view, the anti-*a contrario* argument is not convincing. It is not convincing to maintain that the possibility of a tribunal exercising jurisdiction over territorial issues connected to UNCLOS disputes arising out of a party's conduct in a maritime area would necessarily have been somehow anathema to the UNCLOS drafters. The drafters included provisions that serve public order by expressing the principle of non-aggravation of disputes in maritime areas (Article 74(3), Article 83(3)). A jurisdictional scheme that deters a state from engaging in conduct in disputed maritime areas that might aggravate the dispute serves the exact same purpose of public order. If UNCLOS jurisdiction embraces territorial disputes connected with residual UNCLOS disputes—as I believe it might—then the jurisdictional scheme deters the state from imposing itself in the disputed maritime area: it opens the door to an adjudication that the state would prefer to avoid.

Put differently, Articles 74(3) and 83(3) in effect declare: *Do not aggravate maritime disputes*. And jurisdiction over ancillary territorial disputes deriving from the residuum of UNCLOS disputes reinforces that declaration: *Do not aggravate maritime disputes, or else be ready to answer a claim about a subject matter that is likely even more important to you*. The state's interest in territory is not a consideration *against* the Kateka–Wolfrum *a contrario* argument; it is a consideration *for* it. Moreover, that argument, understood in this light, accords with the drafters' clearly expressed intention to dissuade conduct that might lead to clashes at sea.

The 'minor issue'

In the final paragraph of the section rejecting jurisdiction over Mauritius's claim challenging the United Kingdom's status as the coastal state in the

35 American constitutional lawyers might recognize a familiar relation here, that which Professor Amar suggested in his reading of the Bill of Rights as an instrument 'in which structure and rights mutually reinforce.' Akhil Reed Amar, 'The Bill of Rights as a Constitution' (1991) 100 YLJ 1131, 1201. Part XV, section 2, procedures correspond to the structure; Arts. 74(3) and 83(3) (non-aggravation) correspond to the rights.

Chagos, the majority said as follows: 'The Tribunal does not categorically exclude that in some instances a minor issue of territorial sovereignty could indeed be ancillary to a dispute concerning the interpretation or application of the Convention.'[36]

This concession gives rise to the logical problem that I identified above. The tribunal said that Article 288(1), the global 'any dispute' provision, is the source of the exclusion of territorial issues from UNCLOS jurisdiction. But, because it is a global provision, Article 288(1) has only global effect. It is not the source of a qualified territorial exclusion in the UNCLOS framework.

If a qualified territorial exclusion exists—as the tribunal said it does—then the provision in which to look for it is Article 298(1)(a)*(i)*. Where the tribunal majority said, in effect, that Article 298(1)(a)*(i)* was beside the point, the majority was, at best, confused. Article 298(1)(a)*(i)* had been the *entire* point for decades of inveterate denial that Part XV, section 2, could embrace territorial issues, and it was central to Mauritius's pleading. The United Kingdom sought to deflect the point, and the tribunal majority was only too ready to oblige.

Be that as it may, the award in *Chagos Maritime Protected Area*, with the majority's concessionary closing paragraph, shifts the ground and establishes that, at least in certain circumstances, Part XV, section 2, procedures might address territorial issues when settling maritime claims. However, serious questions remain unanswered, not least of all as regards the meaning of 'minor issue' and of 'ancillary' in the setting where a party invokes a territorial issue in an attempt to prevent the exercise of jurisdiction over a maritime dispute. Chapter 6 considers these matters in connection with the 21 February 2020 Award on Preliminary Objections in *Coast State Rights*.

Judges Kateka and Wolfrum dissent

As I have noted, Judges Kateka and Wolfrum appended a separate opinion in *Chagos Marine Protected Area* in which they dissented in part and concurred in part. The separate opinion holds interest for present purposes, because in it Judges Kateka and Wolfrum found serious fault with the majority's characterization of the dispute over the creation of an MPA, and thus with the majority's conclusion that jurisdiction under Article 288(1) does not embrace the dispute. They also found fault with the majority's reading of Article 298(1)(a)*(i)* and thus with the majority's conclusion that Part XV, section 2, jurisdiction does not embrace territorial issues such as those that Mauritius's claim entailed.

36 Award, ¶ 221.

The majority's mischaracterization of the dispute

As will be recalled, the majority in the *Chagos* case came to the view that Mauritius was, in effect, attempting to obtain an award on the long-subsisting territorial dispute over the Chagos Archipelago. Quite apart from whether Part XV, section 2, procedures might address territorial issues, Judges Kateka and Wolfrum recalled that an arbitrator or adjudicator is duty-bound to 'giv[e] particular attention to the formulation of the dispute chosen by the Applicant' in a case.[37] Judges Kateka and Wolfrum's observation here is based on well-established jurisprudence. Applying the jurisprudence to Mauritius's claim, Judges Kateka and Wolfrum recalled that Mauritius did not request dispositive relief from the Annex VII tribunal in regard to territorial sovereignty; and Mauritius *did* request relief in regard to rules expressly contained in UNCLOS addressing rights and obligations in the maritime area. Mauritius 'emphasized and re-emphasized in the written, as well as in the oral, proceedings' the limited scope of its claims.[38] Nothing in Mauritius's claims requested any relief in regard to the exercise of territorial sovereignty over the Chagos.[39]

Judges Kateka and Wolfrum recalled moreover that Mauritius had raised the territorial issues earlier—before instituting Annex VII proceedings—and had expressed itself satisfied with the United Kingdom's assurance that, in time, the United Kingdom would restore the Chagos Archipelago to Mauritius's effective control.[40] The transactions regarding the territory thus evinced that the claim that Mauritius put forward in the Annex VII proceedings—the claim that the United Kingdom's declaration of a maritime protected area constituted a breach of UNCLOS—was in truth not a claim about territory in disguise. Indeed, the *non ultra petita* principle, to which Judges Kateka and Wolfrum allude without calling it by name, would have prevented the tribunal from deciding on sovereignty over the territory.[41]

37 Kateka & Wolfrum, ¶ 6, quoting *Fisheries Jurisdiction (Spain v. Canada)*, Judgment, ICJ 1998 at p. 449 ¶ 30.
38 Kateka & Wolfrum at ¶ 10.
39 *Ibid.* at ¶ 13.
40 *Ibid.* at ¶ 11.
41 *Ibid.* at ¶ 14. The *non ultra petita* principle, which is widely applied, confines the decision to the legal claims that the parties have raised. See, for example, *Groupe Danone v. Commission of the European Communities*, Case C-3/06 P, Opinion of the Advocate General (Poiares Maduro), 16 November 2006 at [46]; *Guzzardi v. Italy* (6 November 1980), Dis. Op. Judge Sir Gerald Fitzmaurice at ¶ 4: (1980) 3 EHRR at 377–378; *Request for Interpretation of the Judgment of 15 June 1962 in the* Case Concerning the Temple of Preah Vihear (Cambodia v. Thailand) *(Cambodia v. Thailand)*, Judgment, ICJ 2013 p. 281, p. 307 ¶ 71; *Status and Use of the Waters of the Silala (Chile v. Bolivia)*, Decl. Judge Charlesworth, ICJ 2022 p. 667, p. 670

It is true that a tribunal is not bound to accept a party's completely artificial characterization of claim. Sir Christopher Greenwood (one of the members of the *Chagos* majority) in academic settings has admonished lawyers about attempting to fit an 'ungainly foot' of a substantive dispute into a 'glass slipper' of a narrow jurisdictional clause.[42] However, Sir Christopher's admonition assumes that the adjudicator has taken a reliable measure of the foot. Pronouncing it ungainly, and thus too large for the jurisdictional clause, does not in itself make it so. I return to the 'glass slipper' metaphor in Chapter 6 and the Conclusion.

The Kateka–Wolfrum dissent also reminds us of one of the main elements of the jurist's art: making distinctions between proximate but separable legal issues. According to Judges Kateka and Wolfrum, 'the issue of sovereignty over the Chagos Archipelago is merely an element in the reasoning of Mauritius and not to be decided by the Tribunal.'[43] The maxim the 'land dominates the sea' does not mean that territorial disputes and maritime disputes have no separate identity. The distinction that Judges Kateka and Wolfrum drew, but that the *Chagos* majority ignored, is that between a claim that is so suffused and permeated by an issue that the tribunal, if adjudicating the claim, adjudicates the issue; and a claim that the tribunal can adjudicate without depriving the issue its separate identity as an unsettled question between the parties.

The majority's unsupportable territorial exclusion

Judges Kateka and Wolfrum also differed with the majority in regard to the proper interpretation of the scope of Part XV, section 2, jurisdiction over territorial issues. The dissenting judges said that 'the reasoning of the Tribunal [as to the scope of jurisdiction] is not fully coherent.'[44] As the reader will infer from my earlier critique, this was an understatement.

Judges Kateka and Wolfrum rightly took the majority to task for having declared that the interpretation of Article 298(1)(a)*(i)* was beside the point.[45] The dissenters point out that '[t]here is no reasoning by the Tribunal' addressing Mauritius's argument that territorial issues may be subject to jurisdiction when they have a 'genuine link' to a dispute concerning the

¶ 8 (1 December), citing *Arrest Warrant of 11 April 2000 (Democratic Republic of Congo v. Belgium)*, Judgment, ICJ 2002 at p. 19 ¶ 43 (14 February).

42 Cited by Waibel, 'Investment Arbitration: Jurisdiction and Admissibility,' University of Cambridge Faculty of Law Legal Studies Research Paper Series, Paper No 9/2014 (February 2014) 11.

43 Kateka & Wolfrum at ¶ 17.

44 *Ibid.* at ¶ 27.

45 *Ibid.* at ¶ 26.

interpretation or application of UNCLOS.[46] The dissenters said that Article 288(1) implies limits on the scope of jurisdiction but that the limits are spelled out in specific terms in Articles 297 and 298.[47] Judges Kateka and Wolfrum then observed that the plain text of Article 297, which must be read as part of 'the system of exceptions [to jurisdiction] in the Convention seen as a whole,'[48] gives no support to the majority's view that territorial issues are excluded. According to Judges Kateka and Wolfrum:

> On the basis of a purely textual analysis of Article 297 ... it is evident that its exclusion of the jurisdiction of international courts and tribunals under Part XV ... does not embrace the exclusion of disputes for the reason that the decision on them would involve the consideration of any unsettled dispute concerning continental or insular land territory.[49]

Resisting the majority's assertion that Article 298(1)(a)(*i*) did not matter in the case, the dissenters noted that, in fact, it did. It was the United Kingdom's position 'that this clause could be read into Article 297 of the Convention on exceptions to ... jurisdiction.'[50] The United Kingdom's position was at loggerheads with both the text and the drafting history. As I related in Chapter 3, the territorial exclusion clause was deliberately placed elsewhere, *not* in Article 297. Judges Wolfrum and Kateka recalled the negotiating history, in particular the failure of explicit attempts to add territorial issues to the Article 297 exceptions to jurisdiction.[51] They concluded that 'one cannot read an additional exception into Article 297.'[52]

Turning to Article 288(1), Judges Kateka and Wolfrum advanced the *a contrario* argument—and reached the right conclusion: 'If such an inherent restriction for ... jurisdiction ... under Part XV ... existed, it would not have been necessary to include it in Article 298(1)(a).'[53] They found that it is 'not sustainable' to say that Article 298(1)(a)'s territorial clause 'is of a declaratory nature only': the drafters placed the clause there deliberately, and in so doing rejected insistent calls by participants in the Third Conference to place it in the exceptions provision, Article 297.[54] It is apposite here to note that Judges Kateka and Wolfrum are not the only jurists who have discerned this relationship between Articles 297 and 298(1)(a) and Article

46 *Ibid.* at ¶ 28.
47 *Ibid.* at ¶ 29.
48 *Ibid.* at ¶ 31.
49 *Ibid.* at ¶ 32.
50 *Ibid.* at ¶ 35.
51 *Ibid.* at ¶¶ 36–38.
52 *Ibid.* at ¶ 37.
53 *Ibid.* at ¶ 40.
54 *Ibid.* at ¶ 41.

288(1); a number of writers have drawn attention to it as well,[55] and the *Chagos* majority, though in a qualified and contradictory way, conceded that the relationship supports at least certain inferences as to the scope of Part XV jurisdiction.

A final point in the dissent that merits emphasis, and one that has enduring significance for the Convention, is that many disputes under the Convention 'require a decision on the existence of competences or their scope and thus on the sovereignty of the State concerned.'[56] While it is from territory that a state's maritime jurisdiction projects, maritime jurisdiction entails fine distinctions among rights and obligations. Leaving aside internal waters, which present special questions,[57] a state's jurisdiction over maritime areas is not assimilable to full sovereignty. It is, instead, a jurisdiction limited to the particular legal régimes for which the modern law of the sea provides. The 'existence of competences' of the state, or of the 'scope' of those competences, both in the sense of their spatial extent and their substantive content, is central to interpreting and applying the core provisions of UNCLOS. The core provisions become, in effect, impossible to apply if antecedent sovereignty questions remain unanswered. The three arbitrators of the *Chagos Marine Protected Area* majority, like other exponents of a broad territorial disputes exclusion, lay emphasis on the gravity of territorial disputes but ignored the gravity of a jurisdictional theory that all but renders large parts of UNCLOS a dead letter in a world of recrudescent territorial claims.

Concluding points on territory in the *Chagos Arbitration*

Unsatisfactory as the *Chagos* award is, visible in it are two limiting principles. First, there is the limitation in the tribunal's concession that *some* territorial issues yet might fall to be addressed under a Part XV, section 2, procedure. Second, there is the limitation in the tribunal's reasoning as regards the long tenure of the Chagos territorial dispute and the 'relative weight' of the dispute in the overall contestation between the parties. Both limitations, I argue below, are significant, but, as will be seen, the Annex VII tribunal in

55 See, for example, Forteau in Forteau & Thouvenin (eds.) (2017) 1006–1007. Also drawing an inference on the basis of *a contrario* reasoning from Article 298 (albeit on a somewhat different jurisdictional point) see Caflisch, 'The Delimitation of Marine Spaces between States with Opposite or Adjacent Coasts' in Dupuy & Vignes (eds.), vol. 1 (1991) 425, 492–493.

56 Judges Kateka & Wolfrum at ¶ 42.

57 Opinion is divided as to the degree to which internal waters are juristically assimilated into the land territory of the state. See Chapter 2, pp. 77–78, 90–91.

Coastal State Rights observed neither when circumstances called for their observance.

One might suppose that the majority opinion in the *Chagos Marine Protected Area Arbitration* at least puts the final nail in the coffin of the most extreme version of the exclusionary thesis. The extreme version is no straw man; exponents of the territorial exclusion have insisted upon that version of the exclusion for forty years. It is therefore noteworthy that the *Chagos* tribunal, dogmatic as it was, '[did] not categorically exclude that in some instances a minor issue of territorial sovereignty could indeed be ancillary to a dispute concerning the interpretation or application of the Convention.'[58] In light of that reservation, perhaps in an appropriate future case a future tribunal will place a more convincing interpretation on Part XV, section 2, in relation to territorial disputes. As we will see in Chapter 6, however, in *Coastal State Rights*—the case since *Chagos* that most clearly invited a fresh look at the scope of jurisdiction against the backdrop of a territorial issue—the tribunal did nothing of the sort.

58 *Chagos Marine Protected Area Arbitration*, ¶ 221.

5

Separating the land from the sea: South China Sea Arbitration (Philippines v. China)

The next case under a Part XV, section 2, procedure to call on arbitrators to consider land territory and its relation to jurisdiction, the *South China Sea Arbitration*, presented territorial questions in a rather different setting from the *Chagos* case.[1]

The South China Sea contains a number of small islands and other features subject to competing claims by the coastal states of the region, including the Philippines and China.[2] Unlike Mauritius in the *Chagos* case, the Philippines, as the applicant in *South China Sea*, did not ask the tribunal to say

1 For the main critique, see Talmon, *The South China Sea Arbitration: Jurisdiction, Admissibility, Procedure* (2022). See also Odom, 'South China Sea Arbitration Ruling: The U.S. Perspective 2016–2020' (2021) 97 *International Law Studies* 122–187; Tanaka, *Peaceful Settlement of International Disputes* (2018) 241–242; McGarry, 'Third Parties and Insular Features after the *South China Sea* Arbitration' (2017) 35 C(T)YBIL 99, 125–128; Parlett, 'Jurisdiction of the Arbitral Tribunal in Philippines v. China under UNCLOS and in the Absence of China' (2016) 110 AJIL Unbound 266–272; Sheng-ti Gau, 'The 2015 Award on Jurisdiction and Admissibility of the South China Sea Arbitration' (2015) 33 C(T)YBIL 62–108; Thi Lan Anh, 'The July 12 Award on the Historic Titles, Historic Rights and Impacts on State Practices in the South China Sea' (2016) 34 C(T)YBIL 39–55; Zou, 'China's Approach to UNCLOS and its Application to Disputed Issues in the South China Sea' in Barrett & Barnes (eds.), *UNCLOS as a Living Treaty* (2016) 363–382; essays in (2016) 110 AJIL Unbound 263ff. with an introduction by Boisson de Chazournes; Reed & Wong, 'Marine Entitlements in the South China Sea: The Arbitration between the Philippines and China' (2016) 110 AJIL 746–760; Serdy in *Proelss Commentary* (2017) 1918 at 1928–1930; Office of the Staff Judge Advocate, U.S. Indo-Pacific Command, 'The South China Sea Arbitration Award' (2021) 97 *International Law Studies* 62–68; Rothwell (2022) 27–37, 56–57, 120–121, 171–174; Kunoy (2021) 119–123.

2 For the geopolitical *mise en scène*, see Kraska & Pedrozo, *International Maritime Security Law* (2013) 313–354. See also chapters in Song, Zou, & Wu (eds.), *Major Law and Policy Issues in the South China Sea: European and American Perspectives* (2014). See also United States Department of State, Bureau of Oceans and International Environmental and Scientific Affairs, *Limits in the Seas. No. 150. People's Republic of China: Maritime Claims in the South China Sea* (January 2022). Cf. *Limits in the Seas. No. 143, China's Maritime Claims in the South China Sea* (December 2014).

which state is the 'coastal State' in regard to a feature subject to competing claims. It asked instead for a series of determinations clarifying, *inter alia*, whether there is any coast at all; and where a coast exists, which entitlements in appurtenant maritime areas may the sovereign with title to the land behind the coast assert. In aggregate, the determinations that the Philippines sought in regard to land aimed to open the jurisdictional door to further determinations in regard to China's conduct in the sea: they aimed to open the door to adjudicating the Philippines' claims that China's conduct constituted violations of the Philippines' maritime entitlements. To a significant extent, the Philippines convinced the tribunal that its claims indeed were subject to UNCLOS jurisdiction.

The *South China Seas* awards (that on jurisdiction and admissibility dated 29 October 2015 and the final award of 12 July 2016) held that a number of important questions of territorial status are subject to Part XV, section 2, jurisdiction. At least as noteworthy, the awards held that questions of sovereignty *as such*—that is, which among claimants to a territory has title to the territory—have a distinct juridical character and, because they are distinct questions, a tribunal well may address other sovereignty questions without settling those.

Disputed existence: is there land at all?

The principal maritime entitlements recognized under the modern law of the sea—the territorial sea, the EEZ, and the continental shelf—emanate from the land, and so, before asking whether a state has a maritime entitlement, one must ask whether a state has sovereignty over the land. There is however a prior question still: is there any land at all? The prior question arose in two forms in the *South China Sea* case. The Philippines asserted that certain features in the South China Sea, though exposed at low tide, are submerged at high tide, which, in accord with UNCLOS Article 13, would entail their categorization as low-tide elevations (LTEs) instead of islands; which, in turn, would entail that they generate no territorial sea of their own but only a 'parasitic' entitlement arising when they are wholly or partly within twelve nautical miles of land.[3] The Philippines also asserted that China had built artificial 'islands' in places where no naturally occurring islands exist, which under UNCLOS Articles 60 and 80 similarly entails that no land exists in

3 As to the description 'parasitic,' see Schofield, 'Defining the "Boundary" Between Land and Sea: Territorial Sea Baselines in the South China Sea' in Jayakumar, Koh, & Beckman (eds.), *The South China Sea Disputes and Law of the Sea* (2014) 21, 41.

those places for purposes of generating maritime entitlements under the Convention. Let us take each of these matters in turn.

Status of features as above or below water at high tide (Article 13)

UNCLOS Article 13 provides as follows:

> Article 13
>
> Low-tide elevations
>
> 1. A low-tide elevation is a naturally formed area of land which is surrounded by and above water at low tide but submerged at high tide. Where a low-tide elevation is situated wholly or partly at a distance not exceeding the breadth of the territorial sea from the mainland or an island, the low-water line on that elevation may be used as the baseline for measuring the breadth of the territorial sea.
>
> 2. Where a low-tide elevation is wholly situated at a distance exceeding the breadth of the territorial sea from the mainland or an island, it has no territorial sea of its own.[4]

The *South China Sea* Annex VII tribunal made a number of observations regarding the interpretation of Article 13 and of the material evidence that a party might adduce to establish whether or not an LTE exists in a given place.[5] The tribunal then proceeded to apply Article 13 to the evidence to determine that certain features in the South China Sea are LTEs and others 'high-tide features.'[6] (UNCLOS does not use the expression 'high-tide feature,' but the expression is a sensible shorthand.)[7]

The tribunal determined that Hughes Reef, Gaven Reef (South), Mischief Reef, and Second Thomas Shoal are LTEs.[8] It said that the evidence was too ambiguous to say for sure whether Subi Reef is an LTE or a high-tide feature but that the difference would not matter. This was because Subi

4 1833 UNTS at 403. See generally Müller, 'Les limites des espaces maritimes' in Forteau & Thouvenin (eds.) (2017) 529, 534–536; Churchill, Lowe & Sander (2022) at 61–62.

5 *South China Sea Arbitration*, Award (Merits), ¶¶ 305–322.

6 For forensic issues that arise when a dispute arises as to the existence of an LTE, see Grant, 'Islands, Rocks, Low-Tide Elevations' in Heidar (ed.), *Maritime Challenges in Asia* (2017) 221, 226–223.

7 The expression 'high-tide feature' reflects, in inverse, the definition of LTE in Art. 13(1), that definition referring in part to a feature 'above water at low tide but submerged at high tide'; and it is consonant with Art. 121(1) which defines an 'island' as 'a naturally formed area of land, surrounded by water, which is above water at high tide.'

8 *South China Sea*, Award (Merits), ¶¶ 358, 366, 378, 381.

Reef is within the territorial sea of an undoubted land feature (Thitu), and even if Subi Reef were a high-tide feature, this would not affect the scope of the territorial sea in the area, because no other possible LTE exists close enough to Subi Reef (i.e., within twelve nautical miles) to generate a more extensive territorial sea 'parasitic' on Subi Reef.[9]

How does a determination under Article 13 that a feature constitutes an LTE affect sovereignty? It is, perhaps, open to dispute in some cases, but the position now adopted by both the ICJ and at least one Annex VII tribunal—the *South China Sea* tribunal—is that an LTE is not susceptible to sovereign claim as land territory.[10] Writers largely agree.[11] A determination that a feature is an LTE thus entails in most cases, probably all, that a state may not assert sovereignty over it. In itself, this negative consequence is a determination in respect of a land territory issue: a state might assert that land territory exists in a certain place in the sea, but a determination that there is no land there and only an LTE (or that the place is fully submerged even at low tide) defeats the assertion of sovereign title. The existence of an LTE possibly affects the rights of the sovereign in further ways as well, for if the LTE is located within the breadth of the territorial sea of a sovereign's territory, then the LTE may serve as a baseline for measuring the breadth of the sovereign's territorial sea. This is the LTE's 'parasitic' effect, whereby it may generate a further twelve nautical mile extension of the territorial sea, and, with it, a further extension over that distance of those incidents of national sovereignty embodied in the territorial sea entitlement. Thus, latent in a determination that a feature is an LTE are juristic effects directly relevant to sovereignty: (1) the negative effect that a sovereign claim to the LTE as such is inadmissible; and (2) the potential affirmative effect that the sovereign may assert a further twelve nautical mile belt of territorial sea from the LTE, where the LTE is close enough to the sovereign's territory in accordance with Article 13.

Artificial islands and attempted sovereign appropriation

According to the *South China Sea* Annex VII tribunal, '[a]s a matter of law, human modification cannot change the seabed into a low-tide elevation or a low-tide elevation into an island. A low-tide elevation will remain a low-tide elevation under the Convention, regardless of the scale of the island or

9 *Ibid.* at ¶ 373.

10 *Nicaragua v. Colombia*, ICJ 2012 at p. 641 ¶ 26; *South China Sea Arbitration*, Award, ¶ 309 (12 July 2016). See also for analysis prior to those decisions Lavalle, 'The Rights of States over Low-tide Elevations' (2014) 29 IJMCL 457–479.

11 See, for example, Müller in Forteau & Thouvenin (eds.) (2017) 535.

12 *South China Sea Arbitration*, Award, ¶ 305 (12 July 2016).

installation built atop it.'[12] So, too, an 'area of seabed cannot be legally transformed into an island through human efforts,' and 'a rock [i.e., an island that does not generate the full suite of maritime entitlements] cannot be transformed into a fully entitled island through land reclamation.'[13] As the tribunal noted, these observations follow from the plain language of Articles 13 and 121.[14] Article 13(1) defines 'low-tide elevation' as 'a *naturally* formed area of land ... [etc.]' (emphasis added); Article 121(1) defines an 'island' as 'a *naturally* formed area of land ... [etc.]' (emphasis added).

At Mischief Reef, China had been engaged for some time in the construction of an artificial island. The tribunal, having found that Mischief Reef is an LTE, not a rock or island, further found that no fully entitled island exists close enough to Mischief Reef to generate a potential Chinese maritime entitlement in the area. On the basis of these findings, the tribunal determined that Mischief Reef is located in the Philippines' EEZ and on its continental shelf. The tribunal's reasoning here was as follows: the Philippines' territory (over which no sovereignty dispute existed) is within 200 nautical miles of Mischief Reef and, so, a potential EEZ and continental shelf entitlement extends to the reef; there is no land under any other state's sovereignty, or under disputed sovereignty, at Mischief Reef, or close enough to Mischief Reef to project any potential maritime entitlement into the reef and its vicinity; and so, Mischief Reef is part of the Philippines' EEZ and continental shelf.[15]

The tribunal's determination that Mischief Reef is within the Philippines' maritime jurisdiction had a significant impact on China's claims. It opened the door to the tribunal to adjudicate the Philippines' rights in Mischief Reef under Articles 56 and 60 of the Convention. Under Article 56, the coastal state in the EEZ has 'jurisdiction as provided for in the relevant provisions of [UNCLOS] with regard to: (i) the establishment and use of artificial islands, installations and structures.' Under Article 60, the coastal state has the '*exclusive* right to construct and to authorize and regulate the construction, operation and use of: (a) artificial islands' in the EEZ (emphasis added). Article 60(8) makes clear what Articles 13 and 121 well may be read to imply: '[a]rtificial islands, installations and structures do not possess the status of islands. They have no territorial sea of their own, and their presence does not affect the delimitation of the territorial sea, the exclusive economic zone or the continental shelf.' Article 80 provides that 'Article 60 applies *mutatis mutandis* to artificial islands, installations and structures on the continental shelf.' The *South China Sea* tribunal observed that '[t]hese

13 *Ibid.* at ¶ 508.
14 *Ibid.* at ¶¶ 305, 508.
15 *Ibid.* at ¶ 1030.

provisions speak for themselves.'[16] China's construction activities at Mischief Reef, which China conducted without permission from the Philippines, without notifying the Philippines, and against the protests of the Philippines, the tribunal determined constitute a 'manifest' violation of China's obligations under the Convention.[17]

Again, as with the tribunal's determination under Article 13 that certain features constitute LTEs, the tribunal's determination under Articles 60 and 80 that China's artificial island is in the Philippines' EEZ has latent or second-order implications for sovereignty. The artificial island generates none of the maritime entitlements that a sovereign might enjoy as projected from the sovereign's land domain. The artificial island entails an international law violation, because it intrudes in the EEZ and on the continental shelf of another sovereign.

A further point of interest in the *South China Sea* tribunal's treatment both of LTEs and of artificial islands is the tribunal's approach to evidence. China did not participate in the proceedings, thus depriving the tribunal of party submissions.[18] Moreover, China did not permit in-person observation of the features concerned. Most strikingly in respect of the artificial islands, direct observation of the natural characteristics of the features would have been impossible anyway: 'human modifications ha[d] obscured the[ir] original status.'[19] Conduct of the respondent state at the scene, whether or not the respondent state intended it to, created forensic challenges for the adjudicator.

A temptation, perhaps, would seize an adjudicator in a situation such as this to resort to avoidance strategies. For example, the adjudicator might declare that the factual questions do not matter. The adjudicator, to similar effect, might declare that the factual questions that the claimant has raised exceed the adjudicator's jurisdiction. The *South China Sea* tribunal, however, far from avoiding the factual questions, addressed them head-on. According to the tribunal, 'it [is] important that the absence of full information not be permitted to bar the conclusions that reasonably can be drawn on the basis of other evidence.'[20] Thus, for example, the tribunal turned to expert evidence, which was 'unequivocal' that recent construction activities had had massive and harmful effects on the marine environment.[21] The tribunal concluded that China's artificial island-building activities 'have caused

16 *Ibid.* at ¶ 1035.
17 *Ibid.* at ¶ 1038.
18 See generally Yu, 'China's Informal Participation in the Annex VII Philippines v. China Arbitral Tribunal's Proceedings' (2015) 30 IJMCL 54–92.
19 Award, ¶ 321.
20 *Ibid.* at ¶ 321.
21 *Ibid.* at ¶ 978. Cf. *ibid.* at ¶ 980.

devastating and long-lasting damage to the marine environment.'[22] The tribunal also relied on satellite imagery (albeit with special caution),[23] nautical charts, and sailing directions to determine which features were above, and which below, water at high tide.[24]

It might seem a commonplace to say that adjudicators, in accordance with the evidentiary principles that apply to their procedure, should ask for evidence as necessary, and scrutinize it, to reach conclusions as to the matters that the parties have placed in issue. However, as we will see in Chapter 6, not all adjudicators have done so with equal fidelity to their fact-finding function.

Disputed status: what maritime entitlement does the land generate? (Article 121(3))

Not all land under the sovereignty of a state generates the full suite of potential entitlements in the sea. Whether the sovereign has a potential entitlement to an EEZ or continental shelf in relation to an island turns on whether the island satisfies terms set out under UNCLOS Article 121(3). Article 121 is entitled the '[r]égime of islands.' Paragraph 1 of Article 121 defines 'island' as 'a naturally formed area of land, surrounded by water, which is above water at high tide.' Paragraph 2 provides that an island generates a territorial sea, an EEZ, and a continental shelf in the same way as other land territory—subject to paragraph 3, which expresses an exception. Under paragraph 3, '[r]ocks which cannot sustain human habitation or economic life of their own shall have no exclusive economic zone or continental shelf.'[25] The Convention contains no provision defining the terms 'sustain human habitation or economic life of their own.'

As is evident from the text of paragraph 3, read together with paragraphs 1 and 2 of Article 121, a rock is a special case of 'island.'[26] A rock is an island that generates a potential entitlement to the territorial sea but not

22 *Ibid.* at ¶ 983.

23 See *ibid.* at ¶ 326.

24 See generally *ibid.* at ¶¶ 322–332; and for evidentiary analysis as to specific features, ¶¶ 333ff.

25 1833 UNTS at 442. See generally Caflisch, 'Les espaces marins attachés à des îles ou rochers' in Forteau & Thouvenin (eds.) (2017) 477 at 482–489; Churchill, Lowe, & Sander (2022) at 89–99. For a summary of aspects of the drafting history, see Anderson, 'Islands and Rocks in the Modern Law of the Sea' in Nordquist, Moore, Soons, & Kim (eds.), *The Law of the Sea Convention: US Accession and Globalization* (2012) 307, 308–309.

26 See Colombia, Rejoinder, 18 June 2010, ¶ 3.10; *Territorial and Maritime Dispute (Nicaragua v. Colombia)*, Judgment, ¶ 139 (19 November 2012); *South China Sea Arbitration*, Award, ¶ 280 (12 July 2016).

to an EEZ or continental shelf. Paragraph 3, however, requires a wider investigation before a judge or arbitrator places a definite interpretation on it or applies it to a particular claim.

In the *South China Sea* case, the régime of islands, especially the interpretation and application of Article 121, paragraph 3, was a matter of contestation. The Philippines and China disputed the categorization of a number of features under the régime of islands. The features in dispute were among those subject to sovereignty disputes between China and the Philippines (and other states as well). If a feature were determined to be a mere rock, then the direct juridical consequence would be that the feature 'shall have no [EEZ] or continental shelf.' A further juridical consequence would be that, in the geography of the South China Sea, the feature would not generate a potential maritime entitlement overlapping with a potential maritime entitlement of another state. This is because the features in dispute are too far from other land territory and from other disputed features that might be land territory for their potential maritime entitlements to overlap—provided that the features in dispute generate no more than the twelve nautical mile belt of territorial sea. Thus, if the tribunal were to conclude that the features are mere rocks, then that conclusion would disentangle the parties from what otherwise would be a series of maritime delimitation disputes.

Disentangling the parties from maritime delimitation disputes—that is, demonstrating that there are no such disputes between them—was essential to the Philippines' theory of the case. China, as is its right to do under Article 298, excludes maritime delimitation disputes from compulsory procedure. The Philippines sought to demonstrate that their claims alleging that China's conduct violated the Philippines' maritime rights could be settled *without* adjudicating any maritime delimitation disputes.[27]

Prior to the *South China Sea* case, a number of cases had led courts or tribunals to touch on Article 121, but no plain guidance had emerged in regard to the interpretation or application of paragraph 3.[28] Roger O'Keefe called paragraph 3 'a curious and cryptic provision, a poorly drafted compromise text.'[29] The interpretative practice has been addressed

27 See *South China Sea Arbitration*, Award on Jurisdiction and Admissibility (29 October 2015), ¶¶ 368–369, 394. See also Award (12 July 2016), ¶ 162(b). For a critical view of this part of the Award, see Gau, 'Article 121(3)' (2019) 50 ODIL 49–69.

28 *South China Sea*, Award, 12 July 2016, ¶ 474: 'Article 121 has not previously been the subject of significant consideration by courts or arbitral tribunals ... [T]he scope of application of its paragraph (3) is not clearly established.'

29 O'Keefe, 'Island Dependencies' (1996) 45 ICLQ 408, 411. See to similar effect Oude Elferink, 'Article 121 (3)' in Pratt & Allison-Brown (eds.), *Borderlands under Stress* (2000) 393–394. Cf. Crawford, 'Islands as Sovereign Nations' (1989) 38 ICLQ 277, 294–295.

elsewhere.[30] For present purposes, it suffices to recall that the *South China Sea* Annex VII tribunal engaged in detailed examination of the text,[31] and then applied the text to the complex facts pertaining to the land features that the Philippines and China disputed.[32] The tribunal concluded that the largest disputed features of the South China Sea—Itu Aba, Thitu, West York, Spratly Island, South-West Cay, and North-East Cay—'are not capable of sustaining an economic life of their own within the meaning of Article 121(3),' and that 'the other, less significant high-tide features in the Spratly Islands, which are even less capable of sustaining economic life' are not fully entitled islands either.[33] In consequence, these features generate no potential EEZ or continental shelf for any state, which is to say that no state may validly claim such entitlements on the basis of the features.[34] In turn, the absence of overlapping potential EEZ or continental shelf claims meant that the Philippines and China had no relevant delimitation disputes. The absence of delimitation disputes, in turn, opened the door for the tribunal to adjudicate a range of claims that the Philippines had advanced against China for China's conduct in the South China Sea.

We should recall here that, when the adjudication of a dispute requires a definition of an UNCLOS term that UNCLOS does not define, tribunals have considered sources extrinsic to UNCLOS in order to define it. As I noted in Chapter 2, recourse to extrinsic sources was visible in *Duzgit Integrity* and *Arctic Sunrise*.[35] In *South China Sea*, the undefined terms in Article 121(3)—'human habitation,' 'economic life of their own'—similarly occasioned the tribunal to employ this interpretive technique.

Finally, the Annex VII tribunal, in light of China's nonappearance in the proceedings, 'consider[ed] it imperative to examine *proprio motu* whether any further exception to its jurisdiction follows from Article 298.'[36] The tribunal here noted that it was obliged by Article 9 of Annex VII 'to satisfy itself that is has jurisdiction over the dispute.'[37] Two further optional exceptions

30 See, for example, Grant in Heidar (ed.) (2017) 234–246; Song, 'The Application of Article 121(3) of the Law of the Sea Convention to the Five Selected Disputed Islands in the South China Sea' (2009) 27 C(T)YBIL 43–66; Hafner, 'Itu Aba versus Clipperton' (2016) 34 C(T)YBIL 1–19; Guilfoyle, 'The Regime of Islands in the Aftermath of the South China Sea Arbitration' (2018) 112 ASIL Proc. 7–10; and, earlier, Charney, 'Rocks That Cannot Sustain Human Habitation' (1999) 93 AJIL 863–877. See also writings on the *South China Sea Arbitration*, Chapter 5, nn. 1, 2.

31 *South China Sea Arbitration*, Award (12 July 2016), ¶¶ 475–553.

32 *Ibid.* at ¶¶ 554–624.

33 *Ibid.* at ¶ 625.

34 *Ibid.* at ¶ 626.

35 See Chapter 2, pp. 71–72, 78–82, 86, 88.

36 *South China Sea,* Award on Jurisdiction and Admissibility, 29 October 2015, ¶ 367.

37 *Ibid.*

applicable to China under China's 2006 Declaration under Article 298 that the tribunal considered to that end merit a brief word for present purposes:[38] the exception of disputes 'concerning the interpretation or application of articles 15, 74 and 83 … involving historic bays or titles' (Article 298(1)(a)*(i)*) and the exception of disputes 'concerning military activities, including military activities by government vessels and aircraft engaged in non-commercial service.'

Disputed nature and validity of claim: does the 'historic title' exception apply?

In addressing the possibility that the exclusion of disputes involving historic bays or titles would prevent the exercise of jurisdiction over claims of the Philippines, the *South China Sea* tribunal recalled that it needed to determine 'the nature and validity of any claim by China to historic rights in the South China Sea,' for it is not the case that every claim to historic rights is one that corresponds to the concept of 'historic bays or titles' embodied in the Article 298(1)(a)*(i)* exclusion.[39] In other words, just because a party makes a claim does not mean that the claim is one embraced by the exclusion. The same observation applies to the other limiting terms of Article 298(1)(a)*(i)*, including those that exclude 'any dispute that necessarily involves the concurrent consideration of any unsettled dispute concerning sovereignty or other rights over continental or insular land territory.' The 'nature and validity of any claim' that such a dispute exists is not a matter that a tribunal can settle on purely formal grounds; it is a matter into which the tribunal must inquire. As will be seen in Chapter 6, however, the Annex VII tribunal in *Coastal State Rights* did little, if anything, to inquire when the claims in the case raised the question whether a sovereignty dispute existed. By contrast, the *South China Sea* tribunal inquired with care into the 'nature and validity of any claim by China to historic rights in the South China Sea.'

The *South China Sea* tribunal started by acknowledging the lack of clarity in China's position about alleged historic rights.[40] The tribunal stated that

38 People's Republic of China, Declaration under Article 298 (25 August 2006), 2834 UNTS 327.

39 *South China Sea*, Award, 12 July 2016, ¶ 162(a). See generally Symmons, *Historic Waters and Historic Rights*, 2nd edn. (2019).

40 As to which, see Symmons (2019) at 213–215, 217, 223–224 and as to problems of ambiguity in other possible instances of historic claims *ibid.* at 213–216, 217–223, 225–230. Yoshifumi Tanaka notes that even the number of dashes is uncertain. Tanaka, 'Reflections on Historic Rights in the South China Sea Arbitration (Merits)' (2017) 32 IJMCL 458, 462.

this would not prevent it from reaching a conclusion about those alleged rights: 'Certain facts,' the tribunal stated, 'can ... be established.'[41] The tribunal proceeded to consider in detail China's so-called nine-dash line,[42] and what China's invocation of the line might mean for China's claim to historic rights.[43] In proceeding with confidence that '[c]ertain facts can ... be established' about China's 'nine-dash line,' the tribunal did not accept China's invocation of the line at face value. It did not accept without scrutiny China's position that the line expresses a legal claim that would bar the tribunal from exercising jurisdiction over maritime claims that the Philippines had articulated. Instead, the tribunal proceeded to perform the forensic function that parties expect an adjudicator to perform. In this, the tribunal acted consistently with its approach to other contested issues in the case, such as the status of certain low-lying features where China's artificial island-building had effaced much of the physical evidence. Obscurity, where it is the result of the conduct of a party that seeks procedural advantage from it, should not disadvantage the other party.

What did the tribunal conclude about China's assertions in respect of alleged historic rights in the South China Sea?

For one thing, the tribunal determined with no difficulty that the South China Sea is not a bay and, so, it cannot be an 'historic bay.'[44] The question, therefore, was whether China made a claim to 'historic title' in the Article 298(1)(a)*(i)* sense.[45] The tribunal, in approaching the question, undertook a detailed review of China's claims practice.[46] The tribunal, on the basis of that review, understood that China had made no claim to territorial sea or internal waters, other than claims that would project from islands in the normal UNCLOS way.[47] The tribunal, after further analysis of the meaning of 'historic title' and of China's conduct, concluded that 'China does not claim historic title to the waters of the South China Sea, but rather a constellation of historic rights short of title,' and, thus, that China's claims are not embraced by the 'historic title' exclusion.[48]

41 *South China Sea*, Award, 12 July 2016, ¶ 180.
42 *Ibid.* at ¶¶ 181–187. As to China's nine-dashed line generally (also known as 'China's U-shaped line'), see contributions in (2012) 43 ODIL 1–69.
43 *South China Sea*, Award, 12 July 2016 at ¶¶ 200–201.
44 *Ibid.* at ¶ 205. As to historic bays generally, see Churchill, Lowe, & Sander (2022) 81–83; Symmons (2019) at 104–111.
45 *South China Sea*, Award, 12 July 2016, ¶ 205.
46 *Ibid.* at ¶¶ 207–214.
47 *Ibid.* ¶ 214.
48 *Ibid.* at ¶ 229. See further Kopela, 'Historic Titles and Historic Rights in the Law of the Sea in the Light of the South China Sea Arbitration' (2017) 48 ODIL 181–207; Tanaka (2017) 32 IJMCL at 463–466.

In other words, China's assertions about the waters of the South China Sea did not come up to the level of an 'historic title' claim for purposes of Article 298(1)(a)*(i)*. China's assertions undershot the mark.

But what about assertions that go too far? What is an adjudicator to do if a state asserts an 'historic title' so far-reaching that it would overturn what almost everybody understands to be a settled modern legal right? The tribunal was clear that it was *not* determining how to address 'expansive claims to historic title extending well beyond those that may have been anticipated when the Convention was concluded in 1982.'[49] The tribunal nevertheless drew attention to expansive claims as a problem for UNCLOS adjudication. In so doing, the tribunal suggested that it is at least open to question whether 'expansive claims,' potentially of an extra-legal nature, would be properly treated as triggering the Article 298(1)(a)*(i)* jurisdictional exclusion.

The tribunal's analysis of China's assertion of a 'constellation of historic rights short of title' suggested, further, that the answer might well be negative—that is, that 'expansive claims' might fall outside the *legal* claims that UNCLOS allows and, thus, even if an objecting party asserted such claims with perfect clarity, they would not prevent a tribunal from exercising jurisdiction. The tribunal observed that '[n]o article of the Convention expressly provides for or permits the continued existence of historic rights to the living or non-living resources of the exclusive economic zone.'[50] Considering the matter further, the tribunal concluded that 'the text and context of the Convention [are] clear in superseding any historic rights that a State may once have had in the areas that now form part of the exclusive economic zone and continental shelf of another State.'[51]

This conclusion—that UNCLOS has superseded certain kinds of rights—is of considerable importance to general public order. It affirms, in the setting of the law of the sea, that not every *assertion* of right constitutes a legally valid *claim* to a right. A modern law has developed that affirms certain maritime entitlements of states—and removes certain earlier claims from the law. As Chapter 1 recalled, international law since 1945, in similar fashion, removes claims to change a boundary by force. The law of the sea, in this way, is congruent with a longer train of legal development.

49 *South China Sea*, Award, ¶ 229. As to the untenability of expansive claims (with particular reference to China's South China Sea claims), see Symmon (2019) at 97–99, 100, 102.
50 *South China Sea*, Award, 12 July 2016, ¶ 239.
51 *Ibid*., ¶ 247.

Disputed use: does the 'military activities' exception apply?

Turning to the Article 298(1)(b) exception of disputes 'concerning military activities, including military activities by government vessels and aircraft engaged in non-commercial service,' the tribunal drew attention to 'China's repeated statements that its installations and island construction are intended to fulfil civilian purposes.'[52] The tribunal would 'not deem activities to be military in nature when China itself has consistently resisted such classifications and affirmed the opposite at the highest level.'[53] Accordingly, the 'military activities' exception did not prevent the tribunal from addressing claims of the Philippines.

If, instead, China had asserted a change in character of its activities, from civilian to military, then the assertion would have required further scrutiny. As noted above, where China did assert a state of affairs that would have placed a Philippine claim within one of the exceptions to jurisdiction, the tribunal inquired into the evidence. The tribunal based its conclusions, not on party assertion, but on evidence, as regarded the physical characteristics of low-lying features for purposes of Article 13; the socioeconomic characteristics of small islands for purposes of Article 121; and the existence of an 'historic title' claim for purposes of the relevant branch of Article 298(1)(a)*(i)*. It is to be suggested that, where recent practice by an objecting party runs *against* the party's objection, the need for evidence, if a tribunal is to accept the objection, is all the more pronounced. We will see in Chapter 6 that recent practice by the party objecting to jurisdiction in *Coastal State Rights* baldly contradicted that party's assertion—indispensable to its objection—that a sovereignty dispute exists between it and the applicant state. But the tribunal accepted the objection with practically no evidence at all.

South China Sea: assessment

The *South China Sea* tribunal reached consequential legal determinations against the backdrop of well-known territorial disputes in the South China Sea. Distinct from various disputes in regard to the maritime areas in the region, several coastal states of the region maintain claims to some or all of the small islands in the South China Sea. China and Vietnam maintain claims to all or most of the islands, the Philippines, Malaysia, and Indonesia

52 *Ibid.*, ¶ 1027.
53 *Ibid.*, ¶ 1028.

to some of the islands.[54] The Philippines, wary of the limitations widely imputed to jurisdiction under Part XV, section 2, 'stated at all stages of [the] arbitration that it [was] not asking [the] Tribunal to rule on the territorial sovereignty aspect of its disputes with China.'[55]

Tullio Treves, in the *Proelss Commentary*, agrees that the Philippines' claims indeed were limited in that way: 'the Philippines ... had couched its requests in such a way as to avoid raising questions of sovereignty.'[56] The Philippines recalled that, in *Chagos Marine Protected Area*, Mauritius had asked for a determination in regard to which state was the coastal state in the Chagos Archipelago. The Philippines distinguished its own claims in this regard, emphasizing that it asked the tribunal for no determination as to sovereignty over any land feature in the South China Sea.[57] In other words, the matter of the scope of the sovereignty exclusion simply did not arise in the *South China Sea Arbitration*, or at least not in the frontal way that some writers and China insist that it did.

The Philippines also took care to fashion its claims so as to avoid any request to delimit areas of overlapping potential maritime entitlement. As noted, China excludes all maritime boundary delimitations from its acceptance of compulsory dispute settlement.[58]

China, through its position paper,[59] sharply differed with the Philippines' characterization of its claims. China submitted that the Philippines' submissions included requests for the tribunal to adjudicate a dispute over land territory (sovereignty) and maritime boundary delimitation. In particular, China argued that '[u]ntil and unless the sovereignty over the relevant maritime features is ascertained and maritime delimitation completed, this category of claims of the Philippines cannot be decided upon.'[60] China said that the Philippines' claims presented issues that 'constitute an *integral part* of maritime delimitation' as well.[61]

54 Articulating Vietnam's territorial claims see Note Verbale from the Permanent Mission of the Socialist Republic of Vietnam to the United Nations to the Secretary-General of the United Nations, No. 86/HC-2009 (8 May 2009): www.un.org/depts/los/clcs_new/submissions_files/mysvnm33_09/vnm_chn_2009re_mys_vnm_e.pdf

55 *South China Sea Arbitration*, Award on Jurisdiction and Admissibility (29 October 2015), ¶ 8. See also *ibid.* at ¶ 26.

56 Treves, 'Article 286' in *Proelss Commentary* (2017) 1848.

57 *South China Sea Arbitration*, Award on Jurisdiction and Admissibility at ¶ 142.

58 *Ibid.*

59 China did not appear in the proceedings but, instead, communicated its views as a non-participating party.

60 Award on Jurisdiction and Admissibility, ¶ 137, quoting China's Position Paper, ¶ 27.

61 *Ibid.* at ¶ 366 (emphasis added).

The fault in China's objections is that they read into the Convention a series of dependencies among substantive provisions that are not visible in the text. To say whether a feature is a 'rock' or a fully entitled island requires the interpretation and application of Article 121. Nothing in Article 121 makes its terms dependent upon the question of which state holds sovereignty over the feature in question. Similarly, where no overlapping potential entitlements can exist, because no relevant coasts are close enough to one another, the juridical situation is evident from the interpretation and application of the rules defining the breadth of the territorial sea and EEZ and the extent of the continental shelf, applied to the geographic facts of the maritime area concerned. An adjudicator can interpret and apply those rules independently of the question which state is sovereign. Nor does Article 13 subordinate its definition of low-tide elevation to a determination as to which state holds sovereignty (if the feature in question turns out to be a rock) or entitlement in the maritime area (if the feature turns out to be an LTE or less).[62] In respect of the features that the Philippines' pleadings addressed, the tribunal did not need to determine which state holds sovereignty over the disputed coasts of the region to recognize that there are no overlapping potential entitlements. The tribunal could apply the law to the geographic facts without settling the outstanding disputes over geo*political* facts.

The tribunal was careful to avoid dicta that expressed a position of law on the scope of the territorial exclusion under Part XV, section 2. The care that the tribunal took in this regard is visible in several passages in the *South China Sea* awards. For example, in assessing whether a section 1 procedural deficiency existed that would have barred jurisdiction over the Philippines' Article 121 claims,[63] and in concluding that no such deficiency existed, the tribunal said as follows: 'This dispute is not barred from the Tribunal's consideration by any requirement of Section 1 of Part XV.' In the same sentence, the tribunal went on to say that this 'is not a dispute concerning sovereignty over the features, which would remain entirely unaffected by the Tribunal's determination.'[64] It used similar formulations in respect of other parts of the case. For example, regarding the Philippines Article 13 claims, the tribunal said that there was no bar raised 'by any requirement of Section 1 of Part XV' and that '[t]his is not a dispute concerning

62 Of course, sovereignty matters in the application of Art. 13 where a state asserts a further territorial sea envelope on the basis of an LTE as a baseline: the LTE generates an entitlement in that situation only in 'parasitic' fashion upon sovereign territory. However, asserting that a state has a particular maritime entitlement based on an LTE is plausible only where there is an LTE; determining whether there is an LTE is logically prior to the potential entitlement.

63 See above pp. 59–60, 62.

64 Award on Jurisdiction and Admissibility (29 October 2015), ¶ 404.

sovereignty over the features.'[65] The tribunal thus emphasized the point that sovereignty was not in issue.

The tribunal also engaged here in a subtle distinction in phrasing that reinforces the point—and, moreover, avoids affirming the thesis that UNCLOS jurisdiction does not embrace sovereignty questions. In referring to the requirements of jurisdiction under Part XV, section 1, the tribunal referred to the specific text in the Convention expressing them. In referring to sovereignty disputes, by contrast, the tribunal did not say that the absence of sovereignty disputes is a requirement of jurisdiction, and it did not refer to sovereignty disputes with reference to any Convention text. It simply said that there were no sovereignty disputes that needed to be settled for present purposes, because the Philippines' claims were severable from the sovereignty disputes that exist in the region. In short, the tribunal acknowledged certain UNCLOS provisions that could require it to refrain from exercising jurisdiction, where the exclusionary purpose of those provisions is self-evident on the Convention text (i.e., disputes not adequately negotiated in accordance with Part XV, section 1), but it did not say, and it avoided implying, that any UNCLOS provision requires it to refrain from exercising jurisdiction in respect of territorial issues.

On this point—the absence in the *South China Sea* awards of affirmation of the putative sovereignty exclusion—a degree of confusion has arisen. As we will see in Chapter 6, arbitrators in later cases have indicated that the *South China Sea* awards join the *Chagos Marine Protected Area* award in affirming the putative exclusion, and jurists writing in academic capacity have indicated the same.[66] The *South China Sea* awards, however, on the better view, do not affirm the exclusion.

China, immediately after the final award in the *South China Sea Arbitration*, declared that the award was not a legal instrument but 'null and void.'[67] China's sometimes-advisors or publicists denounced the award prolifically. Stefan Talmon, for example, before the tribunal adopted its final award, lamented the 29 October 2015 jurisdiction and admissibility award. According to Professor Talmon, despite long and patient support for UNCLOS, China now learned that the 'provisions [of UNCLOS] on

65 *Ibid.* at ¶ 403.

66 See, for example, Kunoy (2021) 126.

67 Campbell & Salidjanova, U.S.-China Economic and Security Review Commission, Issue Brief, *South China Sea Arbitration Ruling: What Happened and What's Next?* 4 (12 July 2016), quoting China's Ministry of Foreign Affairs, Statement of the Ministry of Foreign Affairs of the People's Republic of China on the Award of 12 July 2016 of the Arbitral Tribunal in the South China Sea Arbitration Established at the Request of the Republic of the Philippines, 12 July 2016. www.fmprc.gov.cn/mfa_eng/zxxx_662805/t1379492.shtml

compulsory dispute settlement [...] may be exploited by other states for political reasons.'[68] Talmon, who was writing in one of China's state-run English-language outlets,[69] suggested that China's 'territorial sovereignty' might be 'undermined by a decision of an arbitral tribunal established under the Convention' and said that this would be good reason for China to denounce the Convention.[70]

Following the final award, the National Institute for South China Sea Studies published a *Legal Critique of the Award of the Arbitral Tribunal in the Matter of the South China Sea Arbitration*.[71] The first 'core' conclusion of the *Critique* was as follows: 'The principal issues at stake in establishing China's maritime entitlements in the South China Sea are inextricably linked to questions of territorial title over land and maritime areas in the South China Sea—issues that are clearly excluded from compulsory international dispute settlement under UNCLOS.'[72]

According to the critics, the readiness of the tribunal to address and settle issues that concerned territory, even though in settling those issues the tribunal left open the question of *title* to territory, overstepped the limits of Part XV, section 2. Unsurprisingly, the *Critique* invoked Article 298(1)(a)*(i)*, asserting that the 'land territory' clause (tertiary though it is in the architecture of Part XV, section 2) requires the complete ouster of any claim addressing any UNCLOS provision concerning land.[73] Indicative of the breadth of the assertion in the *Critique*, its authors said that 'sovereignty' claims excluded by Article 298(1)(a)*(i)* extend to claims to 'waters which are beyond 12 NM [nautical miles] of the [Spratly] islands.'[74] Evidently, the half-hearted attempt by the Annex VII tribunal in *Chagos Marine Protected Area* to sweep Article 298(1)(a)*(i)* under the carpet did not convince China. It was in that UNCLOS provision that China seems to have understood a sweeping sovereignty exclusion to reside.

68 Stefan Talmon, 'Denouncing UNCLOS Remains Option for China after Tribunal Ruling,' *Global Times* (English edition), 3 March 2016. www.globaltimes.cn/content/971707.shtml

69 And one known for 'war-mongering' and 'bellicose' editorials. See Larson, 'China's Fox News: Meet Global Times, the Angry Chinese Government Mouthpiece that Makes Bill O'Reilly Seem Fair and Balanced,' *Foreign Policy* (31 October 2011).

70 *Ibid.*

71 The article appeared in the *Asian Yearbook of International Law* and described itself as 'an independent article' and the output of a 'research team ... formed ... under the direction of Dr. Shicun Wu, President of NISCSS and ... composed of international law scholars, lawyers, historians and technical experts from the United Kingdom, the Netherlands, the United States and China.' (2018) 24 Asian YBIL 151, 151.

72 *Ibid.* at 151. See also *ibid.* at 156.

73 *Ibid.* at 157.

74 *Ibid.* at 162.

As to China's assertion of a 'sovereignty' claim to waters 'beyond 12 NM of the [Spratly] islands,' this makes no sense under the modern law of the sea. China's 'sovereignty' claim to such ocean areas are per se exorbitant and insupportable.[75] But it is difficult to know for sure *what* claims China espouses. If the Annex VII tribunal in *South China Sea* understood China's claims correctly, then China was *not* asserting 'sovereignty' in waters 'beyond 12 NM of the [Spratly] islands.' It is to be asked, then, whether the *Critique* expresses a formal Chinese position. If the *Critique* expresses a formal Chinese position, then it extends China's claims into 'expansive claims to historic title extending well beyond those that may have been anticipated when the Convention was concluded in 1982.'[76] As I noted above, the tribunal did not take a position as to what to do about sovereignty claims of that exorbitant kind, but it suggested that they are incompatible with modern law and, thus, are insufficient to trigger the exclusion of jurisdiction under Part XV, section 2. The tribunal suggested, in short, that such claims are to be rejected. Whether on their substance or as a stratagem of jurisdictional objection, claims that exceed the plain limits of modern international law are not claims that an adjudicator should treat as generating legal effects under that law. A lesson may be discerned here for claims practice broadly, extending to maritime areas and to land territory as well. An assertion that does not constitute a claim belonging to the relevant legal system should not stand in the way of adjudication.

Not all of China's claims in the South China Sea are exorbitant. Many, if not most, of China's claims to islands in the South China Sea are more or less ordinary territorial claims. However, even those claims China, or China's advocates in the post-award *Critique* and elsewhere, have characterized in an expansive way. Central to the critics' reading of the *South China Sea* awards was the critics' premise, largely unspoken, that a tribunal cannot separate issues that Part XV, section 2, embraces from those that it does not. This is the premise visible where the critics say that a tribunal has no authority to determine whether a feature is a rock or a fully entitled island for purposes of Article 121(3) without trespassing against the supposed bar

75 See U.S. Department of State, Bureau of Oceans and International Environmental and Scientific Affairs, Limits in the Seas, No. 150 (January 2022), People's Republic of China: Maritime Claims in the South China Sea, 11–14, and regarding China's 'historic rights' claims, *ibid.* at 27–29. See also Office of the Staff Judge Advocate, U.S. Indo-Pacific Command, 'U.S. Protests China's Maritime Claims in the South China Sea' (2021) 97 *International Law Studies* 89–94; Secretary of State Michael R. Pompeo, U.S. Position on Maritime Claims in the South China Sea, Press Statement (13 July 2020). https://2017–2021.state.gov/u-s-position-on-maritime-claims-in-the-south-china-sea/index.html

76 *South China Sea*, Award, ¶ 229.

prohibiting adjudication of sovereignty disputes. The premise is doubtful. Even if the supposed bar is as extensive as the *Chagos* majority said, it would take an expansive reading of Article 121(3) to conclude that applying that UNCLOS provision necessarily entails deciding a sovereignty dispute.

The *South China Sea* tribunal treated the more or less ordinary territorial disputes in the South China Sea as distinct from the disputes that the Philippines sought to adjudicate. The tribunal relied on well-known jurisprudence to justify its method here. The tribunal recalled that 'it is entirely ordinary and expected that two States with a relationship as extensive and multifaceted as that existing between the Philippines and China would have disputes in respect of several distinct matters.'[77] Quoting the ICJ in *United States Diplomatic and Consular Staff in Tehran*, the tribunal said that there are 'no grounds to "decline to take cognizance of one aspect of a dispute merely because that dispute has other aspects, however important."'[78] The tribunal emphasized that the Philippines had 'not asked the Tribunal to rule on sovereignty' expressly, and the tribunal accepted that none of the Philippines' claims required 'an implicit determination of sovereignty' in order for the tribunal to settle them.[79] The tribunal also understood that determining what, if any, potential entitlement is generated by a given feature in the sea does not necessarily require delimiting overlapping potential entitlements. The two operations are juristically separable. Thus, determining a potential entitlement did not trespass against China's Article 298(1) exclusion of delimitation from compulsory dispute settlement.[80] The claims that the Philippines made were separable from other aspects of the overall relationship between the parties, including disputes over territorial sovereignty.

With the well-tested concept of separability in mind, the tribunal distinguished the Philippines' claims from those that Mauritius had advanced in *Chagos Marine Protected Area*: 'The Tribunal understands the majority's decision in [the *Chagos*] case to have been based on the view both that a decision on Mauritius' first and second submissions would have required an implicit decision on sovereignty and that sovereignty was the true object of Mauritius' claims.'[81] In other words, the *Chagos* majority found that Mauritius's claims that required a decision in regard to sovereignty were not separable from those that did not require a decision in regard to sovereignty. The *South China Sea* tribunal, drawing attention to this finding in *Chagos*, lay emphasis on the difference between Mauritius's claims and the

77 *South China Sea Arbitration*, Award on Jurisdiction and Admissibility, ¶ 152.
78 *Ibid.*, quoting ICJ 1980 p. 3, pp. 19–20, ¶ 36.
79 *Ibid.* at ¶ 153.
80 *Ibid.* at ¶ 157.
81 *Ibid.* at ¶ 153.

Philippines' claims: the former 'required an implicit decision on sovereignty'; the latter required no decision on sovereignty at all. The *South China Sea* tribunal thus avoided engaging with the *Chagos* majority's exposition of a putative territorial exclusion from Part XV, section 2, procedures. That exposition was of no relevance to the *South China Sea* case.

What *South China Sea* did engage with is the separability of issues. The tribunal was clear that certain issues were within its jurisdiction, and that these were analytically distinct from others that might not be. This element of the tribunal's reasoning involved, in turn, a careful examination of the Philippines' claims. The tribunal concluded that it was open to it to address the Philippines' submissions regarding Article 13. It determined that a dispute as to whether certain features are LTEs is 'not a dispute concerning sovereignty over the features.'[82] The tribunal also concluded that it was open to it to address the Philippines' submissions regarding Article 121. It determined that a dispute as to whether an island is a mere rock or fully entitled 'is not a dispute concerning sovereignty over the feature' concerned (nor one concerning delimitation of overlapping potential entitlements).[83]

The National Institute *Critique* of the Award insisted, instead, that these issues are inextricably intertwined. Regarding Article 121, the *Critique* referred in particular to a 1990 article by Alfred H. A. Soons, who served as one of the five arbitrators on the *South China Sea* Annex VII tribunal. In the 1990 article, Professor Soons had addressed the relationship between Article 121 and maritime delimitation.[84] The *Critique* suggested that Professor Soons' 1990 article endorsed China's position that Part XV, section 2, bars a tribunal from determining the status of a feature under Article 121(3) where a party has elected to exclude adjudication of maritime delimitation disputes.[85]

In the 1990 article, however, which was relatively early in Soons' career and co-authored with Professor Barbara Kwiatkowska, Soons was more cautious than the *Critique* suggests. He and Professor Kwiatkowska concluded that '[i]f Article 121, paragraph 3 has any role to play, it would seem to consist in signaling the necessity of giving the question of "rocks" careful consideration, with the implementation of the rocks-principle rightly remaining *in most cases* a matter for the application of equity to maritime boundary delimitation in which islands are involved.'[86] An initial observation here is

82 *South China Sea Arbitration,* Award on Jurisdiction and Admissibility (29 October 2015), ¶ 403.

83 *Ibid.*, ¶ 402. See also ¶ 404.

84 24 Asian YBIL at 156 n. 8.

85 *Ibid.* at 156–157.

86 *Ibid.* at 181 (emphasis added).

that there should be no '[i]f' about it: under the principle of effective interpretation, paragraph 3 *must* have a 'role to play.' Indeed, practically in the same breath Soons and Kwiatkowska identified a role for paragraph 3; *and* they left open the possibility that in some cases it might play other roles as well. In their interpretation, as they stated it, Article 121(3) '*would seem*' to have the 'signaling' function that they identified (i.e., in regard to equity); and it would be limited to that function 'in *most* cases,' which is to say not necessarily in *all* cases. As to the 'signaling' function, they said that this would operate through 'the application of equity,' itself an open-textured principle (or set of principles). It would take a great deal of reading between the lines to find in this early academic writing by Soons and Kwiatkowska an endorsement of the Chinese view that parties have forbidden adjudicators from determining, when a sovereignty dispute exists, whether a feature is a rock or a fully entitled island for purposes of Article 121(3). The issues are distinct from issues of sovereignty (and from issues of delimitation), and an adjudicator well can settle one without settling the other.

In any event, belaboring points in an award for supposed inconsistencies with an academic piece that one of the five arbitrators wrote over a quarter century before is not a promising approach.

Lawyers and judges and arbitrators alike are often called on to discern between things that are highly proximate. Saying whether related things are too closely related to allow the jurist to consider them separately is an essential part of legal reasoning. There is, it is true, the old admonition to avoid the lawyer's urge to 'distinguish the indistinguishable.'[87] It is not convincing, however, to say that the *South China Sea* arbitrators failed to perform their function when they judged that the interpretation and application of Article 121(3) is distinguishable from maritime delimitation. To say that a given legal situation is capable of giving rise to an entitlement is not the same as saying that a state has asserted the entitlement. Still more remote is adjudicating the consequences of a state having asserted it.

The Convention text supplied manifest grounds for exercising jurisdiction over China's artificial island sovereignty claims, jurisdictional claims based on natural non-land features, and exorbitant assertions that the smallest land features of the South China Sea generate an EEZ. All of these land-related questions had plain linkage to Part XV, section 2. Article 288(1) extends jurisdiction under Part XV, section 2, to 'any dispute concerning the interpretation or application' of UNCLOS. Article 288(1) is subject, of course, to the limiting terms of sections 1 and 3, but the tribunal considered the limiting terms carefully. None applied.

87 Grant Gilmore, 'Legal Realism: Its Cause and Cure' (1961) 70 YLJ 1037, 1042.

It is true that several of the claims that the Philippines advanced related to provisions of UNCLOS that concern land and that identify their concern with land explicitly—especially Article 121(3). The provisions of UNCLOS that identify the rights and obligations of states in one another's areas of maritime entitlement, as Chapter 2 pointed out, are also dependent upon land territory. The maritime entitlement provisions are a large part of the Convention's substantive content. If their logical and textual dependence on land territory compelled arbitrators and judges to refuse to exercise jurisdiction over disputes regarding their interpretation and application, then adjudication of a large part of the Convention would be excluded wherever some territorial dispute subsisted—or where a state, whether in good faith or otherwise, invoked a dispute with such a convenient disposition as to 'inextricably link' it to other disputes over which the state would prefer to avoid compulsory proceedings. The surprising—nay, astonishing—result would have been that upon which China's *Critique* insisted: a tribunal resiling from the dispute settlement function and declaring itself unable to address land territory issues at all.

Also important here is the competence of a tribunal to consider the evidence and to reach factual determinations grounded on the evidence. As noted, the *South China Sea* tribunal raised several questions *proprio motu* that required it to exercise that competence. The questions regarding, *inter alia*, 'historic bays or titles,' islands that 'cannot sustain human habitation or economic life of their own,' and 'military activities' each depended on the facts, and so the tribunal deferred consideration of each until the merits phase of the proceedings.[88] Moreover, the tribunal did not over-read the exclusions of Article 298(1)(a)*(i)*. It *might* have done so; it *might* have treated Article 298(1)(a)*(i)* as a bar against asking questions to test the jurisdictional objections that China had raised (or might have raised). But to have treated Article 298(1)(a)*(i) that* way would have foreclosed rational engagement with China's argument. As the tribunal observed with regard to the exclusion of maritime delimitations, '[t]he exception in Article 298(1)(a)(i) of the Convention does not reach so far as to capture a dispute over the existence of entitlements that may—or may not—ultimately require delimitation.'[89] In an objection against the exercise of merits jurisdiction under Article 298(1)(a)*(i)*, it is the objecting party that has asserted the existence of an entitlement—or of an historic bay, or of a military activity—or of a sovereignty dispute. It is unconvincing for the objecting party to argue that the jurisdictional exclusion bars the adjudicator from scrutinizing the premise on which its objection relies.

88 *South China Sea*, Jurisdiction and Admissibility, ¶¶ 393, 394, 396.
89 *South China Sea*, Award, 12 July 2016, ¶ 204.

At the start of this chapter, I recalled that the potential entitlements of a state to a territorial sea, an EEZ, and a continental shelf emanate from the land, and, so, before asking whether a particular state has one or more of those entitlements, one must ask whether that state has sovereignty over the land. The prior question, then, is critical: is there any land? Under the absolutist view of the territorial exclusion from Part XV, section 2, jurisdiction, a tribunal would have to abstain from addressing even the prior question, from which abstention all the other questions, too, would fall away from compulsory dispute settlement. Jurists who see UNCLOS as an instrument partaking at least to a degree in the character of a constitutional settlement for the world's oceans find it difficult to sustain the absolutist view. That view simply excises too much from compulsory dispute settlement to be credible.

Jurists who examine the Convention with a formalist's eye to the text find a significant fault in the absolutists' reasoning as well. Excluding all issues of land territory entails excluding adjudication of disputes concerning the interpretation or application of the range of Convention articles that explicitly concern land territory and that connect land territory in terms with the rights and obligations of sovereigns in the sea. The absolute exclusion of territorial issues, moreover, would prevent adjudicators from placing jurisdictional objections under the evidence-based scrutiny they warrant.

6

A 'sovereignty dispute' by force: Coastal State Rights in the Black Sea, Sea of Azov, and Kerch Strait (Ukraine v. Russia)

Ukraine on 14 September 2016 instituted proceedings against Russia under UNCLOS Annex VII. According to Ukraine, the proceedings would serve 'to vindicate [Ukraine's] rights as the coastal state in maritime zones adjacent to Crimea in the Black Sea, Sea of Azov, and Kerch Strait,' zones in which Ukraine stated that 'Russia has usurped and interfered with Ukraine's maritime rights.'[1] The Annex VII tribunal constituted to adjudicate *Coastal State Rights*, as the case that Ukraine instituted was captioned, adopted an award on 21 February 2020 addressing Russia's preliminary objections.

In the award of 21 February 2020, the Annex VII tribunal declared that it lacks jurisdiction over a significant part of Ukraine's case.[2] In particular, the tribunal determined that it lacks jurisdiction 'over the dispute as submitted by Ukraine to the extent that a ruling of the Arbitral Tribunal on the merits of Ukraine's claims necessarily requires it to decide, expressly or implicitly, on the sovereignty of either Party over Crimea.'[3] The tribunal said that its

1 Statement of the Ministry of Foreign Affairs of Ukraine on the Initiation of Arbitration Against the Russian Federation Under the United Nations Convention on the Law of the Sea, MINISTRY FOREIGN AFF. OF UKR. (15 September 2016), http://mfa.gov.ua/en/press-center/news/50813–zajava-mzs-ukrajini-shhodo-porushennya-arbitrazhnogo-provadzhennya-prot i-rosijsykoji-federaciji-vidpovidno-do-konvenciji-oon-z-morsykogo-prava. For assessment of the case prior to the award of 21 February 2020, see Volterra, Mandelli, & Nistal, 'The Characterisation of the *Dispute Concerning Coastal State Rights in the Black Sea, Sea of Azov, and Kerch Strait*' (2018) 33 IJMCL 614. For an interesting account of the earlier history of sovereign competition in the Black Sea, see Oral, '*Ukraine v. The Russian Federation:* Navigating Conflict over Sovereignty under UNCLOS' (2021) 97 *International Law Studies* 478, 481–486. As to the award of 21 February 2020, Schatz, 'Status of Crimea and the Sea of Azov,' EJIL Talk! (20 March 2020) and the passing reference in Merrills & De Brabandere (2022) 279. For a more detailed discussion, see Kunoy (2021) 123–126.

2 *Dispute Concerning Coastal State Rights in the Black Sea, Sea of Azov, and Kerch Strait (Ukraine v. Russian Federation)*, PCA Case No. 2017–06, Award, Preliminary Objections of the Russian Federation (21 February 2020).

3 *Ibid.* at ¶ 197.

determination 'affects many, but not all, of the claims articulated in different forms' in Ukraine's case.[4]

Quoting, curiously enough, *Methanex Corp. v. United States*, a decision adopted under a different instrument in a different juristic and factual setting, the tribunal said that 'the Russian Federation is "entitled to know precisely the case advanced against it."'[5] I say more in Chapters 7 and 8 about the influence of different decisions on one another. For present purposes, the point of interest is that the tribunal, to let Russia 'know precisely the case,' required Ukraine to revise its Memorial 'so as to take full account of the scope of, and limits to, the Arbitral Tribunal's jurisdiction as determined in the present Award, before the Russian Federation is called upon to respond in a Counter-Memorial.'[6]

Having thus recast the proceedings and constrained the scope of the claims, the tribunal adopted a procedural order the same day as the award setting out a new timetable for the written submissions.[7] The procedural order directed Ukraine to submit a revised version of its Memorial. Russia was directed to submit a Counter-Memorial. The order gave Ukraine the option of submitting a reply and invited Russia to submit a rejoinder.

It was four years before the next public statement in the case. A Permanent Court of Arbitration (PCA) Press Release of 7 August 2024 indicated that a hearing on the merits and remaining issues of jurisdiction and admissibility would be held from 23 September 2024 to 5 October 2024. Shortly before this book went to press, the parties gave oral presentations to the tribunal,[8] and the parties' written submissions, with redactions, were made available at that time.

In the time elapsing between the award on preliminary objections and Russia's rejoinder, Russia launched an all-out invasion of Ukraine and seized much of the remaining coast that it had not already seized in its earlier armed intervention. Russia now purported to annex and integrate into Russia the entire Sea of Azov coast of Ukraine and further parts of the Black Sea coast of Ukraine. Russia in its Counter-Memorial of 14 October 2022 told the Annex VII tribunal that there had been a 'change in circumstances substantially affecting' the dispute.[9] Russia's pleading on the point merits quoting at length, because it makes clear that the defects in the 21

4 *Ibid.* at ¶ 198.

5 *Ibid.*, quoting *Methanex Corp. v. United States of America*, NAFTA/UNCITRAL, Partial Award on Jurisdiction and Admissibility of 7 August 2002, ¶ 162.

6 *Coastal State Rights* at ¶ 198.

7 Procedural Order No. 6, 21 February 2022.

8 https://pcacases.com/web/sendAttach/9342 (visited 10 October 2024).

9 PCA Case No. 2017–06, Counter-Memorial of the Russian Federation, 14 October 2022, p. 6.

February 2020 award that it is the aim of the present chapter to elucidate continue to demand a full account and critique.

According to Russia:

> 25. The Russian Federation submits that since the date of the filing of Ukraine's Revised Memorial [20 May 2021], new circumstances have arisen that substantially affect the issues under consideration in the present arbitral proceedings. The changed circumstances should be taken into account when considering the matters that are pertinent to the resolution of the dispute in front of this Tribunal.
>
> 26. Specifically, on 30 September 2022, following the referendums held in the DPR ['Donetsk People's Republic'], the LPR ['Luhansk People's Republic'], the Zaporozhye Region and the Kherson Region, these areas, as a result of their accession to the Russian Federation, became part of the sovereign territory of the Russian Federation pursuant to the treaties on the accession of the same date. On 4 October 2022, a set of Federal Constitutional Laws was enacted that envisaged a legal framework regulating various aspects of the process of accession, including the status of new territories as the subjects of the Russian Federation and their borders.
>
> 27. Importantly, since the accession to Russia of the areas that are littoral to the Sea of Azov—the DPR (including the Port of Mariupol), the Zaporozhye Region (including the Port of Berdyansk) and the Kherson Region—Ukraine ceased to be a coastal State with regard to the Sea of Azov. Regardless of Ukraine's stance on these events, they remain a matter of reality and, as such, are not to be disregarded by the Tribunal.
>
> 28. In light of the above described circumstances, the Russian Federation respectfully submits that the conclusions that this Tribunal reached in the 2020 Award, in relation to the lack of its jurisdiction over the matters that require the Tribunal to decide on the sovereignty over Crimea, are fully applicable to the present situation with the DPR, the Zaporozhye and Kherson Regions.[10]

Russia's annexation of Donetsk, Luhansk, Zaporozhye, and Kherson in 2022 followed a massive enlargement of the armed action by which Russia had annexed Crimea in 2014. It will be recalled from Chapter 1 that pleading 'changed circumstances' will not result in the change of a settled boundary between states.[11] True, Russia was not asking an Annex VII tribunal to adjudicate a boundary on the merits. It was, however, asking the tribunal to accept a jurisdictional objection on the basis of Russia's assertion that Russia's boundary with Ukraine *might* change—due to 'changed circumstances.' To assert that a boundary might change through a modality that cannot change a boundary is to assert a proposition that, to put it generously, needs more than ordinary logic to prove.

10 *Ibid.* pp. 6–7, ¶¶ 25–28.
11 See Chapter 1, p. 31. See also pp. 49, 54.

When the present book went to press, it remained to be seen how the Annex VII tribunal in *Coastal State Rights* would respond to Russia's new assertions of claim to Ukrainian territory, in particular whether the tribunal would accept Russia's enlarged objection to jurisdiction and, so doing, enlarge the scope of the exclusion of Ukraine's maritime claims. If accepted, the objection would exclude not just 'many' but most of Ukraine's maritime claims.

The present chapter considers in detail how the tribunal, in its 2020 Award, reached the conclusion that a dispute as to sovereignty in Crimea had arisen in 2014 and that such dispute prevents the adjudication of the maritime claims that Ukraine had advanced. I explore here a range of dispute settlement practice, including the cases that I considered in Chapters 4 and 5. I argue that the tribunal's approach in *Coastal State Rights* is at stark variance with well-established method, as well as with legal principle.

The chapter starts by summarizing the argument that Ukraine made in favor of the exercise of jurisdiction over certain maritime disputes involving the conduct of Russia in the Black Sea, Sea of Azov, and Kerch Strait, Russia's objection to jurisdiction, and the tribunal's stated grounds for accepting Russia's objection.[12] I then make a number of critical observations about the tribunal's conclusion and the approach that it took to get there.

I start by considering the tribunal's interpretation of UNCLOS jurisdiction in respect of sovereignty disputes. The tribunal offered little fresh analysis on the point. It did, however, I argue, introduce further confusion.

My next observation concerns claims in international law. An adjudicator does not need to *settle* a claim in order to affect the state of affairs in which the claim is involved. The adjudicator's acknowledgment that a claim exists as a *legal* claim itself affects the rights, obligations, and conduct of states. The *Coastal State Rights* tribunal was not convincing when it declared that its conclusion that Russia has a legal claim to sovereignty over Crimea is a legally neutral act.[13]

However, the most striking defect in the *Coastal State Rights* award of 21 February 2020 is the paucity of evidence-based reasoning behind it. Following the premise that an UNCLOS tribunal shall consider no sovereignty issue, the *Coastal State Rights* tribunal refused to engage in fact-finding in regard to Russia's assertion that there is a sovereignty dispute. Even if the premise were beyond question that UNCLOS jurisdiction does not reach any sovereignty disputes *as a matter of merits*, the competence of a tribunal to settle disputes as to the scope of its merits jurisdiction is a different matter. The *Coastal State Rights* tribunal, though not stating that this is what it was doing, in effect treated *that* competence to be no less confined

12 See below pp. 177–185.
13 See below pp. 190–192.

and limited by the putative exclusion of sovereignty issues than merits jurisdiction is said to be. The tribunal thus turned a theory of merits exclusion into a far-reaching bar to the dispute settlement function, having the effect, in the tribunal's words, that it 'has no jurisdiction to adjudicate' the alleged 'developments' upon which Russia's jurisdictional objection hinged.[14] In this, its chief failure, the tribunal refused to scrutinize Russia's contentions that local inhabitants had faced annihilation by Ukraine, chose to accept Russia's succor and, three weeks later, annexation, and that by that alleged course of events in March 2014, a sovereignty dispute in regard to Crimea had arisen.[15] These contentions were placed in issue only by Russia's jurisdictional objection. As we will see, no other international fact-finder believed them. And, yet, without considering evidence of their truth or falsity, the tribunal upheld the jurisdictional objection that relied on them.

Worsening the effects of the tribunal's refusal to consider the realities behind the jurisdictional objection that Russia advanced, the tribunal took a superficial view of what constitutes a 'sovereignty dispute.' As I recalled in Chapter 1, it is fundamental to modern international law that use of force does not give rise to a sovereignty claim, because international law rejects that a state may change a settled international border by use of force.[16] The tribunal did not ask whether Russia's assertion of a sovereignty claim against Ukraine had anything behind it other than the use of force. In this omission, the tribunal ignored a distinction that long has informed international dispute settlement practice: not all international acts are acts on the international legal plane.[17]

Finally, of a piece with its departure from legal principle and from ordinary methods of adjudication, the tribunal also ignored the effects that its decision will have on international public order at large.[18]

Crimea in dispute?

Crimea is a region of Ukraine. Up until March 2014, Russia agreed. Russia articulated no claim that would have cast doubt on Ukraine's sovereignty in Crimea.[19]

14 *Coastal State Rights*, Award, ¶ 181.
15 See below pp. 222–244.
16 See above pp. 25–58.
17 See below pp. 199–205.
18 See below pp. 234–237, 246–247.
19 *Coastal State Rights* at ¶ 181. To the same effect, *Oschadbank v. Russian Federation*, PCA Case No. 2016–14, Award, 26 November 2018 (Williams, President; Brower and Perezcano Díaz, arbitrators) ¶ 198.

Since the award of 21 February 2020, some three-quarters of the countries of the world have affirmed that they recognize Crimea to form part of Ukraine's sovereign territory,[20] and the Council of Europe, the principal regional intergovernmental organization to which both Ukraine and Russia belonged at the time the proceedings began,[21] also understands there to be no dispute as regards sovereignty over Crimea.[22] The UN Security Council, also in the time since the award, has convened the General Assembly in Emergency Special Session in order to consider Russia's invasion of Ukraine.[23] (This is the first Emergency Special Session that the Security Council has convened in forty years.)[24] The General Assembly, by GA resolution ES-11/4 of 12 October 2022 on the 'Territorial integrity of Ukraine,'[25] reaffirmed that Ukraine's territory is that contained within the boundaries universally recognized in December 1991[26] and recognized by Russia up until March 2014. The resolution received the affirmative votes of 143 states,[27] these states thus expressly rejecting as void and of no effect the annexations that Russia adverted to in its Counter-Memorial of 24 October 2022. Apart from Russia, and it seems Belarus, Cuba, Nicaragua, Sudan, and North Korea, none of the 193 UN member states have expressly accepted the annexations.

There is no doubt that Russia's deployment of armed forces against Ukraine, which started in the last days of February 2014 and was rapidly followed by the forcible seizure of Crimea and the putative absorption of that territory into Russia, is in violation of international law.[28] However, the

20 The casting of a vote in favour of GAR ES-11/4, 12 October 2022 (Territorial integrity of Ukraine: defending the principles of the Charter of the United Nations) necessarily implies recognition that Ukraine comprises all territory within its 1991 boundaries. The resolution was adopted 143–5–35 (see A/ES-11/PV.14). The vote-casting of a state as a measure of the state's attitude is a matter distinct for these purposes from the effects of the adopted resolution. See further below ##–##.

21 The Council of Europe subsequently expelled Russia. See CoE Committee of Ministers Decision of 25 February 2022; Decision of 16 March 2022.

22 See, for example, PACE resolution 1988 (2014), 9 April 2014, ¶ 16.

23 SCR 2623 (2022), 27 February 2022.

24 UN Briefing: Emergency Special Session of the General Assembly on the Russian invasion of Ukraine (28 February 2022): https://una.org.uk/news/un-briefing-emergency-special-session-general-assembly-russian-invasion-ukraine

25 A/ES-11/PV.14, 12 October 2022, 143–5–35.

26 The General Assembly '*[r]affirm[ed] its commitment* to the sovereignty, independence, unity and territorial integrity of Ukraine within its internationally recognized borders, extending to its territorial waters': GAR ES-11/1, 2 March 2022 (Aggression against Ukraine), ¶ 1; GAR ES-11/4, 12 October 2022 (Territorial integrity of Ukraine: defending the principles of the Charter of the United Nations), ¶ 1.

27 A/ES-11/PV.14 (143–5–35).

28 Grant, *Aggression against Ukraine* (2015) 23–33, 43–61; Grant, 'Annexation of Crimea' (2015) 109 AJIL 68, 71–87. Cf. the review by Ruys (2016) 110 AJIL 602–609.

illegality of the invasion as such is a conclusion separate and independent from the proper assessment of Russia's assertion that a sovereignty dispute exists in respect of Crimea. As Chapter 1 recalled, if a state has a legally cognizable claim to a territory, then the claim subsists whether the state pursues it through lawful means or otherwise. Conversely, an invasion, lawful or not, does not change a peacefully settled boundary between states.

These considerations notwithstanding, the Annex VII tribunal constituted to address Ukraine's claims against Russia for alleged violations of a number of provisions of UNCLOS concluded that a dispute exists as to which state is sovereign in Crimea and that the dispute has such legal character that the tribunal was obliged to treat it as precluding the exercise of jurisdiction over claims of Ukraine in regard to Russia's conduct in the appurtenant maritime areas. Let us start by setting out the formal steps that led the tribunal to its conclusion in the February 2020 award.

Ukraine's case on jurisdiction

As would be expected when a state institutes proceedings under an UNCLOS Part XV, section 2, procedure, Ukraine anticipated the main possible objection that the respondent state would raise. Ukraine anticipated that Russia would seek to convince the Annex VII tribunal that a sovereignty dispute existed and that the putative sovereignty dispute barred the exercise of merits jurisdiction over some or all of Ukraine's maritime claims. Ukraine's case on jurisdiction had the following argumentative structure:

- While it is well known that Ukraine opposes Russia's presence in and putative annexation of the land area of Crimea,[29] Ukraine seeks relief from the tribunal only in regard to maritime disputes,[30] not in regard to the land area of Crimea.[31]

29 See Ukraine's Written Observations, ¶ 56. See also Ukraine's official statements: President of Ukraine Official Website, President: We Will Do Everything to Return Crimea via International Legal Mechanisms, 6 December 2015, produced in Annex 38 to Russia's pleadings; Ministry of Foreign Affairs of Ukraine Official Website, Statement of the Ministry of Foreign Affairs of Ukraine on the Initiation of Arbitration against the Russian Federation under the United Nations Convention on the Law of the Sea, 14 September 2016, produced in Annex 44 to Russia's pleadings; Statement of the Delegation of Ukraine at the Special Committee on the Charter of the United Nations and on the Strengthening of the Role of the Organization United Nations, 20 February 2018, produced in Annex 49 to Russia's pleadings.

30 *Coastal State Rights*, Award (21 February 2020), ¶¶ 58, 61; Ukraine's Written Observations, ¶¶ 17, 56; Ukraine's Rejoinder, ¶ 8.

31 *Coastal State Rights,* Ukraine's Written Observations, ¶ 58; Ukraine's Rejoinder, ¶ 49; Award ¶ 125. Cf. *ibid.* at ¶ 62.

- To the extent that the tribunal nevertheless were to understand that Ukraine's case concerns a land dispute,[32] the tribunal has jurisdiction to resolve such land dispute to that extent.[33]
- On the better view, there is in regard to sovereignty in Crimea no land dispute having such legal character as a court or tribunal might address it,[34] only the question of how to bring an end to Russia's legally baseless physical presence in Crimea;[35] Ukraine does not ask the tribunal physically to remove Russia from Crimea;[36] only that it treat Ukraine's sovereignty in Crimea as settled law,[37] as most states,[38] the UN General Assembly, and the Council of Europe do.[39]

As is visible in this structure, Ukraine fashioned its case so that it would remain viable under whichever divergent interpretation of the sovereignty disputes exclusion the tribunal adopted.

Russia predicated its jurisdictional objection on a particular interpretation of the Convention. Russia predicated its objection on the interpretation that holds that an adjudicator under UNCLOS Part XV, section 2, is barred from addressing any issue of territorial sovereignty. Ukraine argued that, in the event the tribunal were to find a sovereignty dispute to exist, the sovereignty disputes exclusion is more nuanced than that. Ukraine relied, in part, on the observation that the *Chagos* tribunal had been split, three-to-two, and that even the majority had struggled with how to characterize the applicant state's claim—as a claim regarding maritime issues or as a claim regarding the territorial dispute over the Chagos Archipelago.[40] Ukraine argued that, in the proceedings that it instituted against Russia, there was no legal issue as to sovereignty over Crimea; and therefore that even if the tribunal were to accept Russia's categorical interpretation, Russia's objection in fact would fail. Secondarily, in the alternative, Ukraine argued that, even if a sovereignty issue existed, Ukraine's maritime claims plainly form the predominant element in Ukraine's case; and UNCLOS does not completely bar an adjudicator from addressing at least *some* territorial issues.

32 *Coastal State Rights*, Award, ¶ 136; Ukraine's Rejoinder, ¶ 41.
33 Award, ¶¶ 77, 137–140; Ukraine's Rejoinder, ¶ 42 (citing *Chagos* Award, ¶ 220); Ukraine's Written Observations, ¶ 36.
34 Award, ¶¶ 99–107, 115–125, 144; Ukraine's Written Observations, ¶¶ 34, 189; Ukraine's Rejoinder, ¶ 39.
35 I.e., the only question regarding Crimea is how to get Russia out.
36 Award, ¶ 144; Ukraine's Rejoinder, ¶ 50.
37 Award, ¶¶ 85, 99, 107; Ukraine's Written Observations, ¶¶ 26–27, 39; Ukraine's Rejoinder, ¶¶ 17, 50.
38 See summary of state practice by region, Ukraine's Written Observations, ¶ 29.
39 Award, ¶¶ 85, 100–102, 125; Ukraine's Written Observations, ¶ 5, 18, 29; Ukraine's Rejoinder, ¶ 14.
40 Ukraine's Rejoinder, ¶ 42; Ukraine's Written Observations, ¶ 36.

In its pleadings, Ukraine addressed the scope of Article 298(1).[41] The chief concern for Ukraine in respect of that provision was the limitation on law enforcement matters and delimitations. However, in respect of delimitations, Ukraine's concern with Article 298(1) also involved the territorial exclusion clause. Recalling the *South China Sea* case, Ukraine noted that only where there are overlapping potential entitlements does delimitation come into play and, thus, only there does the Article 298(1)(a)*(i)* delimitation exclusion matter.[42] To say whether there are overlapping potential entitlements, one must know whether two or more states have coasts that generate potential entitlements that overlap. And, to know whether a state has a coast, one must know whether the state has sovereignty over the land behind the coast.

The application of the exception under Article 298(1)(b)—'disputes concerning military activities' and 'disputes concerning law enforcement activities'—is also linked to the question of sovereignty over land. The link is via Article 297, paragraphs (2) and (3). These paragraphs identify limitations in regard to disputes involving the exercise by a coastal state of rights in its EEZ and continental shelf, and those rights emanate from sovereignty over land. The linkage in Ukraine's pleadings between the delimitation exception and the military activities/law enforcement exception, on the one hand, and the question of the scope of the territorial exclusion clause, on the other, was indirect, but it was necessary to the logic of the pleadings.

The parties disagreed as to the scope of Article 298(1)(a)*(i)*. Ukraine argued that 'Russia's expansive reading' of the provision is unconvincing and that the exclusion of sovereignty disputes contained in the provision is limited to the issues and circumstances that the provision specifies.[43] According to Ukraine, because no question of sovereignty exists in regard to Crimea, Russia's arguments 'about the proper interpretation of Article 298 [were] academic.'[44] This was to say that, on Ukraine's main theory of the case, there was no need to determine whether Article 298 expresses a general territorial exclusion, because Ukraine's claims present no sovereignty dispute for the tribunal to address.

If the tribunal disagreed and found that there *is* a sovereignty dispute in the case, then the 'proper interpretation of Article 298' would *not* be merely 'academic.' So, to address the risk that the tribunal might find that there is a territorial dispute, Ukraine added that Russia's arguments '[about Article 298] are ... incorrect.'[45] In other words, Ukraine joined issue with Russia

41 See esp. Ukraine's Rejoinder, ¶¶ 109–114; Ukraine's Written Observations, ¶¶ 110–119.
42 Ukraine's Rejoinder, ¶ 109.
43 *Ibid.*, ¶ 113.
44 *Ibid.*, ¶ 112.
45 *Ibid.*

as to the breadth of the territorial exclusion in Article 298(1)(a)*(i)*. A broad exclusion of territorial sovereignty questions was very much what Russia's case strategy required, and Ukraine confronted Russia on the point.

As will be seen, the tribunal had practically nothing to say in response to the confrontation between the parties over Article 298(1)(a)*(i)*. The tribunal, instead, rejected Ukraine's case on jurisdiction by accepting that Russia's armed seizure of Crimea in 2014 created a dispute as to which state is sovereign in Crimea—and by treating the question of the scope of the sovereignty dispute exclusion as already closed and settled.

Russia's objection to jurisdiction

In its preliminary objections, the Russian Federation argued that the jurisdiction of the Annex VII tribunal does not extend to any of Ukraine's claims and called on the tribunal to declare itself without jurisdiction 'in respect of the dispute submitted ... by Ukraine.'[46] Russia advanced a number of arguments to that end grounded, *inter alia*, on agreements between Ukraine and Russia purportedly committing them to use other dispute settlement procedures (i.e., procedures other than those under Part XV, section 2),[47] on the assertion that Ukraine failed to satisfy the negotiation requirement of UNCLOS Article 281,[48] and on the parties' declarations under Article 298 excluding disputes concerning military activities or law enforcement activities.[49] The objection to which Russia gave priority, however, was that grounded on the assertion that a sovereignty dispute exists in regard to Crimea. '[T]he real issue in this case,' Russia asserted, 'concerns sovereignty over land territory (i.e., sovereignty over Crimea).'[50] All other objections in Russia's pleading were 'without prejudice to this first objection, which Russia consider[ed] of *fundamental and systemic importance*.'[51]

Turning to the scope of jurisdiction under Part XV, section 2, Russia referred to *Chagos Marine Protected Area*. No doubt having anticipated Ukraine's nuanced interpretation, Russia conceded that the award in *Chagos Marine Protected Area* held open the possibility that 'in some instances, a

46 PCA Case No. 2017–06, Preliminary Objections of the Russian Federation (19 May 2018), ¶ 265.
47 *Ibid.* at ¶¶ 18, 19; ¶¶ 198–214; 215–231.
48 *Ibid.* at ¶ 19; ¶¶ 232–264. On the tribunal's treatment of this objection, which he observed was incomplete, see Kunoy, 'Compulsory Jurisdiction and Exceptions Thereto' (2021) 58 Can. YBIL 78, 87–88.
49 *Ibid.* at ¶ 16; ¶¶ 137–153.
50 *Ibid.* at ¶ 13.
51 *Ibid.* at ¶ 14 (emphasis added).

minor issue of territorial sovereignty could indeed be ancillary to a dispute concerning the interpretation or application' of UNCLOS.[52] Russia said that '[t]he territorial sovereignty issue in the current case is plainly not a "minor issue" that is "ancillary" to some broader dispute.'[53]

In Russia's view, the existence of a dispute is established by a syllogism. In Russia's words:

> (a) Ukraine considers that it is sovereign over Crimea and thereby exercises the rights in the appertaining maritime zones, whilst
> (b) Russia considers that it is sovereign and that, as a consequence, it enjoys the relevant rights, and it has repeatedly set out its position with respect to the lawfulness of its activities in Crimea and on the status of Crimea,
> (c) the two States are engaged in a dispute over this critical issue of sovereignty.[54]

According to Russia, Ukraine was incorrect to say that 'a *bona fide* territorial dispute may not be a consequence of aggression against a sovereign State.'[55]

Russia 'vigorously challenge[d] and denie[d]' the accusations that its presence in Crimea is the result of armed aggression.[56] According to Russia, certain facts on the ground in Ukraine supplied a justification as a matter of international law for the seizure of Ukrainian territory and its putative absorption into Russia. Russia prefaced its recital of the alleged facts by stating that '[i]nsofar as certain matters of a factual nature are referred to herein, this is done solely for the purpose of Russia's contentions on jurisdiction.'[57] Russia proceeded to assert that there was a coup d'état in Kyiv in February 2014; that this provoked 'the authorities of Crimea' to hold a 'referendum'; that the 'referendum,' held on 16 March 2014, had a turnout of 83.1 percent, of whom 96.77 percent said they would like 'reunification with Russia.'[58] Russia further alleged that '[a] large portion of the population' of Ukraine 'did not support the nationalist takeover with ensuing violence and political chaos' and that 'their dissent was brutally repressed by right-wing radicals.'[59]

52 *Ibid.* at ¶ 56, citing *Chagos Marine Protected Area (Mauritius v. United Kingdom)*, Award, 18 March 2015, ¶ 221.
53 Preliminary Objections of the Russian Federation, ¶ 56.
54 *Ibid.* at ¶ 61.
55 *Ibid.* at ¶ 61 n. 91, quoting Ukraine in Transcript of Russian–Ukrainian Consultations on the United Nations Convention on the Law of the Sea, Minsk, 11 August 2016, reproduced with Russia's Preliminary Objections as document RU-41.
56 Preliminary Objections of the Russian Federation, ¶ 7.
57 *Ibid.* at ¶ 9.
58 *Ibid.* at ¶ 11.
59 *Ibid.* at ¶ 10.

The Annex VII tribunal would note that Russia 'does not contest that before March 2014 [Russia] had recognised Ukraine's sovereignty over Crimea.'[60]

As will be seen, the factual contentions that Russia advanced in its Preliminary Objections in *Coastal State Rights* were restrained compared to statements elsewhere that Russian officials made alleging an explosion of violence and disorder and neo-Nazi provocation.[61] Russia advanced the contentions nevertheless, and they were indispensable to Russia's jurisdictional defense. They supplied the entire substance of Russia's assertion that a sovereignty dispute had arisen in 2014 in respect of Crimea where for decades there had been none.

In presenting factual contentions such as did Russia, a state in a dispute settlement proceeding would seem to open the door to their testing through the ordinary methods of fact-finding. I return to this point later.

The tribunal affirms Russia's objection

The tribunal organized its analysis of jurisdiction in three parts: one dealing with the nature or characterization of the dispute that Ukraine instituted proceedings to settle;[62] a second, dealing with the scope of jurisdiction under UNCLOS Article 288(1);[63] and a third, dealing with the question whether Ukraine's sovereignty to Crimea is a settled matter or, instead, a matter subject to legal dispute.[64] However, the structure of the tribunal's analysis in effect reduces to two matters: the tribunal considered whether Article 288(1) allows the tribunal to adjudicate a sovereignty dispute; and then it considered whether, in the case at hand, a sovereignty dispute existed.

The tribunal placed the burden on Ukraine to prove that Ukraine is sovereign in Crimea. Considering the procedural setting in which sovereignty was placed in issue in the case, it is surprising that the tribunal made the matter one for Ukraine. True, the party asserting that jurisdiction exists has the burden to show that it does. But, here, *the party objecting to jurisdiction* advanced its objection by placing sovereignty in issue. The tribunal itself understood that '*the key question upon which it should focus* [was] whether

60 *Coastal State Rights*, Award, 21 February 2020, ¶ 181. See also to the same effect *Oschadbank v. Russian Federation*, PCA Case No. 2016–14, Award, 26 November 2018 (Williams, President; Brower and Perezcano Díaz, arbitrators) ¶ 198: 'There is no dispute that, until sometime in February or March 2014, the region fell within the territory of Ukraine.'

61 See Chapter 8, p. 195.

62 Award, ¶¶ 151–154.

63 Award, ¶¶ 155–161.

64 Award, ¶¶ 162–196.

a dispute as to which state has sovereignty over Crimea exists.'[65] This was against a factual/legal matrix that the objecting party conceded was not in the least promising to the objection: up until March 2014, Russia had accepted its boundaries with Ukraine to be defined, settled, and final.[66]

The tribunal, despite acknowledging Russia's long-settled acceptance of its boundaries, placed those boundaries at the center of the proceedings and, more striking still, characterized the boundary settlement as a matter that it was for Ukraine to prove. According to the tribunal, 'the fact remains that a significant part of Ukraine's claims under consideration rests on the premise that Ukraine is sovereign over Crimea, the validity of which is challenged by the Russian Federation.'[67] The tribunal thus, from the start, positioned the case as a test of the long-standing recognition that Ukraine is sovereign over the territory within its internationally recognized borders. The tribunal indeed, in the same paragraph, said that determining sovereignty 'is a prerequisite to' the settlement of the claims that Ukraine had brought.[68] From there, the tribunal reasoned that, to determine jurisdiction, it had to answer two questions: 'first, the scope of the jurisdiction of the Arbitral Tribunal under Article 288, paragraph 1, of the Convention; and second, the existence *vel non* of a sovereignty dispute over Crimea.'[69] On that reduced basis, the tribunal proceeded to reject Ukraine's argument.

The manner in which the tribunal reached its conclusion, as much as the conclusion itself, deserves careful consideration. In the sections that follow, I consider in particular how the tribunal answered the question whether a 'sovereignty dispute' existed, how the tribunal allocated burden of proof, and how it conducted its testing of evidence and finding of fact. Before we turn to these matters, let us consider the tribunal's interpretation of the limits of UNCLOS jurisdiction in respect of sovereignty disputes.

The tribunal's interpretation of the sovereignty dispute exclusion

The tribunal rejected that its jurisdiction might permit it to address a sovereignty dispute. The tribunal conceded that nothing in UNCLOS clearly supported its conclusion that jurisdiction does not embrace sovereignty disputes: 'the text of the Convention provides no clear answer to this question.'[70] The tribunal proceeded to find that it is in Articles 297 and 298

65 *Coastal State Rights*, Award, 21 February 2020, ¶ 188 (emphasis added).
66 *Ibid.*, ¶ 181.
67 Award, ¶ 153.
68 *Ibid.*
69 *Ibid.*, ¶ 154.
70 *Ibid.*, ¶ 156.

that the answer is found, and that those provisions prevent a tribunal from exercising jurisdiction over a sovereignty dispute. According to the tribunal,

> in light of Article 297, which carves out certain categories of disputes relating to the exercise of sovereign rights and jurisdiction in the exclusive economic zone, and Article 298, paragraph 1, which allows States to exclude three categories of disputes, such as disputes concerning such sensitive matters as the delimitation of maritime boundaries, from compulsory dispute settlement procedures, a sovereignty dispute, which is mentioned in neither provision, may not be regarded a dispute concerning the interpretation or application of the Convention.[71]

The tribunal's treatment of Articles 297 and 298 is, at best, opaque. With all respect to the distinguished jurists who comprised the Annex VII tribunal, where they asserted that 'a sovereignty dispute … is mentioned in neither provision,' Article 297 or Article 298, they were outright wrong. The much-analyzed sovereignty dispute exclusion is in Article 298, paragraph 1.

Even putting aside the tribunal's erroneous statement that 'neither provision' mentions a sovereignty dispute, the tribunal's reasoning here is hard to follow. Precisely because it is the locus of *the* limitations on the applicability of Part XV, section 2, procedures, Article 297 is the most logical place to look for the answer to the question of how far the limitations go. Land territory is not one of the limitations.

I considered in detail in Chapter 3 the contentious differences of interpretation of the territorial disputes clause in Article 298 and the significance of the 'any disputes' clause of Article 288(1). I also considered the drafting history that reflects that the Third Conference was deliberate in *not* placing a territorial disputes clause in Article 297. And in Chapter 4, I recalled the split decision in the *Chagos* Annex VII proceedings, in which a three-arbitrator majority concluded that Part XV, section 2, generally excludes territorial issues from adjudication but that *some* territorial questions nevertheless might be subject to jurisdiction. The *Coastal State Rights* tribunal offered no analysis of this difficult matter of interpretation, even though Russia's jurisdictional objection turned upon it.

The tribunal then said a few words about the decided cases that have addressed the territorial exception and the question of how far the exception extends. The tribunal declared that '[t]hose arbitral tribunals'—by which the *Coastal State Rights* tribunal was referring to the authors of the *Chagos* majority award and of the *South China Sea* unanimous awards—'were circumspect and generally answered the … question in the negative, except for a situation where a sovereignty issue is "ancillary" to a dispute concerning

71 *Ibid.*, ¶ 156.

the interpretation or application of the Convention.' I considered *South China Sea* in Chapter 5; it did not 'answer [...] the ... question in the negative.' It did not answer the question at all. Even if one ignores the *Coastal State Rights* tribunal's over-reading of *South China Sea* and takes the tribunal's observation here on its own terms, there is little substance in it. To say that a 'sovereignty issue' could be addressed by an UNCLOS tribunal only where it is '"ancillary" to a dispute concerning the interpretation or application of the Convention' is to replace analysis with truism and to engage in question-begging. It is a truism to say that a dispute is not subject to UNCLOS dispute settlement procedures if it is neither 'a dispute concerning the interpretation or application of the Convention' nor a dispute ancillary to such a dispute. Nobody says otherwise. It is question-begging when the tribunal only restated the question for which an answer is sought: the tribunal said that an ancillary issue might be subject to jurisdiction—but did not say why 'sovereignty issues' are not themselves issues of the interpretation or application of the Convention when many Convention provisions concern sovereignty or what would make a 'sovereignty issue' an 'ancillary' one.

The *Coastal State Rights* tribunal, after stating the obvious—that sovereignty disputes cannot be addressed under Part XV, section 2, if they are not associated with maritime disputes—proceeded to offer its gloss on the *Chagos* majority's proviso that some sovereignty disputes might be subject to jurisdiction. According to the *Coastal State Rights* tribunal, a sovereignty dispute is not subject to jurisdiction when settling the dispute is 'a prerequisite to the ... decision on ... claims' that a party has advanced.[72] The *Chagos* majority, however, said nothing of the sort.

To recall from Chapter 4, paragraph 220 of the *Chagos* majority award started by observing that 'where a dispute concerns the interpretation or application of the Convention, the jurisdiction of a court or tribunal ... extends to making such findings of fact or ancillary determinations of law as are necessary to resolve the dispute presented to it.'[73] The *Chagos* majority here placed emphasis on the scope of jurisdiction, not the scope of an exception. It was after emphasizing the scope of jurisdiction that the *Chagos* majority articulated a limit. UNCLOS jurisdiction excludes sovereignty disputes, the *Chagos* majority said. It then said that 'minor' and 'ancillary' sovereignty issues could be subject to UNCLOS jurisdiction. This was the proviso. As to the scope of the proviso—'minor' and 'ancillary' issues—the *Chagos* majority was vague. It supplied no definition of 'minor' or 'ancillary.' It did, however, make clear that it would *not* preclude an issue being 'minor' or 'ancillary' that the issue is a *necessary* one to resolve a dispute. The

72 *Coastal State Rights* award, ¶ 195.
73 *Chagos* Award, ¶ 220, quoted at *Coastal State Rights*, ¶ 158.

jurisdiction of a tribunal, the *Chagos* majority said, 'extends to making such findings of fact or ancillary determinations of law *as are necessary to resolve the dispute presented to it.*'[74]

With these carefully chosen words, the *Chagos* majority said the exact *opposite* of what the *Coastal State Rights* tribunal said it said. The *Coastal State Rights* tribunal declared that an issue is *not* minor in the *Chagos* proviso sense when it is 'a prerequisite to the ... decision on ... claims' that a party has presented.[75] On a plain reading of the *Chagos* majority award, it is clear that the arbitrators there did *not* understand 'minor' to mean *irrelevant to the decision*. That, however, is how the *Coastal State Rights* tribunal read the *Chagos* majority.

Reduced to its essentials, the *Chagos* majority postulated a limit on jurisdiction derived from the manner in which the 'real issue' in a case is defined,[76] not from a general exception to land territory issues. One *might* argue for a general exception. In Chapter 3, I addressed the writings of prominent jurists who argue precisely for that. As I also noted, the *Chagos* majority, in accepting the United Kingdom's Article 288(1) argument, seems to have interpreted UNCLOS to exclude *all* sovereignty issues. I suggested that this is an internal contradiction in the *Chagos* majority, because it contradicts the proviso that *some* sovereignty issues can be adjudicated.[77]

The *Chagos* tribunal had wrestled with the interpretation of Article 298(1)(a)*(i)* and its relation to Article 288(1). Judges Kateka and Wolfrum were compelled to dissent because they could not reach a shared interpretation with the majority. The *Coastal State Rights* tribunal not only offered no fresh analysis of jurisdiction in this regard; it offered no analysis at all. Nor did the tribunal say anything about the dissent. But for a footnote in its summary of Ukraine's argument about the relative weight of land territory as an element in the dispute,[78] reading the *Coastal State Rights* award of 21 February 2020 one would not be aware that *Chagos* was a split award. Taking paragraph 220 of the *Chagos* award on its own, one hardly gets a confident or complete interpretation of Article 298(1)(a)*(i)* or Article 288(1). Taking it as it is—the product of a heavily divided tribunal—it deserves less weight still. Yet on that passage of the *Chagos* award the *Coastal State Rights* tribunal places the onus in regard to the putative effect of the territorial exclusion.

74 *Ibid.*, ¶ 158 (emphasis added).
75 *Coastal State Rights* award, ¶ 195.
76 *Chagos* Award, ¶ 220.
77 See above pp. 134–144.
78 *Coastal State Rights*, Award, ¶ 271 n. 482.

And, even then, the *Coastal State Rights* tribunal misread the *Chagos* award, portraying it as a declaration that the only territorial issues that a tribunal might consider under UNCLOS are those that are unnecessary to the claims that a party has presented. To say that the only sovereignty issues not excluded under UNCLOS jurisdiction are irrelevant issues—that is, issues not a 'prerequisite to the ... decision'—effectively is to say that *all* sovereignty issues are excluded. A tribunal has no business addressing irrelevant matters. The *Coastal State Rights* tribunal, in its faulty reformulation of paragraph 220 of the *Chagos* award, in effect voided the proviso that the *Chagos* majority had painstakingly expressed.

The *Coastal State Rights* tribunal did no better with *South China Sea* than with *Chagos*. In reference to *South China Sea*, the tribunal merely stated the negative point that the awards there already acknowledged: the Philippines had not asked for a determination in regard to which state is sovereign over particular land territories.[79] The *South China Sea* tribunal offered no definitive view about the scope of a territorial exception in Part XV, section 2. Invoking *South China Sea* in no way aided the *Coast State Rights* tribunal in its seeming quest for an ouster of Ukraine's maritime case.

After this unavailing foray into the jurisprudence, the tribunal declared, in effect, that the limits to its jurisdiction under Article 288(1) are self-evident and require no analysis. The tribunal said as follows:

> The Arbitral Tribunal does not consider that there exists a serious disagreement between the Parties regarding the interpretation of Article 288, paragraph 1, of the Convention *per se* ... As the Arbitral Tribunal sees it, the essence of the position of Ukraine is not that this Arbitral Tribunal is competent under Article 288, paragraph 1, of the Convention to decide any sovereignty dispute, but that there is no sovereignty dispute between the Parties over Crimea.[80]

It is certainly true that Ukraine argued that no sovereignty dispute exists in regard to Ukraine's territory of Crimea. Emphasizing what was (and remains) a matter of national priority to Ukraine—that Crimea is the sovereign territory of Ukraine—was a natural case strategy. However, as recalled above, Ukraine and Russia also joined issue over Article 288, paragraph 1.

Perhaps Ukraine voiced the point in muted tones. A party has every right to place the emphasis on those parts of its case that it wishes. In defending its internationally recognized sovereignty over Crimea, Ukraine did not surrender the interpretive question on Article 288(1), however. Ukraine advanced its interpretation of Article 288(1) expressly; and Russia advanced

79 *Ibid.*, ¶ 160.
80 Award, ¶ 161.

a different one. The difference mattered. It mattered for reasons of scoping UNCLOS jurisdiction: you cannot say whether a dispute fits within a jurisdictional provision until you know the scope both of the dispute and of the provision.

The parties' difference over Article 288(1) also mattered for the conduct of proceedings in accordance with basic considerations of rule of law. The tribunal mischaracterized the parties' difference when it said that 'there exists [no] serious disagreement' between them regarding the interpretation of Article 288(1). There most certainly was a disagreement; it was serious; the parties expressed it; but the tribunal ignored it.

We might leave the *Coastal State Rights* award of February 2020 at that. However, visible in the award are a number of further faults both of legal doctrine and of legal method. The idiosyncrasies in the tribunal's approach in this case, if adjudicators were to imitate them in future cases, would have damaging effects on international dispute settlement more widely. Accordingly, it falls to consider *Coastal State Rights* in further depth.

The salience of claims in international law

The crucial element in the *Coastal State Rights* award of February 2020 is the tribunal's declaration that a legal dispute exists as to which state is sovereign in Crimea. Necessary to the declaration that the legal dispute exists is a prior proposition—namely, that Ukraine is not the only state with a legal claim to be sovereign.

A great deal of state practice will never be put to the test of adjudication. In a system of law without central organs of legislation or courts with general jurisdiction, assertion and counter-assertion comprise in many encounters the totality of legal process. That the vast majority of claims between states are subject to no compulsory and binding procedure of dispute settlement entails that claims *qua* claims have a significance that assertions of right or obligation by a party in a fully developed national legal system do not. In part for this reason, James Crawford called the prevalence of the process of claim and counter-claim '*[t]he* core point' in international law.[81]

A paraphrasis is in order on this point—the salience of claims in international law—before we turn to consider how the *Coastal State Rights* tribunal came to the conclusion that Russia has a sovereignty claim and thus that a sovereignty dispute in regard to Crimea exists.

81 Crawford (2014), at 22 (emphasis added). Cf. *ibid.* 240.

In the international legal system, the claims that a state espouses predict the conduct that the state pursues. A state's espousal of a claim aligns the many parts of the state behind the claim.[82] As the opportunities for effective enforcement against the state are limited, the espousal—the act of claim articulation—increases the chances that the state, or parts of it, will engage in conduct predicted by (i.e., following the shape and contour of)[83] the claim.[84] This pattern of behavior is not absent among private actors subject to a national legal system, but in the international system it is more conspicuous.

The *Coastal State Rights* tribunal supplied a clear exposition of its own understanding of claims under international law. The tribunal deprecated its award as 'the *mere* recognition of the objective fact of the existence of a dispute over Crimea.'[85] According to the tribunal, its 'recognition of the existence of a dispute over the territorial status of Crimea in no way amounts to recognising *any* alteration of the status of Crimea.'[86] The tribunal's declaration that its 'recognition' entailed no 'alteration of … status' is, at best, formally correct but beside the point: the tribunal was not purporting to transfer sovereignty to Russia, or to find that Russia had sovereignty and transfer it to Ukraine. Nobody thought that the tribunal could do either, and Ukraine explicitly did not ask for the latter. Ukraine was clear that sovereignty had not changed. Russia was clear that it did not pursue a merits award on sovereignty.

However, to say that the tribunal's 'recognition of the existence of a dispute' entailed no 'alteration of … status' is arguably not even formally correct. In any legal system, identifying a legal claim is not a legally neutral act. In the international legal system, it affects the parties in a fundamental way. The tribunal declared that Russia '*simply* asks [it] to recognise the reality that it claims sovereignty over Crimea,'[87] but in that 'simple' request,

82 Exceptions, such as the *Breard* and *Avena* cases presented, tend to prove the rule. Seeming non-alignment between the central government in a federation and its constituent units on a point of international law likely will be referred to a theory and practice of internal sovereignty under which the latter are not bound by a claim or position of the former.

83 I use the term 'prediction' here, not in the colloquial sense of 'forecast,' but in the statistical sense of pattern-matching now brought to prominence by machine learning. See Grant & Wischik, *On the Path to AI: Law's Prophecies and the Conceptual Foundations of the Machine Learning Age* (2020) 45, 55–57.

84 Which is not to say that a state readily comes to a clear articulation of claim. See 'Round Table: New Proposals for Increasing the Rôle of International Law in Government Decision-Making' (remarks of Theodore Sorensen) (1971) 65 ASIL Proc. 285, 288–289.

85 *Coastal State Rights*, Award, ¶ 177 (emphasis added).

86 *Ibid.* ¶ 178 (emphasis added).

87 *Ibid.* ¶ 178.

Russia sought to alter the landscape of claim and thus to redefine legal relations between the parties and beyond. The tribunal obliged.

The formal understanding in law that claim affects the law is not an artifact isolated to legal thinking. One of the central insights of modern times in the natural sciences, the observer effect in quantum theory, resembles that understanding. In quantum theory, the observer effect results from 'the interaction between observer and object' and it 'causes uncontrollable and large changes in the system being observed.'[88] By analogy from quantum theory, the observational act of a judge or arbitrator affects the state of being of the object he observes.[89] To declare that an object exists, where, previously, nobody thought one did, is itself to bring about change in the system concerned. It is implausible to say that an adjudicator performs a neutral act when the adjudicator 'simply' recognizes as a 'reality' that one party claims another's territory. It runs against the proper understanding of the process of claim in international law; and it runs against the modern view of the world at large. As we will see below, to declare that a *territorial* dispute arises 'simply' from 'objective' juxtaposition of rival assertions also contradicts well-settled claims practice.

To summarize so far, we see that the Annex VII tribunal in *Coastal State Rights* thought that finding a legal claim to exist has no great consequence in international law. In the tribunal's view, Russia had made a 'simple' request, and granting it, the tribunal thought, was a 'mere' recognition of something that as a matter of 'objective fact' was true.

Now let us consider the tribunal's understanding of what constitutes a 'sovereignty dispute' for purposes of international law and the tribunal's approach to its forensic function, when the tribunal determined that the parties' opposing assertions constituted a 'sovereignty dispute.'

How the tribunal found a 'dispute'

To the ends that I just identified, I start in the pages that follow by describing how Russia purported to establish that a dispute had arisen,[90] and by suggesting that the tribunal failed adequately to interrogate Russia's assertion that a dispute had arisen.[91] I then turn to the formal definition of 'dispute'

88 Heisenberg, *The Physical Principles of the Quantum Theory* (1930) (Eckart & Hoyt, trans.) 3.

89 A quantum analogy may be found in Tribe, 'What Lawyers Can Learn from Modern Physics' (1989) 103 HLR 1.

90 See pp. 193–194.

91 See pp. 194–196 and pp. 229–234.

that guided the tribunal's analysis,[92] limits to the formal definition,[93] and the approach to fact-finding that the tribunal should have applied,[94] the existence of a dispute being, in some circumstances, not purely a formal matter but one that an adjudicator must consider with reference to factual evidence as well.[95] Pitfalls arise for the dispute settlement process if an adjudicator confines itself to formal indicia of a dispute when more than that is needed.[96]

The 'developments' leading to a 'dispute'

No dispute existed before March 2014 as to which state is sovereign in Crimea, a state of affairs that Russia expressly acknowledged and did not contest. Indispensable, therefore, to Russia's assertion that a dispute exists today was the antecedent proposition that a dispute had come into being—that is, that 'there was a change in the situation of Crimea and that [Russia's] claim of sovereignty was a response to that change.'[97]

It is instructive here to keep in view how recently, how rapidly, and in what unusual circumstances the putative change—and thus the putative dispute—had arisen. The tribunal acknowledged that, quite recently, there had been no dispute at all. To recall, '[t]he Russian Federation,' the tribunal said, 'does not contest that before March 2014 it had recognised Ukraine's sovereignty over Crimea.'[98] It was after that—sometime between the end of February 2014 and the third week of March to be exact—that something changed. Again, the tribunal's recital of Russia's argument is worth repeating, because this is the full extent of the tribunal's reasoning on the matter: 'there was a change in the situation of Crimea and ... [Russia's] claim of sovereignty was a response to that change.'[99] The 'change,' as far as practically every state and intergovernmental body that has a clear position on the matter agrees, was that Russia used force to seize part of Ukraine.

This practice should have given the tribunal pause but did not. The tribunal, at paragraph 181 of its award, said that

> [the tribunal] considers that the principles of good faith and estoppel do not operate so as to bar the Russian Federation from maintaining that a dispute concerning sovereignty over Crimea has arisen since March 2014, as the basis

92 See pp. 197–199.
93 See pp. 199–202, 202–205.
94 See pp. 206–207, 209–211, 211–220.
95 See pp. 207–209.
96 See pp. 220–222.
97 *Coastal State Rights*, Award, ¶ 181.
98 *Ibid.* ¶ 181.
99 *Ibid.*

> of the earlier statements [recognizing Ukraine's sovereignty] has been substantially and materially changed by developments upon which the Arbitral Tribunal has no jurisdiction to adjudicate.[100]

But whether good faith or estoppel operated to bar Russia from 'maintaining' the assertion was not the question that mattered. The question that mattered was whether the assertion reflected the existence of a legal dispute.

At the very least, the volte face between Russia's position circa January 2014 and March 2014—that is, Russia's change from understanding that *no* sovereignty dispute existed to Russia's insistence that one did—and the suddenness of the change, should have led the tribunal to turn a skeptic's eye to Russia's putative 'dispute.' Whether the 'basis' of Russia's long-standing statements recognizing Ukraine's sovereignty had 'substantially and materially' changed was the question on which Russia's jurisdictional objection hinged. To say that that 'basis' was changed by 'developments' and to declare in the same breath that jurisdictional limits bar exploring what those 'developments' were is inadequate. In place of reasoned inquiry, the tribunal substituted an anodyne term of avoidance—'developments'—and proceeded uncritically to accept that a settled boundary between states had somehow ceased to be settled.

Reasons to scrutinize Russia's 'developments': preliminary observations

To answer the question whether a legal dispute had arisen, the correct starting point was to ask whether, under the circumstances, *the* dispute to which Russia had alluded had arisen. Namely, the adjudicator should have asked, is there a dispute as to which state is sovereign in Crimea?

It does not suffice to answer in the abstract or on strictly formal grounds a question such as that which Russia's jurisdictional objection posed. Under the principle that a settled boundary between states does not change by force, and on the rule that *rebus sic stantibus* does not apply to treaties that have settled boundaries,[101] no ordinary 'developments' would have given rise to a legal dispute as to Ukraine's settled boundary. It is true that facts often change in the relations between states, and sometimes a change in the facts gives rise to a dispute under the law. In principle, it is possible between two states that a territorial dispute arises where not long before the states understood their boundary to have been settled. In some cases, states have asserted the existence of a sovereignty dispute after a significant period in which their spatial relations had remained settled. In cases such as those, adjudicators looked into the matter before they reached conclusions.

100 *Ibid.*

101 VCLT Art. 62(2)*(a)*. Cf. *Gabčíkovo-Nagymaros Project (Hungary/Slovakia)*, Judgment, ICJ 1997 at pp. 64–65 ¶ 104 (25 September).

I consider examples below. It suffices here to observe that, to conclude that a sovereignty dispute has arisen, an adjudicator must say what, precisely, happened that gave rise to the dispute. In some circumstances, purely formal evidence—the existence of contradictory assertions—suffices to demonstrate that a dispute exists, though, even in such circumstances, as I recall in a moment, the assertions must be *legal* assertions. In other circumstances, formal indicia do not suffice: the factual allegations on which a state grounds its assertion that a dispute has arisen must be proved.

The Council of Europe, to take one example from the international practice regarding Crimea, had no difficulty dismissing the factual allegations that Russia made in its attempt to demonstrate that a sovereignty dispute had arisen. According to the Parliamentary Assembly of the Council,

> none of the arguments used by the Russian Federation to justify its actions hold true to facts and evidence. There was no ultra-right takeover of the central government in Kyiv, nor was there any imminent threat to the rights of the ethnic Russian minority in the country, including, or especially, in Crimea. Given that neither secessionism, nor integration with the Russian Federation, was prevalent on the political agenda of the Crimean population, or widely supported, prior to Russia military intervention, the Assembly considers that the drive for secession and integration into the Russian Federation was instigated and incited by the Russian authorities, under the cover of a military intervention ... The so-called referendum that was organised in Crimea on 16 March 2014 was unconstitutional ... In addition, its reported turnout and results are implausible.[102]

Practice such as this is relevant, not because the judgments of one international organ necessarily bind another international organ; there is no general international rule or principle to such effect. The practice is relevant, because it demonstrates that international organs are not helpless in the face of factual questions.[103] The *Coastal State Rights* tribunal failed in its refusal to credit any of the surrounding international practice, a matter that I take

102 PACE resolution 1988 (2014), 9 April 2014 (Recent developments in Ukraine: threats to the functioning of democratic institutions), ¶¶ 15–16. Among writers in accord with this assessment, see Raimondo, 'Did Crimea Have the Right to Secede?' in Acconci, Cattin, Marchesi, Palmisano, & Santori (eds.), *Essays in Honor of Flavia Lattanzi* (2016) 535–548.

103 Nor must tribunals refrain from considering the plausibility of the assertions that a party places before them. For a useful review of cases in which adjudicators warn about overstepping jurisdictional limits in applying plausibility tests, see Tanaka, '*ARA Libertad* and *Ukraine* v. *Russia* cases' (2020) 96 *International Law Studies* 223, 239–242. As to the risk of prejudgment, see Lando, 'Jurisdiction Ratione Materiae of the International Court of Justice in Compromissory Clause Cases' (2023) 139 LQR 52, 72–74. But plausibility tests carry the risk of misapplication both ways.

up in Chapter 7; but it failed as well in its refusal to carry out meaningful forensic inquiry of its own. The tribunal left untested Russia's surprising premise that a territorial dispute had sprung to life in Crimea after decades of domestic and international peace.

The tribunal's default to 'objective dispute'

According to the *Coastal State Rights* tribunal, '[o]n the record before the Arbitral Tribunal ... it is clear that the Parties are in disagreement on various points of law and facts relating to the question as to which State is sovereign over Crimea.'[104] On the tribunal's understanding, Russia presented a formal 'record' of a 'legal dispute' and, in so doing, Russia satisfied the only requirement that is needed to show that a putative dispute exists. The 'record' consisted of statements in which Russia asserted that it is the sovereign in Crimea, and statements in which Ukraine asserted that Ukraine is the sovereign in Crimea. The tribunal treated the contrasting assertions as sufficient to demonstrate that a legal dispute exists.

The *Coastal State Rights* tribunal took the view that the 'developments' of February and March 2014 were outside its knowledge and beyond its power to inquire. This was in paragraph 181, which I quoted above, where the tribunal declared that 'the basis of [Russia's] earlier statements [recognizing Ukraine's sovereignty] has been substantially and materially changed by developments *upon which the Arbitral Tribunal has no jurisdiction to adjudicate*.'[105] The tribunal's abstention from fact-finding is one of the most perplexing aspects of the award.

An explanation for the tribunal's abstention lies in the tribunal's unreasoned acceptance of the putative exclusion of sovereignty issues from UNCLOS jurisdiction. Having expressed no reasoning of its own on the matter, the tribunal merely referred to *Chagos Marine Protected Area* and *South China Sea*. I have pointed out the ambiguities in the former as to the scope of jurisdiction over sovereignty disputes and the clarity in the latter that it was not offering a definition of the scope of jurisdiction over sovereignty disputes.[106] Reading these awards as totemic for a proposition that they scarcely support, the tribunal then seems to have exaggerated even *that* proposition: the tribunal declared all but *haram* rational fact-finding in regard to a sovereignty question.

Unsurprisingly, in light of this self-imposed constraint, when called on to address Russia's assertion that a sovereignty dispute exists the tribunal was at a loss what to do. Instead of directing the necessary inquiry toward

104 *Coastal State Rights*, Award, ¶ 165.
105 *Ibid.* (emphasis added).
106 See above Chapter 4, pp. 143–144; Chapter 5, pp. 162–165.

the assertion, the tribunal invoked the concept of the 'objective dispute.' The understanding of the concept that the tribunal applied also conspired toward fact-finding abstention.

Let us consider the term 'objective dispute' as adjudicators have used it, and let us consider its limits and the risks that arise from its misapplication. I then consider the evidence-based approach that, in certain circumstances, an adjudicator should apply when called on to say whether a dispute exists.

The 'objective dispute' and its limits

The concept of the 'objective dispute' entered the canon of international judicial and arbitral decision-writing a long time ago.[107] It is no stranger to law of the sea jurisprudence.[108] Asked to say whether two states have juxtaposed legal claims and thus constituted a legal dispute, a decision-maker must satisfy itself that the claim on each side is, in truth, a legal claim. A situation in which a state's assertion of interest is in conflict with another state's like assertion, without more, is not a situation in which legal claims are 'positively opposed' to one another. This is an observation that the ICJ made as long ago as the *South West Africa Cases*: '[n]or is it adequate to show that the *interests* of the two parties to such a case are in conflict.'[109]

Even earlier, the Permanent Court, in the *Mavromatis Concession* case, said that for there to be a dispute in a legally relevant sense there must be 'a disagreement on a point of law or fact, a conflict of legal views or of interests between two persons,'[110] a formulation that jurists have come to invoke on the assumption that the 'interests' at stake, if a difference concerning them is to be justiciable, must be *legal* interests.[111] Professor Tanaka noted that 'the time-honoured formula [in *Mavromatis*] appears to be too broad in its scope in the sense that it includes "conflict of interests" in the category of disputes. If there are always differences of interest behind international disputes, a mere disagreement of interests does not automatically create a dispute in a legal sense.'[112]

107 See McIntyre, 'The Role of the Dispute Requirement in Assessing Jurisdiction and Admissibility before the International Court' (2018) 19 Melbourne JIL 546, 549–555.

108 Harrison, 'Defining Disputes and Characterizing Claims' (2017) 48 ODIL 269, 270–273.

109 *South West Africa Cases (Ethiopia v. South Africa); Liberia v. South Africa)*, Preliminary Objections, ICJ 1962 p. 319, p. 328 (21 December).

110 *Mavromatis Palestine Concessions*, Judgment on Objection to Jurisdiction, 1924 PCIJ Ser. A No. 2 p. 11 (30 August).

111 See Kolb's review of the cases invoking *Mavromatis*. Kolb, *The International Court of Justice* (2013) 301–303.

112 Tanaka, *The Peaceful Settlement of International Disputes* (2018) 8.

Professor Kolb, whom Professor Tanaka cites with approval,[113] agrees: 'It is not right ... to convey the impression that all such disputes can be heard by the Court. It can hear only "legal disputes"';[114] it 'cannot address itself to factual issues unless they are bound up with points of law';[115] and, finally,

> [The *Mavromatis* definition] is entirely appropriate as regards a political body capable of deciding both types of dispute: the political and the legal. From the perspective of judicial jurisdiction, however, the definition has to be restricted, because the Court (or any tribunal deciding according to law) can decide only 'legal disputes.' It is therefore needful that the claimant under a unilateral application, or the parties together (in the case of a joint one), put forward claims based on rights and obligations arising under international law.[116]

From the proposition that two discordant legal claims are needed to constitute a legal dispute, it follows as a corollary that a party does not have a legal dispute with another, if it makes a legal claim and the other does not. As two sets of non-legal interests in collision do not in themselves make a legal dispute, so, too, one state's legal claim facing another state's non-legal assertion does not make a legal dispute either. Legal claims are what must be in opposition to make a legal dispute, such as a dispute in respect of sovereignty over territory.[117] There must be a legal claim on each side of the contestation.

113 *Ibid.*, 8 n. 32.

114 Kolb (2013) 303. Kolb also states that '[a]ccording to an old tradition, which has rightly been abandoned, the question must in addition be justiciable, that is, must be essentially legal in nature and not essentially political.' *Ibid.* 298. But, to the extent that Kolb rejects the legal–political distinction, Kolb rejects it in a specific setting only. The setting is that in which the parties have submitted a dispute to the ICJ on the basis of party consent. The setting is *not* that in which the parties dispute the characterization of a dispute that they have *not* consented to submit. Kolb elucidates the distinction in a short quotation from Hans Kelsen's *The Law of the United Nations* (1951) 478, where Kelsen said that Article 36(1) of the ICJ Statute, providing that 'the jurisdiction of the Court comprises all cases which the parties refer to it,' should be interpreted to mean 'that the parties may bring before the Court any dispute whatever. In so doing the parties make the dispute a legal dispute.' Quoted at Kolb (2013) 298 n. 480. The formula presupposes that the parties have consented to that characterization.

115 *Ibid.* 304.

116 *Ibid.* 306. Professor Schreuer, addressing the matter in respect of investment claims, agrees that *Mavrommatis*, if one attempts to apply it as a test for the existence of a dispute in the legal sense, is not up to the task. See Schreuer, 'What Is a Legal Dispute?' in Buffard, Crawford, Pellet, & Wittich (eds.), *Festschrift in Honour of Gerhard Hafner* (2008) 959, 960–961. Schreuer points out that Hafner agrees as well.

117 Recall the legal sense in which we speak as international lawyers of 'sovereignty': pp. 23–24.

This brings us to one of the limits of the concept of 'objective dispute': assertions of political character—and we will be reminded that force is an extension of politics by other means[118]—do not suffice to constitute a legal dispute.

Legal and extra-legal assertions distinguished

International law is a legal system that functions, if it is to function at all, in an arena where political action and sovereign discretion continue to influence the relations of its subjects.[119] If states, which are the main subjects of international law, ever are to give up those habits of statecraft, then they are not poised to do so anytime soon.[120] Accordingly, international law for the time being must keep a heightened awareness of the distinction between politics and law. The distinction indeed suffuses international law. It arises when tribunals ask whether a legal dispute exists. It arises in other international law settings as well. The settings are as diverse as they are familiar.

In the *Continental Shelf* cases, the ICJ famously considered the practice of states in regard to the possible development of a rule of customary international law that would require the equidistance method of delimitation. The Court said that 'there is no lack of *other reasons* for using the equidistance method, so that acting, or agreeing to act in a certain way, *does not of itself demonstrate anything of a juridical nature.*'[121] In other words, the conduct of a state is not necessarily indicative of an understanding by the state that a legal obligation requires the conduct—and, in consequence, the conduct of a state does not necessarily have legal effect as concerns the formation of customary international law. The process by which customary rules of international law emerge is one of the most important processes of international law. If an adjudicator is asked to say whether a customary rule has emerged, then the adjudicator must have careful regard to the evidence

118 See p. 220.

119 On the relation between politics (or force or power) and international law, the writings are vast. Among examples across recent decades, see Scott, 'International Law and International Politics' (1994) 5 EJIL 313, 323; chapters in Byers (ed.), *Essays in International Relations and International Law* (2001); and Reisman's 2007 Hague Lectures and Crawford's of 2013: Riesman, *The Quest for World Order and Human Dignity in the Twenty-First Century: Constitutive Process and Individual Commitment* (2012) 351 Hag. Rec. 8–479; Crawford, *Chance, Order, Change: The Course of International Law* (2013) 365 Hag. Rec. 9–369.

120 See Koskenniemi, *The Gentle Civilizer of Nations* (2001) *passim* and esp. 413–509. See also Schreuer in *Hafner Festschrift* (2008) at 959.

121 *North Sea Continental Shelf Cases (Federal Republic of Germany/Denmark; Federal Republic of Germany/Netherlands)*, Judgment, ICJ 1969 at p. 44 ¶ 76 (20 February) (emphasis added).

adduced. If a party's conduct is the result of 'other reasons'—that is, reasons other than the conviction that the conduct is obligatory as a matter of law—then the conduct 'does not of itself demonstrate anything of a juridical nature.' The conduct might be conspicuous in other ways. For example, it might have important effects on geopolitics and security. However, that does not entail in itself that the conduct has the relevant legal effect. The distinction between legal and extra-legal conduct, legal and extra-legal assertion, is fundamental in this way to international law.

To identify a rule of customary international law is, obviously, not the same thing as to apply UNCLOS Part XV, section 2, but the ICJ in the *Continental Shelf* cases addressed a matter that has general relevance. To restate the matter in general terms, not all conduct evinces a change in *legal* relations. This observation is just as applicable to the *Coastal State Rights* case as it is to the formation of a customary rule. Armed invasion does not demonstrate the existence of a territorial dispute sounding in law. Along with many other examples of conduct, some benign, some hostile, conduct does not on its own reshape the legal landscape around it.

The distinction between legal and extra-legal arises in practically all phases of dispute settlement and every situation in which parties might try to juxtapose legal claims. Discussing a request by a third state to intervene in contentious proceedings, Judge Weeramantry said that the state making the request must demonstrate that it has 'an interest of a legal nature' in the matter, *not* 'a merely political or social interest.'[122] Judge *ad hoc* Franck, in the same case, said: 'Even if ... all the Applicant's evidence were to be wholly confirmed, its interest would still be solely political: perhaps susceptible of historic, perhaps of political, but in any event not of judicial, vindication.'[123] Discussing remedies, Judge Simma, writing in an academic capacity with Dirk Pulkowski, distinguished between a remedy 'which operates on the political rather than the legal plane.'[124]

The political–legal distinction arises in treaty-making, too. States enter agreements that are legally binding, agreements that have only political effects, and agreements that mix the legal and the political;[125] Richard Baxter

122 *Sovereignty over Pulau Ligitan and Pulau Sipadan (Indonesia/Malaysia)*, Application by the Philippines for Permission to Intervene, Sep. Op. Judge Weeramantry, ICJ 2001 at p. 647 ¶ 30 (23 October).

123 Sep. Op. Judge Franck, ICJ 2001 at p. 658 ¶ 18.

124 See Simma & Pulkowski, '*Leges* Speciales and Self-Contained Regimes' in Crawford, Pellet, Olleson, & Parlett (eds.), *The Law of International Responsibility* (2010) 139, 153.

125 See Grant, 'The Budapest Memorandum of 5 December 1994' (2014) 34 Pol. YBIL 89–114. See also *The Queen on the Application of Melli Bank Plc v. HM Treasury & Foreign and Commonwealth Office* [2008] EWHC 1661 (Admin) ¶ 16 (Moses LJ).

notably addressed certain World War II-era treaties as political agreements.[126] Arthur Burchard, addressing even earlier practice, assumed that it was well-understood that an act on the international plane might be examined for its legal effects but also for its extra-legal ones, which are a different matter.[127] Olivier Corten, writing in 2024, attests that the distinction remains vital today.[128]

Then there are putative treaties that, owing to some fundamental defect, are not treaties at all. Judge Sir Hersch Lauterpacht's celebrated separate opinion in *Certain Norwegian Loans* concerned an instrument with a fundamental defect. Judge Lauterpacht observed that even an instrument with the *appearance* of constituting an international legal obligation—France's putative Acceptance of the ICJ Optional Clause was the instrument concerned—might be so defective that it is 'incapable of producing legal effects' and thus 'does not constitute a legal obligation.'[129] The instrument surely still existed in *some* sense, but not a legal one.

The thoughtful dissent of Judge Oda in the merits phase of *Military and Paramilitary Activities* is also worth recalling here. Judge Oda said that the Optional Clause of the ICJ Statute, Article 36, paragraph 2, 'affords ... no ground for concluding that voluntary acceptance of the obligation for submission of *legal* disputes to the Court's jurisdiction under that Article equates with the submission of *all* disputes however politically charged they may be.'[130] Judge Oda was reminding the Court of the distinction between legal disputes that, as a matter of their substance, are susceptible to adjudication and *political* disputes that are not. The compulsory settlement of disputes under the Optional Clause embraces 'all *legal* disputes concerning' the categories that the clause enumerates.[131]

Courts rightly refrain from delivering judgments on questions that are purely political, which includes questions the answers to which a party may

126 Baxter, 'International Law in "Her Infinite Variety"' (1980) 29 ICLQ 549, 550, citing McNair, *The Law of Treaties* (1961) at 501–502, 513.

127 'Effect of War on Contracts' (1930) 36 *ILA Reports of Conferences* 59, 106.

128 Corten, *Méthodologie du droit international public*, 2nd edn. (2024) 162–163.

129 *Certain Norwegian Loans (France v. Norway)*, Sep. Op. Judge Sir Hersch Lauterpacht, ICJ 1957 p. 34, p. 44. Expressing a similar point, see *Legal Consequences arising from the Policies and Practices of Israel in the Occupied Palestinian Territory, Including East Jerusalem*, ICJ, 19 July 2024, Dissenting Opinion of Vice-President Sebutinde, ¶ 65.

130 *Military and Paramilitary Activities in and Against Nicaragua (Nicaragua v. United States of America)*, Dis. Op. Judge Oda, ICJ 1986 at p. 236 ¶¶ 48–49 (27 June) (emphasis added).

131 Statute of the ICJ, Art. 36(2): 'a. the interpretation of a treaty; b. any question of international law; c. the existence of any fact which, if established, would constitute a breach of an international obligation; d. the nature or extent of the reparation to be made for the breach of an international obligation.'

put only to political use. The ICJ stated the matter in *Northern Cameroons* like this: '[A]fter a judgment is rendered, the use which the successful party makes of the judgment is a matter which lies on the political and not on the judicial plane. But it is not the function of a court ... to provide a basis for political action if no question of actual legal rights is involved.'[132] In other words, the judgment must have at least the possibility of being put to use in the system of law in which the court functions.

It is to be submitted that the *Coastal State Rights* award, in its determination that a sovereignty dispute exists between Russia and Ukraine, has no possibility of being put to use in the system of international law. As to the 'political ... plane' where it might be put to use, and as to the 'political action' which the prevailing party on that matter might take, the postscript to the award offers no comfort. Russia surely did not decide to launch an all-out invasion of the largest country in land area in Europe[133] solely because Annex VII arbitrators said that Russia's armed seizure of Crimea gives rise to legal claims with legal effects. However, surely too, not a word in the *Coastal State Rights* award of 21 February 2020 did anything to dissuade the aggressor.

A dispute as to which state is sovereign over a territory is a dispute about legal claims, sovereignty being a term, in this setting, denoting the legal rights and obligations that title in respect of territory entails. Not all *assertions* of sovereign right evince legal claims; not all acts in pursuit of control over territory are legal acts such as a state might juxtapose against another state in order to constitute a legal dispute. The distinctions involved here are not abstractions. Their function is indispensable to legal dispute settlement. There must be a *legal* claim on each side of a contestation if the contestation is to be addressed in a dispute settlement procedure under law.

Acts on different legal planes

A further basic point, but one that merits recalling, is that an act with legal effects in one legal order does not necessarily have effects in another. The famous result in *Barcelona Traction* followed from the ICJ's understanding that an act with legal effects in the national legal order of Belgium (the acquisition by Belgian citizens of shares in a Canadian company)[134] did not have the effect that the Belgian citizens had hoped it would in the international legal order (the establishment of standing on the part of Belgium to pursue

132 *Northern Cameroons (Cameroon v. United Kingdom)*, Preliminary Objections, ICJ 1963 at p. 37 (2 December).

133 I.e., 233,062 square miles (603,549 square kilometers) wholly in Europe.

134 As to the national law effects, see *Barcelona Traction, Light and Power Company, Limited (New Application: 1962) (Belgium v. Spain)*, ICJ 1970 at pp. 34–35, 38 ¶¶ 42, 52 (5 February).

a claim against Spain to vindicate their legal interest in those shares after Spain nationalized the company).[135] The ICJ held that Belgium had no such standing.[136] The limitation of effects between legal planes might operate the other way too, as it did in the *International Tin Council* case, the relations between the International Tin Council and its constituent members having existed on the international law plane, not on that of domestic law.[137]

To give an example of a somewhat different kind, but going to the same point, namely that particular acts may be confined in their effects to particular legal planes, Rwanda adopted national legal acts that evinced the intention to withdraw its reservation to the compromissory clause of the Genocide Convention (Article IX), but the ICJ found that, because Rwanda had failed to notify other parties of withdrawal of the reservation, 'as a matter of international law' the national law decree did not 'effect a withdrawal.'[138] True, the matter is naturally associated with the distinction between acts of policy and acts of law and also with defects in effectiveness of putative international acts.[139] It equally illustrates that acts in one legal order do not necessarily have effects in another.

The ICJ's *Kosovo* advisory opinion contains the archetypal statement that a particular act might have its only significance and effects outside the legal order. Considering what, if any, legal effects the declaration of independence of Kosovo had in the legal order that the UN Security Council had constituted for Kosovo during the territory's interim phase, the Court said as follows:

> The declaration of independence ... was not intended by those who adopted it to take effect within the legal order created for the interim phase, *nor was it capable of doing so*. On the contrary ... the authors of that declaration did not act, or intend to act, in the capacity of an institution created by and empowered to act within that legal order but, rather, set out to adopt a measure the significance and effects of which would lie outside that order.[140]

135 As to the lack of international law effects, see ICJ 1970 at p. 48 ¶ 52.

136 ICJ 1970 at pp. 37–38 ¶¶ 50–54 (no formal grounds to find standing); p. 50 ¶ 101 (no standing on basis of equity). Cf. as to the reverse question, holding a corporation to account on the international plane: Jeremy Carver, 'Remedies for Wrongful Acts of Transnational Corporations: Alien Torts, BITs or International Compensation' (2004) 71 *ILA Reports of Conferences* 430, 431.

137 *J. H. Rayner (Mincing Lane) Ltd v. Department of Trade and Industry* [1990] 2 AC 418, 476–477, 499–500 (Templeman LJ).

138 *Armed Activities in the Territory of the Congo (New Application: 2002) (Democratic Republic of the Congo v. Rwanda)*, ICJ 2006 at p. 26 ¶ 43 (3 February).

139 *Ibid.* at pp. 26–28 ¶¶ 45–55, esp. p. 29 ¶ 53.

140 *Accordance with International Law of the Unilateral Declaration of Independence in Respect of Kosovo*, Advisory Opinion, ICJ 2010 at pp. 445–446 ¶ 105 (22 July) (emphasis added).

Acts, even those with powerful effects in their given sphere, do not necessarily have *legal* effects. As the Court said, certain acts are not even capable of having legal effects.

It spurs natural revulsion to compare a peaceful declaration to brute force, but states practice politics along a spectrum of means. War is a political tool, no less than is a declaration of independence. Politics in any form, from pacific to warlike, has legal effects, but it is a duty of organs that apply the law to be clear about where those effects meet their limits. It is submitted that, as the ICJ in *Kosovo* recognized that a declaration of independence did not bring about effects on the legal plane concerned 'nor was it capable of doing so,' the *Coastal State Rights* tribunal should have recognized that there are things that an armed invasion can do and things that it cannot.

The *Jurisdictional Immunities case (Germany v. Italy)* reminds us that even assertions that are undoubtedly legal sometimes speak past one another. Stefan Talmon cogently argues that the distinction between substantive and procedural rules, even where the substantive rules are *jus cogens*, makes sense and should not be abandoned.[141] Talmon acknowledges that writers who criticize *Germany v. Italy* are discomfited by the result of strict application of the distinction. Pleading the distinction, parties have avoided adjudication, and allegations of a serious breach of *jus cogens* rules have been left unaddressed. In *Coastal State Rights*, the Annex VII tribunal reached a result that discomfits many observers in much the way Talmon acknowledges, but, in reaching that result, the tribunal not only ignored the results-oriented concern that animated the critics of *Germany v. Italy*. It also ignored the formal separation between the categories of political-military assertion and of legal claim. The result that the tribunal reached and the manner in which this happened thus for this reason are both unsatisfactory.

Writers who found merit in the refusal of the *Coastal State Rights* tribunal to exercise jurisdiction had little or nothing to say about the distinctions that I have addressed here—between legal acts and those outside the law altogether and between acts on different legal planes. Valentin Schatz, writing shortly after the 21 February 2020 award, said as follows:

> [T]he arbitral tribunal (in my view, convincingly) consistently distinguished between considerations of legality at the level of substantive law and the objective identification of a dispute for the purposes of jurisdiction. In other words, that Russia's annexation of Crimea may have been clearly unlawful and sovereignty may still rest with Ukraine as a matter of substantive law is irrelevant for the question of jurisdiction, which only requires a dispute.[142]

141 See Talmon, '*Jus Cogens* after *Germany v. Italy*' (2012) 25(4) Leiden JIL 979.
142 Schatz, 'Status of Crimea and the Sea of Azov,' *EJIL Talk!* (20 March 2020).

This formulation raises doubt in two respects. First, in the circumstances, there is no question whether Russia's seizure of territory *might* have been unlawful, and no question whether Ukraine *might* still hold sovereignty. Under modern international law, and as was readily appreciated on the evidence, the answer to both is not only clear; it is unavoidable. To the extent that either question had any substance, it would have been so marginal in substance that no great exercise of fact-finding or of legal logic would have been necessary for the tribunal to have answered it. These questions, to use the term from *Chagos Marine Protected Area*, are 'minor' in a very meaningful sense: there is little doubt as to their answer. The over-reading of the exclusion of territorial issues from Part XV, section 2, unfortunately has led adjudicators to believe that even at the margins a question touching on sovereignty is not to be examined, much less given the answer it deserves. And some international law writers, though of the highest caliber, regrettably have concurred.

But Schatz's formulation raises doubt in a further respect, more fundamental than the first. For there to be a legal dispute between two parties, 'the level of substantive law' on which each party's assertion exists must be the same as the other party's. A legal assertion that exists only in one system of law and a legal assertion that exists only in a different system of law are not in contestation with one another in the relevant sense for them to constitute a legal dispute. Equally, an assertion that exists outside *any* system of law does not supply the requisite material for a legal dispute at all. The 'objective identification of a dispute for the purposes of jurisdiction'—to use Schatz's words—means in the setting concerned in *Coastal State Rights* a dispute in respect of sovereignty over territory. A sovereignty dispute in that setting means a dispute as to legal entitlement to territory. For such a dispute to arise, the parties must oppose competing *legal* claims to territory, one legal claim against another. Where one party's putative claim owes its substance to physical weight or military incursion, that party has no claim, and thus there is no *legal* dispute. It says nothing as to legal title to a territory that a party has invaded and occupied it. The conduct might have *evidentiary* value, if a decision-maker is considering the situation in the round with other forms of evidence or is trying to probe a party's state of mind. But, in themselves, invasion and occupation do not constitute an expression of legal claim.

Defining the particular dispute concerned

A further consideration missing from the *Coastal State Rights* tribunal's analysis of the 'objective dispute' is one of definition. The question that the tribunal needed to answer was whether a particular dispute existed that a particular UNCLOS term embraces. The particular UNCLOS term is that in Article 298(1)(a)*(i)*—an 'unsettled dispute concerning sovereignty or other rights over continental or insular land territory.' UNCLOS does not define that term. The proper course would have been to define the term and only then proceed to consider evidence to discern whether or not *that* kind of dispute existed. The tribunal did neither of these things. To uphold Russia's jurisdictional objection, it was not enough to say that a dispute existed *in abstracto*, but that in effect is what the tribunal did.

I observed in Chapter 2 that adjudicators in diverse settings, including under UNCLOS, have turned to other law sources in order to clarify the meaning of undefined terms in a treaty.[143] This is what the Annex VII tribunal constituted in *Duzgit Integrity* did. It considered 'foundational or secondary rules of general international law,' because without those rules it would not have been able 'properly to interpret and apply particular provisions of the Convention.'[144] It is to be submitted that the principle that sovereignty does not change by use of force is a foundational rule that necessarily limits the definition of the UNCLOS term 'unsettled dispute concerning sovereignty.'

To limit the definition, the tribunal did not even have to look outside UNCLOS. As I recalled in Chapter 2,[145] Article 301 obliges every state party in exercising its rights and performing its duties under UNCLOS to refrain from the 'threat or use of force against the territorial integrity or political independence of any State.' A limiting effect on the definition of 'sovereignty dispute' is visible in Article 301.[146]

Make of it what one might, Article 301 in any event is not necessary to the point. To construe an UNCLOS term in a manner that does violence to the foundational rule of non-acquisition of territory by force is unsustainable.

Fact-finding and dispute-finding

In the preceding subsections, I recalled that, for a dispute to exist for purposes of international law, two or more parties each must make an assertion of legal character, where the assertions are in contestation with one another and are within the same legal system, that is, on the same legal plane.

143 See pp. 86–88.
144 *Duzgit Integrity* at ¶ 208.
145 See p. 78.
146 Separately, one reflects that exercising a putative right in a maritime area that the state party grounds on an armed invasion and forcible annexation of another state's territory does not sit well with Art. 301. If Art. 301 does not supply a basis for claim in the circumstances of *Coastal State Rights*, then it would be challenging to formulate a factual hypothesis under which it did. Ukraine seems not to have invoked Art. 301 in its pleadings, and the tribunal did not address it. See Kunoy (2024) 367–372 for an interesting discussion of Art. 301 and Ukraine's missed opportunity to invoke it.

To satisfy itself that a dispute between parties displays this required symmetry, a decision-maker must have a method for distinguishing between a legal claim and a mere interest. It does not make a mere interest a legal claim that the interest happens to arise from perfectly lawful conduct (Professor Tanaka supplies an example from international trade),[147] nor does it necessarily deprive a legal claim its character as such that it arises out of a breach of international law (an illegal invasion, for example, might give rise to a legal claim for reparation). What matters is whether the parties have a dispute comprising contradictory assertions, each of which is predominantly, and not only incidentally or superficially, of legal character.

Insufficiency of the formal approach

It would seem natural, in seeking to answer the question whether a dispute exists in a particular case, that an adjudicator would have recourse to factual evidence relevant to the question. However, according to a considerable body of opinion, the existence of a dispute is a formal matter and factual inquiry has nothing to do with it. To give an eminent example, Professor Schreuer said the following: 'It follows from the practice [in investment claims] that the legal nature of a dispute depends not on the factual circumstances of a case but on the position taken by the claimant. If the claimant presents its claim in terms of rights and legal remedies, the argument that the dispute is not legal will be to no avail.'[148]

Professor Schreuer's approach places a great deal of weight on the form by which a party gives expression to a putative dispute. There are reasons to ask whether that approach might be too categorical. In some circumstances, an adjudicator must say whether a legal dispute exists, because the adjudicator has been called upon to adjudicate *that* (putative) legal dispute. But the adjudicator might have to answer the question for other reasons. The adjudicator might have to answer it, because the existence of a legal relationship constituting a dispute is a necessary predicate to some other legal process or conclusion.

A legal dispute is a kind of legal relationship. The existence of a legal dispute can have a variety of consequences in different circumstances. It might open the door to adjudication, because a party must show that a legal dispute exists in order for the adjudicator to address it. But so too it

147 Tanaka, *Peaceful Settlement of International Disputes*, 8: 'For example, an exporting country of petrol usually attempts to export it at a high price, while an importing country of petrol has an interest in buying it at a low price. Here there is a difference concerning economic interests between States. Nonetheless, this is not a dispute in international law, unless there is an obligation to fix the price of petrol.'

148 Schreuer in *Hafner Festschrift* (2008) 970.

might close the door, as where a jurisdictional instrument bars adjudication of certain kinds of legal disputes, such as disputes over sovereignty.

Before an adjudicator draws conclusions as to the legal consequences arising from a legal relationship of any kind, the adjudicator must satisfy itself that the legal relationship exists. Many situations arise in which a formal approach does not settle the matter. A number of illustrations may be offered.

Legal consequences follow from the existence of a filial relationship. For example, a parent under some national tax laws may claim a tax deduction or other benefit for certain expenses associated with raising a child if the parent demonstrates the expenses in a prescribed way and within prescribed limits. An individual might dispute with the tax authorities an administrative determination disallowing a particular deduction or benefit that the individual claimed, and the authorities then call on the individual to make a more detailed submission about the expenses (school invoices, evidence of the child's school attendance, etc.). However, the authorities might ask the prior question too—that is, whether the filial relationship exists.[149] To answer *that* question will require different evidence. Factual evidence might well be among the evidence required. Without the factual evidence, the party will not have proved the existence of the legal relationship from which the party hopes to draw certain legal consequences.

Or, to take a situation from ordinary commercial relations, two parties might differ as to the interpretation of a contract that they agree they have properly concluded and remains in force between them. Let us call this an 'interpretive dispute.' Two parties readily advance contradictory claims of legal character under a contract and thus constitute an interpretative dispute. The existence of the interpretative dispute well might be established in the purely formal way that Schreuer describes: 'Under our contract, you owe me $100,' says Party A; 'No, I don't,' says Party B. 'Under our contract, I owe you only $50.'

Take, by contrast, a situation where the parties differ as to whether they agreed at all—that is to say, they differ as to whether a contract exists. Let us call this the 'existential dispute.' True, the existential dispute, too, is a dispute of legal character. However, it is a different legal dispute from the one that arises out of a contract the validity of which no party challenges. To prove that a contract exists, a party must make certain factual demonstrations. The existential dispute thus will require the adjudicator to engage in fact-finding.

149 The hypothetical example here is not unrealistic. See Rosie Jempson, 'Benefit Fraudsters Who Pretended to Have 18 Children to Claim 300k Only Have to Repay 2,' *Daily Express*, 16 September 2024.

On reflection, we see that the existential dispute embraces the interpretative dispute to this extent: the existence of the interpretative dispute—which is the one that the claimant wants to settle, because the claimant hopes to win a judgment ordering the other party to pay money (allegedly) due under the putative contract—depends on the existence of the contract. The existence of the interpretative dispute thus depends on factual circumstances as well: there is no interpretative dispute, if the contract that a party wants to interpret does not exist. Determining the facts, in that setting, is a necessary predicate to saying whether the dispute that the claimant wants to adjudicate exists. To say that 'the legal nature of [the] dispute depends *not on the factual circumstances* ... but on the position taken by the claimant' is either false or, if true, true only in a trivial way. Without the factual evidence that a contract exists, the party will not have proved the existence of the legal relationship from which the party hopes to draw certain legal consequences.

Questions of the existence of a contract in municipal law no doubt arise more often than questions of the existence of a sovereignty dispute in international law. But the distinction between determining the consequences of a legal relationship and determining whether the legal relationship exists is just as salient in the latter (rare) cases as in the former (commonplace) ones. On the prevailing view of UNCLOS Part XV, section 2, the adjudicator has no authority to settle a sovereignty dispute, and so the consequence of the existence of that legal relationship—that is, of a sovereignty dispute—is automatic and requires little analysis. The same cannot necessarily be said of the adjudicator's determination whether the legal relationship exists. As with other kinds of legal relationships that a party asserts exist, demonstration of the existence of a putative dispute might require factual evidence and, thus, evidentiary inquiry by the decision-maker.

These observations about the existence of contract disputes, being by way of analogy, necessarily go only so far. However, as we will see below,[150] cases in which adjudicators have had to say whether *sovereignty disputes* exist also refute the postulate that the mere articulation of contradictory assertions necessarily demonstrates the existence of a dispute.

Disentangling the legal from the extra-legal in a situation involving both

At least two challenges arise for the decision-maker whose task it is to determine whether a contestation forms a legal dispute. First, a contestation having no legal character in itself might well have legal consequences, and therefore the decision-maker must discern between the contestation and its sequelae. Second, a contestation is likely to have at least *some* element of legal character, and, even where it does not, the party contending that the

150 See pp. 211–220.

contestation forms a legal dispute likely will say that it does. So the decision-maker must disentangle the legal and the non-legal elements of the contestation and then judge whether the former are adequate to impart to the whole sufficient legal character to make a legal dispute. To do this reliably requires that the adjudicator test the evidence. Let us consider each of these challenges in turn.

The legal sequelae of Russia's armed seizure of Crimea are numerous. Nobody would contend that invasion and occupation have not affected the sovereign's enjoyment of title, or that these acts otherwise entail no legal effects. Ukraine has experienced consequences from Russia's seizure of Crimea, including legal effects. The effects arise under international humanitarian law, the law of investment protection, and the law of human rights, as well as the *jus ad bellum* or prohibition of use of force, under which Russia, if any court had jurisdiction to hear the matter, likely would be held internationally responsible for injuries to Ukraine that the breach of that law has caused.[151] As we will see in Chapter 8, the ECtHR and a number of tribunals under the Russia–Ukraine BIT have addressed some of the human rights and investment law breaches: Russia is responsible for injuries caused by Russia's authorities in Crimea. But none of these legal effects entail a change of sovereignty or the creation of a legal claim to sovereignty.

Analytic clarity here requires keeping in view the distinction between a claim and the means that a party might employ to pursue a claim. A dispute arising out of a valid legal claim, even a claim that is likely to prevail on the legal merits, does not justify use or threat of force as a means to vindicate it.[152] As Professor Serdy observes in connection with Guyana's claim against Surinam for unlawful use of force and threat, '[t]he fact that the location in question was on Guyana's side of the boundary later awarded by the tribunal had no discernible effect on this finding: the strength of a State's claim in the underlying dispute does not render a non-peaceful means either peaceful or lawful.'[153] A similar observation could be made in view of the Costa Rica–Nicaragua dispute over Nicaragua's dredging works at Isla

151 As to the illegality of Russia's use of force, see Grant, *Aggression against Ukraine* (2015) 43–61.

152 See, for example, the situation at Badme: *Eritrea/Ethiopia*, PCA Case No. 2001–02, Eritrea–Ethiopia Claims Commission (van Houtte, President; Aldrich, Crook, Paul, and Reed, arbitrators), *Jus ad Bellum* (Ethiopia's Claims no. 1–8), Partial Award (19 December 2005) ¶ 10 and for comment Milano & Papanicolopulu (2011) at 597–598; Klein & Koutroulis in Kohen & Hébié (eds.) (2018) at 254–256.

153 Serdy, 'Article 279' in *Proelss Commentary* (2017) 1813, 1817. See also the Doklam incident between India and China: Yiallourides, Gehring, & Gauci (2018) 67–70, ¶¶ 130–135.

Portillos: 'The fact that Nicaragua considered that its activities were taking place on its own territory does not exclude the possibility of characterizing them as an unlawful use of force.'[154]

And just as the unlawfulness of a use of force does not invalidate a state's claim to sovereignty,[155] so is the converse true: the *lawfulness* of a use of force does not *validate* a state's claim to sovereignty. The two matters are analytically distinct. Professors Klein and Koutroulis stated the matter succinctly: 'issues relating to the determination of sovereignty, on the one hand, and to responsibility ensuing from a recourse to force, on the other' an adjudicator or other decision-maker must 'appraise on [their] own merits.'[156]

It follows from these observations that there was no need in *Coastal State Rights* to say whether Russia's use of force against Ukraine was lawful or not. Nobody maintains that the use of force in a land area is a circumstance that, without more, precludes dispute settlement jurisdiction in respect of claims concerning an appurtenant maritime area. Nor was there any need for the tribunal to be apprehensive that an inquiry into Russia's assertion of a sovereignty claim would draw the tribunal into an adjudication about state responsibility for use of force. The question of the legality of Russia's use of force, to the extent that there was a question, was separable from the question whether Russia's assertion of sovereignty constituted a legal claim.

Identifying legal disputes: the evidence-based approach

In *Coastal State Rights*, the fact was undisputed that Russia exercised effective control in Crimea. However, that state of affairs was consistent with divergent conclusions. A party might in fact exercise effective control, whether or not the party has a legal claim to that which it controls. The task that the *Coastal State Rights* tribunal was called on to perform was to say how the state of affairs in Crimea had come about. Was Russia's effective control there conjoined with a legal claim? Was it purely an expression of armed force? Or, if it was a mixture of the two—of legal claim and force—which was the predominant element?

The ICJ, in 2024 in its judgment on preliminary objections in the *Ukraine v. Russia* case under the Genocide Convention, would recall that 'it is an integral part of [the] judicial function to establish the facts in light of the

154 *Certain Activities Carried out by Nicaragua in the Border Area (Costa Rica v. Nicaragua)/Construction of a Road in Costa Rica along the San Juan River (Nicaragua v. Costa Rica)*, Judgment, ICJ 2015 p. 665, p. 704 ¶ 97 (15 December).

155 Though it might have relevance as *evidence* of the claim's validity, including of the State's good faith in asserting the claim.

156 Klein & Koutroulis in Kohen & Hébie (eds.) (2018) at 260.

evidence presented.'[157] In the same judgment, the ICJ also would recall that the 'determination of the existence of a dispute is a matter of substance, not of form or procedure.'[158] The ICJ here supplied welcome reminders.

Acts, including unlawful acts, are not in all situations readily disentangled from legal claims associated with them. But even in the hard cases—that is, the cases where the legal and extra-legal are most entangled—the adjudicator has the methodological tools to address the matter. The act and the claim in some situations form a nexus, a situation, the parts of which cannot be clinically isolated one from the other. Where act and claim have such a relation, the adjudicator applies the evidence-based approach to discern how, exactly, act and claim relate. Are they in equilibrium (or nearly so)? Or does one part predominate? Judging what constituent element predominates in a thing of mixed character is one of the adjudicator's routine tasks.[159]

As we saw in Chapter 4, the *Chagos Marine Protected Area* majority performed the routine task. It judged whether the UNCLOS element predominated in a dispute of mixed character between Mauritius and the United Kingdom. The *Chagos* majority said that to determine whether a dispute is one concerning the interpretation or application of UNCLOS—there was no doubt that Mauritius and the United Kingdom had a dispute that at least *in part* concerned the interpretation or application of UNCLOS—a tribunal must determine 'where the *relative weight* of the dispute lies.'[160] In saying that a tribunal must determine 'where the relative weight ... lies,' the *Chagos* majority knew that it is a mainstay of adjudicators' work to

157 *Allegations of Genocide under the Convention on the Prevention and Punishment of the Crime of Genocide (Ukraine v. Russian Federation: 32 States Intervening)*, ICJ, Preliminary Objections, ¶ 103 (2 February 2024).

158 *Ibid.* at ¶ 45.

159 Illustrations from municipal and international jurisdictions are many. For example, courts called on to say whether admiralty jurisdiction embraces a particular claim have to judge whether the 'contracts, claims, [or] services' concerned are '*essentially* maritime' (emphasis supplied): *Ex parte Easton*, 95 U.S. 68, 72 (1877) (Clifford, J). Courts called on to say how to apply the Harmonized Tariff Schedule to a product have to judge on the basis of an 'essential character analysis' which component of the product 'predominates over the others': *Nature's Touch Frozen Foods (West) Inc. v. United States*, 639 F.Supp. 3d 1287, 1305 (U.S. Court of International Trade) (Vaden J.) (2023) (internal quotations omitted). In diplomatic protection, adjudicators consider a range of evidentiary factors to judge whether the *dominant* nationality of an individual or entity is that of the state espousing its claim. See McLachlan, Shore, & Weiniger, *International Investment Arbitration: Substantive Principles*, 2nd edn. (2017) 163. In investment claims practice, where it is a *ratione personae* requirement of jurisdiction that the claimant have the nationality of the other state party and not of the respondent state, adjudicators in some circumstances apply a test of dominant nationality as well—e.g., under the 2012 US model BIT: *ibid.* 175.

160 *Chagos Marine Protected Area*, Award, ¶ 211 (emphasis added).

discern when a situation is mostly one thing or mostly another. I suggested in Chapter 4 that there are better ways to think about the operation than as taking the measure of 'relative weight,' but that is in the setting of a legal instrument (UNCLOS) in which the two disparate things (maritime terms and territorial terms) are both present and both *legal* things. In that setting, both things well might be connected to one another in a juridical sense. I suggested that, there, it would be better to reason about the matter as one of connectedness between things than one of 'relative weight' between them. Here, by contrast, our task is to describe a situation that mixes legal and *political* things. We seek a way to discern whether the legal or the political predominate. The two kinds of things might be connected to one another in an *effective* or *empirical* sense—for example, particular legal situations might arise from particular political acts. But the two kinds of things are not connected to one another on the legal plane. They are not connected in a juridical sense. With an assertion such as Russia's about Crimea, it is the very *extra*-legal character of the assertion that we seek to weigh against any possible legal element that the claim might embody. The weighing operation is therefore apposite.

Russia said that the situation in Crimea is one thing—a dispute under law as to which state is sovereign. The evidence suggested that it is another—an attempt to change a settled boundary between states by force. The *Coastal State Rights* tribunal, in considering the question which thing predominates, failed to scrutinize the evidence or even consider it. As a result, the tribunal ignored the relative weight in the situation between law and force. As fraught as the situation between Russia and Ukraine is, the proper approach for the tribunal was to perform this routine task: examine the evidence and reach a judgment as to the predominant character of a thing of mixed character. The tribunal failed to do what courts and tribunals routinely do.

It was open to the *Coastal State Rights* tribunal, if it had exercised the adjudicator's routine discernment, to determine that Russia's imposition of control over Crimea had nothing to do with law at all. One of the investment tribunals constituted under the Russia–Ukraine BIT to address claims arising out of Crimea appears to have determined something very much like that. According to the tribunal in *Naftogaz v. Russian Federation* in its partial award of 22 February 2019, '[t]he vulnerability of Ukrainian investments (and thus the need for Treaty protection) in Crimea is wholly the result of Russian military action.'[161] An inference to be drawn from the tribunal's observation is that it was not an enlargement of Russia's sovereignty (i.e., legal title to Crimea) or of a legal claim to sovereignty (i.e., a legal claim to title) that led to '[t]he vulnerability of Ukrainian investments.' The inference

161 *Naftogaz v. Russian Federation*, Partial Award, 22 Feb 2019, ¶ 202.

follows because a thing that is *wholly* one thing contains no other thing. The 'vulnerability' was '*wholly* the result of Russian military action.' The form of words in the *Naftogaz* partial award is very close, arguably equivalent, to saying that the power that Russia exercised over Ukrainian investments in Crimea came from an assertion of force, not from a legal right or legal claim. *Naftogaz* concerned an example of what I referred to above as 'legal sequelae.' It is true that the *consequences* of 'Russian military action' included legal incidents, including legal claims, that is, legal claims by Ukrainian investors based on the potential legal responsibility of Russia for violation of the BIT in regard to Ukrainian investments. But military action itself is not action on a legal plane. The *Naftogaz* tribunal's words nicely respect the distinction between force and law, and its conclusion was that Russia's assertion of power in Crimea (and over persons and assets in Crimea) relied wholly on force and not at all on law.

The failure of the Annex VII tribunal in *Coastal State Rights* to engage with the evidence and scrutinize the factual premises behind Russia's supposed 'sovereignty dispute' is a puzzlement. The tribunal's abstention from the fact-finding function, as I suggested earlier in this chapter, was a serious error. Examples of adjudicators willing to engage in fact-finding on ancillary issues are found throughout international dispute settlement practice. As I recalled in Chapter 2, the ICJ examined a range of factual allegations concerning matters that were, at best, ancillary to its merits jurisdiction in *Nicaragua* and *Oil Platforms*.[162] It distinguished legal from political 'justifications' in *Nicaragua* and elsewhere. Even an investment tribunal (in *Naftogaz*)—as a 'mixed' tribunal, a step further removed from the public order concerns that sometimes influence interstate dispute settlement—recognized the facts of the matter. The Annex VII tribunal in *Coastal State Rights* should have examined how Russia came to be present in Crimea, but it did not do so.

Russia's use of force—the invasion of Ukraine and forcible seizure of Crimea—is self-evidently the predominant part in Russia's assertion against Ukraine. The non-legal character of Russia's assertion of a 'sovereignty dispute' would have been evident to the *Coastal State Rights* tribunal, if it had looked. Instead, the tribunal gave a wan recital of a Russian 'claims' practice. Russia, the tribunal said, made statements about its 'claim' to sovereignty over Crimea in 'various *fora*, including the United Nations and the International Maritime Organization since 2014.'[163] There is nothing more to the tribunal's analysis on the point than that. *That* is the formal basis which the tribunal declared 'would seem to be sufficient for a conclusion

162 See pp. 83–86.
163 *Coastal State Rights*, Award, ¶ 165 and above pp. 182–184.

that a sovereignty dispute exists between the Parties.'[164] The *Coastal State Rights* tribunal, almost sheepishly, acknowledged that Russia's evidence for a legal claim was 'not as abundant as [that submitted] in *Chagos*.'[165] This was an understatement. To interpolate a term into Stalin's infamous quip, lack of quantity has a quality all its own.

Did the *timing* of Russia's evidence raise any doubts for the arbitrators? The tribunal referred to statements '*since 2014*' (emphasis added). That was the year when Russia seized Crimea by force. A judge in a territorial dispute would have heavily discounted—most likely, given no weight at all—to evidence of *effectivités* submitted by a state in the dispute if that evidence was from a date after the dispute 'crystallized.' This principle, the principle of 'critical date,' is that acts 'occurring after [the] date [when the dispute crystallized] ... "are in general meaningless ... having been carried out by a State which ... could have taken those actions strictly with the aim of buttressing"' its argument.[166] True, the concern in the 'critical date' jurisprudence is not with evidence advanced to support a claim that a dispute over sovereignty exists. The concern, instead, is with evidence advanced to support a *claim to sovereignty*. It is not clear, therefore, whether evidence of the existence of a dispute is 'in general meaningless' if it comes late in a dispute over the existence of a dispute. Yet evidence consisting of unilateral acts by one party performed only after that party has started to assert that a dispute exists does not seem satisfactory. Whether or not the 'critical date' principle might be adapted to such a situation, it at least calls for explanation why the only evidence that Russia adduced to support its position that a dispute exists consisted of unilateral acts by Russia performed only after Russia had seized the territory by force. As the ICJ has said, '[i]n determining the evidential weight of any statement ... the Court necessarily takes into account its form and the circumstances in which it was made.'[167] That approach is surely proper for international adjudicators to follow generally.

The timeline—the sudden appearance in Russian diplomatic practice of claims to Crimea nearly the instant that Russia used armed force to seize

164 *Ibid.* ¶ 166.

165 *Ibid.* ¶ 165.

166 *Territorial and Maritime Dispute (Nicaragua v. Colombia)*, Judgment, ICJ 2012 p. 625, p. 652 ¶ 67 (19 November), quoting *Territorial and Maritime Dispute between Nicaragua and Honduras in the Caribbean Sea (Nicaragua v. Honduras)*, Judgment, ICJ 2007 at pp. 697–698 ¶ 117 (8 October).

167 *Application of the Convention on the Prevention and Punishment of the Crime of Genocide (Croatia v. Serbia)*, Judgment, ICJ 2015 p. 3, p. 78 ¶ 196 (3 February), quoted in *Certain activities carried out by Nicaragua in the Border Area (Costa Rica v. Nicaragua)/Construction of a Road in Costa Rica along the San Juan River (Nicaragua v. Costa Rica)*, Judgment, ICJ 2015 p. 665, p. 701 ¶ 83 (16 December).

Crimea—should have raised questions in the minds of the arbitrators and received reasoned answers in their award.

The *Coastal State Rights* tribunal also might have looked to other situations in which parties contest whether a territorial dispute exists. Yiallourides, Gehring, and Guaci in a 2018 British Institute of International and Comparative Law (BIICL) study on *The Use of Force in Relation to Sovereignty Disputes over Land Territory* drew attention to the position of Greece in respect of Turkey's assertion that certain Aegean islands, islets, and rocks are in dispute between the two states.[168] In a letter transmitted to the UN Secretary-General on 25 May 2022, Greece reiterated that 'Greece's sovereignty over the islands, islets and rocks in the Aegean ... was definitely attributed to Greece by the Lausanne Peace Treaty of 1923 and the Paris Peace Treaty of 1947.'[169] Greece further observed that 'once a treaty has established a boundary or fixed a territorial situation, the result is no longer dependent on the treaty.'[170]

The ICJ has drawn similar conclusions from similar practice. Referring to the islands of San Andrés, Providencia, and Santa Catalina in the Caribbean Sea, the ICJ concluded that 'it can dispose of the issue of the three islands ... That matter has been settled by the Treaty [of 1928 between Colombia and Nicaragua].'[171] No intervening event, no 'developments'—and Nicaragua pleaded that there were several, including an alleged 'material breach' by Colombia[172]—changed the conclusion that followed from the plain reading of the instrument concerned. There is a parallel here to the long course of treaty practice between Russia and Ukraine confirming their boundary, and Russia's acknowledgment in the *Coastal State Rights* proceedings[173] (and in *Oschadbank v. Russian Federation*, one of the other BIT proceedings that private Ukrainian parties instituted against Russia)[174] that there was no dispute before March 2014. The parallel is not strict, but it nevertheless suggests a degree of likeness among the situations.

168 Yiallourides, Gehring, & Gauci (2018) p. 7 ¶ 9.
169 Letter from Maria Theofili, Permanent Representative of Greece, to the Secretary-General of the United Nations, 25 May 2022, Ref. No. 40.1.184/AS 1487 chrome-extension://efaidnbmnnnibpcajpcglclefindmkaj/https://www.amna.gr/files/202205/26-161733OHE.pdf
170 *Ibid.*
171 *Territorial and Maritime Dispute (Nicaragua v. Colomba)*, Preliminary Objections, ICJ 2007 p. 832, p. 861 ¶ 90 (13 December).
172 *Ibid.* at p. 847, ¶ 36; pp. 857–859, ¶¶ 73–82.
173 *Coastal State Rights* at ¶ 181.
174 *Oschadbank v. Russian Federation*, PCA Case No. 2016–14 (Williams, President; Brower and Díaz, arbitrators), Award, 26 November 2018, ¶ 198.

As for the Aegean, the situation there bears further likeness to Crimea, in that armed incidents have occurred—and should be seen as having no independent effect as such on the existence of sovereignty claims. Greece has observed that, after its sovereignty over the Aegean islands was confirmed by treaty, transactions concerning the islands, including armed incidents, did not change their disposition or introduce a sovereignty dispute.[175] In particular, an armed incident at Imia/Kardak islet during the 1995–1996 crisis between Greece and Turkey did not, on Greece's view, reflect a dispute as to sovereignty over the islet. The Aegean sovereignty issue has not been submitted to comprehensive settlement by any third party, and so a definitive account of the legal claims—including of the question whether there is a dispute as to sovereignty—is lacking. Nevertheless, the fact of an armed incident involving a land feature does not demonstrate the existence of a legal dispute as to sovereignty over the feature. Such an incident might have evidentiary significance, but even then at most of only relative weight, to be measured in light of the totality of the circumstances.

Situations in which 'the existence of a territorial dispute [is] not ... self-evident and ... may itself be disputed (ie "a dispute whether there is a dispute")'[176] are not unheard of in third-party dispute settlement procedure. *Coastal State Rights* is not the first example of such a situation. Again, the Annex VII tribunal in *Chagos Marine Protected Area* considered a dispute whether there is a dispute and did so with care, even as the difficulties that the question raises divided the tribunal. As Chapter 8 relates, an ITLOS Special Chamber in *Mauritius/Maldives* faced the same question and examined it exhaustively, even though the difficulties in that case led the Special Chamber to take a frustratingly indirect approach. In neither case, however, did the adjudicators act as though the ordinary legal methods did not apply.

When cases have involved disputes as to whether there are disputes, the ICJ, too, has proceeded diligently to apply the ordinary methods of fact-finding and discernment. When Colombia and Nicaragua presented contradictory assertions as to sovereignty over the islands of San Andrés, Providencia, and Santa Catalina, the Court recognized that the assertions on their own were not enough by which to judge 'whether there is an extant dispute between them.'[177] The Court gave over fifty paragraphs of its preliminary

175 Congressional Research Service, *Greece and Turkey: The Rocky Islet Crisis*, CRS Report for Congress, 96–140 F, March 7, 1996, pp. 2–3.

176 Yiallourides, Gehring, & Gauci (2018) p. 7 ¶ 9, quoting Thirlway, *The International Court of Justice* (2016) 53.

177 *Territorial and Maritime Dispute (Nicaragua v. Colombia)*, Preliminary Objections, ICJ 2007 p. 832, p. 847 ¶ 33 (13 December).

objections judgment to considering the evidence.[178] In *Certain Activities in the Border Area*, when Costa Rica asserted a legal claim to Isla Portillos, the ICJ could judge the plausibility of the claim only 'after a careful examination of the evidence and arguments.'[179]

Adjudicators have also found that fact evidence is necessary when a case requires them to say when a dispute has crystallized,[180] a question that is a close congener to whether there is a dispute at all.

To identify disputes in other settings, too, for example where a party maintains that a dispute exists as to the interpretation of a judgment, the ICJ has turned to the facts when it asks whether there is a dispute.[181]

All of these determinations about the existence of putative disputes relied upon the adjudicators' conclusions of *fact* and, so, *pace* Professor Schreuer,[182] adjudicators do entertain questions of fact when they are called on to say whether a legal dispute exists. Of this rich judicial practice one finds no trace in the 2020 *Coastal State Rights* award, but the issue that it elucidates is the issue on which the award turned. The formalist approach that the

178 *Ibid.* at pp. 847–861, ¶¶ 33–90. The Court further concluded that the absence of a dispute required it to accept Colombia's objection to jurisdiction under the Optional Clause: *ibid.* at pp. 872–875, ¶¶ 132–140. Contrast, *ibid.* at pp. 861–865, ¶¶ 91–104, respecting Roncador, Quitasueño, and Serrana, over which the Court concluded that there was a dispute extant at the time of proceedings.

179 *Certain Activities carried out by Nicaragua in the Border Area (Costa Rica v. Nicaragua)*, Request for Provisional Measures, Order, ICJ 2011 p. 6, p. 19 ¶ 58 (8 March).

180 See, for example, the ICJ's reasoning as to critical date in *Territorial and Maritime Dispute (Nicaragua v. Colombia)*, Judgment, ICJ 2012 pp. 624, 652–653 ¶¶ 67–71 (19 November); *Territorial and Maritime Dispute between Nicaragua and Honduras in the Caribbean Sea (Nicaragua v. Honduras)*, Judgment, ICJ 2007 p. 659, pp. 697–701 ¶¶ 117–131 (8 October). Even where the parties' disagreement as to the critical dates of their disputes is readily resolved, adjudicators have considered the matter closely and specified the date(s). See *Sovereignty over Pedra Branca/Pulau Batu Puteh, Middle Rocks and South Ledge (Malaysia/Singapore)*, Judgment, ICJ 2008 p. 12, p. 28 ¶¶ 33–36 (23 May).

181 *Request for Interpretation of the Judgment of 15 June 1962 in the Case concerning the* Temple of Preah Vihear (Cambodia v. Thailand) *(Cambodia v. Thailand)*, Provisional Measures, Order, ICJ 2011 p. 537, p. 546 ¶ 37 (18 July). Singapore and Malaysia appear to have agreed on the point: *Request for Interpretation of the Judgment of 23 May 2008 in the case concerning* Sovereignty over Pedra Branca/Pulau Batu Puteh, Middle Rocks and South Ledge (Malaysia/Singapore) *(Malaysia v. Singapore)*: Written Observations of the Republic of Singapore, 30 October 2017, p. 22, ¶ 2.6; Written Observations by Malaysia in Response to Singapore's Written Observations Contesting Jurisdiction and Admissibility, 15 February 2018, pp. 21–22, ¶ 57. The case was discontinued before judgment and withdrawn from the list: Order, ICJ 2018 p. 288 (29 May).

182 See p. 207.

Coastal State Rights tribunal applied to identify a 'sovereignty dispute' was inadequate.

The ordinary and expected approach to dealing with the question would have been an evidence-based approach. The tribunal would have examined evidence of Russia's assertion of sovereignty to distinguish whether Russia grounded the assertion on force or on law.

Maritime Delimitation and Territorial Questions between Qatar and Bahrain (Qatar v. Bahrain) contains a particularly apposite illustration of how an adjudicator distinguishes between an act of force and a legal claim when one party says that a dispute exists as to sovereignty and the other party disagrees. One of the territorial questions in *Qatar v. Bahrain* was sovereignty over Zubarah, an area on the northwest coast of the Qatar peninsula opposite Bahrain. Bahrain noted that the Sheikh of Doha (Qatar) in 1937 had used force to evict from the area of Zubarah certain tribesmen loyal to Bahrain. According to Bahrain, this was a 'use of force from which no legal rights could arise.'[183] It followed, according to Bahrain, that any 'factual occupation' of Zubarah by Qatar 'did not give rise to a valid title of sovereignty over Zubarah.'[184] In short, Bahrain argued in regard to Zubarah much as Ukraine would a decade and a half later in regard to Crimea: use of force supplies no ground for territorial claim.

Whether Qatar, in truth, relied only on force in Zubarah was a matter for the Court to judge by reference to the evidence. The Court examined in detail a long course of transactions and incidents relating to Zubarah, going back to the eighteenth century, including between Britain, which exercised protectorates in the Gulf at the relevant time, and the Ottoman Empire, which held sovereignty to the Nejd.[185] The ICJ took over a dozen paragraphs to consider the evidence in regard to Zubarah. In the event, the Court concluded that Qatar has sovereignty over Zubarah.[186]

Unsurprisingly, as the question of Zubarah did not turn on the point, the Court did not reject Bahrain's statement of international law: a use of force is an act from which sovereign title does not arise. Qatar's sovereignty arose from a process of gradual consolidation between the 1868 and 1937, not from a use of force against a territory belonging to another state.[187]

Modern international law indeed entails, as Bahrain contended, and as Chapter 1 in this book recalls, that use of force, without more, does not

183 *Maritime Delimitation and Territorial Questions between Qatar and Bahrain (Qatar v. Bahrain)*, Judgment (Merits), ICJ 2001 p. 40, p. 65 ¶ 76 (16 March).

184 *Ibid.*

185 ICJ 2001 at pp. 66–69, ¶¶ 82–95.

186 *Ibid.* at p. 69 ¶ 97.

187 *Ibid.* at p. 69 ¶ 96.

change a boundary peacefully settled between states. The deficiency in Bahrain's argument was not that Bahrain had misstated a point of law; it hadn't. It was that Bahrain had no convincing answer to the wide-ranging evidence that supported Qatar's claim. The Court examined that evidence—in detail—and concluded that it gave the definitive answer to the question for purposes of the case. Qatar's claim had a century of ordinary practice behind it. Use of force was not the agency of its consolidation.

In considering whether a dispute had arisen over sovereignty in Crimea, the *Coastal State Rights* tribunal had, on the one hand, a scanty dossier of statements in legal form communicated in this or that intergovernmental organization over a short period of time and after the fact. On the other hand, it had the fact: the armed seizure of a province. For Qatar in Zubarah, the evidence of sovereignty existed, and then Qatar turned to arms. For Russia in Crimea, it was the other way around: Russia turned to arms and then called the evidence into being. The relation of Russia's putative claim-at-law to Russia's use of force is even weaker than mere dependency. Upon use of force the 'claim' is entirely parasitic. The circumstances of the claim very much allowed, if not compelled, the inference that the legal 'evidence' was a fiction, introduced 'with the aim,' to borrow the 'critical date' expression, 'of buttressing' a feeble case. The tribunal should have concluded the obvious: Russia has no 'legal claim' to Crimea and, thus, no legal dispute exists in regard to Ukraine's sovereignty. The putative dispute that the *Coastal State Rights* tribunal said barred it from exercising jurisdiction did not result from a juxtaposition of legal claims. It resulted from the collision of force against law.

'Developments' by force and the absence of law

War, following Clausewitz's oft-repeated formula, is the extension of politics by other means.[188] Clausewitz did not say that war extends *law* by other means. For Clausewitz, the interchangeable terms were politics and war—that is to say, politics and force. If, as the ICJ said in *Military and Paramilitary Activities*, 'justifications, advanced solely in a political context' are naturally not for an adjudicative organ to admit as a source of legal effect,[189] then a 'sovereignty claim' that derives its substance from making war—that is to say, from use of force—is not either.

188 The full expression is as follows: 'We see, therefore, that war is not merely an act of policy but a true political instrument, a continuation of political intercourse, carried on with other means.' Von Clausewitz, *On War*, Book I, chapter 1 (1976) (Howard & Paret, eds. & trans.) (original *Vom Kriege* (1832)) 87.

189 *Military and Paramilitary Activities in and against Nicaragua (Nicaragua v. United States)*, Judgment, ICJ 1986 at p. 134 ¶ 266 (27 June) (emphasis added).

In a study of the repetitive use of well-known blocks of text in the decisions of courts and tribunals, Niccolò Ridi suggests that judges and arbitrators might be participating in a process of 'reiterat[ing] and bolster[ing] the authority of specific formulations' but failing to conduct the process of reasoning by which 'to apply their outcome to a new case.'[190] The 'objective dispute' formulation Ridi counts as one of the most often, and most reflexively, employed in judgments and awards.[191] Terms that jurists use as mere reflex all too often come at a cost to legal reasoning and forensic rigor.

True, there is a place for rules-of-thumb and shortcuts. An arbitral award in which the tribunal must determine whether Russia has a legal claim to the territory that it has seized in Ukraine is not such a place. This was not a situation in which an abstract 'dispute' sufficed to support a jurisdictional objection. Needed was a particular kind of dispute identified in a particular treaty term—'unsettled dispute concerning sovereignty'—and that treaty term needed a definition if the tribunal was to apply it coherently. The *Coastal State Rights* tribunal acknowledged the gravity of the question that it had to answer. According to the tribunal, 'the *key question* upon which it should focus [was] whether a dispute as to which State has sovereignty over Crimea exists.'[192] The tribunal recalled that the Permanent Court of International Justice (PCIJ) and ICJ over decades set out formulations of a definition of 'dispute,' and the tribunal 'consider[ed] that those formulations are flexible enough to leave considerable room for judgment on its part in verifying the existence of a dispute.'[193] But *those* formulations are a shortcut, and one for answering a different question. They answer whether a dispute exists *as such*, not whether a particular kind of dispute exists, the definition of which is shaped and confined by fundamental international law rules.[194] Whether or not 'those formulations are flexible,' they were not relevant formulations in the case at hand.

Even if 'those formulations' *are* relevant and the right ones to apply, and even if there is 'considerable room for judgment' in applying them, an adjudicator still must exercise judgment. To exercise judgment, the adjudicator must have some raw material on which to exercise it. '[T]he threshold for establishing the existence of a dispute is rather low,' the tribunal said.[195] But whether the threshold is high or low or in between, the 'room for

190 Ridi, 'Ratio, Obiter, and the Textualization of International Precedent' (2019) 10 JIDS 361, 391.
191 *Ibid.* 390, Table 2.
192 *Coastal State Rights,* Award, 21 February 2020, ¶ 188 (emphasis added).
193 *Ibid.*
194 See above pp. 205–206.
195 *Coastal State Rights,* Award, 21 February 2020, ¶ 188.

judgment' cannot be so capacious that the adjudicator acts without regard to fact or law.

The *Coastal State Rights* tribunal went on to say, in concessionary tone, '[c]ertainly a mere assertion would be insufficient in proving the existence of a dispute.' On this understanding, it is fair to ask, what *would* be sufficient? A 'mere assertion' accompanied by armed invasion? Or does the asserting state also need to commit multiple atrocities to elevate the matter to the tribunal's threshold? I put the question with rhetorical emphasis, because this passage merits particular critique. The tribunal here lay conceptual groundwork for its finding that a territorial dispute existed and, with that finding, concluded that it lacked jurisdiction to address some of Ukraine's principal claims. It is a pivotal passage in the award. And so the question that it raises needs an answer. But in the award no answer is found. The award concedes that 'mere assertion' will not suffice to demonstrate that a dispute exists, but Russia's 'mere assertion' satisfied the tribunal that an 'objective dispute' had arisen. The Annex VII tribunal used the concept of 'objective dispute,' as it used the word 'developments,' not as an aid to analysis but as an instrument of avoidance.

Let us now consider the tribunal's insistence that Russia's assertions about a 'sovereignty dispute' were not to be tested for plausibility; then, in the balance of this chapter, I offer some further illustrations of why and how the tribunal should have tested them.

The tribunal's denial of plausibility

At the close of the passage about the threshold for concluding that a legal dispute exists—the 'mere assertion' passage that I just considered—the *Coastal State Rights* tribunal declared that 'it does not follow that the validity or strength of the assertion should be put to a plausibility test *or other test* in order to verify the existence of a dispute.'[196] When read together with the tribunal's seeming concession that a 'mere assertion' does not establish the existence of a dispute, the tribunal's denial that a test exists for that purpose is incoherent. What does 'mere' mean, if the arbitrators cannot test the assertion? How do they distinguish a 'mere' assertion from an assertion that is more than 'mere'? The answer is that they test the assertion, or at least they *should*.

A research team of the BIICL, investigating state practice in regard to UNCLOS Articles 74(3) and 83(3), expressed disquiet over 'plausibility,'

196 *Ibid*. (emphasis added).

too.[197] The disquiet is natural. It arises because an inattentive adjudicator might misapply a test of the plausibility of claims and summarily dismiss meritorious claims. In conclusion, however, the BIICL team added a crucial caveat, and one directly relevant to *Coastal State Rights*. They acknowledged that a case could arise in which 'one State considers there to be a dispute over territory which, if taken into account, would greatly enlarge the disputed maritime area'—a case that would 'raise [...] the issue of the plausibility of claims.'[198] Behind the BIICL team's caveat is the realization that an adjudicator who allows a non-existent territorial sovereignty dispute to exclude maritime claims would bring about an unfair and unintended exclusionary effect just as would the adjudicator who applies a plausibility or other test without due caution.

A major deficiency in the *Coastal State Rights* award of February 2020 is that the tribunal did nothing to test Russia's assertion of a sovereignty dispute. Testing a party's assertions against evidence is a well-recognized part of the adjudicator's function. As I suggested in the previous section, a number of decided cases illustrate that adjudicators do precisely that when a party asserts that a sovereignty dispute exists.

Two further cases, one that I have already touched on, merit close readings, as both illustrate in detail how adjudicators test a party's assertions about sovereignty disputes.

In *Pulau Ligitan and Pulau Sipadan (Indonesia/Malaysia)*, the ICJ rejected flimsy assertions of a sovereignty claim,[199] and in *Certain Activities Carried out by Nicaragua in the Border Area (Costa Rica v. Nicaragua)* the ICJ accepted sound assertions of a sovereignty claim.[200] Let us turn to consider these cases, why their lessons should have been applied in *Coastal State Rights*,[201] and how the tribunal should have applied them.[202]

From North Borneo to south Ukraine: plausibility and alleged disputes

Assertion-testing is precisely what the ICJ did when the Philippines in *Pulau Ligitan and Pulau Sipadan*, like Russia in *Coastal State Rights*, attempted to shift the course of the proceedings by asserting that a dispute existed in

197 Barrett et al. (2016) at p. 31 ¶ 105; p. 38 ¶ 129.
198 *Ibid.* at p. 60 ¶ 204.
199 See pp. 223–226.
200 See pp. 226–228.
201 See pp. 228–239.
202 See pp. 239–244.

respect of sovereignty.[203] The Philippines requested the Court to allow it to intervene on the basis of a putative sovereignty claim by the Philippines over North Borneo, a territory long settled to form part of Malaysia. Unlike Russia, which raised its putative claim to Crimea only in 2014 when it used armed force to seize the territory, the Philippines had said over the years that North Borneo belongs to the Philippines. The ICJ nevertheless placed the burden on the Philippines to demonstrate that its putative claim in respect of North Borneo had substance.

In response to the Philippines' request to intervene in the proceedings between Indonesia and Malaysia, the ICJ said as follows: 'a State which ... relies on an interest of a legal nature other than in the subject-matter of the case itself necessarily bears the burden of showing with a particular clarity the existence of the interest of a legal nature which it claims to have.'[204] In short, the Court required the Philippines to 'explain with sufficient clarity its own claim of sovereignty in North Borneo.'[205] Judge Kooijmans, recognizing its importance, repeated the Court's language word for word on the point: '[I]t is highly relevant that the Court has explicitly stated that a State which relies on an interest of a legal nature other than the subject-matter of the case itself necessarily bears the burden of showing with a particular clarity the existence of the interest of a legal nature which it claims to have.'[206] A rational approach in *Coastal State Rights*, too, would have been to place the burden, not on Ukraine to show that there was no dispute of a legal nature, but on Russia to show that there was one. This the tribunal did not do.

The failure of the *Coastal State Rights* tribunal in regard to allocation of burden misshaped its approach to the finding of fact. The distortion that resulted is readily discerned when we compare the tribunal's approach to the ICJ's. In response to the Philippines' attempted intervention in *Indonesia/Malaysia*, the ICJ, in contrast to the *Coastal State Rights* tribunal, approached fact-finding with rigor. The ICJ allocated the burden on the party that pled a putative sovereignty dispute. Moreover, it affirmed that to satisfy the burden that party must 'itself ... show [...] *with a particular clarity*' the factual predicates necessary to sustaining the credibility of its plea.[207] Judge Kooijmans again underscored the point: '[T]he Philippines has ... failed to make its claim sufficiently plausible by not providing answers to

203 See generally about the case Ong, 'Pulau Ligitan and Pulau Sipadan' (1999) 14 IJMCL 399–414.

204 *Sovereignty over Pulau Ligitan and Pulau Sipadan (Indonesia/Malaysia)*, Application by the Philippines for Permission to Intervene, ICJ 2001 at p. 598 ¶ 59 (23 October).

205 *Ibid.* at p. 598 ¶ 60.

206 Declaration of Judge Kooijmans, ICJ 2001 at p. 629 ¶ 15.

207 ICJ 2001 at p. 598 ¶ 59 (emphasis added).

highly pertinent questions which were put during the oral proceedings.'[208] The *Coastal State Rights* tribunal asked scarcely *any* questions of Russia in regard to the plausibility of Russia's claim, much less 'highly pertinent' ones that would have put Russia's claim to an appropriate test. Quite the opposite: the tribunal declared that neither a 'plausibility test' nor 'other test' had any place in its procedure.[209]

The Philippines was not asking the ICJ to terminate proceedings. The Philippines was asking to intervene. *A fortiori*, a state advancing a claim that, if accepted, would bring the proceedings to a close (or at least would silence key claims that the applicant sought to adjudicate) must satisfy a burden as exacting as that which the ICJ rightly placed on the Philippines. Russia, however, did not come even close to 'establish[ing] with fully convincing arguments' the existence of a dispute that it asserted must bar the tribunal from exercising jurisdiction.[210] But, then again, the tribunal did not ask Russia to do so.

In respect of the Philippines' attempted intervention in *Indonesia/Malaysia*, the ICJ had no doubt about the test that the Philippines needed to satisfy; and the ICJ put the Philippines to the test. The Court devoted some forty-five paragraphs to considering the Philippines' assertion that it had an interest of a legal nature for purposes of intervention under Article 62 of the Statute of the Court.[211] And the Court construed the expression 'interest of a legal nature' liberally—that is, in favor of the Philippines.[212] The Court found that the Philippines failed to demonstrate that the alleged interest was plausible.

It is true that Russia's jurisdictional objection was different from the Philippines' request to intervene. These are different procedural devices serving different ends, and the arguments put forward by the two states reflect the difference. However, the cases turned on the same juridical object: if its respective argument were to prevail, it was essential for each state to demonstrate that a sovereignty dispute existed. Where the ICJ referred to 'the burden of showing with a particular clarity the existence of the interest' (and placed that burden on the requesting party, the Philippines), the *fons et origo* of the 'interest' to which the ICJ referred was the putative sovereignty dispute.

208 Declaration of Judge Kooijmans, ICJ 2001 at p. 629 ¶ 16 (emphasis added).
209 The tribunal's refusal to consider whether Russia's assertion of a claim was in good faith also contrasts with the ICJ's approach when the Court has considered whether to assign responsibility to a state for a violation of territorial integrity. See Milano & Papanicolopulu (2011) at 594–595.
210 Declaration of Judge Kooijmans, ICJ 2001 at p. 629 ¶ 16.
211 *Sovereignty over Pulau Ligitan and Pulau Sipadan (Indonesia/Malaysia)*, Application by the Philippines for Permission to Intervene, ICJ 2001 at pp. 589–604 ¶¶ 38–83.
212 *Ibid.* at p. 596 ¶ 47.

An incautious reading of *Indonesia/Malaysia* might lead one to conclude that the ICJ rejected the Philippines' request for intervention because the Philippines had spoken past the case in which it sought to intervene. It is true that much of the evidence that the Philippines had adduced concerned geographic locations that the parties in the case had not called on the Court to address. However, the Court was clear that there was more to the Philippines' failure than that. The Court was clear that the Philippines had failed to present plausible evidence of a territorial dispute: 'Not only are they [the documents that the Philippines adverted to in support of its assertion that a territorial dispute exists] not, for the most part, at the centre of the Court's attention in the case between Indonesia and Malaysia, *but they are not themselves sources of title for the Philippines*.'[213]

Members of the Court stated the matter in their separate opinions as well. Judge Kooijmans said: 'The Court should, for reasons of judicial policy … give special attention to the plausibility of the claim and thereby to the specificity of the legal interest.'[214] Judge *ad hoc* Franck said: 'To allow the Philippines to proceed to intervene in the merits phase of this case, when the legal interest it claims would have *no chance of succeeding* by operation of law, cannot discharge the Court's duties.'[215] One notices an overtone in Judge Weeramantry's separate opinion, too, suggesting that the Philippines' plea for intervention was deficient in substance. '[O]ne is left with a sense of inadequacy,' Judge *ad hoc* Weeramantry said, 'as to the particulars of the legal interest which the Philippines wishes to protect.'[216]

Requests for intervention in bilateral proceedings are one example of a procedural setting in which a party might contend that it has a 'legal interest.' Requests for provisional measures are another example. A claim to sovereignty over territory was a legal interest that Costa Rica asserted in its request for provisional measures in *Certain Activities Carried out by Nicaragua in the Border Area*. Isla Portillos, a modest territory at the boundary between Costa Rica and Nicaragua, was the territory in question. Nicaragua had been dredging a canal at Isla Portillos. Costa Rica asked the Court to order Nicaragua to stop. Crucial to Costa Rica's request, Costa Rica said that it, and not Nicaragua, holds sovereign title to the territory. '[A]t this stage of the proceedings,' said the Court, 'the Court cannot settle the Parties' claims to sovereignty over the disputed territory.'[217] Read in isolation, this form

213 ICJ 2001 at p. 604 ¶ 83 (emphasis added).
214 Declaration of Judge Kooijmans, ICJ 2001 at p. 629 ¶ 15.
215 Sep. Op. Judge Franck, ICJ 2001 at p. 658 ¶ 18 (emphasis added).
216 ICJ 2001 at p. 648 ¶ 35.
217 *Certain Activities carried out by Nicaragua in the Border Area (Costa Rica v. Nicaragua)*, Request for Provisional Measures, Order, ICJ 2011 p. 6, p. 19 ¶ 57 (8 March).

of words would suggest that the Court *presumed* that Costa Rica had an extant legal claim in respect of the territory in question. However, in the same paragraph, it becomes clear that the Court was *not* presuming the existence of Costa Rica's claim. The Court stated that it '*needs ... to decide* whether the rights claimed by the Applicant [Costa Rica] on the merits, and for which it is seeking protection, are plausible,'[218] and, in the next paragraph, concluded that '*after a careful examination of the evidence and arguments* presented by the Parties, ... title to sovereignty claimed by Costa Rica over ... Isla Portillos is plausible.'[219]

A necessary inference, when one reads this passage in its entirety, is that, for the Court to reach its conclusion that a legal claim by Costa Rica over the territory in question existed, it was not enough for Costa Rica merely to have asserted the claim in formal terms. Costa Rica had to prove that the claim existed. To satisfy itself of the proof, the Court conducted 'a careful examination of the evidence and arguments.' In other words, it was not a foregone conclusion that the 'disputed territory' was subject to a dispute in the sense required for the Court to grant the provisional measures that Costa Rica had requested. As a required step before the Court granted provisional measures, the Court needed to satisfy itself that the 'title to sovereignty claimed by Costa Rica' in respect of that territory was 'plausible.'

Generalizing from these examples, where a juridical result requires a territorial claim to exist in the legal sense of a claim, the adjudicator needs to test the plausibility of the relevant party's assertion of claim. There is no dispute without competing claims, and no plausible assertion of a dispute without a plausible assertion of competing claims.

In both these matters—the Philippines' failed request to intervene and Costa Rica's successful request for provisional measures—a claim in form alone did not suffice. Needed was a claim in substance, and to tell whether such a claim existed, the adjudicator tested the assertion of the party that said it existed. Without applying a test—whether a 'plausibility test' or some 'other test'—an adjudicator indulges in discretion unencumbered by law and freed from the obligation to give reasons for the conclusions reached. To use again the words of the *Coastal State Rights* tribunal, an adjudicator has 'room for judgment.' But the adjudicator does not have as much room as the *Coastal State Rights* tribunal took for itself.

When the ICJ, in the Nicaragua-Colombia territorial and maritime dispute, observed that a party, after it has raised preliminary objections, will 'have these objections answered at the preliminary stage of the proceedings unless the Court does not have before it *all facts necessary to decide the questions*

218 *Ibid.* (emphasis added).
219 ICJ 2011 p. 6, p. 19 ¶ 58 (emphasis added).

raised,' the principle behind the observation was that giving an answer requires a reliable grasp of the facts.[220] The Court did not mean that, in the absence of 'all facts necessary,' the adjudicator is to throw up its hands and accept the objecting party's premise. The Court meant that the adjudicator is required to find the facts, including if necessary by adapting the sequence of its procedure. Closer still to home, the Court in the *ICSFT and CERD* case between Ukraine and Russia identified its task as 'to consider the questions of law and fact that are relevant to the objection to its jurisdiction.'[221] The *Coastal State Rights* tribunal decided Russia's objection to its jurisdiction without considering any such questions at all.

The tribunal's avoidance of fact-finding on the question that the tribunal itself described as the 'key question' in the case should raise concern. It should raise concern as a matter of general principle and of legal method. It also should raise concern when viewed retrospectively in light of Russia's litigation strategy in other cases. In the *Ukraine v. Russia* proceedings instituted in 2022 under the Genocide Convention, one of Russia's objections to jurisdiction was that it is 'incompatible with the judicial function' for the ICJ to 'act as a fact-finding body.'[222] The Court had little difficulty in rejecting this objection. The *Coastal State Rights* tribunal, by contrast, so far avoided fact-finding as to suggest that it agreed that fact-finding is 'incompatible' with the role that it was to perform.

Why the tribunal should have tested the evidence

Lawyers, policymakers, and the wider public rightly approach proposals for omnibus controls on 'misinformation' with caution,[223] but an adjudicator

220 *Territorial and Maritime Dispute (Nicaragua v. Colombia)*, Preliminary Objections, ICJ 2007 p. 832, p. 852 ¶ 51 (emphasis added). See also *South China Sea*, Jurisdiction and Admissibility, 29 October 2015, ¶ 390.

221 *Application of the International Convention for the Suppression of the Financing of Terrorism and of the International Convention on the Elimination of All Forms of Racial Discrimination (Ukraine v. Russian Federation)*, Preliminary Objections, ICJ 2019 p. 558, p. 584 ¶ 58.

222 *Allegations of Genocide under the Convention on the Prevention and Punishment of the Crime of Genocide (Ukraine v. Russian Federation: 32 States Intervening)*, ICJ, Preliminary Objections, 2 February 2024, ¶ 85.

223 See, for example, Lahmann, 'Infecting the Mind: Establishing Responsibility for Transboundary Disinformation' (2022) 33(2) EJIL 411–440; Jones, 'Protecting Political Discourse from Online Manipulation' (2021) 1 *European Human Rights Law Review* 68–79; discussants Wilson & Robertson, 'The Promise and Limits of Cyber Power in International Law' (2020) 114 ASIL Proc. at 132, 133. The concern over international propaganda is not new. McDougal, Lasswell, & Reisman addressed it under the rubric 'ideological strategy': McDougal, Lasswell, & Reisman (1969) 126–128.

in the procedure it superintends has a duty to preserve control over the evidence that the parties introduce and to reach conclusions from that evidence that are at least minimally credible. The *Coastal State Rights* tribunal failed to perform that duty. It refused to scrutinize an assertion that no other relevant authority had accepted and many had explicitly rejected: to wit, that a self-determination movement, pushed to *extremis* by a Ukrainian government bent on 'genocide,' had seceded of its own will from Ukraine and then elected for Russia to absorb it.

The practice of other international institutions is relevant here, *not* because it is a source of binding determination for an Annex VII tribunal, but because it demonstrates that international institutions are perfectly capable of carrying out the requisite scrutiny of fact evidence. The practice also suggests that Russia's assertion that 'developments' had given rise to a 'sovereignty dispute' in Crimea called for forensic scrutiny, not mere acceptance on formal grounds.

The credibility of Russia's assertions

A number of international organs by the time of the February 2020 award in *Coastal State Rights* had already reached determinations casting doubt on the credibility of Russia's assertions about its armed takeover of Ukraine's territory. In Chapter 7, I consider a number of these determinations,[224] because the failure of the *Coastal State Rights* tribunal to take account of them undermined systemic coherence. A few words are in order in this chapter about them as well, because they illustrate that other decision-makers had no difficulty in engaging in such fact-finding as was necessary to scrutinize Russia's factual assertions.

As this book went to press, a merits judgment in the *Ukraine v. Russia* proceedings under the Genocide Convention was still awaited,[225] but the 2024 judgment on preliminary objections in that case had already indicated the ICJ's willingness to perform its ordinary fact-finding function and to place due scrutiny on Russia's assertion that Ukraine was a perpetrator of genocide.[226] It is true that any conclusion that we draw from provisional measures in the case must be qualified, too. However, if Russia's invasion had had real justification—that is, if Ukraine's conduct had been threatening the very existence of ethnic populations in Ukraine—then that circumstance would have invited the Court to say more than it did. Instead, the Court

224 See pp. 258–281.

225 Russia in its Counter-Memorial of 18 November 2024 made counter-claims, and the Court set time limits of 20 May 2025 and 22 September 2025 for Ukraine and Russia, respectively, to submit 'views on the matter.' ICJ Rpess Release 2025/5 (31 January 2025).

226 *Allegations of Genocide (Ukraine v. Russian Federation)*, Preliminary Objections, ICJ 2024, ¶ 151 (2 February).

confined itself to requiring that Russia 'immediately suspend the military operations.'[227] At the very least, one would have expected the Court to have addressed an obligation to Ukraine to stop whatever conduct might have plausibly constituted genocide. That the Court addressed no such obligation to Ukraine suggests that no such conduct existed. Moreover, the Court found Ukraine's claim in the case plausible. This was Ukraine's 'reverse' genocide claim, to the effect that Russia's allegations against Ukraine under the Genocide Convention are false. The ICJ's finding that 'Ukraine has a plausible right not to be subjected to military operations ... for the purpose of preventing and punishing an alleged genocide'[228] casts doubt on Russia's asserted 'developments' that Russia said gave rise to a 'dispute' over Ukraine's territory.

In the earlier *Ukraine v. Russia* proceedings, those under the International Convention for the Suppression of the Financing of Terrorism (ICSFT) and the Convention on the Elimination of All Forms of Racial Discrimination (CERD), the ICJ seems to have recognized that Russia adduced no credible evidence that Ukraine had committed atrocities, or any human rights violations at all, against individuals of Russian ethnic background in Crimea. In its 2017 provisional measures order in the *Ukraine v. Russia* proceedings under the ICSFT and CERD, the ICJ directed that Russia refrain from measures against the rights of the Crimean Tatar community and assure access in Crimea to Ukrainian language education. In directing these measures the Court said nothing to suggest that it accepted Russia's contention that Russia was present in Crimea to rectify a human rights problem. To the contrary: the inference instead was that Russia's presence there *was* the problem.[229] When it adopts provisional measures, the ICJ more often adopts measures that address both parties, if not in exactly equal part then in at

227 *Allegations of Genocide (Ukraine v. Russian Federation)*, Provisional Measures, Order, ICJ 2022 p. 211, pp. 230–231 ¶ 86(1) (16 March).

228 ICJ 2022 at p. 226 ¶ 60.

229 *Application of the ICSFT and CERD (Ukraine v. Russian Federation)*, Order, Indication of Provisional Measures, ICJ 2017 p. 104, p. 140 ¶ 106(1) (19 April). It was Russia's contention that the problem in Crimea was that the Tatars were engaged in 'extremist acts aimed at violent change of the foundations of the constitutional order and violating the integrity of the Russian Federation': Preliminary Objections submitted by the Russian Federation (12 September 2018) p. 234, ¶ 464 and *ibid.* n. 642. The ICJ subsequently, on the merits, found that Russia violated CERD Art. 2(1)*(a)* and Art. 5*(e)*(v) 'by the way in which it has implemented its educational system in Crimea after 2014 with regard to school education in the Ukrainian language' but rejected all other CERD claims that Ukraine had advanced. Judgment, 31 January 2024, ¶ 404 (3) and (4). Curiously, the Court also found that Russia, by maintaining restrictions on the Crimean Tatar assembly, the *Mejlis*, violated paragraph 106(1)*(a)* of the provisional measures Order of 19 April 2017: *ibid.* at ¶ 404 (5).

least rough symmetry. As in its *Genocide* provisional measures in March 2022, its provisional measures in the *ICSFT/CERD* case gave specific direction only to Russia.[230] That the Court singled out Russia is telling.

In 2019, the Court held that it had jurisdiction to adjudicate Ukraine's claims under the CERD that Russia has 'engaged in a sustained campaign of racial discrimination, carried out through acts repeated over an appreciable period of time starting in 2014, against the Crimean Tatar and Ukrainian communities in Crimea' and that those claims are admissible.[231] The outcome of Ukraine's claims was mixed on the merits. In its judgment of 31 January 2024, the ICJ found that Russia had breached Articles 2(1)*(a)* and *5(e)*(v) of CERD by failing to implement Ukrainian language education in Crimea,[232] but it rejected all other CERD claims that Ukraine had brought.[233] The proceedings would have been a natural occasion for Russia to counter-claim, so as properly to advance its own assertions that Ukraine had committed a range of gross violations. However, Russia did not counter-claim.

The 'developments' that the *Coastal State Rights* tribunal alluded to as giving rise to a 'legal dispute' in respect of sovereignty in Crimea had no factual reality. They were a figment of Russia's false assertions, made after the fact of Russia's invasion, that Ukraine had instigated a human rights crisis in Crimea and that only Russia's intervention could stop it.

That the heart of the matter was Russia's armed attack, and that no antecedent human rights crisis had supplied even a tincture of a justification for it, did not escape others either. The UN High Commissioner for Human Rights was one of several multilateral bodies that concluded that Russia's assertion that 'developments' in Crimea gave rise to a territorial dispute in 2014 was an assertion with no factual substance behind it.[234]

The Universal Periodic Review (UPR) is another relevant source. In December 2012, Russia made submissions in the UPR in regard to Ukraine. Surely, if the Crimean area of Ukraine really had been on the precipice of

230 ICJ 2017 at p. 140 ¶ 106(1). The Court adopted a general direction of 'non-aggravation' to both parties: *ibid.* at ¶ 106(2).

231 *Application of the ICSFT and CERD (Ukr. v. Russ. Fed.)*, Preliminary Objections, ICJ 2019 p. 558, p. 606 ¶¶ 130, 133 (8 November).

232 *Application of the ICSFT and CERD (Ukr. v. Russ. Fed.)*, Judgment, ICJ 2024, ¶ 404(3) (31 January).

233 *Ibid.* at ¶ 404(4). The Court also declared that Russia violated ICSFT Art. 9(1) but rejected all other submissions by Ukraine under the ICSFT. Art. 9(1) provides, 'Upon receiving information that a person who has committed or who is alleged to have committed an offence set forth in article 2 may be present in its territory, the State Party concerned shall take such measures as may be necessary under its domestic law to investigate the facts contained in the information.' *Ibid.* ¶¶ 404(1), (2).

234 See at Socher, *Russia and the Right to Self-determination in the Post-Soviet Space* (2021) 166–167.

Kosovo-levels of atrocity and strife, then there would have been some precursor, some evidence that would have spurred Russia to raise alarm? Alas, no. In the UPR in December 2012, only a year and three months before Russia said that 'developments' had arisen to throw into doubt the very sovereignty of Ukraine in Crimea, Russia's submissions about Ukraine were broadly favorable and, in any case, contained no allegation about putative human rights violations against ethnic Russians in Crimea. According to Russia, welcome 'progress [had been] made [in Ukraine] reforming legislation, the judiciary, law enforcement and the penitentiary system, as well as the work done to combat all forms of intolerance, xenophobia and racial discrimination.'[235] Russia also 'welcomed the creation of the Ombudsman for children under the Office of the President' and 'noted the improvement in conditions of detention centres.'[236] True, a clean bill of human rights health in December 2012 does not equate to the same in February 2014. But to overturn a settled border between states—even to create a legal claim to that result—credible evidence would have to exist of a very serious and exceptional state of affairs. And even a state of affairs such as that could give rise to a sovereignty dispute only to the extent that one accepts that a 'remedial' right to secession exists under international law. Russia has been clear that any such right 'should be limited to truly extreme circumstances, such as an outright attack by the parent state threatening the very existence of the people in question.'[237] The evidence in respect of Crimea, instead, pointed the opposite way: there was no basis for complaint, much less for radical territorial revision.[238] At the very least, the circumstances should have led the *Coastal State Rights* tribunal to do more than declare that 'developments' had created a 'legal dispute' as to sovereignty over the territory. The circumstances should have led the tribunal to question the credibility of Russia's assertions.

Another determination that might have raised questions in the mind of the tribunal as to the credibility of Russia's assertions was that by a panel constituted in 2017 under Articles 4.7 and 6 of the WTO Dispute Settlement

235 Human Rights Council, Report of the Working Group on the Universal Periodic Review, Ukraine, 20 December 2012, ¶ 28: A/HRC/22/7, p. 6.

236 *Ibid.*

237 *Accordance with international law of the unilateral declaration of independence in respect of Kosovo*, ICJ, Advisory Proceedings, Written Statement of the Russian Federation, 17 April 2009, pp. 31–32, ¶ 88.

238 As to deficiencies in a 'remedial' claim for secession, see Shany, 'Self-Determination in Light of the 2014 Events in Ukraine' (2014) 21(1) *The Brown Journal of World Affairs* 233, 239–240. Professor Shany also notes that the international response was rather muted.

Understanding in *Russia—Measures Concerning Traffic in Transit*. In the proceedings before the panel, Russia invoked Article XXI(b)(iii) of the General Agreement on Tariffs and Trade (GATT 1994). Article XXI(b)(iii) states that '[n]othing in [the GATT 1994] shall be construed ... to prevent any contracting party from taking any action which it considers necessary for the protection of its essential security interests ... taken in time of war or other emergency in international relations.' The panel, in a panel report of 5 April 2019, said that the 'emergency in international relations' to which Russia alluded—and Russia, the panel noted, was 'allusive' in its pleading on the point[239]—'is very close to the "hard core" of war or armed conflict.'[240] To support this conclusion, the panel referred to the practice of the UN General Assembly in and after 2014 in respect of Russia's seizure of Crimea. According to the panel, the '2014 emergency' is one 'that has been recognized by the UN General Assembly as involving armed conflict, and which affects the security of the border with an adjacent country and exhibits the other features identified by Russia.'[241] The panel's conclusion was the one that Russia was looking for—that is, that trade measures that Russia had taken against Ukraine are covered by GATT Article XXI(b)(iii).[242] The reasoning that the panel applied to reach the conclusion was *not* that which Russia was looking for. The panel reasoned that the General Assembly resolutions condemning Russia's illegal occupation of Crimea demonstrated that a wartime situation existed.[243]

In panel proceedings, parties have the opportunity to request amendments to panel reports. Russia requested that the panel amend its report to read that only 'certain countries' understood the situation between Ukraine and Russia to involve armed conflict; and to state the number of countries that voted against one of the General Assembly resolutions (GAR 71/205 of 19 December 2016) on which the panel relied.[244] Russia also seemed to want the panel report to reflect that 'Russia ... is not a party to any armed conflict that Ukraine is involved in.'[245] The panel did not adopt the changes that Russia requested. The panel noted that the relevant General

239 *Russia—Measures concerning traffic in transit (Ukraine v. Russian Federation)*, Panel (Abi-Saab, Chair; Araki and Saeed, members), Report of the Panel, WT/DS512/R (5 April 2019) ¶ 7.137.

240 *Ibid.* ¶ 7.136.

241 *Ibid.* ¶ 7.137. See also *ibid.* ¶¶ 7.122–7.123.

242 *Ibid.* ¶ 7.149.

243 *Ibid.* ¶ 7.8.

244 *Russia—Measures concerning traffic in transit*, Interim Review, WT/DS512/R/Add.1, Annex E-1, ¶ 2.64.

245 *Ibid.*

Assembly resolution, the Assembly having adopted it 'with the constitutionally required majority,' stated 'the position of the UN General Assembly,' and that position was—in the Assembly's words, as quoted by the panel—that Russia is in '"temporary occupation of part of the territory of Ukraine".'[246] So Russia prevailed in part of a trade dispute but, by necessary implication from the panel's reasoning, was identified as a *temporary* occupant in time of war, not as the sovereign claimant that in other proceedings it claimed to be. In explaining its decision not to adopt the changes that Russia had requested to the report, the panel gave the distinct impression that, in relying on the General Assembly, it was intentionally delivering a parting sting to Russia.

Klein and Parlett, in their study *Judging the Law of the Sea*,[247] perhaps take a 'technocratic' view of UNCLOS adjudicators and support a 'procedural approach' that emphasizes the limits of jurisdictional consent.[248] However one characterizes their insights, they do not counsel that adjudicators ignore the fact-finding that other adjudicators have performed. 'It might be expected,' they write, 'at least that third-party proceedings may look to the factual determinations in one case to draw analogies to other fact patterns leading to similar legal conclusions.'[249]

Despite the wealth of factual determinations and analogies readily to hand, the *Coastal State Rights* tribunal accepted Russia's after-the-fact account, unscrutinized, as sufficient to demonstrate that a legal claim by Russia to Crimea exists. The *Coastal State Rights* award of 21 February 2020 is not only at almost complete variance with the determinations of other international institutions in its *result*. It also demonstrates a conspicuous failure of fact-finding that practically no other major international institution seised of these issues has replicated.

The danger of passivity in the face of evidence

H. L. A. Hart observed a long time ago that a characteristic of aggression by one state against another is that it is a largely visible act and, so, international law, whatever its weaknesses, could count as a moderating influence on states' awareness that they cannot hide the worst violence that they might do.[250] Russia engaged in ruses, but these seem to have convinced few

246 *Ibid.* ¶ 2.66.

247 Klein & Parlett, *Judging the Law of the Sea: Judicial Contributions to the UN Convention on the Law of the Sea* (2022).

248 Guilfoyle & Mossop's description of Klein & Parlett: Guilfoyle & Mossop (2024) at 651.

249 Klein & Parlett (2022) 29–30.

250 Hart, *The Concept of Law* (1961) 219.

to whom Russia addressed them.[251] The *Coastal State Rights* arbitrators are among the few.[252] The *Coastal State Rights* tribunal rewarded Russia for its efforts to hide the violence that it did. Considering that the means to hide the source of harm have increased with the rise of cyberspace,[253] and might further increase with autonomous weapon systems,[254] the tribunal's failure to come to grips with Russia's armed takeover of an entire province does not augur well for the machinery of international dispute settlement or international public order. Its 'hybrid' aspects notwithstanding, Russia's seizure of Crimea was essentially conventional and scarcely hidden,[255] and the formal annexation that followed—the BIT tribunal in *Naftogaz v. Russian Federation* had it right when it observed that 'nothing screams louder'[256]—was an overt act if ever there was one.

There are many situations in which an adjudicator is called upon to test the reasonableness of a party's assertions. The *Coastal State Rights* tribunal invites future adjudicators to be dangerously passive. Instead of considering the facts of the parties' claims and assertions and applying ordinary standards of good faith and reasonableness to evaluate them, the tribunal accepted the respondent state's objection to jurisdiction at face value.

Milano and Papanicolopulu in 2011 considered the situation in which activities of a state in an area might attract responsibility for the violation of another state's sovereignty or sovereign rights. To judge whether a state

251 For example, they did not convince the ECtHR. The ECtHR comprehensively rejected Russia's assertion that local groups in Crimea took hold the territory from Ukraine and organized referendums on independence. See *Crimea case* (ECtHR, 16 December 2020) ¶¶ 339, 331, 338. See also *MH17 case* (ECtHR, 25 January 2023) ¶46. For my earlier reflections on fact-finding in situations such as Russia's intervention in Crimea, see Grant (2019) 298–300.

252 As to the lack of evidence behind Russia's assertions that a self-determination movement existed in Crimea, and that circumstances in Ukraine justified such a movement, see Grant (2015) 28–33.

253 Noting problems of attribution in a cyberattack, see Walton, 'Low-Intensity Cyber Attacks' (2017) 126 YLJ 1460, 1463, 1501–1502, 1514; Schmitt, 'In Defense of Due Diligence in Cyberspace' (2015) 125 YLJ 68, 74; Schmitt, 'Cyberspace and International Law' (2013) 126 HLR 176, 179.

254 See generally Lewis, 'The Case for Regulating Fully Autonomous Weapons' (2015) 124 YLJ 1309; Thurnher, 'The Law that Applies to Autonomous Weapons Systems,' (2013) 17(4) ASIL Insights.

255 As to its hybrid aspects and how the law can deal with them, see Grant, 'Intervention, Interveners, and Their More Subtle Means' in Grant (ed.), *International Law and the Post-Soviet Space*, vol. 2 (2019) 290.

256 *NJSC Naftogaz of Ukraine, PJSC State Joint Stock Company Chornomornaftogax, PJSC Ukrgasvydobuvannya and others v. Russian Federation*, PCA Case No. 2017–16, Partial Award, 22 February 2019 (Binnie, President; Stanivuković and Poncent, arbitrators), ¶ 223.

is responsible for such activities, the adjudicator must measure the reasonableness of the state's assertion that the area was subject to a legal dispute. The writers reasoned that '[t]he only possibility to claim responsibility seems to be the case of a manifestly unreasonable claim.'[257] Milano and Papanicolopulu were concerned with maritime claims, and so they suggested that 'manifestly unreasonable,' in that setting, describes a claim 'not supported by any of the elements used in the law of maritime delimitation to draw the boundary.'[258] The instances where a state has pursued reparation for a violation of its sovereignty or sovereign rights in a disputed area are not many, and few of those have prevailed, but possibilities exist.[259] Milano and Papanicolopulu gave some illustrations: claims 'not based on a coastal front' (i.e., where the claimed maritime entitlement has no coast behind it at all), claims 'disregarding the geographical configuration of the area' (e.g., failing to take into account the concavity of a coast), a claim that ignores in its entirety an independent island state (i.e., Italy's claim in its dispute with Malta), a claim to extended maritime areas that 'negates' part of another state's territorial sea (e.g., Turkey's claim to areas west of longitude 32° 16′ 18″ that 'negates portions of territorial sea [of] Cyprus'); a claim that asserts the full potential entitlement projecting from its own coast while according very little or none to another state's opposite coast (e.g., the EEZ claim about which the ICJ remonstrated with Denmark in *Jan Mayen*).[260]

If the *Coastal State Rights* tribunal, as UNCLOS tribunals have done in the past, had engaged in fact-finding in regard to use of force, then it readily would have rejected Russia's pleading that 'developments' had overridden the universal recognition of Ukraine's international borders. There were multiple ways in which rigorous fact-finding would have led the tribunal to reject Russia's pleading. The tribunal might have taken a step back from the arid understanding of good faith that tacitly undergird its conclusion,[261] and declared that Russia's jurisdictional objection was, in truth, based on an armed attack. It might have recalled the famous Lagergren award in which the eponymous sole arbitrator refused to allow a pair of crooks who had defrauded the Argentine Republic to exploit the arbitral function to cover their tracks.[262] It might have declared Russia's assertions about a

257 Milano & Papanicolopulu (2011) 630.
258 *Ibid.*
259 *Ibid.* at 631–632.
260 *Ibid.* at 630 n. 142, citing *Jan Mayen*, Judgment, ICJ 1993 p. 38, p. 69 ¶ 70 (14 June).
261 *Coastal State Rights*, Award, ¶¶ 181–182.
262 International Chamber of Commerce (ICC) case no. 1110 (Lagergren, sole arbitrator), Paris, 1963, ¶ 20 (reprinted with redactions in 1994 *Arbitration International* 282 *et seq.*).

sovereignty dispute inadmissible and implausible, as Ukraine invited it to do.[263] It might have found, as I suggested earlier in the present chapter,[264] that there is no sufficient legal element in Russia's assertions for Russia to have demonstrated the existence of a legal dispute: the 'objective dispute' doctrine is not a license to ignore reality on the ground. But it did none of these things.

Observing the adjudicator's ordinary method

Another reason that the *Coastal State Rights* tribunal should have tested the evidence of the putative 'sovereignty dispute' is that, having done so, it would have done what parties expect. It would have observed the adjudicator's ordinary method. Judging whether a claim of legal right is plausible, or credible, or reasonable—there are nuances among the terms but a shared core element—is a commonplace task of the adjudicator.

There is nothing remarkable in suggesting that a tribunal examine the situation with care when a party asserts that a dispute exists. To the contrary: it is a tribunal's duty to examine the situation with care. The Special Chamber in *Mauritius/Maldives* did not accept that formal expressions of claim, unaccompanied by any other evidence, establish that a legal dispute exists: 'the fact that the United Kingdom and Mauritius continue to make their respective claims to the Chagos Archipelago,' the Special Chamber said, 'is beside the point.'[265] A claim in that setting, even repeated over and over, 'cannot be considered anything more than "mere assertion".'[266] An adjudicator therefore looks behind the assertion. It is what the ICJ in *Fisheries Jurisdiction* said has to be done: the adjudicator considers the parties' assertions but must consider 'other pertinent evidence' as well.[267]

263 See, for example, Ukraine, Rejoinder on Jurisdiction (28 March 2019) at ¶¶ 37–40: https://pcacases.com/web/sendAttach/2620#page=23 The Tribunal's dismissive treatment of Ukraine's pleadings about 'inadmissibility' has not gained credibility since. The ICJ, in its advisory opinion of 19 July 2024 in respect of *Policies and Practices of Israel in the Occupied Palestinian Territory*, referred to 'the *inadmissibility* of the acquisition of territory by force.' Advisory Opinion, ICJ 2024, ¶ 276 (19 July) (emphasis added).

264 See Chapter 6, pp. 209–210, 213.

265 *Mauritius/Maldives* (Prelim. Obj.), ¶ 243.

266 *Ibid.* The phrase 'mere assertion' the Special Chamber took from *South West Africa (Ethiopia v. South Africa; Libera v. South Africa)*, Preliminary Objections, ICJ 1962 p. 319, p. 328 (21 December).

267 *Fisheries Jurisdiction (Spain v. Canada)*, Jurisdiction, ICJ 1998 p. 432, p. 449 ¶¶ 30–31 (4 December). See also *Arbitral Award of 3 October 1899 (Guyana v. Venezuela)*, Declaration of Judge *ad hoc* Wolfrum, ICJ 2023 p. 300, p. 303 ¶ 12 n. 11 (6 April), quoting *South China Sea* (Jur. & Adm.), ¶ 150.

To give another example of a question that called for inquiry into the facts, the question in *Indonesia/Malaysia* was whether to grant a third state's request to intervene. There, too, the adjudicator did not accept the Philippines' factual assertions at face value. The Court put the Philippines' asserted basis for intervention to the test of evidence. Finding that it failed, the Court denied the Philippines' putative sovereignty claim legal effect in the proceedings. I have also adverted to the evidence-based inquiries in cases involving requests for interpretation and in cases where the adjudicator had to identify the starting date of a dispute. As we saw in *Certain Activities Carried out by Nicaragua in the Border Area*, testing a party's assertions is the usual course in provisional measures practice as well.[268] It is the proper approach in diverse settings but, with nary a word as to why it was not the approach to apply in *its* setting, the *Coastal State Rights* tribunal refused to apply it.

Each of the examples that I have considered here involved a closer judgment than the *Coastal State Rights* tribunal was called on to reach. Russia's assertion in regard to Crimea is much less reasonable than the ones to which Milano and Papanicolopulu adverted,[269] and Russia made the assertion in a procedural setting—the jurisdictional phase—where the adjudicator exercises extensive powers of decision. In the *Costa Rica v. Nicaragua* border activities case, Costa Rica's evidence of a plausible sovereign claim concerned relatively obscure border areas of modest size—a claim intrinsically more challenging to evaluate than Russia's notorious assertion against the entirety of a neighboring province. If an adjudicator cannot take the measure of *that* assertion, in *that* setting, then the adjudicator will be incapable of judging credibility in cases where the parties' competing assertions are much more nearly balanced. The February 2020 *Coastal State Rights* award, if its refusal to test party assertion against evidence were generalized, would introduce serious difficulty in a wide range of dispute settlement settings in face of a

268 Adjudicators have affirmed the need for evidence-based fact-finding in provisional measures practice in other situations as well, not just where putative sovereignty disputes are concerned. See *Dispute concerning delimitation of the maritime boundary between Ghana and Côte d'Ivoire in the Atlantic Ocean (Ghana/Côte d'Ivoire)*, Provisional Measures, Order, ITLOS 2015 p. 25, p. 159 ¶ 62 (25 April): 'Côte d'Ivoire has presented enough material to show that the rights it seeks to protect in the disputed area are plausible'); *The 'ARA Libertad' Case (Argentina v. Ghana)*, Provisional Measures, Joint Sep. Op. Wolfrum and Cot, ITLOS 2012 p. 363, p. 367 ¶ 16 (15 December): 'it is not sufficient that an applicant merely invokes provisions which, read in an abstract way, may provide theoretically a basis for the jurisdiction of the court or tribunal in question. On the contrary, it is necessary for the adjudicative body to take into account the facts which are known to it.' See also *The 'Enrica Lexie' Incident (Italy v. India)*, Provisional Measures, Order, ITLOS 2015 p. 182, p. 197 ¶¶ 84–85 (24 August).

269 See above p. 236.

wide range of claims. Failure to follow the ordinary adjudicative method of testing assertion against evidence thus potentially undermines the dispute settlement function at large.

Professor Park, in the inaugural issue of the *Journal of International Dispute Settlement,* addressed arbitration in its commercial and investment treaty setting, but his observations about facts and fact-finding hold just as much for arbitration under UNCLOS:

> Accuracy in arbitration means something other than absolute truth as it might exist in the eyes of an omniscient God. In examining the competing views of reality proposed by each side, arbitrators aim to get as near as reasonably possible to a correct picture of those disputed events, words, and legal norms that bear consequences for the litigants' claims and defences. They recognize that some answers are better than others, even if perfection proves elusive.[270]

The Annex VII arbitrators in *Coastal State Rights* did not need omniscience to identify Russia's assertion of a 'sovereignty dispute' to arrive at the better answer. Nor did they need to attain the elusive 'perfection.' If they had tested the evidence in the way that parties expect arbitrators to do, then they would have arrived nearly enough at 'a correct picture' of the events that Russia had placed in issue. Those events did not give rise to a sovereignty dispute.

How the tribunal should have tested the evidence: burden of proof and standard of proof

The jurisprudence is well known that addresses how an international adjudicator is to test factual assertions.

As to burden of proof, the ICJ said in *Pulp Mills* that, 'in accordance with the well-established principle of *onus probandi incumbit actori,* it is the duty of the party which asserts certain facts to establish the existence of such facts.'[271]

It was Russia that asserted the existence of a legal dispute over territory based upon a putative humanitarian crisis in Ukraine. The ordinary expectation is that the tribunal would have placed the onus on Russia to 'establish the existence of such facts' as would have given substance to Russia's assertion.

Adjudicators long have hesitated to impose on a party the burden of proving that something does *not* exist. Proving a negative is notoriously

270 Park, 'arbitrators and Accuracy' (2010) 1(1) JIDS at 26. See also Corten (2024) 290.

271 *Pulp Mills on the River Uruguay (Argentina v. Uruguay)*, Judgment, ICJ 2010 p. 14, 71, ¶ 162 (20 April) (with citations to decided cases). See generally Corten (2024) 289–293.

difficult in a wide range of legal relations.[272] The ICJ developed the point in *Diallo*,[273] and affirmed it in the *Croatia v. Serbia* case under the Genocide Convention.[274] According to the ICJ, 'it cannot as a general rule be demanded of the Applicant that it prove the negative fact which it is asserting.'[275] It having been Russia that, in support of a jurisdictional objection, alleged a sovereignty dispute over Crimea, the tribunal should not have placed the onus on Ukraine to 'prove the negative fact'—that is, that no such dispute exists. Yet that is what the tribunal did. Calling on the applicant to prove the negative was all the less appropriate, considering that Russia itself conceded that there had been no sovereignty dispute until Russia resorted to armed force to seize the territory.

Writing in *Ocean Development and International Law*, James Harrison observed that '[t]he burden of proof rests with the applicant to demonstrate that a dispute does in fact exist.'[276] Professor Harrison meant the state instituting proceedings but added that the allocation of burden here is 'in line with the general rule that it is up to the party advancing a particular claim to prove it.'[277] The general rule is one that applies when a party places

272 As the Court of King's Bench asked, rhetorically, 'Is not the Statute of Anne [5 Ann. C. 14, s. 2] in effect a prohibition on every person to kill game, unless he brings himself within some one of the qualifications allowed by law; the proof of which is easy on the one side, but almost impossible on the other?' *The King v. Turner* (1816) 5, Maule and Selwyn 206, 210 (Lord Ellenborough C.J.). A logician once suggested that '[t]he reason that the negative appears more difficult to prove in law is that a legal case is more likely to turn on an existential claim, and the negative of that claim is a universal'—that is to say, to prove a negative in the typical legal case, one must show that the statement is *universally* true that 'situation X does not exist.' Saunders, 'What Logic Can and cannot Tell Us about Law' (1998) 73 *Notre Dame Law Review* 667, 678. Put differently, a negative proof 'may depend on complete induction': Van Atten, 'Objections to the Proof Interpretation' in Zalta & Nodelman (eds.), *Stanford Encyclopedia of Philosophy* (2023).

273 *Ahmadou Sadio Diallo (Republic of Guinea v. Democratic Republic of the Congo)*, Merits, Judgment, ICJ 2010 p. 639, pp. 660–661 ¶ 55 (3 November).

274 *Application of the Convention on the Prevention and Punishment of the Crime of Genocide (Croatia v. Serbia)*, Judgment, ICJ 2015 p. 3, p. 73 ¶ 72 (3 February): 'there may be circumstances in which the Applicant cannot be required to prove a "negative fact"'; and *ibid.* at pp. 73–74 ¶ 174: 'It is not for Serbia to prove a negative fact, for example the absence of facts constituting the *actus reus* of genocide within the meaning of Article II of the Convention in localities to which Croatia called the Court's attention.'

275 ICJ 2010 at pp. 660–661 ¶ 55. See also detailed consideration at *Armed Activities on the Territory of the Congo (Democratic Republic of the Congo v. Uganda)*, Reparations, Sep. Op. Judge Yusuf, ICJ 2022 at pp. 146–154, ¶¶ 3–21 (9 February).

276 Harrison, 'Defining Disputes and Characterizing Claims' (2017) 48 ODIL 269, 270.

277 Harrison (2017) 270. See also Corten (2024) 289.

a matter in contention, not just when a party starts a case. In short, the *Coastal State Rights* tribunal should have applied the rule to Russia but did not. It should have asked Russia what developments, precisely, gave a legal basis after March 2014 for the boundary settlement between Russia and Ukraine to be ignored and a sovereignty dispute to have arisen in its place.

There is also the matter of standard of proof. Since its earliest days, the ICJ has been clear that an adjudicator's scrutiny of evidence must be especially rigorous where a state advances the evidence to support an allegation of 'exceptional gravity.' This goes back to *Corfu Channel*,[278] and the Court has sustained the point through recent decades, including in the *Genocide* cases that Bosnia and Croatia instituted against Serbia.[279] The allegation essential to Russia's putative territorial claim is an allegation of 'exceptional gravity.'

By Russia's description, Russia's claim to territory emerged in 2014 because, according to Russia, Ukraine had instigated a humanitarian crisis in Crimea and other parts of the country tantamount to genocide against the Russian ethnic population. Forming the link between that factual allegation and Russia's putative claim is the controversial proposition that a remedial rule exists, under which the presumptive stability of boundaries might be set aside in order to protect people who are victims of the most extreme forms of abuse and where remedy under the government of the existing territorial sovereign has proved unattainable. The factual evidence that would activate the remedial rule (to the extent that a remedial rule applies in international law) is conspicuous. Genocide, in modern conditions, is hard to hide. So, too, failure to remedy the complaints of a population subject to such crimes is out in the open, not secreted in obscure places. States express 'radically different views' as to whether a right to 'remedial secession' exists.[280] None believe that a group has a right to secession absent abuses of the most serious and visible kind.

In *Corfu Channel*, the ICJ rejected 'circumstantial evidence' that Yugoslav naval vessels had laid the mines that had damaged two British destroyers and killed forty-four British naval personnel. 'A charge of such exceptional gravity against a State,' the Court said, 'would require a degree of certainty that has not been reached here.'[281] Russia's 'charge' in regard to Crimea is

278 *Corfu Channel*, ICJ 1949 at p. 17.

279 *Application of the Convention on the Prevention and Punishment of the Crime of Genocide (Bosnia and Herzegovina v. Serbia and Montenegro)*, Judgment, ICJ 2007 p. 43, p. 129 ¶ 209 (26 February): 'claims against a State involving charges of exceptional gravity must be proved by evidence that is fully conclusive.'

280 *Kosovo*, Advisory Opinion, ICJ 2010 p. 403, p. 438 ¶ 82 (22 July).

281 *Corfu Channel (United Kingdom v. Albania)*, Judgment, ICJ 1949 p. 4, p. 17 (9 April).

easier to address than was Britain's in regard to the *Corfu Channel* mines. In *Corfu Channel*, a single act was at issue, and that act was of a kind that state actors readily conceal. Correspondingly, to identify the actor responsible for the act—that was the ICJ's task in *Corfu Channel*—was difficult. A 'degree of certainty' was required that mere circumstantial evidence did not achieve. By comparison, in *Coastal State Rights* the task was easy. The events that the tribunal alluded to as 'developments' leading to a sovereignty dispute would have been impossible to conceal. Russia needed to establish that a humanitarian crisis existed in Crimea of a magnitude that might have sustained a plea that separation of Crimea was a necessary remedy. No serious exponent of the view that international law contains a right of 'remedial secession' contends that the right is activated by anything less than a crisis of extreme magnitude—and for which resolution is stubbornly elusive. Quite apart from the legal uncertainty here—that is to say, uncertainty as to the extent to which international law admits of 'remedial secession' if at all—the *factual* question that Russia's assertion raised was eminently determinable. There was not a scintilla of evidence to prove that a crisis existed in Crimea even approaching the magnitude that would have triggered the remedial right as those who posit the right say is required. All that the tribunal needed to do in order to satisfy itself that this was the case was to exercise the adjudicator's ordinary fact-finding function and to allocate the burden of proof in the ordinary way.[282]

In effect, the *Coastal State Rights* tribunal reasoned that the onus belonged on Ukraine to prove a negative—that is, to prove that there was *not* a crisis in Crimea. The equivalent in *Corfu Channel* would have been for the ICJ to demand of Albania proof of *its* negative—that is to say, proof that Albania or its then treaty partner Yugoslavia *did not* lay mines in the channel. Demanding that a party prove such a 'negative fact' the Court refused in 1949 to do,[283] and has refused since.[284]

Placing the burden of proof on a party in the manner that the *Coastal State Rights* tribunal did on Ukraine is tantamount to turning the other party's allegation into a presumption. International courts do not allocate the burden that way. If they did, then the party that makes an allegation

282 The tribunal would not have needed to settle whether a 'remedial secession' rule exists or its scope. It would have needed only waive Russia's own earlier *Kosovo* objection and assume the legal position most favorable to Russia for purposes of judging Russia's *Coastal State Rights* objection—that is, it would have assumed, to favor Russia, that 'remedial secession' is a legal rule.

283 *Corfu Channel*, ICJ 1949 at p. 18: 'This fact, by itself and apart from other circumstances, neither involves *prima facie* responsibility [of Albania] nor shifts the burden of proof [to Albania].'

284 See p. 240 nn. 273–275.

would gain tremendous advantage. The party's allegation would be presumed to be true—and the adjudicator would accord the party every advantage that follows from the presumption of the truth of the matter contained in the allegation. Allocating the burden of proof this way would have a pronounced effect on dispute settlement procedure. The effect would be especially pronounced where a jurisdictional bar is activated, as it is under a great many jurisdictional instruments, by the existence of certain circumstances. The mere assertion that those circumstances exist would place the burden of proving a negative on the party seeking to adjudicate a claim. Proving a negative is nearly impossible in many cases. Thus, the mere assertion would require the adjudicator in many cases to conclude that it lacked jurisdiction to adjudicate. The objecting party in those cases would have an unlimited option to vitiate its own jurisdictional consent.

Lest the reader mistake these considerations to be limited to the extraordinary case of armed aggression or genocide, an example from a prosaic case illustrates that their relevance is general. Under BITs providing for arbitration of investment disputes, a requirement of jurisdiction *ratione personae* is that the claimant *not* be a national of the state party against which the claimant institutes proceedings. Like the requirement (as interpreted) under UNCLOS that there *not* be a sovereignty dispute, the 'negative nationality' requirement supplies to a respondent state a possible ground of jurisdictional objection. Assuming that there is evidence that the claimant, in truth, is a national of the respondent state, it is open to the respondent state to object to the exercise of jurisdiction. However, even where the applicable treaty provides no definition of 'dominant nationality,'[285] adjudicators have not merely accepted a respondent's assertion that a claimant had the wrong nationality to proceed with its claim. In *Siag v. Egypt*, the arbitrators did not merely accept Egypt's assertion that the claimants were its own nationals. The tribunal inquired into the assertion and, having done so, rejected it.[286] To conduct the inquiry, the tribunal carefully considered evidence in regard to Egyptian nationality law and the facts of the particular claimants' status under that law over time.[287] The respondent's assertion about nationality,

285 See p. 212 n. 159. See also *Ballantine v. Dominican Republic*, PCA Case. No. 2016–17 (Ramírez Hernández, Presiding; Cheek & Vinuesa, Arbitrators), Final Award (3 September 2019), ¶ 541.

286 *Siag v. Egypt*, ICSID Case No. ARB/05/15 (Pryles, President; Williams and Orrego Vicuña, arbitrators) (Vicuña, dissenting), Decision on Jurisdiction, 11 April 2007, ¶¶ 195, 199.

287 Considering the parties' pleadings on the matter, and setting out its own reasoning and conclusions, the tribunal devoted the largest part of its Decision on Jurisdiction to the negative nationality question. *Ibid.* ¶¶ 142–201.

made in an attempt to avoid dispute settlement, required careful testing—and received it.

Nobody in *Siag* said that the applicable treaties—the Egypt–Italy BIT and the International Convention on the Settlement of Investment Disputes (ICSID)—create a jurisdiction for the settlement of disputes over a person's nationality. They obviously do not. Reaching dispositive results on disputes over a person's nationality is not a function of an investment tribunal constituted under such treaties. It *is* a function of an investment tribunal to determine the scope of its own jurisdiction. A respondent state's invocation of a 'negative nationality' requirement implicates that function. To perform it, the tribunal must do more than passively accept the respondent state's objection.

The claims in investment cases are usually of less moment than war and peace. Yet the inquiry that investment tribunals make as to nationality is arguably *more* exacting and *more* intrusive against a respondent state, nationality being a matter classically reserved to domestic jurisdiction, than asking whether a respondent state is a real claimant to sovereignty in a territory, claims to territory being intrinsically matters for international law. If a tribunal refuses to use ordinary forensic tools to discern whether as conspicuous an international rupture has occurred as Russia's invasion of Ukraine, then it will be all the easier for a tribunal to refuse to answer questions such as the nationality questions that are often necessary to the successful operation of investment dispute settlement. If tribunals widely adopt the *Coastal State Rights* approach, then unilateral assertion will suffice in a diverse range of settings to prevent adjudicators from performing the tasks which parties have entrusted them. The objector's *ipsa dixit* should not suffice to trigger a jurisdictional bar. If dispute settlement jurisprudence comes to accept that it *does* suffice, then we will have traveled full circle to self-judging reservations, an unhappy turn and one against which Judge Sir Hersch Lauterpacht admonished long ago.[288]

Article 288(4) and the missing facts

As I related in Chapter 2, Peter Tzeng and others doubt whether UNCLOS tribunals should use Article 293, the applicable law provision, to reach questions such as those raised when parties allege an unlawful use of force.[289] But Article 288(4) is clear. It requires tribunals to determine the scope of

288 See pp. 340–341.
289 See pp. 74–83.

their own jurisdiction.[290] Russia grounded its objection to jurisdiction on the assertion that a putative remedial claim to secession in Crimea had given rise to a legal dispute over sovereignty. True, the 'developments' that the tribunal said were the basis of Russia's sovereignty claim were ancillary to a law of the sea dispute. But Russia pleaded those 'developments' for a purpose absolutely central to the law of the sea dispute of which the tribunal was seised. It pleaded them for the purpose of disposing of the dispute. The posture of Russia's assertion of a sovereignty dispute places it squarely within Article 288(4).

The competence to decide the scope of its jurisdiction is an essential element of a tribunal's function. It is a competence which, in some situations, is not properly exercised unless the adjudicator enters into questions of fact. Indeed, an adjudicator might have to defer reaching a conclusion as to the scope of its jurisdiction until it has 'before it all facts necessary to decide the questions raised.'[291] The refusal of the *Coastal State Rights* tribunal to address the facts of Russia's assertion of a sovereignty dispute ran against the grain of the UNCLOS use of force cases (and other use of force cases such as *Oil Platforms* and *Military and Paramilitary Activities*), where adjudicators did not hesitate to engage with parties' assertions regarding ancillary questions. Whatever one's view of those cases and their accordance with the doctrinal separation of choice of law from jurisdiction, the cases exist, and prominently so. But even if one steadfastly rejects them (perhaps in the conviction that rejecting them is a necessary corrective), there is still the duty of the tribunal to determine the scope of its jurisdiction. The refusal of the *Coastal State Rights* tribunal to scrutinize the facts of the putative sovereignty dispute constitutes a failure to carry out the mandatory determination that Article 288(4) directs and the fact-finding that the adjudicator's function necessarily entails.[292]

Does Article 288(4) entail unlimited discretion for an adjudicator to explore ancillary issues that might have some bearing on the adjudicator's jurisdiction? Obviously not! No more does Article 288(1) establish a general power of adjudication. However, as the UNCLOS cases in which tribunals

290 See pp. 62–66.

291 *Territorial and Maritime Dispute (Nicaragua v. Colombia)*, ICJ 2007 p. 832, p. 852 ¶ 51 (13 December) See also *South China Sea Arbitration* (Jur. & Adm.), ¶¶ 392–396 (finding that it had to address a range of factual and legal issues before it could reach conclusions as to jurisdictional objections under UNCLOS Arts. 297 and 298). *Compare Obligation to Negotiate Access to the Pacific Ocean (Bolivia v. Chile)*, Preliminary Objections, ICJ 2015 p. 592, p. 610 ¶ 53 (24 September) ('the Court considers that it has all the facts necessary to rule on Chile's objection').

292 Regarding fact-finding under UNCLOS procedures and its relation to the adjudicator's function, see Klein & Parlett (2022) 27–30.

considered the scope of the exclusion of territorial issues attest, the limits remain unclear. It is to be hoped that future cases, even if only step by step, will clarify the limits.

Clarifying the limits of a legal rule requires facts. If the adjudicator eschews factual inquiry, then the facts will be missing. Eschewing factual inquiry, as the *Coastal State Rights* tribunal did, thus impedes clarification of rules and, in turn, deprives rules the predictability that a developed legal system seeks to impart to them. If a state of affairs prevails in which the facts remain missing, then, to negate the words of Oliver Wendell Holmes, Jr. in *The Common Law*, perforce the 'facts will [*not*] have taught their lesson.'[293]

Managing public order effects in the law of the sea: some lessons from hydrocarbon practice

As I have argued in this chapter and develop further in Chapter 7, the award in *Coastal State Rights* of 21 February 2020 contains a range of formal defects. The award is further unsatisfactory because its result—the determination of the existence of a 'sovereignty dispute'—is likely to give rise to damaging effects on public international order.

The Annex VII tribunal in *Coastal State Rights* should have taken into account the effects of its decision on public order.

To have taken the public order effects into account would have broken no new ground in law of the sea jurisprudence. Lest my point here be mistaken for telling future adjudicators to untether their reasoning from established approaches, let us be clear: adjudicators addressing maritime disputes have evinced concern over public order in situations where the threat to public order is far more speculative than it is in the situation with which the *Coastal State Rights* was concerned.

We find an example in the jurisprudence regarding hydrocarbon practice—that is, the practice of states in granting concessions to explore for and exploit oil and gas deposits in disputed maritime areas and of concessionaires in placing vessels, personnel, and infrastructure in such areas.[294] Courts and tribunals in most cases have given little weight to hydrocarbon practice.[295] The caution toward hydrocarbon practice is so characteristic of the approach

293 Holmes, *The Common Law* (1881) 150.

294 See generally Chandra & Morss, 'UNCLOS and Maritime Boundary Disputes in Areas of Hydrocarbon Potential' (2022) 53 ODIL 1–18.

295 *Guyana v. Suriname*, Award, Annex VII/PCA (Nelson, President; Franck, Hossain, Shearer, and Smit, members) ¶ 390 (17 September 2007).

that adjudicators have taken that it rightly can be counted among the important features of the jurisprudence. According to the ICJ, 'oil concessions and oil wells are not in themselves to be considered as relevant circumstances justifying the adjustment or shifting of the provisional delimitation line. Only if they are based on express or tacit agreement between the parties may they be taken into account.'[296]

The 'marked reluctance'[297] to accord significance to hydrocarbon practice evinces concern over public order. Where a genuine dispute exists as to the limits of two states' maritime jurisdiction, and the states have plausible overlapping claims, then a jurisprudence that credited unilateral activity in the area would give each state an incentive to enlarge the geographic scope and intensify the frequency and character of its activity in the area. Such an incentive would endanger peaceful relations between the states. They would compete to 'out-practice' one another, which, in this setting, would mean increasing the risk of incidents between them, including between their armed forces.[298]

Courts and tribunals are largely consistent in attributing little weight to hydrocarbon practice or requiring convincing reasons to do otherwise. They have expressed the basis for this approach in strictly formal terms. An unstated premise exists behind the formalism, however. The premise is that if states relied on the raw fact of physical presence to advance, or to impede, legal entitlements in the seas, then general public order in the seas would cease to exist. The *Coastal State Rights* Annex VII tribunal, faced not merely with a risk of international friction but with an armed invasion, ignored the implications for public order that followed from the approach that it adopted.

296 *Land and Maritime Boundary between Cameroon and Nigeria (Cameroon v. Nigeria: Equatorial Guinea intervening)*, ICJ 2002 at pp. 447–448 ¶ 304 (10 October), with reference to *Delimitation of the Maritime Boundary in the Gulf of Maine Area (Canada/United States of America)*, ICJ 1984 at pp. 310–311 ¶¶ 149–152; *Continental Shelf (Tunisia/Libya)*, ICJ 1982 p. 18, p. 83 ¶ 117. See also *Delimitation of the Maritime Boundary in the Atlantic Ocean (Ghana/Côte d'Ivoire)*, Judgment, ITLOS 2017 p. 4 ¶ 147 (23 September).

297 *Guyana v. Suriname* ¶ 390, with reference to *Barbados/Trinidad and Tobago* (2006) 45 ILM 788 ¶ 364.

298 Though, as far as I am aware, the concern is unstated between Lebanon and Israel, Israel's restraint suggests the concern is real that difficulties could arise from oil concession practice in an undelimited area subject to the two states' potential maritime entitlements. See Ioannides, 'The Legal Framework Governing Hydrocarbon Activities in Undelimited Maritime Areas' (2019) 68 ICLQ 345, 351–353.

7

The institutional setting and a tribunal in isolation

The analogy is familiar between international law and a string of islands and archipelagos stretched out across a sea.[1] International law consists of distinct incidents and institutions, jurisdictions and régimes, and wide spaces separate one from the other. To speak of the 'fragmentation' of international law has become a commonplace since Martti Koskenniemi led the International Law Commission in a study of the matter.[2]

Yet the *Coastal State Rights* award widened the 'anomic' spaces and took fragmentation to new extremes.[3] A number of striking instances are visible in the award of 21 February 2020 in which the tribunal refused to accord weight to determinations reached by other courts or tribunals and other public international institutions, misinterpreted them, or ignored them altogether, notwithstanding their relevance to the case at hand.

Let us start by considering the idiosyncratic approach that the tribunal took toward recognition in international law—the decentralized institution that serves to express collective judgment in regard to the emergence and transformation of states—before turning to the tribunal's sharp departure from the practice of a range of international organizations, including adjudicative bodies, that had rejected Russia's putative claims as incompatible with modern international law.

1 See the Hague Lectures in which W. Michael Reisman extended the metaphor: Reisman, 'The Quest for World Order and Human Dignity in the Twenty-First Century: Constitutive Process and Individual Commitment' (2010) 351 Hag. Rec. 31, 34, 38, 42, 43, 90, 96, 163–164, 329, 355. Cf. Reisman, 'Canute Confronts the Tide: States vs. Tribunals and the Evolution of the Minimum Standard in Customary International Law' (2015) 109 ASIL Proc. 12, 127. To similar effect, see Hakimi, 'The Work of International Law' (2017) 58 HILJ 1, 24–25 (regarding the law's 'fragmented normative structure'). Cf. with reference to jurisdictional instruments in particular, Pauwelyn, 'The Role of Public International Law in the WTO' (2001) 95 AJIL 535, 552–553.

2 See pp. 277–278, 284, 285.

3 'Anomic' spaces is Reisman's term. See Reisman (2010) at 31.

Recognition and non-recognition in international law

In responding to Russia's jurisdictional objection, Ukraine drew attention to the General Assembly practice rejecting Russia's putative annexation of Crimea and calling for non-recognition of that act and declaring it to have no legal effect.[4] Ukraine observed that '[w]ithout precedent or reason, Russia has asked [the] Tribunal to ignore the General Assembly, to ignore the international community's determination that the international law principle of non-recognition applies, and to treat a settled part of Ukrainian territory as being subject to ... competing legal claims.'[5] As we have seen, the tribunal disagreed with Ukraine and did as Russia asked. It found that 'competing legal claims' exist in regard to the question which state is sovereign in Crimea. The tribunal concluded that it 'does not consider the UNGA [United Nations General Assembly] resolutions to which Ukraine refers can be read to go as far as prohibiting it from recognising the existence of a dispute over the territorial status of Crimea.'[6]

In its reasoning, the tribunal said that 'at the centre of the contention between the Parties are the legal effect and meaning of the UNGA resolutions' addressing Russia's unlawful attempted seizure of the territory.[7] The tacit assumption behind this characterization—'at the *centre* of the contention'—is that General Assembly resolutions are *the* source of an answer to the question whether Ukraine's sovereignty is recognized, or whether, instead, Russia's assertions now place Ukraine's sovereignty in doubt.

Recognition as decentralized response

The problem is, few if any states, and few if any writers, say that the General Assembly is the 'center' that settles questions of recognition.[8] The tribunal's premise that the contention over Ukraine's sovereignty is centered in the General Assembly is unsupported. Having begun with that dubious premise, the tribunal then ignored a wider practice that, in this setting on this point, deserved the tribunal's careful regard.

4 Written Observations and Submissions of Ukraine on Jurisdiction, 27 November 2018, ¶¶ 17–32.
5 *Ibid.* ¶ 33.
6 Award, ¶ 177.
7 *Coastal State Rights*, ¶ 171.
8 On decentralized determinations in respect of non-recognition, see Thomas D. Grant, 'East Timor, the U.N. System, and Enforcing Non-recognition in International Law' (2000) 33 *Vanderbilt Journal of Transnational Law* 273, 307–309.

One of the characteristic features of recognition is its decentralization.[9] It is this feature that an adjudicator must consider when inquiring into the effects of recognition and non-recognition on sovereignty claims. Addressing General Assembly practice as the locus of the matter, the *Coastal State Rights* tribunal instead steered its analysis to questions of the institutional authority of the Assembly,[10] and of the discretion of a tribunal to interpret or reject Assembly resolutions.[11] As I argue below (in the section 'General Assembly practice and the lessons of *East Timor*'), the tribunal got its relationship to General Assembly practice wrong, but, in treating *that* practice as the pivot of the matter, the tribunal got another matter wrong: the tribunal conflated the role of the General Assembly, which has never asserted an exclusive role, or even a leading role, in regard to recognition, with the role of the decentralized community of states. It is *there*, in that decentralized community, not in organized institutional settings, that the decisions that count in regard to recognition most often have emerged.

Crawford wrote: 'It is one thing to say that statehood is regulated under law; quite another to claim that it has been bureaucratized under the auspices of an international organization.'[12] This observation, expressed in regard to the decentralized character of recognition of the sovereignty of a state for general purposes—that is, recognition of statehood—applies equally to recognition for the specific purpose of identifying legal claims of sovereignty over particular parts of the territory of a state. The General Assembly may add to the evidence of recognition, and in regard to Ukraine's territorial

9 See, for example, *Application for Revision of the Judgment of 11 July 1996 in the Case concerning Application of the Convention on the Prevention and Punishment of the Crime of Genocide (Bosnia and Herzegovina v. Yugoslavia), Preliminary Objections* (Yugoslavia v. Bosnia and Herzegovina), Dis. Op. Judge Dimitrijević, ICJ 2003 p. 65 ¶ 45 (3 February). The decentralized character of recognition is a particular, and key, case of the overall character of international law as a 'form of *praxis* involving diffuse, decentralized but nonetheless observably real authority.' Crawford (2013) 365 Hag. Rec. at 22. Writers have connected its decentralized character to recognition in international law, including recognition of territorial claims. See, for example, Moon, 'Recognition, Rewards, and Regime Change' in Giorgetti & Klein (eds.), *Essays in Honour of Lea Brilmayer* (2019) 130, 142. See also Reporters' Note to similar effect in *Restatement (Third)* § 202.

10 *Coastal State Rights*, Award, ¶ 172–174.

11 *Ibid.* ¶ 176.

12 Crawford, *Creation of States*, 2nd edn. (2006) 193. McDougal and Reisman referred to the 'unorganized process of decision,' which they understood to be a characteristic of international law indispensable to understanding that law. McDougal & Reisman, '"*The Changing Structure of International Law": Unchanging Theory for Inquiry*' (1965) 65 Colum. LR 810, 820. See also McDougal, Lasswell & Reisman (1969) 73, 80.

integrity, it added considerably. But the General Assembly is not a general clearing house of recognition.

The approach that the tribunal in *Coastal State Rights* took toward recognition displayed a number of further idiosyncrasies. These, too, merit remark.

Distinguishing recognition from customary international law identification

Recognition is the act by which a state takes formal cognizance of a situation. It is not a legislative act that *creates* a situation, such as the act, composed of the composite acts of two or more states, that, when combined with *opinio juris*, creates a rule of customary international law.[13] The *Coastal State Rights* tribunal, however, addressing recognition, posited that the practice of states in their participation in the General Assembly sometimes evinces customary international law.[14] The tribunal left the point essentially unremarked, which would leave the reader to puzzle over what the tribunal meant by it.

Perhaps the tribunal meant that the General Assembly practice regarding a putative 'dispute' over Crimea did not evince the formation of a customary international law rule. If that is what the tribunal meant, then it was confused. Recognition of a territorial claim is a different process from emergence of customary international law. A small number of states resisting the emergence of a rule of customary international law may prevent its emergence or exempt themselves from its application if it emerges. By contrast, a minority of states does not prevent a state from emerging by withholding recognition from it; nor do third states overturn a settled territorial entitlement by

13 Tellingly, the ILC in its 2018 draft conclusions and commentaries on identification of customary international law gave examples of outcomes—rules—to be identified by reference to the processes of customary international law formation, but it did not mention recognition in the sense of the institution with which we are concerned here. See 2018 ILC Yearbook, vol. II, Part Two. In five successive reports of the Special Rapporteur on the topic, while the reports refer to 'recognition' of norms and rules and offer a great many further examples from state practice (see, e.g., A/71/10, 2016 ILC Report at p. 300, ¶ 114), no example addresses statehood or a sovereignty claim as a norm or rule subject to 'recognition' in the sense that the reports use the term when addressing customary international law formation. Unsurprisingly, the reports discuss the rule of non-recognition and non-assistance in relation to serious breaches of *jus cogens* norms (see, e.g., A/73/10, 2018 ILC Report at p. 228, ¶ 108), but their concern is with recognition of *the rule* requiring non-recognition and non-assistance, not with indicia from state or institutional practice that a particular state of affairs is one to which the rule shall be applied.

14 Award, ¶¶ 173–174.

declaring it to be in dispute. Recognition of a territorial status and formation of a rule of customary international law are different processes.

The tribunal's confusion between recognition and customary international law formation led the tribunal to impute consequences to abstentions in the General Assembly that abstentions do not have in regard to the matter of territorial title here at issue. According to the tribunal, the General Assembly resolutions calling for non-recognition of Russia's claim to territorial title 'were not adopted unanimously or by consensus but with many States abstaining or voting against them.'[15] The tribunal's conjunction between abstention and negative votes is evasive, and it is a serious error. It is evasive, because it fails to note how very few negative votes there were. When the General Assembly voted on the draft that became resolution 68/262 of 27 March 2014, Russia mustered a mere total of eleven votes against it, in contrast to 100 in favor.[16]

As for the abstentions (there were fifty-eight), these might have reflected an important body of opinion—if this had been a resolution with law-making ambitions behind it, or if the purpose in adverting to it was to find evidence, in the balance of votes, that a customary rule was emerging.[17] But that is not what it was, and that is not why the vote record is relevant. The resolution rejected Russia's putative claim to Crimea and affirmed Ukraine's long-standing title. In so doing, it reaffirmed the spatial settlement between Russia and Ukraine that had prevailed without protest or reservation since 1991. Seen in their proper light, the members' votes may be likened to the international practice of objection and acquiescence in regard to territorial claim. To recall the second clause of Rule 86 of the General Assembly Rules of Procedure, 'Members which abstain from voting are considered as not voting.'[18] The states that abstained, their conduct seen in that light, acquiesced in the General Assembly's affirmation that Ukraine is sovereign. If they thought otherwise, then this was 'an occasion that called for a reaction in order to affirm or preserve' their position 'in the face of an obvious rival'

15 *Ibid.*, ¶ 175.

16 GAR 68/262, 27 March 2014 (Territorial Integrity of Ukraine) (100–11–58).

17 For classic observations as to the relevance of GA vote patterns in regard to customary rule emergence, see Professor Dupuy, as Sole Arbitrator, in *Texaco v. Libya*, Award on the Merits, 19 January 1977, 53 ILR 422, 484–493 ¶¶ 80–88; and, in part by way of reply, Schwebel, 'The Effects of Resolution of the U.N. General Assembly on Customary International Law' (1979) 73 ASIL Proc. 301–309.

18 A/520/Rev.20. See generally Wolfrum, 'Article 18' in Simma, Khan, Nolte, Paulus, & Wessendorf (eds.), *The Charter of the United Nations: A Commentary*, vol. 1, 3rd edn. (2012) ¶ 17.

view.[19] One hundred states joined the 'obvious rival' view, and another fifty-eight stayed silent in face of its articulation. The abstentions in this setting have opposite the effect that the tribunal imputed to them. They reflect that Ukraine's sovereignty was undisturbed.

Erga omnes *character of territorial title and claims*

There is also a mismatch between the bilateralism of the tribunal's approach to identifying whether a legal dispute exists and the *erga omnes* character of territorial rights and claims. To be sure, one of the classic judicial opinions addressing identification of disputes addressed bilateral relations. In *South West Africa*, the ICJ said that '[i]t is not sufficient for one party to a contentious case to assert that a dispute exists with *the* other party.'[20] In *Cessation of the Nuclear Arms Race*, the ICJ said that to establish the existence of a dispute requires 'that the claim of one party is positively opposed to the other and that the *two* sides "hold clearly opposite views" concerning the question of the performance or non-performance of certain international obligations.'[21] Territorial title, however, while it entails important consequences in bilateral legal relations, and from time to time is settled through adjudication between two parties, has an *erga omnes* character. The boundaries that fix the territorial limits of two states address other states as well.

The *erga omnes* character of territorial title is visible in judicial practice. According to the ICJ when it adjudicated the Malaysia/Singapore boundary dispute, '[c]ritical for the Court's assessment of the conduct of the Parties is the central importance in international law and relations of State sovereignty over territory and of the stability and certainty of that sovereignty.'[22] The 'stability and certainty' that the Court identified as having 'critical' importance concerns not only the relations of a state and an immediate neighbor (i.e.,

19 *Temple of Preah Vihear (Cambodia v. Thailand)*, Merits, ICJ 1962 p. 6, p. 31 (15 June). When the ILC considered the effect of acquiescence in the identification of customary international law rules, it said that silence in response to practice matters only where 'a reaction to the practice in question would have been called for.' Conclusion 10 (Forms of evidence of acceptance as law (*opinio juris*), Comment (8): A/73/10, p. 142. Tellingly, the examples that the ILC gave where a reaction was called for were from 'a different context'—a dispute as to sovereignty and a dispute as to a special territorial regime: *ibid.* n. 737.

20 ICJ 1962 at p. 328 (emphasis added).

21 *Obligations Concerning Negotiations Relating to Cessation of the Nuclear Arms Race and to Nuclear Disarmament (Marshall Islands v. India)*, Jurisdiction and Admissibility, ICJ 2016 p. 255, p. 269 ¶ 34 (emphasis added).

22 *Sovereignty over Pedra Branca/Pulau Batu Puteh, Middle Rocks and South Ledge (Malaysia/Singapore)*, ICJ 2008 p. 12, p. 51 ¶ 122 (23 May).

a state adjacent to it). It also concerns the world at large. The need for quiet title arises in the bilateral relations of a state not just for the sake of the state's neighbor but also because that state and any other(s) with which it 'undertake[s] official acts with regard to the territory in question' must do so 'with confidence that those acts would be given legal effect by outside powers or institutions.'[23] Judge Skubiszewski, to whose dissent in *East Timor* I return later in this chapter, observed that '[t]he status of a territory, in view of its objective nature, is opposable not only to each of [the member states of the UN] but also to non-Members.'[24]

It follows from the concern of the international community as a whole with the stability of territorial title that considering only the bilateral dimension of relations concerning territory is inadequate. The *multilateral* response of the international community that takes shape through recognition or non-recognition of a putative title or legal claim, decentralized though the response is, plays an essential part. 'Recognition is an institution of State practice that can resolve uncertainties as to status and allow for new situations to be regularized.'[25]

The *Coastal State Rights* tribunal adduced no evidence that any intergovernmental organization or meaningful group of states outside a small handful in Russia's orbit wished to 'regularize' the 'new situation' in Crimea that Russia's use of force had created.

International responsibility, non-recognition, and UNCLOS Article 304

The tribunal itself nevertheless took a step toward regularizing the 'new situation.' In concluding that Russia's assertions about Ukraine's territory constitute sovereignty claims receivable as such on the international law plane, the Annex VII tribunal arguably clashed with the existing and developing rules of international responsibility, for those rules require non-recognition of situations such as Russia's putative annexations. UNCLOS expressly provides that its own rules are without prejudice to those rules.

Under UNCLOS Part XVI—the 'general provisions' Part—Article 304 envisages the risk of discordance between UNCLOS rules and the general

23 Martti Koskenniemi, Chairman, Report of the Study Group on Fragmentation of International Law: Difficulties arising from the Diversification and Expansion of International Law, 2006 ILC Yearbook, vol. II, Part One, p. 18 ¶ 51.

24 *East Timor*, ICJ 1995 p. 248 ¶ 78 (30 June). See also Bjorge's observation that boundaries between states are 'essentially objective as opposed to relative,' with citations to classic authorities: Bjorge, 'Opposability and Non-opposability in International Law' (2021) BYIL 12–14.

25 Crawford (2006) 27. Cf. Crawford (2013) 147.

international law of state responsibility and tries to mitigate it. Article 304 provides as follows: 'The provisions of this Convention regarding responsibility and liability for damage are without prejudice to the application of existing rules and the development of further rules regarding responsibility and liability under international law.'[26]

The ITLOS Seabed Disputes Chambers in its Advisory Opinion on *Responsibilities and Obligations of States Sponsoring Persons and Entities with respect to activities in the Area* (2011) observed that the expression in article 304 'existing rules and ... further rules regarding responsibility and liability under international law' refers to the secondary rules of international responsibility.[27] Article 304, by its terms, extends to the 'provisions of this Convention,' meaning all UNCLOS provisions, 'regarding responsibility and liability for damage.' Article 304 thus embraces the dispute settlement provisions, it being a principal function of those provisions to supply a procedural framework in which parties can seek determinations of responsibility and liability for damage. When asking whether 'responsibility and liability' exist in a specific factual setting, states do not find an answer merely by reading the plain text of UNCLOS. (Treaties do not attempt to specify the facts and outcome of every conceivable dispute that might arise under their terms.) To find an answer to the question whether responsibility or liability exists, states may apply UNCLOS provisions to the facts under one or another decision-making procedure. Accordingly, dispute settlement procedures under Part XV, section 2, when states parties use them to determine responsibility and liability for damage, operate 'without prejudice to the application of existing rules and the development of further rules regarding responsibility and liability under international law.'[28]

The general law of international responsibility is not silent as regards a situation in which there has been a serious breach of an obligation arising under a peremptory norm of general international law. According to Article 40 of the ILC Articles on Responsibility of States for Internationally Wrongful Acts, a breach of an obligation of that kind is 'serious' when it involves 'a

26 1833 UNTS at 517. See Tams & Devaney, 'Article 304' in *Proelss Commentary* (2017) 1961–1967; Churchill, Lowe, & Sander (2022) 448; *Virginia Commentary*, vol. v, at 163, according to which the text was introduced anonymously at the Third Conference and '[n]o interpretative material appears on the record.'

27 ITLOS Seabed Disputes Chamber, *Responsibilities and Obligations of States Sponsoring Persons and Entities with respect to activities in the Area*, Advisory Opinion, ITLOS 2011 p. 10, pp. 30–31 ¶¶ 64–71 (1 February).

28 In this light, I do not believe that Churchill, Lowe, and Sander identify the scope of Article 304 completely, when they indicate 'the various provisions of UNCLOS concerned with liability' and do not indicate the dispute settlement provisions. See Churchill, Lowe, & Sander (2022) 448.

gross or systematic failure by the responsible State to fulfil the obligation.'[29] In accordance with Article 41, paragraph 1, where any serious breach exists in that sense, 'States shall cooperate to bring [it] to an end through lawful means.' In accordance with Article 41, paragraph 2, '[n]o State shall recognize as lawful a situation created by a serious breach [in that sense], nor render aid or assistance in maintaining that situation.'[30] The ILC Commentary makes clear that the core examples of 'serious breach' are attempts to seize territory by force.[31] The Seabed Disputes Chamber in *Responsibilities and Obligations of States Sponsoring Persons and Entities with respect to activities in the Area* recognized that the ILC's work on state responsibility is indeed pertinent to Article 304: 'account will have to be taken of such rules under customary law, especially in light of the ILC Articles on State Responsibility.'[32]

The ILC Articles on State Responsibility do not indicate any specific modality of decision-making by which an adjudicator might determine that a state's conduct constitutes a serious breach. And questions remain as to whether, and if so to what extent, the propositions set out in the 2001 ILC draft Articles on Responsibility of States for Internationally Wrongful Acts (ARSIWA) Articles 40 and 41 are to be treated as general rules of international law. But UNCLOS Article 304 is concerned not only with 'application of existing rules ... regarding responsibility and liability under international law.' It also is concerned with '*the development of further rules* regarding responsibility and liability under international law.' The Seabed Dispute Chamber's advisory opinion on *Responsibilities and Obligations* placed emphasis on this extended meaning. According to the Seabed Disputes Chamber, 'article 304 ... refers not only to existing international law rules on responsibility and liability, but also to the development of further rules.'[33]

A general international law rule along the lines of ARSIWA Articles 40 and 41 might, or might not, have crystallized in full. It is certainly not in its merest infancy however. It is a rule at a further stage in development.

29 ARSIWA Art. 40: 2001 ILC Yearbook vol. II, Part Two, p. 112.

30 *Ibid.* 113–114.

31 See Art. 41, Comment (6), referring to Manchurian crisis of 1931–1932 and non-recognition of Japan's putative annexations in China; Comment (7), referring to Iraq's invasion of Kuwait in 1990 and non-recognition (and forcible reversal) of that act of aggression; and Comment (8), referring to South Africa's putative partition of the country into 'Bantustans,' which also were refused recognition. *Ibid.* 114–115.

32 ITLOS Seabed Disputes Chamber, *Responsibilities and Obligations of States Sponsoring Persons and Entities with respect to activities in the Area*, Advisory Opinion, ITLOS 2011 p. 10, p. 56 ¶ 168 (1 February).

33 ITLOS 2011 p. 10, p. 56 ¶ 169 (emphasis added).

The two limbs of Article 304 cover the propositions set out in ARSIWA Articles 40 and 41.

The *Coastal State Rights* tribunal had things to say that had direct bearing upon the existing rules and rules development that it is the purpose of Article 304 to protect. The tribunal's award prejudices the application and development of rules regarding responsibility and liability under international law. The award of the *Coastal State Rights* tribunal, denying as it does any general obligation to withhold recognition from the consequences of Russia's aggression against Ukraine, thus sits uncomfortably with Article 304 and with the Seabed Disputes Chamber's understanding of that provision.

Ukraine seems not to have invoked Article 304 in its written submissions.[34] This was a missed opportunity. It is possible to read Article 304 as *not* obliging a tribunal to adopt conclusions that accord with the international law rules that it is the purpose of that provision to protect, but reading it in that limited way is not self-evidently correct. Tams and Devaney, for example, say that '[i]n addition to delimiting spheres of influence between different legal regimes, a "without prejudice" clause such as Art. 304 can also be read as a *renvoi* to the separate legal regimes referred to.'[35] Plainly, Article 304 is not an invitation to UNCLOS adjudicators to ignore the law of international responsibility or to imagine that general international law is not affected by their judgments. As the Seabed Disputes Chamber said, 'account *will have to be* taken of such rules.'[36] To have observed that Article 304 provides for the dispute settlement provisions of UNCLOS to operate without prejudice to the general law of international responsibility (and to the development of that law) would have focused the Annex VII arbitrators on their relationship to the wider legal landscape to which their tribunal belonged. The tribunal's self-isolation from the wider legal landscape is one of the most serious defects in its approach.

Courts and tribunals as addressees of the obligation not to recognize

International practice expressly addressing the general obligation of non-recognition to international courts and tribunals outside the UN system is scarce. For its part, the ICJ, though the principal organ of the UN system, has implied that entities belonging to that system are not the only ones that

34 See Written Observations and Submissions of Ukraine on Jurisdiction (27 November 2018); Rejoinder of Ukraine on Jurisdiction (28 March 2019).

35 Tams & Devaney in *Proelss Commentary* (2017) at 1964.

36 *ITLOS Seabed Disputes Chamber, Responsibilities and Obligations of States Sponsoring Persons and Entities with respect to activities in the Area*, Advisory Opinion, ITLOS 2011 p. 10, p. 56 ¶ 169 (1 February) (emphasis added).

the obligation addresses. 'The duty of non-recognition,' the Court said in the 19 July 2024 advisory opinion on *Policies and practices of Israel*, 'applies to international organizations, *including* the United Nations,'[37] a form of words from which one infers that the duty applies to international organizations in addition to the UN.

A riposte that adjudicative bodies constituted under treaty are not 'international organizations' is not entirely convincing. Such bodies are not constituted under national law. What are they, if not international? It is true that a definitive answer is hard to find in state or international organization practice, but it is at least as hard to formulate an argument that they are anything else.

Writing on the point is scarce. Sebastian Wuschka, one of the few who has addressed it, considered the ICSID system of investment arbitration and concluded that 'because of the system's roots in international law,' investment tribunals under ICSID 'must not render an award that is in conflict with … the obligation of non-recognition.'[38] Wuschka reached this conclusion from considerations of international public policy, but one detects in his analysis a concern to maintain systemic consistency as well. 'Put differently,' Wuschka wrote, 'in the delocalized system of the ICSID framework, the reason why the obligation of non-recognition bears importance will be immanent to that system and its roots.'[39] The same reason would apply with at least as much strength to the UNCLOS dispute settlement framework.

As I posited in the Introduction to this book, treaty-based arbitration and adjudication are difficult to imagine retaining their vitality in a world as uncertain as that which existed before modern international law, with its presumption of spatial stability, took shape. It inheres in treaty-based dispute settlement that legal mechanisms serving to preserve spatial stability apply. Among such mechanisms, non-recognition is a paramount example.

Institutional decisions relevant to *Coastal State Rights*

As I just observed, the developing law of international responsibility, in particular its principle of non-recognition, was not well-reflected in the idiosyncratic approach that the *Coastal State Rights* tribunal took in its 2020 award. The tribunal further is to be faulted for its refusal to have

37 Advisory Opinion of 19 July 2024, ICJ, ¶ 280 (emphasis added).

38 Wuschka, 'Procedural Aspects of the Obligation of Non-recognition before International Investment Tribunals' in Fach Gómez, Gourgourinis, & Titi (eds.), *International Investment Law and the Law of Armed Conflict* (2019) 149.

39 *Ibid.* at 133.

regard for the practice of other international institutions that already had addressed Russia's putative claims against Ukraine.

General Assembly practice and the lessons of East Timor

The *Coastal State Rights* tribunal did not attribute much significance to the practice of the General Assembly in respect of Crimea. In explaining its approach, the tribunal made the observation, which is a banality, that General Assembly resolutions are not binding. The observation is also potentially misleading, because, in its setting, it might suggest that General Assembly practice is relevant only if it results in a proscription—that is to say, only if the Assembly somehow were to 'go as far as *prohibiting* [the tribunal] from recognizing the existence of a dispute.'[40] One discerns here an all-or-nothing attitude—either an institution has a superior position in a hierarchy and thus commands the tribunal (and the tribunal must obey) or it is irrelevant. I have already argued that a more nuanced attitude is sometimes called for, as when, for example, the voting pattern of states in an international organ reflects acquiescence in a proposition on the organ's agenda.

In its consideration of General Assembly practice, the *Coastal State Rights* tribunal referred to the ICJ judgment in *East Timor.* The tribunal indicated that the judgment provides grounding for a tribunal to ignore the General Assembly practice in respect of Crimea. *East Timor* however does nothing of the kind.

Before considering what the ICJ said in *East Timor*, why that case has largely been discredited, and how the General Assembly practice in respect of East Timor differed materially from that in respect of Crimea, let us summarize what the General Assembly has said since 2014 about Crimea.

As I recalled above,[41] the General Assembly, by 100 members to 11, on 27 March 2014 affirmed the territorial integrity of Ukraine.[42] The Assembly '[u]nderscore[d]' that Russia's illegal referendums have 'no validity' and 'cannot' change the international status of Crimea.[43] The Assembly also 'call[ed] upon all States, international organizations and specialized agencies not to recognize any alteration of the status of [Crimea] ... and to refrain from any action or dealing that might be interpreted as recognizing any such altered status.'[44] The General Assembly in Resolution 71/205 of 19 December 2016 condemned the human rights abuses by Russia in

40 *Coastal State Rights*, Award, 21 February 2020, ¶ 177 (emphasis added).
41 See p. 252.
42 GAR 68/262, 27 March 2014 (Territorial Integrity of Ukraine) (100–11–58).
43 *Ibid.*, ¶ 5.
44 *Ibid.*, ¶ 6.

Crimea,[45] recalled resolution 68/262, and 're-affirm[ed] the non-recognition' of Russia's purported annexation of Crimea.[46] Similar resolutions followed in successive sessions of the General Assembly: Resolution 72/190 of 19 December 2017;[47] Resolution 73/263 of 22 December 2018,[48] along with a separate resolution on the '[p]roblem of the militarization' of Crimea and 'parts of the Black Sea and the Sea of Azov';[49] Resolution 74/168 of 18 December 2019,[50] and a companion resolution on militarization;[51] and in like form Resolutions 75/192 of 16 December 2020,[52] and 75/29 of 7 December 2020,[53] the 2020 resolutions being the first adopted after the February 2020 *Coastal State Rights* award.

As the *Coastal State Rights* Annex VII proceedings continued, the General Assembly adopted similar resolutions in 2021.[54] The resolution addressing militarization in Crimea and parts of the Black Sea and Sea of Azov[55] took note of an order of ITLOS granting provisional measures in the *Detention of three Ukrainian naval vessels (Ukraine v. Russian Federation)* (as the case was captioned in provisional measures phase),[56] and of the first procedural

45 GAR 71/205, 19 December 2016 (Situation of human rights in the Autonomous Republic of Crimea and the city of Sevastopol, Ukraine) (70–26–77), op. ¶ 1.
46 *Ibid.*, preamble ¶¶ 5, 6.
47 GAR 72/190, 19 December 2017 (Situation of human rights in the Autonomous Republic of Crimea and the city of Sevastopol, Ukraine) (70–26–76).
48 GAR 73/263, 22 December 2018 (Situation of human rights in the Autonomous Republic of Crimea and the city of Sevastopol, Ukraine) (65–27–70).
49 GAR 73/194, 17 December 2018 (The problem of militarization of the Autonomous Republic of Crimea and the city of Sevastopol (Ukraine), as well as parts of the Black Sea and the Sea of Azov) (66–19–72).
50 GAR 74/168, 18 December 2019 (Situation of human rights in the Autonomous Republic of Crimea and the city of Sevastopol, Ukraine) (65–23–83).
51 GAR 74/17, 9 December 2019 (Problem of the militarization of the Autonomous Republic of Crimea and the city of Sevastopol, Ukraine, as well as parts of the Black Sea and the Sea of Azov) (63–19–66).
52 GAR 75/192, 16 December 2020 (Situation of human rights in the Autonomous Republic of Crimea and the city of Sevastopol, Ukraine) (64–23–86).
53 GAR 75/29, 7 December 2020 (Problem of the militarization of the Autonomous Republic of Crimea and the city of Sevastopol, Ukraine) (63–17–62).
54 GAR 76/179, 16 December 2021 (Situation of human rights in the Autonomous Republic of Crimea and the city of Sevastopol, Ukraine) (65–25–85); GAR 76/70, 9 December 2021 (Problem of the militarization of the Autonomous Republic of Crimea and the city of Sevastopol, Ukraine, as well as parts of the Black Sea and the Sea of Azov) (62–22–55).
55 GAR 76/70, 9 December 2021, preambular ¶ 17.
56 *Detention of Three Ukrainian Naval Vessels (Ukraine v. Russian Federation)*, Provisional Measures, Order, ITLOS 2019 p. 283 (25 May). Under UNCLOS Art. 290(5), pending constitution of an Annex VII tribunal, and where the parties do not indicate a different tribunal of their choice for this purpose, ITLOS may receive a request for and prescribe provisional measures: *ibid.* ¶ 12.

order of the Annex VII tribunal constituted in that case.[57] The cognate resolution of 2020 also noted the ITLOS and Annex VII orders in the *Detention* proceedings.[58] Neither the 2020 resolution nor the 2021 resolution mentioned the *Coastal State Rights* award, nor has any resolution since.[59]

After 2021, Russia's vastly enlarged aggression provoked the Security Council to convene the General Assembly in Emergency Special Session,[60] under which authority the General Assembly adopted a series of further resolutions. The Emergency Special Session resolutions, *inter alia*: condemned Russia's aggression against Ukraine;[61] stressed the humanitarian impact of Russia's siege of Ukrainian cities;[62] suspended Russia from the Human Rights Council;[63] condemned Russia's fake referendums in regard to four Ukrainian provinces and attempted illegal annexations;[64] called upon all states, international organizations, and UN specialized agencies not to recognize any of the territorial changes that Russia attempted to impose on Ukraine and to 'refrain from any action or dealing that might be interpreted as recognizing any such altered status';[65] declared Russia's purported annexations to 'have no validity under international law';[66] recognized that Russia must be held to account for its aggression and for any other violations of international law against Ukraine and recommended that member states establish 'an international register of damage to serve as a record, in documentary form, of evidence and claims information';[67] and reiterated its demand that Russia 'immediately, completely and unconditionally withdraw all of its military forces from the territory of Ukraine within its internationally recognized borders.'[68]

57 *Detention of Ukrainian Naval Vessels and Servicemen (Ukraine v. the Russian Federation)*, PCA Case No. 2019–28, Procedural Order No. 1, 22 November 2019.
58 GAR 75/29, 7 December 2020, preambular ¶ 17.
59 As to the inference that we might draw from the silence, see below ##–##.
60 SCR 2623 (2022), 27 February 2022 (noting Provisional Measures, Order, ITLOS 2019 p. 283 (25 May); and Annex VII tribunal Procedural Order of 22 November 2019).
61 GAR ES-11/1, 2 March 2022 (Aggression against Ukraine) (141–5–35).
62 GAR ES-11/2, 24 March 2022 (Humanitarian consequences of the aggression against Ukraine) (140–5–38), op. ¶ 8.
63 GAR ES-11/3, 7 April 2022 (Suspension of the rights of membership of the Russian Federation in the Human Rights Council) (93–24–58).
64 GAR ES-11/4, 12 October 2022 (Territorial integrity of Ukraine: defending the principles of the Charter of the United Nations) (143–5–35).
65 *Ibid.* op. ¶ 4.
66 *Ibid.* op. ¶ 3.
67 GAR ES-11/5, 14 November 2022 (Furtherance of remedy and reparation for aggression against Ukraine) (94–14–13) op. ¶¶ 2, 4.
68 GAR ES-11/6, 23 February 2023 (Principles of the Charter of the United Nations underlying a comprehensive, just and lasting peace in Ukraine) (141–7–32) op. ¶ 5.

The Assembly in 2022 adopted a further resolution in ordinary session on the human rights situation in Crimea.[69] In 2023, in connection with the topic of 'cooperation between the United Nations and the Council of Europe,' the General Assembly adopted a resolution, *inter alia*, '*[r]ecognizing* … that the unprecedented challenges now facing Europe following *the aggression of the Russian Federation against Ukraine, and against Georgia prior to that*, and the cessation of the membership of the Russian Federation in the Council of Europe, call for strengthened cooperation between the United Nations and the Council of Europe.'[70] Surprisingly, considering the reference in the resolution to 'aggression of the Russian Federation,' China did not abstain but, instead, voted in favor of the resolution, as did Russia's nominal treaty allies Armenia and Kazakhstan.[71]

The resolutions adopted after 21 February 2020 obviously were not on the mind of the arbitrators when they adopted the award of that date, but they are part of the landscape in which the award and its reasoning now may be considered. They are further relevant in light of Russia's enlarged request for jurisdictional exclusions in 2024 in the *Coastal State Rights* proceedings following Russia's enlarged seizure of territory in 2022 in Ukraine.[72]

In the award of 21 February 2020, the tribunal, summarizing Russia's argument, said that Russia '*points to* a "notable dwindling" in support for subsequent UNGA resolutions on this issue.'[73] It would be pedantic to ask whether this form of words conveys that the tribunal was *agreeing* with Russia that support was 'dwindling' and, if so, whether the tribunal judged the dwindling to be 'notable', or if the tribunal was just reporting that Russia had said so. The fact remained that the General Assembly continued to adopt strongly worded resolutions, and these passed with significant majorities, if not as large as they had been at the start.

In its reasoning about the role of General Assembly practice in respect of non-recognition, the tribunal gave pride of place to the *East Timor* case. Let us consider what the tribunal said about *East Timor*.

To recall the background to this well-known case, Portugal, which was the administering power in respect of East Timor, instituted proceedings against Australia in 1991 after Australia had entered into a maritime delimitation treaty with Indonesia in regard to the maritime area between East

69 GAR 77/229, 14 December 2022 (Situation of human rights in the temporarily occupied Autonomous Republic of Crimea and the city of Sevastopol, Ukraine) (82–14–80).

70 GAR 77/284, 26 April 2023, preambular ¶ 9 (emphasis added).

71 See A/77/PV.69, under item 127(I) (26 April 2023).

72 See Chapter 6, pp. 174–176.

73 *Coastal State Rights*, Award, ¶ 89 (emphasis added).

Timor and Australia. Indonesia had forcibly occupied East Timor and purported to absorb it after Portugal had evacuated the territory in 1975. Portugal, in the proceedings that it instituted against Australia, drew attention to General Assembly resolutions recognizing that Portugal remained, for juridical purposes, the administering power in respect of East Timor, and argued that Australia had no right to conclude a treaty with Indonesia in respect of the maritime areas appurtenant to East Timor.

The ICJ was not convinced by Portugal's argument that the General Assembly resolutions obliged a third state to deal exclusively with Portugal. The ICJ said as follows:

> The Court finds that it cannot be inferred from the sole fact that the above-mentioned resolutions of the General Assembly and the Security Council refer to Portugal as the administering Power of East Timor that they intended to establish an obligation on third States to treat exclusively with Portugal as regards the continental shelf of East Timor. The Court notes, furthermore, that several States have concluded with Indonesia treaties capable of application to East Timor but which do not include any reservation in regard to that Territory ... Without prejudice to the question whether the resolutions under discussion could be binding in nature, the Court considers as a result that they cannot be regarded as 'givens' which constitute a sufficient basis for determining the dispute between the Parties.[74]

The Court's conclusion that General Assembly practice at the time did not constitute a set of 'given' legal effects was not the conclusion on which the judgment turned, however. The judgment turned on the absence in the proceedings of Indonesia, the country that had invaded and purported to annex East Timor. The ICJ 'would necessarily have [had] to rule upon the lawfulness of Indonesia's conduct as a prerequisite for deciding on Portugal's contention that Australia violated its obligation to respect Portugal's status as administering Power [etc.].'[75] The Court recalled the *Monetary Gold* principle,[76] and, reasoning that 'Indonesia's rights and obligations would ... constitute the very subject-matter of [the] judgment [that Portugal requested] in the absence of that State's consent,'[77] judged that it lacked jurisdiction to reach the merits of Portugal's claim.[78]

74 *East Timor (Portugal v. Australia)*, ICJ 1995 p. 90, p. 104 ¶ 32 (30 June).
75 *Ibid.* ¶ 33.
76 *Monetary Gold Removed from Rome in 1943 (Italy v. France, U.K., U.S.)*, ICJ 1954 p. 19, p. 32 (15 June): the Court shall not exercise jurisdiction where an absent party's 'legal interests would not only be affected by a decision, but would form the very subject-matter of the decision.'
77 *East Timor*, ICJ 1995 p. 105 ¶ 34.
78 *Ibid.* ¶ 35.

Indonesia's alter ego in *Coastal State Rights* was Russia, the state that carried out the invasion and purported to annex the territory in question. But, unlike Indonesia in *East Timor*, Russia was not an absent third party in *Coastal State Rights*. The *ratio decidendi* in *East Timor (Portugal v. Australia)* has no application whatsoever in *Coastal State Rights (Ukraine v. Russia)*.[79]

The conduct of which the applicant state in *East Timor* complained was a bilateral international act by the respondent state with a third state. Russia, as noted, is not a third state in the *Coastal State Rights* case. Revealingly, Russia is also not a party with third states to treaties in regard to Crimea. As the ICJ noted, states were transacting with Indonesia in regard to East Timor, including for the purpose of parceling out East Timor's maritime resources. What state in 2020 was ready to take similar steps with Russia in regard to Crimea? Neither Russia nor the *Coastal State Rights* tribunal identified any.

It is to be asked whether even the narrow dictum in *East Timor* on which the tribunal fixed its gaze—that is, that General Assembly resolutions were not to be treated as 'givens'—supports the tribunal's conclusion that General Assembly practice may be ignored. One consideration casting doubt on the tribunal's conclusion is that the Court decided to *accept* and *emphasize* certain aspects of General Assembly practice—in particular, the affirmation of East Timor's non-self-governing status.[80] The analogue to that affirmation in the General Assembly's resolution on Ukraine is the affirmation of Ukraine's status as a self-determination unit within its 1991 boundaries—that is, a unit that includes Crimea.

Another consideration, also casting doubt on the *Coastal State Rights* tribunal's reliance on *East Timor*, is that the point on which the tribunal relied was a tertiary one—an applicant's attempt to rebut a respondent's argument after the respondent's argument already had prevailed. The ICJ's refusal to accept that General Assembly practice evinced a general requirement of non-recognition of Indonesia's presence in East Timor, such as would have invalidated Australia's treaty with Indonesia, was the ICJ's response to 'an *additional* argument [by Portugal] aiming to show that' Australia's

79 That the principle of the absent third party was the *ratio* has not been doubted. Crawford identified it as the crux of the case. James Crawford, 'Chance, Order, Change: The Course of International Law' (2014) 365 Hag. Rec. 1, 44 (2014). Moreover, it was 'Australia's principal objection': *East Timor*, ICJ 1995 p. 100 ¶ 23. See also *Arbitral Award of 3 October 1899 (Guyana v. Venezuela)*, Judgment, ICJ 2023 p. 262, p. 281 ¶ 62 (6 April), quoting *East Timor*, ICJ 1995 at p. 105 ¶ 35 on *Monetary Gold* point.

80 ICJ 1995 p. 102 ¶ 29.

Monetary Gold objection was not credible.[81] By the stage of the argumentation where the Court reached this matter, the Court had already concluded that the 'absence of the consent of Indonesia' was fatal to Portugal's claim.[82] That ground had priority in the sequence of the Court's reasoning, and it was self-sufficient.

The *East Timor* case of 1995 has been widely viewed in its result as an embarrassment to the Court. Iain Scobbie called the Court's reasoning 'threadbare and frequently proceed[ing] on the basis of bare assertion rather than reasoned conclusion.'[83] An Annex VII tribunal is under no obligation to concern itself with academic discourse, and there are ample reasons for caution before drawing conclusions in a dispute settlement procedure from the writings of academics.[84] However, subsequent events in East Timor are not a matter of speculation or theorizing. At tremendous cost in human lives and suffering, Indonesia indeed persisted in its unlawful presence in and doubtful claim to East Timor, and even after all that Indonesia did not prevail. East Timor's eventual independence (in 2002) was the conclusion of a difficult series of events, which included mass murder and other atrocities.[85]

81 ICJ 1995 p. 102 ¶ 29 (emphasis added).

82 *Ibid.* p. 102 ¶ 28. The parties' written pleadings confirm the sequence of argument. Portugal's Memorial did not address *Monetary Gold:* see *Mémoire du Gouvernement de la République Portugaise* (18 November 1991). Australia articulated the *Monetary Gold* objection in its Counter-Memorial: see Counter-Memorial of the Government of Australia (1 June 1992) 92–95, ¶¶ 191–195. Australia having raised the objection, Portugal then addressed it in its Reply: *Réplique du Gouvernement de la République Portugaise* (1 December 1992) 226–236, ¶¶ 7.47–7.63; together with argument on the duty of non-recognition and the *erga omnes* character of East Timor's self-determination right that Portugal maintained rendered the *Monetary Gold* objection ineffective in the circumstances: *ibid.* 179, ¶ 6.42; 208, ¶ 7.14.

83 Scobbie, 'Self-determination Undetermined: The Case of East Timor' (1996) 9 Leiden JIL 185, 192. See also Burchill, 'The ICJ Decision in the Case concerning East Timor' (1997) 2(1) *Journal of Armed Conflict Law* 1; Lu, 'The Case concerning East Timor and Self-determination' (2004) 11(2) *Murdoch University Electronic Journal of Law* at sec. 20. Cf. Simpson, 'Judging the East Timor Dispute' (1994) 17 *Hastings International and Comparative Law Review* 323. See also, with summary of the dissents and writers who understood that no institutional decision was needed to activate an obligation of non-recognition in regard to Indonesia's presence in East Timor, Grant (2000) 307–309.

84 A point that the ILC shares: Draft conclusions on identification of customary international law, with commentaries, Conclusion 14 (Teachings), Comment (3): ILC Yearbook 2018, vol. II, Part Two, p. 151. Cf. Barnes, 'Law of the Sea Scholarship and Practice' (2023) 38 IJMCL 1–10; Ridings, 'The Influence of Scholarship on the Shaping and Making of the Law of the Sea' (2023) 38 IJMCL 11–38.

85 *Ibid.* See also Epps, 'Self-determination after Kosovo and East Timor' (2000) 6 *International Law Students' Association Journal of International and Comparative Law* 445, 453.

Portugal's position, in the end, was largely vindicated. The *Coastal State Rights* tribunal was oblivious to the widespread rejection of the *East Timor* judgment by writers, but, worse, it gave no indication that East Timor had a history past the date of the judgment.[86]

The dissenting opinion of Judge Skubiszewski in *East Timor*, unlike the judgment, has stood the test of time. Judge Skubiszewski in his dissent wrote as follows:

> By taking cognizance of the status of East Timor in United Nations law, resolutions included, the Court would not be passing upon any Indonesian territorial or other rights, duties, jurisdiction or powers ... Interestingly enough, the Judgment qualifies the Indonesian action as intervention ... Will this have its effects? Intervention (particularly military) is by definition unlawful *and produces no rights or title* until there is a decision by the United Nations validating its consequences or until there is universal recognition.[87]

As Judge Skubiszewski's careful dissent made clear, the General Assembly resolutions were *included* in the relevant practice, but 'taking cognizance of the status of East Timor'—and of the fact that Indonesia's presence there was the result of 'intervention'—was available on general appreciation of the facts as well.[88] As I observed earlier in this chapter, the General Assembly is not a general clearing house of recognition.

The Court, in face of Judge Skubiszewski's observation that armed force 'produces no rights or title,' did not disagree. Instead, it noted that Indonesia was not present in the proceedings and that Portugal's case called on the Court 'necessarily ... to rule upon the lawfulness of Indonesia's conduct.'[89] The Court's conclusion that neither the General Assembly practice nor the facts at large settled the matter in Portugal's favor, in effect, reiterated its conclusion as to third-party consent. Indeed, it was in the part of its reasoning addressing the effect of General Assembly practice that the Court underscored that '*several States* have concluded *with Indonesia* treaties capable of application to East Timor but which do not include any reservation in regard to that Territory.'[90] The Court appeared concerned that a judgment invalidating

86 For the history in convenient summary, see Crawford (2014) 43–45.
87 *East Timor*, ICJ 1995 p. 248 ¶ 77 (emphasis added).
88 For an admiring retrospective on Judge Skubiszewski's dissent, see Hilpold, 'Krzysztof Skubiszewski and the Right to Self-Determination' (2019) 39 Pol. YBIL 21, 25–31.
89 See above p. 263.
90 *Ibid.* 104, ¶ 32 (emphasis added). As to states in treaty relations with Indonesia, Portugal itself conceded that it would present a *Monetary Gold* problem if the validity of their treaties were put in question in proceedings to which they were not party: *Réplique* at p. 201, ¶ 7.03. For the text of the Treaty between the Government of Australia and the Government of the Republic of Indonesia Establishing an Exclusive Economic Zone Boundary and Certain Seabed Boundaries,' see Prescott, 'Current Legal Developments: Australia/Indonesia' (1997) 12 IJMCL 533, 535–547.

Indonesia's treaty practice in respect of East Timor would have had far-reaching and disruptive effects. The third-party problem plainly worried the Court, the Court drew attention to it repeatedly, and on it the Court's judgment turned. One would not know that, though, from reading the *Coastal State Rights* award of 21 February 2020.

Nor would one know, if reading only the *Coastal State Rights* award, that the ICJ had acknowledged that East Timor's right to self-determination had general effects (i.e., *erga omnes* effects) and that that right emerged *from General Assembly practice.*[91] Far from ignoring General Assembly practice, the ICJ said that the General Assembly affirmed East Timor's non-self-governing status for purposes of UN Charter Chapter XI.

Not only did the *Coastal State Rights* tribunal ignore what the General Assembly affirmed about East Timor. It also ignored that, after a time, the General Assembly had stopped addressing East Timor altogether. The tribunal failed to note that, in the decade prior to the *East Timor* proceedings, the General Assembly had not adopted a single resolution addressing the territory in question. At least as glaring among its omissions, the tribunal did not mention that state practice in those years had shifted in favor of Indonesia's de facto presence in the territory. One writer summarized the state of affairs as follows: '[t]he attitude of third States and the United Nations towards the Indonesian action in East Timor ... consist[ed] of apathy that amounts to effective tolerance of the presence of Indonesia in the territory.'[92] The Court itself noted that, when Portugal instituted proceedings, quite some time had passed since the Assembly's last resolution on East Timor.[93] The fact that the General Assembly had fallen mute on East Timor influenced the ICJ's reasoning but this, too, went unmentioned in *Coastal State Rights*.

The General Assembly in regard to Crimea, by contrast to its long silence on East Timor, continued to adopt resolutions up to and through the proceedings concerned. And there were few states, if any, even before 2022 when Russia enlarged its aggression, that treated Russia's presence in Crimea as lawful or accommodated it on pragmatic grounds. When Canada said, in 1991, that it 'considers that Indonesian sovereignty over East Timor is a fact,'[94] this was no anomaly. Equivalent statements about Crimea are difficult to find.

91 ICJ 1995 p. 102 ¶ 29.

92 C. Antonopoulos, 'Effectiveness v. the Rule of Law Following the East Timor Case' (1996) 27 Neth. YBIL 75, 97 (1996).

93 ICJ 1995 p. 97 ¶ 16.

94 House of Commons Debates, 18 September 1991, p. 2310, in 'Canadian Practice in International Law, 1991–1992' (1992) 30 Can. YBIL 366, quoted in Antonopoulos (1996) 98. As to ASEAN States' support for Indonesia's invasion of East Timor, see Southgate, *ASEAN Resistance to Sovereignty Violation: Interests, Balancing and the Role of the Vanguard State* (2019) 25. Relevant in that light, the East European States do not support Russia's invasion of Ukraine but, instead, oppose it in word and with substantial money and materiél.

The judgment in *East Timor*—concluding that the ICJ could not exercise jurisdiction[95]—it goes without saying did not weaken Indonesia's practical resolve or sense of entitlement. It would not be fair to lay at the Court's doorstep Indonesia's persistence and brutality in East Timor in the years immediately following the judgment, but there was little in the judgment to have dissuaded Indonesia.[96] Richard Burchill submitted that 'the Court's decision ... [went] a long way in showing a legal acceptance for the situation in East Timor.'[97] Gerry Simpson shortly before the judgment said that Indonesia would 'seize on [a win] as a vindication of its policies in East Timor over the past eighteen years,'[98] a forecast that subsequent events proved correct. Indonesia intensified its efforts to rule East Timor by force through the latter part of the 1990s.

That Indonesia in time at least tacitly accepted Portugal's position further diminishes the ICJ's judgment as a source of guidance for future decision. The clouds over *East Timor* did not dissuade the *Coastal State Rights* tribunal, however.

For the reasons noted, *East Timor* is not convincing support for the decision of the tribunal in *Coastal State Rights* to ignore the resolutions of the General Assembly calling for non-recognition of Russia's annexation of Crimea.

Security Council practice and Charter Article 27(3)

Practice in the Security Council offered an altogether more formal ground to doubt whether a 'sovereignty dispute' indeed existed between Russia and Ukraine but a ground that the *Coastal State Rights* tribunal nevertheless might have considered. Neither Russia nor anybody else attested in the Security Council to a legal dispute over sovereignty in respect of Crimea when the Charter rules on Security Council voting supplied an obvious opportunity to do so.

Charter Article 27, paragraph 3, provides as follows:

> Decisions of the Security Council on all other matters shall be made by an affirmative vote of nine members including the concurring votes of the permanent members; provided that, in decisions under Chapter VI, and under paragraph 3 of Article 52, *a party to a dispute shall abstain from voting*. (Emphasis added)

No state sought to suspend Russia's vote in the Security Council when the matter of Russia's intervention in Crimea was put to a vote, and Russia did

95 ICJ 1995 p. 105 ¶ 15.
96 See Antonopoulos (1996) 97.
97 Burchill (1997) 15.
98 Simpson (1994) 347.

not refrain from voting.[99] The body of states condemning Russia's aggression in 2014 was significant—an overwhelming voting majority in the General Assembly. It should at least have given the adjudicator pause that none of those states drew attention to the obligatory abstention that applies to a real disputant.

In an article not long after Russia's purported annexation of Crimea, Enrico Milano suggested that, through long disuse, Article 27(3) perhaps has fallen into desuetude;[100] or that 'systemic non-fulfilment,'[101] or a kind of dormancy or abeyance,[102] had placed it on the sidelines for an indefinite hiatus.[103] Among the several alternative positions at which Professor Milano arrived, one is that the practice of not invoking Article 27(3) and of members in fact not abstaining 'has released them of the obligation to abstain when they are parties to a dispute under consideration.'[104] If one accepts that position, then Russia's Security Council votes (and vetoes) do not in themselves evince anything about the existence of a 'dispute' by reference to Article 27(3). However, amid the heightened alertness that prevailed in 2014 to the conundrum that Russia's Security Council veto presents, it is still surprising that *no* state, even among the large number that sought Security Council action,[105] drew attention to a 'dispute' such as would have placed the matter under the Article 27(3) duty to abstain.[106]

Spurred, perhaps, by the anomaly of Russia casting vetoes on draft resolutions that would have addressed Russia's aggression against Ukraine, the General Assembly in April 2023 held a debate in which representatives, at last, addressed Article 27(3).[107] This was the first significant floor time that Article 27(3) appears to have received in a principal UN organ since the first years of the Charter.[108] A number of representatives, referring to Article

99 Russia on 15 March 2014 vetoed a draft resolution that forty-two members had put forward and that would have had the Security Council condemn Russia's anticipated 'referendum' in Crimea: UN Doc. S/PV.7138(2014).

100 Milano, 'Whither the Duty to Abstain under Art. 27(3) of the UN Charter?' (2015) 75 ZaöRV 215, 224–228. For an earlier assessment, see Stavropoulos, 'The Practice of Voluntary Abstentions by members of the Security Council under Article 27, Paragraph 3' (1967) 61(3) AJIL 737–752.

101 Milano (2015) at 228–229.

102 *Ibid.* 229.

103 After the early 1950s, there was practically no discussion at all about Art. 27(3)—until 26 April 2023, as to which see nn. 107, 109–110.

104 Milano (2015) 230.

105 See n. 99.

106 *Ibid.*

107 See GA/12500 (26 April 2023).

108 But see the rather abstruse arguments of Portugal and South Africa after SCR 221 (1966), discussed by Stavropoulos (1967) at 738.

27(3), challenged the propriety of a permanent member using the veto in regard to a resolution addressing a dispute to which the member is party.[109] In the course of the debate, Germany stated, 'the Russian Federation ... violated Article 27(3) of the Charter of the United Nations.'[110]

But nobody doubts that Russia's invasion has given rise to disputes. The question is whether the invasion has given rise to a kind of dispute that might prevent the exercise of jurisdiction under UNCLOS Part XV, section 2.

In Russia's own participation in the Security Council, Russia readily could have declared that a dispute exists in regard to sovereignty over Crimea. Russia could have invoked Article 27(3) and refrained from exercising the veto when the Security Council came to address Crimea. In fact, Russia exercised the veto.[111] It lies ill in Russia's mouth, having exercised a right in one organ, where that right depended upon their being *no* dispute, to have exercised a right in another organ, where *that* right depended upon their *being* a dispute. In its Security Council participation, Russia further evinced that as to sovereignty in Crimea there is no legal dispute of which an international dispute settlement apparatus properly takes cognizance.

ICJ advisory opinion on the Chagos

The General Assembly by resolution 71/292 of 22 June 2017 requested an advisory opinion from the ICJ in answer to the questions whether the separation of the Chagos Archipelago from Mauritius before that country's independence in 1965 had been lawful, and what international law consequences arise from the United Kingdom's present-day administration of the Chagos. The Court, in the advisory opinion of 25 February 2019 that it delivered in reply, concluded that 'the process of decolonization of Mauritius was not lawfully completed when that country acceded to independence in 1968, following the separation of the Chagos archipelago.'[112] The Court

109 See GA/12500 (26 April 2023): Rytis Paulauskas (Lithuania); Mark Zellenrath (Netherlands); Cornel Feruţă (Romania); Jochen Hans-Joachim Almoslechner (Austria); Vanessa Frazier (Malta); Lachezara Stoeva (Bulgaria); Arian Spasse (Albania).

110 *Ibid.* Michael Hasenau (Germany).

111 S/PV.7138, 15 March 2014. Russia vetoed the draft resolution (S/2014/189), which would have declared that Russia's 'referendum' in Crimea 'can have no validity, and cannot form the basis for any alteration of the status of Crimea' and would have called upon 'all States, international organizations and specialized agencies not to recognize any alteration of the status of Crimea on the basis of this referendum and to refrain from any action or dealing that might be interpreted as recognizing any such altered status.' The draft received thirteen affirmative votes.

112 Chagos Adv. Op., ICJ Rep. 2019, p. 140, ¶ 83(3). As to which see Eichberger, 'The *Mauritius/Maldives* Delimitation Case' (2021) 22 Melbourne JIL 383, 400; Webb, 'The United Kingdom and the *Chagos Archipelago* Advisory Opinion' (2021) 21

reasoned that the right to self-determination is 'an obligation *erga omnes*' and, so, 'all Member States must co-operate with the United Nations' to bring the United Kingdom's administration to an end.[113]

But for a glancing reference to the fact that Ukraine had noted that the ICJ in the *Chagos* advisory opinion had treated General Assembly resolutions as a crucial part of the practice regarding the decolonization of Mauritius,[114] the tribunal had nothing to say about the advisory opinion. Yet the ICJ, in the advisory opinion, had reasoned that the General Assembly had 'acted within the framework of the Charter and within the scope of the functions assigned to it' when it had pronounced upon the United Kingdom's obligations in regard to the decolonization of Mauritius.[115] Moreover, the Assembly 'consistent[ly] ... adopt[s] resolutions' where non-self-governing territories are concerned.[116] The Court then said as follows: 'the obligations arising under international law and reflected in the resolutions adopted by the General Assembly during the process of decolonization of Mauritius require the United Kingdom, as the administering Power, to respect the territorial integrity of that country, including the Chagos Archipelago.'[117]

The logic of the Court's statement merits reflection. Mauritius had been a non-self-governing territory, recognized as such for purposes of Chapter XI of the UN Charter.[118] The Court drew attention to this legal status and concluded that a specific consequence followed from it: Mauritius, according to the Court, was a single unit within the boundaries of the colony that the United Kingdom administered. Even with a form of consent (the Lancaster House Agreements), according to the Court it was not open to the United Kingdom to separate the territory from Mauritius prior to the colony's independence. If one accepts that conclusion, then it is *a fortiori* the case that a fully independent state, where nobody had contested its borders, is not to be dismembered where no form of consent whatsoever has been displayed. The achievement of self-determination of Ukraine was a completed act, and until March 2014 everybody understood that Ukraine maintained

Melbourne JIL 726–748; Allen, 'Self-determination, the Chagos Advisory Opinion and the Chagossians' (2020) 69 ICLQ 203–220; McCorquodale, Robinson, & Peart, 'Territorial Integrity and Consent in the Chagos Advisory Opinion' (2020) 69 ICLQ 221–238; Bordin, 'Chagos Advisory Opinion' (2019) 78 *Cambridge Law Journal* 253–257; Burri & Trinidad (eds.), *Chagos Advisory Opinion* (2021); Rothwell (2022) 66–67, 226–229.

113 *Chagos,* Adv. Op. at p. 139, ¶ 180. See also *ibid.* p. 140, ¶ 183(5).

114 *Coastal State Rights*, Award, ¶ 103.

115 *Chagos,* Adv. Op. at p. 136, ¶ 167.

116 *Ibid.*

117 *Ibid.* p. 137, ¶ 173.

118 *Ibid.* ¶144.

its self-determination as the territorial unit defined by the boundaries that existed in December 1991.

It would not have been hard for the *Coastal State Rights* tribunal to dismiss Russia's assertion that Crimea had a self-determination claim. In Chapter 6, I addressed the serious failure of the tribunal in its function as a finder of fact. The tribunal failed to direct any scrutiny to Russia's assertion that 'developments' in Ukraine had given rise to a 'sovereignty dispute.' The failure to scrutinize Russia's assertion is all the more astonishing in light of the General Assembly practice, not because the General Assembly practice is binding on an Annex VII tribunal (it is not), but because that practice should have raised questions. The practice consisted not only in the General Assembly's resolutions indicating that Russia's annexation is null and void; it also had an altogether negative element, an element of silence. In particular, what the General Assembly said about other situations, and what it *did not say* about Crimea, should have led the tribunal to ask whether Russia's assertion about Crimea had any reality behind it. The General Assembly knows full well how to address legal obligations to states in regard to their relations with territories whose peoples have a right to independence; it addressed such obligations to the United Kingdom, and the ICJ drew conclusions from that practice.[119] It also knows how to address situations in other territories—that is, where the inhabitants are not a colonial people in the Chapter XI sense. Kosovo is an example.[120] The General Assembly had nothing to say to suggest that Ukraine's conduct in Crimea raised any concern, whether of self-determination or of human rights.

The *Coastal State Rights* tribunal did not so much as mention the *Chagos* advisory opinion. It accepted Russia's assertions about self-determination without scrutiny. If the tribunal had not ignored the international practice in regard to decolonization, then it would have compared Crimea to *real* self-determining territories. On the basis of the comparison, an attentive adjudicator would have readily rejected Russia's position that a sovereignty dispute in Crimea has its genesis in self-determination.

This is not to say that we should expect the General Assembly to address an integral part of an independent state the same way that it addresses Chapter XI Non-Self-Governing territories. UN decolonization practice concerns a discrete (and evidently closed) category of territories—the overseas dependencies chiefly of European states, Australia, New Zealand, and the United States. However, the General Assembly has not been silent in respect

119 See also for overview of earlier practice regarding non-self-governing territories, Grant (2015) at 77–78.

120 See p. 273 n. 121.

of other internal crises. Kosovo was the subject of resolutions of the Assembly for over a decade before it declared independence.[121] In respect of Crimea, the putative annexation of the territory took place mere weeks after Russia had taken hold of it by force, and nothing in General Assembly practice (or the practice of any international organization) suggested that the inhabitants had a self-determination grievance, much less that they were being driven to seek an independent exercise of self-determination.[122]

The Annex VII tribunal constituted to adjudicate the *Chagos Marine Protected Area* dispute between Mauritius and the United Kingdom, as we saw in Chapter 4, had taken an equivocal view as to the scope of its jurisdiction to address territorial sovereignty issues.[123] The ICJ in the *Chagos* advisory opinion, while disclaiming any authority to adjudicate a contentious case regarding the Chagos, concluded that the unity of a colonial territory is guaranteed as a matter of international law and that this proposition, in effect, answered the question presented. The transactions of 1965 between the United Kingdom and the pre-independence government of Mauritius fell short of what the ICJ understood to be required to express consent to the disruption of the territorial integrity of the colony, and, so, the ICJ concluded that the separation of the Chagos from Mauritius entailed that Mauritius in 1968 had not attained decolonization in full.

The ICJ's advisory opinion, while formally free-standing and in no way binding on other dispute settlement organs, had obvious potential relevance in *Coastal State Rights*. Essential to Russia's jurisdictional objection was the thesis that the boundaries of Ukraine had changed through a free act of self-determination. Without such an act there had been no change and, thus, no sovereignty dispute had arisen. The *Chagos* advisory opinion made clear that the consent needed to bring about such a result must be genuine.

121 See, for example, GAR 52/139 (Human rights situation in Kosovo), 12 December 1997; GA Res. 53/164 (Human rights in Kosovo), 9 December 1998; GAR 53/241 (Financing of United Nations Mission in Kosovo), 28 July 1999; GAR 61/285 (Financing of United Nations Interim Administration Mission in Kosovo), 29 June 2007.

122 See also as to reasons for rejecting Russia's analogy to Kosovo, above p. 32, and Socher, *Russia and the Right to Self-determination in the Post-Soviet Space* (2021) 158–160; Grant (2015) 27, 171–183.

123 As to the two *Chagos* decisions—the Annex VII award (*Chagos Marine Protected Area*, Award) and the ICJ Advisory Opinion (*Chagos*, Adv. Op.)—see Fahner, 'Reconciling the Advisory Opinion with the Res Judicata Effect of the UNCLOS Award' in Burri & Trinidad (eds.), *Chagos Advisory Opinion* (2021) 71, 71–94. As will be seen (Chapter 8), in *Mauritius/Maldives*, an Annex VII tribunal regarded the *Chagos* advisory opinion with considerably more care than the *Coastal State Rights* tribunal had done.

'Consent' in mere form does not suffice. The ICJ applied an exacting standard. To say whether consent was genuine, it scrutinized the evidence. Russia, in respect of the seizure of Crimea, presented no evidence even approaching the weight of that which the United Kingdom had presented in respect of the separation of the Chagos. Nothing in the record in the proceedings permitted any inference other than that Russia had annexed Crimea by force. The *Coastal State Rights* tribunal did not even look for evidence to the contrary.

The ICJ's readiness in *Chagos* to involve itself through its advisory procedure in a bilateral dispute remains open to critique. However, the substantive legal question—whether Mauritius had consented to the change of boundary—and the exacting standard that the ICJ applied to answer the question are instructive. I submit that, if the well-documented Lancaster House Undertakings, which were concluded after a period of negotiation at a time of peace, did not suffice to demonstrate consent, then the unmonitored 'referendum,' which took place practically at the moment of Russia's armed takeover, is incapable per se of demonstrating consent. As for the obscure grievances to which Russia alluded, these had left no trace in the diplomatic record, and no international organ had known anything of them. A sovereignty claim against Ukraine's settled territorial title did not arise from a self-determination act, because there was none, and it *could* not arise from Russia's armed assault, because modern international law accepts no claim to the territory of a state by force.

With the *Chagos* advisory request and opinion, the General Assembly and the ICJ had opened the door to a colloquy with the UNCLOS dispute settlement system. The *Coastal State Rights* tribunal did not join the conversation. I compare this, in Chapter 8, with the very different approach that the ITLOS Special Chamber took in *Mauritius/Maldives*.

Ukraine's ICJ proceedings

I addressed in Chapter 6 the proceedings that Ukraine instituted against Russia at the ICJ, first under the ICSFT and CERD, then under the Genocide Convention.[124] The *Allegations of Genocide* case remained *sub judice* as this book went to press. The ICJ's judgments and orders in those proceedings cast doubt on the factual assertions that Russia advanced to support the legal assertion that a dispute arose as to which state is sovereign in Crimea. The *Coastal State Rights* tribunal had nothing to say about the ICJ proceedings.

124 See pp. 229–231.

Practice of other intergovernmental organizations

Stephen Allen has written that '[i]nternational governmental organizations have been unequivocally welcomed as vital additions to the architecture of the international system.'[125] Professor Allen did not say *by whom*, however. The *Coastal State Rights* tribunal did not participate in the welcoming. The tribunal barely acknowledged that other intergovernmental organizations exist. It limited itself to a pared-down paraphrase of part of Ukraine's argument, in which Ukraine had observed that non-recognition of Russia's putative claim to Crimea 'has been reaffirmed by several resolutions adopted by the UNGA *and other international organisations* since 2014.'[126] Ukraine had noted the wide range of international practice on the matter, extending to all parts of the inhabited world.[127]

Particularly striking was the tribunal's silence in regard to the practice of the Council of Europe, the principal regional body to which the states of Europe, including Russia and Ukraine, had belonged at the time of Russia's armed seizure of Crimea, which is to say before Russia enlarged its invasion of Ukraine and the Council expelled Russia.[128] As far as one would know, if the award were one's only source, no other institution had addressed the events and legal issues that they raised.

The Council of Europe Committee of Ministers on 2–3 April 2014 determined that the 'illegal referendum held in the Autonomous Republic of Crimea and the city of Sevastopol on 16 March 2014 and the subsequent illegal annexation by the Russian Federation cannot form the basis for any alteration of the status [of Crimea].'[129] The Parliamentary Assembly of the Council of Europe in resolution 1988 (2014) of 9 April 2014 declared that '[t]he outcome of this referendum and the illegal annexation of Crimea by the Russian Federation ... *have no legal effect* and are not recognised by

125 Allen, 'Reflections on the Treatment of General Assembly Resolutions in the Chagos Advisory Opinion' in Burri & Trinidad (eds.) (2021) 41.

126 *Coastal State Rights*, Award, ¶ 167 (emphasis added) without citation to pleadings.

127 Written Observations and Submissions of Ukraine on Jurisdiction, 27 November 2018, ¶¶ 29–30.

128 See Committee of Ministers (by the Ministers' Deputies), 'Measures to be taken, including under Article 8 of the Statute of the Council of Europe,' CM/Del/Dec(2022)1426ter/2.3, 25 February 2022: https://search.coe.int/cm/Pages/result_details.aspx?ObjectId=0900001680a5a360 (decision suspending Russia's rights of representation); Committee of Ministers, CM/Res(2022)2, 'on the cessation of the membership of the Russian Federation to the Council of Europe' (16 March 2022): https://search.coe.int/cm/Pages/result_details.aspx?ObjectID=0900001680a5da51

129 Committee of Ministers, Decision: 'Situation in Ukraine,' 1196th mtg., 2–3 April 2014, ¶ 1.

the Council of Europe.'[130] For only the second time that it yet had taken such a step (the first had been against Russia as well, that time for Russia's destruction of Chechnya),[131] the Parliamentary Assembly of the Council of Europe (PACE) by Resolution 1990 (2014) suspended Russia's voting rights.[132]

The *Coastal State Rights* tribunal ignored other international institutions as well. The Parliamentary Assembly of the Organization for Security and Co-operation in Europe (OSCE) considered Russia's actions 'military aggression,'[133] and it found that from February 2014 onward Russia 'violated every one of the ten Helsinki principles in its relations with Ukraine.'[134] It referred to Russia's assertions of territorial changes against Ukraine 'illegitimate claims.'[135]

The G7 on 12 March 2014 observed that 'international law prohibits the acquisition of part or all of another state's territory through coercion or force.'[136] Declaring that it did not recognize Russia's putative annexation of Crimea,[137] the G7 excluded Russia from its summit.[138]

This is far from a complete summary of intergovernmental practice.[139] As the arbitrators in *Oschadbank v. Russian Federation* said, albeit in passing, 'the international community expressly has refused to recognize Crimea as part of the Russian Federation.'[140] In other words, not only did a wide range of multilateral institutions declare Russia's putative absorption of Crimea to have no legal effect; none said anything to the contrary.

Putting aside the legal effects of Security Council resolutions, no rule in general international law requires intergovernmental institutions that function under their own constitutive instruments to recognize or otherwise treat as binding or persuasive the decisions, judgments, outcomes, or findings of fact of other such institutions. An international court or tribunal in particular must guard its adjudicative function against political interference.

But, equally, in respect of the facts of Russia's presence in Crimea, the intergovernmental practice has evidentiary value. The ICJ has affirmed that evidentiary conclusions reached by international organizations equipped

130 PACE res. 1988 (2014), 9 April 2014, ¶ 16 (emphasis added).
131 See Stéphanie Rabbiler, 'Le pouvoir d'enquête du Secrétaire général du Conseil de l'Europe' (2000) 104 *Revue général de droit international public* 965.
132 PACE res. 1990 (2014), 10 April 2014, ¶ 15.
133 OSCE Baku Declaration (2014), 28 June-2 July 2014, ¶ 12.
134 *Ibid.* ¶¶ 4, 10.
135 *Ibid.* ¶ 6.
136 G7, Hague Declaration, 24 March 2014, ¶ 2.
137 *Ibid.*
138 See www.cnn.com/2014/03/24/politics/obama-europe-trip/index.html
139 See Grant (2015) at 71–83.
140 *Oschadbank v. Russian Federation*, PCA Case No. 2016–14, Award, 26 November 2018 (Williams, President; Brower and Perezcano Díaz, arbitrators) ¶ 215.

to reach them have 'considerable authority.'[141] While the ICJ has not articulated the point in general terms, the ICJ's reliance in practice on evidentiary conclusions reached by intergovernmental organizations evinces its generality.[142]

Their practice demonstrates that intergovernmental bodies, too, are not oblivious to one another or to international courts. For example, the UN General Assembly long has invited the Council of Europe to participate as an observer,[143] and it has '[a]cknowledg[ed] … the contribution of the Council of Europe to the development of international law.'[144] The General Assembly also has '[c]onfirm[ed] its recognition of the key role of the European Court of Human Rights,'[145] a court that we will see in Chapter 8 took a very different approach from the *Coastal State Rights* tribunal to the facts surrounding Russia's putative sovereignty dispute. Apart from a few short passages in which it mentioned the General Assembly (and in terms that were superficial, dismissive, and confused),[146] the *Coastal State Rights* tribunal had nothing to say about the practice of international organizations.

The tribunal did not only ignore the non-recognition of Russia's purported annexation that key organizations expressed. It also ignored a conspicuous absence: no intergovernmental organization of any note formally acknowledged that Russia had a legal claim to Crimea. The tribunal should have found ample signals among intergovernmental organizations that recognition of Russia's putative claim was improper. And it should have noticed the proverbial dog that did not bark in the night: effectively none reached an institutional determination the other way.[147]

Campbell McLachlan in 2024 reflected on the ILC Study Group on fragmentation in international law. Professor McLachlan had collaborated with then ILC member William Mansfield in respect of Vienna Convention on the Law of Treaties 1969 (VCLT) Article 31(3)(c) in connection with

141 *Application of the Convention on the Prevention and Punishment of the Crime of Genocide (Bosnia and Herzegovina v. Serbia and Montenegro)*, Judgment, ICJ 2007 p. 43, p. 137 ¶ 230 (26 February).

142 For example, in *Pulp Mills*, the ICJ accepted without comment environmental data from the International Finance Corporation (IFC): *Pulp Mills on the River Uruguay (Argentina v. Uruguay)*, Judgment, ICJ 2010 p. 14, 97 ¶ 252 (10 April).

143 GAR 445/6, 17 October 1989.

144 GAR 77/284, 26 April 2023, preambular ¶ 4.

145 *Ibid.* ¶ 4.

146 See pp. 249–251, 251–253.

147 Such silence has been consequential in respect of contentions over territory elsewhere too. See, for example, SCR 1244 (1999), 10 June 1999, as concerned 'the territorial integrity of … Yugoslavia *beyond the interim period*' (emphasis original), Mr. Koh (for the United States), *Kosovo* advisory proceedings, ICJ C.R. 2009/30 (8 December 2009) p. 32 ¶ 26.

the fragmentation project.[148] Professor McLachlan recalled that the eventual Study Group report 'chose to eschew institutional questions, taking the view that "[t]he issue of institutional competencies is best dealt with by the institutions themselves."'[149] Professor McLachlan went on to say that 'such questions have persisted, and have not been resolved.'[150] The *Coastal State Rights* award of 2020 is a conspicuous illustration of the persistence of the institutional questions and of the consequences of failure to resolve them. It is one thing for the adjudicator to observe the independence of the adjudicator's function. It is another to proceed oblivious to evidence. Where well-equipped institutions have studied, and drawn confident and unanimous conclusions on points of fact pivotal to the case that the adjudicator must decide, the adjudicator must give reasons if it reaches contrary conclusions, just as surely as it must give reasons in any event. Alluding to judicial or arbitral independence and leaving it at that is a non-answer in that setting.

Charter Chapter XI, decolonization, and the existence of a dispute

As I noted earlier in this chapter, the *Coastal State Rights* tribunal relied on the ICJ's widely impugned *East Timor* judgment to justify its disregard for the practice of the General Assembly. Disregarding the General Assembly practice eased the tribunal's path to concluding that a dispute exists as to sovereignty over Crimea. The tribunal also referred to *East Timor* for the judgment's express pronouncements about ascertaining the existence of a dispute.

The tribunal quoted *East Timor* in this context: '[T]he Arbitral Tribunal recalls the statement of the ICJ in *East Timor* that Portugal, similarly to the Russian Federation in this case, "has *rightly or wrongly*, formulated complaints of fact and law against Australia which the latter has denied. By virtue of this denial, there is a legal dispute".'[151] But Russia 'formulated complaints' against Ukraine after it carried out an armed seizure of Ukraine's territory. Portugal had not seized anybody's territory in hundreds of years. The tribunal's analogy here is worse than inapt. It is preposterous.

148 McLachlan, 'The Principle of Systemic Integration and Article 31(3)(c) of the Vienna Convention' (2005) 54 ICLQ 279–320.
149 McLachlan (2024) p. 5, § 1.08, quoting Martti Koskenniemi, Chairman, Report of the Study Group on Fragmentation of International Law: Difficulties arising from the Diversification and Expansion of International Law, 2006 ILC Yearbook, vol. IIv Part One, p. 5, ¶ 8.
150 McLachlan (2024) p. 5, § 1.08.
151 *Coastal State Rights*, Award, ¶ 178, quoting *East Timor*, ICJ 1995 p. 100 ¶ 22 (emphasis added by tribunal).

A more subtle fault in the tribunal's reliance on this passage of *East Timor* is that it ignores the legal consequences of the status of East Timor at the time of the ICJ proceedings. East Timor, at that time, was a non-self-governing territory for purposes of Chapter XI of the UN Charter. This status, which is a juridical status carrying legal effects,[152] was not controverted in the proceedings. The ICJ indeed affirmed that East Timor was a non-self-governing territory: 'The Court recalls in any event that it has taken note in the present Judgment ... that, for the two Parties, the Territory of East Timor remains a non-self-governing territory and its people has the right to self-determination.'[153] Portugal's claim was predicated on that status.[154]

The contrast to Russia's claim about Crimea could not be clearer. Russia's claim about Crimea has no support from any intergovernmental institution. Portugal's claim that East Timor was a non-self-governing territory, by contrast, was well-supported: the General Assembly said that East Timor was precisely that.[155] This state of affairs gave rise to an obvious legal question between Portugal and Australia after Australia, ignoring Portugal, purported to conclude a treaty with Indonesia to delimit East Timor's continental shelf. Portugal's side of the contestation was based on the non-self-governing status of the territory. Even though the Court judged that it could not adjudicate Portugal's claims in the absence of Indonesia, East Timor's status, which the General Assembly affirmed, gave legal substance to those claims.[156] By contrast, Crimea is a territory partaking in *no* status that an international institution affirms, except its status as sovereign territory of Ukraine, which no international institution doubts.

The tortured reading that the *Coastal State Rights* tribunal placed on *East Timor* confused the tribunal's assessment of Russia's putative sovereignty claim. In the nature of a non-self-governing territory, there were open questions about the eventual *final* status of East Timor. Those questions were embedded in the institutional determination that East Timor was a non-self-governing

152 See n. 156.

153 ICJ 1995 at pp. 105–106 ¶ 37. Cf. *ibid.* p. 102 ¶ 29.

154 Portugal, Application Instituting Proceedings, 22 February 1991, p. 3, ¶ 1: https://icj-cij.org/sites/default/files/case-related/84/6809.pdf

155 See Chapter 7, n. 80.

156 The ICJ's later practice, in particular its advisory opinion of 2019 on the Chagos, affirmed that Non-Self-Governing status entails legal consequences. See *Chagos* Adv. Op., 131 ¶ 144; 134–135 ¶ 161. No doubt, in a general way, this was correct. However, in the particular application of the law to the Chagos, the ICJ opened itself to considerable doubt. As to points in the advisory opinion that merit scepticism, see Richard Ekins & Tom Grant, 'Handing Over the Chagos Islands Is a Grave Mistake,' *The Spectator*, 4 October 2024. For a sympathetic take, see James Summers, 'Chagos, Custom and the Interpretation of General Assembly Resolutions' in Burri & Trinidad (eds.) 9–40.

territory. Indonesia's armed seizure of East Timor almost surely was unlawful in itself,[157] and the armed occupation would have impugned any popular consultations that Indonesia might have conducted there. However, Indonesia might yet have become, at length, sovereign over East Timor, if the inhabitants of East Timor had freely chosen that result, for example through a plebiscite validated within an international framework.[158] The possibility was contemplated in the same institutional determination under which Portugal was the administering power for the time being. Under the Colonial Declaration, the final disposition of territories under Chapter XI of the UN Charter is to be 'in accordance with [the] freely expressed will and desire' of the people of those territories,[159] and '[i]ntegration with an independent State' is one form of final disposition that the people might elect.[160] No determination exists in regard to Crimea that makes the disposition of that region a matter yet to be determined. Crimea's inclusion as part of Ukraine is its final disposition. No analogy between East Timor and Crimea supports the *Coastal State Rights* award.

Other decisions under international dispute settlement procedures

Chapter 2 discussed the line of cases under UNCLOS Part XV, section 2, procedures addressing use of force and other issues, including human rights.[161] The *Coastal State Rights* tribunal had nothing to say about those cases. In light of the posture in which Russia's jurisdictional objection placed the case, the tribunal's silence in this regard is surprising.

Russia asserted that a sovereignty dispute exists in respect of Crimea. Russia conceded that there was *no* sovereignty dispute up to March 2014. According to Russia, a change of circumstances in Crimea—to which Russia in the Annex VII proceedings only alluded in vague terms—gave rise to the putative dispute. It was at least *plausible* that the change of circumstances in Crimea in March 2014 was Russia's use of force, not some antecedent crisis of self-determination. As we saw in Chapter 6, courts and tribunals in a variety of procedural settings have rejected claims that seek to justify

157 Christine Gray, *International Law and Use of Force*, 4th edn. (2018) 74.

158 This is how Indonesia had established sovereignty over West Irian. See Agreement of 15 August 1962 between the Republic of Indonesia and the Kingdom of the Netherlands concerning West New Guinea (West Irian); GAR 1752 (XVII), 21 September 1962; GAR 2504 (XXIV), 19 November 1969.

159 GAR 1514 (XV), 14 December 1960 (Declaration on the granting of independence to colonial countries and peoples) ¶ 5.

160 GAR 1541 (XV), 15 December 1960 (Principles which should guide members in determining whether or not an obligation exists to transmit the information called for under Article 73 e of the Charter) Annex, Principle VI(*c*).

161 See above pp. 66–88.

use of force. There was no principled reason for the *Coastal State Rights* tribunal to accept Russia's claims without having subjected them to the ordinary process of forensic scrutiny.

A tribunal is obliged to refrain from adjudicating issues that a state has not consented to adjudicate, but Russia is the party that placed the matter of a sovereignty dispute in contention. Moreover, a state does not have a right to have its jurisdictional objections accepted without scrutiny. The tribunal's complete silence about the use of force cases, where adjudicators exercised *merits* jurisdiction over questions of use of force, not just competence to determine the scope of their merits jurisdiction, is therefore all the more striking. To have examined Russia's assertion that 'developments' in Crimea had engendered a sovereignty dispute would have been a modest step compared to the merits awards that UNCLOS tribunals have adopted on issues of use of force. The tribunal thus isolated itself even from the dispute settlement procedures most closely related to it.

In closing this point, we should recall that UNCLOS tribunals have not hesitated to borrow from the practice of other international adjudicators. For example, in the *South China Sea Arbitration*, the Annex VII tribunal constituted in that case relied on the ICJ's application of Article 79(9) of the ICJ Rules of Court when applying Article 20(3) of its own Rules of Procedure.[162] The *Coastal State Rights* tribunal itself relied on *East Timor*, an ICJ case, albeit in an unconvincing way. The *Coastal State Rights* tribunal was happy to reach even further afield, quoting a North American Free Trade Agreement (NAFTA) case, *Methanex v. United States*, to support its decision to require that Ukraine comprehensively refashion its case after the tribunal affirmed Russia's jurisdictional objection.[163] It is to be expected that UNCLOS tribunals will inform their decisions by reference to other (relevant) dispute settlement organs. The *Coastal State Rights* tribunal, however, when it came to the question on which the case turned, acted in isolation.

'Without-prejudice' clauses in UNCLOS and other rules and institutions

Jurisdictional instruments exist that expressly limit the effect of determinations by other bodies on a court or tribunal's decision-making. For example,

162 *Philippines v. China*, PCA Case No. 2013–19, Award on Jurisdiction and Admissibility (29 October 2015) ¶¶ 380–382.

163 *Coastal State Rights* quoting *Methanex Corp. v. United States of America*, NAFTA/UNCITRAL, Partial Award on Jurisdiction and Admissibility of 7 August 2002, ¶ 162.

paragraph 9 of Article 15 *bis* (exercise of jurisdiction over the crime of aggression (state referral, *proprio motu*)) and paragraph 4 of Article 15 *ter* (exercise of jurisdiction over the crime of aggression (Security Council referral)) of the Statute of the International Criminal Court (Rome Statute) provide that '[a] determination of an act of aggression by an organ outside the Court shall be without prejudice to the Court's own findings under this Statute.'[164]

The *absence* of a without-prejudice clause by no means necessarily results in determinations by outside organs binding a court or tribunal. For example, no provision of the Statute of the ICJ declares determinations 'by an organ outside the Court' to be without prejudice to the Court's own findings, yet the ICJ in *East Timor* might be described as having treated General Assembly resolutions as without prejudice to the Court's findings or at least to some of them. The ICJ understood the General Assembly resolutions—such as they were: the General Assembly had stopped speaking of East Timor over a decade before Portugal instituted proceedings—not to have settled the question whether Indonesia might have a legally cognizable claim to East Timor.

UNCLOS, though it contains a number of without-prejudice clauses, contains none quite like that in the Rome Statute. No without-prejudice clause in UNCLOS refers expressly to the legal determinations of dispute settlement organs outside the UNCLOS system.[165] A number of without-prejudice provisions in UNCLOS, however, do preserve the effects of legal commitments that states parties have entered into, or might enter into, outside the Convention and of other international rules. For example, UNCLOS Article 226, paragraph 1(c), provides that a state may refuse or make conditional the release of a vessel that it has detained '[w]ithout prejudice to applicable international rules and standards relating to the

164 Under Art. 13 of the ICC Statute, the Court may exercise its jurisdiction with respect to any of the crimes referred to in article 5—the crime of genocide, crimes against humanity, war crimes, the crime of aggression—if '[a] situation in which one or more of such crimes appears to have been committed is referred to the Prosecutor by the Security Council acting under Chapter VII of the Charter of the United Nations.'

165 UNCLOS Article 189 could be described as requiring the Sea-Bed Disputes Chamber to confine its pronouncements so as to avoid prejudice to certain acts of the Authority, but, however Article 189 is described, it concerns intramural relations among UNCLOS organs, not the relations between those organs and others outside the UNCLOS system. Article 189 requires the Sea-Bed Disputes Chamber to refrain from 'pronounc[ing] itself on the question of whether any rules, regulations and procedures of the Authority are in conformity' with UNCLOS, and further requires that the Chamber refrain from 'declar[ing] invalid any such rules, regulations and procedures.' 1833 UNTS at 477.

seaworthiness of vessels.'[166] To give another example, Article 237, paragraph 1, provides that the provisions of UNCLOS Part XII (Protection and Preservation of the Marine Environment) are without prejudice to obligations of states 'under special conventions and agreements concluded previously which relate to the protection and preservation of the marine environment'; and to obligations of states 'in furtherance of the general principles set forth' in UNCLOS.[167] There is also the 'without-prejudice' provision in Article 304, which I addressed earlier in this chapter.[168] As I noted, the *Coastal State Rights* tribunal refused to join the widespread understanding that no recognition is to be accorded to Russia's claims in respect of Crimea. As provided by Article 304, the provisions of UNCLOS regarding responsibility and liability for damage are 'without prejudice to the application of existing rules and the development of further rules regarding responsibility and liability under international law,' and those rules include ARSIWA Articles 40 and 41, which address non-recognition.

Obviously, for a court to treat the decisions of a *political* organ as having power to bind it in an adjudication would be incompatible with judicial independence. The concern to 'guarantee [...] the judicial independence in the application of the substantive law' appears to have animated the Working Group on the Crime of Aggression in 2010 when it recommended the without-prejudice clause in Articles 15 *bis* and 15 *ter* of the ICC Statute.[169] The independence of judicial determinations also may serve to keep *individual criminal responsibility* for aggression distinct from state responsibility in the international criminal law setting. (Megan Wong in connection with the *Genocide case* notes the importance of the distinction.)[170] Even as regards the possible effects of decisions by one judicial or arbitral organ on another—where concerns about independence from political decision-making do not arise—judges and arbitrators are not formally constrained by any general international law rule requiring their decisions to maintain consistency.

However, courts and tribunals do not exist in a public law vacuum, and facts as notorious as Russia's armed invasion of Ukraine are not mere assertions that shift and change relative to the procedural frame in which an observer views them. Judges and arbitrators should act accordingly. At

166 UNCLOS Art. 226(1)(c): 1833 UNTS at 491.
167 UNCLOS Art. 237(1): 1833 UNTS at 494.
168 See above pp. 254–257.
169 See Aggression RC/WGCA/3, ¶ 5 (RC-WGCA-3-ENG-06062010).
170 Wong, 'Aggression and State Responsibility at the International Criminal Court' (2021) 70(4) ICLQ 961, 971, referring to *Application of the Convention on the prevention and punishment of the crime of genocide* (*Bosnia and Herzegovina v. Serbia and Montenegro*), ICJ 2007 p. 43 ¶ 173.

the very least, they should not suspend the ordinary methods of legal reasoning and forensic inquiry but to the contrary, if reaching results at variance with consensus, should apply those methods all the more exactingly.

A concluding word on systemic consistency

Implicit in the points that I have raised in this chapter is that adjudicators should prefer systemic consistency over fragmentation, at least all else being equal. Plainly, it is not always the case that all else is equal. The formal jurisdictional bounds of each dispute settlement proceeding are the indispensable starting point for adjudicators if they are faithfully to perform the function with which the parties have entrusted them.

But the jurisdictional mandate entails the ordinary forensic function of fact-finding, and it entails reaching well-grounded conclusions of law. If relevant international organs have found certain situations of fact to exist (and others not to), and if they have reached well-reasoned conclusions of law, then a future decision that accords with their dispositions at least has merit in that it avoids surprise. All the more so where no meaningful procedure has reached a contrary disposition, and the decision-maker's own procedure presents no obvious grounds to depart from a consensus that has emerged among other decision-makers, parties should not be surprised when the decision-maker adopts a decision that accords with the consensus. Within those constraints, it is not in tension with, but instead complementary to, the duties of the adjudicator within the formal bounds of one adjudication to regard systemic consistency as a *desideratum*.

Achieving the desired consistency will be difficult or impossible in some circumstances. For example, issues in the case and in prior cases might *appear* the same or closely analogous but, on reflection, are very different. Or the adjudicator might have to conclude that earlier decisions (which do not formally bind her) were wrong as a matter of law or fact. Or she might function in a decisional landscape already characterized by conflicting judgments and conclusions in respect of the case at hand. It takes more than one adjudicator to attain systemic results.

Consistency across international procedures was placed in issue, at the margins, in the *Qatar v. United Arab Emirates* case. Qatar had instituted proceedings against the United Arab Emirates (UAE) at the ICJ under Article 36(1) of the Statute of the Court and under the compromissory clause of the CERD (CERD Article 22). Qatar had also made a communication to the CERD Committee under CERD Article 11. The UAE asked the ICJ to grant provisional measures that would have required Qatar to suspend the

CERD proceedings.[171] In its provisional measures order of 14 June 2019, the ICJ rejected the UAE's request.[172] Jean-Pierre Cot, serving as Judge *ad hoc* in the ICJ *CERD* proceedings, dissented. Among Judge *ad hoc* Cot's grounds for dissent was that an adjudicator should have regard for consistency among international procedures, or at least more regard than the order rejecting provisional measures implied. The judge *ad hoc* observed that 'it is not clear that it is only conflicting binding decisions that pose problems in international relations and that contradictory non-binding decisions need not be resolved or avoided' too.[173]

In Professor Cot's view, '[i]t would be too formalistic to assume that a State party ... could ignore a recommendation of an *ad hoc* conciliation commission or the recommendation of the CERD Committee when it contains a conclusion that differs from any decision of the Court.'[174] Reading Judge *ad hoc* Cot's dissent, we should take care to remember that the formal posture of a matter is not to be ignored: the parties' arguments have to be understood in light of the procedural purposes that they served in their setting. However, we should also take to heart the objection to excess formalism. To ignore the systemic effects of 'a conclusion [in one organ] that differs' from a conclusion in another organ on important points of fact and law indeed 'pose[s] problems in international relations.'

It is to be hoped that jurists, where appropriate, continue to consider how they might avert such problems or resolve them if they arise. The 'fragmentation' of international law is relative, and the extent to which adjudicators pursue consistency is an important factor in its measure. So it has been since the first days of UNCLOS adjudication,[175] and so it remains.[176]

171 Among provisional measures that the UAE had requested was that the Court order Qatar 'immediately [to] withdraw its Communication to the CERD Committee.' Request for the Indication of Provisional Measures submitted by the United Arab Emirates (22 March 2019) p. 33, ¶ 74.

172 ICJ 2019 p. 361, 371 ¶ 32.

173 Dis. Op. Judge *ad hoc* Cot, ICJ 2019 at p. 404 ¶ 9.

174 *Ibid.* at p. 405 ¶ 10.

175 See Oxman and Bantz's observation in relation to *M/V 'Saiga' (No. 2)* about 'assuag[ing] those concerned ... about the effect that a multiplicity of international tribunals may have on the law': Oxman & Bantz (2000) 94 AJIL 148.

176 See Boisson de Chazournes, 'Plurality in the Fabric of International Courts and Tribunals' (2017) 28 EJIL 13, 34.

8

After *Coastal State Rights*: repairing the damage

The award of February 2020 in *Coastal State Rights*, which Chapters 6 and 7 critiqued, calls for reflection in light of subsequent developments, including subsequent decided cases, of which a number address related issues of procedure, of substance, and of legal method.

UNCLOS jurisprudence and the decision-making method of UNCLOS adjudicators, like all jurisprudence and legal method, are not static. Parties and the community at large should hope that they are stable enough to serve the ends of fairness and predictability that must be ends of the legal system if the system is to flourish. To the extent that jurisprudence and method change, the influences that instigate them to change are to be considered with care. It would be regrettable if *Coastal State Rights* were to influence UNCLOS jurisprudence and the decision-making method of UNCLOS adjudicators.

As I have argued, the *Coastal State Rights* award exhibits deficiencies in legal interpretation and in forensic method. Rather than ask for evidence that a 'sovereignty dispute' had arisen after decades of territorial stability—stability founded in treaty after treaty as well as in practice—the tribunal declared that it lacked the authority to examine the matter. The tribunal further understated the significance of *claim* in international law: rather than appreciate the gravity of a decision that Russia has a claim under international law to a territory that Russia seized by force, the tribunal said that its decision was 'mere recognition' of an 'objective fact.'[1] And the tribunal paid no heed to the effects of its decision on public order. In light of these and further defects that Chapters 6 and 7 considered, the February 2020 award should be counted among the larger failures of international adjudication in recent times.

What are the consequences, if the *Coastal State Rights* award, rather than recede into justified obscurity, were to influence the development of

1 *Coastal State Rights*, Award, ¶ 177 (emphasis added).

UNCLOS dispute settlement? What is the 'damage' that I have in mind that now must be repaired?

There is the obvious impact on Ukraine's struggle in face of Russia's aggression. Acceptance at the international level that Russia has a legal claim to Ukraine's territory would be a setback for one country. It would also erode the principle that title to territory, when settled between states, does not change by force or threat. Eroding the principle would have far-reaching effects, because many situations exist in which states have territorial ambitions, or latent ones, that they might prosecute by force or threat. The long stability of spatial relations among states, I suggested in chapter 1, supplies the foundation for much that has developed in international law since 1945. If we lose the stability, then we lose the foundation.

The risks, if the *Coastal State Rights* award does not receive the critique that it deserves, thus include the breakdown of the rules and institutions that stable spatial relations support. Nobody says that the adjudicator's task is to save the legal system, still less the party counsel's task. It *is* the task of adjudicator and counsel alike to apply rules and methods of the legal system. In performing that task, adjudicators and counsel necessarily participate in a process that, over time, has effects on the legal system. International law is not the common law, but the accumulation of decided international cases shapes international jurisprudence nonetheless.[2]

It also shapes the collective sense of how we are to reason about legal questions. We have no formal canon telling us precisely what constitutes proper legal method and, so, we look to decided cases to learn our method. The *Coastal State Rights* award is a poor teacher. It fails to reflect the ordinary method that parties expect adjudicators to apply—fact-finding, allocation of burden, exercise of *compétence de la compétence*, respect for other international institutions, observance of long-practiced distinctions in legal reasoning, and others besides. *Coastal State Rights* has too many lapses for us to allow it to influence our method.

The former (the risk of systemic decay) is heightened by the latter (the methodological lapses). In particular, an approach to the adjudicator's method that eschews ordinary fact-finding invites parties to fashion jurisdictional objections that touch supposed forbidden ground. It does not help matters, if future tribunals treat the exclusion of sovereignty questions from UNCLOS jurisdiction as so far-reaching as to prevent reasoned treatment of jurisdictional objections. A ready stratagem for the objecting party will be to invoke a

2 See Klein & Parlett (2022) 26, with reference to *Request for an Advisory Opinion submitted by the Sub-Regional Fisheries Commission (SRFC)*, Advisory Opinion, Sep. Op. Judge Lucky, ITLOS 2015 p. 88, p. 92 ¶ 10 (2 April).

'sovereignty claim' and, therein, find safe harbor against well-pleaded maritime claims.

The *Coastal State Rights* tribunal allowed Russia's assertion of a 'sovereignty claim' to obstruct the orderly settlement of Ukraine's maritime claims. The 'sovereignty claim' there was an exorbitant claim, a claim surpassing the boundaries of what the law accepts. The exorbitant 'sovereignty claim' and the tribunal's wan response are significant to public order more broadly still, because the strategy of jurisdictional objection that Russia used in *Coastal State Rights* is not limited to assertions of title by force on land. 'Sovereignty claims' such as Russia's have an analogue in maritime spaces.

In this chapter, let us begin by considering the potential damage if adjudicators allow exorbitant claims to intrude on dispute settlement procedure. Then let us turn to subsequent decisions that suggest that adjudicators are already distancing themselves from *Coastal State Rights* and further suggest that we might as yet repair some of the damage or at least prevent this anomalous case from doing more.

Exorbitant claims on land and at sea

Difficult cases, even cases freighted with geopolitical implication, do not necessarily lead to anomalous results.

Chapter 5 considered the *South China Sea Arbitration*. The Annex VII tribunal constituted to decide that case had to say whether certain claims by China were claims within the modern law of the sea or, instead, of such a geographic scope and substantive character as to exceed what that law might accept. It is worth recalling what *South China Seas* said about claims that exceed the claims that the modern law of the sea might accept.

According to the *South China Sea* tribunal:

> Having concluded that the exception to jurisdiction in Article 298(1)(a)(i) is limited to disputes involving historic titles and that China does not claim historic title to the waters of South China Sea, but rather a constellation of historic rights short of title, the Tribunal holds that it has jurisdiction to consider the Philippines' Submissions No. 1 and 2. As China has not made such a claim, the Tribunal need not consider whether there would be any limit to the application of Article 298 to expansive claims of historic title extending well beyond those that may have been anticipated when the Convention was concluded in 1982.[3]

3 *South China Sea*, Award, ¶ 229.

Similar to Russia's objection under cover of a putative 'sovereignty claim,' China's objection was that the tribunal could not adjudicate the Philippines' claims because to adjudicate those claims (China maintained) the tribunal would have to adjudicate claims of 'historic title,' and claims of historic title are beyond the scope of jurisdiction.[4]

The *South China Sea* tribunal rejected China's objection. The tribunal's reason for rejecting it was that 'China does not claim historic title.'

The 'historic titles' that a state might claim in lawful fashion are residual rights having their origins in legal relations that predate UNCLOS.[5] To recall, the *South China Sea* tribunal concluded that 'the text and context of the Convention [are] clear in superseding any historic rights that a State may once have had in the areas that now form part of the exclusive economic zone and continental shelf of another State.'[6] The possibility that the tribunal had to consider was that China was making 'historic title' claims, not only to near-shore areas proximate to China but also to a large part of the EEZ and continental shelf of the Philippines. The *South China Sea* tribunal, as I noted in Chapter 5, examined China's claims, including those related to the so-called nine-dash line, a cartographic figure that encompasses significant parts of the Philippines' EEZ and continental shelf (as well as of the EEZs and continental shelves of the other South China Sea littoral states). This was a fact-intensive inquiry, and the tribunal did not shrink from it.[7] The tribunal concluded (as I quoted immediately above) that China was not making claims of historic title in respect of areas that the 'nine-dash line' encompasses 'but rather a constellation of historic rights short of title.' On the facts, then, an exorbitant claim—that is, a claim past that which the UNCLOS historic title *residuum* embraces—was not involved, because China had not made it.

4 See Position Paper of the Government of the People's Republic of China on the Matter of Jurisdiction in the South China Sea Arbitration Initiated by the Republic of the Philippines, 7 December 2014. See also *Statement of the Ministry of Foreign Affairs of the People's Republic of China on the Award of 12 July 2016 of the Arbitral Tribunal in the South China Sea Arbitration Established at the Request of the Republic of the Philippines*, 12 July 2016, ¶ 2.

5 Award, ¶¶ 223–226.

6 *South China Sea*, Award, 12 July 2016 ¶ 247.

7 To discern the meaning of China's claim to 'relevant rights in the South China Sea, formed in the long historical course' (Award, ¶ 206, quoting *Statement of the Ministry of Foreign Affairs of the People's Republic of China on the Award on Jurisdiction and Admissibility of the South China Sea Arbitration by the Arbitral Tribunal Established at the Request of the Republic of the Philippines*, 30 October 2015), the tribunal scrutinized China's conduct in detail: Award, ¶¶ 207–214.

And yet the tribunal strongly suggested that a case might arise in which an exorbitant claim *is* involved. Thus, the tribunal's dictum acknowledging that a state might confront a future tribunal with 'expansive claims of historic title extending well beyond those that may have been anticipated when the Convention was concluded in 1982.'

The *South China Sea* tribunal did not quite say so, but a logical reading of its award, of the Convention, and of the development of the law of the sea in respect of historic title together suggest that 'expansive claims of historic title extending well beyond those that may have been anticipated when the Convention was concluded in 1982' are unreceivable, nullities under modern international law. In a manner analogous to the exclusion of claims to sovereignty over land territory by force, modern international law, it would be submitted, has excluded such 'expansive claims' at sea.

The *South China Sea* tribunal examined China's claims with care, in particular China's claims related to the 'nine-dash line.' A failure to approach China's claims with the full rigor of the adjudicator's method would have had serious effects. It would have allowed mere assertion to trigger the jurisdictional exclusion of Article 298(1)(a)*(i)*. The tribunal considered extensive evidence regarding the 'nine-dash line' and other elements of China's practice that were relevant to China's objections. In other words, it scrutinized China's objection. Whether or not the *South China Sea* tribunal reached the right conclusion, the conclusion that it reached it reached the right way.

The difference between *South China Sea* and *Coastal State Rights* is instructive on this point. Russia, unlike China, plainly made an assertion which, if accepted as a legal claim, would trigger a jurisdictional exclusion under Part XV, section 2 (at least on the sovereignty disputes exclusion as jurists widely understand it). The *Coastal State Rights* tribunal, unlike the *South China Sea* tribunal, accepted the relevant exclusionary assertion. But the most significant difference is that it accepted the assertion without scrutiny.

If future tribunals accept exclusionary assertions such as Russia's with as little care as Russia's received, then they will have significantly changed the dispute settlement process. Failing to insulate the process from exorbitant claims, tribunals will have curtailed much of the intended scope of their jurisdiction. Accepting such assertions also will affect public order more widely. Modern international law places limits on territorial claim (through the principle that boundaries settled between states do not change by force) and limits on maritime claim (through the exclusion of claims to sovereign title in maritime areas beyond the internal waters and territorial sea of the state). In placing these limits on claim, the law ensures stability and predictability in the spatial relations of states, and these are the relations that matter the most in international public order. Adjudicators who either ignore the limits or deny that they have the jurisdiction or forensic means to apply them thus will do damage to dispute settlement procedure. They will also do damage to the wider public order of which dispute procedure forms part.

A consensus takes shape?

A number of cases decided since the February 2020 *Coastal State Rights* award suggest that a consensus is taking shape that accords with the argument that I have put forward here: the award does not articulate a satisfactory approach to the problems that it addressed or to the conduct of dispute settlement under UNCLOS in general.

In his 2016 commentary in the *Yale Law Journal* on use of force and UNCLOS cases, Peter Tzeng observed that it is rare for jurists who serve as UNCLOS adjudicators to criticize one another.[8] Mutual respect prevails among UNCLOS adjudicators, along with diplomatic tact. We therefore must read between the lines if we are to discern what judges and arbitrators comprising UNCLOS tribunals *really* think about the work that their colleagues in earlier cases performed.

The judges of the ITLOS Special Chamber in *Mauritius/Maldives*, writing eleven months after the *Coastal State Rights* award, displayed characteristic reserve. Nevertheless, the conclusions that they reached, and much of the reasoning that they expressed, disown the *Coastal State Rights* award. They are not the only jurists to have engaged in damage control in response to the award of 21 February 2020.

After considering *Mauritius/Maldives*,[9] let us consider a different dispute settlement organ, the ECtHR, because that organ, too, turned a cold shoulder to *Coastal State Rights*. Unlike the *Coastal State Rights* tribunal, the ECtHR confronted the fabrications on which Russia based its jurisdictional defense.[10] There have also been a number of investment claims against Russia, brought under the Ukraine–Russia BIT. Awards resulting from these claims started to come to light after February 2020. Human rights claims and investment claims are, self-evidently, different from UNCLOS claims, but the ECtHR cases and BIT cases arose against the backdrop of the same public order challenge as *Coastal State Rights* and presented related questions of legal method. How the adjudicators addressed those questions merits consideration here.

8 Tzeng (2016) 257.
9 See below pp. 293–300.
10 See below pp. 300–302.

Not all adjudicators have rejected *Coastal State Rights*. An Annex VII tribunal in an award of 27 June 2022 on the Preliminary Objections of Russia in *Dispute concerning the Detention of Ukrainian Naval Vessels and Servicemen* seems to have accepted the conclusion in *Coastal State Rights* that,[11] with nothing more than assertion, an objecting party can satisfy an adjudicator that a sovereignty dispute exists. The *Detention* Annex VII tribunal stated that 'the present dispute arises in the context of competing claims to sovereignty over the land and maritime areas in the vicinity of the Kerch Strait, matters that are outside the jurisdiction of the Arbitral Tribunal.'[12] The tribunal's statement here was only in passing and, by its own admission, unnecessary to the matters that fell for the tribunal to address. It would have been better if the tribunal had refrained from stating that the dispute had anything to do with 'competing claims to sovereignty.' Perhaps stating that there were 'competing claims' was to maintain comity with the *Coastal State Rights* tribunal. Whatever the reason, stating so was a mistake.

After considering these cases, I conclude the chapter with observations on three thematic matters and suggestions in regard to each that might contribute to the corrective that I argue we need in the aftermath of *Coastal State Rights*. Adjudicators and academic writers give interpretative deference to post hoc accounts that participants in the Third UN Conference on the Law of the Sea sometimes proffer in respect of the sovereignty disputes exclusion; we might consider tempering the deference (1). Situations exist in which a strictly formal definition of 'legal dispute' might suffice, but courts and tribunals will be ill-equipped to deal with exorbitant claims if they do not apply ordinary methods of fact-finding to scrutinize party assertions; we should place assertions about the existence of 'disputes' under the scrutiny appropriate to the settings in which parties make the assertions (2). And, finally, there are specific future procedural steps that the Annex VII tribunal in *Coastal State Rights* might take in regard to the maritime disputes that Ukraine sought to settle under UNCLOS Part XV, section 2; but there too we should be mindful of unintended consequences (3).

11 As to which see Kunoy (2021) 132–136.

12 *Dispute concerning the Detention of Ukrainian Naval Vessels and Servicemen*, PCA Case No. 2019–28, UNCLOS Annex VII tribunal (McRae, President; Eiriksson, Wolfrum, Golitsyn, and Greenwood, members), ¶ 42. The tribunal elsewhere in the Award referred to 'conflicting positions on sovereignty over Crimea,' this too 'as a matter of context': *ibid.* at ¶ 110.

Mauritius/Maldives

In *Mauritius/Maldives*, as I noted in Chapter 2 in connection with UNCLOS Article 288(4),[13] the Maldives asserted that a sovereignty dispute exists in regard to the Chagos Archipelago and that the putative dispute should bar the ITLOS Special Chamber from exercising jurisdiction over a delimitation between the Maldives and Mauritius.[14] The Special Chamber disagreed. It concluded that no such dispute exists, and it proceeded to exercise jurisdiction.

The Special Chamber did not arrive at its conclusion through purely formal steps. According to the Special Chamber, an assertion by one party of 'the matter-of-fact existence of a sovereignty dispute,' without more, does not suffice to sustain a jurisdictional objection.[15] Whether or not on the facts the Special Chamber was right to conclude that the sovereignty dispute between Mauritius and the United Kingdom no longer existed (there are reasons to be skeptical),[16] the scrutiny that the Special Chamber applied to the question is welcome. In contrast to the Annex VII tribunal in *Coastal State Rights*, the Special Chamber did not accept that a juxtaposition of contradictory statements, without more, necessarily establishes the existence of a dispute.

Yet the Special Chamber suggested that it took the same approach as *Coastal State Rights*. It suggested that it was not delving into the intricacies of a sovereignty dispute.[17] In this paradox—doing precisely what the *Coastal State Rights* tribunal did *not* do,[18] yet suggesting that it adhered to *Coastal State Rights*—the Special Chamber seemed at pains to demonstrate that its judgment was joining a supposedly consistent jurisprudence.[19] A tension is immediately visible here. If the Special Chamber did not accept the Maldives' assertion of 'the matter-of-fact existence of a sovereignty dispute,' *and* it took the *Coastal State Rights* approach, under which the fact evidence of

13 See above pp. 62–66.
14 See above pp. 63–65. See also Introduction, pp. 10–11, 15. Further to the *Mauritius/Maldives* preliminary objections award, see Thomas Burri & Jamie Trinidad, 'Introductory Note' (2021) 60 ILM 969–971.
15 *Mauritius/Maldives* (Prelim. Obj.) ¶ 245.
16 See *Mauritius/Maldives* (Prelim. Obj.) (Oxman Sep. & Dis. Op.), ¶¶ 6–7. Judge *ad hoc* Oxman relates his concern, in part, to the principle of non-aggravation of disputes, notably in both the first and the final paragraphs of his dissent: *ibid.* ¶¶1, 49. Further to non-aggravation, see Chapter 8, pp. 325–329).
17 *Ibid.* ¶ 214 (indicating that the *Chagos Marine Protected Area* tribunal, and by implication the Special Chamber too, 'lacked jurisdiction to entertain' the sovereignty dispute and contrasting the tribunal to the ICJ).
18 Professor Kunoy agrees that the Special Chamber did not follow the *Coastal State Rights* approach: Kunoy (2021) 129.
19 *Mauritius/Maldives* (Prelim. Obj.) ¶¶ 110–111. See Conclusion, p. 337 for reasons to doubt whether there is a *jurisprudence constante* on this matter.

an alleged dispute was not put to a 'plausibility' test or to any test at all, then how, exactly, did the Special Chamber reach the conclusion that there was no sovereignty dispute?

The Special Chamber, in reaching the conclusion that the Maldives had not shown a sovereignty dispute to exist in respect of the Chagos Archipelago, said that it reached the conclusion by interpreting the ICJ's *Chagos* advisory opinion of 2019.[20] This casts further doubt on the Special Chamber's suggestion that it followed *Coastal State Rights*. The *Coastal State Rights* tribunal neither credited the findings of another international organ (see Chapter 7) nor engaged in fact-finding that looked beyond a party's assertion of 'the matter-of-fact existence of a sovereignty dispute' (see Chapter 6).

The relation between the Special Chamber's engagement with the question of the existence of a dispute and the advisory opinion is subtle. To see what the Special Chamber *really* did, let us take a closer look at its judgment and what it said about the 2019 advisory opinion.

Having invoked *Coastal State Rights* to say that it could not address an alleged dispute over sovereignty, the Special Chamber said, instead, that it would inquire into the meaning of the ICJ advisory opinion.[21] The Special Chamber's engagement with the advisory opinion was no mere passing glance. It devoted *seventy-five* paragraphs of the *Mauritius/Maldives* preliminary objections judgment to the advisory opinion. Whatever meaning the Special Chamber derived from the advisory opinion, the meaning evidently did not jump off the page of the ICJ Reports unambiguously and in full form.

The ICJ's reasoning in the advisory opinion turned on the facts of the contested relations of Mauritius and the UK in regard to the Chagos. It is to be submitted that the Special Chamber did not accept the *Chagos* advisory opinion at face value. Instead, it examined the opinion itself as an evidentiary object. The Special Chamber examined the advisory opinion on the premise—albeit an unstated premise and arguably not an entirely sound one—that the advisory opinion was the best source available on which to base its own fact-finding. In effect, the Special Chamber wrapped scrutiny of the evidence about the sovereignty dispute in a study of the advisory opinion.

The wrapping exercise—placing its own forensic and cognitive operation under the mantle of the ICJ's—served as a declaration of consistency, in particular with *Coastal State Rights*. It was a declaration that the Special

20 As to which see above Chapter 2, pp. 63–64.
21 *Mauritius/Maldives* (Prelim. Obj.) ¶¶ 167, 243, 245.

Chamber, imitating the *Coastal State Rights* tribunal, was not examining a 'sovereignty dispute.' The Special Chamber would have done better without the declaration. The Special Chamber indeed readily could have done without declaring that it followed the *Coastal State Rights* approach to sovereignty disputes, because, in truth, that is not the approach that it followed. Instead, it scrutinized the evidence about the sovereignty dispute.

The Special Chamber knew full well that the advisory opinion is not binding, and even if somehow it were, the consent-based jurisdiction under which the Special Chamber addressed the dispute between Mauritius and the Maldives does not entail automatic deference to another adjudicator's judgment. It would have served the interests of clarity for the Special Chamber to have stated directly what it was that it did. The Special Chamber, while having paid careful regard to the advisory opinion, inquired independently into the facts and reasoning that Mauritius advanced to argue that no dispute as to sovereignty over the Chagos now exists.

I submit that the key to *Mauritius/Maldives* is not the advisory opinion but the Special Chamber's competence to settle a dispute as to the scope of its jurisdiction. This is not a purely speculative submission. The Special Chamber drew attention not once, but twice, to Article 288(4), the provision that indicates that, in the event of a dispute as to whether it has jurisdiction, an UNCLOS tribunal shall settle the dispute. It is true that, in this too, the Special Chamber was rather obscure. The Special Chamber suggested that the only thing that Article 288(4) does is *permit* an UNCLOS tribunal to study *other adjudicators' opinions*: it '[did] not consider that the Parties' disagreement on the consequences of the *Chagos* advisory opinion falls outside its jurisdiction.'[22] The Special Chamber's affirmation here of *compétence de la compétence* was nervously diffident and strange in its negative formulation. The Special Chamber said only that it did not lack jurisdiction to consider a disagreement about the advisory opinion. But the parties' disagreement about the advisory opinion was not for its own sake. They disagreed *about what the opinion meant for their dispute*, which is to say, they disagreed about what the opinion meant for Mauritius and the *United Kingdom's* dispute. The real question for the Special Chamber was whether *that* dispute still existed. If the Special Chamber had answered the question simply by transposing a result from the advisory opinion, then it would not have used seventy-five paragraphs to do so. I consider in a moment the answer that the Special Chamber derived from that lengthy excursus.

22 *Ibid.* ¶ 190. Cf. ¶ 115; see Chapter 2, n. 24.

Sometimes, to make a point more memorable or persuasive, jurists use analogies[23] and even allegories.[24] When reading *Mauritius/Maldives*, one is reminded of the opening passage of Thomas Mann's *The Magic Mountain*,[25] in which Mann alerted the reader that he was about to tell a long and detailed story about a young man who holds little intrinsic interest; the story is not for *his* sake, however, but to elucidate other matters that are largely outside the story's literal bounds. The story, in truth, is a disquisition in allegorical form about the state of Europe and of humankind on the eve of World War I. So too is the Special Chamber's long account of the advisory opinion about something else—but, unlike Thomas Mann, the Special Chamber did not admit what it was doing. The Special Chamber said that it was merely interpreting the *Chagos* advisory opinion, but, in truth, from the advisory opinion it distilled an answer to a question that is outside the advisory opinion's formal bounds and for the purposes of adjudicating a different dispute. Saying that the Special Chamber addressed a 'disagreement' *about the advisory opinion* is no more insightful than saying that Thomas Mann wrote 700 pages about a fictional character's visit to a sanatorium.[26]

It is worth asking what *else*, besides the 'Parties' disagreement' about the *Chagos* advisory opinion, the Special Chamber '[did] not consider falls outside its jurisdiction.' The Special Chamber knew full well that adjudicators consider issues of fact when exercising their competence to settle a dispute as to the scope of jurisdiction.[27] The Special Chamber might have inquired further than it did when settling the dispute as to the scope of its jurisdiction.

23 We also use analogy as a tool of legal reasoning in a stricter sense of legal method, as to which see Fernando Lusa Bordin, *The Analogy between States and International Organizations* (2018) 15–48. See also An Hertogen, 'The Persuasiveness of Domestic Law Analogies in International Law' (2019) 29(4) EJIL 1127–1148.

24 Allegory in legal argument is not without its risks. See *Maritime Delimitation in the Area between Greenland and Jan Mayen (Denmark v. Norway)*, ICJ, CR 93/10 (25 January 1993), Mr Lynge (for Denmark) p. 55.

25 Thomas Mann, *The Magic Mountain* (original *Der Zauberberg*, 1924) (Vintage, 1996) (John E. Woods, trans.) 1.

26 Indeed, '[o]ne may wonder whether the Special Chamber made the ICJ's Advisory Opinion binding through the backdoor' or at least *tried* to make it so: Fabian Simon Eichberger, 'The Legal Effect of ICJ Advisory Opinions Redefined? The *Mauritius/ Maldives* Delimitation Case—Judgment on Preliminary Objections' (2021) 22 Melbourne JIL 383, 400. Naturally, by contrast, in summary accounts of the *Mauritius/ Maldives* case writers have been satisfied to describe the Special Chamber's decision precisely as the Special Chamber described it—that is, as a decision to apply the holdings that the ICJ reached in the *Chagos* Advisory Opinion. See, for example, Merrills & De Brabandere, *Merrill's International Dispute Settlement*, 7th edn. (2022) 274–275.

27 See p. 293 and n. 15. See also Chapter 6, nn. 170, 172, 177–181.

UNCLOS Article 288(4) obliged the Special Chamber to settle that dispute. In particular, the Special Chamber, in applying Article 288(4), might have asked more about the state of relations between the UK and Mauritius in respect of the Chagos. Even before they opened negotiations in 2022, the UK and Mauritius differed as to whether bilateral talks or multilateral dispute settlement is the appropriate course but agreed that the Chagos presents an open question.[28] These circumstances are difficult to understand except as a manifestation of a continuation of at least *some* dispute relative to sovereignty in the Chagos. The aversion of the *Coastal State Rights* tribunal to fact-finding unfortunately left a mark on *Mauritius/Maldives*. The Special Chamber would have done better, if it had spoken not in allegory about an advisory opinion but directly to the jurisdictional question that confronted it. Nevertheless, unlike the *Coastal State Rights* tribunal, the *Mauritius/Maldives* Special Chamber inquired past the objecting party's mere assertion. It subjected that assertion to scrutiny. This was a noteworthy difference in decision method between *Coastal State Rights* and *Mauritius/Maldives*.

The difference in outcome between the two cases merits remark as well. In finding that no territorial dispute exists in regard to the Chagos, the Special Chamber, even as it paid regard to the ICJ *Chagos* advisory opinion, said in its own words that the separation of the Chagos from the colony of Mauritius under the Lancaster House Agreements was 'not based on the free and genuine expression of the will of the people concerned.'[29] According to the Special Chamber, the separation was *per se* a violation of international law, because the Chagos 'was clearly an integral part of Mauritius in 1965' when the separation took place.[30] The Special Chamber here advanced two propositions: first, that there was no 'free and genuine expression' to accede to the change in territorial boundaries; and second, that the change had disrupted a territorial unit that enjoyed the presumption of integrity under international law. If those propositions are valid in connection with the separation in 1965 of the Chagos from Mauritius, then it is beyond cavil that homologous propositions are valid in regard to the putative separation of Crimea in 2014 from Ukraine. Let us consider each proposition in turn.

In favor of the United Kingdom's view that the people of Mauritius had freely and genuinely expressed their acceptance of a change in the

28 See Statement of Sir Alan Duncan, Minister of State, Foreign and Commonwealth Affairs (26 June 2017): https://questions-statements.parliament.uk/written-statements/detail/2017-06-26/HCWS10

29 *Mauritius/Maldives* (Prelim. Obj.) ¶ 171.

30 *Ibid.*

boundaries of the colony,[31] there are two considerations. First, there was a 'people' so defined. This follows from the status of Mauritius as a non-self-governing territory for purposes of Chapter XI of the UN Charter, a status that necessarily entailed the right of the people of Mauritius to exercise self-determination independently from any other territory or polity.[32] In other words, a Mauritian actor existed for international law purposes, and it had the right *ipso facto* to determine the future status of Mauritius, a status which at that stage was yet to be settled.[33] And, second, the colony had undergone years of constitutional development, including the establishment of organs of self-government that had represented the colony through the 1950s and 1960s in the negotiations preliminary to independence. The Special Chamber noted the constitutional development,[34] even if it did not trace that development or the Lancaster House negotiations in as much detail as the *Chagos* Annex VII tribunal had done.[35] In short, Mauritius was a territory that had an international law status permitting its people to choose the fate of the territory; and the people in fact chose the separation of the Chagos as their fate.

Nothing resembling these considerations was visible in relation to Crimea. Crimea is an integral part of Ukraine, a state of affairs that Russia itself recognized up until March 2014.[36] Its inhabitants exercise *their* self-determination as and together with the citizens of Ukraine. But, *quod non*, even if a people of Crimea did have an international law right similar to that of the people of Mauritius, there was nothing in the factual record even approximating the negotiations and agreement that had preceded the separation of the Chagos from Mauritius. In contrast with the transactions of 1965 in regard to the Chagos, there was not a trace of negotiation or agreement surrounding Russia's putative annexation of Crimea in 2014. Nor was there any evidence that Crimeans on their own had the institutional machinery with which to represent themselves in a negotiation if one had

31 At least as the UK's view was at the time of the *Chagos Marine Protected Area* Annex VII proceedings and ICJ advisory proceedings. The UK and Mauritius held negotiations on 23–24 November 2022, 11–12 January 2023, and 23–24 February 2023 in regard to 'the exercise of sovereignty' in the Chagos. See Statement by Lord Goldsmith of Richmond Park, UK House of Lords: https://questions-statements.parliament.uk/written-statements/detail/2023-03-17/hlws630

32 See *Chagos* Adv. Op. 107–108, ¶ 29.

33 GAR 1541 (XV), 15 December 1960, Principle VI. Cf. the famous dictum of Judge Dillard: 'It is for the people to determine the destiny of the territory and not the territory the destiny of the people.' *Western Sahara*, Advisory Opinion, Sep. Op. Judge Dillard, ICJ 1975 at p. 122 (16 October).

34 *Mauritius/Maldives* (Prelim. Obj.) ¶ 58.

35 *Chagos Marine Protected Area*, Award, ¶¶ 64–68, 69–85.

36 *Coastal State Rights*, Award, ¶ 181.

taken place. Ukraine had such machinery—but had nothing about which to negotiate and no time to negotiate even if it had, such was the pace of events. As to Russia's suggestion that people in Crimea had expressed a self-determined choice in a 'referendum,' this suggestion is one that the *Coastal State Rights* tribunal should have tested. As we will see shortly,[37] the ECtHR did not hesitate to find that the putative three-weeks-long march to annexation was *not* the result of a self-determination movement but of external armed force.[38] The *Chagos Marine Protected Area* tribunal, the ICJ in the 2019 advisory opinion, and the *Mauritius/Maldives* Special Chamber each scrutinized the 1965 transactions concerning the Chagos. This kind of forensic operation is perfectly familiar. Yet the *Coastal State Rights* tribunal refused to perform any operation like it.

As to self-governing territorial units, the General Assembly, which plays a special role in decolonization,[39] has stated that a country administering a colony shall respect the territorial integrity of the colony.[40] That consideration plainly animated the Special Chamber in *Mauritius/Maldives*.[41] Post-independence Ukraine, however, certainly no less than pre-independence Mauritius, enjoys a presumption of territorial integrity. Moreover, all parties concerned with Ukraine—at least until Russia's 2014 invasion—agreed that the boundaries of Ukraine were settled and agreed where those boundaries were. It is baffling that the universal obligation to refrain from using armed force to alter the boundaries of an independent state[42] had no effect on the reasoning of the Annex VII tribunal in *Coastal State Rights*.

To summarize the comparison, if the Mauritians had given no 'free and genuine expression' to a desire to divide their territory in 1965, then *a fortiori* the Ukrainians (whether as a body or their Crimean part) had given no 'free and genuine expression' of a desire to absorb Crimea into Russia in 2014; and if Mauritius was a geographic unit enjoying the presumption of territorial integrity, then *a fortiori* so was Ukraine.

If the *Coastal State Rights* tribunal had applied a method similar to the ITLOS Special Chamber's, then it would have scrutinized Russia's assertion that a sovereignty dispute exists in regard to Crimea. Instead, it eschewed

37 See pp. 300–302.

38 As to the measures that Russia alleged gave expression to the self-determination of the inhabitants of Crimea, see Socher (2021) 160–164; and as to the annexation and purported integration of Crimea into Russia, *ibid.* at 167–170.

39 *Chagos* Adv. Op. 135, ¶ 163.

40 *Ibid.* 134, ¶ 160, recalling 'that the self-determination of the people concerned is defined by reference to the *entirety* of the non-self-governing territory' (emphasis added), citing GAR 1514 (XV), 14 December 1960 (Colonial Declaration).

41 *Mauritius/Maldives* (Prelim. Obj.), ¶ 174.

42 See above pp. 25–58.

reasoning and evidence and relied on an arid recital of the doctrine of 'objective dispute.'[43] If it had given weight to the same legal considerations, in particular self-determination and the inviolability of the boundaries of a self-determining territory, then it would have concluded that Russia's assertion was to be rejected *a fortiori*. If it had inquired as carefully into the facts as did these other tribunals, then it would have found that Russia's plea of a 'sovereignty dispute' was premised on violence and fabrication, not on law or fact.

MH17 and *Crimea* cases at the ECtHR

Ukraine, in 2014, lodged a number of applications in the ECtHR alleging that Russia's conduct in eastern Ukraine (Donbas) and Crimea constitutes serious violations of the European Convention on Human Rights, the treaty that established the Court and confers jurisdiction on it to adjudicate interstate claims, as well as the individual claims for which it is better known.[44] The Netherlands lodged an application in 2020 against Russia concerning the destruction of Malaysian Airlines flight MH17, an incident in Donbas in 2014 in which 196 Dutch nationals were killed. The applications were in part separated and in part joined.[45]

In its objections to jurisdiction, Russia asserted that it had nothing to do with events in Crimea or Donbas. The Court, however, considered fact evidence and questioned Russia's factual assertions. The Court found that Russia, in truth, was in control of events in Donbas,[46] and that Russia's forces and operatives, not a putative self-determination movement, had seized Crimea.[47]

As regards Crimea, the Court rejected Russia's attempt to bar the Court from considering 'questions concerning sovereignty.' Russia argued that for the Court to characterize Russia's presence in Crimea as extraterritorial

43 See above Chapter 6, pp. 196–197.

44 As to the jurisdiction of the ECtHR, see generally Schabas, *The European Convention on Human Rights: A Commentary* (2015) 715–722.

45 For the procedural history, see *Ukraine and the Netherlands v. Russia*, Applications nos. 8019/16, 43800/14 and 28525/20), Decision, 25 January 2023, ¶¶ 2–33, 69, 376–382. I address the *MH17* and *Crimea* cases in Grant, 'Sovereignty in Crimea and Donbas at the European Court of Human Rights' (2023) 39(1) *Connecticut Journal of International Law* 47–76.

46 For the Court's factual conclusions, see *MH17 case* (ECtHR, 25 January 2023), ¶¶ 141–142, 147–150, 693.

47 See *Crimea case* (ECtHR, 16 December 2020) ¶¶ 329, 331, 338. See also *MH17 case* (ECtHR, 25 January 2023) ¶ 46 (role of 'unidentified armed men in green military uniforms without insignia').

'would take the Court into questions concerning sovereignty between States that are outside its jurisdiction.'[48] The Court rejected Russia's argument. Instead, it emphasized that Ukraine expressly excluded from its application any request for a determination as to the legality of Russia's physical presence in Crimea or of 'the legality *per se* under international law of the "annexation of Crimea" and, accordingly of [the territory's] consequent legal status thereafter.'[49] The Court made clear that it was not addressing sovereignty over Crimea as a merits matter but, instead, as necessary to determining the scope of the Court's jurisdiction to adjudicate the applicant state's claims.[50]

The Court's conclusion as to Russia's presence in Crimea was a careful but clear rejection of Russia's plea that a sovereignty dispute precludes the exercise of jurisdiction over Ukraine's claims. According to the Court, 'for the purposes of this admissibility decision, the Court will proceed on the basis of the assumption that the jurisdiction of the respondent State over Crimea is in the form or nature of "effective control over an area" *rather than in the form or nature of territorial jurisdiction*.'[51] This conclusion should be read together with the Court's observation that Russia had failed to demonstrate that any change had taken place 'to the territorial integrity of Ukraine in respect of Crimea within the meaning of international law.'[52] Implicit was that Russia is not the sovereign in Crimea and that no dispute on the point exists.

The finding in *Coastal State Rights* that a sovereignty dispute *does* exist in Crimea would seem to have had direct relevance to Russia's jurisdictional objection in the ECtHR proceedings. However, while the European Court in *Crimea* noted the *Coastal State Rights* award, it passed over it without comment.[53]

The Court's silence is telling. The Court, in effect, made understood that it would not allow the award of 21 February 2020 to influence its own approach to Russia's jurisdictional objections. It should be recalled that the General Assembly, too, though it noted other dispute settlement proceedings, ignored the *Coastal State Rights* award.[54] Whether or not these institutions intended their silence to be a signal, they identified nothing in the award persuasive enough to treat as guidance.

48 *Crimea case* (ECtHR, 16 December 2020) ¶ 338.
49 *Ibid.* ¶ 244. See also *ibid.* ¶ 339.
50 *Ibid.* ¶ 341. See also *ibid.* ¶¶ 264–265.
51 *Ibid.* ¶ 349 (emphasis added).
52 *Ibid.* ¶ 348.
53 *Ibid.* ¶ 244.
54 See, for example, GAR 75/29 (Problem of the militarization of the Autonomous Republic of Crimea and the city of Sevastopol, Ukraine, as well as parts of the Black Sea and Sea of Azov), 7 December 2020, preamble.

Having not encumbered itself with *Coastal State Rights*, the ECtHR looked for guidance elsewhere. In particular, it referred to the extensive international practice concerning Donbas and Crimea that the Annex VII tribunal had dismissed or ignored altogether, including UN General Assembly resolutions and Council of Europe practice.[55] It also engaged in thorough fact-finding of its own.[56] Instead of eschewing the adjudicative function, the Court performed it.

Investment claims under the Russia–Ukraine BIT

A number of Ukrainian parties instituted investment treaty claims against Russia following Russia's takeover of Crimea.[57] Proceedings in these cases, which the Ukrainian parties instituted under the Russia–Ukraine BIT of 1998,[58] mostly predate the *Coastal State Rights* award that I critiqued in Chapters 6 and 7. As claimants pursue enforcement against Russia in national courts, a number of the awards resulting from their claims have come to light. Unsurprisingly, the awards did not reach dispositive conclusions in regard to sovereignty over of Crimea. As one of the tribunals noted, a tribunal

55 *MH17 case* (ECtHR, 25 January 2023) ¶¶ 455–458, ¶¶ 596–599, 603.

56 *Crimea case* (ECtHR, 16 December 2020) ¶ 348.

57 For earlier comment, mostly before awards in the cases became public, see Tuzheliak, 'Investors at Conflict's Crossroads: An Overview of Available International Courts and Tribunals in the Crimea Context' (2017) 6(2) *UCL Journal of Law and Jurisprudence* 14–45; Hill-Cawthorne, 'International Litigation and the Disaggregation of Disputes' (2019) 68(4) ICLQ 779, 789–791; Dumberry, 'Claims of Ukrainian Investors against Russia under the Ukraine–Russia BIT' (2018) 9 JIDS 506; Benatar & Schatz, 'The Protection of Foreign Investments in Disputed Maritime Areas' in Ackermann & Wuschka (eds.), *Investments in Conflict Zones: The Role of International Investment Law in Armed Conflicts, Disputed Territories, and 'Frozen' Conflicts* (2021) 176, 196–199 and, in the same volume, De Vriese, 'The Application of Investment Treaties in Occupied or Annexed Territories and "Frozen" Conflicts,' 319, 330–332, 339–343, 346–353. With discussion of the by then published award in *Stabil v. Russian Federation*, see Miles, 'Lawfare in Crimea' (2022) 38 *Arbitration International* 135–150. And, in passing, Zrilič, *The Protection of Foreign investment in Times of Armed Conflict* (2019) 3 and *ibid.* n. 8; Costelloe, 'Treaty Succession in Annexed Territory,' 65(2) ICLQ 343–378; Wuschka in Fach Gómez et al. (eds.) (2019) 149–150. Regarding inter-state dispute-settlement under the BIT, see Grant, 'International Dispute Settlement in Response to an Unlawful Seizure of Territory: Three Mechanisms' (2015) 16(1) *Chicago Journal of International Law* 1, 27–41.

58 Agreement between the Government of the Russian Federation and the Cabinet of Ministers of Ukraine on the Encouragement and Mutual Protection of Investments, 27 November 1998: https://investmentpolicy.unctad.org/international-investment-agreements/treaty-files/2233/download

constituted under the BIT 'is not a tribunal of general jurisdiction.'[59] The awards hold interest here for their incidental observations about the facts of Russia's takeover of the territory and for their approach to the status of Crimea.

In one of the BIT cases, *Stabil et al. v. Russian Federation*, the tribunal in its award on jurisdiction 'note[d] the convergence of the outcomes reached by the different tribunals' in respect of the application of the Russia–Ukraine BIT.[60] The tribunal referred to the jurisdiction awards in *Aeroport Belbek et al. v. Russian Federation*,[61] *Privatbank and Finilon v. Russian Federation*,[62] and *Everest Estate v. Russian Federation*.[63] *Naftogaz v. Russian Federation*[64] and *Oschadbank v. Russian Federation*[65] are further cases arising out of Russia's takeover of Crimea in which tribunals have adopted awards.

While 'convergence' is visible among some of the published awards, distinctions are visible as well. The *Stabil* tribunal said that it 'expresses no view on the legality of Crimea's incorporation into Russia or on the legitimacy of the sovereignty claims over this territory.'[66] It 'observe[d] that the *Belbek* tribunal took a similar view' and then quoted the *Belbek* Decision on Jurisdiction of 24 February 2017: '"this Interim Award does not reach any view on the legality or illegality under international law of the incorporation of the Crimean Peninsula by the Russian Federation or on the sovereignty claims of Ukraine and the Russian Federation in respect of

59 *PJSC CB PrivatBank and Finance Company Finilon LLC v. the Russian Federation*, PCA Case No. 2015–21 (Dupuy, President; Bethlehem and Mikulka, arbitrators), Interim Award, 27 March 2017, ¶ 191 n. 204.

60 *Stabil et al. v. the Russian Federation*, PCA Case No. 2015–35 (Kaufmann-Kohler, President; Price and Stern, arbitrators), Award on Jurisdiction, 26 June 2017 ¶ 95.

61 *Aeroport Belbek LLC and Mr. Igor Valerievich Kolomoisky v. the Russian Federation*, PCA Case No. 2015–07 (Dupuy, President; Bethlehem and Mikulka, arbitrators), Decision on Jurisdiction, 24 February 2017 (not public); Partial Award (liability), 4 February 2019 (not public).

62 *PJSC CB PrivatBank and Finance Company Finilon LLC v. the Russian Federation*, PCA Case No. 2015–21 (Dupuy, President; Bethlehem and Mikulka, arbitrators), Interim Award, 27 March 2017; Partial Award, 4 February 2019.

63 *Everest Estate LLC et al. v. the Russian Federation*, PCA Case No. 2015–36 (Rigo Sureda, President; Reisman and Knieper, arbitrators), Decision on Jurisdiction, 19 March 2017; Award on the Merits, 2 May 2018. The *Everest Estate* awards as of September 2024 had not been widely circulated.

64 *NJSC Naftogaz of Ukraine, PJSC State Joint Stock Company Chornomornaftogax, PJSC Ukrgasvydobuvannya and others v. Russian Federation*, PCA Case No. 2017–16, Partial Award, 22 February 2019 (Binnie, President; Stanivuković and Poncent, arbitrators).

65 *Oschadbank v. Russian Federation*, PCA Case No. 2016–14, Award, 26 November 2018 (Williams, President; Brower and Perezcano Díaz, arbitrators).

66 *Stabil v. Russian Federation*, Award on Jurisdiction, 26 June 2017, ¶ 128.

the Crimean Peninsula."'[67] One might detect a nuance in the *Stabil* tribunal's treatment of the matter absent in the *Belbek* interim award. The *Stabil* tribunal said that it expresses no view 'on the *legitimacy* of the sovereignty claims' (emphasis added). While 'similar' to saying, as the *Belbek* tribunal did, that one takes no view 'on the sovereignty claims,' saying that one takes no view on their legitimacy is open to a different interpretation. The *Stabil* tribunal's statement is open to the interpretation that the tribunal took no view on whether a receivable sovereignty claim had been made in respect of Crimea at all, whereas the *Belbek* tribunal was clear that its agnosticism was about the merits of sovereignty claims, not about their possible irreceivability, inadmissibility, or nullity. The *Stabil* tribunal did not develop the point further, and so one would be exaggerating if one said that the tribunal concluded that Russia has no cognizable claim to Crimea. However, the tribunal's clarity about the use of force in Russia's takeover of the territory—to which I turn shortly—lends support to the conclusion that Russia indeed has no such claim.

In its final award, the tribunal in *Stabil* repeated that it expressed no view about the 'legality of the inclusion of Crimea into the Russian Federation,' adding that this was 'because it need not resolve that issue in order to decide the dispute before it.'[68] The jurisdictional framework in *Stabil* differed in this regard from that in *Coastal State Rights*. The *Stabil* arbitrators could proceed to the merits without reaching a conclusion about the 'legitimacy' of Russia's claim to territory—or, in other words, about the existence of such a claim. In *Coastal State Rights*, the arbitrators, by contrast, on their understanding of UNCLOS jurisdiction, could proceed to the merits only if they first determined that no dispute over territory existed.

Cameron Miles observes that the *Stabil* tribunal went to lengths 'to square the circle,' adjudicating the merits of the Ukrainian investors' claims while also proceeding cautiously in regard to sovereignty.[69] The tribunal chose its approach well. It kept in view both the limits of the jurisdictional instrument concerned (the BIT) and the public order values that an eventual award might affect. The *Stabil* tribunal avoided dictum that might have sanctified Russia's illegal annexation, and even, possibly, depending how one reads the phrase 'expresses no view ... on the legitimacy of the sovereignty claims,' avoided a suggestion that Russia has a sovereignty claim at all.

Other BIT tribunals considering claims by Ukrainians against Russia for injuries in Crimea reached conclusions similar to those in *Stabil* and *Belbek*.

67 *Belbek v. Russian Federation*, Interim Award, 24 February 2017, ¶ 158, as quoted in *Stabil v. Russian Federation*, Award on Jurisdiction, 26 June 2017, ¶ 128 n. 149. The *Belbek* awards as of September 2024 had not been widely circulated.

68 *Stabil v. Russian Federation*, Final Award, 12 April 2019, ¶ 100.

69 Miles (2022) at 147.

'The facts required to establish jurisdiction under the BIT,' said the majority in *Naftogaz v. Russian Federation*, 'do not turn on the legality or illegality of encroachments by one Contracting Party on the territory of the other … [T]he plain terms of the BIT can be applied in their ordinary meaning to the situation in Crimea and Sevastopol at the relevant dates without resolving legal issues such as sovereignty,' which the tribunal understood to be 'extraneous.'[70] In *PJSC CB Privatbank and Finilon v. Russian Federation*, the tribunal likewise proceeded to address the merits of the case without 'reach[ing] any view on the legality or illegality under international law of the incorporation of the Crimean Peninsula by the Russian Federation or on the sovereignty claims of Ukraine and the Russian Federation in respect of the Crimean Peninsula.'[71] The tribunal in *Oschadbank v. Russian Federation* referred 'to the change that occurred in the status of the Crimean Peninsula in February-March 2014, without prejudice to its lawfulness or unlawfulness under international law.'[72] It is to be remarked that to refer to 'the change that occurred in the status' of the territory is question-begging: the very question to be asked—or, as here, the question to be avoided—is *whether* a change occurred in status. The reference in *Privatbank* to 'sovereignty claims' similarly went too far. Nevertheless, a shared approach emerged in these BIT awards, maintaining a (mostly) studied neutrality. It was obvious that from some point in time Russia exerted effective control in Crimea. Whether effective control coincided with sovereignty or even with a sovereignty claim was unnecessary to say.

The BIT tribunals were not unanimous as to the date from which Russia's effective control began. The date was important in the BIT cases, because it was from that date (whatever the adjudicators decided that date to be) that conduct in Crimea was to be attributed to Russia for purposes of attaching legal responsibility for injuries caused to the investors. The tribunal in *Privatbank* considered that it should apply a 'test … of "settled" control signalling a dispensation concerning which there is evidence of sustained character.'[73] The tribunal reasoned that constitutional measures concluded on 21 March 2014 in Russia constituted evidence of the 'sustained character'

70 *NJSC Naftogaz of Ukraine, PJSC State Joint Stock Company Chornomornaftogaz, PJSC Ukrgasvydobuvannya and others v. Russian Federation*, PCA Case No. 2017–16, Partial Award, 22 February 2019 (Binnie, President; Stanivuković and Poncent, arbitrators), ¶ 161.

71 *PJSC CB Privatbank and Finance Company Finilon LLC v. Russian Federation*, PCA Case No. 2015–21, Partial Award, 4 February 2019 (Dupuy, President, Bethlehem and Mikulka, arbitrators), ¶ 171.

72 *Oschadbank v. Russian Federation*, PCA Case No. 2016–14, Award, 26 November 2018 (Williams, President; Brower and Díaz, arbitrators), ¶ 6.

73 *Privatbank and Finilon*, Interim Award, 27 March 2017, ¶ 192.

of Russia's effective control.[74] The *Stabil* tribunal similarly thought that Russia's domestic legal measures are relevant to determining when conduct of public authorities in Crimea should be attributed to Russia: 'having incorporated Crimea into its territory by various legal and constitutional measures, Russia considers that its "territory" encompasses Crimea, which the Tribunal finds relevant for the purposes of its present analysis.'[75] The *Stabil* tribunal concluded that the BIT became opposable to Russia with respect to Ukrainian investments in Crimea 'no later than 21 March 2014.'[76]

The *Naftogaz* tribunal, curiously, identified 18 March 2014 as the date at which Russia became responsible for injuries to Ukrainian investors. The difference in time is small between 18 March and 21 March but the difference in legal implications is large. The *Naftogaz* tribunal referred to the conclusion on 18 March 2014 of the so-called Annexation Treaty between the putative independent Crimea and Russia.[77] The *Oschadbank* tribunal also referred to the Accession Treaty and identified 18 March 2014 as the date from which 'the actions of the Crimean authorities were … attributable' to Russia.[78] A treaty is an act that its parties intend to have effects in a particular legal order, namely the international legal order. The 'Annexation Treaty,' on the better view, had no such effects. The identification of 18 March 2014 as starting point of Russia's effective control is therefore not felicitous. It would have been better to ignore the putative treaty, a nullity for purposes of international law, and focus, instead, either on raw effective control, which began at or around 28 February or 1 March, or on domestic Russian law, which evinced 21 March to be the starting date. The *Privatbank* and *Stabil* tribunals gave sound reasons on the facts to support the conclusion that 21 March 2014 is the starting date. That conclusion also better serves the public order interest in denying effect on the international law plane to Russia's assertion of sovereignty.[79]

The geopolitical background to the BIT cases and *Coastal State Rights* is the same—Russia's forcible seizure of Crimea—but there are significant differences in the jurisdictional instruments that the adjudicators were called on to apply. In the BIT cases, for jurisdiction to exist in respect of certain claims concerning investments in the territory, it was necessary, at a minimum,

74 *Ibid.* at ¶¶ 192–193, 250.
75 *Stabil*, Award on Jurisdiction, 26 June 2017, ¶ 144:.
76 *Ibid.* at ¶ 175.
77 *Naftogaz*, Partial Award, 22 February 2019, ¶¶ 223, 231.
78 *Oschadbank*, Award, 26 November 2018, ¶¶ 271, 272.
79 As to the incorporation of Crimea into Russia for purposes of Russia's domestic law, see Grant, *Aggression against Ukraine* (2015), 18–21; and as to the distinction between that act and the change that Russia sought to bring about under international law, *ibid.* at 21–23, 23–33.

that the respondent state effectively control the territory.[80] By contrast, in *Coastal State Rights*, for jurisdiction to exist in respect of certain claims concerned with conduct in maritime areas it was necessary that the applicant state be the sovereign in the territory as 'sovereign' is understood for general purposes in international law.[81]

It was clear to the arbitrators in two of the BIT cases that Russia took control of Crimea by armed force. This was a finding of fact. In its statement of the facts, the tribunal in *Stabil v. Russian Federation* noted in detail the rapid chain of events on 27 and 28 February 2014 by which Russia deployed its land and naval forces to take control.[82] The tribunal in *Naftogaz v. Russian Federation* expressed the matter plainly: 'On 20 February 2014, the Russian Federation launched a military operation to seize Crimea.'[83] Later in the award, the tribunal concluded that it was 'not good faith' for Russia, 'having taken over Crimea by force of arms,' to suggest that Ukrainian investors there 'by [Russia's] unilateral act' no longer enjoy protection of the Russia–Ukraine BIT. [84] The arbitrators understood that the question which state holds sovereignty in the territory for purposes of international law did not need to be answered in order to answer the question that did need to be answered, namely whether, under the Russia–Ukraine BIT, Russia could be held legally responsible for conduct in the territory. True, a finding that a state holds sovereignty, in a case with ordinary facts, would have answered the necessary question: the state that holds sovereignty, in the ordinary case, can be held legally responsible for conduct in the territory over which it is sovereign. But the Russia–Ukraine BIT cases involved highly unusual facts. It was therefore both helpful and proper for the arbitrators to draw attention to the facts. In drawing attention to Russia's armed takeover, the arbitrators gave a sound reason for the approach that they took, in which they asked whether Russia had effective control in the territory and the intention to maintain it, rather than sovereignty as such.

A distinction between the approaches that the different arbitrators took to the facts is visible among the published BIT awards. In two of the cases,

80 See, above, as to the *Privatbank* and *Stabil* tribunals' adverting to Russian constitutional measures as evidence.

81 See Introduction, Introduction, pp. 23–24.

82 *Stabil v. Russian Federation,* Award on Jurisdiction, 26 June 2017 (Kaufmann-Kohler, President; Price and Stern, arbitrators) ¶¶ 56–57; Final Award, 12 April 2019, ¶¶ 103–105.

83 *NJSC Naftogaz of Ukraine, PJSC State Joint Stock Company Chornomornaftogax, PJSC Ukrgasvydobuvannya and others v. Russian Federation,* PCA Case No. 2017–16, Partial Award, 22 February 2019 (Binnie, President; Stanivuković and Poncent, arbitrators), ¶ 85. See also *ibid.* ¶¶ 86–88.

84 *Ibid.* at ¶ 197.

the published awards display more reticence in regard to the facts than did the awards in *Stabil* and *Naftogaz*. In *Oschadbank*, the tribunal acknowledged that 'Russian military forces were present in the Crimean Peninsula' at the relevant time but did not say what role precisely those forces played in Russia's takeover of the territory.[85] It *did* conclude that Russia's forces, in the course of 'the military intervention in Crimea,' caused damage to the claimant,[86] a conclusion that invites the inference that the takeover of the territory, too, was a result of armed force.

The tribunal in *Privatbank and Finilon* referred to 'armed men in fatigues but without identification' who 'were reported to have' taken over key facilities and infrastructure in Crimea.[87] Suggesting, as the *Privatbank* tribunal here did, that it was unclear who took over is too congenial to the tactics of concealment and ambiguity that constitute 'hybrid' warfare.[88] The award did note that the Russian President later acknowledged 'the involvement of the Russian military in the Crimean Peninsula,'[89] though there, too, the tribunal was unduly cautious, certainly more cautious than the President, who minced no words.[90]

None of this is to criticize the *Privatbank* tribunal for having carefully thread the needle when it came to identifying the critical date for purposes of the attribution of responsibility to Russia for events in Crimea.[91] It is, instead, to suggest that the award would have lost nothing in its cogency or in the faithfulness of its observance of the limits of jurisdiction under the BIT, if it had acknowledged the well-attested reality of the circumstances in which the treaty claims arose.

Draftsmen and undue deference

As I argued in Chapter 3, jurists have read into UNCLOS Part XV, section 2, an enlarged exclusion of sovereignty issues.[92] That reading is not supported

85 *Oschadbank*, Award, ¶ 54.
86 *Ibid.* ¶ 537.
87 *PJSC CB Privatbank and Finance Company Finilon v. Russian Federation*, Interim Award, 27 March 2017, PCA Case No. 2015-21, ¶ 59.
88 Further to which, see above Chapter 6, pp. 234–237.
89 *Privatbank and Finilon*, Interim Award, 27 March 2017, ¶ 71.
90 The President of Russia, as early as 17 April 2014, acknowledged that the takeover was by force of Russian arms. Carl Schreck, 'From "Not Us" to "Why Hide It?": How Russia Denied Its Crimea Invasion, Then Admitted It,' *Radio Free Europe/ Radio Liberty* (26 February 2019).
91 See *Privatbank and Finilon*, Interim Award, 27 March 2017, ¶¶ 191–192.
92 See above pp. 110–117.

by the text, the context, or the drafting history of the Convention. It is nevertheless widely accepted. As I argued in Chapter 6, the enlarged reading of the exclusion frustrated the conduct of proceedings in *Coastal State Rights*. This is not just a matter of excluding sovereignty questions from merits consideration. In that case, as I have argued, the enlarged reading of the exclusion interfered with the operation of *compétence de la compétence*. If adjudicators follow the enlarged reading and insist that they have no authority to scrutinize assertions that a sovereignty dispute exists, then they will have invited such assertions and other exorbitant claims in future cases and, in effect, conferred upon objecting parties a power of auto-revocation of jurisdictional consent. Placing a range of potential jurisdictional objections beyond the reach of reasoned inquiry, the enlarged exclusion of sovereignty issues stands in the way of future adjudications under Part XV, section 2. Moreover, it gives parties an incentive to make exorbitant assertions and, worse, to seek to vindicate them on the ground. A crisis for UNCLOS is emerging, both in the operation of its dispute settlement procedures and in its role in public order.

I also have suggested that, to understand why the view has persisted that Part XV, section 2, lays down a general exclusion of sovereignty issues, we need to consider the role of jurists to whom adjudicators and writers have imputed special authority by reference to their participation in the Third UN Conference. While some lawyers of a more recent generation have continued to advance the exclusionary thesis, the *loci classici* are in the writings and interventions of original UNCLOS specialists. Adjudicators should proceed with caution, however, when they place reliance on interpretative glosses offered after the fact, even when eminent persons offer them.

It is a truism, but worth repeating, that the text of a treaty is the chief source by which we discern the treaty's meaning. Vienna Convention Article 31 reflects this. Vienna Convention Article 32 reflects that supplementary means of interpretation are available in order to confirm the meaning of the text of a treaty or to determine the meaning, where the meaning is otherwise ambiguous or obscure or, if literally interpreted, the text would lead to a manifestly absurd or unreasonable result.[93] Among supplementary means of interpretation, 'preparatory work of the treaty' enjoys priority,[94]

93 VCLT Article 32: 1155 UNTS 340. Drawing attention, however, to the rough edges of the rule stated in Article 32, see Davis Mortenson, 'The *Travaux* of *Travaux*' (2013) 107 AJIL 780, 783–784.

94 Villager, to give one example from the VCLT glossators, calls the 'preparatory work of the treaty ... the most important supplementary means.' Villiger, *Commentary on the 1969 Vienna Convention on the Law of Treaties* (2009) p. 445 § 3.

and, where that work is memorialized in formal records,[95] those are the priority source.[96] As Yves Le Bouthillier observes in the *Corten and Klein Commentary*, 'to be considered as preparatory work, a document ... had to have been in existence before the adoption of the treaty.'[97]

The Third Conference on the Law of the Sea left a set of records remarkable in their detail and scope.[98] A lawyer or judge seeking to resolve a point of interpretation finds in those records a rich source of observations by states and their representatives, including contentious and contrasting positions on a range of issues that the adopted text addresses.[99] Multiple antecedent drafts exist for purposes of comparison. While it is not unheard of to call in aid of interpretation testimony by individuals who were present at the drafting of a treaty, for example as set out in academic articles or seminars or prepared for litigation,[100] they are not the priority source. Eminent though they might be, their after-the-fact recollections and conclusory assertions about the meaning of the text do not override the text itself, nor do they form the first point of reference when one looks to supplementary means of interpretation.

95 Which it not always is: see Kolb, *The Law of Treaties. An Introduction*, 2nd edn. (2023) 154.
96 See Le Bouthillier, 'Article 32' in Corten & Klein (eds.), *The Vienna Conventions on the Law of Treaties. A Commentary* (2011), §24: 'there is no doubt that elements that are intrinsic to the negotiating process leading to a treaty will generally be accepted as preparatory work.'
97 Le Bouthillier, 'Article 32' §27.
98 Thus it took Nordquist and his collaborators six volumes to address them in the *Virginia Commentary*. For a cautionary word about reliance on the commentary in the *Commentary*, as distinct from the drafting history itself, see Kunoy (2021) 93–94.
99 See Chapter 3, pp. 108–109.
100 See, for example, *Içkale Insaat Limited Sirketi v. Turkmenistan,* ICSID Case No. ARB/10/24 (Heiskanen, President; Lamm and Sands, arbitrators), Award, 8 March 2016, where the tribunal was ready to accept eyewitness testimony (*ibid.* ¶207), but 'the preparatory works of the [Turkey–Turkmenistan BIT]' were 'extremely limited' and the 'only relevant evidence' was the eye-witness account (*ibid.* ¶210). In another ICSID case, 'testimony of key actors present during [the treaty] negotiations' only 'amplified' documentary evidence from the negotiations, which itself only confirmed the plain meaning of the treaty. *Hrvatska Elektroprivreda d.d. v. Republic of Slovenia*, ICSID Case No. ARB/05/24 (Williams, President; Paulsson and Brower, arbitrators), Decision on the Treaty Interpretation Issue, 12 June 2009, ¶ 183. Cf. *CEAC Holdings v. Montenegro*, ICSID Case No. ARB/14/8 (Hanotiau, President; Park and Stern, arbitrators), Award, 26 July 2016, ¶108. For an example from a municipal legal proceeding, and the court's skeptical reception, see *Salant Corporation v. United States,* 25 C.I.T. 162, 166 (U.S. Court of International Trade) (2001).

James Crawford observed once that VCLT Article 32 chiefly concerns 'preparatory work,' and this does not embrace 'statements made outside the negotiating forum by one or other individual participant or private conversations, still less recollections or *post hoc* testimony of what individuals, or individual governments, had in mind. The *travaux* must be preparatory work of the treaty. They are not a collection of afterthoughts.'[101] Yet those who posit a broad interpretation of the territorial exclusion in Part XV, section 2, continue to advert to assertions by veterans of the Third Conference.

There is (or should be) nothing sacrosanct about eyewitness testimony in this setting. Adjudicators in other settings have rejected an interpretation when a party relies on one of the treaty's individual progenitors as evidence of the interpretation that the party advances. An ICSID case in which the parties were divided as to the interpretation of Article 25, paragraph 1, of the ICSID Convention supplies an illustration.

Article 25 is the jurisdictional provision of ICSID. In accordance with paragraph 1 of Article 25, '[t]he jurisdiction of the Centre shall extend to any legal dispute arising directly out of an investment, between a Contracting State (or any constituent subdivision or agency of a Contracting State designated to the Centre by that State) and a national of another Contracting State.'[102] In *Cambodia Power Company v. Kingdom of Cambodia, Electricité du Cambodge*,[103] the parties fell into contention over the phrase 'designated to the Centre.' The respondents argued that Cambodia had *not* 'designated' Electricité du Cambodge 'to the Centre,' which, if it had not, entailed that the claimant had no investment in Electricité du Cambodge subject to ICSID jurisdiction and, thus, no claim against that party.[104] The claimant argued that Electricité du Cambodge *was* an entity 'designated to the Centre.' The claimant did not advert, however, to any communication from Cambodia to the Centre expressing a designation; there seems not to have been any. Instead, the claimant relied on an interpretation of Article 25(1). According

101 Further Opinion of James Crawford LLD (Expert Report and Affidavit), ¶30, *Hulley Enterprises Ltd. v. Russian Federation,* U.S. District Court, District of Columbia (3 May 2007).

102 Convention on the Settlement of investment disputes between States and nationals of other States, 18 March 1965, entered into force 14 October 1966: 575 UNTS 159, 174.

103 *Cambodia Power Company v. Kingdom of Cambodia, Electricité du Cambodge*, ICSID Case No ARB/09/18 (Kaplan, President; Beechey and Landau, arbitrators), Award on Jurisdiction, 22 March 2011.

104 Ibid. at ¶ 215.

to the claimant, Article 25(1) 'does not require an act of communication to the Centre.'[105]

In aid of this interpretation of Article 25(1), the claimant referred to the chairman of the Legal Committee on the Settlement of Investment Disputes, Aaron Broches. The eminent jurist,[106] in explanatory notes published in 1993 and addressing the Committee's drafting work of the early 1960s, had indicated as follows: 'Failure of a formal designation should ... not itself defeat jurisdiction if the entity concerned is proved or conceded to be a constituent, subdivision or agency of a contracting state.'[107] Surely, this plain statement by the preeminent eyewitness to the drafting of ICSID settled the matter?

In fact, it did not. The tribunal did not accept Broches' interpretation.

Instead, the tribunal quoted, with approval, the ICSID award in *Government of the Province of East Kalimantan v. PT Kaltim Prima Coal, et al.* According to the *East Kalimantan* tribunal:

> [T]he lack of a valid designation is a bar to ... jurisdiction under the ICSID Convention. While holding so, the Tribunal is mindful of Aaron Broches' view that failure of a formal designation should ... not by itself defeat jurisdiction if the entity concerned is proved or conceded to be a constituent subdivision or agency of a contracting state.' With Christoph Schreuer, the Tribunal considers, however, that Broches' view 'goes too far' and that designation cannot be dispensed with altogether. Accepting jurisdiction in the absence of designation by the state would not be in line with the ICSID Convention, which expressly constrained the possibility for constituent subdivisions to submit to ICSID arbitration within specified limits.[108]

Here is visible a nice professional regard for the late M. Broches, together with an appropriate grounding in the text (and on the work of an accomplished later jurist). The arbitrators in two tribunals thus have done in regard to ICSID what too few jurists have in regard to the putative territorial

105 Ibid. at ¶ 171.

106 See Antonia R. Parra, 'Remembering Aron Broches,' https://oxia.ouplaw.com/page/546

107 *Cambodia Power Company* at ¶ 218, quoting A. Broches, 'Convention on the Settlement of Investment Disputes between States and Nationals of Other States of 1965, Explanatory Notes and Survey of its Application' (1993) 18 *Yearbook Commercial Arbitration* 627, 642.

108 *Government of the Province of East Kalimantan v. PT Kaltim Prima Coal, Rio Tinto PLC, BP P.L.C., Pacific Resources Investments Limited, BP International Limited, Sangatta Holdings Limited, and Kalimantan Coal Limited,* ICSID Case No. Art/07/03 (Kaufmann-Kohler, President; Hwang and van den Berg, arbitrators), Award on Jurisdiction, 28 December 2009, ¶ 201, quoting (with approval) Christoph Schreuer, *The ICSID Convention: A Commentary*, 2nd edn. (2009) (ICSID Commentary) §§ 25–252); and as quoted in *Cambodia Power Company* at ¶ 220.

exclusion of UNCLOS:[109] apply the ordinary tools of interpretation, rather than socio-legal deference to diplomats and draftsmen.[110]

The subtle effects of a 'double hat'

'Double-hatting'—the practice of jurists serving as arbitrator in certain cases and advocate in others—is another part of the social reality of international dispute settlement. It draws criticism, especially in the setting of investor–state dispute settlement.[111] The practice exists in public international dispute settlement as well. A 'double hat' was visible in *Coastal State Rights.*

Vaughan Lowe, formerly Chichele Professor of International Law at Oxford, served as arbitrator on the *Coastal State Rights* Annex VII tribunal. Professor Lowe served as advocate for Qatar in *Qatar v. United Arab Emirates* at the ICJ at the same time.[112] *Coastal State Rights* and *Qatar v. United Arab Emirates* had different parties, and the proceedings took place under

109 But see *Niko Resources (Bangladesh) Ltd. v. Bangladesh Oil Gas and Mineral Corp. (Petrobangla) and Bangladesh Petroleum Exploration and Production Co. Ltd. (BAPEX)*, ICSID Case No. ARB/10/18 (Schneider, President; McLachlan and Paulsson, members). The tribunal, discerning the facts in *Cambodia Power* to have been 'materially different,' took a more permissive approach to designation: Decision on Jurisdiction, 18 August 2013, ¶ 321. An *ad hoc* Committee declined to annul (Zuleta, President of the *ad hoc* Committee; Annacker & Ali Khan, members), Decision on Annulment, 12 October 2023, ¶ 208. Committee Member Makhdoom Ali Khan dissented and said they should have. Ali Khan thought that the tribunal had misread Schreuer (and Amerasinghe too). See Dis. Op. Makhdoom Ali Khan, ¶¶ 72, 199.

110 For a further (and vivid) example, see Myres McDougal's encomium to Sir Humphrey Waldock for 'his very special knowledge of all the circumstances attending the framing of' the VCLT in draft: (1968) 62 AJIL 1021, 1025, and for a critique Gardiner, 'The Vienna Convention Rules on Treaty Interpretation' in Hollis (ed.), *The Oxford Guide to Treaties*, 2nd edn. (2020) 459, 471. There is also a concern here to apply ordinary forensic tools. A writing by an eyewitness, where the eyewitness is not available for cross-examination, presents a problem for the adjudicator. One should ask how an adjudicator is to safeguard the parties' right to procedural justice when it allows an unanswered—and unanswerable—witness to influence its fact-finding. Thanks to Hayk Kupelyants for this point (correspondence between Professor Kupelyants and the author, 14 November 2024).

111 See, for example, in the setting of investor–state dispute settlement, see ICSID UNCITRAL Working Grp. III, Submission from the Government of Bahrain on Its Thirty-Eighth Session, ¶ 5, A/CN.9/WG.III/WP.180 (29 August 2019).

112 Ukraine in its Notification and Statement of claim on 16 September 2016 appointed Vaughan Lowe as one of the arbitrators composing the Annex VII tribunal. Lowe, in the period between having been appointed arbitrator in *Coastal State Rights* and the 21 February 2020 award in the case, also spoke as advocate for Qatar in the *Application of the CERD* case (*Qatar v. United Arab Emirates*).

different jurisdictional instruments. So no issue of formal conflict arose. However, a question that had to be addressed in the Annex VII proceedings also had to be addressed in the ICJ proceedings: what regard should an adjudicator have toward practice of other international organs?

In the role of advocate for Qatar, Lowe argued that the UAE had no legal ground to object to Qatar pursuing claims before the ICJ at the same time that Qatar was making a communication on similar matters to the CERD Committee.[113] The Court in its provisional measures order of 14 June 2019 accepted Lowe's argument and thus rejected the UAE's request for provisional measures to stop Qatar's CERD action.[114]

Jean-Pierre Cot, serving as Judge *ad hoc* in the ICJ *Qatar v. UAE* proceedings, dissented. Concern over the wider impact of Professor Lowe's argument led Judge *ad hoc* Cot to dissent. In the Judge *ad hoc*'s view, an adjudicator should have more regard than the Court did for consistency among international procedures. The judge *ad hoc* observed that 'it is not clear that it is only conflicting binding decisions that pose problems in international relations and that contradictory non-binding decisions need not be resolved or avoided' too.[115] In the judge *ad hoc*'s view, '[i]t would be too formalistic to assume that a State party … could ignore a recommendation of an *ad hoc* conciliation commission or the recommendation of the CERD Committee when it contains a conclusion that differs from any decision of the Court.'[116] Cot's warning was well placed. To ignore the systemic effects of 'a conclusion [in one organ] that differs' from a conclusion in another organ on important points of fact and law 'pose[s] problems in international relations.'

But that was no problem at all for Qatar. It was precisely to convince the Court that it could ignore what was happening at CERD that Qatar wanted. Nine months after arguing the point at the ICJ, Qatar's advocate, now in the role of arbitrator on an Annex VII tribunal, joined in adopting an award in *Coastal State Rights* that declared, in effect, that the Annex

113 *Application of the International Convention on the Elimination of All Forms of Racial Discrimination (Qatar v. United Arab Emirates)*, Vaughan Lowe (for Qatar), C/R 2019/6 (8 May 2019) pp. 21–26, ¶¶ 26–56. Among provisional measures that the UAE had requested was that the Court order Qatar 'immediately [to] withdraw its Communication to the CERD Committee.' Request for the Indication of Provisional Measures submitted by the United Arab Emirates (22 March 2019) p. 33, ¶ 74. Qatar had instituted ICJ proceedings under Article 36(1) of the Statute of the Court and Article 22 of the CERD. Qatar's communication to the CERD Committee was under Article 11 of the CERD.

114 ICJ 2019 p. 361, 370 ¶ 25.

115 Dis. Op. Judge *ad hoc* Cot, ICJ 2019 at p. 404 ¶ 9.

116 *Ibid.* at p. 405 ¶ 10.

VII tribunal could ignore what was happening at the UN General Assembly (and, for that matter, in any international body). There is a subtle, but visible, alignment between Qatar's position and that which the *Coastal State Rights* tribunal reached in regard to General Assembly practice—at a point in time when *Qatar v. UAE* remained *sub judice* and, presumably, fresh in Professor Lowe's mind.

Perhaps one concludes that the ICJ got the matter right and Judge *ad hoc* Cot got it wrong. Still, there are good reasons not to read the ICJ's provisional measures order as stating a general principle. Allowing or disallowing a party to continue proceedings in parallel in a different organ is a procedural decision and, as such, subject to all the variations in procedural rules under which different adjudicators function. But even where an adjudicator has no power to disallow proceedings in another organ, the adjudicator still might adopt an attitude toward the proceedings in the other organ: the adjudicator might ignore evidence that emerged in those proceedings, or the adjudicator might take the evidence into account. The ICJ's decision, albeit at a level of generality, suggests that the adjudicator need not take the parallel proceedings into account at all. The tribunal's disregard for decisions in other international organs finds a certain encouragement in the ICJ's decision and tends to validate it.

The point here is not to impute an intention to Professor Lowe to shape the jurisprudence in favor of a client's case. The ICJ, in any event, adopted the provisional measures order in *Qatar v. UAE* before the Annex VII tribunal adopted the preliminary objections award in *Coastal State Rights*. The hazard of a 'double hat' in this situation and others like it is found not in conscious choices but in the subtler psychology of how we judge.

A basic insight of cognitive science is that our observations, experiences, and interests influence us whether or not we give them much thought. They influence us even if letting them do so in a given setting would be irrational. Consider an experiment described by Daniel Kahneman, who won the Nobel Prize for his work on the psychology of judgment.[117] In the experiment, researchers asked people (test subjects) to say what percentage of the member states of the UN they think are countries in Africa. The researchers asked the test subjects the question after they had had them play a roulette game. The researchers had rigged the roulette game, so that the only possible outcome was the number ten or the number sixty-five. The average reply to the question what percentage of countries are in Africa was 20 percent among test subjects whose roulette ball had landed on the number ten. The average reply to the question was 45 percent among test subjects whose roulette ball had landed on the number sixty-five. So 'winning' the higher

117 www.nobelprize.org/prizes/economic-sciences/2002/kahneman/biographical/

number in a roulette game correlated to the test subjects judging that a higher percentage of countries are in Africa. If we assumed that people reason their way through questions in a purely rational way, then this result is puzzling. The result suggests that our recent experiences exercise an unconscious influence on our judgment.[118]

Did Professor Lowe's experience of winning an important contentious point for Qatar affect how he approached systemic consistency in *Coastal State Rights*? Cognitive science suggests that the question is worth asking. The rules, norms, and culture of adjudication tell us that we should not have to ask: a basic duty of the adjudicator is to manage the adjudicator's own biases and avoid prejudgment. There are settings, however, in which the basic duty is harder to perform, and others in which it is easier. Rule-of-law systems have structured their dispute settlement procedures to make it easier. International law has yet only incompletely structured its dispute settlement procedures that way, even those which address some of the most fraught disputes of our day.

Using the adjudicator's method to address the contested 'dispute'

If adjudicators take to heart the doctrinal position that the existence of a dispute is a matter for *objective* determination, then one would expect adjudicators to rely on fact evidence when they determine whether a dispute exists. When determining whether a sovereignty dispute exists, a number of adjudicators have done precisely that. After engaging with the evidence, the ECtHR concluded that no legal dispute exists as to Ukraine's sovereign title within the recognized borders of Ukraine. When the ITLOS Special Chamber was asked to say whether there was a dispute as to sovereignty over the Chagos, it did not accept that the mere declaration of an 'objective dispute' sufficed to answer the question. It follows that a future tribunal called on to consider an objection to jurisdiction similar to those which Russia and the Maldives put forward, too, should engage with the evidence. That is to say, it should properly perform its forensic function.

I addressed UNCLOS Article 288(4) in Chapter 2 and argued in Chapter 6 that the *Coastal State Rights* tribunal, in deciding Russia's jurisdictional objection without considering fact evidence, erred. Procedural provisions such as Article 288(4) do not exist in clinical isolation from adjudicative method. Instead, it is expected, when an adjudicator applies the provisions, that the adjudicator applies adjudicative method as necessary to answer the questions at hand. When a party makes a jurisdictional objection the validity

118 Kahneman, *Thinking, Fast and Slow* (2012) 67.

of which the adjudicator cannot reliably judge without inquiry into fact evidence, then fact-finding method is called into operation. A tribunal has not done enough, if it concludes that a sovereignty dispute exists and, thus, that it shall not exercise jurisdiction on grounds that a sovereignty dispute exists, but has refused to scrutinize the objecting party's assertion that a sovereignty dispute exists.

The effects of such a failure to apply adjudicative method are not isolated to one kind of alleged dispute. I suggested in Chapter 5 and in the present chapter that a party might raise a similar jurisdictional objection—that is, an objection that pleads an exorbitant claim to spatial entitlement—in respect of maritime areas as well as in respect of land. Another step in repairing the damage done by *Coastal State Rights* will be for adjudicators in a future case, if a party raises a similar jurisdictional objection, to exercise *compétence de la compétence* not as a mere formality but as an adjudicative task entailing use of the adjudicator's ordinary tools.

A riposte to my critique might say that, if the *Coastal State Rights* tribunal had followed the approach that I call for, and if the tribunal had determined that no sovereignty dispute exists, then it would have rendered an award susceptible to misreading: the parties to the case, and future parties in future cases, might read the award as having decided a question of territorial title. The prevalent view of the sovereignty exclusion under Part XV, section 2, precludes deciding territorial questions, and so, the riposte would maintain, it would be improper for tribunals to do as it has been one of my main purposes in this book to suggest that they do, for, if they were to do that, then they would give the impression that they have decided something which the prevalent view holds they have no power to decide.

I do not believe that the riposte is convincing.

Distinguishing what is decided from what is not

Adjudicators know how to mitigate the risk that the parties to a case, or future parties, might misread a judgment or award. Methods to safeguard against misreading a jurisdictional determination as a merits determination in particular are well tested. The methods are familiar in judicial practice, but, as the *Coastal State Rights* tribunal did not use them, they deserve to be recalled.

Judges and arbitrators frequently draw attention to the limited purposes of the conclusions that they reach. This is a tool that adjudicators use when a given thing that they must reach a conclusion about is difficult to separate from another thing that they must *not* reach a conclusion about. Adjudicators no doubt at times go too far with their limitive declarations. 'We chop logic, we split hairs, we distinguish the indistinguishable,' Grant

Gilmore lamented over a half century ago.[119] However, refusing to distinguish the act of determining the scope of a tribunal's jurisdiction from the act of determining the merits of a factual or legal assertion for general purposes in the relations between the parties is to go too far the other way. A tribunal reaching conclusions in order to determine the scope of its own jurisdiction is not hair-splitting when it draws attention to the limited purpose that those conclusions serve. When, as Russia did, a party objecting to jurisdiction has itself declared that, '[i]nsofar as certain matters of a factual nature are referred to herein, this is done solely for the purpose of [the objecting party's] contentions on jurisdiction,'[120] the door is open for the tribunal to use precisely this method of distinction.[121]

Not only is the distinction between jurisdictional determination and merits determination available; it is necessary that adjudicators apply it. Sometimes, to reach a jurisdictional determination, a tribunal must scrutinize assertions by a party that are intertwined with the merits of the case. In *Dispute Concerning the Detention of Ukrainian Naval Vessels and Servicemen*, the Annex VII tribunal had no difficulty determining that it 'needs further elucidation by the Parties before reaching a definitive conclusion on when military activities came to an end' and, thus, postponed its decision on that jurisdictional question to the merits.[122] Tribunals have no trouble postponing the jurisdictional determination in such circumstances to the merits. They do not declare that they are unable to reach a jurisdictional determination. Instead, they rely on a formal distinction: determining the limits of their

119 Gilmore, 'Legal Realism' (1961) 70 YLJ 1037, 1042. There was also Thomas Reed Powell, who reportedly told his students, 'If you can think about something attached to something else, without thinking about what it's attached to ... you have the mind of a lawyer.' Reisman, *The Quest for World Order and Human Dignity in the Twenty-first Century: Constitutive Process and Individual Commitment* (2013) at 39–40, citing William H. Simon, '"Thinking Like a Lawyer" about Ethical Questions' (1998) 27 *Hofstra Law Review* 1, 4.

120 *Coastal State Rights*, Preliminary Objections of the Russian Federation (19 May 2018) at ¶ 9.

121 It remains an undertheorized question, precisely how the factual character of a question affects the exercise of competence by an adjudicator to determine the question as a matter ancillary or incidental to the adjudicator's 'primary' jurisdiction, but decided cases, as noted, indicate that determining the question is part of the adjudicator's function. Ben Love, among the six questions that he identifies as arising when adjudicators consider incidental questions, includes the following: 'Do the answers to these questions differ when the incidental question is one of international law, domestic law, or fact?' Love, 'Jurisdiction Over Incidental Questions in International Law' (2017) 111 ASIL Proc. at 321.

122 *Dispute Concerning the Detention of Ukrainian Naval Vessels and Servicemen*, Annex VII Tribunal (McRae, President; Eiriksson, Wolfrum, Golitsyn, and Greenwood, arbitrators), Award on Preliminary Objections, ¶ 125 (27 June 2022).

own merits jurisdiction is not the same thing as determining the merits of the parties' claims.

As Judge Shahabuddeen observed, in regard to fact evidence that a court appraises in order to determine whether to grant provisional measures, 'the craft of the judge accustoms him to make such an appraisal for ... limited purposes ... without incurring a risk of prejudgment of the merits.'[123] So, too, have ITLOS judges, as in *M/V 'Saiga,'* recognized that an adjudicator, by exercising 'restraint,' enables itself to consider 'the aspects of the merits it deems necessary in order to reach its decision' on a different question. The different question there was whether to grant prompt release. Whether to grant prompt release fell to be decided before 'a case concerning the merits of the situation that led to the arrest of the M/V *'Saiga'* had been submitted.[124] Much the same may be said about fact evidence adduced to determine whether a sovereignty dispute exists, and, equally, a tribunal may consider such evidence without 'incurring a risk' of trespass into merits questions that the tribunal lacks jurisdiction to settle. As it is open to a party to raise 'certain matters of a factual nature ... solely for the purpose of contentions on jurisdiction,' so is it open to the tribunal to scrutinize those 'matters' solely for the purpose of settling the contentions.

Even where a tribunal did not make clear that it addressed a particular matter only for limited purposes, judges and arbitrators in later cases know full well to clarify the limits. Indeed, it is the duty of judges and arbitrators to read the earlier decision in a way that confines its holdings to what the earlier decision-maker decided. This is another axiom that law professors have taught their students for generations, an axiom that forms one of the 'first presuppositions of [your] study' as a lawyer and which 'must be rutted into you till you can juggle with [it] standing on your head and in your sleep':[125] '[e]verything ... big or small, a judge may say in an opinion, is to be read with primary reference to the particular dispute, the particular question before him.'[126] The doctrinal rule of *non ultra petita* is visible here, but the insight about legal method is necessary if we are to give the doctrine

123 *Genocide case (Bosnia and Herzegovina v. Yugoslavia (Serbia and Montenegro))*, Further Requests for the Indication of Provisional Measures, Sep. Op. Judge Shahabuddeen, ICJ 1993 p. 353, p. 359 (13 September).

124 *M/V 'Saiga,'* Prompt Release, Judgment, ITLOS 1997 p. 16, p. 27 ¶ 50 (4 December). See comment by Ferrara, 'Article 292' in *Proelss Commentary* (2017) 1892.

125 Karl N. Llewellyn, *The Bramble Bush: On Our Law and Its Study* (2012; original, self-published, 1930) 42.

126 *Ibid.* at 43. Llewellyn's observation is not confined to American law. The *non ultra petita* principle, noted above, is homologous to it and is one of general application by international courts and tribunals, a point noted in the examples that I gave in Chapter 4 p. 145 n. 41; see also Chapter 2, p. 85 n. 131, p. 97 n. 170.

life in practice. The proper method of reading an opinion remains the method all the way through a lawyer's professional life, including when the lawyer serves as decision-maker. Thus, when confronted with a statement which, taken in isolation, might appear to settle some question that was *not* before the judge in the earlier case, the judge in the later case shall read it only with reference to the 'particular dispute, the particular question' that the earlier judge had been called on to decide. The later judge will point out that the earlier judge addressed the matter only for the limited and permissible purposes necessary to the earlier judge's decision.

It is less than model drafting when a judgment or award contains an ambiguity that a future party might exploit, but it is not the role of judges and arbitrators to render their decisions airtight against every conceivable abuse, however implausible. Ample safeguards exist—both in the proceeding itself and in future proceedings—to prevent a factual or legal determination from affecting legal relations that it was not proper for the tribunal to affect.

Exercising restraint regarding legal relations not placed in question in the dispute

It might be contended that this methodological approach—distinguishing what the tribunal has decided from what it has not—applies equally to the award that the *Coastal State Rights* tribunal in reality adopted as it would apply to a hypothetical award in which, unlike in the adopted award, the arbitrators had *rejected* Russia's jurisdictional objection. It might be contended, in short, that any effect that the *Coastal State Rights* tribunal caused by having held that a dispute exists in respect of sovereignty over Crimea is no greater than the effect that the tribunal *would have* caused if it had it held that no such dispute exists. After all, the limiting tool that I described immediately above and the axiom that everything in a decision must be read with reference to the dispute which the judge or arbitrator properly settled apply both ways.

A number of reflections may be offered in reply.

First, the adjudicator's method that I addressed above—distinguishing what the adjudicator has decided from what it has not—gives future adjudicators no help if they seek to correct the unfortunate decision in *Coastal State Rights* that a sovereignty dispute exists in respect of Crimea. The *Coastal State Rights* tribunal was clear that, on its interpretation of UNCLOS Part XV, section 2, it had to decide whether a sovereignty dispute exists, and it was clear that it decided.

Second, the premise is flawed that the opposite holding—that is, a holding that there is no dispute regarding sovereignty—would have had as much effect on the parties' juristic interests as the holding that the tribunal in fact adopted. Disallowing the objection to jurisdiction in the Annex VII proceedings would not have deprived Russia of any procedural opportunity that Russia otherwise would have had in binding and compulsory dispute settlement. This is because under no jurisdictional argument would it have been open to Russia to seek a merits award in regard to sovereignty over Crimea in the *Coastal State Rights* proceedings. Indeed, Russia did not ask for a merits award on sovereignty, knowing full well that no jurisdictional argument existed to bring the matter within the tribunal's merits jurisdiction. The international law substance of Russia's position would not have changed either. A decision of the tribunal finding that no legal dispute exists would have left Russia as the armed occupier of part of Ukraine. Ousting maritime claims that Ukraine had advanced, by contrast, deprived Ukraine a forum in which Ukraine had a jurisdictional argument for pursuing its claims, its claims having been legal claims under UNCLOS. So the Annex VII tribunal's conclusion—that is, the conclusion that Russia's assertions about Crimea ousted jurisdiction—did not affect Russia and Ukraine equally as a matter of international dispute settlement procedure or international law substance. The effect of the conclusion was asymmetric, and Ukraine bore the brunt of it.

The tribunal gave the appearance of restraint regarding the parties' legal relations but, on reflection, we see that the appearance was illusory. Having refused to engage with the factual assertions that underlay the jurisdictional objection, the tribunal arrived at the conclusion that does more to affect the legal relations of the parties and less to maintain the restraint incumbent on an adjudicator under a limited jurisdictional instrument in a procedure bounded by the parties' substantive claims.

It is a basic error for a dispute settlement organ to say that declaring a legal dispute to exist is a legally neutral act. Law is a system of articulating and settling claims. As I recalled in Chapter 6,[127] claim has particular importance in international law. Whether under international law or domestic law, when a judge or arbitrator says that a claim has legal existence, the judge or arbitrator necessarily implies that the claim has legal effects, is articulable in legal terms, and is susceptible to legal settlement. When a decision-maker concludes that a claim has no legal existence, this leaves the matter outside the dispute settlement process not only in the mechanistic sense that the apparatus of dispute settlement cannot settle the claim but also in the comprehensive sense that the law has nothing to say about it. Some claims are inadmissible or non-justiciable. Others are nullities. Imbuing

127 See pp. 190–192.

such claims with legal life, an adjudicator fails to observe the restraint that parties expect.

Keeping the audience in mind

Even if one thinks that the *Coastal State Rights* tribunal observed due restraint in its approach to the parties' legal relations (I think it did not), there is still to ask how its award affected the audiences who read it.

To bring a legal dispute settlement procedure into operation in respect of a difference between two parties, declaring a legal dispute to exist is the necessary first step. Following the declaration that a legal dispute exists, a sequence of procedural incidents may begin, and a sequence of legal reasoning necessarily begins. The procedural sequence will begin if a party pursues an available procedure.[128] Legal reasoning begins, whether or not a formal machinery of dispute settlement is activated, because the declaratory act of saying that a dispute is legal has many audiences, and, in international affairs, to say with authority that a legal dispute exists over any matter of consequence to a state almost inevitably sets in motion policy-making processes in other states. The declaration that a legal dispute exists in respect of Crimea intruded the decision-maker into the subject matter more than a declaration would have done that either said nothing about the putative dispute or said that it does not exist.

On limited information, we do not know what factors convinced Russia in February 2022 to escalate its aggression against Ukraine, bringing about the largest and bloodiest land war in Europe and one of the costliest in human terms anywhere in the world since 1945, but we may venture that the *Coastal State Rights* award, accepting as it did that a legal claim over Ukrainian territory had emerged in 2014 without evidence

128 Examples include a prosecution pursued by public authorities after an indictment; a claim pursued by a private party after a court of first instance rules against preliminary objections, such as those a defendant makes in a US district court under US Federal Rule 12(b)(6); a claim pursued by an investor after an ICSID tribunal dismisses preliminary objections, including the (seldom-dispositive but available) objection of manifest lack of merit under ICSID Rule 41 (2022 ICSID Arbitration Rules); an application that proceeds at the ECtHR after surviving the 'manifestly ill-founded' test set out in Article 35 sec. 3 of the European Convention; or in English court under the 'reasonable prospect of success' assessment in, e.g., Civil Procedure Rules 6.37(1)(b), or, for that matter, after the ICJ, under Article 79 of the Rules of Court of 14 April 1978 has 'consider[ed] the questions of law and fact that are relevant to [an] objection to its jurisdiction': *Application of the International Convention for the Suppression of the Financing of Terrorism and of the International Convention on the Elimination of All Forms of Racial Discrimination (Ukraine v. Russian Federation)*, Preliminary Objections, ICJ 2019 p. 558, 584 ¶ 58.

other than the fact of Russia's armed occupation, did nothing to dissuade Russia from escalating. One is reminded of Indonesia's intransigence after the ICJ's rejection on jurisdictional grounds of Portugal's claims in *East Timor*.[129]

One is reminded as well of international law as expounded in Russia. G. I. Tunkin, the preeminent Soviet international law publicist, said over a half century ago that '[e]ach State strives to have the principles of its foreign policy reflected and secured as fully as possible in norms of international law which are in the course of being elaborated.'[130] It would be surprising if nobody in Russia read the 2020 award to mean that armed force eventually shapes law, and, if using further force, Russia would eventually pull the law in train to its territorial aims. For a state to go from having no international claim that anybody recognized to having a high-profile treaty tribunal declare that it does have a claim surely places the 'principles of its foreign policy' that animate that claim firmly on 'the course of being elaborated' as law. In its October 2022 Counter-Memorial (that I quoted at the start of Chapter 6),[131] the Russian legal team well nigh demanded that the Annex VII tribunal 'elaborate' as law the subsequent expansion of Russia's 'foreign policy': they pleaded to the tribunal that it attribute jurisdictional preclusive effects to Russia's forcible seizure of three further Ukrainian provinces.

Evidence is available that adjudicators influence strategic-political decisions. Mauritius' decision to pursue an advisory request in the General Assembly offers a case in point. According to one of Mauritius' legal advisors, the outcome in *Chagos Marine Protected Area*, including the separate opinion of Judges Kateka and Wolfrum, 'put diplomatic wind in Mauritius' sails.'[132] In respect of the Chagos, though a situation with none of the sanguinary character of Russia's use of force against Ukraine, one adjudicative outcome seems to have had effect on a later political choice.[133]

Legal advisors, who are the officers in government likely to read international judgments and awards the most closely, exercise influence, even if their influence varies from country to country and from one matter to another. Canadian jurist Ronald St. John Macdonald suggested that 'the legal advising process [in a government] is apt to be most ineffective during

129 See above p. 268.

130 Tunkin, *Theory of International Law* (Butler, trans.) (1974) 273.

131 PCA Case No. 2017–06, Counter-Memorial of the Russian Federation, 14 October 2022, p. 6 ¶ 28.

132 See Guilfoyle, 'The Chagos Archipelago before International Tribunals' (2021) 21 Melbourne JIL 749, 760.

133 I.e., the choice to pursue further legal steps, including an advisory request in the General Assembly.

crisis situations.'[134] Yet Professor Macdonald, referring to Abram Chayes' experience as US Department of State Legal Adviser during the Cuban Missile Crisis, suggested that legal advisors influence statecraft even in fraught circumstances.[135] True, Macdonald was considering the experience of legal advisors in democratic countries.[136] Their experience might not tell us much about a state that functions under very different political controls, bureaucratic arrangements, and legal constraints. Still, even a country that does not seek to validate its contemplated actions for purposes of internal checks and balances does seek reliably to forecast whether those actions will meet with opposition, acquiescence, or approval abroad.[137]

International law does not only, or even primarily, develop in formal proceedings. Political decisions and diplomatic communication exercise important effects on international law. The rigor inherent in judicial reasoning that confines results in a court judgment to the subject matter of the case is often relaxed in the settings where policymakers and diplomats receive, interpret, and draw conclusions from the judgment. It is not for adjudicators to cast nervous glances outside the courtroom while they are hearing and deciding a case, but if a legal procedure is to serve any social purpose, then it is outside the courtroom that it does so.

Having accepted that Russia's assertion of a sovereignty dispute constitutes a legal claim, the arbitrators in *Coastal State Rights* misapplied the formal rules under which Annex VII proceedings take place. They also failed to take account of the integrity of the public order that their decision necessarily would affect. The arbitrators accepted that Russia at least *might* have the authority to prescribe a new territorial disposition in Crimea—and thus took a significant step toward prescription.[138] This result is all the more

134 R. St. J. Macdonald, *The Role of the Legal Adviser of Ministries of Foreign Affairs* (1977) 154 Hag. Rec. 381, 411.

135 *Ibid.* at 411–412, citing Abram Chayes, *The Cuban Missile Crisis* (1974) 45, 102, 106.

136 Macdonald's Hague Lecture considered the legal advisory process in Austria, Canada, West Germany, Japan, the Netherlands, Nigeria, Sweden, Switzerland, the UK, and the USA. *Ibid.* at 414–453.

137 As the late Professor d'Amato said, states seek 'to be legal and thus ward off disapproval of other states': D'Amato, *International Law: Process and Prospect* (1987) 11.

138 As Professor Reisman said, in classic New Haven School terms: 'Augustine remarked that a bandit is a little king and a king a big bandit. There is an important difference, in addition to size. What is missing in the thugs' enactment is … the authority signal, a communication which attends the communication of policy content and control intention and which indicates to the relevant audience that the communicators are the appropriate lawmakers or, in the more functional terms, have the authority to

lamentable when we consider that well-tested legal methods allowed the tribunal to take a different course.

A postscript to *Coastal State Rights*?

Finally, a brief word is in order about a possible postscript to *Coastal State Rights* and how the Annex VII tribunal in the case might itself, at least to a degree, contribute to repairing the damage—but also how it might yet do more harm.

The principle of non-aggravation is one of general international law. Chapter 4 considered how UNCLOS jurisdiction under Part XV, section 2, can be applied to deter conduct in disputed maritime areas that might give rise to friction or even armed incidents between parties. Chapter 4 also noted that UNCLOS, in Articles 74(3) and 83(3), reflects the principle of non-aggravation.[139] The principle of non-aggravation might be the last safe harbor for Ukraine in the final phase of *Coastal State Rights*, though 'safe' only in a relative sense.

If, *quod non*, Ukraine were to accept (as in the confines of the proceedings Ukraine must) that a 'dispute' exists as to sovereignty in Crimea, then, as the applicant state, Ukraine might request an award barring Russia from any activities in the appurtenant maritime areas, on the grounds that activities in those areas, pending settlement of the 'dispute,' aggravate the friction between the parties. Ukraine might make the request with reference to Articles 74(3) and 83(3) of UNCLOS, which, to recall the text, require parties pending a delimitation agreement to 'make every effort ... not to jeopardize or hamper the reaching of the final agreement.' It is arguable that those provisions are not applicable to Ukraine's situation. They are provisions relevant where a delimitation is pending. A BIICL research team studied state practice in respect of Articles 74(3) and 83(3) during 2015–2016, and it concluded that '[c]ases where the maritime boundary dispute is generated *solely* by a sovereignty dispute are not relevant.'[140] Others, however, have suggested that Articles 74(3) and 83(3) indeed might be applied in

prescribe.' Reisman, 'International Lawmaking: A Process of Communication: The Harold D. Lasswell Memorial Lecture' (1981) 75 ASIL Proc. 101, 110. The passage in St. Augustine that Reisman paraphrased was book iv, chapter 4, in *City of God against the Pagans*.

139 See further Milano & Papanicolopulu (2011) at 611–621.

140 Barrett, Burke, Musto, Anderson, Churchill, Nishimoto, & Seta, *Article 74(3) and 83(3) of UNCLOS in respect of Undelimited Maritime Areas* (2016), p. 4, ¶ 21 (emphasis original). See esp. Dr. Nishimoto's observation, *ibid.* at p. 172 ¶ 30.

respect of maritime areas appurtenant to land that an adjudicator understands to be subject to a legal dispute.[141]

A nuanced approach where a maritime area is affected by a concomitant territorial dispute would be to draw attention to the general principle of non-aggravation, Articles 74(3) and 83(3) being instantiations thereof, not its only loci. Milano and Papanicolopulu suggest that the two UNCLOS provisions in this way might apply across the maritime and land domains:

> [T]he importance of Art. 74 para 3 UNCLOS and Art. 83 para. 3 UNCLOS cannot be overstressed: their role as guiding principles and their transversal applicability may be very helpful in determining issues of State responsibility. Their relevance, furthermore, extends beyond maritime boundary disputes since, arguably, the obligation not to hamper or jeopardise the final settlement of the dispute endorses a general principle of due diligence that might be applied to land disputes as well ... [T]o that extent, cross-fertilisation between the law of maritime delimitation and the law of territory could be enhanced.

Further in support of applying Articles 74(3) and 83(3), one might argue that the two provisions are not limited by reference to what difference between the parties has intervened to delay their 'agreement ... to achieve an equitable solution.' A land territory dispute might be the intervening difference. Or so one might argue.

Adjudicators in recent years have held a range of conduct *not* to trespass the 'make every effort ... not to jeopardize or hamper' obligation. *Ghana/Côte d'Ivoire* and *Somalia v. Kenya* are examples.[142] The conduct involved in those cases, however, was considerably more restrained than Russia's.

One of the Annex VII arbitrators in *Coastal State Rights,* Vaughan Lowe, whose role as advocate in *Qatar v. United Arab Emirates* I addressed earlier, has suggested (in academic capacity) that the adjudicators in *Guyana v. Suriname* and in *Ghana/Côte d'Ivoire* were too parsimonious and should have held the conduct there in question to have constituted aggravation.[143] If the conduct in those cases was aggravation, then Russia's conduct necessarily is as well.

As suggested, a difficulty is that common paragraph (3) of Articles 74 and 83 links both provisions to the search for agreement about delimitation.

141 See, for example, Logchem (2021) 244–246.

142 *Delimitation of the Maritime Boundary between Ghana and Côte d'Ivoire (Ghana/Côte d'Ivoire)*, ITLOS 2017 p. 4, p. 169 ¶ 634; p. 175 ¶ 660 (23 September); *Maritime Delimitation in the Indian Ocean (Somalia v. Kenya)*, ICJ 2021 p. 206, p. 283 ¶¶ 211–212 (12 October).

143 See Churchill, Lowe, & Sander (2022) 359–360. As to the latter case, see generally McCreath & Scanlon, 'Delimitation of the Maritime Boundary between Ghana and Côte d'Ivoire (2019) 50 ODIL 1–22.

A weakness in invoking Articles 74(3) and 83(3) is that those provisions do not embrace the situation concerned: the parties are not searching for agreement, much less requesting a delimitation or planning to negotiate one. The tribunal would ask how Ukraine's maritime claims have anything to do with Article 74(3) or Article 83(3).[144]

One might observe, in rebuttal, that the principle of non-aggravation did not have its start in UNCLOS. It is, as noted, a general principle, and courts and tribunals have applied it in diverse situations.[145] In the *South China Sea Arbitration*, the Annex VII tribunal applied the general principle where no question of delimitation was involved.[146] The *South China Sea* Annex VII tribunal referred to Articles 279, 296, and 300 of the Convention, 'as well as ... general international law,' when it declared that China 'breached its obligations ... not to allow any step of any kind to be taken which might aggravate or extend the dispute during such time as dispute resolution proceedings were ongoing.'[147] On these terms, the tribunal's application of the principle of non-aggravation would appear to be connected with—and, seemingly, limited to—powers that an adjudicator exercises during proceedings to ensure their orderly conduct.[148]

As concerns Ukraine, a declaration calling on Russia not to aggravate a dispute would do nothing to repair the harm done. However, in the posture that the *Coastal State Rights* tribunal has placed the matter, that might be the most that the applicant state gets.

And the applicant state should proceed with care before asking for it. A final award that is based on the conclusion that a legal dispute exists in respect of the maritime area has the corollary that settlement of the matter is to be by pacific means. That, at any rate, is what one might say on application of UNCLOS Article 279 and UN Charter Articles 2(3) and 33(1). Ukraine's aims in its war of national self-defense would not be well served by a decided case in which UNCLOS arbitrators maintain, by necessary

144 See *Coastal State Rights*, Award, ¶ 9 (reciting Ukraine's claims).

145 See, for example, *Electricity Company of Sofia and Bulgaria (Belg. v. Bulg.)*, Interim Measures of Protection, Order, 1939 PCIJ Ser. A/B No. 79 at 199 (5 December); *South China Sea Arbitration*, Award of 12 July 2016 (Merits), ¶¶ 1169–1170; Campolieti, 'The Rule of Non-aggravation of the Dispute in ICSID Arbitration Practice' (2015) 30(1) *ICSID Review—Foreign Investment Law Journal* 217, 217–30. Cf. *Ghana/Côte d'Ivoire*, Provisional Measures, Order, ITLOS 2015 p. 146, p. 166 ¶ 108(1)(e) (25 April).

146 *South China Sea*, Award, 12 July 2016, ¶ 1203(B)(16)(d), (e), (f), (g).

147 *Ibid.* ¶ 1203, final unlettered subpara.

148 International law scholars might ask on this point whether the principle of non-aggravation emerges from inherent procedural powers of an adjudicator or, instead, is a part of general international law that the adjudicator shall apply in order to perform its functions as a participant in the wider processes public order.

implication, that the restoration of sovereignty over Crimea, or at least the restoration of maritime entitlements in the appurtenant seas, is to be pursued only in court or through negotiation.[149] A party is well advised to think carefully before bringing a case or requesting a remedy that not only faces the usual risk that it will fail on its own terms but that, further, whether it 'succeeds' or fails might impose new legal *impedimenta* upon the party's interests.

Another risk in tribunals applying the principle of non-aggravation in cases such as *Coastal State Rights* is that it might invite abuse. Consider a party that advances a spurious 'sovereignty dispute' with the goal in mind of obtaining an award that calls for non-aggravation. If a tribunal granted such an award in those circumstances, then the award would prevent the other party from exploiting its own maritime entitlement. In other words, the state willing to engage in a zero-sum game against a neighbor would instigate a 'dispute' and invoke non-aggravation for its spoiling effect. This is no tolerable result for a given adjudication or for the law of the sea at large. The wiser path is that which applies the dispute settlement function as the parties agreed to it and does not accept an objecting party's assertion of a sovereignty dispute where appropriate scrutiny would show none exists.

149 Recall that academic writers have gone so far as to suggest that, even where it is common ground that the territory is under armed occupation by another state, the state that has legal title to the territory, after a time, no longer has a right to use force in self-defense to recover it. See Chapter 1, pp. 40–41 n. 74.

Conclusion

Sir Robert Jennings, commenting in 1989 on the proceedings of the 23rd Annual Conference of the Law of the Sea Institute, suggested that questions of title and boundaries in territorial disputes are to be addressed differently from questions of entitlement and boundaries in maritime disputes.[1] In itself, this was not to say that the difference between the terrestrial and maritime questions would affect the competence of a tribunal. The ICJ has addressed land and maritime questions concurrently.[2] Its competence to do so depends on the jurisdictional instrument, not on differences (or similarities) in the analytic methods that the merits questions arising in a given case call for it to employ.[3] UNCLOS tribunals, too, have addressed a range of different questions. Questions of prompt release, immunities of a warship, use of force, the existence of islands, the sustainability of 'economic life' on an island—these are addressed differently from maritime boundary disputes. All of these are addressed differently from state responsibility for sponsoring activities on the deep seabed or from questions of human rights. Yet tribunals under UNCLOS have addressed such questions as well.

Jurists sometimes mention the proliferation of dispute settlement mechanisms as a reflection of the fragmentation of international law.[4] Thus, for example, it might be that the multiple mechanisms to which parties can

1 Sir Robert Jennings, 'Commentary,' Proceedings of the 23rd Annual Conference of the Law of the Sea Institute, Soons (ed.) (1990) 656.

2 For example, *Territorial and Maritime Dispute (Nicaragua v. Colombia)*, Preliminary Objections, Judgment, ICJ 2007 p. 832; Judgment, ICJ 2012 p. 624; *Land and Maritime Boundary between Cameroon and Nigeria (Cameroon* v. *Nigeria: Equatorial Guinea intervening)*, Judgment, ICJ 2002 p. 303.

3 As to some of the differences, see Oxman, 'Offshore Features Subject to Claims of Sovereignty' in Jayakumar, Koh, & Beckman (eds.) (2014) 8, 10–12.

4 See Martti Koskenniemi (Study Group Chairman), *Fragmentation of International Law: Difficulties arising from the diversification and expansion of international law. Report of the Study Group*, 18 July 2006, Conclusion (28), A/CN.4/L.702, p. 19; and the accompanying *Analytical Study*, 13 April 2006, ¶ 10, A/CN.4/L.682, pp. 12–13.

bring disputes concerning the environment casts doubt on the existence of an 'international environmental law,' or at least on the descriptive purpose in referring to such a law;[5] the development of human rights under regional treaties and their courts might do the same in respect of the concept of 'international human rights.'[6] The differences that distinguish investment arbitration from commercial arbitration and both from dispute settlement under the WTO suggest further divisions.[7] Irina Buga in 2015 mentioned fragmentation specifically in the relationship between UNCLOS and other legal régimes.[8]

International dispute settlement is not, however, an unrelieved landscape of fragments. It might be supposed in view of the long experience of tribunals with land and maritime disputes that questions of territorial sovereignty and questions of maritime entitlement do not belong to entirely separate domains of law. They demonstrably are not so far apart that their settlement under the same apparatus should be excluded as a matter of policy. Judges and arbitrators know how to deal with both together and have done so in a number of cases. From a functional standpoint, the importance of the state's spatial limits to practically all else in international law, and the close connection between territorial sovereignty and maritime entitlement, speak in favor of caution before one clinically separates the land from the sea.

The judge or arbitrator's jurisdictional mandate is the necessary starting point in every case. When applying UNCLOS Part XV, section 2, the court or tribunal must ask whether the dispute submitted to it belongs to a category of disputes indicated in the jurisdictional provision. The assertion has come

5 Boyle & Harrison, 'Judicial Settlement of International Environmental Disputes' (2013) 4 JIDS 245.

6 See, for example, Schreuer, 'Regionalism v. Universalism' (1995) 6 EJIL 477, 485–487. Not to mention the potential of human rights questions to arise under yet other dispute settlement mechanisms, such as investment arbitration: Simma, 'A Place for Human Rights?' (2011) 60 ICLQ 573; or WTO dispute settlement: Hilpold, 'Human Rights and WTO Law' (2007) 45 AdV 485.

7 See, for example, Roberts, 'Clash of Paradigms' (2013) 107 AJIL 45; Pauwelyn, 'The Role of Public International Law in the WTO' (2001) 95 AJIL 535. Cf. Shaffer & Waibel, 'The (Mis)alignment of the Trade and Monetary Orders,' in Halliday & Shaffer (eds.), *Transnational Legal Orders* (2015) 187–230. And the divisions are noted within particular fields as well: see Waibel, 'Coordinating Adjudication Processes' in Douglas, Pauwelyn, & Viñuales (eds.), *The Foundations of International Investment Law* (2014), 499. Bt cf. Alford. 'The Convergence of International Trade and Investment Arbitration' (2014) 12 *Santa Clara Journal of International Law* 35; Schill, 'W(h)ither Fragmentation? On the Literature and Sociology of International Investment Law' (2011) 22 EJIL 875, 883–884, 887–890; McLachlan, 'Investment Treaties and General International Law' (2008) 57 ICLQ 361.

8 Buga, 'Subsequent Practice, Treaty Modification, and Regime Interaction' in Rothwell et al. (eds.), *The Oxford Handbook of the Law of the Sea* (2015) 46, 60–61, 68.

to be widely accepted that territorial issues, even though closely connected to maritime issues, do not belong to any Part XV, section 2, category. This seemingly received view rests on shaky ground. In light of the considerations that I have set out in this book, there are no convincing formal reasons that a court or tribunal must accept a categorical exclusion of territorial issues from UNCLOS jurisdiction. The territorial exclusion in UNCLOS is a narrow one, and its expression in narrow terms was deliberate. The drafters were free to express a general exclusion of disputes regarding sovereignty, if they so chose. The text, context, and negotiating history reflect that they did not.

The Convention was not drafted in a vacuum. When international lawyers observe that '[t]he 1982 Convention ... is a product of its time,'[9] they especially have in mind the stage of development that the rules of the law of the sea had reached at that time. Particularly influential in producing the text that states eventually adopted was the stage of development of the rules defining the permissible scope of national claims to maritime entitlement.[10] However, the ebb and flow of international relations at large produced effects as well, and the drafting reflects them. Albeit in less obvious ways than its expression of particular emergent rules, the adopted text is a product of the geopolitical environment in which international law developed after 1945, and of the assumptions, opportunities, and limits that the environment embodied. A key assumption was that armed aggression no longer may change a settled boundary between states. From that assumption, far more opportunities than limits for international law emerged. To question the assumption is to weaken the foundation on which the law of the sea and much else in international law depends.

The unhappy award

Whether or not Tolstoy was right when he said, 'Happy families are all alike; every unhappy family is unhappy in its own way,'[11] and whether or

9 Scobbie, 'Series Editor's Foreword' in Churchill, Lowe, & Sander, *The Law of the Sea*, 4th edn. (2022) xiv.

10 The *Maritime Dispute case* between Peru and Chile was one in which the stage of development of the rules of the law of the sea was particularly salient. See *Maritime Dispute (Peru* v. *Chile)*, ICJ 2014 p. 3 at pp. 45–47 ¶¶ 112–117; pp. 53–54 ¶¶ 134–135.

11 ['Все счастливые семьи похожи друг на друга, каждая несчастливая семья несчастл ива по-своему.'] Leo Tolstoy, *Anna Karenina* 3 (Constance Garnette trans., 1939) (original in Russian, 1878). It is a favored quotation in family law cases: see, e.g., *Pecore v. Pecore*, 2007 Supreme Court of Canada 17, 2007 CarswellOnt 2752 (S.Ct. Canada), ¶ [77] (Abella J.); *In re Estate of Anna Cantore*, 814 A.2d 331 (S.Ct. of Rhode Island, 22 January 2003). Nowhere near as popular as Humpty Dumpty's

not good legal decisions and every bad one partake of a similar contrast, the infelicities in the award of 21 February 2020 in the *Coastal State Rights* case merit careful reflection. The overarching defect of the 21 February 2020 award in *Coastal State Rights*, which frustrated Ukraine's purpose in instituting proceedings against Russia in 2016,[12] was the tribunal's acceptance that a legal dispute exists in regard to sovereignty over Crimea, a part of Ukraine which Russia purported in 2014 to annex and at that time and since has deployed armed forces effectively to control. The award's defect is clothed in formalism, including approving reference to recent UNCLOS jurisprudence, in particular to the Annex VII award of 2015 in *Mauritius v. United Kingdom*. According to that jurisprudence, as applied in *Coastal State Rights*, adjudicators under UNCLOS Part XV, section 2, are not empowered to decide claims, where the claims 'necessarily involve [...] the concurrent consideration of any unsettled dispute concerning sovereignty or other rights over continental or insular land territory.' Having found that an 'unsettled dispute' exists in the relevant sense in regard to Crimea, the *Coastal State Rights* tribunal further found that a significant part of Ukraine's claims concerning the maritime areas appurtenant to Crimea 'necessarily involve[d]' that putative dispute. On that basis, the tribunal concluded that it had 'no jurisdiction over Ukraine's claims, to the extent that a ruling of the Arbitral Tribunal on the merits of Ukraine's claims necessarily requires it to decide, directly or implicitly, on the sovereignty of either Party over Crimea.'[13]

Some academic writers have welcomed the 2020 *Coastal State Rights* award,[14] which is perhaps a compliment to the formalism. But one wonders whether every note of approval is necessarily about the award as such. Approval of the 2020 *Coastal State Rights* award might instead reflect *disapproval* of incipient trends elsewhere. In particular, there is the ICJ's judgment in the *Marshall Islands* nuclear cases in 2016. The Marshall Islands had asserted that it was in dispute with India, Pakistan, and the United Kingdom in respect of the obligation under Article VI of the Treaty on the Non-proliferation of Nuclear Weapons to 'pursue negotiations' toward

reflections on the open texture of the English language, the records of the ICJ reflect one reference to Tolstoy's 'unhappy family,' that by Mr. Mendelson (for Cameroon) in *Land and Maritime Boundary between Cameroon and Nigeria (Cameroon v. Nigeria: Equatorial Guinea intervening)*, C.R. 2002/6 p. 51 ¶ 16 (public sitting of 25 February 2002, 10 am).

12 By application dated 16 September 2016.

13 *Coastal State Rights*, Award of 21 February 2020, ¶ 492(a).

14 For example, Schatz, 'Status of Crimea and the Sea of Azov,' *EJIL Talk!* (20 March 2020), as to whose observations see above Chapter 6, pp. 204–205.

eventual nuclear disarmament.[15] Considering the matter in the round, the ICJ determined that no dispute existed between the Marshall Islands and any of those states. Embracing the 'objective' approach to the question whether a dispute exists, the Annex VII tribunal in *Coastal State Rights* found that a dispute *does* exist in respect of sovereignty in Crimea. Writers who worry that the ICJ had gone too far in tightening the dispute requirement might take comfort in the arbitrators' approach in *Coastal State Rights* to identifying a sovereignty dispute, an approach which was at least as lax as the ICJ's in *Marshall Islands* was stringent.

There is no small irony if one holds *Coastal State Rights* to be the antidote to *Marshall Islands*. The legal effect of the finding in *Coastal State Rights* is much the same as the legal effect of the finding in *Marshall Islands*: the decision-makers' answer to the question whether a dispute exists, though affirmative in the one case and negative in the other, in both was an exercise of avoidance, for, in both, the answer given required (or, in *Coastal State Rights*, was said to require), in turn, that the dispute settlement organ refrain from exercising jurisdiction over claims that the applicant state had brought proceedings to settle. Avoidance frustrates parties who bargained on adjudicators' addressing their disputes. It also impoverishes the jurisprudence, because, instead of expounding reasoned conclusions about the consequential issues that the parties have raised, the adjudicators pass them by in silence. If there are well-grounded reasons to refrain from exercising jurisdiction, then a court or tribunal should state the reasons. Otherwise, it should exercise jurisdiction.[16]

Unhappier still, not only did the *Coastal State Rights* tribunal avoid the issues that the parties had reason to expect it to settle; it declared that a dispute exists that neither the applicant state nor states at large understood *can* exist under modern international law. Parties do not institute dispute settlement procedures in order to discover disputes that they did not understand they had. Losing a claim is one thing; losing a claim and concluding

15 *Obligations concerning Negotiations relating to Cessation of the Nuclear Arms Race and Nuclear Disarmament (Marshall Islands v. India)*, ICJ 2016 at p. 277 ¶ 56(1); *Marshall Islands* v. *Pakistan*, ICJ 2016 at p. 573 ¶ 56(1); *Marshall Islands v. United Kingdom*, ICJ 2016 at p. 856, ¶ 59(1). As to the dispute requirement as the ICJ addressed it in the *Marshall Islands* cases, see McIntyre, 'The Role of the Dispute Requirement in Assessing Jurisdiction and Admissibility before the International Court' (2018) 19 Melbourne JIL 546–585.

16 But see, with argument in favor of avoidance as a tool at the ICJ, Fouchard, 'The International Court of Justice's Use of Avoidance Techniques' (2020) 33 Leiden JIL 767–787, including with reference to the dispute-denial technique as applied in *Marshall Islands* and elsewhere, *ibid.* at 775–777.

the proceedings with new encumbrances on one's rights is quite another. Parties that contemplate instituting future proceedings will do well to consider the risks that UNCLOS Part XV, section 2, procedures present.

Under the interpretation that now seemingly prevails, a party under the shadow of armed force in particular should take the risks into account. International law offers variegated options for dispute settlement. Procedures other than those under UNCLOS might well be safer in the geopolitical setting in which we now exist, and claims in some cases will be better left outside third-party procedure altogether. If we are concerned to preserve compulsory binding dispute settlement under international law, then we should be more anxious about the demonstrated failure of the *Coastal State Rights* tribunal that was passive in the face of an armed aggressor and less so about tribunals such as those in *Enrica Lexie* that have interpreted Part XV, section 2, to allow the judicious treatment of ancillary issues.[17]

We should also be discomfited by the *Coastal State Rights* tribunal's self-chosen isolation. It is a long time since H. L. A. Hart contrasted international law with a 'developed legal system,' thus suggesting the underdevelopment of the former.[18] International law remains underdeveloped in important respects, but its rules and institutions are far-reaching, and the disputes subject to third-party settlement are in many cases complex and of considerable importance to public order. Private parties seeking pragmatic solutions in commercial settings do not turn to arbitrators because they expect the arbitrators necessarily to demonstrate fidelity to a larger system of rules and institutions, but states parties engaged in a dispute such as that between Ukraine and Russia in respect of the Black Sea, Sea of Azov, and Kerch Strait operate in a different setting. It is not convincing to say that parties in a dispute such as that have no expectation about how the larger system will affect the dispute, or how the dispute will affect the larger system. Only an extremely rudimentary international law would involve no such expectation. That is not the international law states function in today, or at least it is to be hoped.

It thus is to be hoped that the *Coastal State Rights* award of 21 February 2020 does not prove to be the final word on the putative general exclusion of sovereignty issues from Part XV, section 2, procedures. If it does, then it will be a sad denouement. In a world of emboldened aggressors, it would mean that armed domination of the land indeed extends to the sea. From an interpolation into the classic statement of maritime jurisdiction—the 'land dominates the sea'—a new and extra-legal maxim would result, and acts such as Russia's forcible seizure of Crimea would continue to have the

17 See above Chapter 2, pp. 76–78.
18 Hart, *The Concept of Law* (1961) 214.

legal effect of ousting pacific dispute settlement over maritime matters in appurtenant areas. Treating such acts to have such legal effect is hard to reconcile with general legal order. The incentive that it creates is not one that a legal system readily tolerates. It is not an incentive that one would deliberately design a legal system to create. Yet, under UNCLOS procedures, it seems settled for the time being that judges and arbitrators will continue to treat sovereignty issues as a jurisdictional ouster even when an aggressor has imposed its will against another state in an attempt to alter a settled disposition of spatial entitlement.

As I have noted in this book, in Chapters 2 and 8, other dispute settlement organs have addressed questions ancillary to their jurisdiction.[19] The ECtHR, the ICJ, and tribunals under UNCLOS Part XV, section 2, as well have addressed questions of political sensitivity involving use of force over which their jurisdictional instruments grant them no express power to adopt decisions on the merits. Decisions in which they have addressed such questions have drawn criticism, but parties continue to pursue dispute settlement under the procedures that these organs apply. The overreach, whether supposed or real, has not driven parties away.[20]

An adjudicator who truly goes too far is likely to provoke parties to reconsider their adherence to a consent-limited jurisdiction. A race for the exits could also be provoked by an adjudicator who does not go far enough—in other words, one who exaggerates the limits to parties' consent. A striking, albeit not entirely unimpeachable, example is supplied by the decision of an annulment committee in *Malaysian Historical Salvors v. Malaysia*. The committee there annulled the award of an ICSID tribunal that had been constituted to arbitrate the investor's claim. The annulment committee found that the ICSID tribunal had '*exceeded its powers* by failing to exercise the jurisdiction with which it was endowed by the terms of the [UK-Malaysia bilateral investment] Agreement and the [ICSID] Convention, and that it "manifestly" did so.'[21] The Annulment Committee seems, rightly, to have understood that a jurisdictional system needs to apply its own terms, or else parties will not keep faith with it. As the ICJ said some forty years ago, '[t]he Court must not exceed the jurisdiction conferred upon it by the Parties, but it must also exercise that jurisdiction to its full extent.'[22]

19 See above Chapter 2, pp. 83–88; Chapter 8, pp. 300–302.
20 Guilfoyle & Mossop (2024) 666.
21 *Malaysian Historical Salvors SDN BHD v. Government of Malaysia*, ICSID Case No. ARB/05/10 (Schwebel, President; Shahabuddeen and Tomka, *ad hoc* Committee members), Decision on the Application for Annulment, 16 April 2009, ¶ 80 (emphasis added).
22 *Case concerning the Continental Shelf (Libya/Malta)*, Judgment, ICJ 1985 p. 13, p. 23 ¶ 19 (3 June). For discussion and further references see Kunoy (2021) 91.

A similar point is visible in Judge Ndiaye's separate opinion in *M/V 'Louisa.'* Judge Ndiaye suggested that it is error when a tribunal fails to exercise *compétence de la compétence* in respect of the full scope of jurisdictional questions that the parties' pleadings have raised.[23] Judge Ndiaye evidently was concerned that the tribunal had neglected its duty under Article 288(4) when it concluded that it 'is not required to deal with the contention of Spain that Saint Vincent and the Grenadines has failed to satisfy the obligation under article 283 of the Convention to exchange views' and that 'this has precluded its access to the Tribunal.'[24] Judges and arbitrators in the international setting have a duty of fidelity to the treaties that empower them. Their duty sometimes requires them to abstain; it sometimes requires them to act.

With the award in *Chagos Marine Protected Area (Mauritius v. United Kingdom)* in 2015, UNCLOS jurisprudence on territorial issues seemed to reach a turning point. Future tribunals would face a choice between the exclusion of territorial issues that the *Chagos* majority adopted or the dissenting arbitrators' understanding that UNCLOS Part XV, section 2, admits sovereignty issues in adjudication of maritime disputes. Exponents of a broad reading of the territorial exclusion are quick to assert that adjudicators have made their choice.

But the decided cases hardly add up to a settled jurisprudence. In *Coastal State Rights*, the one subsequent case in which the territorial exclusion fell squarely to be addressed, the Annex VII tribunal constituted to decide the case had little to say about it, except to adopt uncritically the *Chagos* majority's view, and, even then, in rather confused terms and with none of the nuance that the *Chagos* majority had been careful to articulate. The 27 June 2022 award on preliminary objections in *Detention of Ukrainian Naval Vessels and Servicemen*, though the issue had no bearing on that case, suggested that there is a sovereignty dispute over Crimea and seemed to accept the *Coastal State Rights* conclusion, which as to the interpretation of Part XV, section 2, by this time was an interpretation second hand and twice-warmed over.[25] Neither in the *Detention* award nor in *Coastal State*

23 *M/V 'Louisa'* (*Saint Vincent and the Grenadines v. Kingdom of Spain*, Sep. Op. Judge Ndiaye, ITLOS 2013 p. 57, pp. 67–68 ¶ 38 (28 May).

24 *M/V 'Louisa,'* Judgment, ITLOS 2013 p. 4, p. 46 ¶ 152 (28 May).

25 *Dispute concerning the Detention of Ukrainian Naval Vessels and Servicemen*, PCA Case No. 2019–28, UNCLOS Annex VII tribunal (McRae, President; Eiriksson, Wolfrum, Golitsyn, and Greenwood, members), Award on Preliminary Objections, 27 June 2022, ¶ 42. The tribunal elsewhere in the Award referred to 'conflicting positions on sovereignty over Crimea,' this too 'as a matter of context' only: *ibid.* at ¶ 110. In at least two of the BIT cases concerning Crimea as well, there were suggestions

Rights does one find any further analysis to justify the interpretation. Both are derivative, in their sourcing from *Chagos*, and exaggerated, in their disregard for the caveats that the *Chagos* majority lay down.

Attempts to cobble together an 'established jurisprudence' on the territorial exclusion by now have become stretched and artificial. As I noted in Chapter 5, the Annex VII tribunal in the *South China Sea Arbitration* took care and largely avoided the matter. *Guyana v. Suriname* has nothing to say about it, though Professor Oxman, one of the most persistent exponents of the exclusion, says that the *Guyana v. Suriname* award belongs to 'the established jurisprudence that eschews the exercise of [UNCLOS compulsory] jurisdiction over issues regarding rights to land territory.'[26] The *Guyana v. Suriname* tribunal in fact said that its 'findings have *no consequence* for any land boundary that might exist between the Parties, and therefore ... this jurisdictional objection [i.e., the objection based on the putative exclusion] does not arise.'[27] Philippe Sands rightly noted,[28] in oral argument in *Chagos Marine Protected Area*, that land sovereignty 'was simply not in issue in that case.'[29] Judge Treves, writing in the *Proelss Commentary*, noted the same,[30] and Bjørn Kunoy, on a slightly different but related point, doubted whether the *Chagos* award itself is 'authoritative,' though more recently he has suggested that adjudicators in future cases are likely to have reference to it when considering whether they might exercise jurisdiction over 'ancillary areas.'[31] This handful of cases is thin material on which to settle a matter of such consequence to the operation of Part XV, section 2, in a world of renewed irredenta and boundary revisionism.

that a dispute exists, and, there, too, not as part of the adjudicators' reasoning. *Oschadbank v. Russian Federation*, PCA Case No. 2016–14, Award, 26 November 2018 (Williams, President; Brower and Perezcano Díaz, arbitrators) ¶ 197 (referring to 'the dispute between the Respondent and Ukraine as to which State has *de jure* sovereignty over the region'); *PJSC CB Privatbank and Finance Company Finilon LLC v. Russian Federation*, PCA Case No. 2015–21, Partial Award, 4 February 2019 (Dupuy, President; Bethlehem and Mikulka, arbitrators), ¶ 171 (referring to 'the sovereignty claims of Ukraine and the Russian Federation in respect of the Crimean Peninsula').

26 *Mauritius/Maldives* (Prelim. Obj.) (Oxman Sep. & Dis. Op.), ¶ 25.

27 *Guyana v. Suriname*, Award, ¶ 308 (emphasis added).

28 Kunoy (2021) 116.

29 *Chagos Marine Protected Area*, Hearing on Jurisdiction and the Merits, 22 April 2014, Mr. Sands (for Mauritius) p. 31, ¶ 23.

30 Treves, 'Article 286' in *Proelss Commentary* (2017) 1848.

31 Kunoy suggests that *Chagos Marine Protected Area* is the final word on the matter but that 'under certain circumstances a court or tribunal [might] exercise jurisdiction in regard to ancillary areas that are not within the explicit *ratione materiae* to which consent is unequivocally indicated.' Kunoy (2024) 354.

Recognizing the ungainly foot when you see it

There is also the matter of alleged 'glass slippers.' None of these cases was a 'glass slipper' in the sense that Judge Greenwood had in mind with his metaphor or that some writers say Georgia's case against Russia at the ICJ had been.[32] The applicants in each case had put forward real claims, comfortably embraced by the jurisdictional instrument. In *Coastal State Rights* in particular, the difficulty was not with the applicant's claims. It was with the tribunal's failure to scrutinize the respondent's jurisdictional objection, a failure attributable to an exaggerated view of the supposed exclusion of territorial issues from Part XV, section 2, procedures. The territorial issues raised in the case were raised by the objecting party. A question to be asked is why this did not constitute consent by the objecting party to a full ventilation of the putative territorial claim, or at least an invitation to a much more probing inquiry into the premises behind the claim. I have barely touched on the question in this book, because my purpose has been to address a question of general relevance not limited to a party's pleadings in one case, namely the question of the scope of consent embodied in UNCLOS Part XV, section 2.

Whether or not the pleadings might have implied an enlarged consent, it is to be asked why the tribunal accepted the objection to jurisdiction with no inquiry into the evidence concerning its circumstances. Nothing in the obligation to exercise *compétence de la compétence* licenses the adjudicator to defer to an objecting party's mere assertion. If one keeps with Greenwood's allusion to feet and slippers, then it goes like this: Russia talked about some *other* sister, one who doesn't exist even in the fairytale, much less real life, and told the adjudicator to ignore Cinderella and take Russia's word that it's really all about that inexistent person. The *Coastal State Rights* tribunal accepted without scrutiny both that the other sister exists and that she is wrong for the shoe.

When a party asserts that a sovereignty dispute exists of such scope and character as to exclude the exercise of jurisdiction under Part XV, section 2, judges and arbitrators must determine whether the putative sovereignty dispute in truth exists. Reaching this determination is indispensable to the functioning of the dispute settlement procedures of Part XV, section 2. The requirement applies whatever a court or tribunal makes of the scope of UNCLOS jurisdiction in regard to sovereignty disputes. A categorical exclusion

32 For reflections on the 'glass slipper' and Ukraine's claims at the ICJ, ECtHR, and under UNCLOS, see Nuridzhanian, '*Ukraine vs. Russia* in International Courts and Tribunals,' *EJIL Talk!* (9 March 2016). See also Zarbiyev, 'On the Judge Centredness of the International Legal Self' (2021) 32 EJIL 1139, 1162–1163.

of sovereignty disputes means that *any* real dispute as to sovereignty entails that the court or tribunal must abstain from settling certain maritime disputes if the claimant has presented them. A more nuanced exclusion would allow the court or tribunal to examine the sovereignty dispute, if one exists, and judge whether it is one that, owing to its subsidiary relation to a maritime dispute, admits of settlement. But regardless of the scope or positioning of the putative sovereignty exclusion, the prior question must be answered: has the objecting party adverted to a sovereignty dispute that really exists?

The *Coastal State Rights* tribunal in its award of 21 February 2020 said that, to answer *that* question—whether a sovereignty dispute exists—a tribunal need do no more than look for formal opposition between the parties in regard to the territory concerned. Taking that approach, a tribunal has nothing to do with the surrounding facts. The shape and substance of the putative dispute, where it came from, and what it signifies—these are matters that a tribunal under the *Coastal State Rights* approach ignores. For the reasons that I have set out in this book, the *Coastal State Rights* approach is flawed.

To determine whether or not a jurisdictional objection grounded on a putative sovereignty dispute has merit, a dispute settlement procedure must distinguish between fact and factitious assertion. To suggest an altogether more apposite foot metaphor, let us recall the Witch in Goethe's *Faust* who failed to recognize Mephistopheles: inattentive, she did not see the demon's cloven hoof.[33] Siebel, by contrast, one of the students in the famous scene in the *Auerbachskeller*, turned a wary eye to the floor and declared, 'That fellow's got a limp—look at his shoe.'[34] A great deal of mischief, and worse, would have been avoided if the tribunal had put aside fairytales and taken a sober look at what Russia's assertion of a 'sovereignty dispute' really stood on.

The argument that I have set out in this book contains two interconnected parts. First, I have argued that we should be skeptical about the position taken by the majority in *Chagos Marine Protected Area* and uncritically applied in the preliminary objections award in *Coastal State Rights*. A categorical exclusion of territorial disputes from adjudication on the merits is not supported by the text of the Convention or its logic.

Second, I have argued that a doctrinaire insistence on that position—the categorical exclusion—has distorted adjudicators' approach to determining the scope of their jurisdiction to address merits questions. Even for the purposes of determining the scope of their jurisdiction, adjudicators have

33 Johann Wolfgang von Goethe, *Faust* (Williams trans.) (2007) (original 1808, 1828–1829) p. 77 lines 2489–1490.

34 *Ibid.* at p. 66, line 2184.

refused to consider the evidence behind an objecting party's assertion that a sovereignty dispute exists. The refusal is all the more remarkable, because *some* adjudicators have had no difficulty in considering such evidence. Nicaragua's assertion of a sovereignty dispute over Colombia's San Andreas islands occasioned careful analysis by the ICJ, as did the Philippines' assertion over North Borneo.[35] Bahrain's assertion about Qatar's Zubarah and Costa Rica's about its own Isla Portillos are still further examples.[36] There were certainly *assertions* in these cases that territory was in dispute, but, on inspection, the adjudicators recognized when there were no disputes.

And the ITLOS Special Chamber in *Mauritius/Maldives*, on a full view of its reasoning, did not merely transpose an ICJ advisory opinion to say whether a dispute existed; it examined the United Kingdom's assertion that one did.[37] Whether the Special Chamber arrived at the more convincing answer is doubtful, but it looked before it answered.

Hazards real and imagined

I have also argued that on wider considerations of international public order, as well as on formal grounds, a more robust approach to the putative sovereignty exclusion is needed than the *Coastal State Rights* tribunal took.

The approach that tribunals take to sovereignty in UNCLOS adjudication can give rise to a moral hazard. By accepting that one state's mere assertion of sovereignty suffices to establish that a sovereignty dispute exists, and then accepting that the existence of a sovereignty dispute prevents a court or tribunal under UNCLOS from exercising jurisdiction, adjudicators give parties incentive to make mere assertions of sovereignty. Elsewhere, the ICJ warned that more than 'mere allegation, as yet unestablished' must be put forward, before an adjudicator is to accept an objection to jurisdiction, otherwise the 'means of defeating jurisdictional clauses would never be wanting.'[38] This was in the 1972 case concerning an *Appeal relating to jurisdiction of the ICAO Council (India v. Pakistan)*. It echoes the observation years earlier by Judge Sir Hersch Lauterpacht, writing separately in *Certain Norwegian Loans*, about an 'automatic reservation' to the jurisdiction of the Court. According to Judge Lauterpacht,

> it [is] legally impossible for the Court to act in disregard of its Statute which imposes upon it the duty and confers upon it the right to determine its

35 See above Chapter 6, pp. 223–228.

36 See above pp. 219–220, 226–227, ##–##.

37 See above ##–##.

38 *Appeal relating to jurisdiction of the ICAO Council (India* v. *Pakistan)*, ICJ 1972 p. 46, p. 54 ¶ 16(b).

> jurisdiction. That right cannot be exercised by a party to the dispute. The Court cannot, in any circumstances, treat as admissible the claim that the parties have accepted its jurisdiction subject to the condition that they, and not the Court, will decide on its jurisdiction.[39]

The incipient jurisprudence on territorial disputes under UNCLOS has opened an easy path to a party to place precisely that condition on its apparent consent—'that *they*, and not the [adjudicator], will decide on [the adjudicator's] jurisdiction.' A party that takes the path—assuming that the adjudicator leaves it open—attains a power of auto-revocation over any jurisdictional clause to which it might be party.[40] Exercising such power, the party reduces the jurisdictional clause to the mere appearance of consent. Where a tribunal applies the putative exclusion of territorial issues in its exaggerated form, as the *Coastal State Rights* tribunal applied it, the tribunal, in effect, vitiates party consent. We should exercise caution before we assume that respecting party consent in every instance equates to adjudicating less rather than more.[41]

The moral hazard in refusing to address issues that the parties have consented to the adjudicator to settle extends well past the four corners of UNCLOS. The adjudicators in *Coastal State Rights* accepted that an assertion of sovereignty, backed only by force, gave rise to a cognizable claim and, as such, exerted juristic effects on the parties. In so doing, those adjudicators have called into question the fundamental rule of the post-1945 legal order: boundaries peacefully settled between states do not change by force. They have communicated to future aggressors that the once-absolute refusal to accept that force might change such boundaries is now relative. The loss of ground here is incremental, but it is cause for concern. If use of force is capable of producing a *claim* to a new boundary, then use of force is capable of producing a new boundary. The auto-revocation that Judge Lauterpacht said was 'legally impossible' to accept involved formal declarations by a state; the problem that now looms is auto-revocation by armed attack.

An argument of slippery slopes—or, perhaps, the more apposite expression would be landslides, the concern expressed being that, if an adjudicator addresses *any* territorial dispute for *any* purpose, then whole territories will fall away under ancillary jurisdiction—is only as plausible as such arguments

39 *Certain Norwegian Loans (France* v. *Norway)*, Sep. Op. Judge Sir Hersch Lauterpacht, ICJ 1957 p. 34, p. 43 (6 July).

40 Cf. Buga, 'Territorial Sovereignty Issues in Maritime Disputes' (2012) 27 IJMCL 58, 89–90, observing that it is untenable to treat exceptions under Article 298 as self-judging.

41 For a thoughtful articulation of the need for a 'more circumspect approach' see Klein & Parlett, *Judicial Contributions to the UN Convention on the Law of the Sea* (2022) 371.

generally are. For example, no neighboring state by pursuing a maritime delimitation claim is going to win a judgment or award assigning it the entire territory of Belize. And, yes, at least one exponent of the territorial exclusion really does argue that Belize *in toto* might fall subject to unchosen territorial dispute settlement. Professor Talmon suggests that, if any territorial question is subject to dispute settlement under UNCLOS, then Belize is in peril.[42] David Colson and Brian Vohrer write in similar vein, offering that '[m]any states parties to the Convention, including major powers, are embroiled in such politically sensitive, not to say explosive, disputes,'[43] by which they meant to suggest, as Talmon does, that opening any aperture for an UNCLOS tribunal to scrutinize assertions about such disputes would be the end of UNCLOS jurisdiction as we know it. Oddly, though anxious about a procedural incident that has not yet occurred, these writers appear at ease about a breakdown of public order that is already underway.

The considered answer to the risk of an unintended aggrandizement of jurisdiction in respect of territorial issues is the same as that for any issue—that is, the answer that the Annex VII tribunal gave in the part of its award in *Southern Bluefin Tuna* that writers less often remember. The tribunal determined that Australia and New Zealand had demonstrated a dispute to exist under UNCLOS, and it did so after meaningfully engaging with the parties' arguments, in particular with Japan's contention that there was no dispute: 'In the instant case, it is for this Tribunal to decide whether the "real dispute" between the Parties does or does not reasonably (and not just remotely) relate to the obligations set forth in the treaties whose breach is alleged.'[44] Where a party asserts that a dispute exists under UNCLOS, and the relation between the dispute, as alleged, and UNCLOS is reasonable (and not just remote), a procedure under Part XV, section 2, well may properly address the dispute even where the dispute is 'centered in the [other

42 See, for example, the slippery slope argument that title to the territory of Belize (*in toto*) would be susceptible to UNCLOS dispute settlement, if any territorial question is: Talmon (2014) at 47–48.

43 Colson & Vohrer, 'In re Chagos Marine Protected Area (Mauritius v. United Kingdom' (2015) 109 AJIL at 851.

44 *Southern Bluefin Tuna (New Zealand-Japan, Australia-Japan)*, Annex VII tribunal (Schwebel, President; Feliciano, Keith, Tresselt, and Yamada, members), Award, 4 August 2000, ¶ 48: (2006) XXIII *RIAA* 1, 39. Judge Keith evidently agreed with this part of the award, his famous dissent having concerned a different issue—the one that is more often written about, and on which Australia and New Zealand lost the case—i.e., whether the other treaty (the Convention for the Conservation of Southern Bluefin Tuna) precluded all other dispute settlement procedures. See Sep. Op. Justice Sir Kenneth Keith, XXIII RIAA at p. 49, ¶ 1, as to which see, e.g., Bjørn Kunoy, 'The Scope of Compulsory Jurisdiction and Exceptions Thereto under the United Nations Convention on the Law of the Sea' (2021) 58 Can. YBIL 78, 85–86.

treaty].'[45] That the dispute involves rules under another treaty—or rules of general international law—does not deprive the dispute of its connection to UNCLOS.

A tribunal under Part XV, section 2, should not adjudicate a dispute about something entirely unrelated to UNCLOS to which an enterprising party has appended a mere vestige of an UNCLOS question. Parties assume that the adjudicators whom they have chosen possess those powers of discernment necessary to tell when that is what a claimant has done. They also assume that the adjudicator knows a reasonable proposition from its opposite and a plausible one from one the chances of which for validation are so remote as to require dismissal out of hand. In tribute to the famous dictum that 'most of the distinctions of the law are distinctions of degree,'[46] relations of this kind—of reasonableness and remoteness—are ones that parties routinely have entrusted adjudicators to discern. It is to be hoped, notwithstanding recent disappointments, that they continue to do so.

For a return to method

I suggested in the preface to this book that one of the unifying strands in a fragmented international law, perhaps international law's most important source of cohesion, is legal method. Method is centrally important to all legal systems, but its importance is heightened in international law. The observance of received techniques of argument, adjudication, and discourse arguably supplies the response, or at least part of the response, to the long-noted incompleteness of international law—the absence in international law of an effective centralized power for law-making and for law enforcement.

Its incompleteness accounts for other features of international law which, if not unique to international law, are, likewise, present in it in heightened form. Not least among these is the distinction international lawyers observe between primary rules of international law (i.e., the obligations of legal substance) and the secondary rules (i.e., the rules that determine the consequences of breach). The ILC's ARSIWA insistently enforce the distinction, which is a central organizing principle of the Articles. Contrast that approach

45 *Ibid.* at p. 41, ¶ 52. Irina Buga, too, has referred to *Southern Bluefin Tuna* for this concept: Buga, 'Territorial Sovereignty Issues in Maritime Disputes' (2012) 27 IJMCL 58, 90.

46 *Panhandle Oil Co. v. Mississippi* ex rel *Knox*, 277 U.S. 218, 223 (1928) (Holmes, J., dissenting). See also *Alabama* v. *King & Boozer*, 314 U.S. 1, 9 (1941), in which Holmes, in Justice Scalia's words, 'was ... vindicated.' Antonin Scalia, 'Essay: Assorted Canards of Contemporary Legal Analysis' (1989) 40 *Case Western Reserve Law Review* 581, 590 n. 14.

with classic positivist descriptions of the law, no more classic example of which do we find than that in Holmes's *Path of the Law*:

> One of the many evil effects of the confusion between legal and moral ideas ... is that theory is apt to get the cart before the horse, and consider the right or the duty as something existing apart from and independent of the consequences of its breach, to which certain sanctions are added afterward. But ... a legal duty so called is nothing but a prediction that if a man does or omits certain things he will be made to suffer in this or that way by judgment of the court; and so of a legal right.[47]

So much for separation of the primary from the secondary. And so much, too, for any distinction between determination of breach and the imposition of coercive penalty: Holmes went on to say that 'it would be better to cease troubling ourselves about [the distinction between] primary rights and *sanctions* altogether.'[48] Holmes' debt to John Austin was in plain view here. To Austin, '[i]t also appears ... that *command, duty,* and *sanction* are inseparably connected terms: that each embraces the same ideas as the others.'[49]

These formulations have been treated many times over, and so I do not belabor them, except, if it be to belabor, to observe that they concern a distinction that international lawyers rely upon and that Austin, Holmes, and jurists in their tradition reject. Their rejection is not incidental. Nor is our reliance. In international law, responsibility and primary rules have distinct analytic identities, because to treat them as one would be to invite a hopeless confrontation of the law with one element of its incompleteness—its lack of a central enforcer with coercive power. The distinctiveness of responsibility and primary rules thus supplies a response to one of international law's chief problems.[50]

47 Holmes, 'The Path of the Law' (1897) 10 HLR 457, 458.

48 *Ibid.* at 462 (emphasis added).

49 Austin, *The Province of Jurisprudence Determined* (1995; 1st edn. 1832) (Rumble, ed.), Lecture I, p. 24 (emphasis original).

50 The ILC, when setting the stage for its Articles on State Responsibility, identified a pragmatic ground and a doctrinal or conceptual ground for 'not attempt[ing] to define the content of the international obligations, the breach of which gives rise to responsibility,' the pragmatic ground being that codifying the primary rules 'would involve restating most of substantive customary and conventional international law.' ARSIWA, *General commentary*, Comment (1), ILC Yearbook 2001, vol. II, Part Two, p. 31, which obviously would have been an impractical task; the doctrinal or conceptual ground being that stated by Roberto Ago in 1970: 'principles' of State responsibility 'maintain[...] a strict distinction' between the two and defining a substantive rule is different from determining whether a party has breached the rule and 'what should be the consequences of the violation.' *Ibid.*, Comment (2) quoting Ago, ILC Yearbook 1970, vol. II, p. 306. The ILC here did not draw attention to *why* 'a strict distinction' is needed or *how* the two differ.

Then there is that other problem of decentralization in international law, the law's variegated and dispersed rule-makers, which is to say, the multiple (and changing) sources that are much involved in international law's fragmentation. Whether or not it is intrinsic to international law that it has no centralized source of law, there is none in fact. In the current stage of its development, international law is a law that is pronounced in the decentralization of the processes by which it is made. If the lack of a single coercive enforcement power invites the distinction between primary and secondary rules in international law, then what response does fragmentation of sources invite? An answer is the one that I suggested in the Introduction, have just recalled here, and which has surfaced in several aspects in the preceding chapters. The response to fragmentation, or the best response that we have, is found in legal method.

Method is a common thread that runs through international law, and it goes further than that, because it connects international law to law at large. The process of argument, decision, and discourse in international law is international law's most reliably legal aspect. We should apply the ordinary techniques of argument, decision, and discourse to the international law with which we engage and to the differences that parties seek through law to regulate. Where a decision or other legal encounter parts ways from the ordinary techniques, we should not refrain from calling for a return.

References

Ahmed, Dirdeiry M., *Boundaries and Secession in Africa and International Law: Challenging* Uti Possidetis (Cambridge: Cambridge University Press, 2015).

Alford, Roger P., 'The Convergence of International Trade and Investment Arbitration' (2014) 12 *Santa Clara Journal of International Law* 35.

Allen, Stephen, 'Article 297 of the United Nations Convention on the Law of the Sea and the Scope of Mandatory Jurisdiction' (2017) 48 ODIL 313.

Allen, Stephen, 'Self-determination, the Chagos Advisory Opinion and the Chagossians' (2020) 69 ICLQ 203–220.

Allen, Stephen, 'Reflections on the Treatment of General Assembly Resolutions in the Chagos Advisory Opinion' in Burri & Trinidad (eds.) (2021) 41.

Alvarez, José E., 'State Sovereignty Is Not Withering Away: A Few Lessons for the Future' in Antonio Cassese (ed.), *Realizing Utopia: The Future of International Law* (Oxford: Oxford University Press, 2012) 26.

Alvarez-Jimenez, Alberto, 'Boundary Agreements in the Court of International Justice's Case Law' (2012) 23 EJIL 495.

Amar, Akhil Reed, 'The Bill of Rights as a Constitution' (1991) 100 YLJ 1131.

American Law Institute, *Restatement (Third) Foreign Relations Law of the United States*, § 201, Comment *b.* ('*Defined territory*') and Comment *d.* ('*Government*') 73 (1987).

Anderson, David H., 'Coastal State Jurisdiction and High Seas Freedoms in the EEZ in Light of the "Saiga" case' in Clive R. Symmons (ed.), *Selected Contemporary Issues in the Law of the Sea* (Leiden: Martinus Nijhoff, 2011) 105.

Anderson, David H., 'Islands and Rocks in the Modern Law of the Sea' in Myron H. Nordquist, John Norton Moore, Alfred H. A. Soons, & Hak-So Kim (eds.), *The Law of the Sea Convention: US Accession and Globalization* (Leiden: Nijhoff, 2012) 307.

Anderson, David H., 'Peaceful Settlement of Disputes under UNCLOS' in Jill Barrett & Richard Barnes (eds.), *Law of the Sea: UNCLOS as a Living Treaty* (London: British Institute of International and Comparative Law, 2016) 385.

Antonopoulos, Constantine, 'Effectiveness v. the Rule of Law following the East Timor Case' (1996) 27 Neth. YBIL 75.

Austin, John, *The Province of Jurisprudence Determined* (Cambridge: Cambridge University Press, 1995; 1st edn. 1832) (Wilfrid E. Rumble, ed.).

Bankes, Nigel, 'The Jurisdiction of the Dispute Settlement Bodies of the Law of the Sea Convention with Respect to Other Treaties' (2021) 52 ODIL 346.
Bardonnet, Daniel, *Les frontières terrestres et la relativité de leur trace (Problèmes juridiques choisis)* (1976) 153 Hag. Rec. 15.
Barnes, Richard, 'Reflections on the Waters: Law of the Sea Scholarship and Practice' (2023) 38 IJMCL 1.
Barrett, Jill, Naomi Burke, Callum Musto, David H. Anderson, Robin Churchill, Kentaro Nishimoto, & Makoto Seta, *Report on the Obligations of States under Article 74(3) and 83(3) of UNCLOS in respect of Undelimited Maritime Areas* (London: BIICL, 2016).
Barriga, Stefan, 'Negotiating the Amendments on the Crime of Aggression' in Stefan Barriga & Claus Kreβ (eds.), *The Travaux Préparatoires of the Crime of Aggression* (Cambridge: Cambridge University Press, 2012) 3.
Bartels, Lorand, 'Applicable Law and Jurisdiction Clauses: Where Does a Tribunal Find the Principal Norms Applicable to the Case Before It?' in Tomer Broude & Yuval Shany (eds.), *Multisourced Equivalent Norms in International Law* (Oxford: Hart, 2011) 115.
Baxter, Richard R., 'International Law in "Her Infinite Variety"' (1980) 29 ICLQ 549.
Beckman, Robert, 'International law, UNCLOS and the South China Sea' in Beckman et al. (eds.), *Beyond Territorial Disputes in the South China Sea: Legal Frameworks for the Joint Development of Hydrocarbon Resources* (Cheltenham: Edward Elgar, 2013) 47.
Beckman, Robert, 'UNCLOS Part XV and the South China Sea' in Jayakumar, Koh, & Beckman (eds.) (2014) 229.
Benatar, Marco & Valentin J. Schatz, 'The Protection of Foreign Investments in Disputed Maritime Areas' in Tobias Ackermann & Sebastian Wuschka (eds.), *Investments in Conflict Zones: The Role of International Investment Law in Armed Conflicts, Disputed Territories, and 'Frozen' Conflicts* (Leiden: Brill, 2021) 176.
Bering, Juergen, 'The Prohibition on Annexation: Lessons from Crimea' (2017) 49 *New York University Journal of International Law and Policy* 747.
Bjorge, Eirik, 'Opposability and Non-opposability in International Law' (2021) BYIL 12.
Boisson de Chazournes, Laurence, Lucy Reed, & Kenneth Wong, 'Marine Entitlements in the South China Sea: The Arbitration between the Philippines and China' (2016) 110 AJIL 746.
Boisson de Chazournes, Laurence, 'Plurality in the Fabric of International Courts and Tribunals: The Threads of a Managerial Approach' (2017) 28 EJIL 13.
Bordin, Fernando Lusa, *The Analogy between States and International Organizations* (Cambridge: Cambridge University Press, 2018).
Bordin, Fernando Lusa, 'Reckoning with British Colonialism: The Chagos Advisory Opinion' (2019) 78 *Cambridge Law Journal* 253.
Boyle, Alan & James Harrison, 'Judicial Settlement of International Environmental Disputes: Current Problems' (2013) 4 JIDS 245.

Broches, A. 'Convention on the Settlement of Investment Disputes between States and Nationals of Other States of 1965, Explanatory Notes and Survey of Its Application' (1993) 18 *Yearbook of Commercial Arbitration* 627.

Brunk, Ingrid & Monica Hakimi, 'The Prohibition of Annexations and the Foundations of Modern International Law' (2024) 118(3) AJIL 417.

Brunk, Ingrid (Wuerth), 'International Law in the Post-Human Rights Era' (2017) 96 *Texas Law Review* 279.

Brunk, Ingrid (Wuerth) & Monica Hakimi, 'Russia, Ukraine, and the Future World Order' (2022) 116(4) AJIL 687.

Buga, Irina, 'Territorial Sovereignty Issues in Maritime Disputes: A Jurisdictional Dilemma for Law of the Sea Tribunals' (2012) 27 IJMCL 58.

Buga, Irina, 'Between Stability and Change in the Law of the Sea Convention: Subsequent Practice, Treaty Modification, and Regime Interaction' in Rothwell et al. (eds.), *The Oxford Handbook of the Law of the Sea* (Oxford: Oxford University Press, 2015) 46.

Burchill, Richard, 'The ICJ Decision in the Case concerning East Timor: The Illegal Use of Force Validated?' (1997) 2(1) *Journal of Armed Conflict Law* 1.

Burri, Thomas & Jamie Trinidad (eds.), *The International Court of Justice and Decolonisation: New Directions from the Chagos Advisory Opinion* (Cambridge: Cambridge University Press, 2021).

Burri, Thomas & Jamie Trinidad, 'Introductory Note (*Dispute concerning delimitation of the Maritime Boundary between Mauritius and Maldives in the Indian Ocean, Preliminary Objections (ITLOS)*)' (2021) 60 ILM 969.

Byers, Michael (ed.), *The Role of Law in International Politics: Essays in International Relations and International Law* (Oxford: Oxford University Press, 2001).

Caflisch, Lucius, 'The Delimitation of Marine Spaces between States with Opposite or Adjacent Coasts' in Dupuy & Vignes (eds.) vol. 1 (1991) 425.

Caflisch, Lucius, 'Les espaces marins attachés à des îles ou rochers' in Forteau & Thouvenin (eds.) (2017) 477.

Campbell, Caitlin & Nargiza Salidjanova, U.S.–China Economic and Security Review Commission, Issue Brief, *South China Sea Arbitration Ruling: What Happened and What's Next?* (12 July 2016).

Campbell, McLachlan KC, *The Principle of Systemic Integration in International Law* (Oxford: Oxford University Press, 2024).

Campolieti, Federico, 'The Rule of Non-aggravation of the Dispute in ICSID Arbitration Practice' (2015) 30(1) *ICSID Review—Foreign Investment Law Journal* 217.

Carter, David B. & H. E. Goemans, 'The Making of the Territorial Order: New Borders and the Emergence of Interstate Conflict' (2011) 65(2) *International Organization* 275.

Chandra, Vivek & John R. Morss, 'UNCLOS and Maritime Boundary Disputes in Areas of Hydrocarbon Potential: Oil under the Troubled Waters?' (2022) 53 ODIL 1.

Charney, Jonathan I., 'Rocks That Cannot Sustain Human Habitation' (1999) 93 AJIL 863.

Chimni, B. S., *International Law and World Order: A Critique of Contemporary Approaches*, 2nd edn. (Cambridge: Cambridge University Press, 2017).

Chimni, B. S., 'The Articles on State Responsibility and the Guiding Principles of Shared Responsibility: A TWAIL Perspective' (2020) 31 EJIL 1211.

Chukwurah, Anthony Oye, *The Settlement of Boundary Disputes in International Law* (Manchester: Manchester University Press, 1968).

Churchill, Robin, Vaughan Lowe, & Amy Sander, *The Law of the Sea*, 4th edn. (Manchester: Manchester University Press, 2022).

Colson, David A. & Brian J. Vohrer, 'In re Chagos Marine Protected Area (Mauritius v. United Kingdom)' (2015) 109 AJIL 845.

Congressional Research Service, *Greece and Turkey: The Rocky Islet Crisis*, CRS Report for Congress, 96–140 F, March 7, 1996.

Coracini, Astrid R. & Pål Wrange, 'The Specificity of the Crime of Aggression' in Claus Kreβ and Stefan Barriga (eds.), *The Crime of Aggression: A Commentary* 338 (Cambridge: Cambridge University Press, 2017) 307.

Corbett, P. E., *Social Basis of a Law of Nations* (1954) 85 Hag. Rec. 471.

Corten, Olivier, *Méthodologie du droit international public*, 2nd edn. (Brussels: Éditions de l'Université de Bruxelles, 2024).

Costelloe, Daniel, 'Treaty Succession in Annexed Territory,' 65(2) ICLQ 343.

Crawford, James, 'Islands as Sovereign Nations' (1989) 38 ICLQ 277.

Crawford, James, *Creation of States*, 2nd edn. (Oxford: Oxford University Press, 2006).

Crawford, James, *Chance, Order, Change: The Course of International Law* (2013) 365 Hag. Rec. 9.

Crawford, *Brownlie's Principles of Public International Law*, 9th edn. (Oxford: Oxford University Press, 2019).

D'Amato, Anthony, *International Law: Process and Prospect* (Dobbs Ferry, NY: Transnational Publishers, 1987).

Damrosch, Lori Fisler, 'The Sources of Immunity Law: Between International and Domestic Law' in Tom Ruys, Nicolas Angelet, & Luca Ferro (eds.), *The Cambridge Handbook of Immunities and International Law* (Cambridge: Cambridge University Press, 2019) 40.

Davis Mortenson, Julian, The *Travaux* of *Travaux*: Is the Vienna Convention Hostile to Drafting History?' (2013) 107 AJIL 780.

De Bailleul, Marine & Sarah Kerc, 'Defining Violations of International Public Policy under French Law: A Confirmed New Standard,' *Baker McKenzie Global Arbitration News* (13 December 2023).

De Brabandere, Eric, 'Non-state Actors in International Dispute Settlement: Pragmatism in International Law' in Jean d'Aspremont (ed.), *Participants in the International Legal System: Multiple Perspectives on Non-state Actors in International Law* (Abingdon: Routledge, 2011) 342.

De la Fayette, Louise, 'ITLOS and the Saga of the Saiga: Peaceful Settlement of a Law of the Sea Dispute' (2000) 15 IJMCL 355.

De Vriese, Kit, 'The Application of Investment Treaties in Occupied or Annexed Territories and "Frozen" Conflicts; *Tabula Rasa* or *Occupata*?' in Tobias Ackermann & Sebastian Wuschka (eds.), *Investments in Conflict Zones: The Role *of International Investment Law in Armed Conflicts, Disputed Territories, and 'Frozen' Conflicts* (Leiden: Brill, 2021) 319.

Denk, Erdem, 'Interpreting a Geographical Expression in a Nineteenth Century Cession Treaty and the Senkaku/Diaoyu Islands Dispute' (2005) 20 IJMCL 97.

Devaney, James G. & Christian J. Tams, 'In re Arbitration between the Italian Republic and the Republic of India concerning the "Enrica Lexie" Incident' (2021) 115 AJIL 513.

Duffy Toft, Monica, 'Territory and War' (2014) 51(2) *Journal of Peace Research* 185.

Dumberry, Patrick, 'Requiem for Crimea: Why Tribunals Should Have Declined Jurisdiction over the Claims of Ukrainian Investors against Russia under the Ukraine–Russia BIT' (2018) 9 JIDS 506.

Dupuy, René-Jean, 'The Sea under National Competence' in Dupuy & Vignes (eds.) vol. 1 (1991) 247.

Dupuy, René-Jean & Daniel Vignes (eds.), *A Handbook on the New Law of the Sea* (Dordrecht: Nijhoff, 1991).

Dzurek, Daniel J. (with Clive Schofield), *Parting the Red Sea: Boundaries, Offshore Resources and Transit* (Durham, NC: International Boundaries Research Unit Maritime Briefing, vol. 3, no. 2, 2001).

Eichberger, Fabian Simon, 'The Legal Effect of ICJ Advisory Opinions Redefined? The *Mauritius/Maldives* Delimitation Case: Judgment on Preliminary Objections' (2021) 22 Melbourne JIL 383.

Elferink, Alex Oude, 'Is It Either Necessary or Possible to Clarify the Provision on Rocks of Article 121 (3) of the Law of the Sea Convention?' in Martin A. Pratt & Janet Allison-Brown (eds.), *Borderlands under Stress* (The Hague: Kluwer, 2000) 393.

Epps, Valerie, 'Self-determination after Kosovo and East Timor' (2000) 6 *International Law Students' Association Journal of International and Comparative Law* 445.

Evans, Malcolm, 'Maritime Boundary Delimitation' in Donald Rothwell, Alex G. Oude Elferink, Karen N. Scott, & Tim Stephens (eds.), *The Oxford Handbook of the Law of the Sea* (Oxford: Oxford University Press, 2015) 254.

Ezenwajiaku, Josephat, *State Territory and International Law* (Routledge, 2020).

Fahner, Johannes Hendrik, 'Two Takes on *Chagos*: Reconciling the Advisory Opinion with the Res Judicata Effect of the UNCLOS Award' in Burri & Trinidad (eds.) (2021) 71.

Ferrara, Pablo, 'Article 293: Applicable Law' in Proells (ed.) (2017) 1893.

Fietta, Stephen & Robin Cleverly, *A Practitioner's Guide to Maritime Boundary Delimitation* (Oxford: Oxford University Press, 2016).

Ford, Christopher A., 'Anything but Simple: Arms Control and Strategic Stability' in Elbridge A. Colby & Michael S. Gerson (eds.) (with foreword by Thomas C. Schelling), *Strategic Stability: Contending Interpretations* (Carlisle, PA: US Army War College, 2013) 201.

Forsberg, Tuomas, 'Explaining Territorial Disputes: From Power Politics to Normative Reasons' (1996) 33(4) *Journal of Peace Research* 433.

Forteau, Mathias, 'The Diversity of Applicable Law before International Tribunals as a Source of Forum Shopping and Fragmentation of International Law: An

Assessment' in Rüdiger Wolfrum & Ina Gätzschmann (eds.), *International Dispute Settlement: Room for Innovations?* (Heidelberg: Springer, 2013) 417.

Forteau, Mathias, 'Le règlement des différends' in Forteau & Thouvenin (eds.) (2017) 989.

Forteau, Mathias & Jean-Marc Thouvenin (eds.), *Traité de droit international de la mer* (Paris: A. Pedone, 2017).

Fouchard, Felix, 'Allowing "Leeway to Expediency, without Abandoning Principle?" The International Court of Justice's Use of Avoidance Techniques' (2020) 33 Leiden JIL 767.

Franchini, Daniel & Russell Buchan, 'The Obligation of Peaceful Settlement of International Disputes: Status, Nature, Content, and Scope' in Russell Buchan, Daniel Franchini, & Nicholas Tsagourias, eds., *The Changing Character of International Dispute Settlement: Challenges and Prospects* (Cambridge: Cambridge University Press, 2023) 15.

Franck, Susan & Bailey Roe, 'The Cost Award' in Katia Fach Gómez & Catharine Titi (eds.), *The Award in International Investment Arbitration* (Oxford: Oxford University Press, 2024) 59.

Franckx, Erik, 'Two More Maritime Boundary Agreements Concluded in the Eastern Baltic Sea in 1997' (1998) 13 IJMCL 274.

Gardiner, Richard, 'The Vienna Convention Rules on Treaty Interpretation' in Duncan B. Hollis (ed.), *The Oxford Guide to Treaties*, 2nd edn. (Oxford: Oxford University Press, 2020) 459.

Gau, Michael Sheng-Ti, 'Issues of Jurisdiction in Cases of Default of Appearance' in Talmon & Jia (eds.) (2014) 81.

Gau, Michael Sheng-Ti, 'The 2015 Award on Jurisdiction and Admissibility of the South China Sea Arbitration and Insurmountable Thresholds' (2015) 33 C(T) YBIL 62–108.

Gau, Michael Sheng-Ti, 'The Interpretation of Article 121(3) of UNCLOS by the Tribunal for the South China Sea Arbitration: A Critique' (2019) 50 ODIL 49.

Georgoula, Danae F., 'The LOSC Renvois as a Source of Untapped Jurisdiction' (2023) 38 IJMCL 228.

Gibler, D. M., 'What They Fight For: Specific Territorial Issues in Militarized Interstate Disputes, 1816–2001' (2017) 24(2) *Conflict Management and Peace Science* 194.

Gilmore, Grant, 'Legal Realism: Its Cause and Cure' (1961) 70 YLJ 1037.

Grant, Thomas D., 'Defining Statehood: The Montevideo Convention and Its Discontents' (1999) 37 *Columbia Journal of Transnational Law* 403.

Grant, Thomas D., 'East Timor, the UN System, and Enforcing Non-Recognition in International Law' (2000) 33 *Vanderbilt Journal of Transnational Law* 273.

Grant, Thomas D., 'The Budapest Memorandum of 5 December 1994: Political Engagement or Legal Obligation?' (2014) 34 Pol. YBIL 89.

Grant, Thomas D., *Aggression against Ukraine: Territory, Responsibility, and International Law* (New York: Macmillan, 2015).

Grant, Thomas D., 'Annexation of Crimea' (2015) 109 AJIL 68.

Grant, Thomas D., 'International Dispute Settlement in Response to an Unlawful Seizure of Territory: Three Mechanisms' (2015) 16(1) *Chicago Journal of International Law* 1.

Grant, Thomas D., 'Islands, Rocks, Low-Tide Elevations, or None of the Above: Some Practical Considerations in Case You Have to Decide' in Tomas Heidar (ed.), *Maritime Challenges in Asia* (Busan: Korea Maritime Institute, 2017) 221.

Grant, Thomas D., 'Intervention, Interveners, and Their More Subtle Means' in Thomas D. Grant (ed.), *International Law and the Post-Soviet Space: Essays on Ukraine, Intervention, and Non-proliferation* (New York/Stuttgart: Columbia University Press/Ibidem, 2019) 290.

Grant, Thomas D., 'Arbitration, Corruption and Post-award Control in French and English Courts' (2022) 71(2) ICLQ 481.

Grant, Thomas D., 'Fraud and the Integrity of Arbitration: Part 1' (2022) 25(3) *International Arbitration Law Review* 177.

Grant, Thomas D., 'Fraud and the Integrity of Arbitration: Part 2' (2022) 25(4) *International Arbitration Law Review* 259.

Grant, Thomas D., 'The "Open System" and Its Gatekeepers: From Complexity in International Law, a Seminar in Honour of James Crawford' (2022) 13 JIDS 41.

Grant, Thomas D. & Damon J. Wischik, *On the Path to AI: Law's Prophecies and the Conceptual Foundations of the Machine Learning Age* (New York: Palgrave Macmillan, 2020).

Gray, Christine, *International Law and Use of Force*, 4th edn. (Oxford: Oxford University Press, 2018).

Guilfoyle, Douglas, 'Remarks: The Regime of Islands in the Aftermath of the South China Sea Arbitration' (2018) 112 ASIL Proc. 7.

Guilfoyle, Douglas, 'The Chagos Archipelago before International Tribunals: Strategic Litigation and the Production of Historical Knowledge' (2021) 21 Melbourne JIL 749.

Guilfoyle, Douglas & Cameron Miles, 'Provisional Measures and the MV Arctic Sunrise' (2014) 108 AJIL 271.

Guilfoyle, Douglas & Joanna Mossop, 'The Extent and Legitimacy of the Judicial Function in UNCLOS Dispute Settlement' (2024) 73(3) ICLQ 641.

Hafner, Gerhard, 'Some Remarks on the South China Sea Award: Itu Aba Versus Clipperton' (2016) 34 C(T)YBIL 1.

Hakimi, Monica, 'The Work of International Law' (2017) 58 HILJ 1.

Hampson, Françoise J., 'The Relationship between International Humanitarian Law and International Human Rights Law' in Scott Sheeran & Nigel Rodley (eds.), *Routledge Handbook of International Human Rights Law* (Abingdon: Routledge, 2013) 185.

Harris, Callista, 'Incidental Determinations in Proceedings under Compromissory Clauses' (2021) 70(2) ICLQ 417.

Harrison, James, 'The Arctic Sunrise Arbitration (Netherlands v. Russia): Background to the Arbitral Proceedings' (2016) 31 IJMCL 145.

Harrison, James, 'Defining Disputes and Characterizing Claims: Subject-Matter Jurisdiction in Law of the Sea Convention Litigation' (2017) 48 ODIL 269.

Hart, H. L. A., *The Concept of Law* (Oxford: Oxford University Press, 1961).

Hathaway, Oona A. & Scott J. Shapiro, *The Internationalists: How a Radical Plan to Outlaw War Remade the World* (New York: Simon & Schuster, 2018).

Hayashi, Moritaka & Roy S. Lee (eds.), *New Directions in the Law of the Sea: Regional and National Developments* (Dobbs Ferry, NY: Oceana Publications, 1995).

Hayton, Bill, 'When Good Lawyers Write Bad History: Unreliable Evidence and the South China Sea Territorial Dispute' (2017) 48 ODIL 17.

Heisenberg, Werner, *The Physical Principles of the Quantum Theory* (Carl Eckart and Frank C. Hoyt, trans.) (Chicago: University of Chicago Press, 1930).

Hertogen, An, 'The Persuasiveness of Domestic Law Analogies in International Law' (2019) 29(4) EJIL 1127.

Hill-Cawthorne, Lawrence, 'International Litigation and the Disaggregation of Disputes: Ukraine/Russia as a Case Study' (2019) 68(4) ICLQ 779.

Hilpold, Peter, 'Human Rights and WTO Law: From Conflict to Coordination' (2007) 45 AdV 485.

Hilpold, Peter, 'Krzysztof Skubiszewski and the Right to Self-Determination: Past and Future' (2019) 39 Pol. YBIL 21.

Hoffman, Leonard, 'Human Rights and the House of Lords' (1999) 62 MLR 159.

Hoffmann, Leonard, 'The Universality of Human Rights' (2009) 125 LQR 416.

Holmes, Jr., Oliver Wendell, *The Common Law* (Boston: Little, Brown, and Company, 1881).

Holmes, Jr., Oliver Wendell, 'The Path of the Law' (1897) 10 HLR 457.

Hong, Nong, *UNCLOS and Ocean Dispute Settlement: Law and Politics in the South China Sea* (London: Routledge, 2012).

Huh, Sookyeon, 'Title to Territory in the Post-colonial Era: Original Title and *Terra Nullius* in the ICJ Judgments on Cases concerning *Ligitan/Sipadan* (2002) *and Pedra Branca* (2008)' (2015) 26(3) EJIL 709.

Irwin, Paul C., 'Settlement of Maritime Boundary Disputes: An Analysis of the Law of the Sea Negotiations' (1980) 8 ODIL 105.

James, Crawford, *Chance, Order, Change: The Course of International law* (The Hague: Brill, 2014).

Jayakumar, S., Tommy Koh, & Robert Beckman (eds.), *The South China Sea Disputes and Law of the Sea* (Cheltenham: Edward Elgar Publishing Limited, 2014).

Jennings, Robert, 'Commentary,' *Proceedings of the 23rd Annual Conference of the Law of the Sea Institute*, Alfred H. A. Soons (ed.) (Honolulu: Law of the Sea Institute, 1990).

Jennings, Robert & Arthur Watts (ed.), *Oppenheim's International Law, vol. 1, Peace*, 9th edn. (Harlow: Longman Group, 1992).

Jia, Bing Bing & Stefan Talmon, 'Introduction' in Talmon & Jia (eds.) (2014) 1.

Jia, Bing Bing, 'The Issue of Admissibility in Inter-State Arbitration' in Talmon & Jia (eds.) (2014) 107.

Jones, Kate, 'Protecting Political Discourse from Online Manipulation: The International Human Rights Law Framework' (2021) 1 *European Human Rights Law Review* 68.

Kahneman, Daniel, *Thinking, Fast and Slow* (New York: Penguin, 2012).

Kamto, Maurice, 'Les différentes catégories d'Etat' in Forteau & Thouvenin (eds.) (2017) 235.

Karagiannis, Syméon, 'The Relationship(s) between Treaties and Territory' in Duncan B. Hollis (ed.), *The Oxford Guide to Treaties*, 2nd edn. (Oxford: Oxford University Press, 2020) 309.

Kelsen, Hans, *The Law of the United Nations* (London: Stevens and Sons, 1951).

Klein, Natalie & Kate Parlett, *Judging the Law of the Sea: Judicial Contributions to the UN Convention on the Law of the Sea* (Oxford: Oxford University Press, 2022).

Klein, Natalie, *Dispute Settlement in the UN Convention on the Law of the Sea* (Cambridge: Cambridge University Press, 2009).

Klein, Pierre & Vaios Koutroulis, 'Territorial Disputes and the Use of Force' in Marcelo G. Kohen & Mamadou Hébié (eds.), *Research Handbook on Territorial Disputes in International Law* (Cheltenham: Elgar, 2018).

Knox, John H., 'A Presumption against Extrajurisdictionality' (2010) 104 AJIL 351.

Kocs, Stephen A., 'Territorial Disputes and Interstate War, 1945–1987' (1995) 57(1) *The Journal of Politics* 159.

Kohen, Marcelo G. & Facundo M. Gómez Pulisich, 'Typologie des espaces marins' in Forteau & Thouvenin (eds.) (2017) 341.

Kolb, Robert, *The International Court of Justice* (Oxford: Hart, 2013).

Kolb, Robert, *The Law of Treaties: An Introduction*, 2nd edn. (Cheltenham: Edward Elgar: 2023).

Kontorovich, Eugene, 'Arctic Sunrise' (2016) 110 AJIL 96.

Kopela, Sophia, 'Historic Titles and Historic Rights in the Law of the Sea in the Light of the South China Sea Arbitration' (2017) 48 ODIL 181.

Koskenniemi, Martti, *The Gentle Civilizer of Nations: The Rise and Fall of International law 1870–1960* (Cambridge: Cambridge University Press, 2001).

Kraska, James, 'The "ARA Libertad"' (2013) 107 AJIL 404.

Kraska, James & Raul Pedrozo, *International Maritime Security Law* (Leiden: Nijhoff, 2013).

Kunoy, Bjørn, 'Jurisdiction of Courts and Tribunals under the UN Convention on the Law of the Sea over Disputed Land Areas' (2024) 39 IJMCL 345.

Kunoy, Bjørn, 'Preservation of Territorial Integrity: A Substantive Rule under UNCLOS?' *EJIL: Talk!* (23 April 2024), https://www.ejiltalk.org/preservation-of-territorial-integrity-a-substantive-rule-under-unclos/

Kunoy, Bjørn, 'The Scope of Compulsory Jurisdiction and Exceptions Thereto under the United Nations Convention on the Law of the Sea' (2021) 58 Can. YBIL 78.

Kupelyants, Hayk & Michael Waibel, 'Applicable Law' in Hélène Ruiz Fabri (ed.), *Max Planck Encyclopedia of International Procedural Law* (Oxford: Oxford University Press, 2022).

Lahmann, Henning, 'Infecting the Mind: Establishing Responsibility for Transboundary Disinformation' (2022) 33(2) EJIL 411.

Lake, David A., 'The State in International Relations' in Christian Reus-Smit & Duncan Snidal (eds.), *The Oxford Handbook of International Relations* (Oxford: Oxford University Press, 2008) 41.

Lando, Massimo, 'Jurisdiction Ratione Materiae of the International Court of Justice in Compromissory Clause Cases' (2023) 139 LQR 52.

Lasswell, Harold D. & Myres S. McDougal, 'Jurisprudence in Policy-Oriented Perspective' (1966–1967) 19 *University of Florida Law Review* 486.

Lavalle, Roberto, 'The Rights of States over Low-Tide Elevations: A Legal Analysis' (2014) 29 IJMCL 457.

Le Bouthillier, Yves, 'Article 32' in Olivier Corten & Pierre Klein (eds.), *The Vienna Conventions on the Law of Treaties: A Commentary* (Oxford: Oxford University Press, 2011).

Letter from Maria Theofili, Permanent Representative of Greece, to the Secretary-General of the United Nations, 25 May 2022, Ref. No. 40.1.184/AS 1487 chrome-extension://efaidnbmnnnibpcajpcglclefindmkaj/https://www.amna.gr/files/202205/26-161733OHE.pdf

Lewis, John, 'The Case for Regulating Fully Autonomous Weapons' (2015) 124 YLJ 1309.

United States Department of State, Bureau of Oceans and International and Environmental and Scientific Affairs, *Limits in the Seas. No. 143, China's Maritime Claims in the South China Sea* (Washington, DC: United States Department of State, Bureau of Oceans and International and Environmental and Scientific Affairs, December 2014).

Lisztwan, Julia, 'Stability of Maritime Boundary Agreements' (2012) 37 YJIL 153.

Llewellyn, Karl N., *The Bramble Bush: On Our Law and Its Study* (Quid Pro Pro Books, 2012; original, self-published, 1930).

Love, Ben, 'Jurisdiction over Incidental Questions in International Law' (2017) 111 ASIL Proc. 316.

Lu, Bingbin, 'The Case concerning East Timor and Self-determination' (2004) 11(2) *Murdoch University Electronic Journal of Law*, https://classic.austlii.edu.au/au/journals/MurdochUeJlLaw/2004/17.html

Malintoppi, Loretta, 'Remarks by Loretta Malintoppi' (2017) 111 ASIL Proc. 131.

Mälksoo, Lauri, *Illegal Annexation and State Continuity: The Case of the Incorporation of the Baltic States by the USSR*, 2nd rev. edn. (Leiden: Brill, 2022).

Marceau, Gabrielle, 'Evolutive Interpretation by the WTO Adjudicator' (2018) 21 *Journal of International Economic Law* 791.

Martens, F. F., *Sovremennoe mezhdunardodnoe parvo tsivilizovannykh narodov*, 2nd edn. (St. Petersburg: Tipo. Ministerstva putei soobschcheniia, 1887), I, 353.

McCorquodale, Robert, Jennifer Robinson, & Nicola Peart, 'Territorial Integrity and Consent in the Chagos Advisory Opinion' (2020) 69 ICLQ 221.

McCreath, Millicent & Zoe Scanlon, 'The Dispute concerning the Delimitation of the Maritime Boundary between Ghana and Côte d'Ivoire: Implications for the Law of the Sea' (2019) 50 ODIL 1.

McDougal, Myres S., and W. Michael Reisman, '"The Changing Structure of International Law": Unchanging Theory for Inquiry' (1965) 65 Colum. LR 810.

McDougal, Myres S., Harold D. Lasswell, & W. Michael Reisman, 'The World Constitutive Process of Authoritative Decision' in Cyril E. Black & Richard A. Falk (eds.), *The Future of the International Legal Order, vol. 1, Trends and Patterns* (Princeton, NJ: Princeton University Press, 1969) 73.

McGarry, Brian, 'Third Parties and Insular Features after the *South China Sea* Arbitration' (2017) 35 C(T)YBIL 99.

McIntyre, Juliette, 'Put on Notice: The Role of the Dispute Requirement in Assessing Jurisdiction and Admissibility before the International Court' (2018) 19 Melbourne JIL 546.

McLachlan, Campbell, 'Investment Treaties and General International Law' (2008) 57 ICLQ 361.

McLachlan, Campbell, Laurence Shore, & Matthew Weiniger, *International Investment Arbitration: Substantive Principles*, 2nd edn. (Oxford: Oxford University Press, 2017).

McNair, Arnold, *The Law of Treaties* (Oxford: Oxford University Press, 1961).

Mégret, Frédéric, 'International Criminal Justice as a Peace Project' (2018) 29 EJIL 835.

Merrills, John & Eric De Brabandere, *Merrill's International Dispute Settlement*, 7th edn. (Cambridge: Cambridge University Press, 2022).

Mikanagi, Tomohiro, 'Establishing a Military Presence in a Disputed Territory: Interpretation of Article 2(3) and (4) of the UN Charter' (2018) 67 ICLQ 1021.

Milano, Enrico, 'Russia's Veto in the Security Council: Whither the Duty to Abstain under Art. 27(3) of the UN Charter?' (2015) 75 ZaöRV 215.

Milano, Enrico & Irini Papanicolopulu, 'State Responsibility in Disputed Areas on Land and at Sea' (2011) 71 ZaöRV 587.

Miles, Cameron, 'Lawfare in Crimea: Treaty, Territory, and Investor–State Dispute Settlement' (2022) 38 *Arbitration International* 135.

Monageng, Sanji Mmasenono, 'The Crime of Aggression: Following the Needs of a Changing World?' (2017) 58 HILJ 7.

Moon, William J., 'Recognition, Rewards, and Regime Change' in Chiara Giorgetti & Natalie Klein (eds.), *Resolving Conflicts in the Law: Essays in Honour of Lea Brilmayer* (Leiden: Brill, 2019) 130.

Moore, John Norton, 'Prolegomenon to the Jurisprudence of Myres McDougal and Harold Lasswell' (1968) 54(4) Virg. LR 662.

Movchan, Anatoly P., *Problems of Boundaries and Security in the Helsinki Declaration* (1977) 154 Hag. Rec. 4.

Müller, Daniel, 'Les limites des espaces maritimes' in Forteau & Thouvenin (eds.) (2017) 529.

Munkman, A. L. W., 'Adjudication and Adjustment: International Judicial Decision and the Settlement of Territorial and Boundary Disputes' (1972–1973) 46 BYIL 1.

Nordquist, Myron H., Shabtai Rosenne, & Louis B. Sohn (eds.), *The United Nations Convention on the Law of the Sea 1982: A Commentary* (Dordrecht: Nijhoff, 1989).

Nuridzhanian, Gaiane, '*Ukraine vs. Russia* in International Courts and Tribunals,' *EJIL Talk!* (9 March 2016).

O'Keefe, Roger, 'Palm-Fringed Benefits: Islands Dependencies in the New Law of the Sea' (1996) 45 ICLQ 408.

Odom, Jonathan G., 'The Value and Viability of the South China Sea Arbitration Ruling: The U.S. Perspective 2016–2020' (2021) 97 *International Law Studies* 122.

Office of the Staff Judge Advocate, U.S. Indo-Pacific Command, 'Archipelagic States' (2021) 97 *International Law Studies* 12.

Office of the Staff Judge Advocate, U.S. Indo-Pacific Command, 'The South China Sea Arbitration Award' (2021) 97 *International Law Studies* 62.

Office of the Staff Judge Advocate, U.S. Indo-Pacific Command, 'U.S. Protests China's Maritime Claims in the South China Sea' (2021) 97 *International Law Studies* 89.
Ong, David M., 'Case between Indonesia and Malaysia concerning Sovereignty over Pulau Ligitan and Pulau Sipadan' (1999) 14 IJMCL 399.
Oppenheim, Lassa, *The Future of International Law* (Oxford: The Clarendon Press, 1921).
Oral, Nilüfer, '*Ukraine v. The Russian Federation:* Navigating Conflict over Sovereignty under UNCLOS' (2021) 97 *International Law Studies* 478.
Oude Elferink, Alex G., 'The *Arctic Sunrise* Incident: A Multi-faceted Law of the Sea Case with a Human Rights Dimension' (2014) 29 IJMCL 244.
Oxman, Bernard H. and Vincent Bantz, 'The M/V "Saiga" (No.2)' (2000) 94 AJIL 140.
Oxman, Bernard H. & Vincent P. Cogliati-Bantz, 'The M/V "Virginia G"' (2014) 108 AJIL 769.
Oxman, Bernard H., 'Offshore Features Subject to Claims of Sovereignty' in Jayakumar, Koh & Beckman (eds.) (2014) 8.
Oxman, Bernard H., 'The Third United Nations Conference on the Law of the Sea; The Ninth Session (1980)' (1981) 75 AJIL 211.
Park, William W., 'Arbitrators and Accuracy' (2010) 1(1) JIDS 25.
Parlett, Kate, 'Jurisdiction of the Arbitral Tribunal in Philippines v. China under UNCLOS and in the Absence of China' (2016) 110 AJIL Unbound 266.
Parlett, Kate, 'Beyond the Four Corners of the Convention: Expanding the Scope of Jurisdiction of Law of the Sea Tribunals' (2017) 48 ODIL 284.
Parra, Antonia R., 'Remembering Aron Broches,' Oxford University Press, 14 October 2016, https://oxia.ouplaw.com/page/546
Parson, Lindsay, 'Article 76: Definition of the Continental Shelf' in *Proelss Commentary* (2017) 587.
Pauwelyn, Joost, 'The Role of Public International Law in the WTO: How Far Can We Go?' (2001) 95 AJIL 535.
Payandeh, Mehrdad, 'The Concept of International Law in the Jurisprudence of H. L. A. Hart' (2010) 21(4) EJIL 967.
Pellet, Alain, 'Peaceful Settlement of International Disputes' in Anne Peters (ed.), *Max Planck Encyclopaedia of International Law* (Oxford: Oxford University Press, 2013).
Platzöder, Renate (ed.), *Third United Nations Conference on the Law of the Sea: Documents* (Dobbs Ferry, NY: Oceana Publications, 1982).
Pobjie, Erin, *Prohibited Force. The Meaning of 'Use of Force' in International Law* (Cambridge: Cambridge University Press, 2024).
Pompeo, Michael R., 'U.S. Position on Maritime Claims in the South China Sea,' Press Statement (13 July 2020), https://2017–2021.state.gov/u-s-position-on-maritime-claims-in-the-south-china-sea/index.html
Pomson, Ori, 'Ukraine Symposium—Russian Preliminary Objections at the ICJ: The Case Must Go On?' *Articles of War* (13 October 2022), https://lieber.westpoint.edu/russian-preliminary-objections-icj-case-must-go-on/
Prescott, Victor, 'Current Legal Developments: Australia/Indonesia' (1997) 12 IJMCL 533.

Prescott, Victor & Clive Schofield, *The Maritime Political Boundaries of the World*, 2nd edn. (Leiden: Martinus Nijhoff, 2005).

Proells, Alexander (ed.), *The United Nations Convention on the Law of the Sea: A Commentary* (Munich: Nomos Verlagsgesellschaft, 2017).

Purcell, Kate, *Geographical Change and the Law of the Sea* (Oxford: Oxford University Press, 2019).

Raimondo, Fabián, 'The Right of Peoples to Self-determination Revisited: Did Crimea Have the Right to Secede from the [*sic*] Ukraine?' in Pia Acconci, David Donat Cattin, Antonio Marchesi, Giuseppe Palmisano, & Valeria Santori (eds.), *International Law and the Protection of Humanity: Essays in Honor of Flavia Lattanzi* (Leiden: Brill, 2016) 535.

Ranganathan, Surabhi, 'Seasteads, Land-Grabs and International Law' (2019) 32 Leiden JIL 205.

Ranjeva, Raymond, 'Settlement of Disputes' in Dupuy & Vignes (eds.) (1991) 1333.

Rao, Judge P. Chandrasekhara, 'Delimitation Disputes under the United Nations Convention on the Law of the Sea: Settlement Procedures' in Thomas A. Mensah, Tafsir Malick Ndiaye, & Rüdiger Wolfrum (eds.), *The Law of the Sea, Environmental Law and Settlement of Disputes: Liber Amicorum Judge Thomas A. Mensah* (Leiden: NijhNoff, 2007) 877.

Redgwell, Catherine & Antonios Tzanakopoulos, 'The Interaction of Treaty and Custom in the Concept of Offshore Archipelagos' (2023) 72 ICLQ 573.

Reisman, W. Michael, 'International Lawmaking: A Process of Communication—The Harold D. Lasswell Memorial Lecture' (1981) 75 ASIL Proc. 101.

Reisman, W. Michael, 'The Other Shoe Falls: The Future of Article 36(1) Jurisdiction in Light of *Nicaragua*' (1987) 81 AJIL 166.

Reisman, W. Micheal, 'In Defense of World Public Order' (2001) 95(4) AJIL 833.

Reisman, W. Michael, *The Quest for World Order and Human Dignity in the Twenty-First Century: Constitutive Process and Individual Commitment* (2010) 351 Hag. Rec. 8.

Reisman, W. Michael, 'Canute Confronts the Tide: States vs. Tribunals and the Evolution of the Minimum Standard in Customary International Law' (2015) 109 ASIL Proc. 12.

Ridi, Niccolò, 'Mirages of an Intellectual Dreamland? Ratio, Obiter, and the Textualization of International Precedent' (2019) 10 JIDS 361.

Ridings, Penelope Jane, 'The Influence of Scholarship on the Shaping and Making of the Law of the Sea' (2023) 38 IJMCL 11.

Roach, J. Ashley, 'Offshore Archipelagos Enclosed by Straight Baselines: An Excessive Claim' (2018) 49 ODIL 176.

Roberts, Anthea, 'Clash of Paradigms: Actors and Analogies Shaping the Investment Treaty System' (2013) 107 AJIL 45.

Rothwell, Donald R., 'The Law of the Sea in the Asian-Pacific Region: An Overview of Trends and Developments' (1994–1995) 13 C(T)YBIL 81.

Rothwell, Donald R., *Islands and International Law* (Oxford: Hart Publishing, 2022).

Saliternik, Michal, 'Expanding the Boundaries of Boundary Dispute Settlement: International Law and Critical Geography at the Crossroads' (2021) 50(1) *Vanderbilt Journal of Transnational Law* 113.

Saunders, Kevin W., 'What Logic Can and Cannot Tell Us about Law' (1998) 73 *Notre Dame Law Review* 667.

Scalia, Antonin, 'Essay: Assorted Canards of Contemporary Legal Analysis' (1989) 40 *Case Western Reserve Law Review* 581.

Scanlon, Zoe, 'Upsetting the Balance? The Legality of Vessel Confiscation under the LOSC after the *M/V "Virginia G" case*' (2018) 33 IJMCL 166.

Schabas, William A., *The European Convention on Human Rights: A Commentary* (Oxford: Oxford University Press, 2015).

Schatz, Valentin, 'The Award concerning Preliminary Objections in *Ukraine v. Russia:* Observations regarding the Implicated Status of Crimea and the Sea of Azov,' *EJIL Talk!* (20 March 2020).

Schill, Stephan W., 'W(h)ither Fragmentation? On the Literature and Sociology of International Investment Law' (2011) 22 EJIL 875.

Schmitt, Michael N., 'Cyberspace and International Law: The Penumbral Mist of Uncertainty' (2013) 126 HLR 176.

Schmitt, Michael N., 'In Defense of Due Diligence in Cyberspace' (2015) 125 YLJ 68.

Schofield, Clive & David Freestone, 'Islands Awash amidst Rising Seas: Sea Level Rise and Insular Status under the Law of the Sea' (2019) 34 IJMCL 391.

Schofield, Clive, 'Defining the "Boundary" between Land and Sea: Territorial Sea Baselines in the South China Sea' in Jayakumar, Koh, & Beckman (eds.) (2014) 21.

Schreuer, Christoph, 'Regionalism v. Universalism' (1995) 6 EJIL 477.

Schreuer, Christoph, 'What Is a Legal Dispute?' in Isabelle Buffard, James Crawford, Alain Pellet, & Stephan Wittich (eds.), *International Law between Universalism and Fragmentation: Festschrift in Honour of Gerhard Hafner* (Leiden: Martinus Nijhoff, 2008) 959.

Schreuer, Christoph, *The ICSID Convention: A Commentary*, 2nd edn. (Cambridge: Cambridge University Press, 2009).

Schwebel, Stephen M., 'The Effects of Resolutions of the U.N. General Assembly on Customary International Law' (1979) 73 ASIL Proc. 301.

Scobbie, Iain, 'Self-determination Undetermined: The Case of East Timor' (1996) 9 *Leiden JIL* 185.

Scott, James C., *Seeing Like a State: How Certain Schemes to Improve the Human Condition Have Failed* (New Haven: Yale University Press, 1998).

Scott, Shirley V., 'International Law as Ideology: Theorizing the Relationship between International Law and International Politics' (1994) 5 EJIL 313.

Serdy, 'Article 279: Obligation to Settle Disputes by Peaceful Means' in *Proelss Commentary* (2017) 1813.

Serdy, 'Article 297: Limitations on Applicability of Section 2' in *Proelss Commentary* 1906.

Serdy, 'Article 298: Optional Exceptions to Applicability of Section 2' in *Proelss Commentary* (2017) 1918.

Shaffer, Gregory, Manfred Elsig, & Sergio Puig, 'The Extensive (but Fragile) Authority of the WTO Appellate Body' (2016) 79 *Law and Contemporary Problems* 237.

Shaffer, Gregory & Michael Waibel, 'The (Mis)alignment of the Trade and Monetary Orders' in Terence C. Halliday & Gregory Shaffer, eds., *Transnational Legal Orders* (Cambridge: Cambridge University Press, 2015) 187.

Shany, Yuval, 'Does International Law Grant the People of Crimea and Donetsk a Right to Secede? Revisiting Self-Determination in Light of the 2014 Events in Ukraine' (2014) 21(1) *The Brown Journal of World Affairs* 233.

Simma, Bruno & Dirk Pulkowski, '*Leges* Speciales and Self-contained Regimes' in James Crawford, Alain Pellet, Simon Olleson, & Kate Parlett (eds.), *The Law of International Responsibility* (Oxford: Oxford University Press, 2010) 139.

Simma, Bruno, 'Foreign Investment Arbitration: A Place for Human Rights?' (2011) 60 ICLQ 573.

Simon, William H., '"Thinking Like a Lawyer" about Ethical Questions' (1998) 27 *Hofstra Law Review* 1.

Simpson, Gerry J., 'Judging the East Timor Dispute: Self-determination at the International Court of Justice' (1994) 17 *Hastings International and Comparative Law Review* 323.

Smith, Robert, 'The Effect of Extended Maritime Jurisdiction on Land Sovereignty Disputes' in Albert W. Koers, Bernard H. Oxman, & Willy Østreng (eds.), *The 1982 Convention on the Law of the Sea: Proceedings, Law of the Sea Institute Seventeenth Annual Conference* (Honolulu: Law of the Sea Institute, 1984) 336.

Socher, Johannes, *Russia and the Right to Self-determination in the Post-Soviet space* (Oxford: Oxford University Press, 2021).

Song, Yann-huei, 'The Application of Article 121(3) of the Law of the Sea Convention to the Five Selected Disputed Islands in the South China Sea' (2009) 27 C(T) YBIL 43.

Song, Yann-Huei, Keyuan Zou, & Shicun Wu (eds.), *Major Law and Policy Issues in the South China Sea: European and American Perspectives* (London: Routledge, 2014).

Sorensen, Theodore, 'Round Table: New Proposals for Increasing the Rôle of International Law in Government Decision-Making' (1971) 65 ASIL Proc. 285.

Southgate, Laura, *ASEAN Resistance to Sovereignty Violation: Interests, Balancing and the Role of the Vanguard State* (Bristol: Bristol University Press, 2019).

St. J. Macdonald, Ronald, *The Role of the Legal Adviser of Ministries of Foreign Affairs* (1977) 154 Hag. Rec. 381.

Stavropoulos, Constantin A., 'The Practice of Voluntary Abstentions by Members of the Security Council under Article 27, Paragraph 3' (1967) 61(3) AJIL 737.

Sumption, Jonathan, 'The Limits of Law,' Sultan Azlan Shah Law Lectures 2013, www.sultanazlanshah.com/pdf/2021/SAS_Lecture_27.pdf

Symmons, Clive R., *Historic Waters and Historic Rights in the Law of the Sea: A Modern Reappraisal*, 2nd edn. (Leiden: Nijhoff, 2019).

Talmon, Stefan, '*Jus Cogens* after *Germany v. Italy*: Substantive and Procedural Rules Distinguished' (2012) 25(4) Leiden JIL 979.

Talmon, Stefan, 'The South China Sea Arbitration: Is There a Case to Answer?' in Talmon & Jia (eds.) (2014) 15.
Talmon, Stefan, 'The Chagos Marine Protected Area Arbitration: Expansion of the Jurisdiction of UNCLOS Part XV Courts and Tribunals' (2016) 65 ICLQ 927.
Talmon, Stefan, 'Denouncing UNCLOS Remains Option for China after Tribunal Ruling,' *Global Times* (English edition), 3 March 2016.
Talmon, Stefan, 'Article 121: Regime of Islands' in *Proelss Commentary* (2017) 858.
Talmon, Stefan & Bing Bing Jia (eds.), *The South China Sea Arbitration: A Chinese Perspective* (Oxford: Hart Publishing, 2014).
Talmon, Stefan, *The South China Sea Arbitration: Jurisdiction, Admissibility, Procedure* (The Hague: Brill, 2022).
Tamada, Dai, 'The Timor Sea Conciliation: The Unique Mechanism of Dispute Settlement' (2020) 31 EJIL 321.
Tams, Christian & James G. Devaney, 'Article 304' in *Proelss Commentary* (2017) 1961.
Tanaka, Yoshifumi, 'International Tribunal for the Law of the Sea: The ARA Libertad Case (Argentina v. Ghana, 15 December 2012), Request for the Prescription of Provisional Measures' (2013) 28 IJMCL 375.
Tanaka, Yoshifumi, 'A Note on the M/V Louisa Case' (2014) 45 ODIL 205.
Tanaka, Yoshifumi, 'Reflections on Historic Rights in the South China Sea Arbitration (Merits)' (2017) 32 IJMCL 458.
Tanaka, Yoshifumi, *Peaceful Settlement of International Disputes* (Cambridge: Cambridge University Press, 2018).
Tanaka, Yoshifumi, 'Release of a Detained Warship and Its Crew through Provisional Measures: A Comparative Analysis of the *ARA Libertad* and *Ukraine* v. *Russia* cases' (2020) 96 *International Law Studies* 223.
Terasaki, Naomihi Hiro, 'The Regime of Islands in International Conventions (Part 1),' *The OPRI Center of Islands Studies* (13 March 2014).
Thi Lan Anh, Nguyen, 'The July 12 Award on the Historic Titles, Historic Rights and Impacts on State Practices in the South China Sea' (2016) 34 C(T)YBIL 39.
Thirlway, Hugh, 'Territorial Disputes and Their Resolution in the Recent Jurisprudence of the International Court of Justice' (2018) 31 Leiden JIL 117.
Thirlway, Hugh, *The International Court of Justice* (Oxford: Oxford University Press, 2016).
Thurnher, Jeffrey S., 'The Law that Applies to Autonomous Weapons Systems' (2013) 17(4) *ASIL Insights*, www.asil.org/insights/volume/17/issue/4/law-applies-autonomous-weapon-systems
Treves, Tullio, 'Article 286: Application of Procedures' in *Proelss Commentary* (2017) 1844.
Treves, Tullio, 'Art. 290: Provisional Measures' in *Proelss Commentary* (2017) 1866.
Treves, Tullio, 'What Have the United Nations Convention and the International Tribunal for the Law of the Sea to Offer as Regards Maritime Delimitation Disputes?' in Rainer Lagoni & Daniel Vignes (eds.), *Maritime Delimitation* (Leiden: Nijhoff, 2006) 77.

Tribe, Laurence H., 'The Curvature of Constitutional Space: What Lawyers Can Learn from Modern Physics' (1989) 103 HLR 1.

Tunkin, G. I., *Theory of International Law* (William E. Butler, trans.) (Cambridge, MA: Harvard University Press, 1974).

Tuzheliak, Natalia, 'Investors at Conflict's Crossroads: An Overview of Available International Courts and Tribunals in the Crimea Context' (2017) 6(2) *UCL Journal of Law and Jurisprudence* 14.

Tzeng, Peter, 'Jurisdiction and Applicable Law Under UNCLOS' (2016) 126 YLJ 242.

United States Department of State, Bureau of Oceans and International Environmental and Scientific Affairs, *Limits in the Seas. No. 150. People's Republic of China: Maritime Claims in the South China Sea* (Washington, DC: United States Department of State, Bureau of Oceans and International Environmental and Scientific Affairs, January 2022).

Van Atten, Mark, 'Objections to the Proof Interpretation' in Edward N. Zalta & Uri Nodelman (eds.), *Stanford Encyclopedia of Philosophy* (2023).

Van Logchem, Youri, *The Rights and Obligations of States in Disputed Maritime Areas* (Cambridge: Cambridge University Press, 2021) 239.

Vasquez, John A. & Emily E. Barrett, 'Peace as the Absence of Militarized Conflict: Comparing the Democratic and Territorial Peace' (2015) 2 *Journal of Territorial and Maritime Studies* 5.

Villiger, Mark E., *Commentary on the 1969 Vienna Convention on the Law of Treaties* (Leiden: Brill/Nijhoff, 2009).

Volterra, Robert G., Giorgio F. Mandelli, & Álvaro Nistal, 'The Characterisation of the *Dispute concerning Coastal State Rights in the Black Sea, Sea of Azov, and Kerch Strait*' (2018) 33 IJMCL 614.

Von Clausewitz, Carl, *On War, Book* I, chapter 1 (Princeton, NJ: Princeton University Press, 1976) (Michael Howard and Peter Paret, eds. and trans.) (original *Vom Kriege* (Berlin: Dümmlers Verlag, 1832)).

Vukas, Budislav, 'The Definition of the Law of the Sea' in Nisuke Ando, Edward McWhinney, Rüdiger Wolfrum, & Betsy Baker Röben (eds.), *Liber Amicorum Judge Shigeru Oda* (The Hague: Kluwer, 2002), vol. 2, p. 1303.

Waibel, Michael, 'Coordinating Adjudication Processes' in Zachary Douglas, Joost Pauwelyn, & Jorge E. Viñuales (eds.), *The Foundations of International Investment Law: Bringing Theory into Practice* (Oxford: Oxford University Press, 2014) 499.

Waibel, Michael, 'Investment Arbitration: Jurisdiction and Admissibility,' University of Cambridge Faculty of Law Legal Studies Research Paper Series, Paper No 9/2014 (February 2014).

Walker, George K., *Definitions for the Law of the Sea: Terms not Defined by the 1982 Convention* (Leiden: Brill, 2011).

Walton, Beatrice A., 'Duties Owed: Low-Intensity Cyber Attacks and Liability for Transboundary Torts in International Law' (2017) 126 YLJ 1460.

Webb, Philippa, 'The United Kingdom and the *Chagos Archipelago* Advisory Opinion: Engagement and Resistance' (2021) 21 Melbourne JIL 726.

Wegen, Gerhard, 'Discontinuance and Withdrawal: Article 88 of the Rules' in Andreas Zimmermann, Christian J. Tams, Karin Oellers-Frahm, & Christian Tomuschat (eds.), *The Statute of the International Court of Justice. A Commentary*, 3rd edn. (Oxford: Oxford University Press, 2019) 1611.

Weisbord, Noah, 'Conceptualizing Aggression' (2009) 20 *Duke Journal of Comparative and International Law* 1.

Whomersley, Chris, 'Offshore Archipelagos Enclosed by Straight Baselines: A Reply to J. Ashley Roach' (2018) 49 ODIL 203.

Wilson, Doug & Sue Robertson, 'The Promise and Limits of Cyber Power in International Law' (2020) 114 ASIL Proc. 132.

Wolfrum, Rüdiger, 'Article 18' in Bruno Simma, Daniel-Erasmus Khan, Georg Nolte, Andreas Paulus, & Nikolai Wessendorf (eds.), *The Charter of the United Nations: A Commentary*, vol. 1, 3rd edn. (Oxford: Oxford University Press, 2012).

Wolfrum, Rüdiger, 'Remarks by Rüdiger Wolfrum: Shifting Baselines—Shifting Maritime Boundaries?' (2021) 114 ASIL Proc. 386.

Wong, Megan S., 'Aggression and State Responsibility at the International Criminal Court' (2021) 70(4) ICLQ 961.

Wood, Michael, 'The Creation of States in International Law (Second Edition): Review' (2006) 55(4) ICLQ 994.

Wood, Michael, 'The International Tribunal for the Law of the Sea and General International Law' (2007) 2 IJMCL 351.

Wuschka, Sebastian, 'Procedural Aspects of the Obligation of Non-recognition before International Investment Tribunals' in Katia Fach Gómez, Anastasios Gourgourinis, & Catherine Titi (eds.), *International Investment Law and the Law of Armed Conflict* (Cham: Springer, 2019) 149.

Ye, Qiang and Keyuan Zou, 'Interpretation and Application of Article 298 of the Law of the Sea Convention in Recent Annex VII Arbitrations: An Appraisal' (2017) 48 ODIL 331.

Yiallourides, Constantinos, Markus Gehring, & Jean-Pierre Gauci, *The Use of Force in Relation to Sovereignty Disputes over Land Territory* (London: BIICL, 2018).

Yu, Mincai, 'China's Informal Participation in the Annex VII Philippines v. China Arbitral Tribunal's Proceedings' (2015) 30 IJMCL 54.

Zacher, Mark W., 'The Territorial Integrity Norm: International Boundaries and the Use of Force' (2001) 55(2) *International Organization* 215.

Zarbiyev, Fuad, 'On the Judge Centredness of the International Legal Self' (2021) 32 EJIL 1139.

Zelman, Beth, 'A Crime Universally Acknowledged' (2020) 51 *Georgetown Journal of International Law* 727.

Zhang, Haiwan & Chenxi Mi, 'Jurisprudential Tenability of the Philippines v. China Arbitration on South China Sea Disputes?' in Talmon & Jia (eds.) (2014) 137.

Zou, Keyuan, 'China's Approach to UNCLOS and Its Application to Disputed Issues in the South China Sea' in Jill Barrett & Richard Barnes (eds.), *Law of the Sea: UNCLOS as a Living Treaty* (London: British Institute of International and Comparative Law, 2016) 363.

Zrilič, Jure, *The Protection of Foreign investment in Times of Armed Conflict* (Oxford: Oxford University Press, 2019).

Index

EU authorised representative for GPSR:
Easy Access System Europe, Mustamäe tee 50,
10621 Tallinn, Estonia
gpsr.requests@easproject.com

www.ingramcontent.com/pod-product-compliance
Ingram Content Group UK Ltd.
Pitfield, Milton Keynes, MK11 3LW, UK
UKHW021037221225
466318UK00007B/165
* 9 7 8 1 5 2 6 1 9 0 6 0 4 *